THE PRACTICE

OF

CHRISTIAN AND RELIGIOUS
PERFECTION.

WRITTEN IN SPANISH,

BY V. F. ALPHONSUS RODRIGUEZ,

Of the Society of Jesus.

IN THREE VOLUMES.

VOL. I.

DUBLIN:

JAMES DUFFY AND SONS,

15 WELLINGTON QUAY,

AND 1 PATERNOSTER ROW, LONDON.

1882.

ISBN: 978-1-7371910-2-5

Published by:
St Athanasius Press
133 Slazing Rd
Potosi, WI 53820
1-608-763-4097
http://www.stathanasiuspress.com
Melwaller@gmail.com

Email can be the best way to contact us. Stores and
retail customers can order via our web site or directly.

For as little as $500, you can help bring a Catholic
Classic back into print. Please contact us to assist us
in bringing solid Catholic books back into print.

Check out our other titles on last page of this book!

CONTENTS.

THE SECOND TREATISE.

THE THIRD TREATISE.

THE FOURTH TREATISE.

LIFE OF ALPHONSUS RODRIGUEZ.

———o———

THE celebrated father, Alphonsus Rodriguez, to whom all devout Christians, as well as the members of the different religious orders of the Church, are so deeply indebted for the rich treasures which he has bequeathed to them in his ascetic writings, was born at Valladolid, in Spain. He commenced his studies at Salamanca; and there, after having attained his degree in the School of Philosophy, he was moved by the apostolic preaching of Father John Ramirez, of the Society of Jesus, and, at the age of nineteen, embraced the religious state in that society. During his noviceship, and in the course of his theological studies, he acquired so high a reputation for virtue, that scarcely was he ordained priest, when he was intrusted with the care of the young religious to train them up in the spirit of their vocation—an employment which is considered of the utmost importance in the society. Amongst those who had the happiness of being under him as master of novices, was the celebrated doctor, Father Francis Suarez, who used frequently to congratulate himself on having been the disciple of one so renowned in spiritual life. He was next appointed Rector of Monterei, where he afterwards remained; and, during the space of twelve years, delivered lectures in Moral Theology with such celebrity that many were anxious to obtain copies of his writings. To the important duties of the theological chair, his zeal associated still greater labours in his endeavours to promote the spiritual welfare of the city in which he dwelt, and of the neighbouring country, by preaching, catechising, and absolving sinners. From Monterei he was removed to Valladolid, to fill the office of domestic casuist in the house of the professed fathers; thence he was summoned to Montilla to instruct the novices, and continued to perform this duty for more than thirty years. He was afterwards deputed to Rome to attend the Fifth General Congregation, where he gave illustrious proofs of his sanctity, prudence, and knowledge of the rules and constitutions of the society. From Rome he returned to Spain, and became Spiritual Father in the college of Cordova. It was during his sojourn here, that, having principally in view to promote the advancement in solid virtue of the entire body of the society, he wrote those admirable Treatises on Christian Perfection, to which the Holy Ghost has imparted such unction, that, read again and again, they never tire. Having gone to Seville, in the year 1606, to assist at a provincial congregation, he was ordered by his superiors to remain there, and was placed once more over the novices. He continued at Seville till his death, devoting his leisure moments to the revisal of his writings previous to their publication. Unceasing labour had by this time greatly impaired his strength; and, during the last two years of his life, he became so decrepid, that he was no longer able to support himself on his limbs to celebrate the holy sacrifice of the mass; but the saintly old man received daily from the hands of another the adorable sacrament of the eucharist. At last, loaded with years and merits, he slept in the Lord, at the advanced age of ninety, in the 70th year of his religious life, and 46 years after his solemn profession. He expired on the 21st of February, 1616.

He was a man who never failed to illustrate in his own person, and by his own example, those lessons of virtue and sublime perfection which he inculcated in his works. His union with God was most intimate; he found a heaven in his cell, and seldom left it unless at the call of charity or obedience. During the last years of his life, being released from those obstacles which are inseparable from offices of authority over others, he used to devote four hours each day to prayer. He took no pleasure in walking about the garden attached to the college; his delight was to remain alone with God. He was the first at every public duty, most punctual in the least little observances of religious life, and a strenuous assertor of evangelical poverty. Even in the last stage of his long life, he would admit of no singularity in his diet; and when he happened to be helped to something likely to gratify his palate, he would contrive to spoil its flavour with water. To the very last, he never omitted to crawl to the church to hear the confessions of the people, and, in his turn, threw himself daily at the feet of his own confessor to obtain absolution himself. It was a most edifying sight to behold this venerable man, at the age of ninety, with the most profound sentiments of humility, stooping to kiss the feet of his religious brethren, as though he was the last and lowest amongst them, and only fit to be trampled under foot by all around him.

TRANSLATOR TO THE READER.

————o————

HAVING, contrary to the ordinary practice, translated this work from the French copy, rather than from the original itself, it is proper to inform the reader, that I do so, yielding to the reasons and authority of competent judges, who understand perfectly the French, Spanish, and English languages. They told me, were they to translate RODRIGUEZ, they would be better pleased to follow the French copy of MONS. DES MARAIS, than the Spanish original—1st, Because the style of M. DES MARAIS' translation is more even than that of the Spanish original, a circumstance which indeed cannot be wondered at, as the author wrote at different and distant periods. 2ndly, Because the French approaches nearer than the Spanish to the English idiom. It is to the observations of those competent judges I am indebted, not only for the first idea I conceived of undertaking this work, but likewise for the preference I gave the French copy.

While engaged in translating it I had the advantage of seriously and frequently perusing this book : and, as usually happens to those who peruse works of merit, the oftener I read, the more I admired it. Besides, the abilities, experience, and application of M. DES MARAIS, who, in France, is admitted to be one of the most eminent critics of the age, will certainly give his translation more than ordinary celebrity. Having thus stated the reasons of my own undertaking, I will proceed to give the following account of the author's Work and Life, extracted from the Preface of M. DES MARAIS.

Lest, says he, the Author's Dedicatory Epistle to the Fathers of the SOCIETY should not convey such idea of his work as to display fully its merits and excellence, I shall add this short eulogy :—It abounds in most solid principles of Christian morality—it is written with that spirit and unction which characterize the scriptures and the writings of the holy fathers. It is historical and learned—it is eminently calculated to conduct all sorts of persons both to and in the way of perfection. Here the man of learning, who wishes to be guided by the great maxims and truths of Christianity, will find suitable subjects for the mind to dwell on. Here those on whom the impulse of

tender and affecting devotion makes deep impression will meet
whatsoever tends to inflame still more the heart of a Christian
already touched with the love of God.   Here, in fine, those
whom God wishes to attract to himself by a happy simplicity
of spirit, will find instructions and examples proportionate to
their capacity and peculiar vocation.

Now to say something of the author himself, and thereby to
give an idea of the value we ought to set on his work, I will
here set down in a few words what the historians of his order
have written of him :—He was born at Valladolid in the year
1526, and in the 20th year of his age he renounced the world to
consecrate himself to God, in the Society of Jesus at Salamanca.   After having been engaged about thirteen years in
teaching moral divinity at Monterey, he was sent to Montille,
in the Province of Andalusia, to be there master of novices ; and
to deliver such spiritual exhortations, as are delivered weekly
in all the houses of the Society.   In these two employments
he acquitted himself for thirty years together, with all possible
zeal and ability, and hereby evinced how skilled he was in the
science of saints, and in the direction of souls.   Being afterwards chosen to go to Rome, to the Fifth General Congregation,
he there also gave marks of exemplary virtue, and consummate
prudence.   At his return he was sent to Corduba, where for
twelve years he had the direction of spiritual things, that is to
say, the care of taking an account of the interior state of all the
religious in the house, and to help them to overcome and root
out of their souls whatsoever opposed their advancement in perfection.   As at Montille so at Corduba, his office was to make
the weekly exhortations; and it was towards the end of the
twelve years he remained here, that collecting together what he
had written upon different subjects, he compiled these three
volumes of the Practice of Christian Perfection.   He did
not, however, publish them till a long time after, when he went
to the Provincial Congregation held at Seville in the year 1606,
where he was ordered to stay to take care of the novices ; and
at the same time to publish this his work.   After having applied
himself for eight years together, without any relaxation, to the
discharge of both these duties, he became so infirm, that he had
neither force to exercise any longer the painful function of
master of novices, nor even to celebrate the holy sacrifice of
mass.   Lest, however, he should be deprived of the precious
body of Jesus Christ, he daily received it from the hand of

another; and having lived two years in this languishing condition, at length, upon the 21st of February, in the year 1616, in a good old age, full of merits, he happily rested in our Lord in peace. His death was not less universally regretted than his sanctity was esteemed. He was a great lover of retirement, an exact observer of rules, and had a very great zeal for the salvation of souls; his self-abnegation was such that in all things he had but God in view. The time in which he was not engaged in the discharge of other indispensable duties, he spent in prayer and spiritual reading, adding to these pious exercises very frequent austerities, which he continued to the end of his life; and when it was represented to him that he could not practise such penances without shortening his days, he answered: "An unmortified religious man is already dead." Behold, in short, the life of this most excellent master of a spiritual life; but the reading his works will still give you a better knowledge of him, for there was nothing he proposed to others to practise, of which he gave not first an example in himself; his life being nothing else than a constant practice of what in his writings he had taught others.

ALPHONSUS RODRIGUEZ

TO THE

RELIGIOUS OF THE SOCIETY OF JESUS.

———o———

St. Gregory being desired to write some spiritual instructions for the conduct of certain religious houses, excuses himself in his 6th Book and 27th Epistle in these terms :—"The exercises of mortification and prayer, practised by religious, produce such a source or fountain of wisdom in their hearts, that they stand not in need of being watered with those few drops our aridity is able to impart to them. For as the fountain in the midst of the terrestrial paradise watered all parts thereof, and kept it continually fresh and green without the help of rain, which it needed not ; so those who are in the paradise of religion have no need of being watered from without, because prayer and mortification produce in them such a source or fountain of grace, as is always sufficient to maintain their virtues in their full splendour and beauty."

I might, RR. FF., upon this account, with far more reason than St. Gregory, excuse myself after the same manner he did, to those faithful souls our Lord has planted in the garden of the Society of Jesus—souls, he has cultivated and watered by the help of that mental prayer they daily make. But though this excuse would doubtless be a very just one, if I imagined you expected anything new from me, yet I am prevented from making it, as I propose to myself nothing else in this work, than to revive in your memories what you already know and daily practise. In doing this, I shall pay obedience to our holy founder, who in one of his Constitutions ordains that, " once a week, or at least, once a fortnight, there should be appointed to lay before our eyes the obligations of a spiritual life, lest human frailty, which daily inclines us to relax in our duties, might cause us to forget and to discontinue them." (Cons. p. 3.) The Constitution, God be praised, is exactly observed through the whole Society, and produces great fruit therein. Having, therefore, above those forty years been employed in the function of exhorting the novices, or other religious ; and having gathered divers things together for this purpose, my superiors, and many other persons to whom I owe a deference, were of opinion that I might render great service both to God and to religion, and that the advantage drawn from my labours would be more lasting, if I should take care to review and put in order what I had already composed.

I considered also, that in the Constitution before cited, St. Ignatius puts this alternative :—" Let there be," says he, " one appointed to deliver these spiritual exhortations to the religious, or at least let the religious be obliged to read them." I was still more encouraged in my undertaking, when I reflected that it is a practice established in the Society, and very much recommended by saints, to read something every day that may promote our spiritual advancement. This being the principal design of the following work, I have for this reason laid before you as clearly and briefly as I was able such things as are more essential, and more common to our profession. These, I trust, will serve us as a mirror, wherein, if we daily view ourselves, we shall be enabled to correct our imperfections, and decorate our souls in such a manner as will render them more pleasing to the eyes of Divine majesty.

Moreover, though my principal intention was to fulfil the particular obligation I have to serve those, whom religion has constituted my fathers and brethren in Jesus Christ ; yet, because we ought to extend, as far as we can, the effects of charity, and being particularly obliged to it by our Institute, I have endeavoured to dispose this work after such a manner, as that it may be useful not only to our Society in particular, but to all other religious, and even to all persons in general, who aspire to Christian perfection. Wherefore that the title may correspond to the work, and may indicate that it is a profitable and useful book for all the world, I have entitled it, Practice of Christian Perfection. I call it *Practice*, because things are treated in it after such a manner, as may render the practice very easy.

I hope, by the mercy of our Lord, that my labours will not be unprofitable ; and that this grain of seed of the word of God, being sown in the good soil of souls aspiring to perfection, will render not only thirty or sixty, but even a hundred-fold.

THE PRACTICE

OF

CHRISTIAN AND RELIGIOUS PERFECTION.

THE FIRST TREATISE.

ON THE ESTEEM AND AFFECTION WE OUGHT TO HAVE FOR WHAT-
EVER RELATES TO OUR SPIRITUAL ADVANCEMENT ; AND ON
MANY OTHER THINGS CONDUCIVE TO IT.

———o———

CHAPTER I.

The great Value we ought to set on Spiritual Things.

" I WISHED for a right understanding of things," says the Wise
Man, " and God gave it me, I called upon him, and he filled
me with the Spirit of Wisdom, which I preferred before scep-
tres and crowns, and believed that riches and precious stones
deserved not to be compared thereunto ; for all the gold and
silver upon earth is nothing but a little sand and clay, in comparison of wisdom." (Wis. vii. 7.) The true wisdom which all
of us ought to desire is Christian perfection. Now, this consists
in uniting ourselves to God by love, according to these words
of St. Paul,—"Above all things I recommend charity unto you,
which is the bond of perfection, whereby we are united to God."
(Colos. iii. 14.) We ought, therefore, set as great value on
perfection, and on everything conducive to its attainment, as
Solomon says he set on wisdom ; and we ought to believe with
St. Paul,—" That if we gain Jesus Christ it is enough ; for all
the rest is nothing but dirt and ordure." (Phil. iii. 8.) This is
the best means we have of attaining perfection. For the degree
to which this esteem ascends in our hearts will be the measure
of our own spiritual advancement in particular, and of that of
religion in general. The reason is, because we desire nothing
but according to the estimation we hold it in. For our will
being a blind faculty that pursues nothing, but what the un-

derstanding proposes to it, that value, which our understanding sets upon any object, becomes of necessity the measure of
our desires.   And our will being the absolute mistress that
commands all the interior and exterior faculties of our souls,
we never exert ourselves for the attainment of any object, but
according to that degree wherein our will is moved to desire
it.   In order, then, that we earnestly desire it, and diligently
exert ourselves for its attainment, it is necessary that we hold
in high estimation whatever relates to our advancement in perfection.   For, these things bear such reciprocal relation, that
the measure of the one is the infallible rule of the other.

To carry on his trade to advantage, a jeweller should know
well the value of precious stones : otherwise he may happen to
sell at a low rate a jewel of great value.   Our traffic is in
precious stones ; " and we are all merchants in the kingdom of
heaven, and seek for fine pearls." (Matt. xiii. 45.)   We should,
therefore, be good judges of the merchandise we trade in, lest,
by a strange abuse, we give gold for dirt, and part with heaven
for earth.   "Let not the wise man," says our Saviour, by the
mouth of the Prophet Jeremy, "glory in his wisdom, nor the
strong man in his strength, nor the rich man in the abundance
of his wealth ; but let him that does glory, glory in his knowledge of me." (Jer. ix. 23.)   The most valuable of all treasures
consists in the knowledge, love, and service of God ; this is our
greatest, and, indeed, our only affair ; or to say better, it is for
this we were created ; for this we entered into religion ; and it
is in this alone, as in our only end, we ought to repose ourselves, and establish our greatest glory.

I wish, therefore, that this esteem of perfection and of
spiritual things conducive to it, would make a deep impression
on the hearts of all men, and particularly of religious; and that
we take care to encourage each other to it, not only by our words,
and ordinary conversation, but much more by our actions, and
the general tenor of our lives.   By this means, those as yet but
novices in the way of virtue, and such as are more advanced in
it, and all in general, must acknowledge, that in religion we
should attach importance to spiritual things only.   In fine, as
St. Ignatius sets forth in his Constitutions : " What we value
most in religious persons is not depth of learning, nor great
talents for preaching, nor any other natural or human endow-
ment ; but it is humility and obedience, a spirit of recollection
and prayer." (Cons., p. 10.)   It is this we must, from the

beginning, imprint on the minds of all who are received into religion, and it is with this milk they, who intend to lead a holy life, must be first fed. When they perceive that, of all things, piety is most valued, that it is the practice those convinced of the vanity of the world are engaged in, and that the pious are chiefly loved and esteemed, then they will presently apply their thoughts, and use their endeavours, not to acquire great learning, or to become famous preachers, but to excel each other in humility and mortification. By this, however, I do not mean, that gaining general esteem or good will should be our motive for embracing virtue. I only assert, that when it shall be known that virtue is the only thing esteemed in religion, we shall be more convinced, that it is the only thing truly deserving of esteem. For every one coming thus to the knowledge of the true way in which he should walk, will devote himself without reserve to virtue—will apply himself solely to his spiritual advancement, and will believe that everything else is but vanity and folly.

From all this, it can be readily inferred, what a dangerous example is set religious societies, by those who introduce no other topic than human science, and who are constantly bestowing praises on such as are eminent for learning. This example is the more dangerous, because seeing them so highly valued by the graver sort of men, new beginners will conclude, that it is by the acquisition of these things they will be entitled to respect and preferment. Upon this account, learning is the only object they propose to themselves, and the desire of acquiring it increasing daily, the love of humility and mortification insensibly decays in their hearts. At length they make so little account of the one in comparison of the other, that from intense application to study, they omit what is of strictest obligation. Hence it comes to pass, that many of them relax, are perverted, and forsake religion. Now, instead of instilling into the minds of these beginners, the vain desire of being reputed men of learning, were it not better to represent to them, how important and necessary a thing it is to acquire virtue and humility, and how unprofitable, or rather how dangerous it is, without humility, to be possessed of talents and learning.

In his Life of St. Fulgentius, abbot, Surius has a passage very applicable to the present subject. He tells us, that among the religious in the monastery of this holy abbot there were some, who laboured hard, and devoted themselves entirely to the service of the community, but who applied not with equal fervour to prayer, spiritual reading, and interior recollection. Now, St. Fulgentius never thought so much of these, as of others. He always showed a far greater love and esteem for those who, though unable, by reason of their weak and sickly constitution, to be of any service to the convent, were yet devoted to spiritual things, and careful to advance in virtue. And doubtless he acted right. For, if we are not humble and submissive to the will of our superiors, what will it avail us to have talents, and other good qualities? If on this ground we claim greater liberties and exemptions, it certainly were far better for us never to have had talents at all. The case were different indeed, if in the account which is, one day, to be demanded of the superior, God should ask him,—"Were his subjects men of study and science?" But no! these are the questions God will ask him,—"Have those committed to your charge improved themselves in the science of saints?" "Have they advanced daily in virtue?" "Have they been employed according to their talents, without suffering their exterior occupations to check their interior advancement?" It is this, in the opinion of a very holy man (Tho.-à-Kempis, xiii. c. 3), for which every particular person also shall be accountable to Almighty God, who, on the day of judgment, will not ask us, what we have read, but what we have done—nor how learnedly we have spoken, but how religiously we have lived?

The sacred text relates, that our blessed Saviour having sent his disciples to preach, they returned full of joy, telling him, "That even the devils were subject to them, in his name." To whom our Saviour answered,—"Rejoice not that you work miracles, and that the devils are subject to you; but rejoice in this, that your names are written in heaven." (Luke x. 17, 20.) We ought, then, to place all our joy and happiness in acquiring the kingdom of heaven, for without that all the rest are nothing. "What will it avail a man to gain the whole world, if he loseth his soul?" (Matt. xvi. 26.)

And if we say, what our Saviour himself says, that these occupations which tend to the conversion of souls ought not to make us forget what we owe to our own salvation, since it were useless to have contributed to save all the world, if we do not endeavour to save ourselves—what may we not, with greater reason, say of other occupations? Certainly, it is unreasonable in a religious man, to be so entirely absorbed in study, or in any other worldly employment, as to neglect his interior—to neglect prayer, examination of conscience, penance and mortification—to give to spiritual things the last and lowest place in his thoughts—to employ in devotion, that time only which remains after the discharge of other duties, and in case he could not compass both, to choose rather to omit his spiritual duties, than to be remiss in the others. This, in a word, were to live not as a religious person, bnt as a man who had no relish for heavenly things.

St. Dorotheus reports, that his disciple Dositheus discharged the duty of infirmarian so well, was so attentive to the sick, made their beds, dressed their rooms, kept all things so neat, and in such good order, that the saint going one day to visit the infirmary, Dositheussaid to him : "Father, I have a thought of vain glory, which tells me, that I do my duty perfectly well in this employment ; and methinks you ought to be perfectly well satisfied with me." But the answer of the good abbot gave a check to the presumption of his disciple. " I allow," said St. Dorotheus, " that you are grown a very good infirmarian, and very careful ; but I do not perceive as yet, that you are become a good religious man." (Patr. tom. 3. Doct. 11.) Let every one, therefore, use his utmost endeavours, that no man may say of him, you are a good infirmarian or a good porter—you are a great scholar, a learned doctor, or a celebrated preacher ; but you are not a good religious man." For in fact, we entered religion only to become true religious. It is this character we ought to prefer to all others—it is this we ought to seek after with the utmost diligence, and have perpetually before our eyes. Indeed all other things, compared to our advancement in piety, ought to be looked upon as accessaries only, according to the words of our Saviour : " Seek first the kingdom of God and his justice, and all those things shall be added unto you." (Matt. vi. 33.)

We read that some of the Fathers in the desert (Cass. lib. 10), unable to apply themselves continually to prayer and spiritual reading, yet resolving not to spend any of their time idly, employed all their leisure hours in making baskets of palms, or in some other manual labour. And at the end of the year many of them burnt what they had made, having laboured only to give themselves occupation and to avoid idleness. So ought we to make what relates to our spiritual advancement our chief business, and to apply ourselves to all our other affairs, even to those which regard the edification of our neighbour, with the same spirit as these holy Fathers did to making their baskets, that is, without weakening, in the slightest degree, our obligations of working out our salvation and aspiring to perfection. We must then proceed upon this ground, and hold it an infallible maxim, that the spiritual exercises conducive to our advancement in piety must ever be preferred to all other things, and that none of these duties must ever be omitted or neglected on any account whatever. For it is that which maintains us and advances us in virtue : and if we are once negligent therein, we shall soon feel our neglect prejudicial to us. We have but too often experienced, that the derangement of our interior proceeds from our growing cold in spiritual exercises. "My heart is withered within me," says the Psalmist, "because I have forgotten to eat my bread." (Ps. ci. 5.) If the food of our souls is wanting, it is certain, we shall become very feeble and languishing. St. Ignatius earnestly recommends this point, and often insists upon it. "The study," says he, in one place, "of novices and of all others ought to be that of self-denial, and of the most proper means of advancing in virtue and perfection." (III. p. 1. § 28, and R. 12. Sum. Const. &c.) And in another place he says, "Let all devote sufficient time to their spiritual exercises, and endeavour to advance daily in virtue, according to the measure of grace God has given them." And elsewhere he adds, "Let every one be as exact as possible in spending well the time allotted for prayer, meditation, and spiritual reading." And these words, "as exact as possible," deserve, no doubt, particular attention.

Here we can readily perceive, that in whatever business we are engaged, whether in discharging the duties of the trust reposed in us, or in obeying our superiors, it is by no means their intention, that, on this account, we omit our usual spiritual exercises. For it cannot be the intention of any superior, that we should fail in the observance of our rules, and particularly of rules so important and indispensable. Let no one, therefore, attempt to excuse the neglect of his spiritual exercises, under the specious pretext of obedience, alleging, that he could not attend to prayer, the examination of conscience, or to spiritual reading, because he was obliged to fulfil the duties of obedience. For after all, it is not obedience, but it is our own tepidity and

the little relish we have for piety, that hinders us from performing these things. St. Basil (Bas. Ser. Per.) says, we ought to
be very exact in giving to Almighty God the time allotted for
our spiritual exercises. And as, whenever it happens, that
we have not had time to eat and sleep in consequence of our
being obliged to watch with a sick person, and to assist him
in dying well, we take great care to refresh immediately our
wearied bodies, and will be sure to find time for doing so ; in
like manner, in case we are hindered from making our prayer
or examination of conscience at the usual hour, we must
ardently desire to supply that omission, and to acquit ourselves
of these duties as soon as we possibly can.

Whenever, during the time of the spiritual exercises, we are,
through necessity, employed otherwise by our superiors, their
intention is not that we neglect, but only that we defer for a
while these spiritual exercises, and afterwards resume and fully
perform them, according to the saying of the Wise Man :—
" Let nothing hinder you from praying always." (Ecclus. xviii.
22.) He does not say, " hinder no man," but " let nothing
hinder you ; " i.e., let no business make you omit your prayers;
and certainly nothing can make a good religious man omit
them, because he will always find sufficient leisure for them.

In the book called *Bibliotheca Patrum*, it is written of St.
Dorotheus, that though he was often obliged to go very late to
bed, and occasionally to rise in the night in order to entertain
strangers and passengers of whom he had the care, yet he never
omitted rising to prayer, at the same hour with the other religious of the convent. When he perceived that, in consequence
of his great fatigues, the brother whose office it was to call up
the rest of the religious did not knock at the door of his cell,
he requested of one of his companions to do him that kindness,
thought he lately had a violent fever, and was not quite recovered
from it. Thus, indeed, he showed a real desire of not omitting
his spiritual duties, and by not, on every trifling indisposition,
dispensing with himself in them, he was enabled to observe his
rule during the rest of the day. We read likewise in the same
book, that an aged holy monk saw once an angel incensing all
the religious who made haste to come to prayer, and incensing
the very seats of those other religious, who, by reason of lawful
avocations, could not be present at this duty : but the angel
did not incense the seats of such as, through sloth, neglected to
come to choir. This is very proper both to comfort those who,

called elsewhere by obedience, cannot assist with the rest at the common exercises of devotion, and to teach us, not, through our own fault, to absent ourselves from them.

———

CHAPTER II.

What a Love and ardent Desire of Perfection we ought to have.

" BLESSED are they," says the gospel, "who hunger and thirst after justice, for they shall be filled." (Matt. v. 6.)   Though the word "justice" is particularly applied to one of the four cardinal virtues as distinct from the rest; nevertheless, it is very applicable to all the virtues, and to sanctity in general. We give the name of justice to righteousness and to holiness of life, and we call those just, who are holy and virtuous.   The Wise Man says, "That the justice of the righteous shall deliver them " (Prov. xi. 6), that is, they shall be saved by their holiness of life. This word is taken in the same sense in several passages of Scripture. " Unless your justice," says our Saviour, "exceeds that of the Scribes and Pharisees, you shall not enter the kingdom of heaven " (Matt. v. 20) ; *i.e.*, you will not be saved unless you have more virtue, more religion, and more sanctity, than they have.   In the same manner, must be understood what our Saviour said to St. John, when he refused to baptize him :— " For so it becometh us to fulfil all justice " (Matt. iii. 15) ; as if he had said, I must do this to set an example of obedience, of humility, and of all manner of perfection.   We must then take in the same sense, those words I have cited in the beginning of this chapter, and believe that Jesus Christ called those blessed, who have so great a love, and so ardent a desire of virtue, as to feel the same pain from it as is felt from hunger and violent thirst.   St. Jerome writing on this passage, says, it is not enough for us to have a weak desire of virtue and perfection, but we must hunger and thirst after it ; so as to cry out with the Royal Prophet :—"As the hart panteth after the fountains of waters, so my soul panteth after thee, O God ! " (Ps. xli. 2.)

This ardent desire is so necessary to us, that, as I have said in the foregoing chapter, all our spiritual advancement depends upon it.   It is the first principle which disposes us to it, and our only means of acquiring perfection. " The beginning of wisdom," which is nothing else than the knowledge and love of God, wherein this perfection consists, " is to have a real and strong desire to obtain it." (Wis. vi. 18.)   It is with great justice said by philosophers, that the end is the first cause which impels us to act ; so that the more strongly we desire this end the more solicitude and ardour we feel to attain it. I repeat, then, this earnest desire of our spiritual advancement is so necessary—it should spring so immediately from the heart—it should, without the aid of anything else, impel us so forcibly— that there are but little hopes of such as feel not its impulse. Let us give an example in the person of a religious, and every man can apply to it himself, according to his peculiar situation. It is very necessary in religion that the superiors should have a watchful eye over their subjects, and that they reprehend and punish those who do amiss.   Now there can be no greater hope of the religious who does his duty through this motive only. For his regularity of life will last no longer, than while the eye of the superior is on him : and hence, unless what he does springs from the heart, and from a real desire of amendment, there is no reason for relying much on it ; and infallibly this man will not persevere.

There is this difference between things put in motion by an extrinsic principle, and things which move of themselves, that, in the former, the motion weakens, the nearer they approach their term, as happens when a stone is thrown upwards; whereas in the latter, as when the same stone falls to its centre, the nearer they approach their term, the more rapid the motion becomes. The difference will prove the very same between those who act through dread of punishment, desire of esteem, or through human respect of any sort, and those who act through love of virtue and a sincere desire of pleasing God.   These remain always firm and constant in the exercises of piety, but those persevering only while they are reprehended or watched, quickly relapse into their former disorders.

St. Gregory (Hom. 38) tells us of his aunt Gordiana, that when her two sisters, Tharsilla and Emiliana, reprehended her for the levity of her manner, and for her not observing that modesty and reserve so requisite in a person of her profession, she, while the reprehension lasted, put on so serious and com- posed a countenance, that she seemed to take the admonition in good part, and with an intention to profit of it ; but in a little time, this feigned reserve entirely vanishing, she resumed her former manners, spent her time in idle conversations, and thought of nothing but of amusing herself with some seculars who were pensioners in the same monastery. Just as the bow, though bent, when the string is loosened quickly restores itself to its natural form, in like manner the impressions made on this young lady's mind were quickly effaced, as they had been made by an external cause, whose source lay not in her heart.

The affair of Christian perfection is not a business to be done by constraint; it is the heart which must undertake it. Speaking to the young man in the gospel, our Saviour tells him, "If thou wilt be perfect" (Matt. xix. 21); in order to show us that the root of perfection is in our will. For if we have not a sincere desire of becoming perfect, all the care and attention of our superiors will avail nothing. Here we can find the answer to the question put by St. Bonaventure, when he asks : Why was one superior sufficient formerly for one thousand religious, nay for four or five thousand, who, according to St. Jerome and St. Austin, lived under one abbot; and now-a-days one superior is scarce sufficient for ten religious, nay even for a smaller number. (Bon. Rel. Per. T. I. c. 39.) The reason is, because formerly the religious cherished an ardent desire of perfection, and this fire kindling in their hearts, they applied themselves, with all possible zeal, to their spiritual advancement. "The just," says the Wise Man, "shall shine, and shall spread like sparks of fire among reeds." (Wis. iii. 7.) By this metaphor, the Holy Ghost explains very clearly, with what ease and speed just men advance in the paths of virtue, when their hearts are once inflamed with this divine fire. "They shall spread like sparks of fire among reeds." Imagine to yourselves how quick the flame rushes among reeds, when they are set on fire, and you will conceive how the just advance in virtue, when their hearts are once inflamed. This was the case with the ancient hermits, who, for this reason, were so far from having need of a superior to spur them on in their duties, that they needed one to moderate their zeal. But if we feel not these desires in our hearts, so far from one superior being sufficient for ten religious, ten superiors, notwithstanding their united efforts, would not make one religious man perfect against his will. For what will it avail to visit his chamber; to see that he makes his meditation and prayer at the time appointed? The visit being past, cannot he amuse himself as he pleases? And even whilst he is on his knees, cannot he

direct his thoughts to his studies, to business, to trifles? When
he is afterwards to give an account of the state of his conscience,
cannot he say what he pleases, and conceal what is most essential
to be revealed? Cannot he make us believe, that his conscience
is in a good state, while, perhaps, it is in a state of all others
the most deplorable? It is in vain, then, we take all possible
care and precaution to make a man virtuous, unless he sincerely
desires, and strenuously endeavours, to become so himself.

The answer of St. Thomas of Aquin to one of his sisters is
very well adapted to the present subject. She asks him, "How
she could save her soul?" (Hist. Pr. v. 37.) He answered, "By
willing it;" if you desire it, you will be saved, if you desire it,
you will make progress in virtue, you will render yourself
perfect. All then depends on our willing it, *i.e.*, on our willing
it seriously and effectually, and on exerting ourselves with all
possible dilligence to secure our salvation. For Almighty God
is always ready to assist us; but if our own will is wanting, all
the exertions of our superiors are unavailing. It is you yourself,
therefore, that must take your salvation to heart—it is your
own affair—it is you alone that are concerned, and it is for this
alone you entered religion. Let every one, then, be persuaded,
that as soon as he begins to grow tepid and negligent in what
relates to his spiritual advancement—as soon as he abstains from
the exact performance of his exercises of devotion, and feels not
interiorly a great desire of making progress in virtue and of
mortifying himself—from that very moment, he conducts badly
the business of his eternal salvation. This doctrine is conformable to a rule laid down by St. Ignatius in the beginning of his
Constitutions. "It is the interior law," says he, "of charity
and of the divine love imprinted and engraven on our hearts by
the Holy Ghost, which ought to support, guide, and make us
advance in the way of God's service." (Proem. Const. § 1.) It
is this fire of his love, this insatiable desire of his greater glory,
which ought continually urge us to elevate ourselves towards
him, and make us advance in virtue.

This desire once truly imprinted in the soul makes us exert
ourselves with fervour and diligence to attain what we wish for.
For we are naturally active in seeking and finding out the
things we have an inclination for; and it is for this reason the
Wise Man says, "The beginning of wisdom is to excite in
our hearts an earnest desire thereof." (Wis. vi. 18.) But in
this we find another advantage also which renders this means

very efficacious; for let the duties be ever so difficult in themselves, a strong attachment to them makes them easy and sweet.
For example, how comes it to pass, that a religious should feel
so little pain on quitting the world, and entering religion, but
because he desired with his whole heart to become religious?
God had inspired him with an exceeding great desire thereof,
which is the grace of vocation, and plucked out of his heart all
attachment to the world, planted therein a love of retirement
and religion, and everything became easy.   On the contrary,
the very same thing appears extremely painful to persons in the
world, because they have not been favoured by God with the
desires, and the grace of vocation, you have been favoured
with.   As, then, what rendered our entrance into religion so
easy and pleasant, was the fervour we had at the time, and
that determined will, which nor parents, nor friends, nor the
whole earth together, could change or pervert; in like manner,
it is by persevering in this original fervour we shall advance
in virtue, and render the practices of devotion easy and
delightful.   So long as this fervour shall last, the performance
of all religious duties will become easy ; but this once cooling,
they will seem painful and insupportable.   What, think you,
is the reason, why the same man is, at one time, dejected and
disgusted, and at another time is content and at ease in the performance of his religious duties? Let him not attach the blame
thereof to the duties themselves, nor to the superiors, but let him
impute this inconstancy to himself, and to the little relish he
has for virtue and mortification.   A strong, healthy man, says
Father Avila, will, with ease, carry that burden, which a child
or sick person cannot raise from the ground.   It is only then
from the different dispositions of our souls, that the difficulty
springs.   The duties are always the same.   They seem to us,
for a time, so easy, that they cost us no trouble ; and if they
appear different now from what they had been before, we are
to blame ourselves, who, instead of being perfect men, as long
since we ought to have been, are still children in virtue—are
fallen sick, and have suffered that fervour to cool, which we
had on entering religion.

———o———

CHAPTER III.

That an ardent Desire of our Spiritual Advancement is a Means and Disposition most proper for obtaining Favours from God.

WHAT renders so very necessary this desire, and as I may say, this hunger and thirst for our spiritual advancement, is, that we cannot have a better disposition than this is for obtaining from God the perfection we aim at. St. Ambrose says, that the Lord is so well pleased with the man who feels this longing desire, that he fills his soul with graces and favours ; and in support of this assertion, he quotes these words of the Blessed Virgin in her canticle : " The Lord has filled the hungry with good things." (Luke i. 35.) The Royal Prophet has said the same before : " The Lord has filled the empty soul, and has satiated the hungry and thirsty soul with good things." (Ps. cvi. 9.)

Here then we see, as has been observed in a former chapter, that, in recompense of their good-will, the fervour whereof is most pleasing in his eyes, God has heaped his favours and riches on those who have had so great a zeal for perfection as, in a manner, to have hungered and thirsted after it. An angel appeared to Daniel, and told him his prayers were heard, because " he was a man of desires." (Dan. ix. 23.) The desire David had of building a temple was so pleasing to God, that though he did not permit him to carry his design into execution, yet, as if he had executed it, the Lord, to recompense him, confirmed the crown to his posterity. In fine, so earnest was Zacheus's desire of seeing the Redeemer, that Jesus first looked up to him in the sycamore tree, saying, " Zacheus, make haste and come down, for this day I must abide in thy house." (Luke xix. 5.) But the truth of this maxim is still more clearly set forth by Solomon, who, speaking of wisdom, which is nothing else than God himself, says : " Wisdom is easily seen by those that love it, and is soon found by them that seek it." (Wis. vi. 13.) But do you know with what facility it is found? "It preventeth them that covet it, and it showeth itself first to them." (Ib. vi. 14.) It is at hand the moment you wish for it. "He that rises early to seek it shall not go far before he meets it, he shall find it sitting at his door." (Ib. vi. 15.) How infinite is the goodness and mercy of God ! He is not content with coming to seek us and to knock often at our door; " Behold," says he, in the Apocalypse, "how I stand at your door and knock?" (Ap. iii. 20);

and in the Canticles, " Open, my sister, the door to me." (Cant. v. 2.) He is not content with all this, but as if he were tired of knocking, he sits down himself at our door, to let us know, that, he would have entered before, had he not found it shut ; and still, instead of going away and leaving us, he chooses rather to sit down and wait for us, that we may be sure of finding him as soon as we open the door. Though you have delayed to open your heart to God and to comply with his inspirations, yet he has not, on this account, gone away. He has too great a desire of entering, to be so easily repulsed ; and therefore he sits at the door and waits till you open. " The Lord waits," says Isaiah, " that he may shew mercy to you." (Is. xxx. 18.) And certainly no friend is so eager to visit an intimate friend, as God is to visit our hearts ; he longs much more to communicate himself, and grant his favours to us, than we long to receive them ; the only thing he requires of us is, to hunger and thirst after them. "To him that thirsts I will give of the fountain of the water of life gratis." (Ap. xxi. 6.) " If any man, therefore, thirsts, let him come to me and drink." (John vii. 37.) He would have us feel an earnest desire of acquiring virtue and perfection, that the object of our desires being granted, we may know how to esteem and preserve it as a most precious jewel. For in general, what-ever is not earnestly wished for is, when obtained, not much esteemed. One of the principal reasons why we make so little progress in perfection is, because we do not desire and long for it so earnestly as we ought ; we have some desires, it is true, but then they are so weak and languid that they vanish almost as soon as they are felt.

St. Bonaventure (Process. iv. Rel. c. 3) says that there are many who intend well, and who conceive the best projects imaginable, yet have not courage enough to offer violence to themselves, and to overcome themselves as far as to carry their good projects into execution. Hence we may say of them what the apostle said of himself : " To will is present with me, but to accomplish that which is good, I find not." (Rom. vii. 18.) These projects without effect are not the productions of a resolute will, and to speak properly they are but mere velleities ; in a word, we will, but we do not will effectually. " The slothful," says the Wise Man, " wills and does not will." (Prov. xiii. 4.) " His desires kill him, for his hands will not work at all. He spends himself all the day long in desires." (Ib. xxi. 25.) " He is a compound of desires," says St. Jerome ; and Father Avila very justly compares him to those who, in their dreams, imagine they do great feats, but when they awake have not courage to undertake anything, as is said by the Prophet Isaiah : " He that is hungry sometimes dreams that he eats, but when he awakes, his soul is empty as before." (Isa. xxix. 8.) This description of persons fancy, while at prayer, that they burn with a desire of suffering, and of being despised, but on the first occasion that presents itself after prayer, they behave in a manner quite different from what they had fancied to themselves; for in fact, it was not a real desire, but a sort of dream they had at the time. By others they are compared to soldiers represented on the canvas, who always brandish their swords over the enemy's head, but never strike ; and this is one of the senses wherein may be taken the following words of the Psalmist : " Men are like images" (Ps. xxxviii. 7)—they hold the arm always raised, but they strike not. Comparing them likewise to women in labour, who cannot be delivered, we may apply to them these words of Ezekias in Isaiah : " The children are come even to the birth, and the mothers have not strength to bring them forth." (Isa. xxxvii. 3.) St. Jerome, explaining these words of St. Matthew : " Woe to such as are with child and give suck in those days" (Matt. xxiv. 19), says, Woe to those souls that have not brought up their buds to the maturity of a perfect man—woe to those, who have not brought forth the good desires they had conceived, but who extinguish them in their breasts ; for when we do not carry them into effect, we do not extinguish them ? And woe to those who pass all their life in wishes, and are surprised by death, before they perform any good work. For then they will derive not only no advantage from having had those good desires, but they shall be severely punished for not having carried them into execution. In fine, they will see their own children they had conceived rise up against them, when, had they brought them forth, they might have derived great advantage from them.

Holy Scripture (2 Kings xviii. 9) tells us, that Absalom had a most comely head of hair ; but it only proved his ruin. For the bough of an oak having, in his flight, caught him by the hair, he hung between heaven and earth, and in that situation was killed by Joab. Death will surprise us in the same manner, while our good desires hold us, as it were, suspended ; and these good desires will make, in part, the subject of our condemnation. St. John says in the Apocalypse (Apoc. xii. 4), that he saw a woman in labour, and that there lay near her a horrible dragon, watching till she should be delivered, that he might devour the child. It is this the devil, with all his power, endeavours to do to us, whenever the soul has conceived a good design. We ought, therefore, be very careful to proceed, as soon as we can, to the execution of any good resolution we have formed. · St. Bernard says, that the prophet Isaiah meant the same thing, by the short and pithy sentence, " If you seek, seek " (Isa. xxi. 12); *i.e.*, be not weary of desiring, be not weary of seeking, for true desires require fervour and perseverance; they must be fervent, they must be efficacious, they must, in fine, be such as, according to the prophet Micheas, may excite in us a continual care always to please God more and more : " I will shew you, O man," says he, " what it is which is good, and what our Lord requires of you. It is to do justice, to love mercy, and to be careful to walk always with your God." (Mic. vi. 8.) Behold these are the desires he expects on our part, in order to bestow on us his graces and treasures. Happy are the souls that feel this hunger and thirst to be, of all things, the most urgent; for they shall be satiated and shall have all their desires most fully accomplished. We read in the Life of St. Gertrude, that our Saviour appearing one day to her, told her, that he had given to every good soul a golden tube, that through it they may imbibe from his sacred side as much grace as they could desire : and that golden tube, as he afterwards declared, was no other than a holy and upright will, whereby we draw down on ourselves all sorts of blessings from God.

———o———

CHAPTER IV.

The more we apply ourselves to Spiritual Things, the more earnestly shall we desire them.

" THEY that eat me shall yet hunger, and they that drink me shall yet thirst " (Ecclus. xxiv. 29), says the Holy Ghost, speaking of wisdom. St. Gregory says, there is this difference between the pleasures of the body, and the pleasures of the soul, that we desire the former with great impatience, when we have them not, and when we have possessed them, we set but little value on them. For example, in the world every man, according to his birth, quality, and profession, longs very much for some civil, military, or ecclesiastical preferment. Scarce, however, does he obtain the object of his desire, when he begins to contemn it, and to fix his eyes on something else, which, when obtained, he is, in like manner, as soon weary of: in short, unable to regulate his ambition or to set bounds to his desires, he still gapes after something new, and never rests satisfied with what he has. But it is not so in spiritual things. For when we have them not, we feel for them disrelish and aversion; but when once we possess them, it is then we begin to know their value; it is then we set still higher value on them, and the more we taste them, the more earnestly we seek after them. The reason of this difference, says this great saint, is, that the enjoyment of temporal goods unfolds to us their vanity and emptiness; so that not finding in them the satisfaction we hoped for, we contemn what we possess; and expecting to find in something else the content we seek after, we suffer ourselves to be carried away by new desires. But still we deceive ourselves—these new desires will meet the same fate as the others. For, as we are not made for this world, there is in it nothing which can fully satiate our appetite. This is what our Saviour taught the Samaritan woman, when he told her, "Whoever drinks of this water shall thirst again" (John iv. 13); because all the pleasures of this life cannot quench the thirst of man, who is created for heaven. But as to spiritual goods and pleasures, we never love or desire them so much, as when we possess them; because then we best know their value, and the more perfectly we possess them, the greater is our desire and thirst after them. The same St. Gregory says, it is not to be wondered that we do not desire spiritual things, when so far from having experienced how sweet they are, we have not even begun to taste them: "For how can any one love that he is ignorant of?" (Hom. 16.) The Apostle St. Peter also says, "If nevertheless you have tasted how sweet the Lord is" (1 Pet. ii. 3); and the Royal Prophet, "Taste and see how sweet the Lord is." (Ps. xxxiii. 9). Because when once we begin to taste the Lord, and to relish spiritual things, we shall experience such sweetness in them, as to render our desires of them insatiable. By these words, then, "those who eat me shall yet hunger, and those who drink me shall yet thirst," we must understand, that the more assiduously we apply ourselves to heavenly things, the more frequently and fervently shall we feel the desire of possessing them.

But you will ask me, how can this accord with what our Saviour says to the Samaritan, " He that shall drink of the water I shall give him shall never thirst ?" (John iv. 13). Here the Son of God says that we shall never thirst, if we drink of the water he shall give ; and the Holy Ghost, by the mouth of the Wise Man, says, " 'That the more we drink, the more we shall thirst." How shall we reconcile one with the other such different assertions ? The holy Fathers reply, that by the words of Jesus Christ to the Samaritan, we are to understand, that whoever drinks of the living water therein described, " shall never thirst after sensual pleasures ;" because the sweetness of spiritual things will give him an absolute disrelish for things of the world, and will render them quite insipid. As when you have tasted honey, says St. Gregory, everything else will seem sour and bitter ; in like manner, when we have tasted God and spiritual things, all that savours of any affinity to and contagion of flesh and blood will become insipid and excite a loathing. But as to the words of the Wise Man, " Those who eat me shall yet hunger, and those who drink me shall yet thirst" (Ecclus. xxiv. 29), we must consider them to relate to spiritual things, and we must understand, that the more we taste them, the more we shall feel our hunger and thirst for them to increase. For being then come to a better knowledge of their worth and having experienced their sweetness, we shall, in consequence, be impelled to be more zealous in seeking after them. It is thus the holy doctors reconcile these two passages.

But then, how can this accord with what our Saviour says again in the Gospel, "Blessed are they that hunger and thirst after justice ; because they shall be filled ?" (Matt. v. 6.) Here he says that he will fill those who shall hunger and thirst after justice ; and there the Wise Man assures us, that such as shall eat and drink of wisdom, shall always find the same hunger and thirst as before. Now, how is it possible that things so opposite can exist together ? how is it possible to reconcile assertions so different ? It is very easy to do it. It is the privilege and the excellence of spiritual things to satisfy, and, at the same time, to excite our appetite ; to quench, and still to excite our thirst ; and, in a word, to cause that the more we eat and drink of them, the more we hunger and thirst after them. But then it is a hunger, which, instead of making us faint and weak, renders us strong and hearty; and it is a thirst, which, instead of pain, imparts great pleasure to us. It is true, that it is only in heaven we shall be perfectly satisfied, according to these words, " I shall be satisfied when I shall see thee in thy glory" (Ps. xvi. 15); and these others, "They shall be inebriated with the plenty of thy house." (Ps. xxxv. 9.) However, the above words of the Wise Man must be understood according to the interpretation of St. Bernard, who says we shall never be in such manner satisfied with the sight of God as to be without a desire of, and thirst after his sight; because, instead of giving us disgust, it will excite in us perpetually a new desire of seeing and enjoying him. In the Apocalypse, St. John, speaking of the blessed who assisted at the throne, and before the Lamb, says, " That they sung as it were a new song." (Apoc. xiv. 3.) This is to show us, that this song will always contain something new, and will excite in us new joy, and new admiration, which will make us continually cry out, as the children of Israel did in first seeing the manna fall in the desert, " Manhu ?" that is to say, " What is this ?" It is just so with spiritual things here below ; for being an emanation from those above, they, in consequence, participate of their qualities and virtue. On the one hand they satisfy and fill our hearts, and on the other, they excite in us extreme hunger and thirst. The more we devote ourselves to them, the more we relish them ; and the more we enjoy them, the more we con- tinually hunger and thirst after them. But then this very hunger will be a kind of satiety, and this thirst a most sweet and agreeable refreshment to the soul. All this ought to excite in us a high idea of spiritual things ; it ought to make us set a great value on them, and devote ourselves to them with such zeal and fervour, that regardless of, and scorning all the allure- ments and vanities of this world, we may say with the prince of the apostles, " Lord, it is good for us to be here." (Matt. xvii. 4.)

CHAPTER V.

That the Desire a Man has of becoming perfect in Virtue, is a great Mark that he is in a State of Grace.

WHAT ought urge us to wish still more ardently for our advance- ment in perfection, and to renew our efforts to please God daily still more and more, and what ought, at the same time, to be of very great consolation to us, is that there can be no mark more certain than this of God's dwelling in a soul, and of the good state it is in. St. Bernard says, that there is no more certain mark of God being present in a man's heart than the desire of still increasing in grace, and he proves it by the saying of the Wise Man, already quoted, "Those that eat me shall still hunger and those that drink me shall still thirst." If then you hunger and thirst for heavenly things, rejoice, since it is an evident sign that God dwells in your soul It is he who excites in you this hunger and thirst; and you have certainly found the true vein of this precious mine, because you constantly adhere so closely to it As the terrier, whilst he meets nothing, beats the field without spirit, but on finding the scent, pursues eagerly, and stops not till he runs down the game; in like manner whoever tastes the sweetness of the divine odour runs after it without ceasing, and cries out with the spouse in the Canticles, "Draw me after thee, we will run in the odour of thy divine perfumes." (Cant. i. 3.) It is God who is within you that draws you thus after him. But if you feel not this kind of hunger and thirst, you may justly fear that God dwells not in your heart; for, as we have already said after St. Gregory, it is peculiar to spiritual things, that when we do not possess them, we love them not, and are no ways concerned about them.

St. Bernard said he trembled, and his hair stood of an end, as often as he reflected on these words of the Holy Ghost, uttered by the mouth of the Wise Man, "Man knows not whether he deserves love or hatred." (Eccles. ix. 1.) This passage is terrible, says this great saint, and I shook with horror as often as I thought on it; never without trembling repeating that sentence, "Who knows whether he deserves love or hatred?" (Serm. 23 on the Cant.) If then this reflection made a great saint tremble, who was, as it were, a living pillar of the Church, what effect ought it to have on us, who, on account of our sins, have so many causes of fear, "who carry within us the answer of death?" (2 Cor. i. 9.) I am certain I have offended God, but am ignorant whether or not he has forgiven me; who would not tremble on making this reflection? But if we could possibly be assured that our sins were remitted, and that we are in God's grace; if we could find a certainty of this, what value ought we not set on it? For though without a particular revelation from God, we cannot have in this life an infallible certainty that we are in a state of grace, yet there are signs that give a moral probability of it, and the surest mark we can have is to feel in our hearts an ardent desire of daily perfecting ourselves more and more in virtue. So that there can be no need of any motive but this to urge us to cherish this desire, since it gives us, in some measure, an assurance that we are in the state of grace, than which nothing in this life can be of greater consolation.

This may be easily confirmed by what the Holy Ghost says in the Proverbs: "The ways of the just are like the sun that rises, and increases both in light and heat till mid-day." (Prov. iv. 18) The farther they proceed, the more they increase in virtue, and to use the words of St. Bernard, the just man never believes that he has fully performed his duty ; he never says it is enough, but always hungers and thirsts after justice; so that if he were to live here always, he would perpetually strive to become more just and more perfect, and to advance always from good to better. (Ep. 253 to Ab. Gaurin.) Again it is written of the just, "they shall proceed from virtue to virtue" (Ps. lxxxiii. 8) ; *i.e.*, they shall continually increase in fervour, and advance in virtue without stopping till they ascend the height of perfection. But the way of the tepid, the imperfect, and the wicked, is like unto the light of the evening, which, decreasing every moment, at length disappears, and leaves us in the darkness of night. "The way of the wicked," says the Wise Man, "is full of darkness, so that they cannot see the precipices into which they fall." (Prov. iv. 19.) They stumble every step they take. Their confusion is so great, and their blindness so deplorable, and they see not their faults, and feel no remorse for them. On the contrary, judging of sins according to their fancy, they will not believe that to be a sin which is so in reality, and will often think that to be but venial which is mortal ; nay, will consider it to be nothing more than a trivial imperfection.

CHAPTER VI.

That not to advance in Virtue is to go back:

It is a maxim received by all holy men, that in the way of God we certainly go back, if we do not advance. This is the point I intend to demonstrate here, that it may be a powerful motive to encourage us daily to make new progress in perfection. For what man is there, that, after having travelled homeward several days, would feel inclined to go back, particularly when he calls to mind the sentence the Saviour of the world pronounces against him, " Whosoever puts his hand to the plough and looks back is not fit for the kingdom of heaven ?" (Luke ix. 62.)   These are the words which should make us tremble ; and the great St. Austin, upon this occasion, says, we cannot possibly prevent ourselves from descending, but by always striving to ascend ; for as soon as we begin to stop, we descend, and not to advance, is to go back ; so that if we wish not to go back, we must always run forward without stopping. (Ep. 113 to Dem. Vir.)   St. Gregory, St. Chrysostom, St. Leo Pope, and many other saints, say the same, and express themselves almost in the same terms.   But St. Bernard enlarges on this subject in two of his epistles, wherein addressing himself to a negligent and tepid religious, who contents himself with leading an ordinary life, and struggles not for his advancement, he thus discourses with him in the following dialogue : "Well ! will you not advance ?   No.   What then ?   Will you go back ?   By no means.   What will you do then ?   I will remain as I am, and grow neither better nor worse.   Then you will do what is impossible, for in this life there can be no state of permanency. This is a privilege appertaining to God alone, " With whom there is no change nor the least shadow of vicissitude." (Jas. i. 17.)   " I am the Lord," says he, "and I do not change." (Mal. iii. 6.)   But all things in this world are subject to a perpetual change.   " All shall grow old like a garment," says the Psalmist, speaking of the heavens, " and as a garment thou shalt change them ; but as for thee, O Lord ! thou art always the self-same, and thy years shall not fail." (Ps. ci. 28.)   Man, above all, according to the testimony of holy Job, is never long in the same condition ; " He passeth like a shadow, and never continueth in the same state." (Job, xiv. 2.)   Jesus Christ himself, as St. Bernard adds, as long as he lived here on earth and conversed with man, was never stationary ; "He grew in wisdom, age, and favour, before God and men. (Luke ii. 52.) That is to say, that as he grew in age, he gave more   signal proofs of his wisdom and holiness, " And prepared himself as a champion to run his race" (Ps. xviii. 7) of labour and sufferings. St. John also declares, that " Whoever saith he abideth in him, ought himself also to walk even as he.walked." (1 John, ii. 6.) But if, while our Saviour runs on, you stop, is it not clear that you will remain behind him instead of approaching near him ?

Holy Scripture (Gen. xxviii. 12) tells us, that Jacob saw a ladder reaching from earth to heaven, on the top of which Almighty God leaned, and that it was full of angels ascending and descending perpetually without ever resting. Now, according to St. Bernard, this is to show us, that in the way of virtue, there is no medium between ascending and descending, between advancing and going back. But as when we work at the lathe, the wheel flies back when we wish to stop it, even so, the very moment you cease to advance in virtue, you must of necessity go back. Abbot Theodore explains the same thought in these terms related by Cassin (Cas. Collat. vi.): We must, says he, apply ourselves without remissness to the study of virtue, and strenuously exert ourselves in the practice thereof, lest ceasing to grow better, we should instantly begin to grow less perfect ; for, as was already said, our souls cannot remain long in the same state, so as not to increase or decrease in virtue ; but not to gain is to lose, and whoever feels not in himself a desire of making progress is in danger of falling instantly.

The same Cassian explains this by a very just comparison, which St. Gregory (Greg. iii. 2. past. adm. 51.) likewise makes use of. Those who lead a spiritual life, says he, are like a man in the midst of a rapid river ; if he stops but for a moment, and strives not continually to bear up against the stream, he will run great risk of being carried down. Now, the course we ought to take is so directly opposite to the current of our nature corrupted by sin, that unless we labour and force ourselves to go on, we shall certainly be hurried back by the impetuous torrent of our passions.

" The kingdom of heaven is to be taken by storm, and it is only the violent that carry it." (Matt. xi. 12.) And, as when you go against the tide, you must always row without ceasing, and when you stop but for a while, you find yourself drifted far from the spot you had rowed to ; so here you must still push forward, and make head against the current of your depraved passions, unless you be content to see yourself quickly carried far back from that degree of perfection which you had before attained. St. Jerom and St. Chrysostom elucidate this truth still more by quoting a point of doctrine universally approved of, and which is stated by St. Thomas (St. Th. ii. 2. 9. 84. ar. 5. ad. 2.) in the following words : A religious life, says he, is a state of perfection : not that a man becomes perfect as soon as he becomes a religious, but because religious have a more strict obligation of aspiring to perfection ; and because he who strives not to become perfect, and who does not apply himself in good earnest to it, cannot be said to be a true religious, as he does not do the only thing for which he should have embraced that profession.   I will not here discuss the question, whether a religious would sin mortally who should say, "I content myself with being faithful to the commandments of God and to my essential vows ; but as for other rules not binding under pain of sin, I design not to observe them." My intention, I say, is not to decide this point, as it is a disputed question.   Some divines maintain that he would sin mortally ; others say he would not, unless he acts through some kind of contempt on the occasion. But what is certain, and what they all agree in, is, that a religious in such a disposition of mind, and who would make such a resolution, would give very bad example, and, morally speaking, would be in great danger of falling into mortal sin.   "For he that despiseth small things will by little and little fall into great." (Ecclus. xix. l.)

To explain this the more clearly, St. Chrysostom gives several familiar examples : If a servant, says he, were not a thief nor drunkard, nor gamester, but trusty, sober, and without vice ; yet, if he should idle his time, sit down all day, without performing the duties of his state, there is no doubt but he would deserve to be severely punished ; for though he did no positive harm, yet it is fault enough to neglect what he ought to do.   Again, if a husbandman, though exceedingly well conducted in every other respect, should nevertheless stand with his arms across, and neither plough nor sow, it is certain, though he did no other harm, he would, on this account alone, be culpable ; for it is fault enough to neglect one's duty.   In fine, if one of our hands gave us no pain, but were paralytic, and absolutely of no use to us, should we not consider that circumstance alone to be of great detriment ?   It is just so in spiritual matters.   If a religious remains idle—if he makes no effort to advance in virtue, he is much to be blamed, because he fulfils not the obligations of his profession.   To conclude, what greater fault can we find with land, than that it is barren and bears no crop, though it had been well tilled ?   In the same manner, if land, like your soul, continually cultivated by so many good instructions, watered by frequent showers of heavenly graces, and warmed by the rays of the sun of justice, produces no fruit, but remains dry and barren, will you not think that dryness and barrenness a great misfortune to yourself? It is of this the Psalmist complains, when he says, "They returned me evil for good, and afforded me nothing but barrenness." (Ps xxxiv. 14.)

Another comparison is also made use of, which suits the present purpose, and strongly confirms what has been already said. As sailors on the main ocean dread nothing so much as a calm, because then they consume all their provisions, and afterwards feel themselves in want of the necessaries of life ; so by those who navigate the tempestuous sea of the world, and steer towards heaven, there is nothing more to be dreaded than an unhappy calm, which stops them in the midst of their course, and prevents them from making sail. Because the small provision they had laid in for their voyage is soon consumed, and the little virtue they had begins to fail them ; and afterwards amidst the storms and temptations which assail them on all sides, they find themselves, even in their deepest distress, destitute of all help, and in the greatest danger of perishing. Woe to such as are surprised by a calm so dangerous. "You did once run well," says the apostle, "who has hindered you from obeying the truth ?" (Gal. v. 7.) You went at first in full sail, what calm or sand-bank has stopped you? Certainly "you are satiated, you are become rich." (1 Cor. iv. 8.) You fancy you have done enough ; feeling yourself tired, you think yourself entitled to repose ; you imagine that your present stock is sufficient. But reflect and consider well, that you have still a great way to go, for "that part of your journey that still remains is very long." (3 Kings xix. 7.) Be persuaded that many occasions will still offer, wherein you will have need of more perfect humility, more courageous patience, more absolute detachment, and more constant mortification ; and perchance you will be surprised and found unprovided, at the time of your greatest distress.

———o———

CHAPTER VII.

That a good Means of attaining Perfection is to continually think on what we are deficient in—without thinking on what we have acquired.

"Let him that is just become still more just, and let him that is holy become still more holy." (Apoc. xxii. 13.) St. Jerome and venerable Bede tell us, that our Saviour in saying, "Blessed are those who hunger and thirst after justice, for they shall be filled," wished to teach us, that we must never think we are just enough, but must always aspire to greater justice, as St. John recommends in the above passage. To this effect St. Paul proposes to us an excellent means he himself had made use of. "Brethren," says he, "I do not count myself to have apprehended. But one thing I do; forgetting the things that are behind, and stretching forth myself to those that are before, I pursue towards the mark for the prize of the supernal vocation of God in Christ Jesus." (Phil. iii. 13.) If, then, the apostle of the Gentiles, the vessel of election, does not believe himself perfect, who will dare think himself so? He believes not that he has attained perfection, but endeavours all he possibly can, to acquire it. For this purpose he forgets all he has done, and only looks to what he is deficient in, and it is to obtain this, that he excites and encourages himself with all his might. All the saints have very much extolled and earnestly recommended this means as having been prescribed and recommended by the apostle. Hence St. Basil and St. Jerome teach, that whoever wishes to be a saint, must forget what he has done, and constantly think on what he has still to do, and that *he* is truly happy who advances daily, and who never thinks on what he did yesterday, but what he has to do to-day in order to make new progress.

But St. Gregory and St. Bernard descend more to particulars, and say, that this means prescribed by St. Paul consists of two principal parts. The first is to forget the good we have done, and never to look back at it. Certainly we stand much in need of this warning in particular; for it is very natural in us to cast our eyes on what is pleasing, and to turn them away from what may be displeasing. Hence taking pleasure in looking at our improvement, and the good we fancy we have done; and on the contrary, feeling it painful to think on our spiritual wants and poverty, we are inclined to dwell rather on the former than on the latter. St. Gregory says, that as a sick man in a burning fever, is always searching for the coolest and softest part of his bed to find a little ease, even so human weakness ordinarily fixes its eye on the good it has done. But St. Bernard says, that there is extreme danger in this. For if you look only to the good works you have done, you will readily yield to vain glory, preferring yourself to others; you will not endeavour to ascend, believing yourself already arrived at a high degree of perfection. In a word, you will begin to grow tepid, and from tepidity falling into negligence, you will quickly bring on your ruin. The example of the Pharisee in the gospel shows us plainly what must befall those who act in this manner. He cast his eyes on the good works he had done, and then enumerating them, he says, " I thank thee, O God, that I am not as the rest of men, extortioners, unjust, adulterers, or such as this publican. I fast twice in the week : I give tithes of all that I possess. And the publican standing affar off would not do so much as lift up his eyes to heaven: but striking his breast, saying, O God be merciful to me a sinner. I declare to you," says our Saviour, " this man went down to his house more justified than the other." (Luke xviii. 11, 14.) Thus we see the one by humbling himself was justified, while the other by his criminal presumption drew upon himself the sentence of his condemnation and of his death. This is the plan the devil has formed against us. By always representing to us the good we have done, his design is to instil into us a high esteem of ourselves, and a contempt of our neighbour, that by yielding to pride, we may bring on our own condemnation.

There is still another danger, as St. Bernard says, in looking back on the good we have done. For we will in consequence, make no effort to advance ; we will grow cold in the business of heaven, and at length fancying that we have done enough we will think only on resting ourselves. As travellers when they begin to grow weary, look behind and consider the journey they have made ; just so when those on the road of perfection begin to get tired, they look back to the journey they have made, and imagining they have advanced a great deal, they content themselves, and through shameful sloth, stop half way.

In order to avoid these inconveniences, we must always think not on what we have already done, but on what still remains to be done. For the former tempts us to stop, while the latter incites us to go on with our work. This is the second branch of the means the apostle teaches us—to have our eyes fixed on what we are deficient in, that we may be encouraged to attain it. St. Gregory explains this by several familiar comparisons, and says, that as a man who owes a thousand crowns does not think his debt discharged by his having paid three or four hundred, but still reflects on what he is still to pay, and cannot be at ease till he has fully satisfied his creditor, so we, who are deeply indebted to Almighty God, ought not to reckon upon what we have paid, but always consider what we are still to pay in order to satisfy the debt that remains, and mind nothing else than applying ourselves continually to find out the means of doing so. Again as men on a road, who travel with a firm resolution of arriving at their journey's end, never look back to see how many miles they have already gone, but consider how far they have yet to go, and think of nothing else till they arrive at the destined place : in like manner, we, who are travellers in this world, and purpose to go to heaven, our native country, ought not to consider how far we have gone, but how far we have yet to go, and how to get thither. When a man, adds he, undertakes a journey to any place, it avails him nothing to have gone a great way, unless he continues to go on till he comes to his journey's end, because it is only at his arrival there he can expect the recompense of all his labour. It is therefore of no avail, that you run well at first, if you get tired in the middle of your course ; and hence the apostle counsels us :— " Run so as you may carry the prize." (1 Cor. ix. 24.) Never look back upon the space you have left behind, but keep your eyes fixed upon the goal you aim at. Consider that it is perfection you ought to aspire to, and think how far you have yet to go to arrive there, and, in consequence, you will make haste still to advance; for, as Chrysostom says, a man never ceases to run whilst he thinks he is not yet arrived at the end of his journey.

St. Bernard says, that we ought to imitate merchants, who, though they have acquired considerable property and encountered much hardship and pain, yet so far from being content with their gain or discouraged by their losses, constantly endeavour to acquire additional property, as if hitherto they had neither done nor gained anything. It is in the same manner, says he, we ought constantly endeavour to increase our store, and to enrich ourseves in humility, charity, mortification, and in all the virtues ; and, in a word, like good merchants for heaven, we ought make no account of the slight pains we have hitherto felt nor of the riches we have acquired. It is for this reason our blessed Saviour, in St. Matthew, compares the kingdom of heaven to a merchant, and commands us, "To traffic till he comes." (Luke xix. 13.)

And the better to explain this example proposed by our Saviour himself, you must observe what great care the merchant always takes not to lose any opportunity of gaining. Let your conduct be the same as his. Lose no opportunity of making some new progress in virtue, and as St. Ignatius says, " Let us encourage one the other never to lose any degree of perfection, which by the mercy of God, it is in our power to attain." (Reg. 15. Sum.)

Suffer nothing to escape without endeavouring to derive some advantage from it. An angry word is said to you ; you are commanded to do something against your will ; an opportunity of humbling yourself is offered—from all these things, if made proper use of, you will derive considerable advantage. We ought to seek after occasions of this nature, and purchase them at any price : and as a merchant never lies down with more satisfaction than after the day on which he made several good and advantageous bargains, so a religious ought to think that he never succeeds better in his profession, and ought never to go to bed with more comfort than after the day whereon he met with many occasions of exercising his humility and patience. A merchant is no ways troubled at the losses of another, nor is he angry with him upon this account, but thinks and often reflects with joy on his own particular gain: in like manner, a religious ought never examine whether another did well or ill in giving him the mortification he received, nor be angry with him for it, but he ought to rejoice at the particular advantage he derived therefrom. If we acted in this manner, we would not so readily lose our peace of mind on such occasions. For when those very things which of their own nature are capable of depriving us of it, and exciting discontent in us, are the only things we seek after and desire, what can happen, that can ever disturb our peace, or cause us any affliction of mind ?

Consider, moreover, with what great care and industry the merchant applies to everything which can promote his own interest ; how he thinks of nothing else, and how ardently he undertakes any affair wherein there is the least appearance or hope of gain ; whether he is at table ; whether he lies down or gets up ; whether he is asleep or awake ; in fine, wheresoever he is, or whatsoever he does, that affair alone engages his thoughts and allows him not to enjoy repose. In the same manner we must proceed in the affair of our salvation, having our mind and heart entirely engaged with it ; and we should be ever attentive to derive some spiritual profit from every even the least occasion that presents itself. This is the thought which should always accompany us, at table, at our going to bed, and getting up ; in all our actions and in all our exercises, at all times, and in all places during our whole life. This is our only business. If we do *this well*, we need desire nothing more, and in fact, it is not worth our while to trouble ourselves even for a moment about everything else. To all this St. Bonaventure (B. II. Rel. Prof., c. i.) adds, that as a good merchant never finds in one country all he wants, but often travels into different countries to find many things; even so a religious ought to seek for his spiritual advancement not only in prayer, meditation, and interior consolations, but also in resisting temptations, in mortifying his senses, in suffering injuries, pain, and labour, and in discharging his duty on all occasions that present themselves.

If we seek, in this manner, after virtue, we shall be rich in a short time. "If you seek for wisdom," says Solomon, "as men seek for riches; and if you dig for it, as you would to find a treasure, you shall then know what is the fear of the Lord, and you shall learn the true science of God." (Prov. ii. 4, 5.) What God demands of us here, says St. Bernard, is not much; since for gaining the treasure of true wisdom, which is God himself, he requires no more exertion on our part than is usually made to gain earthly riches which are subject to a thousand accidents, and whereof the enjoyment is so short and so troublesome. To keep, then, a proportion in things, were it not proper, that as there is an infinite difference between spiritual and temporal goods, so there should also be as great a difference between our manner of seeking the one and that of our seeking the other. It is also a great shame and confusion to us, that worldly men desire those things that are pernicious to them, with more earnestness than we desire those things that are of the greatest advantage, and that they run faster to *death*, than we do to *life*.

It is set down in Ecclesiastical History (Part II. B. VI. c. i) that the holy Abbot Pambo going one day to Alexandria, and meeting with a courtezan very finely dressed, began to weep bitterly, crying out several times : Alas ! what a wretched man I am ! And his disciples having asked him, why he wept so bitterly ? he answered : Would you not have me weep to see this unfortunate woman take more care and diligence to please men, than I do to please God ; and to see her take more pains to lay snares for men, in order to drag them into hell, than I use endeavours to gain them to Jesus Christ, and to conduct them to heaven ? We read also of St. Francis Xaverius that he was ashamed and extremely troubled on seeing that merchants had arrived before him in Japan, and that they had been more diligent to sail thither to sell their merchandise, than he had been to carry thither the treasures of the gospel, to propagate the faith, and to increase the kingdom of God. Let us adopt the same sentiments, and be filled with a holy confusion, on seeing, "That the children of this world are wiser" (Luke xvi. 8), and more careful in the concerns of this life, that we are in the affairs of heaven, and let this prevent us from remaining any longer in our sloth and tepidity.

———

CHAPTER VIII.

To aim at the highest Things is very conducive to the Attainment of Perfection.

IT will conduce much to our spiritual advancement, that we propose to ourselves as objects the highest things, and such as are of more exquisite perfection, according to the counsel of the apostle, " Be zealous for the better gifts. And I yet shew to you a more excellent way." (1 Cor. xii. 31.) This means is without doubt of very great importance ; for our desires must necessarily soar high, if we wish to elevate our actions to that perfection, with which even our indispensable duties should be performed. This may be easily explained by a familiar comparison : when your bow is too feebly bent, you will never be able to hit the mark unless you aim considerably higher ; because the looseness of the string gives to the arrow a downward direction. It is precisely so with us. Our nature is so feeble, and we are so relaxed by the evil habits we have contracted, that we must take our aim considerably higher than the mark, if we wish to reach it. Man is become so weak by sin, that to attain an ordinary degree of virtue, his thoughts and desires must soar much higher. But some will say, " All I propose is to avoid mortal sin : this is the only perfection I aspire to." It is much to be feared that you will not reach this point you propose to yourself, for the string is slack. Perhaps you would have reached this point, had you directed your thoughts higher ; but not having done so, it is probable you will never reach it, and it is very probable you will fall into mortal sin. The religious who intends not only to keep the commandments of God, but likewise endeavours to follow his counsels—the religious who purposes to avoid not only mortal, but also venial sins, and even the least imperfections, as much as he can, adopts a good means of not falling into mortal sin, because he takes his aim considerably higher ; and though his frailty should hinder him from attaining the proposed object, yet at most he will fail only in something of counsel, in an unimportant rule, slight imperfection or venial sin. But he whose object is only not to offend God mortally, will doubtless fall into some mortal sin, if his bow is even in the slightest degree slackened, and if he fails to point at the object. It is thus that seculars fall so repeatedly into most grievous sins, and good religious are by the mercy of God preserved from them. And certainly were there no other advantage in religion, this alone would suffice to comfort us, and should urge us continually to thank the divine goodness for having called us thereunto. For to conclude, I hope that, by the grace of God, you will pass your whole life here without mortal sin, whereas if you had lived in the world, perhaps you would pass scarcely one year, month, or week ; no, not even one day or hour without falling into it.

Hence you may easily infer what danger the tepid religious is in, who scruples not the breaking of his rules, and who is not solicitous to aspire to perfection. It is very difficult for him to retain these sentiments, without being exposed to the danger of committing some great crime. But if you desire to improve in virtue, propose to yourself, for example, to acquire humility so perfect, that you may be able to receive contempts and injuries with joy; and after all this, God grant, you will be able to support them with patience. Resolve with yourself to make an entire submission of your will and understanding to everything ordained by your superiors ; and God grant that, even after this resolution, you will not fail in the duty of obedience, and in the exactness it requires. In fine, resolve to be perfectly resigned on occasions the most arduous and extraordinary ; and you will do not a little, by manifesting this resignation, when even the most easy and common trials occur.

It was well contrived by Almighty God, says St. Austin (Lib. de Perf. tom. vii.), to place the greatest and most perfect of his commandments at the head of all the rest. " Thou shalt love the Lord thy God with thy whole heart, with thy whole soul, with thy whole strength, and with thy whole mind." (Luke x. 27.) " This is the greatest and first commandment." (Matt. xxii. 38.) This is the end for which the rest were given us, according to the words of the apostle : " The end of the precept is charity" (1 Tim. i. 5) ; and the excellence of this commandment is such that the fathers and divines are of opinion, it is only in the other life we shall be able to fulfil it perfectly. For to have our hearts

and minds wholly taken up with God, to be continually absorbed
in him, and to employ all the powers of our soul in only loving
and adoring him, is what cannot be well done by us but in heaven.
In this life the weakness of our nature, and the necessity of supplying the wants of the body, hinder us from attaining so high a
degree of perfection.   However, though this commandment is the
consummation of all the rest, yet God has vouchsafed to place it
at the head of all, that, at first sight, we may know what we ought
to aspire to, and how far we must endeavour to advance. "Why,"
says St. Austin, " are we commanded to love God with all our
heart, which is a command we cannot fully perform in this life?
It is because a man never runs well, if he knows not how far he
has to go." (Lib. de Perf. tom. vii.)   Almighty God has set immediately before our eyes the greatest of all the commandments,
that aiming at an object so sublime, at perfection so complete, we
may constantly endeavour to reach it ; and if, through weakness,
we are unable to reach, the higher we aim, the nearer shall we
approach the object.   St. Jerome explaining these words of the
Psalmist : " Blessed is the man, O Lord, whose help is from thee :
his heart is always thinking how to raise itself higher and higher"
(Ps. lxxxiii. 6) ; says, the just man's heart is always towering
aloft, and the sinner's heart is perpetually sinking. The just man
has his eyes continually raised to the things most sublime in
virtue ; he aspires to increase in perfection ; and it is this he perpetually thinks on, according to the saying of the Wise Man :
" The thoughts of the strong are always carried to an abundant
increase." (Prov. xxi. 5.)   But no thought is less present to the
mind of the sinner than this; he is content to live like the rest
of the world ; at the utmost he proposes to himself but an ordinary
degree of virtue, he grows tepid, his spirits sink, and he attains
not his object.   This, says Gerson (Gers. 3. p. Tract. de Myst.
indust. seu consid. 4), is the language used by many : It is enough
for me to live as people in general live ; I desire only to be saved ;
the sovereign degree of perfection and glory I leave to the
apostles and martyrs ; I do not pretend to soar so high, but am
content to walk upon the plain ground.   Such is the language of
sinners and imperfect men, who, in number, far exceed the just
and perfect : " For many are called," says our Saviour, " but few
are chosen." (Matt. xx. 16.) " And wide is the gate and broad is
the way that leadeth to destruction, and many there are who
enter by it.   How narrow is the gate and strait is the way,
which leadeth to life, and few there are who find it." (Matt. vii.

13.) St. Austin, speaking of such as walk on the broad beaten way
of a loose life, says that those are the men whom the prophet
calls " beasts of the field" (in Ps. viii.), because they always
range in a spacious place, and will not be confined by rule or
discipline. And Gerson says, that by this kind of language, "It is
enough for me to live as others do ; if I be but saved it is sufficient ; I aspire to no greater perfection ;" a man readily mani-
fests the imperfect and bad state of his own interior, since he is
not willing to enter by the narrow gate. He adds, moreover, that
persons who, through sloth and tepidity, think it sufficient to
obtain the lowest seat in heaven, have great reason to fear that
they will be condemned with the foolish virgins who fell asleep
without having made any provision, or with the negligent servant who buried the talent he had received, and took no pains to
improve it. He was cast into exterior darkness, and we read not
in the gospel, that he was condemned for anything else, than for
having neglected the talent his master had entrusted him with.

But to put the shameful and deplorable state of these men in a
still clearer point of view, the same Gerson advances this example. Image to yourself, says he, the father of a family, rich,
noble, having many children, each of whom is qualified to promote the interest and honour of the family. All apply with zeal
to the performance of their respective duties except one, who,
through sloth, leads a loose and shameful life, though, provided
he did but apply himself, he is as well qualified as the rest for
performing virtuous actions. Still he does nothing worthy his
birth and talents, but contents himself, as he says, with a small
fortune, and since he has wherewith to live at ease, he will take
no pains to increase his property, nor will he trouble his mind,
with projects of ambition. His father calls upon him, exhorts,
entreats him to adopt nobler sentiments, reminds him of his
good qualities and noble birth, proposes to him the example of
his ancestors and of the rest of his brothers ; but when he sees
that notwithstanding all he does, he cannot prevail on him to
rise out of his sloth, and to lead an active life, he must needs conceive against him a very just indignation. It is the same with
God. We are all his children and brothers of Jesus Christ. He
would not have us content ourselves with an idle life, but exhorts
us to perfection in these words : "Be ye therefore perfect as your
heavenly Father." (Matt. v. 48.) Consider how holy and perfect
he is ; think on what your birth obliges you to, and endeavour to
shew by your actions, that you are the true children of such a father;

take example from your brothers also, and if you will look upon your eldest brother Jesus Christ, who most freely gave his blood and life to repair the losses felt by all our race, and to restore it to its former splendour. But if so great an example dazzles you, look upon your other brothers who are as feeble as yourself, born in sin as you were, subject to passions, temptations, and evil inclinations as you are. They fought against them constantly; they conquered, and they gained a crown of glory; and our mother the Church proposes these examples to you, and celebrates their feasts in order to encourage you to imitate them. And if you wish to have set before your eyes the example of those still nearer to you, consider your brethren, who were born in the bosom of the same mother you were, i.e., who were of the same order you are of; look upon St. Ignatius, St. Xaverius, St. Francis of Borgia, the great Edmund Campian, and so many others who flourished in the society. Endeavour all you can to imitate them, and do not be a dishonour to your race and society. He that with all these motives cannot be encouraged to perform extraordinary acts of virtue, but will continue to live in the ordinary way, is it not true that he gives just cause of indignation to his Father, who is God himself, and great occasion of scandal to his brethren, and deserves that his heavenly Father should disown him, and his brothers not acknowledge him?

For this reason, therefore, we say it is necessary for us to direct our thoughts high; to raise our eyes and hearts to sublime things, that if unable, through weakness, to reach them, we may not at least be kept back at so great a distance from them. Let us act on this occasion like merchants who ask a great deal more than it is worth, to induce the buyers to give the value of the article; or like referees, who, to bring the parties at variance to a reasonable settlement, demand at first too much, that they may obtain only what is equitable. But what I desire you to demand is not too much; it is just and moderate. Ever keep your eye fixed on it, that you may at least obtain what is absolutely necessary. Propose to yourself the attainment of great treasures that you may be able to acquire a competency. For if you propose to yourself at first only what is of little value, you will be far from acquiring it.

By this discourse we easily see how important it is, that in our spiritual exhortations we speak of that only which is perfect in a sovereign degree. If we preach, for example, on humility, it must be that humility which is most profound, and which reaches to contempt of one's self. If we preach on mortification, it must be on that which subjects all our passions to reason; if we preach on conforming our will to God, we must recommend a conformity which leaves us no will but that of the Almighty, which resigns our will entirely to his, and which establishes all its content and joy in the accomplishment of the divine will.   In fine, with respect to all the virtues, we must convey of them the noblest idea and elevate them to the highest point possible. But why, it will be said, recommend the highest degree of virtue to weak persons who are as yet but novices in spiritual matters? If you propose to them things proportionate to their strength, and such as are easily reduced to practice, and within their reach, they will very probably embrace them; but this sublime perfection you propose, ravishes men to the third heaven, and is proper only for a St. Paul, and for some other few saints whom God has particularly chosen in order to raise them to the highest degree of glory and perfection. But you are exceedingly mistaken in this point; for an exhortation of this nature is better adapted to you than to them, and ought to be addressed to you for the very reason you allege against it : you say you are weak, and that I ought not propose to you such high things as you are not yet able to attain. I answer, because you are weak, I must propose to you the most perfect kind of virtue and devotion, that by your aiming at what is best, you may be able to perform at least what is of strict obligation.   For this purpose, it would be much to your advantage to read the lives of saints, and to observe the most distinguished virtues wherein they excelled ; for, without doubt, the intention of holy Church in proposing to us their heroic actions is to invite us by their example to rouse ourselves, and at least to shake off the sloth and stupid lethargy which have seized us, if we have not sufficient courage and resolution to imitate them in their austere and holy life. There is also another advantage derived from reading the lives of saints, which is, that considering their great purity, and how far we come short of it, we may feel confusion, and have just reason for humbling ourselves. This is the opinion of the great St. Gregory, who explaining those words of Job, " He will look upon other men, and then will say, I have sinned" (Job xxxiii. 27), says, that as a poor man is much more sensible of his own poverty, when he considers the immense treasures of rich men; so the soul humbles herself more lowly, acknowledges her own indigence with more reason, when she reflects upon the great examples set us by the saints, and the glorious actions they have performed. St. Jerome reports that St. Anthony went to visit St. Paul the first hermit, and admiring the holiness of his life, at his return, being asked by his disciples where he had been ? "Alas," replied the holy man, "miserable sinner that I am ! I have no right to bear the name of a religious ; I have seen an Elias, I have seen a St. John the Baptist in the desert, when I beheld Paul in his solitude." We read also of the great St. Macarius, that having seen the sublime perfection of some holy hermits whom he had visited, the blessed man wept, saying to his disciples, " I have seen a real and true religious ; but as for me, I deserve not the name of a religious." What these great saints said out of pure humility, we may say with a great deal of truth, when we consider the example set by themselves, and by many others who lived before and since their time. Let us then seriously reflect on the great perfection they attained, that we may be encouraged either to make efforts similar to theirs, or if our strength fails, that the confusion and shame we may justly feel for being so tardy, may, in some measure, supply what is defective by reason of our frailty; and thus, at all events, the means I here propose cannot but prove of exceeding great advantage.

———o———

CHAPTER IX.

How important it is not to neglect the smallest Things.

" HE that contemneth small things," as it is said in Ecclesiasticus, "shall fall by little and little." (Ecclus. xix. 1.) The doctrine contained in these words is of great importance to all persons, especially to those who aspire to perfection : for we are exact in the performance of great things, as they carry with themselves their own recommendation ; but it is very usual with us to be careless in small things, as we fancy they are of no great consequence. In this, however, we deceive ourselves, because it is very dangerous to neglect and fail in these things ; and therefore the Holy Ghost in this passage of Scripture declares to us, "That he who contemns small things, shall fall by little and little." To convince us then of this truth, and to oblige us to be watchful, it ought to be sufficient that God himself says so : but in order that this may make a deeper impression on our minds, when treated more at large, let us consider what was the opinion of the saints on this subject. St Bernard says, " That those who run into disorders and crimes of the highest nature, begin at first by committing small faults, and no person ever falls or plunges himself all at once into an excess of wickedness." (Bern. de ord. vit. et mor. instit.) That is to say, that commonly speaking, none ever ascend at once to the highest point of vice or virtue, but that good and evil gradually insinuate themselves, and grow insensibly in us. It happens in spiritual as it does in corporal diseases ; both the one and the other increase by little and little ; so that when you see a religious commit some great fault, do not imagine, says the saint, that his disease then begins, for none ever fall on a sudden into an enormous sin, after having a long time led an innocent and virtuous life. But they begin first by negligence in those duties which they consider as unimportant, then their devotion growing cold, it diminishes daily more and more : so that at length they deserve that God should withdraw his hand, and no longer supported by him, they easily yield and fall under the first great temptation that attacks them.

Cassian explains this very well, by a comparison taken from holy Scripture. Houses fall not to ruin on a sudden, but the damage first begins by some gutters out of repair and neglected, through which the rain entering, by degrees rots the timber that sustains the building ; in process of time it penetrates the wall, dissolves the cement, and at last undermines the very foundation, so that the whole edifice tumbles to the ground, perhaps in one night. "By slothfulness," says the Holy Ghost in Ecclesiastes, "a building shall be brought down, and through weakness of hands, the rain shall drop through." (Eccles. x. 18.) Every one knows, that by neglecting to repair a gutter, or to examine the roof carefully in time, the whole building at last falls. It is just so with us, says the same author, a certain natural inclination which we have to evil, first flatters our senses, then gains ground, and insinuating itself into our souls, shakes the firmness of our good resolutions, and at last so weakens and undermines the whole foundation of our piety, that the entire spiritual edifice falls in a moment. A little care and vigilance in the beginning might have easily prevented the growth of the evil; but because we neglected it when it was but small, and did not take care in time to correct such faults, as appeared to us but inconsiderable, it happens that this shameful sloth is the cause, why we suffer ourselves to be overcome by any temptation that occurs ; nay, some thereby abandon their religious order, and become miserable apostates. Would to God that sad experience had not taught us, that these woeful examples are too frequent amongst us ! In truth we have great reason to wonder, and to tremble at the same time, when we consider that the ruin of many, who have fallen into this precipice, had its origin from small and trifling occasions. All this happens by the wile and craft of the devil, who dares not attack those that serve God, by tempting them in the beginning to omit things very essential, but begins by those that seem to be of little consequence, and always insensibly gaining some slight advantage, he succeeds better in this manner, than if he had acted otherwise. For if at first he should propose and tempt us to mortal sin, he would be quickly discovered and repulsed; but insinuating himself by little and little, he through our slight omissions and small faults gets into our souls before we are aware of it. It is for this reason St. Gregory says, "that small faults are in some manner more dangerous than great ones" (Greg. 3, past. adm. 34), because great faults, as soon as we reflect on them, carry such horror along with them, as obliges us to endeavour to arise speedily after we have fallen, and to be very circumspect in avoiding them for the future. But the less we perceive small faults, the less we avoid them, and making no account of them, we fall so often, that in time we acquire such a habit of them, as we seldom or never are able to eradicate; so that the evil which at first seemed nothing becomes, by our neglect and frequent relapses, almost incurable. St. Chrysostom confirms the same, when treating of this subject: "I dare," says he, "advance a proposition which will appear strange and unheard of. It seems to me that men ought to be less vigilant in flying from great sins, than in avoiding small faults; for the enormity of great sins naturally excites in us a horror of them, but we are easily induced to commit little faults, because we fancy them not to be considerable, and the little account we make of them, preventing us from endeavouring to correct them, they become at last so great by our negligence, that we are no longer able generously to resist and put a stop to them." (Chrys. hom. 87. sup. Mat.)

It is for this reason that the devil chiefly makes use of this means to assault religious, and those that serve God, because he knows it will be afterwards more easy for him to make them fail in greater and more essential duties. "It makes no matter," says St. Austin, "whether a ship be sent to the bottom by one great wave, or whether the water entering gradually by the chinks, and be neglected to be pumped, at length sinks the vessel." (Aug. Ep. 118. ad Seleu.) The devil, in like manner, cares not whether he enters the soul by this or that breach, all being equal to him, provided he attains his end, and brings you to a miserable shipwreck. St. Bonaventure says, "That of many small drops of rain great torrents are formed, which undermine and tumble down strong walls ; and that a small chink by which the water gets into a ship, oftentimes causes the loss of the vessel." (Bon. sup. Ps. lxvi.) Wherefore St. Austin tells us, that as when a ship springs a leak, we must immediately pump, in order to get out the water and prevent her from sinking ; so we also, by fervent prayer, and a strict examination of conscience, must continually endeavour to root out of our heart whatever imperfection or impurity had found its way into it, which, if neglected, would at last cause our ruin. This should be the continual exercise of a religious ; he must incessantly labour to amend his faults, and continually put his hand to the pump, otherwise he will be in great danger of perishing. "You are armed," says St. Austin, in another place, " and prepared to defend yourself against great sins; but what care do you take to avoid small faults ? Are you not afraid of them also ? You have already thrown overboard those heavy bales, which would have sunk your ship; but take care that the small heap of sand, still in the hold, does not bring you down." (Aug. sup. Ps. xxxix. 13.) You have happily escaped all the storms raised against you, in the tempestuous sea of the world ; but take precaution lest you be wrecked in the harbour of religion. For as it would avail nothing that a ship should have weathered all the storms, and escaped all the rocks at sea, if she is wrecked in port ; so it would be of no advantage to you to have resisted all the assaults of the strongest temptations, if afterwards you yield to weaker ones and thereby lose your soul.

———o

CHAPTER X.

Another weighty Reason which shows how extremely requisite it is to attach Importance to small Things.

ANOTHER very cogent reason, why we should apply ourselves with great care and attention to the smallest thing conducive to our perfection, is, that if we neglect to perform it, it is to be feared that God will refuse us these special graces, which we stand in need of, both to preserve us from sin, and to assist us in attaining the perfection we aim at, and for want of which graces we shall be exposed to great danger. In order to comprehend this better, we must premise the doctrine of St. Paul, who teaches, that God never refuses that supernatural assistance, which is necessary and sufficient for every one to overcome, if he wishes, the strongest temptation. "God is faithful," says the apostle, "who will not suffer you to be tempted above that which you are able : but will make also with temptation issue, that you may be able to bear it." (1 Cor. x. 13.) Besides this general assistance, the apostle here speaks of, there is another more particular one; and though we could have resisted and overcome the temptation, without this particular grace, if we make the good use we ought of the general, yet it often happens, that we do not overcome the temptation, unless God adds this special grace. It is not but we could resist the temptation, if we wished, because, according to the apostle, the first general grace is sufficient ; so that we fall through our own fault, because we fall wilfully ; yet we would not have fallen, had we been at the time assisted by the special grace. But as this special and efficacious grace is the pure gift of God's great mercy and liberality, he is not pleased to give it to all men, nor upon all occasions, but only to whom he pleases, and to such as act generously and liberally towards him, according to these words of the prophet : "With the holy, you will be holy ; with the innocent you will be innocent ; with the elect you will be elect ; and with the perverse you will be perverted." (Ps. xvii. 26, 27.) Another version has it, "With the meek you will be meek : with the liberal you will be liberal : with those who deal sincerely and candidly, you are sincere and candid : and with those who are perverse, you are also perverse." St. Ignatius in his Constitutions declares the same, where he says : "The stricter union we make with God, and the more liberal we show ourselves to the Divine Majesty, the more bountiful shall we find him to us, and we shall dispose ourselves to receive daily more and more graces from him." (Ign. reg. 19). St. Gregory Nazianzen, and many other fathers of the Church, maintain the same doctrine. (Greg. Naz. hom. 19.)

In order to understand what it is to be liberal towards Almighty God, we need but consider what it is to be liberal towards man. "To be liberal is to give to another more than we owe him, and more than we are obliged to give him :" for to give him barely what is his right, is not called liberality but justice. Whosoever then makes it his chief care to please God, not only in matters of duty and obligation, but also in those things which are of supererogation, and which tend to a more eminent perfection, and this not only in great matters, but even in the smallest, is said to be truly liberal towards God, and in return God will recompense him liberally. For God is always pleased to make those, who are thus faithful to him, his chief favourites, and pours his blessings on them in greater abundance; nor does he confine himself to that general assistance which is sufficient to resist temptations, but he bestows on them special and efficacious graces, whereby they always triumph over the assaults of the devil. But if you are not liberal towards God, how can you expect he should be so towards you, and if you offer your gifts to him with a parsimonious hand, must you not expect that he will treat you in the same manner? If you are afraid of doing much for him, if you hold always the compass in hand to measure what you are obliged to under pain of sin, and examine whether the omission be mortal or only venial; if, in fine, you intend to give God no more than what you think to be precisely his right, you plainly shew you are a miser, and oblige him to be more sparing of his blessings towards you. For he will give you only what he is bound to by his promise, to wit, he will give you the general aid which he grants to every one, *i.e.*, such aid as is necessary and sufficient to overcome temptations; but you have reason to apprehend, that he will not bestow on you that special and efficacious grace, which he usually gives to those who deal more liberally with him, and it is to be feared, that for want of it, you will at last yield to the assaults of the enemy, and fall into some grievous crime.

It is in this sense we are to understand the opinion of divines, and holy men in general, when they say that a subsequent sin is usually the punishment of a former, because by our first sin we render ourselves unworthy of God's particular grace, and thereby easily fall into a second sin. They also say the same of venial sins, and extend it even to very slight faults; they even maintain that a certain negligence, into which we suffer ourselves to fall, is alone sufficient to render a man unworthy of this special and efficacious grace, by aid of which he would have overcome the temptation, and through want of which he miserably falls. Some of them explain in the same manner the words of the Wise Man, " He that contemneth small things, shall fall by little and little" (Ecclus. xix. 1); and say that in consequence of this neglect and contempt we deserve to be deprived of the extraordinary assistance of God's grace, through want of which these cold and tepid Christians afterwards run into great disorders. Divines give the same interpretation of this passage of the Apocalypse: "Because thou art neither cold nor hot, I will begin to vomit thee out of my mouth." (Apoc. iii. 16) God has not as yet entirely rejected the lukewarm man, but he begins to spew him out, in consequence of his inattention, and of the faults he commits with deliberation, which, though they seem to him but small, still cause God to withhold his efficacious grace, without which, a sinner will certainly fall into greater crimes, and will be spewed out, and at last be absolutely rejected.

Let us then consider what great reason we have to fear, lest, by our negligence and indifference, we render ourselves unworthy of God's special favour and assistance. How often do we behold ourselves tempted, and in great danger of falling; how often do we behold ourselves reduced to so great extremities, that we doubt whether or not we have dwelt with complacency on the sinful object—whether or not we have given consent to an evil thought, and whether, by this consent, we have not defiled our souls with the guilt of mortal sin? In this doleful situation, what an advantage would it be for us, if, having been more liberal towards God, we deserved at his hands that special favour and assistance, which is the pure gift of his bounty, and with which we would have infallibly supported ourselves against the violence of the temptation; but without which grace, we will be not only in great danger of falling, but in all probability, we will be actually overcome.

Speaking of our spiritual enemy the devil, and of the continual war he wages against us, St. Chrysostom observes, that the means here described is very proper and efficacious for resisting and overcoming temptations. "You know," says he, "that we have an irreconcilable enemy, from whom we must expect neither peace nor truce; so that if we wished not to be overcome, we must stand continually upon our guard. But what shall we do, not only to prevent ourselves from being overcome, but even to defeat the enemy? Would you know it?" says the saint: "The only means we have to vanish him, is to merit the assistance of Heaven by the purity and innocence of our lives; it is thus we shall be always victorious." (Cor. hom. 60. sup. Gen.) We must remark that the saint does not say it is the *best*, but that it is the *only* means whereby we shall be victorious. St. Basil tells us the same, when he says, "That he who expects assistance from God, must never be deficient in performing his duty in the best manner he is capable of, and if he acts in this manner, divine grace will never be wanting to him ; wherefore, we must be extremely cautious, that our conscience may not accuse us of anything whatsoever." (Bas. in const. mon. cap. ii.) From these words of St. Basil, it is evident we should resolve to perform all our spiritual exercises, and our other actions, with so much attention and exactness that our conscience may have nothing to reproach us with, and that thereby we may obtain that special grace, which is so requisite for our salvation. It is therefore plain, that we ought to set a great value upon small things, if those things can be called small, which are capable either of procuring us so much happiness, or of draw- ing down upon us so much misery.   Hence, " He that feareth God," says the Wise Man, " neglecteth nothing." (Ec. vii. 19.) Because he knows that, from the slightest faults, we fall by little and little into great crimes; and is afraid that if he deals not liberally with God, his Divine Majesty will cease to deal liberally with him.

To conclude—I say that this point is so essential and so neces- sary to be observed by every good Christian that we ought to hold it for a general maxim, that as long as we consider the smallest things in devotion, as matters of great importance, all will go well with us, and we shall attract the blessings and assistance of Heaven.   But, on the contrary, if we neglect them, we shall ex- pose ourselves to great danger ; for it is only by this carelessness and indifference that sin can find entrance into the soul of a re- ligious. This is what our blessed Saviour intimated to us when he said, " He that is faithful in that which is least, is faithful also in that which is greater :—And he that is unjust in that which is little, is unjust also in that which is greater." (Luke xvi. 10.)   When, therefore, you desire to know whether you advance in virtue, upon which you should often reflect with at- tention, examine carefully whether you are faithful in small things, or whether you despise and neglect them ; if you perceive that you make no account of them, and yet that your conscience feels not the remorse she had used to feel on similar occasions, be sure speedily to remedy this evil with all possible care. For St. Basil says, " That the devil, when he cannot prevail on us totally to abandon religion, strains every nerve to dissuade us from aiming at perfection, and to excite in us an indifference for small things ; hoping at least to deceive us, by instilling into us a vain confidence that God, in consequence of such neglect, will not deprive us of his holy grace." (Bas. ser. de renun. &c. spir. perfec.)   But we. on our part, should always endeavour to act in such a manner that it may be as impossible for him to divert us from perfection, as to persuade us to forsake religion; for this purpose we must always aspire to perfection, and set a great value upon the smallest things conducive to it.

———o———

CHAPTER XI.

That the Business and Concern of our Spiritual Advancement are to be undertaken not in a general, but in a particular Manner; and of what great Importance it is to put in Execution the good Intentions with which God inspires us.

THE great masters of a spiritual life tell us that one of the means most conducive to our advancement is not to content ourselves with applying to it in a general manner, but that we must descend to particulars. Cassian relates that the Abbot Moyses, one day in a spiritual conference, asked his religious, "What was it they aimed at by all their praying, fasting, watching, and other austerities?" When they answered, "That it was the kingdom of heaven:" he replied, "I know very well that heaven is your last and great end; but what is the immediate and particular object by which you mean to attain your last end?" (Cass. Col. V. cap. iii. and iv.) For as a husbandman, whose principal view is to reap a plentiful crop, applies, with all possible care, to cultivate his land well and to root out the weeds; because these means are necessary to be taken, in order to attain the object of his desires : and as a merchant, who aspires to nothing but riches, seriously considers what particular commerce may be most conducive to the increase of his wealth, then embarks into that business with his whole stock, and devotes his whole time and industry to it. In like manner, although the chief business of a religious is to work out his salvation, nevertheless, it will not be sufficient for him to undertake it in general, saying, "I intend to save my soul ; I will become a perfect religious ;" but he must consider in particular what vice or passion chiefly opposes his advancement, what virtue he stands most in need of. It is upon these two points he must continually exercise himself, so that advancing gradually, and reflecting with attention, sometimes on one action, sometimes on another, he may more easily attain the perfection he desires. An ancient father of the desert gave the same advice to an anchoret, who, after having a long time persevered with diligence and fervour in devotion, became at last so negligent in the discharge of his spiritual exercises that he fell into a state of tepidity and indifference; at length desiring to recover his former fervour, but imagining that all the avenues to it were closed against him, he knew not where to begin to open a passage. Upon which the good father, in order to console and encourage him, told him this parable : A certain man, says he, having a field, which was all overrun with briers and thorns, sent his son to stub and clear it. The young man, perceiving the laborious task imposed on him by his father, lost courage, and fell asleep the first day, and the second day he did the same, for which his father reprehended him, saying, Son, you must not look upon this work all together, and in the gross, as if you were to do it all at once ; but you must undertake every day as much as you can easily perform. The son followed the father's advice, and in a short time the whole field was cleared.

But the chief obstacle to our advancement in virtue, and to our receiving new graces from God, is our not putting into execution those good desires with which he inspires us ; so that, by the bad use we make of his gifts, we compel him to withhold his hand. In the affair of perfection, he treats us as scholars are treated by a writing-master, who, until they form their first letters well according to the copy already given, will not allow them to get a new one. The longer we refrain from making good use of the graces God has given us, the longer he defers to give us new ones ; and the more we endeavour to put in practice those good inspirations which he sends us in time of prayer, the more he is inclined to bestow on us his heavenly gifts. Doctor Avila says, that he who makes good use of the lights God has given him, shall receive additional ones from him ; but he that neglects to make good use of those already received, can have no pretensions to ask for others ; for he may be justly answered, why do you desire to know the will of God, when you do not accomplish it in these things wherein you already know it ? (M. Avila, lib. i. de las. ep. fol. 241.) If you do not put in practice the good desires which he gives you, how can you expect that he will confer on you greater favours ? With what confidence can you entreat him in your prayers, to bestow on you such a gift, which you stand in need of, if you omit to amend those faults, which, by his holy inspirations, he has so often reminded you to correct ? I cannot comprehend how any person, who wilfully and deliberately persists even in one fault, how trivial soever it may appear, can lift up his eyes, or open his lips, to beg of God new and extraordinary graces. If we desire to obtain them, let us be careful to put in execution the holy inspirations which he sends us.

It is the opinion of all the saints, that he who makes good use of the grace he has received, deserves to obtain new ones ; but on the contrary, he who does not employ the first well, becomes undeserving of any more. Solomon, in the book of Wisdom, gives a good reason why the *manna*, which resisted the violence of fire, dissolved and corrupted as soon as the first ray of the sun appeared. "It is, O Lord," says he, " that it might be known to all, that we ought to prevent the sun to bless thee." (Wisd. xvi. 28.) Thus, in order to punish the indolence of those, who would not rise before the sun, to avail themselves of his benefits towards them, God permitted that the first beam of the sun should deprive them of food for the whole day. The same thing is beautifully represented to us by our Saviour, in the parable of the nobleman, who, going into a far country, to take possession of a kingdom, called his servants, and divided amongst them his money, that they might trade during his absence ; and, at his return, having demanded an account of them, he appointed them governors of as many cities as they had gained talents : to him that gained ten talents, he gave the government of ten cities, and to him that gained five talents, he gave the government of five cities. (Luke xix. 12.) This plainly shews us, that as this nobleman was pleased to recompense the fidelity and industry of his servants with such excessive liberality as to give him who gained ten talents, the government of ten cities ; so, Almighty God, if we faithfully correspond with the inspirations he sends us, will shower down his graces and blessings on us in abundance; but on the other hand, if we do not diligently follow the motions of grace, we will not only be deprived of what we have received, but we will be severely punished, as the unprofitable servant was, who did not lay out to advantage the talent he had received.

It is said of Apelles, that in whatsoever business he was engaged, he never let pass a day without exercising himself in his own profession, by painting something or other. For this purpose he always endeavoured to find out some time amid his other employments, and to excuse himself from going into company, was wont to say, " This day I have not as yet drawn one stroke with my pencil;" so that, by this means, he became a most excellent painter. In like manner, you will become a perfect religious, if you let no day pass without making some advancement in virtue: practise daily some act of mortification—correct some fault you were accustomed to commit, and you will quickly find, that your life will become every day more perfect. When you examine your conscience at noon, and perceive that you have done nothing that morning conducive to your improvement, that you have mortified yourself in nothing, that you have performed no act of humility when occasions offered themselves ; believe that you have lost so much time, and make a firm resolution not to let the remaining part of the day pass in the same manner. You will find it impossible to observe this rule, without gradually advancing, and making in a short time a considerable progress in the way of perfection.

————o————

CHAPTER XII.

In order to attain Perfection, we should never deliberately commit
any Fault, nor be remiss in our Endeavours to become perfect.

In order to attain perfection, to which during life we should continually aspire, it is of the utmost importance never to commit any fault deliberately. This being premised, we must understand that there are two sorts of venial sins : one, into which those who fear God most, often fall, through frailty, ignorance, and inadvertence ; although there is generally a little negligence mixed with these frailties.   They who serve God faithfully and with an upright heart, should find in these faults rather a subject of humiliation than of affliction : for God will not on that account abandon them, but on the contrary will afford them his divine grace, and animate them with fresh courage, when upon these occasions they humbly address themselves to him.   There is another species of venial sins, into which they who are cold and remiss in the service of God wilfully and deliberately fall.   These faults are a very great obstacle to those graces which God in his infinite goodness would have bestowed on us, if we had not committed them.   These are also the cause why we find no comfort or satisfaction in prayer, and that God ceases to impart to us those spiritual consolations and favours, which he was accustomed to bestow.   So that if we intend to advance in Christian perfection, and to engage Almighty God to continue his favours towards us, we must be very careful never to commit a wilful or deliberate fault.   Those we daily commit, through ignorance or inadvertence, are but too many, and therefore we should not multiply greater faults. Our distractions in prayer, springing from the natural inconstancy and wanderings of the imagination, are but too great, without voluntarily diverting our minds to other objects : and the faults which through frailty we often commit, contrary to what is required by the strictness of our rule and profession, are such as we need not aggravate by consent.

St. Basil prescribes another means, which, he says, will in a short time contribute very much to our advancement in perfection. This is never to stop in the pursuit of virtue. There are men, who are sometimes seized with certain fits of zeal and devotion, but stop short on a sudden, and go no farther. Be sure not to imitate these, but advance constantly on your way, and remember that, in your spiritual career, you will become more weary by halting than if you continue your journey. It is not the same in spiritual as in corporal exercises : the body is weakened and exhausted by continual labour ; but the more the soul acts, the more strong and vigorous she becomes, according to the Latin proverb : "The bow is broken by being too much bent, and the mind is corrupted by too much relaxation." (Arcum frangit intensio, animum remissio.)

St. Ambrose says, that as it is far easier to preserve our innocence, than to repent truly : so it is easier to persevere in the fervour of devotion, than to recover it after a short discontinuance. When a smith has taken a bar of iron from the fire, to forge it to the shape he desires, he never permits it to grow quite cold, but puts it into the fire again as soon as possible, that it may grow hot and fit for the hammer to work upon as before. In like manner ought we to be cautious never to suffer the fire of our devotion to be extinguished : for if the heart once grows cold, and begins to harden, we shall find it extremely difficult to warm and soften it again. We find by experience, that though men be very far advanced in virtue, if they once begin to grow remiss, and discontinue their exercises of piety, they lose, in a few days, what they had been a long time acquiring ; and when they endeavour to recover it again, they find so many difficulties and contradictions in the attempt, that they can seldom rise to that degree of perfection from which they had fallen. They, on the contrary, who persevere with fervour in the devotions and spiritual exercises, not only remain with ease in that degree of perfection they had already attained, but in a little time ascend much higher. Thus they never lose time, nor diminish what they have once acquired. They are not like the tepid and negligent, who spend their whole life in alternate fits of tepidity and devotion, destroying by their negligence what they have acquired by their fervour, doing and undoing, building up and pulling down, without ever bringing any of their projects to perfection. But the fervent labour incessantly without repose ; and acquiring new strength by continual exercise, they perform with great facility the most difficult undertakings, and daily advance more and more in virtue. Thus both the one and the other verify in themselves that saying of the Wise Man : "The slothful hand hath wrought poverty ; but the hand of the industrious getteth riches." (Prov. x. 4.) "The soul of those that labour shall grow fat." (Prov. xiii. 4.)

A great servant of God was wont to compare the tepid and fervent religious to two sorts of courtiers. He said that the lukewarm who think themselves entitled on account of their seniority to ease and indulgence, and who labour to advance no farther in perfection, were like those old domestics, who, from their former services, were allowed a place in court, but on account of their present inactivity, receive no further prefer-ment from their prince, or are hardly admitted into his presence ; but the fervent he compares to those wise and active young courtiers, who continually waited upon, and applied all their thoughts to discover what was most pleasing to their prince, and by their diligence and assiduity, insinuated themselves so far into his good graces, that they were at length raised to very high honours and dignities.

----o----

CHAPTER XIII.

Of three other Means which conduce very much to our further Advancement in Virtue.

St. Basil, and many other holy men say, that in order to ac-quire perfection, it is very advantageous to consider attentively the lives of the most perfect, and propose them to ourselves as models for our imitation. St. Anthony also says, that as the bee settles upon, and extracts from every flower its most pure and exquisite substance to make honey ; so a religious ought to observe every man in his community, and learn from one modesty, from another silence, from a third fervour, from a fourth obedience and resignation ; in fine he ought to imitate what he finds most commendable in each, and endeavour to conform in all things to the proposed model. It was thus St. Anthony himself acted, and by this means became so great a saint. Good example is one of the greatest advantages we have in religion. When St. Jerome advised men to live in community, rather than in solitude. "it was," as he said. "to the end that they might learn humility from one, and patience from another; that one should teach us silence, and another meekness and docility." Charillus, King of Lacedæmon, being asked what sort of republic he considered to be the best? "That," said he, "wherein the citizens live without strife or sedition, and strive with emulation who shall become most virtuous." We are all assembled in religion under a happy form of government, which differs from, and far excels all other governments in the world. In the governments of the world, men are eagerly employed in procuring wealth, honours, dignities, and preferment, and scarce make any efforts to acquire virtue. But in religion all their study is to deny their own will; all their application is to discover the means whereby to become more perfect; every man lives in peace and charity, without contention, without murmuring, without complaint; their only emulation is to excel each other in obedience, humility, and virtue. Certainly God has conferred on us no small favour, in calling us to a state where virtue alone is esteemed; where neither doctor nor preacher is valued for extensive knowledge or profound eloquence, but for humility and mortification; where every man endeavours to advance in virtue, and where, in fine, by mutual good example, they encourage each other to live well. Let us then embrace so favourable an opportunity of becoming perfect; and making good use of the examples we daily receive from our brethren, let us consider that we also are obliged to edify them by our example.

This is the second means, which I shall propose in this chapter, as conducive to your spiritual advancement. In order to know its utility and importance, we need only consider in what manner our Saviour speaks of it in the gospel. "Let your light," says he, "so shine before men, that they may see your good works, and glorify your Father who is in heaven." (Matt. v. 16). Every one sufficiently knows the force of good example. A perfect religious does more good in a community by his example, than the most eloquent sermons or pathetic exhortations. Men are much more affected by what they see, than by what they hear; and being easily convinced that the thing is practicable, when they see another perform it, they are strongly encouraged to undertake it. That fluttering of wings, of which the prophet Ezechiel speaks when he says, that "he heard the wings of living creatures striking one against the other," (Ezech. iii. 13), is, properly speaking, the good example by which you touch your brother's heart, move it to piety and compunction, and inspire him with an ardent desire of perfection.

St. Bernard declares, that at first when he entered into religion, the very sight of some religious who were full of zeal and charity, nay, even the remembrance of them when they were absent or dead, imparted so much comfort and joy to him, and so deeply impressed him with sentiments of tenderness for God, that oftentimes tears fell from his eyes in great abundance. "The memory of Josias," says holy Scripture, "is like the composition of a sweet smell made by the art of a perfumer." (Ecclus. xlix. 1.) Such were the good religious of whom St. Bernard speaks, and such ought we endeavour to become, according to the words of the apostle: "We are the good odour of Jesus Christ." (2 Cor. ii. 15.) Let us then be in effect like unto a box of perfumes, which freely communicates its odour, and delights and fortifies all who touch it. Above all, let us be exceedingly careful never to give occasion of scandal, or bad example to any of our brethren. A religious of an exemplary life does a great deal of good in a community. He may edify the rest and induce them to copy his virtues. But a bad religious is the author of incalculable mischief; he alone is capable of destroying an entire community, and will the more easily plunge it into disorder, because our inclinations being much more prone to vice than to virtue, example urges us more forcibly to evil than to good.

We read in Deuteronomy, that when the people of Israel were drawn up in order of battle, Almighty God commanded the captains to have it proclaimed throughout the whole army, "that whosoever was fearful or faint-hearted should depart and return home, lest he make the heart of his brethren to fear as he himself was possessed of fear." (Deut. xx. 8.) The example of a tepid and slothful religious produces similar bad effects in religion. He communicates his negligence to the rest, and renders them feeble in all their efforts to attain perfection. It is therefore very justly remarked by Eusebius, "that whoever has chosen to live in a community either does good to a great many by sanctity, or injures them by his laxity of manners."

To those already mentioned, we can add a third means which is very conducive to our spiritual advancement. This is the obligation we lie under of giving good example not only to our brethren with whom we daily converse, but likewise to all others in general, lest through the scandal given by an individual the whole order should lose its reputation.   For people in the world form a judgment of all the religious from the actions of the individual, and as if his fault were an original sin, or a kind of community-property, they readily impute to the whole order the irregularity of the particular member.   It is therefore the bounden duty of each individual religious to be extremely careful to edify his neighbour, that by this means the reputation of the whole order may be preserved and enhanced.   For this purpose we must imagine that the eyes of the whole world are upon us ; "That we are made a spectacle to angels and to men " (1 Cor. iv. 9), and that although it is unreasonable to censure a whole order for the faults of one man, yet it is certain that the whole body consists of members, and consequently that the growth or decay of that body depends upon the good or bad conduct of each particular member.   Let every one therefore remain firm at his post, like a good soldier ; let him take care that through his fault a battalion so strong and so well formed be not broken.   Let him take heed that religious discipline be not relaxed through his irregularity.   In fine, let him imagine that in religion his mother addresses him in the language wherein the mother of the Machabees addressed her youngest son, encouraging him to suffer and to die courageously for the observance of the law.   " My son," says she, " have pity upon me that bore thee nine months in my womb, and gave thee suck three years, and nourished thee and brought thee up unto this age." (2 Mach. vii. 27.)   The only return I ask is that you do not ruin yourself and me, and that you do not employ against yourself and me those arms which I put in your hands for your own defence and for that of your neighbour.   In fine, I request that what should render you more grateful, more humble, and more virtuous may not render you more ungrateful, more proud, and more irregular.

———o———

CHAPTER XIV.

That we should behave ourselves all our Lifetime in Religion, after the same Manner we did the first day we entered into it.

AN ancient religious, asking the Abbot Agatho how he should behave himself in religion, the good abbot answered him, "That he should remember how he had behaved himself the first day he had left the world, and was received into the convent ; and

that he should continue to do still, as he had done then." **If**
therefore you wish to know the most proper means of continuing
always a good religious and improving much in virtue, reflect
well upon the disposition you were in, when you first left the
world, and entered into religion, and endeavour to continue
always in the same state. Consider with what zeal and courage
you then renounced everything, your parents, your friends,
riches, pleasures, and all the conveniences of this life. Persevere
and still retain the same contempt of the world, the same
forgetfulness of your parents and of all other conveniences of
life, and thus you will become a good religious. Call to mind also
with what earnestness and humility you begged to be admitted
into religion, and remember that the same day you were assured
of admittance, you thought the gates of heaven had been open
to you. Remember what gratitude you then expressed, and
how highly you conceived yourself obliged both to God and to
religion. Persevere in the same sentiments of humility and
spiritual comfort; be convinced that you are still under the
same obligations as you were the first day, and in this manner
you cannot fail of making great progress. In fine, think often
with what modesty and devotion you behaved yourself at first
after your admittance; remember how obedient, how humble,
how fervent, how exact, and how resigned you were then;
continue always the same, and you will daily improve more
and more, and continually advance in virtue and perfection.

This means is much recommended by holy men, as I shall
show hereafter, but first it is very necessary clearly to explain
its import. I do not mean hereby, that you need not be more
perfect now than you were the first day you entered into religion,
or that an ancient religious should content himself with the
virtue of a novice. For religious orders are schools of perfection ; he that has frequented them longer ought to have learned
and improved himself more than he who entered them later; and
as in human sciences, he that has studied ten years ought to
know more than he who newly begins his studies ; so a religious
who has laboured for a long time to advance in virtue ought,
without doubt, to have made greater progress in his profession
than one who is but newly entered into religion. But, as a
young student, who at first was very diligent in his studies, and
afterwards grows idle, is told that if he pretends to become
learned, he must continue to take his business still as much to
heart as he did at the beginning ; so what I intend, by that

which is said before, is, that you should preserve the same fervour you brought with you, when treading the paths of virtue, you first entered into religion. With what zeal and resolution did you then begin to serve God? Nothing could then impede you, nothing seemed hard; re-assume the same fervour now, pursue your great affair with the same courage, and by this means you will make great progress in virtue. This is what holy men would have us understand by the expedient I last spoke of.

St. Athanasius tells us that St. Anthony being desired by his disciples to give them some advice concerning their spiritual advancement, began his discourse to them in these words: "What I first must recommend to you all in general is, that you never relent in that fervour, with which you first embraced a religious life; but that you still go on, always increasing it, as if you did but now begin," (Athan. et Surius, tom. i. p. 386.) He repeated the same advice to them upon several other occasions, and the better to imprint it in their minds, when he was near his death, enjoined them the same thing, as his last will and testament, in such pathetic words as expressed in him the tenderness of a father. "As to me," says he, "my dear children, I am shortly entering into the way of my forefathers, according to the Scripture expression; for our Lord already calls me to him, and I have a longing desire to see my heavenly country; but before I go, I must remind you of one thing. That if you will not lose the fruit of all the time you have already spent, and of all the pains and hard labour you have undergone, ever since you entered into religion, you must imagine that you begin only to-day to embrace a religious life, and must live so, that the fervour and zeal which you had at your first entrance, may daily increase and acquire new strength." If therefore you have a desire to advance in virtue, bear this continually in your mind, and suppose that you are every day to begin anew, and always to continue the same fervour, with which at first you began, by which means you will find it very easy to become a good religious.

St. Austin proposes another means, of which we have treated in one of the preceding chapters; "Forget," says he, "all that is past, and imagine that every day you do but begin." But to return to what we have quoted from St. Anthony, which he was used to explain by a familiar example, and said, that "we ought to apply with the same care and diligence to God's service, as a good servant does to the concerns of his master." A good servant, though he has served his master many years, and taken great pains and care in his affairs, yet he never refuses to do whatever lies in his power for him, but on the contrary rejoices to receive his master's commands, and performs them with the same willingness and readiness, as he did the first day he entered into his service. This St. Bernard practised. He believed that all other religious were arrived at the height of perfection, and being come to the end of their course, they might very well dispense with themselves in many things (which is indeed an excellent antidote against judging rashly of others); but as for himself, he always imagined that he was as yet but a novice, and that it was not for him to take upon him the same liberty, nor to use the same privileges, which others might do, and for that reason he never abated anything of the exactness and rigour of his rule, nor exempted himself from any of the meanest offices of his monastery. He was always the most forward in doing whatsoever obedience prescribed; the first in sweeping the cloister, the first in washing the dishes, and when it happened that he was not well versed in, or could not do something he saw others do, he presently endeavoured to repair that defect by taking some other work in hand that was far meaner than what his brethren were employed in. He either took a spade to dig the garden, or an axe to cleave wood, which afterwards he carried to the kitchen, and took great delight in these offices, because he really believed he had very great need of practising them for his spiritual advancement. There are many now-a-days not of his mind, who, when they are employed in such offices, say that good example may perhaps require it, but in any other respect they do not think these practices necessary. I do not say, but that it is good to do such things for the example and edification of others, but that it were better to believe, that we ought to do them for our own advancement, since St. Bernard was persuaded, that he had need of them for his.

But to elucidate still more what we have already quoted from St. Anthony we must make another observation, which is, that the saint was not satisfied with our not abating anything of that fervour we brought at first: but required that we should continually endeavour to increase it, by growing still better and better, and as if we did then only begin. Just as a man who is but newly entered into God's service, and sees hitherto he has done nothing else but offended him, adds therefore every day penance upon penance, in order to make satisfaction for his past offences, and to render himself worthy of reward for the future.

In the same manner, ought we daily to apply ourselves, to gain and lay up new treasures for heaven, as if hitherto we had gathered no treasures, but rather made every effort to squander and lose them.

This is the means St. Gregory thinks most convenient for all sorts of persons, nay even for the most perfect. And as perfect as the holy prophet David was, he did not, for all that, forbear to make use of it, as he himself signifies in these words, " I said to myself now I do but begin." (Psal. lxxvi. 11.) He had so much fervour and zeal for God's service, that even in his old age he continued the same fervent desire and diligence to serve God, as if he had but then begun to serve him. It is likewise evident from the saying of the Wise Man, " When a man shall have finished his task, then he shall begin anew," (Ecclus. xviii. 6) ; the more the true servants of God advance and approach to their end, which is perfection, the more they increase in fervour and redouble their activity. For, as St. Gregory says, " Men who are digging for a great treasure, the deeper they dig the more earnestly and diligently they go on still in their work ; for hoping they are not far from what they looked for, they imagine that a little more pains will bring them to it ; and by these hopes they encourage themselves to work afresh, without being tired. In like manner those who truly take to heart the great affair of their salvation, the farther they are advanced in the way of perfection, and the nearer they approach, they are still the more pressing to arrive at it. There is but a little earth that hides your treasure from you, dig a little farther and you will discover it, take courage, make haste," (Greg. 1. v. Mor. c. 3), and labour so much the harder, as you see the day nearer to approach (Heb. x. 25), as the apostle counsels the Hebrews ; as if he would say, that the nearer we draw towards our end, the harder we ought to labour. When a stone falls down from above, the nearer it draws towards its centre, the quicker it moves, till it reaches it : so when a man walks diligently in the way of God and proposes no other end to himself, than to please him alone, the more he advances in perfection, and the nearer he approaches to him, who is his centre, and his last end, the more he hastens and labours to arrive thither. Those who live thus, says St. Basil, are perfectly such as the apostle would have them be ; " Perpetually careful, most fervent in spirit, knowing that it is God whom they serve." (Rom. xii. 11.) There are certain religious who

have a great deal of fervour in the beginning, during the first
year of their probation ; but as soon as that is over, they begin
to relent, and rather become tepid and negligent, than zealous
and fervent.   For those who are truly zealous, will never grow
remiss in their devotion, but will always keep up the same
fervour for their religious duties ; and instead of being tired in
God's service, they desire nothing so much, as to serve him still
better and better, according to those words of the royal prophet :
" He who fears the Lord, will have great delight in his commandments." (Psal. cxi. 1.)

---o---

CHAPTER XV.

*That it is very advantageous to consider and often to ask ourselves,
for what End we entered into Religion.*

ANOTHER means, which may assist us very much in acquiring
perfection, is that made use of by St. Bernard himself.   He had
always in his thoughts, says the author of his life, and often in
his mouth, these words : " Bernard, Bernard, for what art thou
come hither ? "   St. Arsenius often asked himself the same
question, and often entering into himself, demanded an account
of his own actions.   "Arsenius," said he, " wherefore hast thou
left the world ?   What was thy intention in quitting it, and
entering into religion ?   Was it not to apply thyself wholly to
please God, and not to be at all solicitous to procure the esteem
and good will of men ?   Be then serious and diligent, in carrying on the design thou hadst at that time, and value not what
opinion men may have of thee.   All desire of honour, praise,
and vanity is, properly speaking, that world thou hast renounced.
Do not suffer thy heart to be seized anew with these follies; for
it will be of no service to keep thy body shut up in a cloister,
if thy heart still sighs and longs for the esteem of men, and so
hurries thee continually back again to the world."   Thus did
these great saints encourage and fortify themselves ; and so
should we in like manner animate and strengthen ourselves
against all the difficulties we can meet with in religion.   When
you find a repugnance to obey a superior in what he orders,
encourage yourself by these or the like words : "Wherefore art
thou entered into religion ?"   Was it to do thy own will ?   Was
it not rather to submit it to the will of another ?   Wherefore

dost thou then pretend to follow thy own? Whenever you find
that any ordinary effects of poverty molest you, encourage
yourself in these terms : Art thou come hither to seek thy own
ease and convenience, and not to suffer the least want of anything? Dost thou not remember that thou camest to religion
to be poor, and to suffer the want of many things, as one truly
poor? Wherefore then dost thou complain? When you
imagine that others have not a sufficient regard and esteem for
you, console yourself by often saying : Hast thou entered into
religion to be respected, or rather hast thou not entered it to be
neglected and forgotten by all men, not at all regarding nor
valuing the opinion and esteem of the world? Why dost thou
now refuse that which thou camest hither to seek? Wherefore
wilt thou run after that which thou hast once quitted? Thou
camest not to do thy own will, but to be truly poor, to live in
want of all sorts of conveniences, and to desire to be neglected,
and scorned by men ; this is to be a true religious, this is to be
dead to the world, and to live wholly to God.

Let us then often call to mind, that it is for this end we entered
into religion, and that it will not at all profit us to be in religion,
unless we perform what we came for. It is not the place, but
our good lives, that must make us saints. The great St.
Austin treats this point excellently well in a sermon, wherein
he addresses himself to those religious, who live in the desert.
" Behold," says he, " we are got into solitude, we are got into
the desert : yet, it is not the place, but our good works that can
make us saints ; it is these will sanctify the place, and us too.
Do not then trust to the holiness of the place ; we may sin in
all places, and may everywhere meet with our damnation. For
the angels sinned in heaven, Adam in Paradise ; and you know
there was no place could be more holy than these. It is not
then the place that makes the saints ; for if the place could
sanctify those that live in it, neither man nor angels could ever
have fallen from their dignities." (Ser. xxvii. ad frat. in Erm.)
I say the same to you : do not imagine that all the work is done,
and that you are already out of all danger, because you are
become a religious; for it will avail you nothing to be a religious,
unless you do those things, for which you have entered into
religion ; for you are not come thither, to be a man of great
learning, nor to become a great preacher, but solely and purely
to become a true and good religious, and to aspire continually
after perfection. It imports but little whether you are more or

less learned, or whether you preach with greater or less eloquence; but that which is of the greatest importance is, that you
become a good and perfect religious, and if that be not the thing
we aim at, and labour to attain, what is it we do? And what
have we done all this while if we have not done this? And to
what have we applied our minds, if we have not studied and
endeavoured to attain that, for which only, and for no other end,
we are come hither? Wherefore examine your conscience, and
ask yourself often this question: "Friend, for what art thou come
hither?" (Matt. xxvi. 50.) What art, or what profession, could
I have made choice of, wherein I should not have rendered
myself perfect, during the same time I have been in religion?
I have made choice of the profession of religious, and hitherto
I have advanced little or nothing in it; so many years are now
past, since I was admitted into this school of virtue, and I have
not yet learned the first rudiments of it; I am yet to learn the
smallest and lowest degree of humility. Others become good
philosophers, and good divines in seven years' space; and I, after
so many years, have not yet learned to be a good religious.
How easy were it, notwithstanding, for us to be so, if we would
but apply with the same care and labour to acquire true virtue,
that we do to become eminent in learning.

Many, says St. Bernard (Lib. de Cons. ca. 2), run after the
splendour and vanity of human learning; and how very few are
there, that study the purity and holiness of a good life? But if
men would apply themselves with the same fervour to virtue,
as they do to be eminent in profane sciences, they would find
the acquisition of it more easy, and its possession much more
advantageous. And yet, would it be at all surprising, if, in
acquiring the science of the cross, and in securing our eternal
salvation, we display as much zeal as we do in acquiring profane
science, and in cultivating our minds? St. Dorotheus, writing
upon this subject, says very well, that he often made a reflection,
which much improved him. When I studied in the world, says
he, I took my studies so much to heart, that I thought of nothing
else; and had it not been for one of my friends, who took care
to provide me something to eat, and to call me at dinner time, I
had never thought of eating. The vehement desire I had to
learn went so far, that when I was at table, I had my book
always open before me, that I might eat and study at the same
time; and at night when I came from school, I presently lighted
my candle, and studied till midnight; and when I lay down to

sleep, I took my book into my bed, and after I had slept a while, I fell a reading again, and was so wholly taken up with this passion of studying, that I could take no delight in anything else. Since I came to be a religious, I have often reflected and said to myself, "If thou didst heretofore take so much pains, and wert so zealous to acquire eloquence, what great pains and care oughtest thou not to take now, in order to acquire true virtue? And this very thought," says he, "was a great help to me, and gave me fresh courage, and new strength." (Doroth. Doct. 10.)

Let us encourage ourselves by the same consideration, and remember that it is of greater concern to become good religious, than great and learned orators. Let all our endeavours and applications, therefore, be, to attain to the knowledge and love of God, which is the greatest, and indeed our only affair in this life. All the time that our blessed Saviour lived amongst us, he had no other intent than to manifest the tender love he had for us, and to procure us the greatest happiness we were capable of enjoying; and to that end he refused not to shed his most precious blood, and even to lay down his life. And shall we think too much, in return for so great goodness, to make it our chief business to love and serve him, and always to promote his honour and glory? "Wherefore lift up your hands that hang down as if tired, and stretch out your loose knees," (Heb. xii. 12): "Let us make haste to arrive at the place of rest," (Ibid. iv. 11), and let us not stop till we go to "Horeb, the mountain of God," (3 Kings xix. 8), that is to say, the highest pitch of glory and perfection. And as a traveller that has slept till late in the morning, makes haste to repair the time he has lost, by mending his pace till he overtake his company, that were gone before; so should we make haste, and never stop in our course, till we have repaired the time we have lost by our negligence. It is to this end, that each of us should always have these thoughts in our mind :—My companions and brethren are already far advanced on their journey, and I alone still loiter behind, notwithstanding I began my journey first, and entered into religion before them. How great a happiness and advantage would it prove to us, if we did truly grieve for all the time we have lost? And what an encouragement would it give us for the future, to advance with more diligence, and make haste without remissness?

Denis, the Carthusian, reports a passage which he takes from the Lives of the Ancient Fathers, saying that a certain woman finding her son desirous to become a religious, endeavoured all she could to hinder his executing this good design, laying before him all she thought might serve to prevent him; but the young man, continuing still firm in his holy resolution, made no other answer to all the difficulties and objections his mother urged, but only this, *I will save my soul*. At last, his mother seeing she could prevail on him neither by reason or importunity, left him to his own choice; and so the young man took the habit of religion. But this first fervour cooling afterwards, he began to live so negligently that there could scarce be found any trace of that zeal he had at first shewn for heavenly things. Soon after his mother died, and he fell sick of a very dangerous fever, in which, lying in a trance, he fancied, that he was carried before God's great tribunal, where he saw his mother, with many others, expecting the sentence of their condemnation; and that his mother, looking upon him, and perceiving that he was of the number of those who were to be condemned; "Alas! son," said she, "what is become of that good resolution, and that sentence you so often heretofore repeated to me, *I will save my soul?* Was it to become a lost soul that you made yourself a religious?" This reproach of his mother put him into so great a confusion, that he could not tell what to reply. At last, awaking from this trance, and permitted by God to recover from that sickness, he began to consider that the vision he had had was certainly a warning from God; which wrought such a change in him, that he spent all the rest of his life in tears, and continual penance. Many endeavoured to persuade him to moderate, and abate some part of his great austerities and mortifications, lest he should destroy his health by them; but he rejected all their advice, saying, "Alas! if I could not bear those reproaches of my mother, how shall I be able to bear those that will be made me by Jesus Christ, and his blessed angels, on the terrible day of judgment?" (Dion. Cart. art. 30 de quatuor novis.)

———o———

CHAPTER XVI.

Of some other Things which may contribute much to our Advancement in Virtue and Perfection.

"Be ye perfect, as your heavenly Father is perfect" (Mat. v. 48), says our blessed Saviour, in that admirable sermon he preached to his disciples on the Mount. In his discourse on these words, St. Cyprian says, "If men feel great pleasure in seeing their children resemble them, and if a father is never better pleased than when all his son's features are like his own ; how much greater joy will our eternal Father feel, when we are so happily regenerated in spirit, that by all our actions, and by our good behaviour, we are known to be truly his children ; what palm of justice, and what crown of glory will it be to you, that God shall have no cause to say, *I have nourished and brought up children, and they have scorned me* (Isa. i. 2) : but, on the contrary, that all your actions tend to the glory of your heavenly Father ? For it is truly his glory, to have children who resemble him in such a manner as that by them he may come to be honoured, known, and glorified."

But how will it be possible for us to render ourselves like to our heavenly Father ? St. Austin teaches us in these words : "Let us remember," says he, "that the more just we become, and the more united with God's will, the better we shall resemble him ; and that the more holy, and the more perfect we are, the greater resemblance we shall have to our heavenly Father." (Ep. 85. ad Consent.) And it is for this reason, that our Saviour so earnestly wishes and desires our holiness and perfection, and so often recommends it to us ; sometimes by himself in St. Matthew, in the passage we have already quoted ; telling us also the same thing by the mouth of St. Paul in these words, "That which God desires of you is, that you be sanctified." (1 Thess. iv. 3) : and also by the Prince of the Apostles, saying, "You shall be holy, because I am holy." (1 Pet. i. 16.) It is a very great comfort to parents to have wise and discreet children ; this truth the Holy Ghost tells us by Solomon, who says, "That a wise son brings great joy to his father : but a foolish son causes grief to his mother." (Prov. x. 1.) If then, by doing so, we attained no other end than to please Almighty God, whose pleasure, honour, and glory should be the chief motive of all our actions; we ought continually to aspire to perfection. But that we may be still more forcibly urged to embrace it, I shall propose several other means, which may serve to the attaining it.

The reason why in holy Scripture we are so often called the children of God, by the mouths of the prophets, who very often repeat this saying, " I will be your father, and ye shall be my children ; " and by St. Paul, who exhorts us to be " followers of God, as his most dear children," (Eph. v. 1) ; and by St. John when he tells us, " See what love the heavenly Father has had for us, insomuch that he would have us called, and be effectually the sons of God," (1 John iii. 1) ; and also in many other places to the same purpose. The reason, I say, why the same thing is repeated to us so often in holy Scripture is, as St. Austin says, " To the end that seeing, and considering the dignity and excellency of our origin, we may conceive and entertain a greater esteem and higher value of what we are ; and, consequently, take greater care not to do anything unworthy our noble extraction. We use great care," says the same father, " to preserve a rich suit of clothes, and to see that it be not stained, and we look carefully to our jewels and other things of great value : so also, when holy Scripture tells us of our dignity ; when it reminds us that we are the sons of God, and that God himself is our Father; it is to the end we should take great care to preserve our hearts pure and clean ; and that we behave ourselves in all our actions, so as becomes those who have the honour to bear the character of the sons of God, and that we never degenerate from the noble and high sentiments with which that great dignity ought to inspire us." (Ep. 243, ca. 19.) The saying also of St. Leo Pope is well adapted to our purpose. "Consider," says he, "O Christian ! what thy dignity is ; and seeing thou art made partaker of the divine nature, suffer not thyself to fall back into thy ancient baseness, by attaching thyself too much to the things of this life; reflect on that head and body, whereof thou hast the honour to be a member." (Serm. 1. de Nat. Dom.) St. Paul represented the same thing heretofore to the Athenians, telling them, "That we descended from God ; and it is from him we derive our origin." (Acts xvii. 28, 29), and thereby he wishes to inspire them with sentiments worthy their noble extraction. But to make a still fuller and a more particular application of what is here said, and of the comparison of the rich robes mentioned by St. Austin, let us consider, that as the smallest stain is more indecent in a fine robe ; and the richer the cloth is, the more the stain appears, inasmuch that what appears very considerable upon cloth of gold or silver can hardly be perceived upon that of a coarser kind; in like manner the stain of a venial sin, nay, many times even that of a mortal sin, is scarce taken notice of amongst seculars, or it is looked upon only as a trifle, there being so great and general a corruption in the world. But in religious, who are the dearly beloved of God, the least imperfection is very considerable—the least immodesty, the least murmuring, the least impatient or hasty word is a very great offence, and gives great occasion of scandal amongst us. But amongst seculars there is so little account made of such things that oftentimes they never reflect on nor take any notice of them. To have dust on our feet troubles us not, but the least particle that gets into the apple of the eye puts us to very great pain. Men in the world are like the feet of the mystical body of the Church, and religious resemble the eyes of the same body ; so that the least fault in a religious is of very great and very bad consequence, because it works a far worse effect in him than it can do in a secular; and for this reason a religious lies under a greater obligation of watching, and taking care of all his actions than others do.

Another means already stated in one of the preceding chapters, which will serve to encourage us still more, is that we should always imagine we have a great way to go, and that as yet we have advanced but very little. Our blessed Saviour also insinuates the adoption of this means by these words, "Be ye perfect as your heavenly Father is perfect." For what, think you, does our Saviour mean by saying so? Can it be that we should ever be able to come near the perfection of our heavenly Father? "Can any man be just in comparison of God?" (Job iv. 17.) No, certainly. Whatever degree of perfection we can possibly arrive at, there will still remain an infinite distance between his perfection and ours. And yet our Saviour says to us, "Be perfect as our heavenly Father is perfect." To let us understand that in the career of virtue there are no bounds, and therefore we should never be satisfied with what we have already done, but should labour continually to acquire what we still want. It is a usual saying with holy men, and with a great deal of reason, that a most certain sign of a person's being far from perfection is that he thinks himself arrived at it. For on the road of a spiritual life, the more a man travels, the more plainly he sees that he has advanced but little. St. Bonaventure says, "That the more a man ascends a hill, the more extensive will be his prospect ; in like manner, the nearer we come to the top of the mountain of perfection, the greater we perceive the extent of virtue to be." (De Prof. Rel. ca. 21.) When we contemplate a high mountain at a distance, we imagine that it reaches so near the heavens, that were we upon the top thereof, we fancy we might be able to touch the clouds with our hand ; but having travelled on, and got up to the very top, we find that we are still far from the heavens ; just so it happens with those who travel in the way of perfection, and advance perpetually in the knowledge and love of God. St. Cyprian, explaining the words of the Psalmist, " Man shall arrive at the greatest height that his heart is capable of, and God will still be more and more exalted," says, " That the higher our souls are by degrees raised to the knowledge of God, the higher he appears still exalted above us. Whatever knowledge of God you have attained, and how great soever your love is of him, there remain still infinite degrees of knowledge and love of him beyond what you have already acquired." (Ad Corn. Pap. Ps. lxiii. 8.) In fine, there will still remain a great way to ascend in the path that leads up to perfection, and whosoever imagines that he has got to the top, is yet very far from it, which makes him so easily imagine he can reach the heavens with his hand.

This may be understood by what is experienced in human sciences, viz., that the more a man knows, the more he finds he has still to learn. This made the wisest of all the philosophers say, " All that I know is, that I know nothing." (Socrates.) And an excellent musician was wont to say, that it grieved him to find he understood nothing of music ; because he discovered in that science things of such vast extent that he perceived he could never arrive at any perfection in it. On the contrary, the ignorant, who are not sensible of their own wants, and who see not how many things they have still to learn, readily imagine that they know a great deal. Just so it is in spiritual science. Those who are best versed in perfection know they have a great way still to go before they can arrive at their end ; and therefore they more they improve in this knowledge, the more humble they become ; because according to that proportion or progress they make in other virtues, they make the same also in the virtue of humility, and in the knowledge and contempt of themselves, which are things inseparable one from the other. For the more knowledge they acquire of the goodness and majesty of God, the more clearly they perceive their own misery and nothingness. " One abyss invokes another "

(Ps. xli. 8), says the Royal Prophet. The great abyss of the knowledge of God, and of his goodness and infinite majesty, discovers to us the depth of our own misery; and it is by the beams of this divine light that we best perceive the many atoms of our imperfections, and how much we still want of being perfect. But he who is yet but a beginner in the practice of virtue, by not knowing how many things are still requisite for its attainment, is apt to fancy that he is already, in a very high degree, become master of it. It many times happens with a man, who has little or no skill in painting, that when he sees a picture, he presently admires it, and discovers no fault; but if an excellent painter happens to view it, and to consider it attentively, he will observe many defects. The same occurs in spiritual matters. He who has not attained to the art of self-knowledge, cannot perceive the faults which lie concealed in the tablet of his own soul; whereas another man, who is better skilled in that art, would quickly discover them.

Let this, therefore, serve to augment in us daily a desire of acquiring the virtue still wanting to us; for, " Blessed are those who hunger and thirst after justice " (Matt. v. 6); that is to say, as St. Jerome explains it, such as never think themselves perfect enough, but always labour to improve in virtue. Thus did the Royal Prophet, when he said to Almighty God: "Wash me still more and more from my iniquity, and cleanse me from my sin " (Ps. l. 4), as if he would have said : It is not enough, O Lord ! that I should be washed ; an ordinary washing and cleansing is not sufficient for me, " But I beseech thee to wash me, so as I may become whiter than snow." (Ib. l. 9.) Let us cry to Almighty God in the same manner : " Wash me, O Lord ! still more and more." Give me more humility, patience, and charity ; more mortification, and a more perfect and absolute resignation to your holy will in all things.

————o————

CHAPTER XVII.

Of the Perseverance we ought to have in Virtue.

St. Austin, explaining the words of St. Paul, " No one is crowned but he who lawfully fights " (2 Tim. ii. 5), says, that to fight lawfully is to fight with perseverance to the end, and that only those who fight in this manner deserve a crown. And upon this occasion he alleges, what St. Jerome also says, that

" Many begin well, but few end well," (Contra Jovin.)   Of this
we have a great example in the Israelites.   Holy Scripture
observes, that there went out of Egypt about six hundred
thousand men, besides women and children ; and that, nevertheless, of all that great number, there were but two that entered
into the Land of Promise.   " It is then," adds the saint, " no
great matter to begin, but the chief thing is to perfect what we
have begun ; for it is in that alone that perfection consists."
(Aug. Serm. ad frat. in Erem.)   St. Ephrem makes use of a very
just comparison on this subject, saying, " That as when you
build a house, the greatest difficulty is not only in laying the
foundation, but in raising the building to its perfect height ; and
that the higher the building is raised, the more the labour and
expenses increase : so in the spiritual building, the hardest task
is not to lay the foundation, but to carry your work on to
perfection." (Exhort. ad. Piet.)   It will avail us nothing to have
begun well, unless we also end well.   " In Christians," says
St. Jerome, " we consider not how they begin, but how they end.
St. Paul began ill, but ended well ; Judas began well, and ended
ill." (Ad Furiam vid.)   What did it avail him to have been an
apostle of Jesus Christ, and to have wrought miracles ?   Wherefore, what will your good beginnings avail, if a miserable end
contradicts and gives them the lie ?   It is to perseverance only
that the crown is promised :   " He who shall persevere to the
end," says the Son of God, " shall be saved." (Matt. xxiv. 13.)
Jacob saw Almighty God, not at the foot, nor in the middle,
but at the top, of the ladder ; to let us know, says St. Jerome,
that " It is not enough to begin well, nor yet to continue to do
well only for a time, unless we hold on and persevere to the
end," (Ep. ad Ab. Gaurin.)   " What does it avail," says St.
Bernard, " to follow Jesus Christ, unless we overtake him at
last ?"   Wherefore St. Paul bids us " Run so as that at last we
may gain the prize." (1 Cor. ix. 24.)   Let thy race, O Christian ! and thy progress in virtue have no other bounds than
what Jesus Christ prescribed to himself :   " He rendered himself
obedient even to death."   It is in vain for you to run unless
you continue your race to the last moment of your life.   Without this, you will never get the prize.

The Son of God gives us a special warning of this, when he
assures us, that " Whoever puts his hand to the plough, and
looks back, is not fit for the kingdom of heaven." (Luke ix. 62.)
As also when, at another time, he bids us " Remember Lot's

wife." (Ib. xvii. 32.) What was it she did? God having brought her out of Sodom, in order to save her from the fire which consumed that city, she stopped upon the way, and turned to look behind her, and immediately in the very place where she turned her head, she was changed into a statue of salt. Would you know, says St Austin, what this signifies? Salt seasons and preserves everything, and our Saviour would have us remember Lot's wife, to the end, that, reflecting upon what happened to her we may preserve ourselves with that salt, which her transformation does furnish us with; that is to say, that taking warning by the example of her punishment, we may go on and persevere in that good course of life, into which we are entered, without stopping or looking behind us, lest we ourselves should be turned also into statues, from which others may take salt, for their own preservation. Alas! how many are there now-a-days, who serve us for statues of salt, like that of Lot's wife? How many are there whose fall may serve us for a warning, and become of very great advantage to us, in order to our eternal salvation? Let us then be wise at other men's cost, and let us endeavour to do nothing that may make others become wise at our expense.

St. Austin and St Jerome farther add and say, that " To begin well and end ill, is to make a monster, as if a painter, after he had drawn the head of a man, should add to it the neck of a horse. (Ad frat. in Erem. ser. 8.) St. Paul, writing to the Galatians, reprehends them very severely for proceeding after this manner. " What," says he, " are you grown to such a height of folly, as that having once begun well in the spirit you will needs end in the flesh? Senseless men! who has bewitched you, thus to rebel against truth?" (Gal. iii. 1.)

But to the end we may obtain God's holy grace to persevere in doing well, we must strive to lay at first a good foundation of virtue and mortification; for if the foundation be weak, the building will quickly come to lean, and so fall to the ground. That fruit into which the worm has once crept, never ripens, but soon falls from the tree; while that which is sound sticks fast to the branch, till it is perfectly ripe; in the same manner if your virtue be not solid, and your heart not wholly possessed by God, and if you still cherish the same worm of presumption, of pride, of impatience, or any other irregular passion; that worm will by degrees corrupt your heart, and consume all its best juice and substance; and to speak more clearly, you will run the danger of not persevering. "Wherefore it is very necessary to confirm and fortify your heart by grace" (Heb. xiii. 9), and in time to lay a solid foundation of true virtue.

Albertus Magnus, explaining by what means we ought to confirm ourselves in virtue, to be the better able to persevere, says, that a true Christian ought to be so well grounded in virtue, and have it so firmly rooted in his heart, that it may be always in his power to practise it, without any dependence upon what other men can say or do to him. There are persons who outwardly seem to have the spirit of meekness and humility, so long as nothing thwarts them, and all things happen as they wish; but upon the least cross accident that occurs, this peace vanishes, and they presently take fire, and discover what they are. Such men as those, says Albertus, have not the virtue of peace and humility in their own, but in other men's minds and humours; so that if your virtue be such as this, it belongs to others and not to you, since it lies in their power to give, or take it from you, whensoever they please. But your virtue, if it be true, must be your own, and not of another's growth, and the fund ought always to be at your own disposal, without any dependence upon another. We may make a very just comparison of such persons as those, to a stagnant water which yields no bad smell or vapour, so long as you do not trouble it; but disturb it once, and it sends forth so intolerable a stench as is enough to poison the standers by. Just so it is with these men. As long as you leave them to themselves, as long as nobody vexes them, they are in profound peace, they seem as quiet as stagnant water that offends nobody; but as soon as they are molested or the least moved, presently such pernicious vapours are raised, as give great scandal, and very bad example to their neighbour. "Touch the mountains" (Ps. cxliii. 5), says the Psalmist, "and they will smoke."

---o---

CHAPTER XVIII.

Of Spiritual Exhortations, and what is requisite to derive Advantage from them.

AMONGST the many means religion furnishes us with for our better assistance and encouragement in our spiritual progress, a principal one is that of sermons, and spiritual exhortations.

On the present occasion, therefore, I intend to shew how, and in what manner we ought to hear them, so as to derive advantage from them; and what I shall say, relating to ourselves in particular, may also serve as a general instruction to all sorts of persons, and teach them how to profit by the hearing of sermons. The first disposition necessary for that end is, that we do not frequent sermons out of custom, nor merely because it is a part of a Christian's duty to do so, but to hear them with a true and earnest desire of improving by them. Let us consider with what zeal the ancient fathers in the desert were wont to resort to these spiritual banquets, and what store of good provisions they carried back with them to their cells. With the like fervour we ought to go to those exhortations that are made for us, and then they cannot fail of doing as great good to our souls, as good meat does to our bodies, which nourishes and strengthens him that sits down to table with a good appetite. St. Chrysostom observes, that as hunger is a sign of the body's being in good health, so a longing desire of being nourished with the word of God is a certain sign of a good and happy disposition of the soul. But if you do not thirst after the divine word, nor find any gust in it, it is a certain sign that you are sick; and that your soul is in a very dangerous condition; seeing it loathes that food which is so proper for its nourishment. Besides, though it were only to hear the preacher speak of Almighty God, that alone should suffice to make us run joyfully to hear him: for, naturally a man is glad to hear another speak well of one he loves. So if you have a true love for God, you cannot but be everjoyed to hear the preacher speak well of him. For, as our blessed Saviour says, "He who is of God, hears the word of God, and the reason why you desire not to hear it is, because you are not of God." (John viii. 47.)

In the second place, if we intend to improve ourselves by the sermons we hear, we must not hear them with a spirit of curiosity; as for example, to observe the good language, the graceful action and pronunciation, the novelty and turn of thought of the preacher, together with his manner of delivery. It is this for which, with great reason, we blame many seculars, and which is the cause of their profiting so little by sermons. But instead of minding such things as these, we must apply ourselves wholly to attend to the substance of the discourse. What should you say of a sick man that was going to be let blood, who instead of letting the surgeon open his vein, should amuse himself in looking upon the lancet, and admiring its workmanship? Would you not persuade him to forbear that idle curiosity, and tell him that it is his business to be let blood ; that what he was to mind now, was to have his vein opened ; and the rest was little or nothing to the purpose.   It is the same with those who, instead of attending to that which is most essential in a sermon, to that whence they could extract the so necessary nourishment of their souls, stop at the rind, and attend to nothing more than to the plan and division of the discourse, to the strength and beauty of the language—in a word, to that which is only an idle ornament and a vain artifice of eloquence. Such men as these may justly be compared to a sieve and a sarse which retain only the chaff and bran, and let all the grain and flour pass through them.   Holy Scripture tells us, that when Esdras (2 Esd. viii.) read the law of God to the people of Israel, all the people were so moved, that reflecting upon their past lives, they wept most bitterly, comparing their actions with the law of God, which ought to have been their rule, and which was delivered to them for that end.   Insomuch that the Levites felt it extremely difficult to suppress their sighing.   It is after this manner we ought to hear sermons, with a wholesome and profitable confusion for our faults ; comparing our lives with the doctrine we hear preached ; examining the difference there is between what we are, and what we ought to be ; considering, in fine, how far we are from the perfection proposed to us to practise.

There is a third point which will confirm still more and more the preceding one, and which being presupposed will also serve as an excellent precaution against the spirit of curiosity, and will dispose us better to derive advantage from what we hear. It is, and the whole world ought to believe it, that exhortations are not made to unfold to us any new extraordinary duties, but only to revive in us the memory of the more common and ordinary duties, and thereby to inspire us with more fervour to put them in practice.   In effect, it is particularly upon this account that St. Ignatius (Part iii. Const. cap. i.) required so frequent exhortations amongst us ; for in the third part of the Constitutions, after he had established the rules set down in the summary ; " Let there be," says he, " some one appointed, who every week or at least every fortnight, may remind us of these Rules, and other such like instructions ; lest, through the weakness of our nature, we may forget them, and at last come to neglect and discontinue their practice." Father Natalis takes a cursory notice of this, in his remarks upon the Constitutions; saying, that though the Constitutions speak only of eight or fifteen days, yet, the custom observed throughout the whole society is to make these exhortations regularly every week. And doubtless none could speak with more certainty on this point than he, who visited almost all the houses of the society, and knew perfectly well all their practices. Hence these exhortations being made on subjects already very well known to us, our facility in forgetting them is the reason why they cannot be too often set before our eyes. But suppose we remember them ever so well, yet it would be in vain that our memories should be faithful, if our wills also be not fervent; and therefore it is to warm and animate us, that the obligations we have contracted by our profession, and the end for which we came to religion, are so often repeated and inculcated to us. The opinion of St. Austin is very true, that "The understanding is quick and ready, but the motion of the will is very slow:" wherefore we ought often to touch and treat upon the same matter, and in a manner rivet it in our minds, as St. Paul endeavoured when he wrote to the Philippians, saying, " Moreover, my brethren, rejoice in our Lord : it is no pain at all to me, but for you it is very necessary, that I often write and repeat the same thing to you." (Phil. iii. 1.) The apostle having been wrapt to the third heaven, without doubt wanted not matter; he had new things enough, and very elevated too, to tell them of : yet for all this, he believed himself obliged to repeat only these things, wherewith he had before entertained them ; because he knew these were more necessary for them than the others. And this ought to be the particular object of him who makes exhortations or sermons. He ought not to think of what may make himself appear more eloquent, or more profound ; for hereby he would rather preach himself, than preach to others. But he should consider what will be most useful to his audience, and. propose only those things from which they may reap most profit. Thus they will not become weary of hearing those common things they already know ; because they will presently perceive, that either they neglect to perform them or at least do not practise them with all possible perfection ; and therefore it is always necessary they should be put in mind of them.

In the fourth place it will be of very great profit, that whatever is said in exhortations. be received by us as particularly said to

ourselves, and not as a thing which regards others ; and let us
not act herein as worldly persons ordinarily do, when they hear
a sermon.   A preacher addresses himself to them, for example,
in this manner—You are like, says he, to those, whose employment it is to carve at great men's tables, and help others, without
taking any meat for themselves.   When you hear me say this,
you cry out ; an excellent reflection indeed, and very proper for
such a one ! this is quite adapted to one of my acquaintance ! if
such a one were here, O how it would answer him !—and notwithstanding after all this carving for others, you keep nothing
for yourself.   In this banquet of the word of God, I would have
all of you to be of the number of guests, and not of the carvers.
" All that a prudent man shall hear, that is good and profitable,
he will practise," says Ecclesiasticus, " and will apply it to himself ; but a vain, ambitious man will not hear but with disgust,
and will cast it behind his back." (Ecclus. xxi. 18.)   Let us then
endeavour to be of the number of guests ; of the number of those
wise men, who so take to themselves what is said, as if it were
spoken to them alone, and to none else.   For perhaps that which
seems to you to be very well applied to another, may be better
applied to yourself, if you knew yourself better than you do ;
and if you were not like those, who can " perceive a mote in
their neighbour's eye, yet see not a beam in their own."   (Mat.
vii. 3.) But though in effect there should be nothing in what is
said, which any way touches or concerns you at present, yet
neglect not to hoard it up in your mind for the future ; perhaps
you will soon come to stand in need of it, and by this means
you can never fail always to take what is said as addressed to
yourself only.
    In the fifth place, the better to explain what we have said, it
is fit that every one should presuppose, that oftentimes in exhortations the preacher reprehends certain faults, not as though
he actually believed them practised by any of his auditors, but
only with a design to hinder the practice or the introduction of
such imperfections for the future.   The physic which by precaution is given to prevent diseases, is no less advantageous than
that which is given to cure them   Wherefore in our exhortations, we ought to have regard to this, following the counsel of
the Wise Man, " Before sickness comes, make use of remedies."
(Ecclus. xviii. 20.)   And as we ordinarily strive to apply the
remedy before the disease is formed, or comes to a crisis ; so we
exhort to virtue and perfection : we blame vice and remissness ;

to the end that being advertised of the danger he is in, every one may the better stand upon his guard, and take care lest he fall. Moreover, as to the preacher, he ought not note or point out any one in particular; for this would be a great imprudence in him, because he would hereby reap less fruit, and give great occasion of scandal. Wherefore it would be very ill done to think, and still worse to express, that this was said for such a one, this for another; and it would be forming a very rash judgment of the preacher to think that he had anything so unreasonable in view. But though, both on the preacher's and the auditor's part, there ought to be a great circumspection in this matter, and that it is always very good that every one takes what is said as said to himself, yet I would not that any one should frame to himself that the preacher had a design to point him out; for such a thought as this must never enter into our minds; but what I desire is, that laying our hands upon our hearts, we confront our life and actions with the doctrine he preaches, and say to ourselves, certainly what he says may very well be addressed to me; I have great need of this warning; it is God that has put this into his mouth for my good. In this manner we shall let nothing pass, from which we may not derive some fruit either for our amendment, or our greater perfection. The gospel takes notice, that after the discourse our Saviour had had with the Samaritan, she said to all she met with, "Come and see a man who has told me all things that I have ever done." (John iv. 29.) When the preacher speaks in this manner to his audience, and tells them what passes in their hearts, then he may securely judge that he effectually makes a good sermon, and that his exhortation becomes fruitful.

In the last place, we ought to be convinced that the word of God is the nourishment and sustenance of the soul; and therefore we should always endeavour, in every exhortation we hear, to carry something away with us, and conserve and lay it up in our hearts, whence we may obtain more strength and force to begin anew. "The grain which is sown in good ground," says our Saviour, "signifies those who hear the word of God with a heart well disposed, and retain the same, and make it bring forth good fruit in due season." (Luke viii. 15.) St. Gregory, explaining this passage, says, that the body is in a very bad state of health when the stomach cannot keep or retain any nourishment, but throws up whatever it takes. (Hom. 15.) In the same manner, the soul is in a dangerous

state, when the heart retains not the word of God. The Royal
Prophet knew this truth very well when he said, " I have hid
thy words in the bottom of my heart, to the end I may not sin
against thee." (Ps. cxix. 11.) And in effect how often does it
happen that we are tempted, and are in danger of yielding to
the temptation, and that then, remembering only some passage
of Scripture, or some holy maxim we heard in a sermon, we
regain new strength, and derive from it very powerful assistance ? And we know that, by three passages of Scripture, our
Saviour overcame the three temptations wherewith the enemy
assaulted him.

By all that has been said, it is easy to comprehend in how
great an error these are, and what prejudice they do themselves,
who go to sermons and exhortations for fashion' sake ; or
suffer themselves to be overcome with sleep and distractions
during the sermon. " The devil," says our Saviour in the
gospel, " comes and snatches the word of God out of their
hearts, lest they should believe and be saved." (Luke viii. 12.)
And it is in this manner that unhappily is verified in them the
parable of the grain which was eaten by the birds as soon as it
was sown. Perhaps one word which you lost when you were
asleep or distracted would have contributed very much to your
spiritual advancement ; and for that reason the devil, who
nourishes a mortal envy and hatred against you, endeavours by
all means possible to prevent this good seed from taking root
in your heart. St. Austin says, " That the word of God is like
a fish-hook which never takes, but when it is taken : and as the
fish remains a prize to the hook, so we remain a prize to the
word of God when we take and receive it." And for this reason
the devil exerts all his powers to hinder us from receiving it,
lest our heart should thereby be engaged, and we should never
be able to get loose or free ourselves. Let us endeavour,
therefore, to go to sermons and exhortations with so requisite
a disposition as this is, and to hear the word of God in such
sort that it take root in our heart, and produce the fruit of
justice. " Practise it," says St. James, " and be not content to
hear it only, thereby deceiving yourself ; for he who hears the
word of God, and practises it not, is like a man that considers
his face in a glass : he views himself, and goes his way, and
soon forgets what kind of man he was." (James i. 22.)
" Those who hear the law," says St. Paul, " are not just before
God ; but those who practise it shall be justified." (Rom. ii. 13.)

In a book called the *Spiritual Meadow*, composed by John Evirat, or, according to some, by St. Sophronius, patriarch of Jerusalem, which is quoted with great respect in the second Council of Nice, we read that a holy man called Eusebius sitting one day in the field with another anchoret, called Amianus, and this Amianus reading one of the books of the gospel, which the other explained, it happened that Eusebius cast his eyes upon the labourers who tilled the ground in an adjoining field, and at the same time this distraction hindered him from attending to what was read; so that Amianus lighting by chance upon a very hard passage, asked him its explanation. Eusebius, who had not attended, desired him to read it the second time; whereby Amianus came to know he had been distracted, and repeating it, told him it was no wonder he had not heard the words of the gospel, since he had distracted himself by looking upon the workmen. Eusebius remained so confounded at this rebuke, that for the future he strictly prohibited his eyes from beholding either that plain or the stars of heaven any more; and presently rising up he took a little by-path, and retired into a poor cell which he never afterwards quitted; living more than forty years in this strait prison, to which he had condemned himself. He confirmed this his resolution by such a kind of necessity, as might force him to keep it. For he bound his reins with a girdle of iron, and put another of a great weight about his neck, and then joined these two together by a great chain, which he fastened to the earth; to the end he might always be constrained to remain in such a bent or bowing posture, that he could not go into the fields round about him, nor so much as look upon them, nor even lift up his eyes to heaven. This was the manner wherein this holy man chastised himself for one light inadvertency, for one single dissipation of mind, whilst the other read the word of God. Is not this sufficient to give us an extreme confusion, seeing the little concern we have for all those distractions, that daily happen to us on the like occasions?

———o———

THE SECOND TREATISE.

———o———

———o———

CHAPTER I.

That our Advancement and Perfection consist in performing well our ordinary Actions.

" PERFORM well what is just " (Deut. xvi. 20), says our Lord in Deuteronomy, to his elect people. It is not sufficient for our advancement and perfection, that we perform our actions, but we must perform them well ; in like manner, it is not enough to be a religious, but we must endeavour to be a good one. St. Jerome understanding that St. Paulinus praised him very much, for living in the place where our Saviour Jesus Christ wrought the mysteries of our redemption, wrote thus to him : " Not the living in Jerusalem, but the living well in Jeruslem, is a subject worthy of praise." (Ep. ad Paul.) This saying became afterwards a proverb amongst the religious, and shewed them that it was not sufficient for their salvation to live in a monastery ; and that neither the place, nor the habit, but purity and sanctity of life, makes a true religious. The chief point therefore consists not in being a religious, but in being a good one; not in performing the exercises of religion, but in performing them well : " He did all things well " (Mark vii. 37), said the people, speaking of Jesus Christ, and it is truly in this *well* that our well-being consists.

It is certain that the good or bad state of our souls depends upon our good and bad works ; because, such as our works are, such shall we also be ; since they alone shew what we are. The tree is known by its fruit, and according to St. Austin, "Man is a tree, and his works the fruit, and therefore by the fruit of his works we may soon perceive what every man is." Our Saviour also, speaking of hypocrites and false prophets, says, " You may know them by their fruits " (Matt. vii. 16) ; and on the contrary, speaking of himself, " The works," says he, " which I do in the name of my Father, give testimony of me ; and if you will not

believe me, believe at least my works; they tell you who I am."
(John x. 25.)   But our actions discover not only what we are in
this life, but also foretel what we must be in the next; for as we
are in this life, such we shall for ever be in the life to come :
because God will recompense every one according to his works,
as the holy Scripture teaches us, in divers places of the Old and
New Testament.   "You, O Lord," says the Psalmist, "will
render to every one according to his works" (Ps. lxi. 13): and St.
Paul writing to the Romans : "Whatever any man," says he, "shall
have sown in this life, that shall he reap after his death in the
next." (Gal. vi. 8.)

But let us descend to particulars, and see what those actions are,
upon which all our good, and all our advancement and perfection
depend.   I say, they are no others than the common and ordinary
actions we perform every day.   It is in making well our prayer
and ordinary examen ; it is in hearing or saying mass with due
respect; in reciting the divine office, and vocal prayers with attention and fervour ; it is in exercising ourselves continually in
penance and mortification ; in acquitting ourselves well of our
charge, and of what obedience imposes on us : in fine, it is in performing well the most common and familiar actions of our life,
that our advancement and perfection consist.   We shall soon become perfect, if we perform these perfectly well; we shall still remain imperfect if we perform them imperfectly.   This then is all,
that properly makes the difference between a perfect and an imperfect religious.   For our perfection arises not from our doing
more things than another does, but from our doing them better ;
and proportionably to the *manner* wherein every one works,
every one will infallibly become more or less perfect.

The Son of God tells us in the parable of the sower, "That
the grain which was sown in good ground, in one place rendered thirty, in another sixty, and in another a hundred-fold."
(Mat. xiii. 8, 23.)   By this, as the saints expound it, our
Saviour would manifest to us the three different degrees of those
that serve God ; that is to say, those that begin, those that have
made some progress, and those that are arrived at the height of
perfection.   We all sow the same grain ; because we all perform
the same actions, and observe the same rule ; all of us have the
same hours for prayer, and examen ; and, from morning till
night, we are all employed according to the prescription of
obedience.   Yet for all this, "What difference is there between
man and man," between one religious and another ?   In some,

the works they sow produce a hundred-fold, because they perform them with an extreme fervour of spirit, and a very great purity of intention ; and these are such as are perfect. In others they render sixty, and these are they who still advance in the way, but are not yet arrived at perfection. And others reap but thirty for one, and these are beginners only in God's service. Let every one therefore see, to which of these degrees he is arrived—see if you be not amongst those who render only thirty-fold ; and God grant that none of us find ourselves of the number of them, of whom the apostle, St. Paul, makes mention : " They have gathered together," says he, " and built upon the foundation of faith, with wood and straw ; to burn in the day of our Lord." (1 Cor. iii. 12.)   Take care, therefore, you do nothing out of ostentation, or human respects, to please men, or to gain their esteem ; for this were to make a building of wood or straw, to burn, at least, in purgatory.   But endeavour to perform all your actions with the greasiest perfection you are able ; whereby " you will," as St. Paul says, " erect a structure, all of gold, silver, and precious stones."

The truth of what I have already said will more clearly be comprehended, by establishing this maxim, that our advancement and perfection consist in two things :   " In doing what God wishes us to do ; and in the manner he wishes us to do it ;" for it is certain, that these two points comprehend all perfection. As to the first, all religious by God's great mercy are thereunto arrived ; and it is, without doubt, one of the greatest advantages and comforts religious have, that they are certain whatever they do through obedience is, without doubt, what God would have them to do.   This proposition is a kind of religious maxim, entirely conformable to the doctrine of saints, and to the gospel itself, as I shall prove more amply, when I speak of obedience. " He who hears you, hears me " (Luke x. 16), says our Saviour. So that by obeying our superior we obey God, and perform his divine will because it is what he precisely demands of us. And as to the second point, which is, that perfection consists in doing the things that God commands, *in the manner* he would have us perform them, as it cannot be doubted, but that he would have us to do them with all possible perfection ; so it is not at all necessary to enlarge upon it, in order to prove a truth so evident in itself.   It is related in the Chronicles of the Cistercian Order, that St. Bernard being with his religious at matins, saw a great many angels, who noted, and wrote down the actions of each one of his religious, and the manner wherein they performed them ; and according to the greater or less attention and fervour in their singing and praying, they noted the actions either in letters of gold or silver, or else with ink or water. But they wrote nothing at all of some, who being present only in body, but absent in spirit, let themselves be carried away with vain and unprofitable thoughts. He perceived also that the angels chiefly at the *Te Deum* were very desirous that the religious should sing it devoutly, and he saw as it were flames issuing from the mouths of those who performed it with fervour. Let each one reflect upon himself, and take notice after what manner he makes his prayer ; to see whether it deserves to be written in gold or silver letters, or with ink or water; or in fine, to see whether it deserves to be noted at all. Let him observe whether the flames of his heart issue through his month by fervorous aspirations, or whether he yawns through laziness and disgust; and in fine, let him reflect, whether he be there present in body only, but elsewhere in mind, having it dissipated with the thoughts of his studies, with the care of his affairs, or with other things still more to be condemned.

---o---

CHAPTER II.

Perfection consists in such easy Matters, that we ought to be extremely encouraged to labour to attain it.

WHEN Father Natalis, who, in the Society of Jesus, was distinguished for learning and virtue, visited the provinces of Spain, the principal thing recommended by him was, that this truth should be perpetually inculcated, viz., that all our advancement and perfection consist not in the performance of very extraordinary things, or in the being employed in the highest and most laborious offices of religion, but only in doing our ordinary actions well, and in acquitting ourselves well of whatsoever obedience employs us in, be it ever so mean or easy. For it is this that God requires of us, and consequently it is upon this alone we are to fix our eyes, if we desire to please him, and to attain perfection. Let us now see and examine at what little expense we can render ourselves perfect. In fact, nothing more is requisite on our part than what we daily perform—a consideration which should be at once a great comfort and encouragement to us.   If, indeed, we could not attain perfection but by the exercise of some great employments, by extraordinary elevations of the soul and by sublime meditations, we might have something to plead for our excuse—we might allege our incapacity and inability to soar so high.   Were it exacted of you to discipline yourself daily to blood, to fast on bread and water; to go barefoot, and to wear a perpetual haircloth; you might answer that you have not strength sufficient to undergo these mortifications.   But it is not this that is asked of you; it is not this upon which our perfection depends: but it consists only in the performing well the very actions you are doing.   By this you may render yourself perfect if you please.   All the expenses are already incurred; there is no necessity of adding any other actions than those you do.   Who will not therefore encourage himself to acquire perfection, since it is thus within our reach, and consists only in such ordinary and easy things?   God, the better to excite his people to serve him, and to fulfil his law, spoke to them in this manner :—The commandment which I give you to-day, consists not in anything above your reach, nor is it far from you; it is not in heaven, whereby you might excuse yourself, saying, who is able to ascend to heaven to bring it from thence, to the end that we may hear and fulfil it? Nor is it anything beyond the sea, so that one may complain and say, who of us is able to cross the seas, to go to bring it, to the end that we may hear and perform what is required of us? But it is a thing very near you, a precept with which you often entertain yourselves, which you have often in your mouth, of which the execution depends upon no other than your own heart.   (Deut. xxx. 11—14.)   We may say the same of the perfection we speak of ; and this is likewise the same means that St. Anthony used to exhort his disciples thereunto.   The Greeks, says he, who devoted themselves to the study of wisdom, undertook great voyages, both by sea and land, underwent great labours and hardships, and exposed themselves to very great dangers to attain it.   But you, to acquire virtue, which is true wisdom, are not obliged to go so far, nor to expose yourselves to so great danger; you need not even to go out of your cells, for there you will find it, or rather, "The kingdom of God is within yourselves." (Luke xvii. 21); it is in such things as are most familiar to you, and that you do every day, in which your perfection consists.

When those times approach that are more particularly consecrated to devotion, as for example, Advent, Lent, Pentecost, and renovation of vows, it is then that ordinarily, in our spiritual conferences, we ask what means we may best make use of to prepare ourselves to be born again with Jesus Christ, to die and rise with him, to receive the Holy Ghost, and to renew our vows; and then our directors fail not to suggest an infinity of most wholesome and proper means, to attain these ends. But the most important of all, and that in which we ought most to confide, is, what we speak of at present; that is, the perfecting ourselves in those things we are accustomed to perform. Correct every day those faults and imperfections you commit in doing these things, and daily apply yourself to do them better and better; and this will be an excellent preparation to compass all you desire. In fine, apply yourself chiefly to this, and look upon all other things as means only to help you to perform it.

———o———

CHAPTER III.

In what the Goodness and Perfection of our Actions consist, and some means to help us to perform them well.

LET us now see in what the goodness of our actions consists, and thereby we may better know the means of performing them well. I say, it consists in two things, of which the first and chief is, that we act purely for God. St. Ambrose (De Inst. Virg. ad Euseb. c. 3) asks the reason why God in the creation of the world, after he had created the living creatures, and all other corporal things, praised them at the same instant ? " He created the plants and trees," says the Scripture, "and he saw that it was good. He created the beasts upon the earth, the birds also, and fishes; and he saw that it was good. He created the heavens, and stars, the sun, and moon ; and he saw that it was good." (Gen i. 10, 12, &c.) ; in fine, he praised everything he created, as soon as he had perfected its creation. But as soon as he had created man, he seems to leave him the only one without praise, because he added not presently, " He saw that he was good," as he had said of the rest. What mystery is there in this ? And what can be the cause of this difference that God makes ? The cause, says this great saint, is this : That the beauty and goodness of beasts and corporal things consist entirely in their external appearance ; and that there is nothing at all, besides what presently appears externally to the eye, that is perfect in them; and therefore they may be praised as soon as they are seen. But the goodness and perfection of man consist not in the exterior, but in what lies inwardly hid : all the glory of the king's daughter is from within (Ps. xliv. 14) : it is this which is pleasing in God's sight. "For man sees only what outwardly appears," says our Lord to Samuel, "but God penetrates to the bottom of the heart." (1 Kings xvi. 7.) He sees with what intention every one performs each action; and it is upon this account that he did not praise man, as he did all other creatures, as soon as he had created him. The intention is the foundation of the goodness of all our actions : the foundations are not seen, and yet they alone sustain the whole edifice. Our intention also does the same.

The second thing required for the perfection of all our actions is, that we do all we can to perform them well. It is not enough that your intention is good, nor to say that you do this for God. But the better to please him, you must endeavour to perform it after the best manner possible. The first means, therefore, to perform our actions well, is to perform them purely for God; for hereby, though our superiors do not behold us, and though men cannot see everything we do, yet the desire we have to please God will make us force ourselves to perform all our actions with all the perfection we are able, and in fine to imitate those who truly work for God. St. Ignatius once asked a brother, whom he saw perform his office very negligently, "Dear brother, for whom do you do that?" "For the love of God," answered the brother. "Then I assure you," replied the saint, "if you do so hereafter, I shall give you a severe penance ; for if you did it for men, it were no great fault to do it with so little care as you do, but since you do it for so great a Master, with so great carelessness, it cannot be excused."

The second means which the saints propose as most efficacious, is always to walk in God's presence. And Seneca himself says, "That when we desire to be virtuous, and to do all things very well, we ought to imagine ourselves in the presence of some person of great merit and quality, and accustom ourselves to say and do all things, as we should do or say, were we actually in his presence." (Ep. 25.) And if this may be sufficient to oblige us to perform our duty exactly, of what efficacy will it be, to place ourselves always in God's presence, and to think every moment that he sees us; especially, since this is not a mere imagination, but a real truth, as the Scripture teaches us in divers places?

"The eyes of our Lord are more glorious than the sun, looking round about upon all the ways of men and upon the bottom of the abyss ; and penetrating the most secret corners of man's heart." (Ecclus. xxiii. 28.)

We shall, in another place, treat expressly of the presence of God ; where we shall make appear how profitable a thing it is and how much recommended by the saints, to place ourselves always in God's presence. What we ought to infer from this subject at present, is to consider how much it will help us, to perform our ordinary actions well. And though it is of so great importance, as we shall prove in its proper place, yet in our continually reflecting on it, we ought not make the presence of God our principal object, but we ought to look on it as only a very proper means or help to perform our actions well. But should it happen, that the attention we pay to the presence of God should cause us to perform our actions negligently, and thereby make us commit several faults, this would not be a good or true devotion, but an illusion. Some even add that the true presence of God, which we ought always to have before our eyes, and which the Scripture and saints recommend unto us, is to take great care that in consequence we do all our actions so, that they may be fit to appear in his sight, and may contain nothing unworthy of his divine presence ; in a word, we ought to perform them, as if we performed them in his holy sight. St. John seems to remind us of this in the Apocalypse, when, speaking of the four beasts he saw before the throne of God, he says, "That within and without, before and behind, and on all sides they were full of eyes" (Apoc. iv. 8); to signify that those who would perfectly serve God, and be worthy of his presence, ought to be very circumspect to do nothing, whereby they may render themselves unworthy to appear before him. You ought to be full of eyes, within and without, in order to take care of all your actions, of your steps, your looks, your words ; of what you hear, of what you think ; and in fine of what you desire, and what you love ; to the end that in all your thoughts, words, and actions, there may be nothing disagreeable in the sight of God, in whose presence you are.

Behold here a most excellent manner of walking in God's presence. Let us also take notice that instead of these words in Genesis : "Enoch walked with God" (Gen. v. 24), that is to say, before God, "and disappeared because our Lord took him ;" Ecclesiasticus and St. Paul say, " Enoch pleased God, and was translated to Paradise" (Ecclus. xliv. 16; Heb. xi. 5); giving us hereby to understand, that there is no difference between *walking with* God, and *pleasing* God; since the Wise Man and the apostle explain both expressions alike, and make them signify one and the same thing. Origen and St. Austin give the same explanation to what is said in Exodus, where when Jethro came to see his son-in-law Moses, Aaron and the chief of the people of Israel assembled "to eat bread with him before the Lord." (Exod. xiii. 12.) The Scripture says, not that they assembled to eat before the tabernacle, or before the ark, because they were not then in being; but they met together to rejoice, and divert themselves with him, by entertaining and feasting him; and kept the same moderation and decency during their mirth and feasting, as they would have done, had they eaten in God's presence : taking care there should be nothing that might offend his sacred eyes. It is after this manner that the just and perfect walk before God in all things, even in the most indifferent actions, and the most necessary for the preservation of life. "Let the just," says the Royal Prophet, "feast and rejoice themselves in God's sight." (Ps. lxvii. 4.) Let them eat, drink, and recreate, so they do it in his sight, and do nothing indecent, or unworthy of his divine presence.

Many saints affirm, that we ought to understand in this sense those words of our Saviour, "We must always pray without ceasing" (Luke xviii. 1); and also these of St. Paul, "pray without intermission" (1 Thess. v. 17); and they, moreover, add that those who perform well what they do, pray always. St. Austin, speaking of these words of the Psalmist, "I will celebrate thy praise all the day long." "Would you know," says he, "the way to praise God always ? Perform well what you do, and you will praise him continually. They pray always," says St. Hilary, "who always perform their actions to please and glorify God, whereby they make their life a perpetual prayer, and they who thus live night and day according to his law, their lives are no other than a continual meditation on the law." St. Jerome, writing upon this verse of the Psalmist : "Sun and moon, praise ye the Lord, and let the light and all the stars praise him" (Ps. cxlviii. 3), asks how the sun and moon, the light and stars can praise God?—and answers the question himself thus : "By never failing to do their duty, and by continually complying with those obligations God imposed upon them at the moment of their creation ; for by this continual service, they render to God a continual praise. Hence, whoever acquits himself well of his charge, and performs well the more ordinary actions, to which his profession obliges him, such a one praises God always and exercises continual prayer. This doctrine may also be confirmed by those words of the Holy Ghost in Ecclesiasticus : " He who observes the law, multiplies prayer. It is a wholesome sacrifice to keep the commandments, and withdraw one's-self from all kind of iniquity." (Ecclus. xxxv. 1.) Such persons as these let us see, of how great perfection it is to perform our ordinary actions well : because hereby we multiply our prayers, we walk always in God's presence, and we offer a continual sacrifice, which is pleasing to him and wholesome and profitable to us.

——o——

CHAPTER IV.

That another means to perform our Actions well, is to imagine each one the only one we have to do.

THE third means of doing our actions well is, to do separately each one, as if it were the only one we had to do—to make our prayer, to say mass, to recite our beads, and divine office, and to do all the rest of our actions, as if in effect we had nothing else to perform but the one we are engaged in. There is nothing to hurry us—let us not be disturbed in what we are doing—let us not suffer our actions to clash with another, but let us apply ourselves totally to what we are engaged in. Whilst we are at our prayers, let us not think of our studies, nor of anything else, nor even of the duties of our office or employment. For these thoughts tend only to divert us from our prayer, and to hinder us from acquitting ourselves well of it. We have the rest of the whole day to study, or to fulfil the other obligations of our charge. All things have their time " (Ecclus. iii. v. l.) ; let us not confound or disturb their order to no purpose, but let us remember our Saviour's words : " That sufficient for the day is the evil thereof." (Matt. vi. 34.) Each day's disquiet and affliction is sufficient to take up our thoughts, without thinking of the evils to come. This is so profitable a means, and so conformable to reason, that the Pagans themselves made use of it, to be able to keep themselves with more profound respect before their false gods and idols ; which gave rise to the ancient proverb : " Let those sit that adore." Let those that adore God in prayer, and thereby entertain themselves with him, do it with repose and attention, and not run about as if they were thinking of something else. Plutarch speaking of the reverence with which priests in his time approached their gods, says, that whilst the priest offered sacrifice, there was one appointed to cry out continually with a loud voice : " Do what you do ;" as if he would have said, think of nothing else but what you are doing, distract not yourself, but apply your mind wholly to your business. It is by adopting the means at present proposed, you will do all things well. Apply yourself closely and entirely to each action alone, as if you had nothing else to do ; attend only to this, apply to it with all your care ; banish all other thoughts, and you will never fail to do well. " Let us do what we are about at present," said Aristippus, " without thinking either of what is past or to come ; " and let us apply ourselves wholly to the present action ; because it is that alone which is in our power ; and what is to come is so uncertain, that we cannot answer whether it will happen or not. How happy should we be, if we could gain so much upon ourselves, and were so much masters of our thoughts and imagination, that we never thought of anything, but what we are at present about ? But then so unsteady is our heart— besides, so crafty and industrious is the devil to avail himself of our natural levity, that when we are employed about anything, he sets before our eyes what we should do at another time, in order to distract our minds, and divert us from doing what we are engaged in at present. This mode of tempting us is the more frequently practised by him, as he sees it to be more dangerous and prejudicial to us ; for by this means he hinders us from ever performing anything well. In time of prayer, he fills our minds with the thoughts of our studies and of other affairs, that we may not be able to pray as we ought ; and as long as he can but take away our attention from what we are about, he ceases not to suggest a thousand excellent means of performing afterwards our other actions well. But when we come to do them, he will not fail to set others before our eyes, that we may not acquit ourselves so well of what we are about at present, endeavouring after this manner continually to deceive us, and to render all our actions imperfect. But since " we are not ignorant of his thoughts " (2 Cor. ii. 11), let us lay aside future affairs ; rejecting them as soon as they present themselves. It will be good to think of them in their due time ; but it is bad to do so when we ought to be taken up with other thoughts. But if the fear of not being able to think afterwards of those things, which now present themselves to your imagination, cause you to dwell upon them; that very circumstance ought to show you, that it is not an inspiration from God, but a temptation of the devil. For God is a friend of peace, and of order; and therefore whatever troubles your repose, and interrupts the order of things, comes not from God, but from the devil, who loves only confusion and disorder. Banish, therefore, whatsoever presents itself to your imagination under this pretence. Be not diverted from what you are doing, and assure yourself if you perform then your duty well, that God will not fail to put you in mind, in due time, of the thoughts you had before banished for his sake, and will fix them again in your mind to your greater advantage. If, for example, it happens that in time of your spiritual exercises you should be surprised with some thought of your studies; and if some convincing reason on a hard point or difficulty, or any light concerning some obscure passage, or a solution of some hard doubt offers itself, cast all equally away, and believe that you will be rather a gainer than a loser thereby. "The knowledge that is despised for the sake of virtue," says St. Bonaventure, "is afterwards acquired by the virtue itself;" and Father Avila advises us, when any business comes into our mind out of due time, to say, God ordains not this at present; wherefore I will not think on it—when he pleases to command me, I will diligently apply myself to it.

------o------

CHAPTER V.

Another Means of doing our Actions well, is to perform each one as if it were the very last Action of our Life.

ANOTHER means which the saints teach us to perform our actions well is, to do them as if each action were to be the last we were to perform in this life. St. Bernard, speaking of the manner wherein a religious ought to comport himself in all he does, says, "That in all his actions, he should often repeat to himself: Were you to die presently, would you do this?" (Bern. in Spir. Monac.) And St. Basil gives us the same counsel, when he says, "Have always your last hour before your eyes. When you rise in the morning, doubt whether you shall live till night; and when you go to bed at night, do not assure yourself that you shall live till next morning; and in this manner it will be very

easy for you to correct all your vices." (Bas. ad fil. spir.) Thomas
a Kempis says as much almost in the same terms. St. Anthony
also gave the same advice to his disciples, to encourage them to
virtue and perfection : and without doubt there is no better
means to help us to do our actions well, than to believe each day
to be our last. If we could put ourselves into this disposition
of mind, and perform everything as if we were to die as soon as
we had done it, we should perform our actions after a far
different manner, and with far greater perfection than we do.
With what fervour would a priest say mass, if he thought it
would be the last action of his life, and that afterwards he
should have no more time to merit, or to perform the least good
work ? What attention and zeal should we not have in our
prayer, if we were persuaded that it were to be our last, and
that we should never have any more leisure to ask God pardon
for our sins, and implore his mercy ? It is for this reason that
we commonly say, there is no better place to pray in than at sea,
because we find our fervour far different, when we have death
before our eye, than when we are in no fright or fear at all.

It is reported of a holy religious who was daily wont to go to
confession before he said mass, that suddenly falling very sick,
and his superior seeing him in great danger of death, acquainted
him with it, advising him to confess as if he were presently to
die :—God be praised, said the sick man, lifting up his eyes and
hands to heaven, it is about thirty years since I daily made my
confession, and if I were to die the next moment, so that there
remains no more at present for me to do, than to dispose myself
to receive my viaticum. It is after this manner we ought to
perform all our actions. Let us confess, let us communicate, as
though we were to die as soon as we had done it ; and by our
doing so, it will not be necessary, at the hour of death, that we
confess in such a manner as if we were to die ; but it will suffice
that we dispose or reconcile ourselves, as we often do a moment
before communion, to put ourselves into a state of receiving
more worthily our Lord's body. If we carry this precaution
along with us, death will always find us prepared, and will never
surprise us. Behold here is the best means we can avail ourselves of, to be preserved from the misfortune of a sudden death.
" Happy," says Jesus Christ, "is the servant whom his master at
his arrival shall find busy in performing his duty." (Matt. xxiv.
46.) Job acted thus, as he himself tells us ;—" From the time
of my combat in this life, I daily attend when my change will

come; you will call me, O Lord, and I will answer you." (Job
xiv. 15.) Call me when you please, in what place or employment soever I am, I am always ready to answer your call.

One of the best means to know certainly whether we walk
uprightly before God is, to consider whether we are in a state to
answer him at what time soever he calls, and in what employment soever we are engaged. I speak not here of an infallible
certainty, because such a one is not to be had in this life, without a particular revelation; but I speak only of a probable
conjecture, which is all we can pretend to, and I say that the
most proper means of obtaining this is, to examine whether in
the condition and present conjuncture we are in, and in the very
action we are about, we should be content to be surprised by
death. Think whether you are as ready to answer God as Job
was, in case he should call you this very moment; try yourself
often in this manner; sound your heart, and ask yourself,
whether in the state you are in you would be content to render
your last account at his tribunal. For my part, when I reflect
and question myself on this subject, if I find that at this very
moment, and in the very action I am doing, I should not fear
death, methinks my affairs go well, and I am content with
myself. On the other hand, if I should not wish to die in my
present state and occupation, but should wish my death to be
deferred for some time, till the things which take up my thoughts
at present, and hinder me from performing my duty, were
finished: I take this for an evident sign that I am not as
solicitous as I ought about my spiritual advancement, and that
I do not satisfy the obligations of a good religious. For,
according to what Thomas-a-Kempis says, " If you had a good
conscience you would not fear death, because it is sin, and not
death, which we ought to dread. Wherefore, since you fear it
so much, it is a sign that your conscience reproaches you with
something, and that your accounts with God are not in a good
state. A steward who has his accounts in good order desires
nothing more than to give them up: but he whose accounts are
not in order is always afraid lest he should be called upon, and
thinks of nothing else than how to gain time, and defer the
giving them up as long as he can.

The best exercise for a religious would be, according to St.
Francis of Borgia, to place himself twenty-four times a day in
the situation of a dying man, and often to repeat to himself, " I
must die this day." In this case, if the religious feel nothing to

trouble him, no doubt his soul would be in a good state. Let every one then enter into himself and examine himself frequently on this point; and if in the moment you make this reflection you are not in the state you would wish to be in were you to die, endeavour to put yourself into it, and dispose yourself well for this dangerous passage. Imagine that you ask God some few days more to prepare yourself for it, and that he grants them you; and endeavour to make good use of the respite he gives you, by living during this time as if you were to die the moment after. Happy is he who is such during his life, as he desires to be at the hour of his death.

We never make a deeper impression upon the minds of men than when we preach this truth forcibly to them, admonishing them not to defer their conversion from day to day; because to-morrow is uncertain, and they know not whether ever they shall live to see it. " He who has promised pardon," says St. Gregory, " to those that repent, has not promised a next day for repentance to those who sin." (Hom. xii. in Evan.) We ordinarily say that there is nothing more certain than death, and nothing more uncertain than the hour in which it will happen. But the Saviour of the world says yet more than this :—" Be ready," says he, " because the Son of man will come at the hour you least expect." (Luke xii. 40.) For though he speaks in this place of the general day of judgment, yet this may be understood also of the hour of death; because then each one shall receive his particular judgment, and such sentence, as being once pronounced, will never be revoked, but confirmed on that great and general day. Jesus Christ does not content himself with saying the hour is uncertain, and we know not when it will come, but he says it will come at an hour when we least expect it, and perhaps when we are least of all prepared for it. St. Paul tells the Thessalonians, " That he will come like a thief in the night " (1 Thess. v. 2.) : and St. John in the Apocalypse, speaking in God's name, says, " I will come to you as a thief, and you shall not know at what hour it will be." (Apoc. iii. 3.) A thief gives no notice when he will come, but awaits the hour when we are least upon our guard, and when the world is buried in sleep; wherefore this comparison made use of by the Son of God is also an instruction to teach us how we ought to prepare ourselves, that death may not surprise us. " Know ye," says he, " that if the father of the family knew at what hour the thief would come, he would watch, and would not suffer him to break open his house." (Luke xii. 39.) But because he cannot foresee the hour, nor whether it will be in the beginning, towards the middle, or in the end of the night, he continually stands upon his guard to hinder himself from being robbed. It is after this manner we ought to be ready at all times, and in all places whatsoever, because death will attack us when we least think of it.

The saints hereupon observe, that it is a very great mercy of God that the hour of death should be uncertain, to the end we might always be prepared for it ; for if we knew its time, this assurance would give us occasion to become more loose, and to sin with greater confidence. If uncertain as we are of the hour of death, we live notwithstanding so greatly negligent, what would we do if we were assured we should not die for some time ? St. Bonaventure says, that God has vouchsafed to leave us in this incertitude, that we might set no value on temporal things; that seeing every hour, nay every moment we may lose them, we might not any ways be attached to them, but aspire to those we shall always possess when we shall once have gained them : "Fool," says the Son of God to the rich covetous man, "this night thy soul shall be required of thee ; and what then will become of all those riches thou hast gathered together ?" (Ibid. xii. 20.)

Now what we preach to others let us apply to our own advantage, that we may avoid the reproach of St. Paul, "you who instruct others, instruct not yourself." One of the temptations the devil most commonly makes use of to deceive worldlings is, to hide as much as he can from them so clear a truth as this, to divert their eyes and their thoughts from it, and to make them believe that there is time enough for all—that one day they will grow better, and live after another manner than they now do. But it is not only worldlings he deludes after the same manner ; but he also deceives many religious, and continually persuades them to defer their spiritual advancement from one day to another ; to be negligent in applying themselves seriously to their duties, or in regulating their spiritual exercises, or in devoting themselves to penance, till they have ended their studies, quitted their present employments, or accomplished the affair they have in hands, which takes up all their thoughts. Unhappy are you, should you die in time of your studies, whilst you are employed in this office, or distracted with this affair! Because the knowledge which you will have acquired, the employments which you shall have exercised, the cares you shall have given yourself, are the cause why you are become lax and tepid in virtue, and will serve only as hay and straw to burn and torment you in the other life. Turn then to your own advantage the advice you give to others. Physician, "cure yourself" (Luke iv. 23), make use of the same remedy you prescribe to others, since you stand as much in need of it as they do.

———o———

CHAPTER VI.

That to perform our actions well, we ought to think of the present Day only.

ANOTHER means which is of the greatest advantage, and will exceedingly encourage us to do our actions well, is to look no farther than the present day; and though at first sight this means seems not at all different from the former, yet in effect it differs very much, as we shall see in the sequel of this discourse. One of the things which is wont most of all to discourage those that enter into the way of perfection, and one of the most ordinary temptations which the devil makes use of for this end, is the consideration of the long time we shall have to live in this severe restraint, in a constant watch over our actions, in mortifications, fasts, and austerities, in the want of all the conveniences of this life, and in the absolute renunciation of our own will. The enemy lays all these things before our eyes, representing the difficulty of them, and by augmenting the difficulties that accompany them, endeavours to excite in us a disgust, and to dissuade us from embracing such a life in which he would persuade us that we shall never be able to persevere. When St. Ignatius retired to Manresa, to live there in the practice of continual penance, amongst many other temptations wherewith he was attacked, this was one of the greatest:—The devil represented these thoughts continually to his mind : " Is it possible you should be able to undergo so hard and painful a life during fifty or sixty years, which probably you have still to live ? " The means we propose to ourselves in this chapter, is a true remedy against this kind of temptation, and is exceedingly proportionate to our weakness. Do not imagine that you have many years, no not even many days, but only this very day alone ; for who is there who will not be able to urge himself to live well one day, and will not do his endeavours to acquit himself well of all his obligations ? Our holy founder ordains that we should follow this method in our particular examens, according to the things in which we find ourselves more subject to fail. To purpose, for example, in the morning to keep silence at least till noon, or to be observant of modesty, or to suffer with patience whatsoever may happen to us till that time shall have expired. By this means all things will become easy and supportable, instead of appearing difficult and insupportable, as would be the case if we should take a different way, by imposing an absolute necessity upon ourselves never to speak out of time, or to live in a continual circumspection, or to offer perpetual violence to our irregular inclinations.

This, as we read in the lives of the fathers, was the means the solitary made use of, who being so much tempted to gluttony, that even at break of day he found himself so very hungry that he was ready to faint ; yet resolving not to break the holy custom of his order, in eating before three in the afternoon, he adopted the following pious *finesse:* —In the morning he said to himself, As hungry as I am, I will fast till 9 o'clock, and then I may eat: at 9 o'clock, Verily, says he, I ought in something to force myself ; therefore I will not eat till noon, I will have patience till then, as I had till now : and after this manner he passed the time till midday, when he put his bread into water, saying, Since I have waited thus long, I will wait at least till my bread soaks, and for two or three hours more or less, I will not break the custom of my brethren. In fine, at 3 o'clock, he took his refection after he had said his prayers. For several days he acted in this manner, deceiving himself by these delays, till it happened that once being ready to eat at the ordinary hour, he saw rise out of the basket, where he put his bread, a thick smoke which went out of the window of his cell ; and this without doubt was nothing else but the wicked spirit that tempted him. From this time forward, he never found the least inconvenience from hunger, nor felt the same appetite which he was accustomed to feel ; but on the contrary, he easily passed two or three days without eating. It is in this manner that our Saviour recompenses our fidelity in such assaults as these, with a victory obtained over them.

But we had said, and with great reason, that this means was proportionate to our weakness ; for thereby we are gradually strengthened, like infirm persons who are wont to be managed lest labour should affright, and overwhelm them at their very first view of it. But if we were strong, if we were fervent, if we truly loved God, it would not be necessary thus to conduct us by degrees, and to hide the labour and difficulty from us ; because a true servant of God is not affrighted either with the length of time, or the difficulty of things ; but in God's service he thinks all the time short, and the pain and labour he undergoes appear to him sweet and easy. " He does not bind himself," says St. Bernard, " for a year or some certain time, as a mercenary does, but consecrates himself for ever to God's service." Hearken to the voice of the just, who says, " I will never forget the commandments, for you have united my salvation to their observance ; I have disposed my heart to observe them for ever." (Ep. 253. ad Abb. Guar.) It is not therefore simply for a certain time, but for ever, like the recompence to be received for it, which is not of a short durance, but for an eternity ; and without doubt the eternal hunger of the just merits to be eternally satisfied. The same saint explains also the words of the Wise Man in the same sense : " He lived a short time, and yet failed not to perform a long course." (Wis. iv. 13.) The just man, says he, lives many years in a few days ; because he has so much love for God, and so much fervour in his service, that if he should live a hundred thousand years, he would employ them all, to serve him better and better ; so that the determined will which he has to do this, is as meritorious in God's sight, as if he had effectually spent them after this manner ; and God, who knows the bottom of his heart, measures the extent of his resolutions, and the greatness of his zeal, and rewards accordingly These are truly firm and courageous men like Jacob, who had so great a love for Rachel, that to gain her, " seven years' service seemed to him but a few days." (Gen. xxix. 20.)

---o---

CHAPTER VII.

That it is exceeding advantageous to accustom ourselves to do all our Actions very well.

PYTHAGORAS, in his excellent advice to his friends and disciples, pointed out to them how they could become virtuous and make the practice of virtue easy and sweet. Let every one, says he, choose an honest state of life ; and in the beginning, let him regard not whether it is hard or painful, because custom will afterwards render it easy and agreeable. Behold here a very important means whereby we ought to help ourselves ; not only because it comes from a very great philosopher, but because the Holy Ghost himself suggests the same, as we shall see afterwards ; and because it is most proper to attain our end. We have already chosen an excellent way of living; or to say better, our Saviour has chosen one for us: "Because it is not we that have made choice of him, but it is he that has made choice of us" (John xv. 16); and we ought to bless and praise him continually for this particular grace. However, you may advance more or less in this state of life in which God has placed you; for according to your conduct therein you may become either a good, or a tepid religious. But if you desire to acquire perfection, accustom yourself to perform all your duties well, to obey punctually, to observe your rules exactly, and to set an high value on even the smallest things. Accustom yourself to recollection, mortification, penance, modesty, and silence; and be not dismayed at the difficulties you shall find in the beginning; for afterwards custom will render these things not only easy, but delightful; and you will not cease to give God thanks for the habit and facility you will have gained by the practice of them.

This doctrine is taught us by the Holy Ghost in divers places of Scripture. "I will show you," says he in the Proverbs, " the way of wisdom" (Prov. iv. 11); that is to say, according to St. Bernard's explanation, who interprets this holy word *wisdom* to be "a delicious knowledge of God," I will show you the way in which you will come to take delight in the knowledge, love, and service of God; "I will lead you by the path of equity, and when you have once entered therein, thy steps shall not be straitened, and when thou runnest thou shalt not meet a stumbling-block." (Prov. iv. 12.) The Holy Ghost calls the way of virtue a path; because our inclinations, naturally bad, make it so very hard in the beginning, that we seem to enter into it by very strait and narrow passages. But when we are once advanced, we find the way more large, and we walk with more ease, and even run therein without meeting any stumbling-block or even the least difficulty. Thus by a most elegant metaphor he teaches us, that though the practice of virtue seems hard in the beginning, yet we ought not to lose courage on this account; because afterwards we shall not only find no difficulty therein, but even an abundance of pleasure, so as to be able to say with the Wise Man: " I have laboured a little, and I have found very great repose;"—and again, "You have scarce taken any pains to gain wisdom, but you begin to taste the fruits it carries along with it" (Ecclus. li. 35; vi. 20):—and St. Paul tell us the same thing, when he says, " All discipline in the beginning seems rather to give trouble than joy; but they who are accustomed

to it, will reap in peace the fruits of justice." (Heb. xii. 11.)
We daily experience this in all sorts of arts and sciences. What
difficulty, for example, do we not find in the beginning of our
studies? So that oftentimes it happens, that we must be drawn
to them by force, and kept to our duty by punishment; whence
comes the proverb, "That knowledge makes a bloody entrance."
But afterwards when we get a habit, and begin to make progress, and have already gained some knowledge, we often take
so much delight therein, that our studies become our chief
pleasure and delight. The same happiness in the way of virtue
and perfection.

This is perfectly well explained unto us by St. Bernard,
writing upon these words of Job: "I am reduced to such an
extremity that the very things I had a horror to touch are at
present become my ordinary food." (Job vi. 7.) "Would you
know," says he, "what power practice or habit has over us? At
first a thing will appear to you insupportable; but if you accustom yourself to it, in time it will seem less hard, afterwards you
will find it easy, and in the end it will give you no pain at all,
but a great deal of joy and delight" (De consid. ad Eug.); so
that you may say with Job—"I now take pleasure in feeding
upon those things, which before I had a difficulty to touch."

All then depends upon the habit, which renders very easy the
things that we perform often; so that if you feel a difficulty in
observing the circumstances which are necessary to make your
prayer and examen well, it is because you are not accustomed
thereunto. If in the morning when you awake, or in the time
of prayer, you cannot call home your imagination, and hinder it
from wandering here and there, it is because you have never
used violence, nor accustomed yourself to restrain it from ex-
patiating upon whatever occurs besides the subject of your meditation. If silence and retirement give you any pain, it is because you have not habituated yourself to them. "We find our
chamber sweet and pleasant," says Thomas-a-Kempis, "when
we stay a long time in it, but we find it very tedious and irksome
when we are not accustomed to keep it." Make retirement familiar to you, and it will become very pleasant and agreeable.
Prayer and fasting seem hard to seculars, because they do not
sufficiently practise them. Saul put his own armour upon
David (1 Kings xvii. 38), when he sent him to fight with the
Philistines; but because David was not accustomed to carry
such a weight, he found it troublesome, and cast it away. Yet

afterwards he became so used to it, that it did not at all hinder him from fighting. What I say of virtue ought to be understood in like manner of vice; for if you let yourself be carried away with any bad habit, the evil will augment, and from day to day gain new strength; and in fine, it will at last become so hard to apply a remedy, that you will be in danger of never being able to obtain a cure whilst you live. But if from the beginning you had accustomed yourself to do things well, how happy would you be at present, and how would you rejoice to see the practice of virtue become so very sweet and easy? Begin therefore at present to accustom yourself thereunto: "It is better to begin late than never." Undertake to do your ordinary actions well, since this is of so great consequence; and if it be necessary, make this the matter of your particular examen, since you can never choose a better or a more profitable one: and thus you will gain a great facility, and will feel very great delight in performing all your actions well.

———o———

CHAPTER VIII.

Of how great importance it is to a Religious not to relax in the Way of Virtue.

By all we have said, it is easy to comprehend of how great consequence to a religious it is to walk always with fervour in the exercise of religion, and never to slacken or relent therein: because afterwards it will be very hard for him to resume his first perfection; and to effect it, he will even stand in need of a sort of miracle. St. Bernard treats this point perfectly well, writing to Richard the abbot of Fontaines and his religious, in whom God had wrought this wonder, that having led a very tepid and loose sort of life, they afterwards embraced a fervent and most perfect one; so that the saint seems astonished and rejoices very much at their change, and congratulating with them on it, he says: " Here is truly the finger of God. Who will make way for me to come to you, to behold, like another Moses, this great and wonderful vision? For in fine, this is no less surprising, and no less pleasing than that of the burning bush. There is nothing more rare and unusual in the world than to see a religious raise himself ever so little above that degree in religion whence by tepidity he had fallen; and it is far easier to find many seculars who are entirely converted to God, after having led an irregular life, than to meet a religious that from a languishing and negligent state passes to an ardent and zealous way of living." (Ep. 96.) The reason of this is, because seculars have not the remedies, either so present or so frequent as religious have; so that when seculars hear an affecting sermon, or when they behold one of their relations or friends die a sudden or unhappy death, this being a novelty to them strikes them the more, and the more easily rouses them to conversion, and to an entire change of life. But a religious who has such helps and remedies always present—who so often frequents the sacraments, so frequently hears spiritual exhortations, who exercises himself continually in meditating upon God and pious subjects—thinking upon death, judgment, hell, and heaven; if with all this he lives loosely and tepidly, what hopes can there be that he will ever amend his life, since he is so insensible as to hear these things, without being at all moved by them; so that what ought to rouse him, and what most affects others, makes no impression at all upon him? It is this that gave occasion to St. Austin, to pronounce this celebrated sentence :—" Since I began to serve God," says he, " as I have seldom seen better Christians than those who have perfected themselves in monasteries, so I have scarce found worse, than those religious who have fallen." (Ep. ad Pleb. Hipp.) St. Bernard says, that there are very few of them who re-ascend to the same degree whence they had fallen. And it is over such as these that the prophet Jeremy weeps and laments, when he says:—"How is the gold obscured? How has it lost its colour and brightness? They who were brought up and nourished in purple, are plunged in filth and ordure." (Lamen. iv. 1, 5.) Those upon whom God bestowed so many graces, who so frequently entertained themselves with him, whose chief desires were in heaven, have defiled themselves with the dung and filth of the earth.

There is then, commonly speaking, very little hope left for a religious, who has begun to deviate from the right way. Now this ought to make all of us tremble; because according to what I have said, what can be expected from such a one, since he grows worse by the use of such remedies as cure others? When physic works no effect upon the sick person, but on the contrary augments his disease, we look upon his condition as desperate. When a physician sees a sickly person in a fainting fit, or finds a great weakness in his pulse, he is no ways alarmed, because it is not extraordinary for such things to happen to one that is weak and infirm. But when he perceives the like symptoms in a healthy and strong man, he looks upon them as very dangerous; since such an accident as this cannot proceed but from a revolution of malignant and predominant humours, which infallibly either prognosticate an approaching death, or a great and very dangerous sickness. If a secular falls into sin, it is not much to be wondered at, as it corresponds to the life of such a one, who perhaps confesses only once a-year and who is continually amidst such occasions as urge him to irregularities. But when a religious, supported by the frequent use of the sacraments, by prayer and other spiritual exercises, notwithstanding all this, happens to fall, it is a sign that some dangerous change and revolution have happened in his soul, that some malignant disease has attacked and even shaken the very foundation of his spiritual life, and that he has great reason to fear. I do not say, says St. Bernard, that this always happens, because I would by no means discourage you, especially if you will endeavour to rise as soon as you have fallen; for the longer you defer to do so, the greater difficulty you will feel in rising. But I say this to the end you may not sin at all, and that you do no ways relent in your fervour. " But if any one sins, we have Jesus Christ the just, for advocate to the eternal Father." (1 John ii. 1.) Wherefore let not any one lose courage, for whosoever returns truly to God with his whole heart without doubt will obtain mercy. If the prince of the apostles, after he had for so long a time frequented the school of Jesus Christ, and received so many favours from him, fell notwithstanding in so foul a manner as he did; and if after a sin so enormous, if after having renounced his Master and God, he was restored to so eminent a state of grace, who is there that can despair of his pardon? Have you, as St. Bernard adds, committed greater sins in the world than St. Paul, or in religion than St. Peter? If the one and the other by their repentance and penance not only merited that God should pardon them, but afterwards raise them to so sublime a degree of sanctity and glory, do you also imitate them in their penance, and thereby you will be able not only to re-ascend to the height you were on before your fall, but also to ascend to a still higher and a more complete perfection.

CHAPTER IX.

Of what Importance it is that Novices employ their Time well, and perform their religious Duties with great Exactness, during their Noviceship.

FROM what has been said, we can infer of how great consequence it is, that novices make good use of the time of their noviceship, and that they accustom themselves to perform, during that period, all their religious duties with great exactness; and what we address to them in particular, may be applied to all those in general who begin to enter on the way of virtue. The first rule we have in the society, relating to the master of novices, states two reasons, which shew of how great consequence this is, and also proves to us that the charge of master of novices ought to be considered as one of the greatest importance in all religious communities. The first reason is, because, probably speaking, all the future progress of a religious depends upon the education he received in his noviceship, and upon his conduct therein. And the second, which is still of greater weight, that all the hopes of religion and all its happiness absolutely depend thereon. But, to come to a more particular discussion of this point, I say in the first place, that the progress or little advancement of a religious does so much depend upon this his first education, and his conduct during his noviceship, that, morally speaking, it is very certain that if he is then negligent and tepid in his spiritual duties, he will continue to be the same during his whole life. For how can we imagine he will afterwards become attentive and fervent, since there is not the least reason for believing there will be such a change; but on the contrary, there are many reasons to persuade us he will still remain in the same state.

To make this truth more clearly appear, let us address our discourse to the novice himself—let us lay our reasons before him, and thereby convince him of this truth, in the following manner:—Now you are in your noviceship, you have a great deal of time to apply yourself to your spiritual advancement, and to the different means conducive thereto. Your superiors think of nothing else than this, and make it the principal object of their efforts. You have the example also of your brethren before your eyes, who apply themselves to nothing else; and example ordinarily makes such an impression upon us, that commonly when we are in the company of those who devote themselves to virtue, and who make considerable progress therein, it is hard, how remiss and sluggish soever we be, not to feel ouselves excited to rise out of this remissness and tepidity. You have, moreover, a heart not engaged by worldly thoughts and cares, but which feels in itself a strong inclination to virtue, from which you have no motive to withdraw yourself, but a thousand to urge you on to embrace it. Now if at present, while you have nothing else to do, you make no progress—if you hoard up no treasure of virtue for the time to come; what will become of you when afterwards your heart shall be filled and divided with a thousand different distractions? If now, when you have so much leisure, such opportunities, and so many helps, you make not your prayer and examen well—if now you use not your utmost endeavours to omit nothing—if now you do not perform very diligently all your spiritual exercises—what will become of you when the care of your studies will take up your thoughts, when you shall be put into office, when you shall be appointed to hear confessions, to preach or to teach? If with so many conferences, so many exhortations, so many examples, and so many solicitations, you do not profit at all, what will become of you when you will meet with impediments and obstacles on all sides? If in the beginning of your conversion, when novelty should increase your fervour and zeal, you notwithstanding languish and become tepid, what will become of you when your ears shall be accustomed and your heart hardened to all things that may touch you or do you any good? In fine, if at present, whilst your passions do but begin with you, and your inclinations are still weak and tender, you have not the courage to oppose them, how shall you be able to resist them, how will you be able to overcome them when they shall be so strengthened by custom, and be so deeply rooted in you, that you will not be able to master them though you use violence even more cruel than death.

St. Dorotheus explains this very well, by an example he relates of one of the fathers in the desert, "who being one day with his disciples in a place full of cypress-trees of every size, commanded one of them to pluck up a little one he pointed at, which his disciple presently did without any difficulty; when he pointed at another somewhat bigger, which he in like manner plucked up the roots, but with far greater difficulty than the former, being forced to put both his hands to it. To pluck up another, which was yet stronger, he was forced to use the help of one of his companions; and, in fine all of them together laboured in vain to pull up another which was much bigger than the former. "Behold," says the ancient father, "how it is with our passions. In the beginning, when they are not yet rooted, it is easy to master them if we take but ever so little pains ; but afterwards, when by a long habit they have taken deeper root in our hearts, it is very hard to pluck them out; then we must use extraordinary efforts, and oftentimes shall not be able even thereby to attain our object."

By what I have said, we may perceive it is a very great abuse, and a very dangerous temptation, to defer from day to day our amendment on the ground that we shall be better able to overcome ourselves in the same things at another time ; or that we have not at present the courage to oppose them, by reason of the great difficulty we feel in them. If, whilst this difficulty is yet small, you dare not undertake to surmount it, what will you be able to do when it shall become greater? And if at present, whilst your passion is but like a lion's whelp, you have not the courage to attack it, how will you be able to do it when it shall be grown a large and furious beast? Hold it therefore as a certain truth, that if now you lead a loose and tepid life, you will hereafter do the same ; if now you be not a good novice—a good apprentice—you will never hereafter be a good religious, nor a good workman. If at present you are negligent in the things relating to obedience, and regard not the observance of rules, you will continue afterwards still to become more negligent ; if at present you are but little solicitious to perform your spiritual exercises well, and if you perform them by piece-meal, you will continue to do the same during your whole life. All therefore consists in beginning well, as St. Bonaventure teaches, when he says :—"The impressions we receive young are seldom effaced ; and he who, in the beginning of a new kind of life, contemns discipline, will not without great difficulty afterwards apply himself to it." (Bon. in spec. discip.) "It is a proverb," says Solomon, "that the course of life a man has followed in his youth, he will never change the same in his old age." (Prov. xxii. 6.) St. John Climacus also says, "That loose and weak beginnings are very dangerous, this being an evident sign of a future fall." It is therefore of very great importance to accustom ourselves to virtue, and to a punctual performance of our spiritual exercises in the beginning ; which the Holy Ghost teaches us, when he says, "that it is good to carry the yoke from our youth" (Lam. iii. 27), because thereby the practice of virtue will become more and more easy, and if he does not practise it betimes, "how will he be able to find in his old age what he has not been careful to hoard up in his youth?" (Ecclus. xxv. 5.)

From this first reason thus deduced, we may draw a necessary induction for the second. For as the future perfection of a particular religious depends upon his first education, so also the advancement of religion in general does consequently depend upon every particular man's perfection. Because it is the religious and not the walls of their houses and churches, that sustain religion; and those that are in the noviceship are they who are to compose the whole body. It is for this reason, that by a wholesome institution, the society has established particular houses of probation, to apply ourselves to abnegation, mortification of our senses, and to the practice of true virtue. And St. Francis of Borgia said that those houses ought to be a Bethlehem for the novices, that is to say, *a house of bread;* because there we make biscuit and provisions for the long voyages or navigations we are to make, after we go from thence. The time you remain there is the time of harvest, the time of fruitfulness and abundance, in which, like Joseph, you should hoard up for the time of scarcity and famine. Had the Egyptians understood what would have happened, or had they had any forecast, they would not so readily have parted with their corn, which with so much care Joseph gathered together. If you can but conceive of how great importance it is, that you should not quit the noviceship without having made a good provision, you would not desire to leave it so soon; but would quit it rather with a deep sense of sorrow, when you reflect that perhaps you are very ill provided with all those virtues, necessary for a religious. Those who are desirous and impatient to leave the noviceship rather soon, shew very clearly, says the same saint, that they want experience; because being to make a long and tedious journey they are not afraid to begin it, though they have not made such provisions as are necessary for it.

St. Ignatius has taken such particular care to have us make sufficient provision of virtues during our noviceship, that in his Constitutions, he supposes it as a thing certain, that every one has done so. He has established and appointed two years of probation, to the end that in that time we should think of nothing else than our spiritual advancement, and devote ourselves to no other study, than to that which would help us so powerfully to acquire a great abnegation of ourselves, and a high degree of perfection. Moreover, being persuaded that a religious leaves the noviceship with the spirit of fervour, mortification, and retirement, and with such a love of prayer and spiritual exercises, that he ought even to be moderated therein, he advises those, who afterwards are to continue their studies, to moderate their fervour, and to devote less time to prayer and austerities than they usually did. Endeavour therefore to leave the noviceship such, as in effect this great saint imagines you should be; manage this precious time very well; think with yourself, that perhaps during your whole life, you shall not have another opportunity so proper to advance yourself, or to heap together all sorts of spiritual treasures. In fine, to make use of the words of Scripture, " permit not so good a day to pass without profiting of it, and lose not the least part of so excellent a gift." (Ecclus. xiv. 14.)

Those whom God calls to religion from their tender years, have great reason to be thankful to him; because then it is very easy to apply themselves to virtue, and to submit to the yoke of religious discipline. It is easy in the beginning to bend a young tree, and make it grow straight; but if it grow crooked, and you let it alone, it will always remain so; and you will sooner break than straighten it. It is the same in persons of a tender age. It is easy to make them take a good turn and apply themselves to perfection: so that being accustomed to it betimes, they afterwards find therein a great facility, and always persevere in it. Cloth that is dyed in the fleece never loses its colour:—How is it possible, says St Jerome, to bring back wool that is dyed scarlet to its first colour? "An earthen pot retains a long time the smell of the first liquor that is poured into it." And the Scripture praises Josias, "for having given himself to the service of God from his youth." (2 Paral. xxxiv. 3.)

Humbertus, a person of note, and general of the order of St. Dominic, reports, that a certain religious, after his death, appeared all in glory to another ; and leading him out of his cell, he shewed him a great number of men clad in white robes, and encompassed with light, who carried very fair crosses upon their shoulders, as they went in procession towards heaven. He shewed them others who followed in the same manner, but who shone far brighter than the former, and carried in their hands far richer and more beautiful crosses. After that, a third procession passed, still far more glorious and admirable than the

two former; for all their crosses were of a very surprising
beauty, and instead of being carried by men, as the former
were, either in their hands or upon their shoulders, each of
these had an angel that carried their crosses before them ; so
that they went with a great deal more ease, and followed with
far greater cheerfulness.   The religious, astonished at the
vision, demanded an explanation.   The holy man answered,
that the first who carried their crosses upon their shoulders,
were those who entered into religion advanced in years; the
second, who held their crosses in their hands, were those that
entered young; and the last, who marched with so much ease
and cheerfulness, were those who from their tender years
renounced all the vanities of the world, and embraced a religious
life.

——o——

THE THIRD TREATISE.

———o———

———o———

CHAPTER I.

That we ought to fly Vainglory in our Actions.

ONE of the things St. Ignatius has most of all recommended to
us, and most frequently repeated in his Constitutions, is, that his
children should endeavour to have a pure intention in all their
actions, and that they never seek anything in them but the will
of God, and his greater honour and glory. He constantly
repeated these words : "To the greater honour and glory of
God," and these, "having ever in view his greater honour and
service." (Reg. iv. Sum. Const.) And as "out of the abundance of the heart the mouth speaks" (Luke vi. 45), so God's
glory was so profoundly rooted in his heart, that he directed
all his words and actions to this end. It is therefore with great
reason, that to the images engraven of this saint they have
affixed these words: "To the greater glory of God;" for they
could not bestow on him greater praise in fewer words—in fact,
therein is comprised the whole history of his life. God's glory
was the soul which animated all his actions—it was his device—
his motto—his arms; and to us it should be the same ; it should
be the rule of our conduct, that by this resemblance we may be
known to be the legitimate children of such a father. That
which renders this point of so great importance is that our
advancement and perfection consist in the perfection of our
actions ; and the more holy and perfect they are, the more
holy and perfect we shall also be. This being supposed as an
infallible truth, we may also assuredly conclude, that our actions
will be more meritorious and perfect, as our intentions will be
more upright and pure; and that we cannot propose to ourselves
a more high and sublime end than God's honour and glory.
For it is the intention which stamps a character and value upon
108

all our actions, conformably to this passage of Scripture :—
" Your eye is the light of your body : if your eye is simple, your
whole body will be enlightened; but if your eye is evil, your
whole body will remain in darkness." (Matt. vi. 22, 23.)   By
the eye the saints understand the intention, which regards and
foresees what we ought to do : by the body is understood the
action following the intention that directs it, as the body follows
the eye that conducts it.   The Son of God would therefore in
this place assure us, that it is the intention that gives splendour
and light to the action: according to this, the action will be
good or bad, proportionably to the goodness or badness of the
intention.   " If the root be holy," says St. Paul, " the branches
will also be holy." (Rom. xi. 16.)   What can we expect from a
tree whose root is unsound, but that it should bear wood which
will scarce have any sap, and bring forth ill-tasted fruit, which
will not keep.   But if the root be whole, all the tree will be
fair, and bring forth good fruit.   The goodness also and the
perfection of our actions depend upon the purity of our intention,
and will become like to the root; and the more pure and
upright the intention is which produces them, the more virtuous
and perfect they will be.   St. Gregory, explaining that passage
of Job : "Upon what are the foundations supported?" (Job
xxxviii. 6) says, that as it often happens that a building is
supported by pillars, and the pillars by their bases ; so in like
manner, a spiritual life is supported by virtue ; the base whereof
is the upright intention of the heart.   But to observe some
method in what I have to say, I will speak first of the end we
ought to avoid in our actions, which is vainglory or human
respects of any kind ; and afterwards, I will treat of the end we
ought to propose to ourselves in our actions ; and shall thus
observe the same method the Psalmist teaches us, when he says :
" Avoid evil, and do good." (Ps. xxxiii. 15.)

All the saints admonish us to be on our guaad against vainglory;
because, say they, it is a cunning thief. which often steals from us
our best actions; and which insinuates itself so very secretly, that
it has given its stroke even before we perceive it.   St. Gregory
says, that vainglory is like a robber, who first craftily insinuates
himself into the company of a traveller, pretending to go the same
way he does, and afterwards robs and kills him when he is least
upon his gaurd, and when he thinks himself in greatest security.
I confess, says this great saint, in the last chapter of his *Morals,*
that when I go about to examine my own intention, even while I

am writing this, methinks that I have no other will than to please
God: but notwithstanding, while I am not upon my guard, I find
that a certain kind of desire of pleasing men intermixes itself, and
methinks that I feel some vain satisfaction for having performed it
well.   How it comes to pass I know not; but what I perceive very
well, that while I go on, what I do is not so free from dust and
chaff as it was in the beginning.   For I know, that I begin it at
first with the best intention in the world, with the sole view of
pleasing God; but now easily perceive other considerations mixing
themselves, which render my intention less upright and pure than it
was before.   The same thing happens to us in eating.   In the
beginning we eat from necessity; but sensuality so cunningly
insinuates itself, that what we begin in order to supply the necessities of nature, and to preserve our life, we continue on account
of the relish and pleasure we feel in eating.   Experience makes
us see but too often the selfsame thing even in our best actions:
we apply ourselves to them at first, to preaching for example, or
such other like practices, solely through a motive of charity, and
for the salvation of souls; and afterwards vanity enters and
unites itself to these intentions, exciting in us a desire to please
men, and to be esteemed by them; so that when we acquire
not this esteem we seem to lose courage, and to be unable to do
anything but with regret.

———o———

CHAPTER II.

In what the Malignity of Vainglory consists.

THE malignity of this vice consists in this; that those who are
infected with it endeavour to rob God of the glory that belongs
to him alone, according to the words of St. Paul: "To God alone
be glory and honour" (1 Tim. i. 17); of which he is so jealous
that he himself says, in the prophet Isaiah, "I will not give my
glory to another." (Isa. xlii. 8; Aug. c. 16. Solil.)   Wherefore
St. Austin, speaking on this subject: Lord, says he, whoever
would be praised for your gifts, and seek not your glory, but his
own, in the good he does, is a robber; and is like the devil himself,
who attempts to rob you of your glory.   In all the works of God
there are two things, utility and glory: as to the utility he leaves
that entirely to men; but he reserves all the glory of them to
himself alone.   "The Lord has wrought all things for himself"

(Prov. xvi. 4,) that is to say, for his glory: "and has created all nations to praise and glorify his name." (Deut. xxvi. 19.) We see that all things preach his wisdom, his goodness, and his providence; and it is for this reason that he inspired the Psalmist to make this petition : " Be thou exalted, O Lord ! above the heavens, and thy glory over all the earth." (Psal. cvii. 6.) When, therefore, it happens, that we seek to attract to ourselves the esteem and praise of men, we pervert that order which God established, and we do him an injury, because in a manner we endeavour to make men, who should have no other employment than to praise and honour him, employ themselves in praising and honouring creatures ; and we endeavour to replenish with an esteem of ourselves, the hearts of creatures which God has made, as vessels to be filled with nothing else than with his own honour and praises. What is this but to rob God of his creatures' hearts, and in a manner, to drive him out of his own house ? Can one commit a greater evil than this ? Or imagine anything worse, than in such a manner to rob God of his glory ? For though by your words you exhort men to regard none but him, yet you wish in the bottom of your heart that they would turn their eyes from him, and fix them upon yourself. He who is truly humble, desires not to live in the heart of any creature, but in the heart of God alone; he seeks not his own glory, but that of God alone ; desires not that any person should entertain himself with him, but with God alone : and in fine, he wishes that all the world should have God so in their hearts, that no other object may ever have the least place in them.

The grievousness of this sin may also be easily understood by this comparison. If a married woman dresses and adorns herself to please any other man than her husband, she would, without doubt, do her husband very great injury. The good works are the dresses and ornaments of your soul; if you do them to please any one but God, who is your spouse, you do him a signal injury. Moreover, imagine what a shame it would be, if any private person should set a great value upon some small service he had done to some mighty king or prince, who had before, through love of him, exposed himself to a thousand pains and dangers ? If, besides this, he should boast all over the world of some small service he had rendered his prince ; whilst the prince, in all he had done for this man, had not received the least assistance from him; but the same man would not have been able to do anything, without the prince's help—to whose services he was also excited, by the great recompense the prince had beforehand promised, and afterwards bestowed upon him. Would not this vanity appear intolerable, and this procedure appear base and unworthy? Every one of us in particular ought to apply this to ourselves, to the end that we may blush at the good opinion which, with so little reason, we have of ourselves; and be ashamed hereafter to praise ourselves for anything whatsoever; because in comparison of that which God has done for us, and of that we ought to do for him, that which we do is so little, that we ought rather to feel a great confusion, than to harbour any vanity for having performed it.

But what sufficiently demonstrates the deformity of this vice is, that the saints and divines rank it amongst those sins ordinarily called mortal, or which are more properly styled capital sins; because they are, as it were, the head and source of all others. Some reckon eight of this nature, and say, that the first is anger, and the second vainglory; but the common opinion of saints, and that which is received by the Church, is, that there are seven capital sins. And St. Thomas, who names vainglory as the first, says, that pride is the root of all the rest, according to the words of the Wise Man: "The beginning of all sins is pride." (Ecclus. v. 15.)

---o---

CHAPTER III.

How prejudicial Vainglory is.

THE prejudice we receive from vainglory is sufficiently explained to us in the gospel, by the Son of God, when he tells us: "Take care not to perform your actions before men, to the end they may take notice of you: otherwise you will have no recompense for them from your heavenly Father." (Matt. vi. 1.) Do not, as hypocrites are wont to do, who perform nothing but to be seen by others, and to gain their esteem. "In truth I tell you, these have already received their reward." (Matt. vi. 5.) You have a desire to gain reputation—this is the motive of your actions, and will also be their reward; but take notice that you must expect no other reward than this. Unhappy are you, who have already received your wages, and for whom there remains nothing else to be hoped for. "The hope of the hypocrite shall perish," says holy Job, "and his folly shall afford him but little satisfaction." (Job viii. 13, 14.) And St. Gregory, explaining this passage, says, that "what the hypocrite hopes for, is the esteem and praise of men, and that all this ends with his life." The saint adds, "that he who by his virtuous actions would gain the applause of the world, resigns at a low rate a thing of great value. And when he might thereby have purchased the kingdom of heaven, he seeks to gain nothing but the transient reward of human applause." (Greg. lib. viii. Mor. c. 13.) What greater abuse can happen than this, and what greater folly can one imagine, than to have taken a great deal of pains, and to have performed many good actions, and yet to find his hands empty in the end? It is this the prophet Aggæus gives us to understand when he says, "Reflect upon your own conduct. You have sown much, and have reaped but little; you have eaten, and you have not been at all satisfied: you have drank, but you have not quenched your thirst : you have clothed yourselves, and you are not warm : and he who has gathered together the greatest reward, has put it into a sack full of holes," which another text calls, "a bushel full of chinks." (Ag. i. 5, 6.) Behold what vainglory does. It puts all things in a bag full of holes ; for what enters at one end goes out at the other : it puts all into a vessel full of chinks; because what is cast into it, runs through the moment it is cast in ; and it gains nothing but what it presently loses. "Wherefore do you lay out your money, and buy not bread," says the prophet Isaiah, " and why do you take pains and not satiate yourselves?" (Isa. lv. 2.) Since you take so much pains to do the thing, do it after such a manner as to profit by it, that you may not lose all the fruit of your labours.

St. Basil enumerates three sorts of evils, which vainglory inflicts on us. The first is, to make us destroy our body by great labour, watchings, and by what is most painful in good actions. The second is, to corrupt or destroy all the merit of our actions, after they are done, and to make us lose all the advantage we might expect from them. This vice, says he, does not hinder us from working, because it would not be so hard for us to be frustrated of our recompense, if we had not laboured at all ; but it waits till we have taken pains to perform many good works, and afterwards it robs us of them, and takes the profit of them from us. It is like a pirate, says he, that attacks not a vessel which is sailing out of port to purchase goods, but waits till it returns home richly freighted, and then fails not to set upon it. But vainglory does still worse—it inflicts on us a third evil, by turning good into bad, and virtue into vice, through the vanity of the miserable end we propose to ourselves ; hence instead of the recompense due to us, it causes us to merit nothing else than chastisements and punishments. In such sort, that we reap bad fruit from good seed; and what should elevate and raise us to heaven, serves only to precipitate us more deeply into hell. Moreover, vainglory does all these things in so sweet and quiet a manner, that we are so far from troubling ourselves at the loss of all these good works, that on the contrary, we even take pleasure in these our losses. And say what you will to a man guilty of this vice—make his losses ever so evident to him, yet he will still yield so far to the desire of human praise and glory, that one would think there were some charm or enchantment in it. It is for this reason that St. Basil called vainglory "A charming thief that robs us of all our good and spiritual actions; a mild and peaceful enemy of our souls. And it is," says he, "by this sweet insinuating flattery, that it attracts and deceives such a multitude of people. For human praise and glory is a thing very sweet and pleasant to such persons as know not what it is." "Take heed of the arrow," says St. Bernard; "it flies silently, penetrates as silently, but I assure you it inflicts a wound hard to be cured, and kills upon a sudden: and this arrow is indeed nothing else than vainglory." It is a sweet scented powder, but it is entirely composed of arsenic.

We read in the life of St. Pachomius, that conversing one night in his monastery with some other ancient fathers, one of his religious carried two little mats he had made that day, and laid them close by his cell, over against the place where the saint was sitting; imagining that when the saint should see them, he would praise his diligence for having made two mats in one day, when the rule obliged to make only one. The saint readily perceived that it was done through a spirit of vanity, wherefore addressing himself to the fathers that were with him, "Behold," says he, heaving a deep sigh, "what pains this brother has taken from morning till night, to offer up in the end all his labour to the devil; having preferred the esteem of men to the glory of God?" And afterwards calling him he gave him a severe reprimand, and ordered him, for his penance, that when all the religious were assembled to make their prayer, he should go with these two mats about him, and with a loud voice tell them, "My dear fathers and brothers, I beg of you all, for the love of God, to pray to our Lord, that he will have mercy upon me, a most miserable sinner, who have more esteemed these two little mats than the kingdom of heaven." Moreover, he commanded him, that when the religious went to eat, he should go into the refectory in the same garb, and stand in the middle of it the whole time of dinner. But the penance ended not here, for he caused him to be imprisoned five whole months in a cell, and to fast on bread and water; he also ordered that none should visit him, and obliged him to make two mats every day. This example, besides the instruction on the present subject which we ought to derive from it, serves likewise to show us what severe penances the ancient fathers inflicted for very light and small faults; and how great was the humility and patience of their subjects, to submit to and undergo such severe penances imposed on them.

——o——

CHAPTER IV.

That the temptation of Vainglory attacks not only those that enter into the Way of Perfection, but even such as are most advanced in it.

St. Cyprian, speaking of the second temptation the devil made use of against Jesus Christ, when he carried him to the top of the pinnacle of the temple, and said to him, "If you be the Son of God, cast yourself down" (Mat. iv. 6), cries out in this manner: "O execrable malice of the devil! this miserable spirit thought, that he who could not be overcome by gluttony, might be vanquished by vainglory;" and therefore he endeavoured to persuade him to cast himself into the air, to the end that, by flying, he should become a spectacle of admiration to all the beholders. The devil imagined that he should have the same success against Jesus Christ, that he had formerly had against others. He had experienced, says St. Cyprian, that he had often overcome by vainglory, such as he could not vanquish any other way; and it was for this reason, that after he had tempted him with gluttony to no purpose, he tempts him with vainglory, as with something more considerable, and which was harder to be resisted. For it is very hard not to be touched with praise; since as there are very few persons that are pleased to hear anything that is said to their disadvantage, so also there are very few but are extremely delighted when they hear what is said to their advantage. So that the temptation of vainglory attacks not only such persons as are beginners in virtue, but also those who are most advanced in it; and it is even such as those, to whom the enemy chiefly addresses himself.

The holy abbot Nilus, who was a disciple of St. Chrysostom, relates, that the most ancient and most experienced fathers of the desert educated and instructed the young religious in a manner very different from that wherein they instructed the others.   To the young they recommended and enjoined temperance and abstinence ; because such as permit themselves to be carried away by gluttony will more easily yield to and be carried away by impurity ; for having yielded to the weaker temptation, there was little appearance that they would resist the more violent. But as to the seniors—they admonished them to take care, and be continually upon their guard against vainglory.   As those who go to sea, ought diligently evade the sand-banks and the rocks in the mouth of the harbour ; because it often happens, that after a most prosperous voyage, a vessel is wrecked in the very haven.   Just so, the most perfect ought to be exceedingly on their guard against vanity ; because it often happens, that when we have sailed very prosperously throughout the whole course of our life, and resisted courageously all the storms and tempests the devil had raised against us ; in fine, when we are come in sight of the harbour, confiding in our past victories, believing ourselves out of all danger, we come at last, by our pride and negligence, to suffer a miserable shipwreck.   It is upon this account that the saints styled vainglory a tempest in the harbour; and others say, that it does to the most perfect Christians, what · a man does who, going on board a ship well provisioned, and richly laden with merchandise, bores a hole in the bottom of it, through which the water enters, and at length sinks it.

So that these ancient fathers thought it was not so necessary to give novices any warning or particular remedy against vainglory, because they supposed, that such as those who came out of the world all covered with the fresh bleeding wounds of their sins, had in themselves sufficient matter of humility and dejection, and therefore it was necessary to speak to them only of abstinence, penance, and mortification.   Indeed the more ancient, who had already deplored their sins, and performed severe penance for them, and who had for a long time exercised themselves in the practice of virtue, ought to be continually on their guard against vainglory. But they who only began—who had not as yet acquired any virtue—who were not yet free from the bad inclinations and evil habits which they had contracted in the world, and who were still employed in deploring their sins, and their so long-continued forgetfulness of the things belonging to God's service, these were supposed to have no need of any precaution against vanity; because they saw in themselves nothing but what was matter of sorrow and confusion. This ought also to confound many persons, who having frequent occasions to humble themselves, do still in very many things permit themselves to be puffed up with pride, for some one thing or other that is commendable in them. This is a very great abuse. One fault alone ought to be sufficient to humble and confound us; because there ought to be nothing defective in what is good; since even the least defect renders anything whatsoever bad and imperfect. We, notwithstanding, act after a different manner. The many faults and many sins we daily commit suffice not to inspire us with humble thoughts; but the least advantage we think we possess, is sufficient to fill us with a great deal of vanity, and make us sigh after the esteem and applause of the world. By this it is very easy to perceive that vainglory is very dangerous, because it spares nobody, and sets upon us without any cause at all. "It is the first thing we give way to, and it is the last we resist." (Aug. sup.) Wherefore, says St. Austin, let us arm ourselves, my dear brethren, and use great precaution against this vice, the danger whereof was very sensibly felt by the Royal Prophet, when he made this earnest petition : "Turn my eyes, O Lord, from beholding vanity." (Ps. cxviii. 31.)

----o----

CHAPTER V.

That those who labour for the Salvation of their Neighbour have more Reason than others to be upon their guard against Vainglory.

ALTHOUGH all the world in general has reason to take precaution against vainglory; yet those who, by their institute and charge, are employed in the salvation of souls, have yet a more particular obligation to be always upon their guard in this respect. For their employment being so sublime, and so exposed to public view, they have a great deal more to be afraid of than others; and they will render themselves far more guilty, if in this function they only regard themselves and seek nothing else than the vain applause of men. This were to make use of the graces and gifts of God as instruments to rebel against him ; and it is for this reason St. Bernard cries out:—" Unhappy are they, who have received the gift of speaking and thinking well of God, if they look upon piety as merchandise, and apply that to the profit and interest of vain-glory, which they received to promote God's honour : if the greatness and generosity of soul that moves them to undertake so high enterprises, be not founded upon true humility of heart, let them truly fear that they are not such as we read of in the prophet Osee : " I have given them silver and gold, wherewith they have made an idol of Baal,"—that is, they have erected my gifts, as an idol to their own vanity.

On this subject, St. Gregory (Greg. lib. ii. Mor. c. 17) relates what St. Paul said to the Corinthians :—" We are not like the great number of those who corrupt the word of God; but we speak with sincerity, we speak as those who are of God, and in his presence, and speak in Jesus Christ." (2 Cor. ii. 17.) This passage, says he, admits of two explanations, and shews that we may corrupt the word of God two ways. The first is, when explaining the holy Scripture after another manner than we ought, we draw thence innumerable falsities, which, like illegitimate children, are produced by our understanding ; for the Holy Ghost being the author and spouse of holy Scripture, it ought to have that true and legitimate sense, which he declares to his Church by the saints and doctors thereof. The second is applicable to our purpose, which this great saint gives us to understand after this manner : There is this difference, says he, between the spouse and the adulteress—the one proposes to have children and the other thinks of nothing else than to gratify her passion : so that he who, by his preaching, intends not to beget spiritual children to God, conformably to the obligation of his office, and according to these words of the apostle, " I have begotten you by the gospel " (1 Cor. iv. 15), but only seeks his own satisfaction, and to gain for himself the esteem of men, is a mere adulterer, who corrupts the purity of the word of God. It is upon this account also that the saints call vainglory *a spiritual luxury;* which as far surpasses carnal pleasure, as the sensibility of the soul is infinitely more exquisite than, and surpasses that of the body. Let us therefore take care not to be adulterers of the word of God, but to do as our Saviour in St. John tells us he did: "For my own part I seek not my own glory." (John viii. 50.) Let us not in effect seek our own ends in our employments, but let us always have the honour and glory of God alone before our eyes. The Holy Scripture relates a very remarkable passage of the conduct of Joab. He kept the king of the Ammonites straitly besieged in his capital city, and having advanced the siege in such a manner, that he was upon the point of taking it by assault, he sent a messenger to David, to let him know the place was reduced to extremity, and that it was time he should come to complete the taking of it: "For fear," says he, "if I press or make an assault upon them at present, the victory should be attributed to myself." (2 Kings xii. 28.) We ought, in all our employments, to have the same fidelity to God he had to his prince, and we ought never desire that any one should attribute to us the glory of the conversion of souls, or any other good success, but refer it always to God alone; according to what the Prophet says: " Give not thy glory to us, O Lord, but to your name" (Ps. cxiii. 9), and according to the canticle the angels sung at our Saviour's birth : " Glory be to God on high." (Luke ii. 14.)

We read in the Life of St. Thomas of Aquin, that he was never touched with the least sentiment of pride ; and that neither his profound knowledge, nor his angelical talents, nor the other favours he had received from God in great abundance, ever moved him to take the least vain complacency in himself. We read also of St. Ignatius, that for many years before his death, he was not the least moved by temptations to vainglory ; because the light of heaven, illuminating his mind, filled him at the same time with such knowledge of his nothingness, and with such contempt of himself, that he was accustomed to say, " that there was no vice he less feared, than that of vainglory." See therefore after what models we ought to form ourselves, and what ought to be the subject of our confusion, when, even in our most frivolous and insignificant actions, we permit ourselves to be carried away by vanity. For if in these small things you shew so little moderation, how would you be transported, if you were eminent for learning—if you had the character of a great preacher—if you had converted and advanced in perfection a great many souls, and if you heard yourself applauded by the whole world ? We ought therefore in small things to accustom ourselves betimes to set little or no value on the praises of men, and to do nothing at all through human respects; to the end that we may more easily do the like on other occasions of greater moment.

CHAPTER VI.

Of several Remedies against Vainglory.

ST. BERNARD, explaining these words of the Psalmist: "You shall walk upon the asp and basilisk, and trample under your feet the lion and the dragon" (Psal. xc. 13), says, that of these beasts some kill by their looks and breath ; others tear in pieces with their teeth and claws, and frighten by their roaring ; and that the devil insensibly inflicts all these evils on man after the same manner.   Afterwards comparing the different properties of these animals to the various temptations and vices made use of by the devil to attack us, he speaks of the basilisk ; and after having said what naturalists report of it ; viz., that it kills by its very looks, he applies this to the vice of vainglory ; and citing the words of Jesus Christ : "Take care you perform not your good actions before men with design they should behold them" (Mat. vi. 1):— have a care, says he, of the eyes of the basilisk ; but know, at the same time, that it only kills those it sees first ; and that if you see it before it perceives you, it will not only do you no hurt, but will presently die itself. It is after this manner, says the saint, that vainglory kills only the inconsiderate and negligent, who expose themselves to be seen by it, and who use no endeavour to see it first and to examine its weakness.   For if you behold it first, you shall not only be free from all fear that this basilisk can do you any harm, but you will destroy it, and make it vanish into smoke.

Behold here the greatest remedy against vainglory, which is, that we take care to see the basilisk first, and to consider with attention that the good opinion of men is but mere wind and smoke ; because it neither gives nor takes away anything from us ; and all they can say of us, whether good or bad, neither makes us anything better or worse.   St. Chrysostom upon these words of the Royal Prophet: "Because you will bless the just" (Psal. v. 14), treats this matter perfectly well, and says, that the prophet hereby encourages the just to contemn the persecutions and calumnies of men.   For what harm can the injuries and affronts which they receive do them, if God blesses and praises them ?   And on the contrary, what good can the praise or applause of men do us, if we have not God's blessing ?   He afterwards quotes upon this subject the example of Job, who sitting upon the dunghill, covered all over with leprosy, ulcers, and worms, persecuted and scoffed by his friends, by his own wife, and even by the whole world, was notwithstanding very happy in this state; because God blessed him, and gave him this testimony: "That he was a sincere and upright man, fearing God, avoiding evil, and persevering in his innocence." (Job ii. 3.) It is this that rendered him truly happy, and truly great, nor could the contempt of men diminish or lessen in the least his merit. St. Chrysostom adds, that what we ought with all zeal and care to procure, is to be esteemed by God: and since the esteem or contempt of men can neither give nor take anything from us, we have no reason to trouble ourselves about what opinion they entertain of us. "I am not in pain," says the apostle, "what judgment you and the rest of mankind make of me, for my true Judge is our Lord." (1 Cor. iv. 3.) Let us add to this a consideration of St. Bonaventure :—Be not angry, says he, with those that speak ill of you: for either what they say is true or false: if it is true, you must not wonder they dare say, what you durst do; if it is false, their detraction can do you no harm. But if, notwithstanding, any motion of anger should arise, repress it, and suffer all with patience, as one suffers the fire, when applied to a wound; for as the fire heals the wound, even so the detraction you suffer will perhaps cure you of some secret pride, which for some time you have entertained and taken pleasure in.

The second means, that will help us very much to attain this end, is what St. Basil, St. Gregory, St. Bernard, and generally all the saints recommend to us; which is to take very great care never to use any expression in praise of ourselves. "Never say anything of yourself that may redound to your praise," says St. Bernard, "though the person you speak to should be one of your most familiar friends; but on the contrary endeavour to hide all your virtues, with more care than you take to hide your vices and imperfections." (Ber. in formulâ honestæ vitæ.) Father Avila used so great circumspection in this matter, that when it seemed necessary for the instruction of his neighbours, to say something of edification that had happened to himself, he related it as of a third person; so that they could not conceive that what he had said was of himself. St. Ignatius practised the same; and we have been informed by a Spanish bishop who knew him at Paris, that this saint one day discoursing of prayer, and the bishop having asked him how, and in what disposition he felt himself at the time of prayer? he made this answer:

" Of that I will say nothing ; it suffices that I entertain you with what is fit and proper for yourself—charity and duty oblige me to this ; but in what you desire of me, there would be a great deal of vanity should I do it."   We read in like manner of St. Francis, that he was so reserved in this matter, that he not only never discovered to others the favours and particular graces God had communicated to him in prayer, but when he went from it, he endeavoured so to compose himself in his words and comportment, that none should be able to perceive the joy and interior satisfaction with which his mind was replenished.

In the third place, we ought not content ourselves with abstaining from what may tend to our praise ; but we must yet go farther, and even hide and conceal, as much as possible we can, the good actions we perform, according to the precept of Jesus Christ in the gospel : " When you would pray, enter into your closet, shut the door upon you, and pray to your Father in secret : he who penetrates the most secret and hidden places, will give you a reward for it." (Mat. vi. 6.)   " When you shall give alms," says he in the same place, " let not your left hand know what your right hand does" (Mat. vi. 3.); as if he would say, you ought yourself, if it were possible, to be ignorant of the good you do ; " and when you fast, anoint your head, and wash your face, to the end that none may perceive that you fast." (Mat. vi. 17.)   Vainglory is a crafty and dexterous enemy, who beholds all our good actions ; and it is for this reason that the Saviour of the world recommends to us so great diligence in hiding them, lest vainglory should rob us of their merit.   It is after this manner, says St. Gregory, that travellers hide their money with a great deal of care, lest they should be robbed of it; and hereupon he relates a passage in the life of King Ezechias, who for having shewn his treasures to the ambassadors of the King of Babylon, gave occasion to the Assyrians very soon after to besiege Jerusalem, and take them away.   See here an example of what happens to those who perform their good works, through a spirit of pride.   The intention with which they perform them makes them lose their merit.   Some have compared them to hens, who make a cackling after they have laid an egg, whereby they cause it to be discovered and lose it in consequence.   It is after this manner, says he, that we lose our good actions, when we ourselves speak of them, or when we endeavour to manifest them to others.

"The true servant of God," says St. Gregory, " is so far

from acting after this manner, that he esteems the good he does as nothing ; and what he cannot hide from the eyes of men, he believes he has already received a kind of reward for, if he adds not other good works, which cannot come to their knowledge." (Greg. lib. xxii. Mor. c. 9.)   St. Jerome relates of St. Hilarion, that perceiving the concourse of people that followed him, and the reputation his miracles had attracted, he was much afflicted, and wept every day very bitterly : and his disciples asking him what was the occasion of his sadness and tears ?   " Methinks," says he, " seeing the esteem that men have of me, that God pays me in this life for the service which I endeavour to render him."   This is a very profitable consideration, on which we ought to set a great value, as being a means well calculated to free us from the danger of vainglory.   Do not therefore aspire to the esteem of men, for fear that God should make them to be the extent of all the recompense of those good actions you were able to perform.   For it is after this manner he is used to treat those that do so, and he himself tells us the same, by the words of Abraham to the rich glutton.   " Remember, son, that you have received your share of rewards whilst you lived."   (Luke xvi. 15.)   It is also for the same reason that the saints counsel us to avoid all sorts of singularity in devotion ; because singular add unusual actions are most remarked, and most spoken of. " And he who does what others do not, draws the eye of all the world upon him" (Gers. et. Guli. Par.); whence arises the spirit of pride and vainglory, which makes us look upon others with contempt.

But, because we cannot always hide our actions, this being impossible for those who are obliged to contribute by their example to the edification of their neighbour ; the first means of defence against vainglory is to rectify in the beginning our intention, and to elevate our heart to God, and offer to him all our thoughts, words, and actions ; to the end, that when vainglory comes to claim a part in them, we may say to it, according to the advice of Father Avila, " You come too late, all is already given to God."   It will also be very good to make use of the answer St. Bernard made to a thought of vainglory, that came to his mind whilst he preached : " I neither began," says he, " for your sake, nor will I leave off for it." (Bern. in vita ipsius.) For we ought not to permit, that the fear of vainglory should make us desist from our good undertakings ; we must only stop our ears, and thereby render ourselves deaf to the praises of men. St. Chrysostom says, we ought to behave to the world, as a father behaves to his son whilst he is yet in his infancy; for whether the son be fond of him, or shews himself peevish to him, it is all the same thing—he laughs as well at the one as at the other; because he looks upon him as an infant, who knows not what he says, nor what he does. Let us look upon the world in the same manner, and believe it is an infant, and as though it had not the sense to know what it says, or what it does. St. Francis Xaverius went still farther, and said, if we attentively considered our faults and sins, and what we truly are in God's sight, we should look upon and receive the praises of men but as so many railleries and injuries.

Let us hence conclude, that the knowledge of ourselves is the most proper remedy against vainglory—it is also the last means we propose to protect us from it. If we enter a little into ourselves, and take an account of what we are, we shall see nothing we can be proud of, but rather many things to humble and confound us. For we are full of defects, not only in regard of our sins, but even in regard of those actions that appear the most just and perfect; for if we examine them well, we shall find occasion enough of humiliation and confusion. It is for this reason St. Gregory frequently repeats this sentence: "All human justice is convicted as guilty of injustice, if we judge to the rigour; for if mercy takes not place in the examination of our actions, those for which we expect the greatest reward will even deserve punishment." (Greg. lib. ix. Mor. c. 11, &c.) And hence Job said, "That he feared all his actions." (Job ix. 28); that is, he had an extreme mistrust of himself, because of the many imperfections and defects which easily intermix with all we do; especially, when we stand not upon our guard, and keep not a diligent watch over ourselves; hence it is that the ignorance of our imperfections is the foundation of our pride, and the source of that vainglory which so puffs up our mind. For if we come to examine ourselves with attention, and at night if we take an exact account of what we have done during the day, shall we not find in ourselves an abyss of miseries, a thousand imperfections, and a thousand faults we have committed in our thoughts, words, and actions, and a thousand omissions we were guilty of? And if it happens that we have done anything that is good, we often find we have corrupted it, and destroyed its merit, either by our vanity or negligence—or in fine, by several other defects we perceive therein; or by an infinity of others we are ignorant

of : in which notwithstanding we ought always to believe ourselves
guilty.   Let us then enter into ourselves—let us have recourse
to the knowledge of our nothingness—and let us, like the pea-
cock, look upon our feet, that is, let us take notice of that wherein
our actions are defective ; and under God, we shall put down
that pride and vanity which self-complacency had before raised
in our hearts.

———o———

CHAPTER VII.

Of the End we ought to propose to ourselves in our Actions.

WE have already shown that our actions ought to be entirely
disengaged from all sorts of vanity and human respects, and
thereby have pointed out how evil is to be avoided.   Now I
shall speak of the end and intention we ought to have in all we
ought to propose to ourselves.   St. Ambrose quotes from naturalists what is very much to our purpose : these relate, that when
the eagle desires to know whether her young ones are legitimate
or not, she takes them in her talons, and holding them suspended
in the air, exposes them to the brightest beams of the sun ; if
they look steadily on the sun, she judges them to be legitimate,
carries them back to her nest, and feeds them as her own.   But
if their eyes twinkle, she looks upon them as illegitimate, and
lets them fall to the ground.   In the same manner, it may easily
be known that we are the true children of God, if we fix our eyes
upon the true Son of justice, who is God—if we refer all our
actions to him ; and if we have no other object than to please
him, and to accomplish his divine will.   This truth is confirmed
by the words of our Saviour in the gospel, when he says,
" Whosoever does the will of my father that is in heaven, he is
my brother, my sister and my mother." (Matt. xii. 50.)

We read of an ancient father of the desert, who was used to
stop a little at the beginning of each action he performed.   And
one day being asked why he did so ?—I believe, says he, that all
our actions have no merit of themselves, if they be not done for
a good end.   Wherefore, as he who fires at a target takes his
aim for some time in order to cover the object ; even so, before
I perform what I purpose, I direct my intention to God, who
ought to be the only object or end of all our actions ; and it is

upon this account, that I always pause or stop a little in the beginning of everything I do. We ought to imitate those archers, who, the better to hit the mark, shut the left and open only the right eye, that the sight, by being less spread on other objects, may be more concentrated and strengthened ; even so we ought to shut the left eye, that is to say, have no human respect, and open the right ; that is, we ought to look to God alone ; and by this means we shall not fail to hit the mark, and infallibly touch the heart of God, as he himself acknowledges in the Canticles : " You have wounded my heart, O my sister ! my spouse, you have wounded my heart with one of your eyes." (Cant. iv. 9.)

To speak more clearly, and to descend more to particulars, I say we ought to endeavour to offer and actually to direct all our actions to God, which we may do with more or less perfection. For first, in the morning, we ought, when we rise, to offer to God all our thoughts, words, and actions of that day, and beg of him, that all these may be performed to his honour and glory ; to the end, that when vainglory shall present itself to desire a part in them, we may answer it with reason : " You come too late, all is already disposed of." But we ought not to content ourselves with this ; we must also accustom ourselves, as much as we are able, to take care not to begin anything without first referring it actually to God's greater glory : and as, in a building, we lay no stone without applying the rule and plumb ; so in every action we do, we ought to apply the unerring rule of the will and greater glory of God. Moreover, as a good workman contents not himself with making use of his rule and square only once, but often applies them, till the stone is fairly placed ; so it is not enough that we have once offered our actions to God, in the beginning of each of them ; but at the very time of performing them we ought to act in such manner, as thereby continually to offer them to God ; saying to him, " Lord, it is for you I do this—I do it because you have commanded me, and because you desire to have it so."

CHAPTER VIII.

*What is requisite on our part, that we may always act with a great
Purity of Intention.*

WHEN the masters of a spiritual life wish to explain to us what
we are to do, in order to raise our actions to a high degree of
perfection, they are wont to make use of a very just comparison.
As the mathematicians, say they, consider in bodies only the
dimension and figure; and always abstract from the matter
because it makes nothing to their purpose; so the true servant
of God ought to think of nothing in all his actions but the will
of God—and for this end he ought to abstract totally from the
matter, that is to say, not at all regard, either in what charge
he is employed, or what he is commanded to do; because it is
not in that in which our perfection consists, but only in performing the will of God, and in seeking his glory in all things.
It is this which the great St. Basil teaches us, as the apostle
St. Paul had done before : " The whole conduct of a Christian,"
says he, " proposes to itself only one 'end, which is, the glory of
God ; wherefore, whether you eat or drink, or whatever you do,
do all to the glory of God."

The Saviour of the world, feeling himself fatigued on his
journey, his disciples went to purchase some food, whilst he reposed upon the well of Jacob, and entertained himself with the
Samaritan woman. At their return they pressed him to take
refreshment ; but he answered them, " I have meat to eat, you
know not of ;" and afterwards when they asked one another,
" Who has brought him food to eat ?" " My food," answered he,
" is to do the will of him that sent me." (John iv. 32.) See here
what ought to be our food in all things we perform. When you
study in private, when you teach in public, or when you preach
the word of God, feed not on the pleasure imparted by your
knowledge, or talents for preaching ; but feed on the pleasure
imparted by doing the will of God, who is pleased that you
should be then employed in those things. But if you be employed in the functions, which regard the temporal service of
your brethren, still have the same intention. The food of the
porter and infirmarian is not different from that of the preacher
and master ; and you ought to be as content in this, your employment, as each one of them is in his. For the fulfilling the

will of God being the only subject of that satisfaction they ought to feel, you may have as much hereof as they; since as a good spiritual mathematician, you stop not at the matter of the action you perform, but you consider only that you do what God requires of you. We ought therefore endeavour to have always in our mouths and in our hearts these words :—" It is for you, O Lord ! I do this—it is for your glory—it is because you desire it ;"—and always continue this exercise till we shall have performed our actions, " as those that serve God, and not men" (Eph. vi. 7); that is to say, till we find ourselves actually inflamed with the love of God in what we do; and till we feel joy in accomplishing his divine will : and, in fine, till all our actions savour of nothing else than the effects of that divine love which animates us.

Father Avila adduces a familiar comparison very applicable to our purpose. He says, that in all our actions we ought to resemble the affectionate wife, who seeing her husband return from a great journey all covered with dust, quite spent and weary, washes his feet herself, and feels joy in this service she does him ; so that we clearly see it is love moves her to what she does. If we can perform our actions in this manner—if we can find this treasure hidden in the fields, this treasure so exposed, and yet so hid at the same time ; how rich should we become, and how soon should we be perfect ? This is truly the philosopher's stone, which changes iron and brass into gold ; because how mean soever any action is of itself, it renders it very precious. Let us, therefore, for the future, thus strive to convert all things into most pure gold, since it is so much in our power to do so. And as, in the temple of Solomon, there was nothing but what was of gold, or covered with gold ; so let there be nothing in you, which is not either an act or an effect of the love of God.

———o———

CHAPTER IX.

That our Distractions and Remissness ought not to be ascribed to our exterior Occupations, but to our Negligence therein.

FROM what has been said we may easily see that if our employment happen sometimes to distract us, and make us relent in our fervour, the fault is not in our employments, but in ourselves, who know not how to acquit ourselves of them. If you stop at the rind or exterior of the action, you will fatigue both mind and body to no purpose. The will of God, which is, as it were, the interior, the marrow and the substance of all things, ought to be your food and nourishment. Break the rind and penetrate to the marrow like the eagle, which Ezechiel speaks of, " which carried away the marrow of the cedar" (Ezech. xvii. 3), and say with the Psalmist : "Lord, I will offer unto you holocausts full of juice and marrow" (Psal. lxv. 14) ; and by this means you will constantly advance in perfection. Martha and Mary are sisters—one neither hurts nor hinders the other; that is, action and contemplation prejudice not each other. But, on the contrary, prayer well made helps us to perform each action well ; and each action well done helps us very much to pray well. If you feel, therefore, any trouble and disquiet in what you are about, it is because the help and assistance of prayer are wanting : " Martha, Martha, you torment and trouble yourself about many things." (Luke x. 40, 41.) Martha is troubled because her sister Mary does not help her ; and, therefore, desiring her assistance, addresses herself to our Saviour, saying, "Speak to her to help me." Do you also endeavour to gain assistance from Mary, that is from prayer and meditation, and you will find that all your disquiet will soon vanish. The holy living creatures that appeared to Ezechiel "held their hands hid under their wings" (Ezech. i. 8), to let us understand, that those who make profession of a spiritual life ought not to act but under the shadow of contemplation ; and must unite meditation and action in such a manner, that the one be never separated from the other. Cassian says, that the ancient anchorets of Egypt ceased not to practise contemplation, though they were most attentive to their work ; and as long as their hands were employed in the duties of Martha, their hearts were entirely engaged in the exercises of Mary. And St. Bernard, speaking of this subject, says : " The principal care of those who devote themselves to spiritual exercises is to employ themselves in exterior things, in such manner that the interior head of devotion do not at all cool ; but that the same function which weakens the body serves to give new strength to the mind." (Bern. Ser. ad Solit.) It is, therefore, by no means true that exterior occupations impede devotion and interior recollection ; on the contrary, they contribute thereto. For they, giving employment but to the body, the mind is quite at liberty to think constantly on God. It is for this reason, an ancient religious, very much advanced in virtue, was used to say, that in religion, he envied extremely two sorts of persons, novices and lay-brothers ; the first, because they were employed in nothing but in promoting their spiritual advancement ; and the second, because not having their minds embarrassed by care, they might have it always disengaged, and free for prayer.

St. John Climacus relates, that in a monastery near Alexandria he found a cook who was exceedingly occupied in his employment, because he was every day to prepare meat for two hundred and thirty religious persons, besides strangers : and yet amidst all these his exterior labours, he failed not to be always recollected in himself, and to shed tears in very great abundance. St. John Climacus, much astonished at this, pressed him to tell him how, amidst so many embarrassments, he was able to preserve so great recollection of mind, and to obtain the gift of tears. I always imagine to myself, answered the brother that it is God whom I serve, and not men ; wherefore, I believe that I ought not to give myself any respite or repose ; and the sight of the material fire furnishes me with a continual fountain of tears, by setting continually before my eyes the violence of the fire of hell. We read in like manner of St. Catherine of Sienna, that the persecution of her parents, who would oblige her to marry, went to such an excess, that believing the spiritual exercises she practised were what most of all hindered her from marrying, they deprived her of all liberty of being able to apply herself in secret to prayer ; and employed her in the meanest offices of the house, putting her into the kitchen in the place of a slave whom they took out of it. But this holy virgin, instructed by the Holy Ghost, built herself a retreat in the bottom of her heart, and proposed to herself never to quit it, and she performed faithfully what she had proposed ; so that though she was not permitted to remain in the apartment, which she before had in her parents' house, any longer than they thought fit ; yet she never left that she had made within her heart ; so that though it were easy to deprive her of the one, it was impossible for them to put her out of the other. For when she was employed in the most servile offices of the house, she looked upon her father and mother as representing Jesus Christ and the Blessed Virgin ; and in the persons of her brethren, and the rest of the family, she represented to herself the apostles and the disciples of our Saviour.

Thus having her mind always filled with this idea, she performed all things with joy, thinking that it was Jesus Christ she served; and placing herself always in God's sight, she enjoyed continually his presence, and shut herself up with him in the sanctuary of her heart. Hence she was wont to say to her confessor, when he was charged with any temporal employments, or had any journey to make; "Dear father, make within yourself a retreat, and endeavour never to forsake it." Let us take this counsel to ourselves, and we shall find by experience, that all exterior employments that can be imposed upon us, so far from impeding, will, on the contrary, help us to interior recollection and continual prayer.

———o———

CHAPTER X.

How advantageous it is to perform our Actions after the Manner already described.

ACTIONS performed after the manner aforesaid are called full and perfect—and St. Jerome and St. Gregory say, that when the holy Scripture speaks of those that have lived after this manner it expresses itself, "That they have thus lived entire and full days : and that they died full of days" (Isa. xxxviii. 10), though they died very young. It is this the Wise Man teaches us, when he speaks of the just : "That in the short time they lived, they fulfilled a great space or length of time." (Wisd. iv. 13.) But how can it be that one should live a great while in a short time, and that in a few, he should complete many years? Would you know how? It is by performing his actions full and entire, and by passing perfect and whole days. "Full and entire days shall be found in them" (Psal. lxxii. 10)—these words of the Psalmist explain the foregoing text. To the true servants of God every day is twenty-four hours; they suffer not one moment of this time to pass unprofitably. The day is always full and entire to them, because they employ it totally in doing the will of God. The very hours of eating, recreating, and sleeping are fruitful to them, because they refer all their actions to the greater glory of God; and because they do them conformably to his divine will. They eat from pure necessity, not for pleasure ; and seek not their satisfaction in anything. On the contrary, they would desire, if it were God's will, to be able to live without eating, sleeping, or recreation—they would never be employed but in loving God, and they earnestly desire with the Royal Prophet: "That he would deliver them from their necessities" (Psal. xxiv. 17); that is, that they might be disengaged from the miseries of the body, and the necessity of supplying nature, to the end they might be always absorbed in the love and contemplation of God.

I know very well that this is what none can arrive to in this life; and that the just ought to suffer with patience all the infirmities of human nature; yet they cannot accommodate themselves to them but with sorrow; of which the testimonies of Job and David are clear proofs. The one says, ". I sigh before I eat" (Job iii. 24); and the other, "That he mixed his drink with his tears" (Psal. ci. 10); and again, "That he washed his bed every night, and watered it with his tears." (Psal. vi. 7.) It is ours to do the same; as soon as we lie down in bed we ought in tears to say to God: Must I, O Lord! be so long a time deprived of thinking of you? "Why are my exile and banishment prolonged" (Psal. cxix. 5), when will you be pleased to put an end to them? "Draw my soul out of its prison" (Psal. cxli. 18), draw it out of the prison of this miserable body, to the end that it may never more be employed but in blessing and praising you eternally. It is after this manner that all our actions and all our days become full and entire—it is after this manner that the just live a long while in a short time, and that a few days of life make many years of merit. But says St. Gregory, whoever has not well employed his time, and has neglected to do good works during his life; how long soever the course of his life may be, we can say of him, that he dies void and destitute of days, because he has permitted his days and years to pass unprofitably; and he himself may truly say, that the "days of his pilgrimage have been short and evil." (Gen. xlvii. 9.)

St. Jerome, speaking of these words of King Ezechias, related by the prophet Isaiah: "In the midst of my days I will go to the gates of hell" (Isa. xxiii. 10), makes this remark, that the saints and just, even such as Abraham was, do entirely accomplish the multitude of their days. "He died in a happy old age, and full of days"(Gen. xxv. 8), says the holy Scripture, but the wicked die in the midst of their days, and even go not so far; because they let many years pass unprofitably. "The men of blood, and the deceivers," says the prophet, "shall not live half their days." (Psal. liv. 17.) It is upon this account, and for the same reason that the holy Scripture calls a sinner an infant of an hundred years ; because he lives not as a man, but as a child. " An infant died of an hundred years of age," says Isaiah, " and the sinner of an hundred years old shall be cursed." (Isa. lxv. 20.) Hence it is, that the wicked are always surprised by death, and cut down whilst they are green ; and when it happens thus, they complain that it happens too soon, and beg some respite that they may have leisure to do penance. We say the same of tepid religious; for be it ever so long since they took the habit, yet they have lived but very few days in religion.

We read in the Chronicle of St. Francis, that a good old man, being asked by a secular, how long he had been religious, answered him, " That he had not yet been one moment." But the old man seeing him scandalised at this answer, which he did not rightly comprehend, added : " I know very well that it is seventy-five years since I put on the religious habit, but I know not how long I have been a true religious by the due performance of all my actions." God grant that none of us may say of ourselves with truth, what his humility alone made this holy man say. Because it matters not to have been a long while in religion, and to have grown old therein, but it is of importance, to have lived well in religion ; and what does it profit us to count many years from the day of our conversion, if we be not at all grown better ? A few days of a pure and holy life are of greater value, than many days of a dissolute and tepid one. Hence before God we reckon not the years of our life, but those of a good life ; nor the years that are passed in religion, but those in which we have lived as good religious. The holy Scripture furnishes us with an excellent example of this truth in the first book of the Kings, when he says, that Saul " was an infant of a year old, when he began to reign, and that he reigned two years over Israel." (1 Kings xiii. 1.) Yet it is very certain that he reigned forty years; and St. Paul clearly states this in the Acts of the Apostles in these words : " Afterwards they asked a king, and God gave them Saul, the son of Cis, of the tribe of Benjamin, during the space of forty years." (Acts xiii. 21.) Why then, in the history of the Kings, is there mention made of only two years ? Because in God's annals we count only the years that we have lived well ; and therefore of the whole time that the reign of Saul lasted, the holy Scripture only counts two years, because he reigned only those two years

as a just prince, and a true king. The gospel also teaches us,
that although those, whom the father of the family had sent last
of all to his vineyard, had wrought only an hour, yet they had
the same recompense as those who had wrought all the day long.
And without doubt, he treated them after this manner, because
in the short time they had laboured, they had merited as much,
if not more, than the others had done the whole day. Let us,
therefore, regulate our account after this manner, and let us
mark accordingly how long we have lived in religion.

Eusebius Emissenus describes this admirably well, when he
says: " It is by the number of years that we ordinarily measure
the time we have lived ; but take care you deceive not yourself
by counting from the time of your entrance into religion.   Because you ought not to count any other days than those in which
you have renounced your own will ; or resisted your passions ;
or wherein you have done nothing contrary to the exact observance of your rules ; reckon also that day as one of your life,
which received its light from the purity of your mind and holy
meditations.   Make, if possible, some years of this sort of days,
and measure hereby the time you have lived in religion : fearing
lest otherwise the same reproach be made to you that was made
to the Bishop of Sardis in the Apocalypse: " Write to the
angel of the church of Sardis," says our Lord, "I know all your
actions ; I know they say that you live, and notwithstanding you
are dead ; wherefore stand upon your guard, because I find your
actions are not full in the sight of God." (Apoc. iii. 1.) Believe
that nothing is hid from the knowledge of God ; he sees in you
that which men cannot discover ; they believe you live, when,
alas ! you are dead ; you bear the name of a Christian ; you
bear the name and habit of religion, but have not the qualities
of a religious.   All your actions accord very ill with the name
you bear : they are entirely void of God ; and if they are full of
anything it is of yourself—you seek only yourself in all things
you do—you seek your own particular interest, your own glory,
honour, and reputation.   Let us, therefore, watch ourselves
carefully—let us endeavour that our actions be full and complete, and that our days be full and entire, to the end that
after this manner we may live a great while in a short time,
and that we may merit very much before God.

———o———

CHAPTER XI.

The Rectitude and Purity of Intention we ought to have in all our Actions, more fully explained.

IT is customary to instruct those who are engaged in promoting the salvation of their neighbour, how they are to conduct themselves in the discharge of their duties. Now the advice we give them, and which we take from the doctrine of the fathers of the Church, will show us how to purify our intention in all things ; and with what simplicity and disinterestedness we ought to seek God in everything we do. When, say they, you undertake anything, whence any spiritual advantage may arise to your neighbour, let not the good success of your enterprise, but only the fulfilling of the will of God, be your principal end and intention. And hence, when we hear confessions, when we preach, and when we teach, we ought not to have chiefly in view the conversion, the amendment, and the profit of our neighbour ; but above all, our intention ought to be to do the will of God in whatsoever he employs us, and to perform it in the best manner we are able, purely to please him. And after we have done this, whether we succeed or not in our undertaking, whether any one is improved by our instruction, or derives advantage from our sermons, it is God's affair and not ours. " I have planted," says the apostle, " Apollo has watered, but God has given the increase." (1 Cor. iii. 6.) That which we are able to do is to plant and water as the gardener does ; but to make the plant grow, and to make the tree bring forth fruit, is not his work, but the work of God alone. The fruit of souls, which is their conversion, their amendment, and their progress in virtue, can come from none but God ; and it is not on these fruits that the merit and perfection of our actions depend. Behold the purity of intention we should endeavour to have ; behold the means which will enable us to enjoy a profound peace in everything we do. For then, if to a laudable action and to the advantage expected from it, there is opposed any obstacle, we shall not be at all troubled, if the end we propose to ourselves in our enterprise has not the wished for event, but we shall rest satisfied in having done the will of God, by having performed our duty in the best manner we were able to please him. But if when you preach, hear confessions, and treat with your neighbour for his salvation, you have in view the producing much fruit by this means—and if you make this your chief end, you will infallibly feel great trouble of mind, if your design happens to be thwarted; and sometimes you will lose not only your interior peace of mind, but your patience also, and perhaps permit yourself to be transported still farther.

" St. Ignatius was accustomed to explain this by a very proper comparison : " Do you know," says he, " how we ought to behave towards our neighbour in the employments that concern the salvation of souls? As the angel guardians behave towards those of whom God has given them care." They give them all the good counsel they are able—they defend, conduct, enlighten, excite, and help them to do well; but if men make a bad use of their free will, and resist their good inspirations, the angels afflict not themselves for this—the felicity they enjoy is not at all diminished ; but they say with Jeremias : " We have used all our care and industry to cure Babylon ; and it is not healed : let us leave and abandon it." (Jer. li. 9.) It is after this manner we ought to do what we can for the conversion and amendment of our neighbour ; but when we have carefully performed our duty, we must keep our minds in peace, and not permit it to give way to any disquiet, because the sick person is not, nay even will not be cured.

The disciples, sent by Jesus Christ to preach, could not forbear, at their return, expressing the joy they felt in having wrought miracles and cast out devils. But the Son of God reprimanded them thus : " Do not rejoice at this, but rejoice that your names are written in heaven." (Luke x. 20.) Let not your joy and contentment depend upon your success, though ever so great, but see whether you perform your actions so as to merit that your name be registered in the kingdom of heaven. See that you exactly fulfil the obligation of your charge ; and let the doing so be all your ambition and all your joy ; since the happy issue, the extraordinary conversions, and the other wonders God shall enable you to work, shall not be looked upon as your own—your reward shall not be regulated by these—for whether men be converted or not, the pains you shall have taken with them shall be the due measure of your recompense. On the contrary (and this will let us also see more clearly the truth of this proposition), should the whole world by your means be converted, " What will it profit you to have gained the whole world, if you suffer the loss of your own soul?" (Mat. xvi. 26.) And hence believe likewise that though you should not convert one person, your recompense shall not be anything the less, provided you do everything in your power. Whereas were our reward to depend upon accidents, and our satisfaction to be derived from them, certainly the apostle St. James had been very unhappy, because, as they say, in all Spain he converted not more than eight or nine persons; yet the little success he had did not at all diminish his merit, nor render him less acceptable and pleasing to God than the rest of the apostles were.

We have, moreover, in what has been said, a great subject of consolation; because, hence it follows, that not only God will not ask of us, whether or not by our preaching we have produced great fruits? Or whether we have preached well? Because it is not that which he commands, nor to which our merit is annexed. That which he requires of us is, that we do what we are able, according to the talents he has given us. He desires but little of us, if we have received little : "But of him," says the gospel, "to whom he hath given much, he also requires much." (Luke xiii. 48.) St. Chrysostom explains admirably well this doctrine, when, discoursing upon the parable of the talents, he asks,—why the servant who had gained two talents was as well treated as he who had gained five? The gospel says, that when the master came to take account of his servants, of the talents divided amongst them, he to whom he had given five presented himself, saying, My lord, you gave me five talents, behold here are five others I have gained. "Well done, good and faithful servant," says his master, "because you have been faithful in small things, I will place you over many: enter thou into the joy of your Lord." (Matt. xxv. 21.) Then, he who had received two talents presented himself, saying, My lord, you trusted me with two talents, and I have gained two more. His master made him hereupon the same answer he made the other, and promised him the same recompense. "It is with justice," says this great saint, "that he rewarded them equally; because the more or less gain the one or the other had made, proceeded not from the care of the one, nor from the negligence of the other, but from the sum committed to their charge. As to the care thereof, it was the same in them both ; and it is for this reason that they received an equal reward." (Chrys. hom. xli. sup. gen.) This point is of great advantage and extreme consolation; because it may be applied to all things, and all sorts of employments and functions. So that he who labours and takes as much care as another, to perform what is commanded him, merits as much, though perhaps he performs not so great things. For example, if I take as much pains as you in preaching, and yet I preach ill, and you well, it may happen that hereby I merit as much as you, nay, perhaps, more; because I do all that I am able, and perhaps you may be able to do more than you perform. It is the same as to studies; although he who studies with you succeeds not well in them, and you make great progress, so that he remains very ignorant, and you become very learned; it may happen, nevertheless, that he merits more in his ignorance than you with your learning. In like manner, in matter of employments; if I perform not mine as well as you do yours, and my strength is not able to extend itself so far as yours, it may happen that there may be more merit in the little I do, than there is in all you perform. And without doubt this consideration will also help very much both to repress the motions of vainglory in those that have better qualities than others, and will hinder those who have less genius and talents from losing courage through a consciousness of their own weakness and incapacity.

St. Jerome's opinion is very conformable to what I have already said, who speaking of the same parable :—" In fine," says he, " the master gave the same kind of reception to his servant who had increased his five talents to ten, as to the other who had increased the two talents he had received to four ; and without taking notice of the great gain they had made he considered only the great zeal and diligence they had thereby manifested." It is not the value of the oblation, says Salvin, but it is the affection with which it is offered, that renders it pleasing to God. He regards not how much we give, says St. Gregory, but the good will with which we give it—he esteems not the present, but accepts of the heart that bestows it : so that we may even do less than another, and yet often please him more, if we act with a greater extent of charity. It is in this that the greatness of God appears, that all the service we are able to do him is inconsiderable in his sight, unless on account of the excess of love wherewith it is performed. For he wants not our goods ; since he cannot increase in riches, or in anything else, " and all our good actions can give him nothing he has not." (Job xxxv. 7.) All he desires of us, therefore, is, that we love him, and that we do all in our power to manifest it. We have a formal example of this in the two mites which the widow in the gospel offered. The Son of God standing near the treasury in the temple, took notice that the Pharises and rich people put very great alms into it, and that a poor widow approaching put in only two mites. Our Saviour hereupon turning towards his disciples said, " Verily, this poor widow hath given more than all the rest; for they cast in of their abundance, but she of her want cast in all she had, even her whole living." (Mark xii. 43, 44.) In this manner God judges of our actions; "and as he rewarded the widow," says St. Chrysostom, " so he will reward those that instruct others." He will act in the same manner towards those who preach, study, labour, or employ themselves in other religious duties—he will not take so much notice of what they do, as of the charity and fervour with which they do it.

———o———

CHAPTER XII.

Several Marks to know when we act purely for God, and when we seek ourselves in what we do.

St. Gregory proposes to us an excellent mark to know whether, in our functions which relate to the salvation of our neighbour, we seek purely the glory of God, or have our own glory also in view. Take notice, says he, whether or not you feel the same joy when another preaches well, is numerously attended, and produces great fruit in souls as if you performed all this yourself. For if you rejoice not as much at his performance as at your own; but on the contrary feel a sort of trouble and envy; it is an infallible sign that you do not purely seek the glory of God, as the apostle St. James tells us in express terms : " If you have a bitter jealousy and nourish in your heart the feelings of contention and envy, your wisdom comes not from above, but is earthly, it savours of creatures, and is diabolical." (James iii. 14.) You are not jealous of God's honour, but of your own, and of attracting to yourself that esteem and reputation which you perceive another has gained. For if you desire the glory of God and not your own, you would be glad that there should be many excellent persons, and able workmen in the vineyard, and that another should do more than you are able to do yourself. It is thus Moses acted when Josue wished to make him prevent several persons from prophesying in the camp. He answered very angry, and much moved at such a proposal: "What zeal," says he, "do you arrogate to yourself upon my account? Would to God that all people were able to prophesy, and that our Lord would impart his spirit to them all!" (Num. xi. 29.) A true servant of God ought in like manner to say: Would to God that all preachers were very excellent, and that our Lord would give them the spirit of eloquence and persuasion, that they might be the better able to extend his glory throughout all places, and that his name might be known and sanctified by the whole world!

Father Avila has set an edifying example in this respect. It is related of him, that on his hearing that the Society of Jesus was established through the exertions of St. Ignatius, and understanding what its end and institution were, he declared that this was the object he had aspired to for many years, but that he could not attain it. He added, that on the occasion, it happened to him as to a child who at the foot of a mountain should endeavour to roll a heavy burden to the top of it, but who by reason of his weakness could not effect his purpose—at length there came a giant, who took up the same burden, and with all the ease imaginable, carried it where he pleased. Thus this holy man looked upon himself as a child, whilst he compared St. Ignatius to a giant. But to come to what is more to our present purpose—the establishment of our society gave him as great joy as if he had been the founder and institutor of it himself; because therein he regarded only the glory of God and salvation of souls. Behold here how the faithful ministers of God "think not on their own interests, but on those of Jesus Christ" (Phil. ii. 21, 4); and it is after this manner, that those who serve him ought to be so detached from themselves, that when the divine Providence should advance its glory, and procure the salvation of souls by the means and help of others, they ought to be as well satisfied, as if it had made use of their assistance. It is therefore a very laudable practice, adopted by some servants of God, very zealous for the conversion of souls, to pray after this manner: "Lord, so that these sinners correct their ill courses, that this soul converts itself to thee, that this good happens, that the increase and progress of Christianity takes place, it is all that I desire; let it be performed by what means and assistance you please, it is all equal to me; for my part I desire that nothing thereof be ascribed or attributed to my efforts." This in effect is to have a pure and upright intention, to act with an entire disengagement from all things that relate to ourselves, and to have no other object than God's greater honour and glory.

The same may be said of our own and our brethren's spiritual advancement. Whoever is disgusted, or dejected, because he sees his brother advance before him in the way of virtue, seeks not purely the greater glory of God. For though it be true that a faithful servant of God ought to have his heart deeply pierced with sorrow on seeing that he serves not so great a master as diligently as he ought and could; yet it does not therefore follow that he needs must disquiet himself or repine, because another makes greater progress than he. On the contrary, in the sorrow he ought to feel at not serving God better than he does, it should be a great comfort to him to see, that though he himself complies not entirely with his duty, yet there are others at least, who acquit themselves of theirs, as he would wish to acquit himself of his : and who serve and glorify God as they ought. So that the disquiet and trouble into which any person is cast upon this account, comes from nothing else than self-love or some secret motion of pride and envy. For if we desired truly the honour and glory of God, and desired to serve him upon this account alone, it is certain we should exceedingly rejoice on seeing others increase in virtue and perfection ; though the idea of our not serving him as well as they ought to give us great sorrow and confusion.

A second mark that we do our actions purely for God, is when a religious embraces the office allotted him, and executes his orders in such a manner, that he is wholly indifferent whether they prescribe one thing or another : whether they employ him in one function or another, and in whatsoever office he is employed, he is always equally pleased and content. For this indifference and evenness of mind spring from his thoughts being entirely engaged in doing the will of God, without troubling himself about anything else. But if he does not acquit himself as willingly of a mean and painful, as he does of an easy and honourable employment; it is sign that he acts not purely for God, but that he regards himself, and seeks his own satisfaction and particular interests. Wherefore, a holy man had great reason to say, that whatever way it shall please the divine Providence to dispose and order things, we should always equally rejoice at all events, if God's will be truly the motive of our desires. (Thomas-à-Kempis.)

But when a religious wishes very much that his superiors

should know what he does, and what pains he takes; when he desires to be praised by them, or at least to receive some remark of approbation from them; and when on this being withheld, he is presently discouraged : it is an evident sign that the love of God is not the sole motive of his actions; but that there is a considerable share of human respects mingled with it. If you act purely for God, the praises of men would be of no value in your eyes : but on the contrary, if you reflected that when your superior expresses approbation of your conduct, it is merely because he feels for your weakness and imperfection, which stand in need of his encouragement, certainly you would be ashamed and confounded at it, instead of being pleased; and bewailing yourself you would cry out, Is it possible that I should be still so imperfect as to cause my superior to treat me after this manner? Shall I always remain a novice, and appear so little advanced in virtue, as to stand in need of being excited to it by so poor and imperfect a motive as this?

We read, in the *Spiritual Meadow*, that the abbot John, disciple of St. Amon, served for the space of twelve years one of the ancient fathers of the desert, who was extremely infirm, and though during this time he applied himself with all imaginable care and affection to serve him, yet he never received the least comfortable word from him, but on the contrary, was often received very rudely, and treated unkindly by him. At length the old man finding himself near his death, in presence of a great many ancient hermits that came to visit him, he called to him the holy man, who during this space had served him with so much patience and humility; and taking him by the hand he thrice repeated these words : " Remain constant in God's service"—and recommending him to the most ancient fathers present, in order to move them the more, he says, Believe me it is not a man but an angel I recommend to you, since during the twelve years he has served me in my sickness, he has never had a good word from me; and yet he never failed to serve me with all possible diligence and affection.

———o———

CHAPTER XIII.

What is requisite on our part to obtain every Day a greater Purity of Intention.

St. Ignatius, explaining in his Constitutions, after what manner we ought daily to increase in rectitude and purity of intention,

says : " Let all our study be, to have an upright intention, not
only in our state of life in general, but also in all our actions in particular ; proposing nothing else to ourselves, than to serve and
please God ; and this rather through love and gratitude for the
benefits we have received, than through fear of punishment, or
hope of reward, though nevertheless these two motives are very
good, and may profitably be made use of by us." There are
several ways of seeking and serving God. To serve him through
fear of punishment, is to seek him, and to do a good action ; because fear, though servile, ceases not to be good, and to be a gift
of God; and therefore the Royal Prophet begged it of God, when
he said, " Penetrate my flesh, O Lord, with your fear." (Psalm
cxviii. 120.) But if we should truly say to ourselves, and in
effect had the same sentiments in our hearts, that "if there were
no hell, and I were not afraid of being punished, I would offend
God :" divines hold that such an act as this is a new sin, because
this were actually to have our will very ill disposed. However,
to avail ourselves of the fear of punishment, with the apprehension of death, and the fear of God's judgment, in order to
excite ourselves the better to serve God, and to abstain from
offending him, cannot but be laudable; because it is upon this
account that the holy Scripture frequently recommends this very
thing to us, and holds out such terrible threats as it does.

It is, moreover, to seek God, if we serve him for the recom
pense which we hope for in glory : and it is also to seek him after
a more perfect manner than the former ; because there is more
perfection in doing our actions with a view to recompense, than
through a motive of fear.   Moses acted after this manner, as St.
Paul teaches us when he says, " that it was by faith that Moses,
after he became of age, renounced the title of Pharaoh's daughter's
son ; desiring rather to be afflicted with the people of God, than
to enjoy the transitory advantages of sin ; and preferring the ignominy of Jesus Christ before all the riches of the Egyptians ;
because he fixed his thoughts upon the recompense to come."
(Heb. xi. 24.)   It is also upon the same aacount, and with the
same intention, that the Psalmist said, " I have disposed my
heart to observe continually your commandments, because of the
recompense I thereby hope for." (Ps. cxviii. 112.)

Wherefore the two motives of fear and hope are very good; and
we can avail ourselves of them in order to excite ourselves to do
good and to avoid evil.   But St. Ignatius will have us go farther,
and desires we should still elevate our hearts, and entertain higher

thoughts: " Aspire to greater gifts, and I will show you a more excellent way." (1 Cor. xii. 31.) He is not content that we seek and serve God after an ordinary manner, but he teaches us a more perfect way; he will have us seek him, and serve him purely for himself, upon account of his infinite goodness, and because God is God ; and in this is comprised all we can imagine to be excellent, great, and sublime.

The fathers of the Church, St. Basil, St. Chrysostom, and St. Gregory, treat this matter excellently well. Those who serve God through hope of reward, they compare to Simon the Cyrenean, who carried the cross of Jesus Christ for a certain price or reward, which had been agreed on. They do not wish that this should be the spring of our actions. " We ought not," say they, " to be like those servants, who have little or no affection to their masters, and regard only the recompense they are to receive; because this is to act rather like a mercenary or hireling, who thinks of nothing else but his own interest, than like a servant that has a love for his master." It is their wish, therefore, that we should be influenced by a more noble motive, and that we should serve God as his children, purely for love of him. There is a great deal of difference, as they add, between the service of a slave, or of a hireling, and that of a son. The slave serves his master only through fear of punishment—the hireling through hope of recompense; and if he be careful to serve well, it is because he believes that by this means he shall be more amply rewarded. But the son acts after a different manner; it is out of pure love he serves his father—and when he takes great care to do nothing that may displease him, it is not that he fears any punishment, nor that he hopes for any reward; but it is because love naturally gives him this tenderness of affection and attention ; and, thus, though his father be poor and able to leave him nothing, yet he serves and honours him nevertheless, because the quality of father obliges him to it ; so that if his father be but pleased, he believes himself sufficiently rewarded for all his pains and services. We ought to serve God after the same manner, say these great saints; not as slaves, through fear of punishment, nor as hirelings, who regard nothing but gain and recompense; but, as the true children of God, since he has done us the favour to raise us to that dignity. " Behold what love the Father has for us," says St. John, "that he is pleased we should style ourselves children of God, and be so in effect." (1 John iii. 1.) Since, therefore, we are truly such, and since it is not without reason that we call God our Father, and Jesus Christ our Brother ; let us love and serve him as it becomes true children of his; let us honour and respect him as our father ; and as a father so worthy and deserving our obedience and respect. Let it be only for his love that we act, let it be purely to please him, and because he deserves it by being what he is ; and because his infinite goodness deserves still a thousand times more than we can do ; though we had a thousand hearts, and a thousand lives, to devote to his love and service.

"If you have ever been worthy to do anything pleasing to God," says St. Chrysostom, "and if you seek any other recompense than to have deserved to please him ; you are, without doubt, ignorant how great a good it is to please God ; because if you knew it, you would never desire any other recompense." (De compun. cor.) In effect what greater good can we wish for, than to please him? "Be ye imitators of God," says St. Paul, "as his most dear children, and make it your business to love him as Jesus Christ has loved us." (Eph. v. 1.) Let us also add to this, the reflection St. Bonaventure makes when he says : "Consider that God, your benefactor, imparts to you his gifts after such a manner, that he desires nothing of you, having no need either of you, nor of any other creature whatsoever." And he not only desires nothing of us ; and it is not only without any interest of his own that he loves us, and heaps upon us so many favours; but what he bestows upon us is purchased at the inestimable price of his most precious blood, and even the loss of his life. Behold here after what manner we should love God purely for himself, and without any mixture of our own particular interest. Nor are we to wish for virtues or any other supernatural gifts, for our own advantage and satisfaction, but purely for his sake alone, and for his greater glory; *i.e.*, that we may have something to make ourselves more agreeable and pleasing to him, and to enable us to serve him the better. Nay we ought to go still farther, and not even desire eternal glory but upon that account; in such sort, that when to excite ourselves to virtue, we set before us the recompense annexed to good works; it is not that which we ought to propose to ourselves as our principal motive ; but our last end ought always to be to love and praise God, and to think that the higher we shall be elevated in glory the more we shall be able to glorify and praise him.

It is this which is called a true love of zeal and charity, and a true and perfect love of God ; and this is properly to seek God alone, and his greater glory. Everything else is, to speak the truth, only to seek and love ourselves. This will more easily be perceived by the difference divines and philosophers make between that perfect love they call the love of amity, and the love of concupiscence. The one moves us to love for the good of our beloved, and for the love of virtue, without having any regard to our own interest ; and the other moves us to love, but it is for the advantage we hope to derive from it ourselves. It is after this manner we ordinarily love rich and powerful persons, and attach ourselves to them through the sole motive of interest. And it is very easy to perceive that this kind of love is so far from being perfect, that it is full of self-love ; because instead of loving the friend, it is rather loving ourselves and seeking our own interest. Those who serve God, either through fear of punishment or hope of reward, do the same thing; all their sentiments are mingled with self-love, and hence they do not seek him in a pure and disinterested manner. It is this Jesus Christ tells us in St. John, when after he had wrought that great miracle of feeding five thousand persons with five loaves and two fishes, turning himself towards the people, who followed in great crowds, he said to them :—"Verily, verily, I say unto you, you do not seek me, for the signs and wonders you have seen, but by reason of the bread you have eaten, and because you have been satisfied. Labour not to obtain the food that perishes, but to gain that which will last for ever." (John vi. 26.) But this food that Jesus Christ speaks of is what he calls his own food, which is purely to do the will of God. It was a very judicious and holy answer which Gerson relates a servant of God made who practised very great penance, and was continually in prayer. The devil, jealous of this holy man's progress in perfection, and anxious to divert him from it, one day tempted him very violently in the matter of predestination, causing him in imagination to hear these words frequently repeated :—Why do you torment yourself in this manner? Why do you take so much pains? Do what you will, you will never be saved." To whom this holy man answered :— "It is not for recompense I serve God, but it is for his sake alone I serve him." By this answer he freed himself completely from this importunate temptation, and confounded the devil.

But St. Bernard goes still farther, and would have us think so little of ourselves in all our actions, and be so disengaged from all self-interest, that we should not think it sufficient to love and serve God as children love and serve their fathers ; but he requires of us a still mure pure, perfect, and more elevated

affection :—" For in fine," says he, " it is true that children love
their fathers, but they also look to their inheritance; and the
more they are afraid of being on any account disinherited, perhaps the more respect they pay those from whom they expect the
inheritance, but perhaps they also love them the less. This indeed may be called love ; but may very well be suspected when
it seems to live on the hope of gain. It is also very weak, when
it can either relent or be extinguished, on the hope of advantage
being diminished or removed ; and it is less pure when it is
capable of desiring anything besides the beloved. Pure love is
not mercenary ; pure love and true charity presume not upon
hope, nor feel or receive any damage from despair." (Bern. serm.
lxxxiii. sup. Cant.) The saint would teach us that this pure
love wants neither hope nor recompense to excite it to labour,
and to move it to serve God. And though a soul inflamed with
this love should certainly know she could gain nothing by it,
yet she would never lose the least courage, nor desist from daily
doing her duty ; because it is not interest, but only tenderness
of love, which is the rule and motive of all she does. But what
love is there that can be so perfect and elevated, as to surpass
that of children for their parents ? " Would you know," says
this great saint, " what this love is ? It is the love that the
spouse has for her beloved " (De Dilig. Deo) ; for true love is
content with itself alone, and bounds its desires and recompense
within the limits of the object it loves; in fine, this love between
the spouse and her beloved is such that it entirely satisfies itself
with the object it loves ; it searches nothing out of it, nor desires anything else :—" This is the only affair of true lovers,
and it is after this manner," says St. Bernard, " that all of us
ought to behave ourselves in our love for God, the beloved of
our souls. Let us love him for himself, and let all our joy and
satisfaction be in loving him : for love is sufficient for itself—it
pleases by itself and for itself; it is both its own merit and
recompense ; it neither seeks any motive to love, nor out of
itself does it look for any advantage in loving. But the fruit
and exercise of this love is, I love, because I love ; I love,
purely to love."

" But do not think," says St. Chrysostom, " that because you
have it not in view, your recompense will be the less on that
account." On the contrary, it shall for that very reason become
greater ; and the less you look on your own interest the more
considerable will be your gain. For it is certain, that the more

our action is free from and void of all sort of self-interest, the more pure and perfect it is; and it never becomes so meritorious as when there is no mixture at all of self-love. If you turn away your eyes therefore entirely from yourself—if in all you do, you propose to yourself nothing else than to please God, and if it is not the hope of reward that moves you to act; be assured your reward will be greater, and far more precious. For not having laboured as a mercenary to whom nothing more is given than the salary promised, you shall be treated as a son, who is heir of all the treasures of his father. "For if we be the children of God, we are by consequence heirs; heirs of God, and co-heirs of Jesus Christ" (Romans viii. 17), with whom we shall enter on the enjoyment of our heavenly Father's possessions. The daughter of Pharao gave money to the mother of Moses, for nursing Moses. Yet it was not for this recompense, but for the natural love she bore him, that this mother nursed her son.

———o———

CHAPTER XIV.

Of three Degrees of Perfection, by which we may elevate ourselves to a great Purity of Intention, and a most perfect Love of God.

FROM the doctrine of the holy fathers, and chiefly from that of St. Bernard, we infer that there are three degrees of perfection, by which we can elevate ourselves to a very great purity of intention, and to a most perfect love of God. The first is to seek nothing but the glory of God; so that in all we do, we must keep the mind absolutely detached from all earthly things, and fixing our content on God alone, we must confine our thoughts to the accomplishment of the divine will. Do you desire, says St. Bernard, to have an excellent mark to know, as far as it is possible in this life, whether or not you love God perfectly? See if there be anything out of God that can give you joy and satisfaction; and thereby you will perceive the progress you have made in loving God. Certainly as long as I am capable of receiving any comfort or satisfaction elsewhere, says he, I dare not affirm that God exclusively possesses the tender affection of my heart. St. Austin is of the same opinion when he says: "Lord, he loves you less, who loves anything with you, which he loves not for you." (Lib. x. Conf.) This sort of love is far from the excellence and purity of the love of that great queen, who, in the midst of the pomp and glory of her royal majesty, said to God : " You know, O Lord, that from the time I was brought hither, to this very day, your servant has taken no satisfaction but in you, O Lord, the God of Abraham." (Esth. xiv. 18.) Behold here, without doubt, a most perfect and pure manner of loving God.

Writing on these words of Job, " who build themselves solitudes" (Job iii. 14), St. Gregory asks, what it is to build a solitude ? He answers, that whatsoever is so detached from all creatures, and has put off all affection to earthly things so absolutely, that even amidst the greatest amusements he ceases not to feel himself alone; such a one, he says, has built a solitude; because he is not affected by any of these things. For having placed all his satisfaction in God, he can find amusement or consolation in nothing else. We daily experience, that when our affection is placed on any person, if we happen to lose him, either by absence or death, we are then in a mournful solitude, even amidst the best company ; because we have not him in whose company we felt so much pleasure. The same happens to him who has entirely banished all creatures from his heart, to fill it only with God. Amidst the greatest pleasures, and greatest assemblies, he feels himself alone, because he takes no pleasure in the things of the world, and because there is nothing, save the object of his love, which can yield him pleasure. Persons, says St. Gregory, arrived at this point of perfection, enjoy a most perfect tranquillity and peace of soul. Nothing disquiets or troubles them—they are not cast down by adversity, nor are they puffed up by prosperity. For as they have no attachment to this life, all the changes occurring therein produce no change in them; and framing to themselves an happiness which depends not on events, they feel superior to vicissitudes. Do you know, says he, who was raised to this height of this perfection, and who built himself such a solitude as this ? He who said, " One thing I asked of our Lord, which I will never cease to ask till I have obtained it, which is to live all the days of my life in the house of our Lord." (Ps. xxvi. 4.) For after all, what else is there either in heaven or earth worth our desiring or seeking ? "And what is at present my expectation but God ? " (Ibid. xxxviii. 8.) The holy abbot, Sylvanus, likewise attained this degree of happiness : for they relate of him, that on rising from prayer all earthly things seemed so contemptible to him, that putting his hands before his eyes, he said: "Shut yourselves,

O my eyes, shut yourselves, for there is nothing that is worth your beholding." We read in like manner of St. Ignatius, that sometimes lifting up his eyes to heaven, and his heart to God, he cried out, " Alas ! how contemptible does the earth appear, whilst I contemplate heaven."

The second degree by which we may ascend to the perfection we speak of is suggested to us by St. Bernard, in his Treatise on the Love of God. It is, not only to forget all things of this world, but even to forget ourselves, and not to love ourselves but in God and for God. For if we wish to be truly perfect, we ought to be wholly and entirely forgetful of ourselves, and of everything regarding ourselves or our interest—we ought to love God in so pure and elevated a manner, that in all the gifts we receive from his hands, whether those of grace or those of glory, it is not the advantage we derive from them, but the accomplishment of his divine will in us, that ought to constitute our content and our joy. This is the practice of the blessed saints in heaven. They rejoice more at the will of God accomplished in them, than at the height of glory they are placed on; and love God in so sublime a manner, and are so transformed into him, and united to his divine will, that amidst the ineffable delights they abound in, it is more for God's sake than their own, that they love the felicity they possess. It is in this manner we ought to love God, says St. Bernard, and it was in that the Royal Prophet loved him, when he said, " Bless our Lord, because he is good." He says not, " because he is good to me," but only, " because he is good " (Ibid. cxvii. 1) : he does not love or praise him upon his own account, and for self-interest, as he did of whom he speaks in another place, " He will bless you because you have done him good :" but he loves and praises him, because he is good in himself : because God is God, and because his goodness is infinite.

The third and last degree of perfection, says St. Bernard, is to do our actions not only to please God, but because God is pleasing to us, and pleased with what we do. So that without thinking any more upon ourselves than if we were not in the world, we should look only upon the sole contentment and satisfaction of God. Behold here a most pure and perfect manner of loving. " This love," says the saint, " is truly the mountain of our Lord, a high mountain, very fat and fertile." Ps. lxvii. 16.) For this expression of the mountain of God, in Scripture, means nothing else than the aggregate of all sorts of excellency and perfection. "Who, O Lord, shall ascend this mountain?" (Ib. xxiii. 3, and liv. 7.) "Who will give me the wings of a dove, that I may fly thither, and there take my repose?" But, alas! says this great saint, the very worst of all is, that, in this land of exile, I can never be so happy as entirely to forget myself; "Miserable man that I am, who will deliver me from this body of death?" (Rom. vii. 24.) "Lord, I suffer violence, answer you for me." (Is. xxxviii. 14.) When shall I die entirely to myself, that I may live only to you? "Why must my banishment be prolonged?" (Ps. cxix. 5.) "When shall I come and present myself before the face of God?" (Ib. xli. 2.) When, O Lord! will it come to pass, that I shall be totally united to thee, and transformed by love into thee, and be so entirely disengaged from myself, that I may become one spirit with thee; that in fine, I may love nothing in myself nor for myself, but love all in you and for you? For not to seek, nor find ourselves in what we do, any more than if we were as I may say, lost in ourselves; or if as one were not in being; nor even feel ourselves at all, but be as it were altogether perfectly annihilated; is the effect of that love the blessed saints enjoy, and which has no mixture of human or terrene affections. It is for this reason the Royal Prophet said, "I shall enter into glory, and into the power of our Lord, and then I will remember, O Lord, nothing else but your justice." (Ib. lxx. 16.) When we shall have thus acted like faithful servants, we shall enter into the joy of our Lord, and shall be inebriated with the abundance of his love, and transformed into him, that we shall think upon, or remember nothing at all that belongs to ourselves.

"Then we shall be like to him, for then we shall see him as he is in himself." (1 John iii. 2.) Then the creature shall entirely transform itself into its Creator; "and as he made all things for himself" (Prov. xvi. 4), as the Scripture testifies; so also we shall love nothing but him—we shall not even love ourselves, but in him, and for him. So that neither the misery from which we shall be freed, nor the happiness which we possess, but the will of God accomplished in us, shall be the only object of our joy. Behold here the manner of entering into the joy of our Lord.

O holy and chaste love! cries out St. Bernard in this place, sweet and tender affection! O pure and upright intention of the will! Intention so much the more upright and pure, by how much it is purified from any mixture of self-interest! Affection so much the more tender and sweet, by how much it is moved or touched by nothing but what is divine ; and to be moved and affected after this manner, is to be deified. (Bern. de Dilig. Deo.) And the saint, desirous to explain to us how afterwards we shall be deified and transformed into God, makes use of three comparisons, and says, as a drop of water loses all its properties, when it is cast into a great vessel of wine ; or as a red-hot iron in the furnace has no appearance of iron but only of fire ; or in fine, as the air, enlightened by a ray of the sun, becomes so bright as though it were the light itself ; so when we shall be in glory, we shall wholly lose our first qualities, we shall be deified and transformed into God, and then we shall love nothing but him, and in him. Otherwise how will it come to pass, "that God shall be all things in us;" should there remain anything of man in us ? Wherefore there shall then be nothing in us that shall be ours. (1 Cor. xv. 28.) The joy and glory we shall possess shall be the joy and glory of God, and not our own, according to the words of the Psalmist : "You are my glory, it is you that have exalted me." (Psalm iii. 4.) And in fine, we shall not place our satisfaction in our own happiness, but it will be in God alone, in whom we shall place all our content and comfort. But though in this world we can never arrive at so high a degree of perfection, yet we ought often to endeavour to have our eyes continually fixed upon it ; because the nearer we approach to this end, the closer shall our union be with God. Wherefore let us conclude with this great saint, and say : O Lord ! it is only in this union that the will of your Son does consist, and live in us ; it is this he asked of you in that prayer he made for us when he said : " Grant, that as you and I are one, so they may be one in us." That is to say, that they love you for yourself ; and that they love not themselves but in you. It is this which is truly the end, consummation, and perfection of all things ; this is the peace, this is the joy of the Lord, this is the joy of the Holy Ghost, the calm and repose of the blessed saints in heaven.

———o———

THE FOURTH TREATISE.

---o---

OF UNION AND FRATERNAL CHARITY.

---o---

CHAPTER I.

Of the Merit and Excellency of Union and Fraternal Charity.

"BEHOLD," says the Royal Prophet, "how good and pleasing a thing it is for brethren to live together in union!" (Ps. cxxxii. 1.) How estimable is union and harmony amongst brethren !—St. Jerome says, that this passage is addressed peculiarly to religious assembled together in the same community. And in truth, says he, it is a very great good, and a very great comfort, that for one brother we have left in the world, we find an infinity of brethren in religion, who love us better than our brothers could do. For ordinarily speaking, the affection our relations have for us is not sincere—it is very often grounded on interest ; and it is only upon this account that they show kindness to us. Take from them this interest, and they are seldom concerned for us—perhaps my own brother feels less affection for my person than he feels for my estate. But as to our spiritual brethren, who have contemned and abandoned all they possessed, they are far from desiring or sighing after the possession of others ; it is not your riches, but the salvation of your soul, they desire; see here what is most justly entitled to the name of *love.* The great St. Ambrose also teaches us, that brotherhood in Jesus Christ is far more excellent than that of blood ; because the one may perhaps produce some likeness of body, but the other produces a likeness and union both of heart and soul, according to what is affirmed in the Acts of the Apostles : " The multitude of the believers had but one heart and one soul." (Acts iv. 32.)

St. Basil, reflecting on this strict union between religious persons, says : what can we figure to ourselves more pleasing, happy, and admirable, than to see men of divers nations so strictly united by an exact resemblance of manners and discipline that they seem to have but one mind in divers bodies, and in like manner to see many different bodies become the instruments of one mind only ? It is this that seemed wonderful on our being first established, and in fact, it is a kind of continued miracle in our society ; in which there is so great a harmony and so strict an union between men of so many nations, and so differing in their birth, education, inclination, mind, and temper :—so that whatever difference nature had made between them, grace which unites, " and makes them live in one house, and under one rule " (Psal. lxvii. 7), gives them a perfect conformity of inclinations and will. In this the mercy of God appears so great, that we enjoy not only amongst ourselves this blessing, but it spreads its sweet odour abroad also, to the extreme edification of our neighbour, and to the greater glory of God. Whence it happens, that many of those who enter into the society, when asked the motive of their choice, answer, that it is the union they see in it which most of all moves them to make the election. This perfectly agrees with the idea of St. Austin, who, when speaking of this passage : " how good and profitable a thing it is for brethren to live together in union," says : these words of the Psalter, their sweet sound, their harmonious melody, have given birth even to monasteries. It is by the accents of so charming a voice, that many, awaked from their drowsiness and tepidity, have left both friends and riches, to live together in the union and poverty of a religious life ; and it is at the sound of this trumpet that, assembled from divers parts of the world, they were persuaded that this mutual charity which united them together was the foretaste of a heavenly life. In fine, it is this has peopled so many religious houses, established so many different orders, and attracted so many hearts to Jesus Christ. The Wise Man also, speaking of " three things very precious both in the sight of God and man," puts " concord amongst brethren" (Ecclus. xxv. 1) in the first place.

We have two precepts of charity. The one, "to love God with all our heart, with all our soul, and with all our strength, and this is the first and greatest commandment. The other, which is like to the former, is to love our neighbour as ourselves." (Matt. xxii. 38.) And it is of this second commandment we shall treat at present ; because it is the origin of that fraternal union we intend to speak of. For this union of minds and hearts is the effect of charity ; whose property, says St. Denis, is to join and unite things together. St. Paul likewise calls it

the " bond of perfection." (Col. iii. 14.) For it attracts and
unites together things which had been before widely separated
one from the other—of many wills it makes one—it prompts
me to desire that for another which I desire for myself, by
making me love him as myself. This makes me look on my
friend as my *second self*, and on me as a *second self* to him ; and
in fine, of us both it makes only one. It is for this reason St.
Austin praises very much the expression of the poet of old who
called his " friend the one-half of his soul ; " as if he and his
friend had had but one soul which animated both their bodies.

But that we may know the value and excellency of charity and
love of our neighbour, and in what esteem our Saviour holds it,
let us examine the words of Jesus Christ already cited.   St.
Chrysostom reflecting on these, and considering that after our
Saviour had spoken of the first commandment, which is "to love
God," he presently adds that the second, which is " to love our
neighbour, is like unto the first:" Behold, says he, the extreme
goodness and bounty of our Lord, who notwithstanding the infinite difference and distance there is between God and man,
would have us love man with the very self-same love, with which
we ought to love God—this methinks is to give the same measure
and extent to the love of our neighbour, as to the love of himself;
since that he ordains us to love himself with all our heart, and
with all our soul, he also commands us to love our neighbour as
we love ourselves. When we have an intimate friend, whom we
desire to recommend extremely to another, our ordinary expression is: "by the love you show to him you will express your love
to me." In the same manner, says St. Chrysostom, when our
Saviour said, the second commandment was like the first, he
would have us to understand, that if we love our neighbour we
love God himself, and it is in this sense that he said to St. Peter:
" If you love me feed my sheep " (John xxi. 17)—as if he would
say, if you love me take care of mine, and thus I shall know
whether it is true or not, that you really and effectually love me.

Of our charity towards our neighbour there is yet another
measure, of which Jesus Christ himself gave the model, when he
said to his disciples : " I give you a new commandment, that you
love one another as I have loved you." (John xiii. 34.) As our
Saviour has loved us purely for God, he will have us also love
our neighbour purely for God. Behold here, says St. Austin, the
commandment he calls *new ;* not only because he then issued a
new ordinance, or because he had lately taught it, by word as

well as by example ; but because it is effectually a new mode of loving, which he exacts from us. Natural love, which is founded upon flesh and blood, and upon the considerations of interest or pleasure, is a very ancient love, and as old as the world ; a love that is no less in practice amongst the bad than it is amongst the good ; and which is equally common to men and beasts ; according to the common saying, " Every animal loves his own kind." But the love with which Christ would have us love our neighbour is a *new* love, because he would have it to be a spiritual and supernatural one, which makes us love our neighbour for God, and with the same love and charity wherewith we love God. The divines and holy fathers take notice, that the virtue of charity which makes us love God for God, is the same that makes us love our neighbour for God. And they say, moreover, that as this love of God is a theological virtue, that is to say, a virtue wholly divine, which has God for its object : so that charity towards our neighbour is also a theological virtue, inasmuch as it is for God that we love our neighbour ; and that the same infinite bounty and goodness of God, which deserves we should love it for itself, deserves also that for it we should love our neighbour.

In fine, we cannot find anything in the whole Scripture more earnestly recommended to us, or so often inculcated, as this union and fraternal charity. For the Son of God recommends it himself to us more than once in his sermon at the last supper. " The precept which I give you," says he, " is, that you love one another, as I have loved you " (John xv. 17) ; and a little after, " that which I command you is, that you love one another." By this we see how much he desires that this charity should take deep root in our hearts ; and without doubt it can never take sufficient, because it is upon this that the whole law depends ; and this is the fulfilling of all the other commandments, according to these words of the apostle ; " He who loves his neighbour has accomplished the law." (Rom. xiii. 8.) The beloved disciple, who had imbibed the same doctrine from the very bosom of his Master, scarce speaks of anything else in all his canonical epistles ; and St. Jerome relates of him, that being so worn out with old age, that he was not able to go to church, unless he was carried, he continually repeated to his disciples these words, " Children, love one another." They, tired out with his continual repetition of the same advice, asked him one day the reason why he so often recommended the same thing ;

to whom he made, says St. Jerome, this answer, truly worthy of St. John : " because it is the precept of our Lord, and this alone is sufficient, if well observed." St Paul declares the same when he says : " The whole law is comprised in this commandment— you should love your neighbour as yourself." (Gal. v. 14.) Accomplish this but perfectly well, and you have fulfilled all the rest. St. Austin, reflecting on this precept, says, that our Lord adds so great a weight unto it, that he sticks not to make it the distinctive mark of his disciples, when he says : " by this all will know you to be my disciples, if you love one another."

But the Son of God does not stop here ; and it is a remark of St. Chrysostom, that in the prayer he made to his eternal Father, after the last supper, he was not content that charity should be only the mark and badge of his disciples, but he would also that there should be such a union amongst them, that the world should be thereby convinced of the truth of his being sent. "I pray not only for them," says he, "but for those also that shall believe in me, by their help and ministry: and I beg of you that they become one ; and that as you, my Father, are in me, and as I am in you, so they may be also as one in us, that the world may believe that you have sent me." (John xvii. 20, 21.) Can any one extol the excellency of this fraternal union higher than to say, that it ought to be sufficient to convince the world of the coming of the Son of God, and oblige it to receive his doctrine?

The truth of this will be perfectly understood in what happened to St. Pacomius, when he was yet a pagan, and served in the army of Constantine the Great. He embarked with new levies, who were sent against Maxentius, and they arrived in very great distress, in a town where the inhabitants gave them all sorts of provisions with so much cheerfulness, that Pacomius, astonished at it, asked who those persons were, that had such a wonderful inclination to help and assist others. They answered him, they were Christians, whose institution was to help and succour all the world, as much as they were able. Upon this he found himself interiorly touched with so ardent a desire of embracing the profession of Christianity, that lifting up his hands to heaven, and calling God to witness, he embraced it forthwith. So that the example alone of the fervent charity of these Christians was a sufficient motive to convert him, and make him believe that their religion was excellent.

But there is still another thing, which ought to be a great comfort to us, in the prayer of the Son of God to his Father,

wherein he says : "And that the world may know that you have
sent me ; and that you have loved them, as you have loved me
myself." (John xvii. 23.)   One of the chief marks, to know
that God particularly loves any congregation, and cherishes it
with a love approaching to that he bears his Son, is when he
pours forth upon them the grace of fraternal union ; as he did
in the primitive Church, upon the Christians, that enjoyed the
first-fruits and first blessings of the Holy Ghost.   Wherefore,
" if we love one another, God will dwell in us, and will love us
with a perfect love." (1 John iv. 12.)   And seeing he has promised, " that where two or three are together in his name, he
will be in the midst of them." (Matt. xviii. 20.)   What effects
ought we not to hope for, from his divine presence, amongst so
many persons met together in his name, and for his love ?   That
we may therefore enjoy the great benefits he has promised, and
that we may have an assured pledge, and earnest, that he remains with us, and that he loves us with a special affection, let
us endeavour always to maintain ourselves in the spirit of
union and fraternal charity.

———o———

CHAPTER II.

*Of the Necessity of maintaining the Spirit of Union and Charity,
and of the Manner of doing so.*

ST. PAUL, writing to the Colossians, after having recommended
to them the practice of many virtues, says : " But above all
things, have charity one with another, which is the bond of
perfection." (Col. iii. 14.)   St. Peter also expresses the same in
his first canonical epistle.   After having therein touched on
some points, he says : " But before all things entertain a continual and mutual charity one with another."   (1 Peter iv. 8.)
Hence we may judge of how great importance it is, that we
should always exercise the spirit of charity and union, since
these great apostles, these two princes of the Church, recommend
it to us, "above and before all things ;" and would have us prefer it before all things else.   Herein we see in effect that nothing
is more generally necessary than this ; for what religious community or human society can ever be formed, or be able to subsist, without this union and charity ?   Take away this union or
bond from any assembly whatsoever, and it will presently be-

come a Babylon, and present nothing but discord and confusion. The common saying is, that "where there is a multitude of people, there is also confusion :" but this ought only to be understood of a multitude that is not well united; for that which is perfectly united is a heavenly hierarchy upon earth. Moreover, there is no society or commonwealth in the world, how barbarous soever it be, where there is not some kind of union ; whether they live under one head, or whether the government be composed of divers heads. We also see this verified amongst irrational creatures, and this not only amongst bees, to whom nature has given an admirable instinct of union and order ; but even amongst the most savage beasts, amongst wolves and lions ; in whom the same principle that prompts them to self-conservation moves them also to maintain a certain kind of union, by a sort of knowledge or instinct they have that division will cause their destruction. It is for the same reason that even the devils themselves, who are spirits of division, and the sowers of cockle and discord, keep a kind of union amongst themselves; "For if Satan be divided against himself, says Jesus Christ, "how will his kingdom be able to subsist ?" (Luke xi. 18.) And he afterwards confirms it by this maxim, which the example of all ages has ever held up as an infallible principle of policy, " That a king-dom divided against itself shall become desolate." (Luke xi. 17.) Hence Plato says, that there is nothing more pernicious to a commonwealth than discord and disunion, nor anything more useful or profitable than peace and a good understanding amongst the inhabitants.

St. Jerome still more forcibly says the same of a religious life. It is charity, says he, that makes religious, and assembles them under one and the same discipline and government : without this monasteries are a hell, and those that are in them devils ; but with this, monasteries become a paradise upon earth, and their inhabitants angels incarnate. Moreover, to speak the truth, what greater hell can we imagine, than to be continually to-gether, and always to have different wills, and judgments op-posite one to the other ? While, on the contrary, what is the living in union of wills, but to live the life of angels here below, and to begin to taste in this world the peace and tranquillity they enjoy in heaven ? This truth is confirmed by St. Basil, who, speaking of religious, says : " Those that live in the true spirit of a community, imitate, in a manner, the lives of angels, amongst whom there are no law-suits, no disputes, no quarrels.

And St. Laurence Justinian affirms, that nothing in this world represents so well that admirable assembly of the heavenly Jerusalem, as a society of religious, who are perfectly united together by charity. The life they lead is truly heavenly and angelical : " Our Lord is truly amongst them : the place they live in is no other than the house of God, and the gate of heaven." (Gen. xxviii. 17.)

But to treat this matter in less general terms, I will come to the particular necessity we ourselves have of living in this union and fraternal charity. It is for this reason that St. Ignatius, speaking of the means conducive to the good and spiritual advancement of the society, says that one of the chief things that can conduce or contribute to it is the spirit of union and charity. We have already touched on some general reasons, sufficient to show us how necessary it is in all religious communities; yet besides these, we have particular considerations, which render it far more necessary amongst us. The first is, that our society is like a battalion of soldiers, which God has sent as a reinforcement to his Church, to aid and assist it, to sustain the holy war it wages against the devil and the world, and to gain souls to heaven. It is this that the patent of our institute makes mention of ; it is this that the Church proclaims in its bull for the confirmation of our society : " Whosoever desires to fight under the standard of the cross, and enrol himself in the service of God alone, or in that of the Church his spouse, must abound in charity." (Bul. Julii. cxi. anno 1550.) And it is this which is given us to understand by the name of *Company* or *Society*, which we have taken. We are a company of soldiers; we beat our drums, we display our colours, we obtain recruits, and enlist new soldiers to fight against the enemies of the cross. If the battalion is well united, and if it marches in good order, it will surmount all obstacles and vanquish whatsoever opposes its power. And it is for this reason that the Holy Ghost, speaking of the Church, says, that it is " terrible as an army ranged in battle." (Cant. vi. 3.) It will not, therefore, be possible to break through this battalion, if it be always well united, if the soldiers observe exact discipline, and always firmly keep their ranks; because it is by this means, and after this manner, they defend one another. But if they are disunited it will be presently broken, and entirely defeated. David having obtained a signal victory over the Philistines, "The Lord," says he, " has divided my enemies before me, as waters are divided." (2 Kings v. 20.) And the field of battle was called *Baal-pharasim*, that is, *the*

Place of Division. This shews that to divide and to overcome is one and the self-same thing, and that the place of division is taken for the place of victory. In effect, those who have written on warlike affairs say, "that troops marching irregularly, go rather to the butchery, than to a battle;" and there is nothing more recommended in military discipline, than to keep the ranks well, and take care that the battalion be so united, that all the soldiers mutually succour one another, remaining always firm at their post. This alone makes it invincible, and this secures not only the general good of the whole corps, but the particular good of every soldier, whose success or misfortune is inseparably attached to the victory or defeat of the battalion. We may say the same of our society. If we preserve the spirit of union, if we assist one another, if we march well united, and set upon our enemies in good order ; we shall infallibly overcome, and be under no apprehension of defeat in any encounter. " The brother that is assisted by his brother, is a strong city" (Prov. xviii. 19), says the Wise Man ; and " it is hard to break a triple cord." (Eccles. iv. 12.) All the little threads, of which the string of a cross-bow is made, are very weak of themselves, if taken one by one ; yet when they are united and interlaced one with another, they are able to bend a bow of steel. Even so will religious be strong, when they are all united with one another by the bond of fraternal charity.

St. Basil, desirous to encourage us to this virtue, bids us consider what that union of the Machabees was, when they fought for the Lord. Consider, says he, what was that of the Israelites also, who having levied an army of more than three hundred thousand men, "marched," says the Scripture, "as if all of them had been but one man," (1 Kings xi. 7.) That is, they marched all with the same resolution and courage ; and hence it came to pass, that they struck fear into their enemies, and gained most signal victories over them. We ought to fight after the same manner, in the spiritual warfare we sustain for our Lord ; and by this means we shall advance in perfection, and fill our enemies with terror. The devil himself will tremble, and will not dare to attack us ; and as long as he sees so many persons united against him, he will lose courage, and despair of doing us any harm.

Our holy founder, speaking of the chief reason for which it is necessary we should live in perfect union, says in one place, we ought to take very great care to preserve a strict union amongst ourselves, without permitting it to be wounded or hurt in anything; that being thus united by the bond of fraternal charity, we may employ ourselves more efficaciously in the service of God, and of our neighbour. He says in another place, that without this union, the society cannot long subsist, nor attain the end for which it was instituted. And indeed it is evident, if there be any division, any caballing or dissensions amongst us, we shall be so far from attaining the end for which our society was instituted, which is to gain souls to God, that we shall not be even able to maintain or preserve ourselves. If the soldiers destined to fight the enemy, turn their arms one against another, it is not to be doubted but that, instead of overcoming them, they will infallibly destroy themselves. " Their hearts are divided," says Osee, "and they will presently perish." (Osee x. 2.) And the apostle, writing to the Galatians, says, " If you bite or devour one another, take care that you come not to be destroyed amongst yourselves." (Gal. v. 15.) Behold what is to be feared in religion. For as to other things we have nothing to fear from without; and all the persecution and tempests which the world can excite will never be able to hurt us, so long as charity and peace shall be established amongst us.

It is this which St. Bernard says, when speaking to his religious upon this subject, " What can there be from without," says he, " that can contristate or trouble you, if you be in a good state within, and if you enjoy fraternal peace ?" And " who can do you any harm, if you are animated with a true zeal, and a holy emulation ?" As long as we are what we ought to be, and live in a perfect union one with another, all contradictions from without are so far from doing us any hurt, that, on the contrary, they will contribute to our good and advancement. Thus when the Church was persecuted in the first ages, it received no more damage than the vine does when it is pruned ; because for one branch which was cut off, there sprouted out many ; and as a holy martyr said heretofore very well to the tyrant, whilst he caused him to be torn to pieces by the executioners, that in shedding the blood of Christians, he only watered the earth, to make it produce greater abundance of fruit.

In the first book of the Machabees, the Holy Scripture praises the Romans very much, for living in great union amongst themselves. " They commit," says the Scripture, "every year the supreme authority to one man, whom all obey ; and there is no envy nor jealousy amongst them." (1 Mac. viii. 16.) So that being united after this manner, they overcame all their enemies, and became masters of the world : but when they began to be embroiled in civil wars, they destroyed themselves ; which gave rise to that saying, "That little things are augmented by concord, and the greatest ruined and destroyed by discord."

But besides what we have already said, there is still another particular reason, for which our society has greater cause than all other orders to live in closest union. And it is what St. Ignatius alleges in his Constitutions ; because we in particular meet with many difficulties and obstacles, which hinder our living in union ; and consequently we ought to take more care to establish it amongst us, and to seek proper remedies against whatsoever may prejudice it. The difficulties we meet with are reduced to three :—The first, says he, is, that our society being spread over the whole world, as well amongst the faithful as infidels, and all its subjects being thus separated one from another, it is very hard to know one another, or have any communication, whereby to maintain or exercise ourselves in this union. Moreover, that as it embraces so many different nations, amongst which there seem to be such natural oppositions and antipathies, it is very hard so to overcome this aversion, with which we were born, and in which we were a long time brought up, as that we should bring ourselves to look upon a stranger not as a stranger, but as our brother in Jesus Christ, and a child of our holy mother the society. The second obstacle is, that the greatest part of our society ought to be persons of learning. And we know that knowledge ordinarily puffs up the mind of man, and fills him with an esteem of himself, and contempt of others, and attaches him very much to his own opinion : and it often happens, that "the learned," as St. Thomas says, "are less devoted to piety, than the simple and illiterate ;"—so that there is great reason to fear lest all this should impede union and fraternal charity ; and that every one desirous to follow his own opinion should go a particular way, and have in view only his own interest and reputation ; and thus division would begin to introduce itself into the society. The third difficulty, which is not at all less than those already mentioned, is, that the very persons of whom we have spoken, looking upon themselves as persons of merit, and endowed with such peculiar talents as are requisite for the world, avail themselves of all this to enter into familiarity with princes and great men, and to form particular connexions and friendships with magistrates and persons in authority. Hence arise particularities, claims to exemptions

and privileges, and a desire that distinction should be made between them and others ; all which cannot but exceedingly prejudice union and fraternal charity.   But as great precautions
ought to be taken in order to prevent great inconveniences, so
St. Ignatius carefully marks in the same place those remedies we
ought to make use of in order to surmount these difficulties.
The first of all, and that which should be the foundation of the
rest, is, not to receive, nor retain in the society, any one who has
not a firm resolution to govern and overcome his passions, and
who does not effectually apply himself to it.   For if we have
not the spirit of mortification, we are incapable of the spirit of
discipline, union, or regularity ; without this spirit, if we acquire
learning, or any other superior advantage, we shall be carried
away with vainglory, contempt of our neighbour, a desire to be
preferred before him, and a presumptuous belief that we have
right to dispensations and privileges.   Without this spirit we
shall always court the favour of princes, endeavour to be intimate
with persons of distinction, and we shall wish to have amongst
them some particular patron to shew us kindness.   Now these
singularities and distinctions will produce nothing else in the
end but the bad fruits of jealousy and division.   The more
learning, merit, or distinguished qualifications a man has, if he
has not also the true sentiments of virtue and mortification, he
will have just reason to fear that these endowments will be an
occasion of division and scandal ; and that, at some time or other,
he will excite great disturbance in religion.   Knowledge and great
talents in a man that wants the spirit of mortification and
humility, are like a sword in a madman's hand, who turns it
against himself as well as against others.   But if knowledge be
accompanied with humility, if the learned, instead of seeking
themselves, " seek none but Jesus Christ" (Phil. ii. 21); then
all things will go well ; and their example being of great power,
will attract others to follow it, and we shall see peace and union
flourish abundantly.   See here the first and chief remedy ; and
if we apply this well, it will not be necessary to recur to any of
the rest.

Nevertheless, St. Ignatius proposes to us other means of ob-
viating the inconvenience we have touched on.   As for example,
to take care that distance of place hinder us not from having a
knowledge of and holding communication with each other, he
ordains that we entertain ourselves reciprocally with pious letters, and these full of edification, whereby, one understanding

what the other does, we may animate each other to similarity of conduct, as far as diversity of nations will permit. And this, without doubt, is a very proper means to conciliate and cement together that union which is necessary for us.

But one of the most important means to keep ourselves in union is, that which the same saint farther prescribes, and which consists in an exact observance of all that obedience shall enjoin. For it is obedience that assembles, and binds religious together, and is the cause that divers wills and different judgments make but one will and one judgment; insomuch, that particular persons being deprived of their own wills by obedience, there remains nothing but the will of the superior, to which all others accede and conform themselves. Moreover, the subjects being conformed and united to their superior, they are also in like manner conformed and united one to another, according to the infallible rule, " that things which are equal to a third are also equal amongst themselves;" and the greater conformity they have with their superior, the more perfect also that will be which they have amongst themselves. Obedience, religious discipline, and observance of rules make all alike, and thereby establish a great order and admirable union. Amongst the ancient Egyptians, the hieroglyphic of union was a *lyre;* for as this sort of instrument produces a wonderful harmony, when all the rest of the strings accord well with the first; and, on the contrary, if any of these strings happen to break, or loosen, there is no longer harmony but discord; even so in a community, when subjects agree well with their superior, this good understanding produces a perfect harmony. But one who agrees not well with his superior, is sufficient to disturb all the harmony of this delightful union. This, perhaps, is what induced some to say, the word *concord* is derived from *cord,* or string, but those who take its etymology from the word *cor,* or heart, shew more discernment; because, in effect, by concord nothing else is understood than union and conformity of hearts, according to those words in the Acts of the Apostles, " the multitude of believers had but one heart and one soul."

St. Bernard says, that if a vessel springs a leak, it is, ordinarily speaking, because the planks are not firmly joined; in like manner, a community will destroy and ruin itself unless the members be well united together by the bond of charity. Father Aquaviva, also our general, in a letter he wrote on union and fraternal charity, says, that we ought most studiously promote this charity and union amongst ourselves, and believe that upon this all the good and advantage of the society depend. It was this spirit of union and concord which Jesus Christ, the night before his passion, begged of his Eternal Father for the elect, as a thing absolutely necessary for their salvation, when he said:—" Holy Father, preserve in your name those that you have given me, that they may be one as we ourselves are." (John xvii. 11.) The comparison which he makes in these words, *as we*, merits, no doubt, particular attention. He desires that as the Father and Son are but one by nature, so we should also be but one by love. It is this will preserve us for ever.

—— o ——

CHAPTER III.

Certain Reasons taken from Holy Scripture, which evince the obligation we are under of living in the Spirit of Union, &c.

SAINT JOHN having spoken of the exceedingly great love God testified to us, by giving his only Son, concludes thus : " But if God has thus loved us, we ought also to love one another." (John xvii. 11.) We may with reason here object and ask, why the conclusion he draws from the love that God has for us is, that we ought to love our neighbour ; since it would seem a more just and natural one to infer, that we are obliged to love God, because he has in so extraordinary a manner loved us ? To this objection many answers may be given. The first is, that the apostle speaks in this manner to let us see the excellency of the love of our neighbour, and what a great value God sets on it. It is for this reason that, as St. Matthew relates, a doctor of the law asking our Saviour Jesus Christ, " What was the greatest commandment in the law ?" our Saviour answered, " You shall love the Lord your God with all your heart, with all your soul, and with all your mind ; behold here the first and greatest of all the commandments : as to the second, it is like the first, you shall love your neighbour as yourself." (Matt. xxii. 36.) They asked him only about the first commandment ; why therefore does he speak of the second ? It is to show the excellency of the love of our neighbour, and in what esteem God holds it.

The second answer that may be given is, that the love of God and the love of our neghbour are like two rings joined together, and put upon a finger, one of which rings cannot be taken off without the other ; but both must be pulled off together. The love of God and the love of our neighbour are, in like manner, inseparable. The one can never subsist without the other : so that it is but one love of pure charity which makes us love God, and our neighbour for God. We can therefore neither love God without loving our neighbour, nor love our neighbour with the love of pure charity, without loving God himself ; because the motive we have to love our neighbour is God. Wherefore the same apostle, wishing to show us that we cannot love God without loving our neighbour, presently adds: " If we mutually love each other, God remains with us, and his charity is perfect within us." (1 John iv. 12.) And afterwards, to show us also that the love of our neighbour is included in the love of God : " It is a commandment," says he, "which we have received from God, that he who loves God must also love his brother." (1 John iv. 21.)

One evident proof, that God loves man exceedingly, and that he desires we should in like manner love one another, is, that we cannot love God without loving our neighbour, nor offend our neighbour without offending God. If a king loved one of his subjects so well, as to interpose himself between all the blows that should be aimed at him, so that they could never hurt his subject without first hurting himself, would not this be a very great love ? This is what God does to man ; he always so interposes himself, that you cannot offend your neighbour without offending God : and he does this to hinder you from offending your brother, through fear of offending him. " Whosoever shall touch you," says our Lord, " touches me in the very apple of my eye." (Zach. ii. 8.) So that by offending our neighbour we offend God ; and by loving our neighbour we love God, and by loving God we love also our neighbour. But because the love of God and the love of our neighbour go always together, and are included one in the other, and can never be divided, St. John might as well have concluded in behalf of the one as of the other love ; because the obligation we have to love the one, necessarily implies our obligation to love the other. But he would rather conclude in the behalf of the love of our neighbour, than in behalf of the love of God ; because the love of God is a truth and principle known of itself, and principles are not proved, but admitted. Wherefore he passes to this conclusion, that we ought to love our neighbour ; and expressly does so; because perhaps another would not have drawn this consequence from the proposition he had advanced.

The third answer is, that St. John speaks in this epistle, not of a dry and sterile, but of a fruitful and profitable love—of a love that is accompanied with benefits and good works. " Dear children," says he, " let us not love in words, and in our tongue, only ; but let us love in effect and in truth." (1 John iii. 18.) And in order to inform us that it is for the good of our neighbours and brethren that God desires we should perform these works, according to the passage repeated in the gospel, out of Osee, "I desire mercy and not sacrifice" (Matt. xii. 7) ; he draws no other conclusion from his proposition than the love of our neighbour. It happens very often that a creditor, who is absent, writes thus to his debtor :—You will do me a favour by paying to such a one what you owe me ; and what you shall give him I shall consider as received by myself. It is after this manner that St. John, speaking in God's behalf, to whom we owe so much for the many obligations and benefits received, says to us : " If God has loved us in so extraordinary a manner, we ought also to love one another." The love which each of us owe him is a debt he has transferred to our neighbour ; and the charity you exercise towards your brother, you exercise towards God, who receives it as if it were done to himself. It is this which Jesus Christ declares in these words : " Verily, I say unto you, that whatsoever you do to the least of my brethren, you have done it unto myself." (Ibid. xxv. 40.) And without doubt this ought to be a powerful motive to excite us to love our brethren, and to do them all the good we can ; because though it seems to us that we do it to those to whom we owe nothing, yet if we look upon God, and reflect upon the infinite obligations we have to him, and consider that he has transferred all his right to them, we shall find that we are indebted to them for all we have. Father Avila, therefore, speaking on this subject, says, when the carnal man that is within you shall represent to you, what great obligations have I to such a one, to move me so far as to do him any favour ? And how can I be able to love him, since he has so much injured me ? Answer him, that perhaps you should give ear to what he says against your neighbour, if your neighbour were the only motive, object, or cause of this your love ; but that Jesus Christ himself is the cause and object thereof, and it is he himself who receives the good you do to your neighbour, and who looks upon the pardon you bestow upon your neighbour as if it were a favour and a pardon you bestowed upon himself ; and thus, whosoever your neighbour is, and whatsoever injury he can have done you, yet there is nothing that ought to cool your charity towards him or hinder its effects, since it is not him, but Jesus Christ, you ought to consider in all your thoughts and actions. Wherefore, it is a most just consequence that St. John draws, who, after he had proved the great love that God has for us, infers the obligation we therefore have to love our neighbour. We ought to observe farther, that to move us the more, he takes notice of the mystery of the incarnation of the Son of God, in the same proposition from which he draws this conclusion. For, setting before our eyes, "That God hath sent his only Son into the world" (1 John iv. 9), he gives us occasion to consider, that God has allied himself to men, and consequently would have us think that since they are allied to God, and brothers of Jesus Christ, we ought to love them as such.

———o———

CHAPTER IV.

What this Union is, which we ought to have with our Brethren.

St. Basil and St. Austin in order to explain what that union is which ought to be amongst religious, makes use of what St. Paul says, on the union and correspondence there is between the members of a man's body. Behold, say they, how they serve and help one another. The eyes direct the feet, the hands defend the head, and all jointly endeavour to succour and help the weakest part, as experience sufficiently teaches us, when we have received a wound or any other hurt. In the distribution that is made of nourishment, each member receives so much as is necessary for it, and leaves the remainder for the other members. Besides, there is such a sympathy between them, that the stomach, for example, cannot be out of order, but also the head suffers and feels for it. " All the members interest themselves one for another. The pain of one communicates itself to all the rest, and is no sooner cured but all the others are eased and comforted." (1 Cor. xii. 25, 26.) St. Austin explains this admirably well. It happens, says he, that the foot treads upon a thorn : what is more remote from the eyes than the feet? It is indeed, by situation, very far off, but it is very near by the mutual and charitable correspondence with all the rest of the members. Wherefore, as soon then as the foot is pricked with the thorn, the eyes presently go to find it out, the body stoops to facilitate their approach, the tongue asks where it is, and the hands endeavour to pull it out. Yet the eyes, the hand, the body, the head, and the tongue are all well, nothing ails them, and the foot itself is hurt only in one place. It is therefore because all the members are in pain one for another, and feel the pain the others suffer. See how we ought to conduct ourselves towards our brethren; we ought to have as great a care of them as we have of ourselves : that is, we must rejoice as much at their good fortune as at our own, and we must feel as much for their misfortunes and sufferings, as we do for our own.

St. Basil says that the two chief marks of the love of charity are, to be sorry, as well for the spiritual, as for the corporal sufferings of our neighbour ; and to feel joy when anything fortunate happens to him, according to the words of the apostle : " Rejoice with those that rejoice, and weep with those that weep." (Rom. xii. 15.) In like manner, St. John Climacus says, that in order to try whether we truly love our neighbour, we must see whether or not we deplore the faults he commits, and rejoice at the grace and favours he receives from God, and at the progress we perceive he makes by corresponding with them. St. Angela was wont to say, that God had rewarded her with more and greater favours, after she had lamented the sins of her neighbour, than after she had deplored her own. But we are not hence to understand, that we ought in reality be touched with more sorrow for the sins of our neighbour, than for our own ; but this exaggeration should convince us that charity towards the neighbour is most agreeable to Almighty God. The two effects it produces are, in St. Bernard's opinion, the two breasts of the spouse, between which her beloved reposed : " And the one and the other," says he, " have a proper and particular milk ; the one of joy and congratulation, the other of sweetness and consolation." (Ser. x. sup. Cant. i. 12.)

But what is still to be considered in St. Paul's comparison is, on the one hand, the diversity of members, their congruities, qualities, and different functions ; and, on the other, their strict union, mutual correspondence, and the satisfaction which each one takes in its distinct use and employment, not at all envying the higher employments the other has. Thus we ought to do— each of us ought to be content with the charge and employment we are in, without envying those that are in greater and more honourable offices. Moreover, as in the body, a superior or more noble member despises not the inferior, but, on the contrary, esteems, conserves, and helps it as much as it can, so those that are established in the chief employments of religion ought not to contemn, or to have a meaner opinion of those in inferior offices; but, on the contrary, they ought to esteem, and carefully assist them in their necessities, and consider them as members absolutely necessary. For "the eye cannot say to the hand, I want not your help; nor the head, in like manner, say to the feet, I have no need of you; but those members that to us seem the most contemptible and the weakest, are in effect those that we stand most in need of." Take notice, for example, how necessary our feet are, and to what distress we should be reduced, should we want them! And God, in his infinite wisdom, has disposed things in this manner, "to the end," says St. Paul, "that there be no division nor disunion in the body." (1 Cor. xii. 25.) It is the same in a religious body or community; one is the head, another the eyes, and the head cannot say that it stands not in need of the hands, nor the eyes that they stand not in need of the feet. But it appears, on the contrary, that each one properly seems to be that we stand most in need of in religion; and without doubt the providence of God would have things disposed and ordered in this manner, that there might be no schism or division amongst us, and that we might always live in a strict union of minds, and in a perfect charity of hearts.

Behold here the model of a holy union and true fraternal charity; and hence we ought to learn to assist and serve one another, because there is no means more proper than this to conserve and augment this union; it being what the apostle St. Paul so earnestly recommends to us, when he says : "By charity of spirit serve one another." (Gal. v. 13.) Moreover, it is a most commendable thing in religious to be condescending, kind, and always ready to oblige every one, because by this we show that we have the spirit of charity, humility, and mortification. But we show quite the contrary when, through an unwillingness to mortify ourselves, or to suffer the least pain, or to lose a single moment of our pleasure, we cannot find in our heart to please our brethren, or accommodate ourselves to them. It is most certain, that in the action our Saviour did in washing his disciples' feet, he would give us an example of humility; nay, even of such an active humility as applies itself to the exercise of charity towards our neighbour : "If then I have washed your feet," says he, "I, who am your Lord and Master, you ought also to wash the feet of one another; for I have given you this example, that you do to one another as I have done unto you." (John xiii. 14).

CHAPTER V.

*What Fraternal Charity particularly requires of us, and the most
proper Means of preserving it.*

" CHARITY is patient," says the apostle St. Paul, " it is benign, it
envies not, it deals not perversely, it is not puffed up with pride,
it is not ambitious, nor seeks its own particular profit." (1 Cor.
xiii. 4.) As it is certain that all vices are an obstacle to fraternal
charity, and that pride, envy, ambition, impatience, self-love,
stubbornness, and the like, are so many enemies which continually
fight against it, so it is very true that the practice of all the virtues
is necessary for its preservation. And this is what St. Paul
teaches us in those words I just now cited ; " Charity is patient,
charity is benign." Behold two things very essential ; and in
effect nothing can be of greater importance, and more necessary
to preserve this union with one another, than to suffer patiently
from every one, and to do good to all the world. We are all of
us men, and consequently full of faults and imperfections, so that
we all afford our neighbour sufficient matter of patience. But
as we are in like manner very weak and infirm, we have also need
of their assistance to do us good, according to St. Paul's precept :
" Carry one another's burdens, and by this means you will fulfil
the law of Jesus Christ." (Gal. vi. 2.) St. Austin, explaining
these words, adduces an excellent comparison on this subject : he
says, naturalists report that when stags would pass over an arm of
the sea to seek fresh pastures in any island, they observe this
order. Their horns being very heavy, with which their heads
are charged, they put themselves all in a line one after another,
and each one, to help the other, rests his head upon that which
goes before him, and so they all swim after this manner without
any fatigue at all, except the first, which carries its head in the
air, and willingly bears the burden for the ease of its companions.
But that this one alone may not feel all the difficulty, as soon as
it begins to be weary, it passes from being the first and becomes
the last of all, and then that which followed it conducts all the
rest ; and thus they change place by turns, till they get to the
other side. We ought, in like manner, reciprocally assist and
solace each other ; and as charity requires this of each of us, so
it is deeply wounded when we avoid labour, and suffer the whole
burden to lie heavy upon our neighbour. Let us consider that
the more pains we take the greater will be our merit, and con-

sequently that we labour for ourselves no less than for our neighbour.

St. Austin says also in the same place, that one of the things which imparts the greatest beauty and splendour to charity is to know how to support the ill-humour and imperfections of our neighbour :—" Bear with one another," says St. Paul to the Ephesians, " and be careful to conserve a perfect union of spirit in the bond of peace." (Eph. iv. 2.)   Because " charity," says he in another place, suffers all, charity bears all." (1 Cor. xiii. 7.) But if you are able to suffer nothing from your brethren, and have not sufficient sweetness of disposition to support patiently their defects, be assured that what reflection soever you may make, what means soever that you may use, and what remedies soever you may apply, you can never be able to preserve charity.   If a love that has no other source than flesh and blood is able to accommodate itself without any pain, to whatsoever it suffers in assisting a sick person, as we daily learn from what mothers continually undergo in bringing up their children, or in assisting a sick husband ; without doubt spiritual love, which has its origin in God himself, should prompt us to undergo the infirmities and weaknesses of our brethren, with all patience and sweetness possible.   But you say it is a very difficult task so to accommodate ourselves, as continually to support their defects ; but remember, says St. Austin, that it is an employment that cannot last always, and that we shall have nothing to suffer in the other life.   Wherefore, let us suffer at present in this, to be happy in the other life ; let us not lose the good opportunity offered us ; the pain we undergo will not be long, and the recompense we merit will never have an end.   It is of so great importance, says the same saint, to bear with our neighbour, and to assist him as far as we are able, that the whole of a Christian life is contained in these two points.   And he advances this proposition not without great reason; because a Christian life being founded upon charity, and the perfection of charity being the fulfilling of the law, by consequence the consummation or perfection of charity is the consummation or perfection of a Christian life.

" Charity," says the apostle, " is not puffed up with pride ;" and St. Ambrose says, " that friendship knows not what pride is."   (B. iii. c. 16.)   And it is for this reason that the Wise Man tells us, " We ought not to be ashamed to salute a friend." (Ecclus. xxii. 31.)   For amongst friends there is no standing upon ceremony ; and without studying who should be first to

salute, each should endeavour to anticipate the other. Friendship is a stranger to these sorts of ceremonies—it has more
frankness, simplicity, and equality, in its manner ; and it is for
this reason that Aristotle will have "friendship to be amongst
equals ;" and a Latin poet says that "love and majesty agree
not well together, nor live under the same roof." The elevation
of a throne does not very easily stoop or accommodate itself to
friendship ; and whoever wishes to maintain true friendship
must stoop and put himself on an equality with his friend—he
must make him *another self.* It is after this manner that the
love which God has borne to men wrought so much upon him,
that it made him debase himself so far, as to render himself like
them, "he became in some manner inferior to the angels."
(Ps. viii. 6), and made himself man like unto us. For which
reason he says, "He calls us not servants, but friends" (John,
xv. 15) ; to signify, as it were, an equality between himself and
us, in which we cannot too much admire the great excess of
his love.

For in fine, let a subject be ever so high in favour with his
prince, let his rank be ever so elevated, yet they never say of
him, that he is the prince's friend—No ! they call him nothing
more than *favourite;* because the word *friend* imports an equality.
Notwithstanding, God, whose majesty is infinite, renders himself
so familiar with us, and loves us with so great a tenderness, that
instead of treating us as his servants, he openly gives us the
title of his friends. It is therefore necessary, in imitation of his,
that our charity in religion should be so remote from any sort
of pride, that in all things it should introduce an extreme
equality ; and this same equality, being an effect of charity and
love, will contribute very much to augment charity and union ;
for the one ordinarily maintains itself by the other. Hence it is,
that when the spirit of humility and equality reigns in any
place, it is a sign that the spirit of union and fraternal charity
reigns there also. Wherefore as we see that, by the mercy of
God, charity shines forth in a particular manner in our society ;
so we perceive also that the spirit of equality and simplicity is
carefully preserved in it ; each one following what is prescribed
in our rule. "In preferring others before himself, and esteeming
them as if they were his superior." (Reg. xxix. Sum. Con.)
He, who was a man of rank and consequence in the world, says
St. Austin, glories more in the alliance with his brethren in
religion, though poor, than he does in being born of rich parents ;

for, persuaded that in religion no account ought to be made of anything but virtue, he easily contemns all things else. But the better to confirm what I have said, and to show more clearly how conducive equality is to the preservation of charity, we shall conclude by repeating the words of St. Ambrose :—" We never," says he, " strengthen charity more, than when, in obedience to the doctrine of the apostle, we yield one to the other—when every man esteems his neighbour better than himself—when inferiors feel pleasure in serving, and superiors abstain from domineering—when the poor are not angry that the rich be preferred to them, and the rich are content that the poor be made equal to them—when nobility renders not the higher orders proud, and equality renders not the lower orders vain. In fine, when we attach not more consideration to riches than to morals ; and set not greater value on the power and pomp of the wicked, than on the equity and simplicity of the virtuous." (Ep. lxxxiv. ad Demet.)

———o———

CHAPTER VI.

Of two other Things that Charity still requires of us.

" CHARITY is not envious," says the apostle ; but on the contrary, he who truly loves another wishes him as much good as himself, and rejoices as much at the good fortune and preferment of his friend as at his own. St. Austin confirms this by the example of Jonathas, who loved David, in such a manner, as the Scripture says, " That his soul seemed to be glued to the soul of David, and that Jonathas loved him as his own soul." (1 Kings xviii. 1.) Whence also it happened that though he was the son of Saul, yet he rather desired to see the crown upon David's head than upon his own. " You shall reign," says he to David, " and I will be first after you in the kingdom." (Ibid. xxiii. 17.)

This effect of charity is still more particularly explained by the example of the blessed, proposed to us by many holy men. In heaven, say they, those who enjoy a less degree of beatitude envy not the happiness of the others : but on the contrary, each one of them desires to see, if it were possible, the felicity of the others increased, and would even give them part of their own ; and this in such a manner, that they desire that the least of all were in as great, if not more elevated glory than they themselves.

So that every blessed soul feels as great joy at another's glory as at its own. And this is not hard to comprehend; for if love in this miserable world makes us as much interested in the good of our children as in our own, ought we not, with greater reason, suppose similar feelings to exist in the blessed, whose love is incomparably more perfect and more purified than that of nature? Charity, says St. Austin, ought to work the same effect in us : and to encourage us to practise it he says, it is peculiar to charity, that without robbing another of what belongs to him, and by rejoicing only in the good the neighbour does, she makes all his merits, and all the good actions he performs, her own. Nor is there anything in this to be wondered at; for if it be true that we become guilty of the sin of another when we rejoice at it, it is not strange that the joy we take at the good of our neighbour should make us participate in his merit; and this chiefly because God is more disposed to reward than to punish. Let us then consider, on the one hand, how excellent charity is, and what advantage we may derive from it; since by its means and by the joy alone we shall take in the good actions of our brethren, we may appropriate all of them to ourselves; with so much the greater certainty, by how much more we are freed from all occasions of vainglory, which here can have no place. And on the other hand, let us take notice, how detestable and pernicious envy is; since it makes the prosperity of another our own punishment. Influenced, then, by these different motives, let us be as careful in flying the one, as we are zealous in embracing the other.

From what we have said, it necessarily follows, as the apostle adds, that " charity is not ambitious, and seeks not its own advantage " (1 Cor. xiii. 5); so that though it makes the advantage of another its own, it is yet far from entertaining any thought of self-interest or ambition. Nothing is more contrary to charity and union than self-love, and that attachment we naturally have to ourselves, and to our ease. Wherefore St. Ignatius calls self-love the mortal enemy of all kind of order and union; and the learned Humbertus calls it the plague of a religious life, and the bane of all communities. It also infects and ruins all things—and though it is true that it is the common enemy of all virtues in general, yet it is also very often the particular enemy of charity. The very name of self-love gives us to understand this; because the word *self* imports a formal exclusion of all kind of communication, and consequently renders self-love entirely opposite to charity ; which seeks nothing more than to communicate itself. Self-love wraps itself up totally within itself, and introduces division everywhere else ; it thinks of nothing but itself, and endeavours always to turn all things to its own particular interest—all which is directly contrary to charity and union.

The holy Scripture relates, that Abraham and Lot had such numerous flocks of sheep, that the land in which they were not being able to furnish sufficient pasture for them, and their shepherds daily quarrelling on this head, it was necessary at last, for the preservation of peace, that they should separate one from the other. The reason of this, says St. Chrysostom, is, that wheresoever we make the distinction of *mine* and *thine,* there also arises a continual source of quarrels, and a perpetual occasion of disputes. But where all is in common, there reigns a constant peace, and an inviolable concord. (Hom. xxxiii. sup. Gen.) Thus, in the primitive Church, there was so great an union amongst them, that they had but *one heart and one soul*: and this happened, adds the saint, " because no one of them possessed anything to himself ; but all things were in common amongst them." (Acts iv. 32.) All religious societies likewise, instituted and inspired by God, and founded upon the holy Scripture, have laid poverty for their foundation ; and it is of this we make our first vow, that as we have nothing amongst us, which any particular person can say is his own, self-love will find nothing to unite itself unto, and we shall all of us have but one heart and one soul.

There is no doubt but, for the conservation of charity and union amongst us, it is a very great point entirely to divest ourselves of all property in temporal things. But it is not sufficient that we have no property in these alone ; we must with respect to everything else do the same, without which it will be impossible that union and charity should flourish amongst us. For if you desire to attract esteem to yourself, if you desire to be honoured, if you aspire to great employments, if you seek your own ease and convenience, you will thereby detach yourself from your brethren. It is this, which ordinarily annoys charity ; it is from this springs that sort of envy we feel, because another displays the talents he has received, and because he is esteemed and praised for them. For we would rather attract and appropriate this esteem and praise to ourselves, and look upon that which another receives as a theft. It is from this proceeds that malignant and base joy, or at least that secret satisfaction we feel in our souls, on another's not succeeding in his affair. For then we imagine that this will humble him, and his humiliation will add to our reputation. In fine, it is on account of this that we sometimes endeavour to lower our brother's character, by striving either to confound him in some argument, or to mortify him by some expression which our heart, full of envy, prompts us to utter unawares. Now all this is the irregularity of self-love, which ambition, pride, and envy make use of to destroy utterly union and charity. Because " charity," says the apostle, "rejoices not at evil, but is overjoyed at good" (1 Cor. xiii. 6); it rejoices not at the humiliation of our neighbour, but on the contrary, wishes his prosperity ; and the greater this is, the greater also is its joy. " You are our brother, prosper therefore, and let your increase amount unto millions" (Gen. xxiv. 60); increase in virtue, in reputation, and in honour—your increase and your success are so much mine, that it is impossible I should not always feel a most sensible pleasure in them. When a man enters into partnership with others, their talents for business and their profits, so far from being a cause of sorrow, are a cause of joy to him ; becauseall goes to the common stock, on which he draws for his own part. It is in this manner we ought to act, and rejoice as much at the virtues, good qualities, and advancement of our brethren; because all turns to the advantage of that society whereof we are members, and in whose prosperity we individually participate.

———o———

CHAPTER VII.

That we ought to feel and testify a great Esteem of our Brethren; and always speak well of them.

But the charity we entertain one for another ought to be not only interior, but must also appear exteriorly in our actions, according to the words of St. John : "Whosoever shall see his brother in any necessity, and shall shut his bowels of mercy against him, how does the charity of God remain in him ?" (1 John iii. 17.) When we shall be in heaven, and stand in need of nothing, then our actions, says St. Austin, shall be no longer necessary to conserve charity. Fire, when it is in its sphere, has no need of fuel to conserve itself, but here below it is extinguished as soon as it wants a supply ; so also in this world charity soon grows cold, if not cherished by action. St. Basil alleges to this purpose, what St. John says in his first epistle, "In this we have known the charity of God, because he has given his life for us ; and we, according to his example, ought also to give our life for our brethren." (1 John iii. 16.) Hence he very justly infers, that if the love which Jesus Christ would have us bear towards our brethren, ought to be so great as to give our lives for them, it ought therefore, with far greater reason, to extend itself to innumerable other things which daily present themselves, and which are far easier to be performed.

One of the chief things which charity requires of us, and which will serve very much to preserve and increase it, is to have an esteem for our neighbour; and it is upon this foundation that the magnificent building of charity is raised. For charity is not a blind passion, nor a love, nor the effect of a mere tenderness of heart ; but it is a love of reason, a love of the superior part of our souls, of which all the motions are spiritual and heavenly. It is called the love of esteem, which springs from that we have for God ; and which prompts us, esteeming God above all things, to esteem our neighbour as one belonging to him. The esteem we conceive for our brethren moves us to love, honour, and respect them, and to perform towards them all the duties which charity requires of us ; and as this esteem increases in us, even so charity, and all those other sentiments which it inspires, will increase. The apostle also, writing to the Philippians, exhorts them to live "in humility, alway esteeming their neighbour above themselves" (Phil. ii. 3); and in like manner recommends to the Romans, " To prevent one another with testimonies of civility and respect." (Rom. xii. 10.) Whereupon St. Chrysostom takes notice, that St. Paul would not have them barely honour one another, but even obliges them reciprocally to prevent each other with testimonies of kindness. We ought not to wait till another begins, and first expresses his civility in advancing towards us, but we must endeavour to advance before him; we ought to show him the way, " and be glad," as St. Ignatius says, " to prevent one another on all occasions." (Reg. xxix. sum.)

But to give more particular instructions upon this matter, one of the things wherein we ought most of all to testify the esteem we have for our brethren, is always to speak of them in such manner, as to make known to others the esteem we ourselves have for them. We read in the Life of St. Ignatius, that he always spoke so well of all persons whomsoever, that every one immediately conceived himself to be a particular favourite of his ; and upon this account, he was in like manner beloved and respected by all.   There is nothing so much inflames our charity towards our brother, or better conserves it, than to know he loves us, has a good opinion of us, and speaks to our advantage on all occasions.   Let every one reflect and think on the satisfaction he himself feels, when one tells him that such a one has a kindness for him, or has done him any good office or favour ; let him call to mind, how he instantly resolves on making a return, and on saying all the good he can of his friend.   We cannot sufficiently extol the great and good effects this produces ; and Seneca knew very well the nature of love when he said, " If you will be loved, love ;" because in effect there cannot be a better means than this, as love can never be better recompensed than by love itself.

It is this which St. Chrysostom very justly infers from these words of our Saviour, " Whatsoever you would that others should do for you, do that also for them." (Mat. vii. 12.) Do you desire, says the saint, that others should do good to you ? Do so to them.   Do you wish to be sympathized with ?   If so, sympathize with others.   Would you be praised ? Praise others. Would you be loved ?   Love.   Do you desire the first place ? Be you the first to yield it.   But what ought to prompt us to speak well of our brethren is, that by thus evincing great union amongst ourselves, we will exceedingly edify our neighbour. Whereas, on the contrary, the least word which directly or indirectly seems to censure any of our brethren ; the least sign we show of not esteeming them ; the least thing in this way which is observable, will be an occasion of scandal.   It will be inferred that there is envy and jealousy amongst us ; and therefore we ought diligently to avoid anything that could in this way give the least ground of suspicion.   Though your brother has his defects, it is hard also if he should not have something commendable in him. Imitate the bee who lights upon flowers only, not minding the thorns that surround them ; and follow not the example of the beetle, which lights upon nothing else but ordure.

————o————

CHAPTER VIII.

That we ought to abstain from relating anything that may anger the Person to whom we relate it.

MY intention is not to speak at present of detraction, because I shall treat of it elsewhere ; but I shall mention here one thing of very great importance, and very apposite to our present subject, and which St. Bonaventure also takes particular notice of. As we ought abstain most scrupulously from speaking ill of another, so when we hear anything said of him which may excite his displeasure or resentment, we ought to take care not to say to him :—" Such a one has spoken thus and thus of you." For this tending only to exasperate their minds, and sow discord amongst brethren, there is nothing so pernicious to the good of religion, nor which God has a greater horror of. " There are six things," says the Wise Man, " that our Lord hates, but his soul has a perfect detestation of the seventh, the sower of discords amongst brethren." (Prov. vi. 16.) When we would express the horror we have of anything, we say we detest such a thing from our hearts, and the Scripture in this accommodates itself to our manner of speaking, that we may the better understand how disagreeable those who cause or foment divisions are in the sight of God. But if they are detested by God, they are detested by man also. " The whisperer, or tale-bearer," says the Wise Man, " defiles his own soul, and shall be hated by all ; and he who lives with him shall become odious to the whole world." (Eccl. xxxi.) Wherefore, says he in another place, " Be not styled a tale-bearer." (Ibid. v. 16.) That is, give no occasion for any one to affix this name to you. And to speak truth, there is no quality so unworthy not only of a religious, but of any man whomsoever. For what is more dangerous in a community than one of a seditious spirit, who is good for nothing else than to create dissensions amongst his brethren, and who thus charges himself with an employment that belongs to the devil, the father of discord and division ?

Here it must be observed, that in order to set two persons at variance, it sometimes is not necessary, that the thing we report be of any consequence. Sometimes a mere trifle is sufficient to do it ; the least thing in the world, that amounts not even to a venial sin, is able to do it. We must, therefore, most cautiously abstain from telling it, not only when the thing is important in itself, but also whenever it is at all capable of giving pain to the person we tell it to, or of making him discontented, and creating a misunderstanding between himself and brother. One has, perhaps, let fall a word that may have somewhat lessened another's wit, capacity, or merit ; and thereupon you tell the person what is said of him, with less consideration than it was spoken at first. What bitterness of heart do you think this will give him against the person that said it ? You think you have done no hurt at all, and you have wounded him to the very heart :—" The words of the whisperer appear simple," says the Wise Man," but they penetrate the bottom of the heart." (Prov. xxvi. 22.) There are certain things that many persons make no account of at all, and I know not which way, or in what manner they look upon them, or whether they take any the least notice of them ; but they appear to be of so great consequence to those who view them through a proper medium, that seeing the inconveniences and the bad effects arising from them, they have reason to fear that they are mortal sins; and of this description are the things we now speak of.

But if it be thus prejudicial to our neighbour, and so displeasing to God, to carry about stories of this sort, and thereby sow discord between brethren, what will it be to sow discord between superiors and subjects, and to cause a division between the head and the members, between a father and his children ? May we not very justly say, that this crime would be more abhorred by God, than the other ? Yet what little care do we take to preserve ourselves from being guilty of it ? The people of Israel were exceedingly attached to David, and had oftentimes given him splendid proofs of affection and obedience : yet on hearing his son Absalom speak ill of him— on hearing him blame his conduct and decry his government, they sometimes rebelled against David. How often has it happened that a religious stood well with his superior, had a high opinion of him, interpreted all his actions in good part, laid open to him upon all occasions even the hidden secrets of his heart ; and yet all this is suddenly destroyed by a word some one has inconsiderately said, and perhaps without the least evil intention ? Hence ensue suspicions, diffidences, dissimulations, rash judgments, detractions, and unkind offices ; and sometimes it happens that the evil increases so much, that one secretly whispering and communicating the matter to another, the contagion spreads itself over the whole community : so that one cannot sufficiently describe how prejudicial these sorts of reports and stories may, and do often prove to religious union, peace and tranquillity.

But some may answer, it is sometimes proper that our brother should know what is alleged against him, that he may stand more upon his guard, and for the future give no occasion of having such things said of him. It is true ; but it is sufficient to tell him the thing, without naming any one, though it should even be said in public ; and so far we are probably excusable, as another might have told him the same. It is the duty of every man to look to himself, " For woe to that man by whom scandal happens." (Matt. xviii. 7.) And how pressing soever your friend may be to prevail on you to discover the author, deny him still, and take care that his importunities, and the great favour you imagine you should do him, extract not what he desires. For this were a dangerous condescension ; and by giving him a mark of your friendship, you would at the same time do hurt to him, as well as to the person of whom you should speak, and to yourself also ; as ever after you should scruple very much the injury you may have done the parties. We shall readily perceive the inconveniences of this practice, if we reflect, that even when one informs the superior of the faults of his brethren, in order that by his paternal care he may be able to apply a remedy, the rule declares that the superior ought not to signify from whence he received this information, and that he ought to take great care to keep it very secret ; lest the knowledge thereof should exasperate them, or cause any change of affection amongst the brethren. But if, when things of this nature are managed with so much prudence and caution, through a spirit of true charity, and with a view to greater good, there are oftentimes many inconveniences to be dreaded, and great circumspection to be used ; with how far greater reason ought we to apprehend these inconveniences, when any one discovers to another the person who has not spoken so well of him ; and this, not in complying with the rule, or through a motive of charity, but in a disobliging manner, through imprudence, and indiscretion, and perhaps through jealousy, and envy also, or in fine, through some other unreasonable motive, or at least that will pass for such in the mind of him you spoke of ? St. Austin praises exceedingly his mother St. Monica upon this account, that when those who were at variance, one with another, came severally to make their complaint to her with a great deal of bitterness, she never told either of them what the other said ; but charitably endeavouring to create a right understanding on both sides, she related only what she thought would sweeten and mollify their hearts, and contribute to their reconciliation. We ought to practise the same, and thus become angels of peace.

CHAPTER IX.

That good and fair Words conduce very much to the Preservation of Charity; while the contrary tends to its Destruction.

ONE of the things very conducive to the preservation and increase of fraternal charity is sweetness in our conversation. "A sweet word multiplies friends, and appeases enemies" (Eccl. vi. 5), says the Wise Man ; and on the contrary, "A harsh word raises up fury" (Prov. xv. 1), and occasions quarrels and dissensions. For being all of us men, words of this sort hurt our feelings ; and when the mind is once incensed, we look upon our brother not as we did before ; but presently find something blameable in his conduct, and often stop not at blaming him in our hearts only ; but go farther, and speak ill of him. It is then of very great importance that our discourse be always so seasoned with sweetness, that thereby we may gain the good will of our brethren, according to that saying of Scripture :— "A prudent man renders himself amiable by his words." (Eccl. xx. 13.) Now to attain this end, it is requisite, that first of all, we should be advertised of one thing, which ought to be the ground or foundation of what we have to say upon this subject ; which is, that we deceive not ourselves by imagining that our brethren, being men of information and virtue, will not notice or be scandalised at a sharp word we may say to them. The question at present is not what they are, but what you ought to be ; and how you ought to conduct yourself towards them. If you say, they will not be angry at so trifling a thing :— "The more trifling it is," answers St. Bernard, "the easier it is for you to abstain from it." St. Chrysostom goes farther, and says, that the parvity of the matter is what aggravates the fault ; because the more easy the victory, the more culpable are you, for not having obtained it. "Is your eye bad," says our Saviour, "because I am good?" (Matt. xx. 15.) And because your brother has a great deal of moderation, ought you to have none at all? It is very true that we ought to have a good opinion of our brethren, and not believe they are so alive to resentment, as to be angry at any small matter ; but still we are bound to converse with them, and to manage them with as much caution and circumspection, as if we knew they were very sensible to the least thing—we ought to be as tender of them, as if they were more brittle than glass ; in a word, be their temper and feelings that they may, we must most scrupulously abstain from giving any cause whatsoever of offence. It is to this we should apply ourselves, as well upon our own as our brother's account ; because the wisdom of our neighbour excuses not our indiscretion ; and because all are not, or at least all are not *always* disposed to take things in the best part, and to overlook offences of this sort, which are given them.

It only now remains to observe, that it is very easy to discriminate the words which may, or may not, offend our brother. Every man can do this by following the rule which the Holy Ghost gives us, by the mouth of the Wise Man :—" Judge of your neighbour by yourself." (Ecclus. xxxi. 18.)   Let every one consult himself, and see whether he be content others should speak coldly of him, that they should answer him sharply, and command him in a haughty and imperious manner ; and if he finds this will hurt his own feelings, let him abstain from the like ; because his neighbour is a man like himself, and may have the same sentiments and feelings as he himself has.   Humility also is a very proper means, to make us never speak but as we ought to do.   For if we be humble, and esteem ourselves the least of all, we need no other precaution than this ; this alone is sufficient to teach us how to behave to every one, so that we shall never speak a hasty word, at which any one may be offended ; but we shall always speak to every one with respect and sweetness.

It is certain, that a simple religious will never take the liberty to speak otherwise to his superior than as it becomes him ; because, considering himself as his inferior, he has a respect for him ; and when it happens that he speaks sharply to his brother, it is because he thinks himself not inferior to him, and therefore respects him not as he otherwise would do.   Let us therefore be humble, and following the counsel of the apostle, esteem ourselves the least of all, and we shall soon learn, both what language we ought to use, and after what manner we ought to speak to others.   But besides these general rules I have hitherto prescribed, I will now speak more in particular of the language, from which, as being directly contrary to charity, we ought to abstain.

———o———

CHAPTER X.

That we ought to abstain from all kind of Raillery, that may offend our Brother, or give him any Displeasure.

WE ought first to abstain from all sharp words, such as are used by those who animadvert upon the neighbour's person, capacity, or anything else belonging to him ; for words of this kind are entirely contrary to charity. Sometimes we utter them in a refined and witty way, to recreate and please ourselves ; and then they become more prejudicial than otherwise they would be ; because the more wit and grace they are said with, the deeper impression they make, and the longer they live in the memories of those that hear them. And that which is still worse, it often happens, that he who speaks them is very much pleased with himself ; thinking he has met with a good opportunity to show his wit, when, in reality, he very much deceives himself, and instead of showing his wit he only evinces his bad inclinations ; because the wit given him for God's service, he employs in speaking such fine things as wound and scandalize his brethren, and annoy peace and charity.

Albertus Magnus says, That as a stinking breath is a sign of a disordered stomach ; so sharp words are a sign of a corrupted heart. But what would St. Bernard say of a religious, that should offend his neighbour by railleries ? For if all sorts of pleasantry appeared to him as so many blasphemies and sacrileges, in the mouth of a religious, what name would he give such jests as offend ? Nothing is more opposite to the spirit of religion than such discourses as these. Everything, therefore, of this kind is to be avoided :—As for example, the inventing ridiculous comparisons, scoffing, playing the mimic ; and in fine, bantering of every kind. All this ought to be so far from the practice of any religious person, that he ought not, either in jest or any other way, to assume to himself any such liberties as these. Let every man judge of himself. Would you be content to be compared to something fantastical, which, on their seeing the likeness between itself and you, would make every one laugh that heard of it ? Since, therefore, you would take no pleasure therein, do not that to another you would not have done to yourself ; because this is the unerring rule of charity. Would you be content, suppose you said anything unhandsomely, that it should be presently repeated, and be divulged also in public? Certainly you would not : wherefore would you then that another suffers that from you which you would not be content to suffer from another, and which you would conceive highly injurious to yourself? The very names also that they use in such sort of jesting and pleasantry sound harshly in the mouth of a religious. Let us then avoid all such kinds of railleries, and exactly observe St. Paul's precept : "Lead such a civil life as becomes saints to do; let none hear out of your mouth such words as fornication or any other kind of impurity, or dishonest actions are explained by, nor in fine, any other foolish speeches or scurrility unbecoming your profession." (Ephes. v. 3.) All which agree not with a religious profession ; and if at the day of judgment we must give an account of all the idle and unprofitable words of our past life, what an account will be required of other words? What will be required of those whereby we have offended our brother, or any way done him any injury or prejudice?

———o———

CHAPTER XI.

That we ought to abstain from Disputes and Contentions with our Brethren, and also from reprehending them.

WE must also carefully avoid entering into any dispute or contention with any one, it being a thing very contrary to union and fraternal charity. St. Paul gives us warning of this, when writing to Timothy, he says, " Do not dispute or contend in words, for it serves for nothing else but to subvert and give scandal to the hearers" (2 Tim. ii. 14) : and a little after he adds,—" A servant of God must not be contentious, but mild and sweet towards all men, and be patient and apt to learn." (Ibid. ii. 24.) All the saints recommend the same thing to us, and St. Ignatius, in particular, has inserted this point in his rules. St. Dorotheus says, that he had rather things should be left undone, than perceive any disputes or contests arise amongst brethren in doing them ; and adds, that should he repeat this sentiment of his a thousand times, he should not repeat it too often. St. Bonaventure also affirms that there is nothing more unworthy or unbecoming God's servants, than to be at variance and to contend one with another about nothing, as women are wont to do. And St. John Climachus, moreover, assures us, that obstinacy, though it be in a matter of truth, can come from none but the devil. The reason is, because that which usually moves a man to maintain his own opinion with any heat, is the desire he has of being esteemed. Hence, it happens, that to appear more able or learned than his adversary, he endeavours to convince him that he is in an error ; and if he cannot be victorious in his dispute, he endeavours at least to make it appear he had not the worst of it; and thus it is always the devil of pride, who is the occasion of this obstinacy.

But in this, two sorts of faults may be committed ; the first and greatest is his who first contradicted the other; because it is he who begins the dispute, and first kindles the fire. And though, for the most part, the subject they dispute about is in reality of so small consequence, that it is no matter whether the thing in debate be the one way or the other; yet, it is of great importance not to lose peace or charity, which ordinarily are very much impaired by these sorts of debates. A man, for example, advances an assertion, which he fancies and firmly believes to be true. Well! leave to him his opinion, because you are not at all interested therein; and according to the counsel of the Wise Man : " Dispute not about what does not concern you." (Ecclus. xi. 9.) The spirit of contradiction is a very bad one : wherefore, endeavour to cast it off, though the thing in question be of consequence; and if you imagine that your brother may indeed receive some prejudice, by adhering to his erroneous opinion, yet you ought to bear with him for the present by not opposing him ; but what remains is, that upon the first occasion you take him aside, and sweetly inform him of the truth, and then in private convince him of his mistake. By this means you will be able to fulfil your duty, or at least to avoid such inconveniences as otherwise may be feared.

The other fault we must avoid is, the maintaining with too much obstinacy what we have once advanced. If, then, it happens that any one contradicts you, insist not much upon it, nor suffer yourself to be carried on by a desire of getting the better of him ; but explain yourself once or twice, with all mildness possible, and show him your idea of the question, and after that, let him believe what he pleases ; and impose silence upon yourself, as if you had nothing more to say about the matter. But do not, as many frequently do, who, though they yield in appearance, yet, either by muttering to themselves, or by some other exterior sign, make it appear that they submit only out of politeness, and that they drop the dispute only for quietness sake, and that they still judge their own opinion to be right, " He that avoids contentions gains honour" (Prov. xx. 3), says the Wise Man, and without doubt, there is a great deal of merit in politely yielding to another, and permitting one's self seemingly to be overcome on such like occasions.   In effect, he that does this exercises at the same time an act of charity towards his neighbour, by avoiding such disquiets and heats as ordinarily accompany these disputes ; he exercises an act of humility by overcoming the desire that all men have to get the better of another, and to attract glory to themselves ; and he exercises also an act of love towards God, by cutting off the occasion of many sins, which are almost inseparable from such sorts of debates, according to what the Wise Man says : " Abstain from all debates, and you will diminish the number of sins." (Ecclus. xxviii. 10.)   On the contrary, he that contests, besides the scandal he gives, is the cause that peace and charity are violated ; he interferes in the debates and disputes of his brethren, whence spring many other inconveniences ; and instead of gaining the esteem he aimed at, he makes himself pass for an obstinate and quarrelsome person, who is tied to his own opinion, and who seeks always to have the upper hand, never yielding upon any account to another.   It is related of St. Thomas of Aquin, that in his disputations he always proposed his opinion with meekness and sweetness, with an unspeakable moderation, without any show of presumption, and without the least offence to any one ; but behaved as a man who regarded not gaining the victory, but merely endeavoured to make known the truth. The affair of the two old men is sufficiently known, who having lived a long time together in one cell, without the least contention, would one day try whether they were able to dispute about a subject ; and casting their eyes upon a brick, which accidentally lay before them in their cell, they resolved to contend, to which of the two it belonged ; but they reciprocally yielding the right to each other could never enter into any dispute.   We ought to have such a disposition of mind as this was, so far estranged from all kinds of debates, as if we were absolutely incapable of them.

Moreover, we must not intrude ourselves into the office of

reprimanding our brother, though we should discharge it with ever so much precaution and charity, for this belongs only to the superior; and though, perhaps, subjects may suffer one or two superiors to reprehend them for their faults, yet they do not willingly permit those who are not superiors to usurp to themselves this authority; and in fine, generally speaking, men are not willing to be reprehended by their equals. We have also a rule that forbids every one either to command or reprehend another, without having express orders from the superior to do so. And in effect it does not become every one to do it; and even the superior himself, if he desires that the reprehension he gives should be well taken, and become profitable to him he reprehends, ought to think well of it beforehand—he ought to wait for a fit opportunity, and consider very well what he will say, as well as in what monner he will do it; since he cannot be too circumspect in this point. And yet a particular person, without reflecting upon anything, out of pretended zeal, will sometimes take upon him to reprehend his brother, without any consideration at all, even as soon as he committed the fault, at which time he is less disposed to hearken to, or profit by, that which is said unto him. This is not the effect of a discreet zeal but what is very contrary to charity, and what is wont to do more hurt than good. For though you may have reason for what you do, yet it is very probable it will exasperate your brother, and make him think within himself, nay, perhaps, even object to you; "Who has set you over us, to be our Judge?" (Exod. ii. 14.) Why do you meddle with what does not belong to you? And if you tell him it belongs to you, because what he does is against the rule, he may answer you very well, it is also contrary to our rules that you should take upon you to correct him.

We read of Socrates, that dining one day with his friends, and happening in a large company to reprehend a little too sharply one of the guests, Plato, who was present, could not refrain from saying to him, would it not have been better for you to have deferred this reprehension to another time, and secretly to have told him of his fault? But would not you also, replied Socrates, have done much better to have told me of mine in private? And thus he answered one reprehension with another, letting him see that he fell into the same fault he admonished him of. Behold here to what little purpose such unseasonable reprehensions as these are made, which for the most part proceed not from a motive of zeal and charity, but are an effect of ill-nature, impatience, anger, and levity of mind, which makes us dogmatize after this manner upon our brother's fault, and oftentimes upon what is no fault at all, so that sometimes we cannot refrain even from telling the corrector himself of it; which, when we have done, our heart seems to be at ease, and we find a satisfaction and content within us. Thus, though we cannot mortify ourselves, or at least will not, yet we desire that others should be mortified. It is good, therefore, that every one should have the spirit of mortification, severity, and rigour towards himself, and the spirit of love, meekness, and sweetness towards his brethren. It is this that the saints recommend to us in their writings; it is this they teach us by their examples; and it is this that helps very much to preserve union and fraternal charity. By what has been said, we may see, that if it is not permitted to reprehend our brother, when it seems to be done with civility, charity, and sweetness, it is far less lawful or permitted when it is done without this circumspection. We must, therefore, abstain from reprehending our brethren, and in general from saying the least word that may give them any mortification.

Cassian reports, that the abbot Moyses, disputing with the abbot Macharius, and having said a cross and mortifying word, God presently chastised him upon the spot, permitting the devil at the same time to possess him, and such a foul devil also, that made him speak all sorts of filthy and impure words; which punishment lasted till the abbot Macharius, by his prayers, rescued him from slavery so wretched. Such a chastisement, in so great a person, and in such a servant of God as the abbot Moyses, who was a man of approved sanctity, very clearly evinces that God extremely abhors such faults as these. We read in the Chronicles of St. Francis, that in imitation of this punishment, an ancient brother, permitting himself to be so transported with anger, as to give some harsh and choleric words to his companion in the presence of a gentleman of Assisium, he presently perceiving that his companion was moved, and the secular also scandalized, resolved to revenge his fault upon himself; wherefore gathering together a great deal of dirt, he crammed it into his mouth, "Let my mouth," says he, "eat this filth, since it has vomited out such gall and poison against my brother." The secular was so surprised at, and so edified by the fervour wherewith this good religious punished his own fault, that he became more attached than ever to those that lived under that rule, and offered both his person and whatsoever belonged to him to the service of the order.

———o———

CHAPTER XII.

Of the Sweetness we ought to have in our Words and Actions, in order to acquit ourselves well of Charity.

St. BASIL gives a very profitable instruction for the conduct of those who are employed in the exterior functions of a religious life. " When it happens," says he, " that you are employed in these sorts of offices, take care that sweetness of words be joined with the labour of the body." (Basil in principio, ii. tom.) It is not enough that you take pains, and torment yourselves very much, but you must also perform the good you do with a good grace ; and take care that there be sweetness and meekness in your words, that others knowing you act with a spirit of charity, your service may thereby be more pleasing to them. It is this that the Wise Man counsels us when he says: "Son, make no complaint whilst you do that which is good ; and whensoever you give anything, mortify none with harsh words. The dew tempers the day's great heats, and a sweet word excels whatsoever you can give ; it is above all other presents." (Eccl. xviii. 15.) The agreeable manner wherewith you serve another, and the sweetness with which you answer him, is more regarded and esteemed than all you can do ; and, on the contrary, what pains soever you shall take, know, that if you appear not to take them with a good will, if you perform not your actions with a good grace, and if your words be not always accompanied with sweetness, all the pains you take will be esteemed as nothing, and you will have laboured in vain. "Let your discourse," says the apostle, " be always seasoned with a certain kind of salt, that may render it agreeable, in such sort, that you understand what answer to give to every one." (Colos. iv. 6);—and this salt is nothing else but that sweetness, of which we speak at present. Though you should be so employed, that you were not able to perform what is desired of you, yet you must not upon this account rudely put off your brother, but on the contrary it is then that you should hearken more mildly to his petition ; it is then you ought to signify that you should be extremely glad it were in your power to do what he desires, and that nothing but the pressing affairs you have in hand could hinder you from doing at present, what you will joyfully do as soon as you are a little more at leisure. Thus his being convinced of your good will will make him retire as satisfied, as though he had obtained what he came for. But if your not having permission to do it is the reason why you do not comply with his request, tell him you will instantly go to the superior and ask the requisite permission. Act thus on all other occasions, and when it is not in your power to perform what is desired of you, endeavour by fair words to supply the want of deeds, that at least they may never doubt but that you have all possible inclination to serve them. "Good words," says the Holy Ghost, "abound in the mouth of a virtuous man" (Eccl. vi. 5) ; and in effect they conduce very much to the maintenance of union and charity in our minds.

It is in the opinion of St. Bonaventure, that when we happen to make an answer to our brother which is capable of giving him offence or the least uneasiness, we ought to be extremely ashamed of it, though what we said were in itself of very small moment, and were only the effect of a sudden and first motion, and the saint adds, that when anything of this kind has happened, we must presently humble ourselves before God, and endeavour to make our brother satisfaction by begging his pardon. We read in the life of St. Dositheus, that he spoke to everyone with great sweetness and charity, and took great care to avoid all kinds of dispute with everyone. But his office of infirmarian obliging him to have to do with a great many, occasioned sometimes some little disputes, as with the cook of the monastery, because he took not that care he should in dressing the meat for the sick ; or sometimes also with the dispenser, because he gave him not what was best for the sick, or made him wait too long for it, or because he carried into the refectory what he wanted for the infirmary ; whereupon it sometimes happened that he spoke louder than ordinary, or a little more sharply than became him. But when this happened, he felt so confused, that retiring to his cell, he there prostrated himself, and wept so bitterly that his superior, St. Dorotheus, was often forced to go to him to ask him what ailed him, and to urge him to tell him the cause of his trouble. "Father," replied Dositheus, weeping anew, "I have spoken with contempt to my brother :" whereupon Dorotheus reprehended him severely for his fault, saying "Fie, is this the humility you ought to have ? You have offended your brother, and yet you do not die for shame to have committed such a fault as this is ?" And having thus chid him, he added, "Well, take courage now and get up, God has pardoned you, let us now endeavour to begin a new life." The good disciple rose at these words with as much joy as if his pardon had been pronounced by the mouth of God himself, and made a new and firm resolution never more to speak rudely to any person whomsoever.

But that those, who are employed in the offices of charity, and those towards whom it is exercised, may equally make their profit, both of the service they render, and that they receive, St. Basil proposes two excellent expedients. Would you know, says he, how you may perform well those services you do to your brother? Make account, says he, that in serving him you serve Jesus Christ, who has assured you, " That what you do to the least of his brethren, you do unto himself." (Mat. xxv. 40.) Do, therefore, your actions as if it were God, and not man, whom you served, and by this means you will never fail to serve your brethren as you should do. But would you be informed, continues the saint, in what manner you ought to receive any service your brother renders you? After the same manner that a servant ought to receive any service that his master is pleased to do him ; and after the same manner that St. Peter received that, which the Saviour of the world was pleased to perform, when he washed his feet, by crying out, full of confusion: "How! What! do you, O Lord, wash my feet ?" (John xiii. 6.) By this means humility will be conserved alike in both the one and the other : because these will not disdain to serve their brothers, when they look upon them as children of God, and brethren of Jesus Christ himself ; nor will the others be puffed up with pride, to see themselves served ; but on the contrary will herein find occasion of humiliation and confusion, when they consider themselves inferior to those that serve them, and when they consider, that those who serve them look not upon them, but upon God himself. What remains is, that fraternal charity, which is so highly recommended to us, will hereby be conserved, and still more and more augmented.

——o——

CHAPTER XIII.

How we ought to behave ourselves towards our Brethren, when there has happened any dispute in which we have given them any cause of Uneasiness.

BUT because we are all of us men, and even the greatest part of us stand not always so much on our guard, but that we occasionally drop a harsh word, which gives pain to our brethren; it is good that I explain here, how we are to behave towards them on such occasions.

First, when it happens that any one has spoken to us after a rude manner, we must not answer him in the same tone or language, but must have so much moderation and humility, as to suffer it with patience, and overlook it with humility. The fire of our charity must not be so weakly lighted, as to be extinguished by a few drops of water; and the apostle St. Paul, speaking of charity, gives it, says St. Basil, for no other reason, the epithet of *fraternal,* but to signify that it ought not to leave so weak an impression on our hearts, as may be easily effaced : but that it ought to be solid, fervent, and strong. (Heb. xiii. 1, and Rom. xii. 10.) It is without doubt very much to be wished, that, neither by word nor action, any one should give the least discontent to his brother, and it is also equally to be desired, that we should not easily take fire, or be incensed ; nor be so alive as to raise our voice, be disquieted in mind, and lose the peace of our soul for nothing. I know very well that it would be much better that none should take upon them to reprehend another, nor interfere in what belongs to another's office ; yet if it happens that any one should take this liberty, we must not upon this account presently reproach him to his face; ask him who gave him this authority, and tell him that our rule forbids us to intrude ourselves into another's office. All this serves only to create disturbance, about that which would not have been worth taking notice of, if, in the beginning, we could have overlooked and not minded it at all, but held our peace. When two hard bodies hit one against the other, they make a great noise; but if a hard body strikes against a soft one, it makes none at all. A cannon ball beats down a tower with a terrible crash ; but if it be shot against a wool sack, its force is deadened and quickly spent. "A civil and meek answer appeases wrath," says Solomon, "but a rude word provokes one to fury." (Prov. xv. 1.)

The Holy Ghost also counsels us " not to contend with a man of haughty words, this being to lay wood upon the fire." (Eccl. viii. 4.) Take heed, therefore, of disputing with him or of incensing him by your replies : but, on the contrary, endeavour to have so much sweetness and moderation, that whatsoever he says, though ever so rude and provoking, may not, on touching you, make noise, or leave impression, but may be hushed and effaced by your meekness.

St. Dorotheus teaches us a mode of answering very humbly ; which we may make use of on such occasions. He says, that when any one speaks very sharply to us, or reprehends us for any fault, or reproaches us for what we have not been guilty of ; we must always receive the correction with equal humility, and say, whether we have wrong done us, or not :—" Dear brother, pardon me, and pray for me." (Dorot. Doct. xv.) He learned this doctrine from an ancient father, who was wont to practise it himself, and to recommend it to others. And without doubt, if we practise this with the like spirit of humility, and if, on the one hand, we endeavour with all possible care to beware of giving our brother any discontent, and on the other if we are disposed to receive all things in good part, we shall live in a strict union, and in an admirable peace and concord.

But nevertheless, if perhaps you chance to fail in this —for example : if you happen to have had any difference or dispute with your brother, because he took the liberty to say something that displeased you, and you had not sufficient discretion and humility to overlook it and bear with it—if there has happened any dissension or dispute between you, and you resented it alternately ; you because he first attacked you ; he because you answered him very sharply ; you ought, says St. Bonaventure, to reconcile yourselves one with another, by a speedy and mutual satisfaction ; in order that " the sun set not upon your anger" (Eph. iv. 26) ; and the means to reconcile yourselves is mutually to beg pardon one of another. St. Ignatius prescribes the same thing in his Constitutions :—We ought not to permit, says he, that any difference or animosity arise amongst us ; but if it happens, either by our own weakness, or by the instigation of the devil, who is never wanting to blow the coal, and kindle the fire of discord between brethren, we must presently endeavour to reconcile those that are at variance, and oblige them to make each other suitable satisfaction. But this satisfaction, as he has defined, in some other spiritual instructions he left written, must be to ask pardon of each other. So that there is nothing but humility, says St. Bernard, that can truly repair a breach of charity ; and therefore we must always have a great facility in demanding and granting pardon ; "Bearing with one another," as St. Paul says, "mutually forgiving all the occasions or subjects of complaints, that may have happened." (Colos. iii. 13.) Nay we must do still more—we must endeavour to prevent our neighbour ; "Lest he take our crown from us" (Apoc. iii. 11) ; for he who first humbles himself, and asks pardon, infallibly gains it. Wherefore the more ancient, and he who either is, or ought to be, the more perfect in the practice of virtue and self-mortification, ought not to take notice whether he be the person offended, or be less to blame than his brother ; but without dwelling upon any human consideration, he must think of nothing else, but to advance in humility, by making the first step to charity. When the shepherds of Abraham and Lot quarrelled about the pastures of their flocks, Abraham spoke first to Lot, and by giving him his choice of the lands before him, he yielded up to him that right he might justly have taken to himself :— "I pray," says he, "let there be no difference between you and me, nor between your shepherds and mine, for we are brothers ; behold the whole land is before you, I beseech you separate from me. If you take the left hand, I will take the right, if you choose the right, I will retire to the left." (Gen. xiii. 8.)

We read in the Chronicles of the Cistercian order, of one of these religious who received this grace and favour from God, that every time he communicated, he felt a sweetness, as it were of an honeycomb, which frequently remained in his mouth for three days together. It happened that having one day repre-hended one of his brethren somewhat sharply, he hereupon went to communicate, without being first reconciled to him, and that day he had his mouth filled with a greater bitterness than that of gall or wormwood ; and this, because he had not complied with that precept of the gospel : "If you present your offering before the altar, and there remember that your brother has anything against you, leave your gift before the altar, and go first and be reconciled to your brother, and then come and offer your gift." (Matt. v. 23.) Hence we see how pleasing a speedy reconcilia-tion with our brethren is to God ; because when we are even at the foot of the altar, and ready to make our oblation to him, we must quit all, to go and be reconciled to our brother.

CHAPTER XIV.

Three things we ought to practise when any one has given us any Subject of Discontent.

FROM all that has been said we may infer, that there are three things, which we must observe when our brother has offended us, or given us cause of being displeased with him. The first is, that we restrain our minds from giving way, in the least, to the spirit of revenge. We are all of us brothers, members of the same body : and it was never heard that one member injured by another ever meditated revenge ; nor ever was there yet any child so foolish, that having bit its own tongue, pulled out its teeth for mere spite. Let us not be then less wise than they ; but when any one has offended us, let us say to ourselves he is a member of the same body with myself, wherefore let us pardon him ; and neither desire, nor do him any further harm; there is mischief enough done already, and, therefore, I will not be the occasion of doing more. But I will follow St. Paul's counsel, which says :—" Let us not render any one evil for evil." (Rom. xii. 17.) I pretend not here to speak of revenge in matters of consequence ; because I suppose no such thing happens among religious ; and that such persons are far from having any senti- ments of this nature ; but I speak of revenge in things of less moment, which we imagine may be lawful to desire or practise, without committing any great sin. Some will say—I would by no means that any evil should happen to my brother, but I must confess, I should be glad to say to him a word or two which he would feel a little, and which would show him that he is in the wrong. Others will rejoice at the reprehension and correction of the person with whom they had a dispute or falling out. The third sort, in fine, will feel a kind of malignant joy, that he, from whom they received some slight displeasure, succeeded ill in some business, or met with some mortification. All this is much to be censured, and may very deservedly be styled revenge ; since whoever has such sentiments as these, has not yet pardoned his brother from his heart, and ought to have a scruple when he prays thus to God : " Forgive us our trespasses as we forgive them that trespass against us." (Matt. vi. 12.) It is also in some kind more criminal in a religious to retain in mind these little rancours, than for a secular to desire a signal revenge upon his enemies. Wherefore if your brother has offended you on any occasion, say not, " I will do to him as he has done to me" (Prov. xxiv. 29) : I will use him as he has used me, for this proceeds from an exasperated mind, that harbours a desire of revenge.

But it is not enough that we harbour no desire of revenge, we must also take great care of another thing, which people of the world look upon as lawful. I do not wish such a one, say they, any mischief, but I will have nothing more to do with him; and thus they conceive such a bitterness and aversion in their hearts, against those by whom they have been once offended, that they cannot afterwards have any feeling for them or converse with them for the future with any satisfaction. But if we condemn this in seculars, so far as to call in question whether they have satisfied their obligation of charity, because hence it often happens that they converse no more together, and give scandal thereby to their neighbour ; how much more is it to be condemned in us, that there should still remain a disgust and bitterness of heart against our brother, by looking upon him no more, " as we did yesterday and the day before ? " (Gen. xxxi. 2.) This is far from the spirit of religion. " Let all sorts of harshness, choler, and indignation be banished from amongst you," says St. Paul, "and be ye sweet and merciful one to another, pardoning one another, as God has pardoned you, through Jesus Christ." (Eph. iv. 31.) That is to say, that you pardon all from the bottom of your heart, for it is after this manner that God pardons us. For when we have truly repented of our sins, and asked pardon of him ; there remains not in him the least sentiment of displeasure against us, but he treats us after the same bountiful manner as he did before—he has the same tenderness for us, as if we had never offended him ; and is so far from reproaching us with our past sins, that he does not so much as remember them. " I will no more remember their sins and iniquities " (Ezech. xviii. 22), says he by the mouth of St. Paul. " He will cast," says the Prophet Micheas, " all our sins into the bottom of the sea." (Mich. vii. 19.) It is after this manner we must pardon our enemies—it is thus we ought to forgive injuries. There must remain no aversion, no animosity against our brother, but we must be the same to him as if he had never offended us, and as if nothing at all had passed between us. If you would have God pardon you after this manner, do you after the same manner pardon your brother ; and if you do not, take heed and be afraid, lest you become like that servant who had no compassion for his fellow-servant, and whom his master delivered over to the sword of justice. " It is after this manner," says our Saviour, " that my heavenly Father will deal with you, if every one of you pardons not his brother from the bottom of his heart." (Matt. xviii. 35.) " Forgive and ye shall be forgiven ; for the same measure you make to others, the same also shall be again made unto you." (Luke vi. 37.)

The third direction is given us by St. Basil, and will help still more to evince the utility of the former. He says, that as we ought not to have any particular attachment to any one, because it is the cause of many inconveniences, as we shall show hereafter : so we must not be prejudiced against any person, because hence also proceed very great inconveniences. Would it not, for example, be a very great evil (which God preserve us from), that any amongst us should say : such and such a one are not well together ; ever since such an accident happened the other day, they live not together as they were wont to do. This alone is enough to destroy religion, and since Jesus Christ desires, that the affection we have for another be the mark that we are his disciples ; it consequently follows, that those who love not their brethren are not disciples of Jesus Christ, nor true religious. To remedy this you must act after the same manner as when you feel a particular inclination to any one ; you must take particular care to cast it off, lest this particular affection take too deep root in your heart, and become master of it ; and as spiritual directors would then have us avoid, as much as possible, the letting it appear, upon account of the scandal that may arise from thence ; so when you find an aversion for any one, you must presently endeavour to root it out, for fear it should take root in your heart ; and you must endeavour that none perceive it ; because those exterior signs that we permit to appear do ordinarily produce dissensions and other bad consequences. It is not, however, sufficient to conceal it from every one else, if you conceal it not from him also, to whom you bear it. But to prove this by adhering to the comparison already proposed ; as there are some people, who, that they may evade all blame and scandal, are very careful to hide from others the particular affection they have for any one, yet either directly or indirectly show the person himself all the marks of this affection in their power, which is of a pernicious consequence; even so, there are some that take a great deal of care, for this reason, to hide from others the hatred or ill-will they have for their brother, but at the same time they signify it to himself, both in their looks and gestures. They avoid his person, keep not company with him as before, affect a kind of moroseness and ill-humour whilst they are with him, and in effect, endeavour to let him see the resentments they retain of the injury they pretend to have received from him. But this being a kind of revenge, is very much to be condemned, and we can never take too much care and precaution to avoid it.

Now to obviate all this—as in time of temptation, when we feel the danger, we, to prevent ourselves from being carried away by the enemy's suggestion, make more than ordinary exertions; just so, when you feel any aversion or displeasure against any one, you must then have a more particular attention and guard upon yourself, lest this aversion or unkindness should provoke you to say or do anything that may let your brother perceive your resentment; and according to the counsel given us in the gospel, you must pray for him, and do him all the kindness you can. "Let not your charity be overcome by the evil that is done you, but overcome evil by good" (Rom. xii. 21), says St. Paul, "do them more good than they did hurt to you: and by this means you will heap burning coal upon the head of your enemy." (Ibid. xii. 20.) You will gather together the coal of his love and charity for yourself, if he receives in good part all the marks of yours; and the coal of revenge against him in the other life, if his heart still continues hardened against you.

Thomas-a Kempis relates that a holy priest who lived in the same monastery with him, going one day about some business to another convent, in his way met with a secular, and both presently entered into familiar discourse. At length coming to speak of God and pious things, the secular told him he would relate to him a passage that had heretofore happened to himself. He was once, he said, hearing mass, and was surprised that he did not see the host in the priest's hand; but imagining that it was owing to his weakness of sight, and to his being at too great a distance from the altar, he approached nearer, and yet could not see it. This extraordinary circumstance continued for the space of a year. In fine, not knowing what cause to attribute it to, and finding himself in a strange perplexity of mind, he resolved to speak of it to a prudent director, who, having examined him closely, discovered that he (the secular) had for a long time hated a neighbour, from whom he received an injury which he would never pardon. The confessor finding so great a hardness in his heart, failed not to represent to him the dangerous state he was in, gave him many reprehensions, and wholesome counsels, and in fine, told him that he need not seek any other cause than this, why he saw not the holy host; and that he hoped in vain to obtain this favour from God, if he did not pardon the injury done him by his neighbour. This man was so touched with these words, that immediately from his heart he pardoned his enemy and having concluded his confession, and received penance and absolution, he went into the church, heard mass, and without any difficulty saw the holy host, and failed not ever after to render due thanks to God for so great a favour, and continually to bless him for those other wonders he daily works for the good of his servants.

——o——

CHAPTER XV.

Of rash Judgments, and in what their Heinousness particularly consists.

" But you," says St. Paul, " what right have you to judge your brother ; or who are you that you should contemn him ?" (Rom. xiv. 10.) Amongst all the temptations that the enemy of our salvation provides himself with, in order to make war against us, one of the chief is that which incites us to judge ill of our brethren. For by judging ill of them, we lose first the good opinion, and secondly, the affection we had had for them ; or at least our charity towards them abates and grows cold. Wherefore we must take all care imaginable to vigorously resist this temptation, which, as it annoys and weakens charity, we must believe to be extremely dangerous. If you will therefore preserve charity in your heart, if you desire to keep yourself in a perfect union with your brethren, " above all things," says St. Austin, " take care you admit no suspicions into your mind ; because they are the poison of friendship." (Lib. de amic. c. xxiv.) St. Bonaventure calls them " a secret plague, but a very dangerous one, because it drives God far from us, and tears in pieces fraternal charity." (In stim. amor. c. x.)

That which is most pernicious in this vice is, that it makes us injure the reputation of our neighbour within our own hearts; so that upon very slight grounds we come to despise him within ourselves, whereby without doubt we do an injury to our brother. But the fault we commit is greater or less, in proportion to the matter upon which we frame our judgments ; and as the ground upon which we frame them is strong or weak. In order to comprehend more clearly the heinousness of this fault, let us speak of another like unto it. Consider how great a sin it would be, if you should lessen your brother's esteem in the opinion of another, and that by staining his reputation, you should ruin the esteem and good opinion he had before conceived of him. You do him as great an injury, when, without reason or sufficient ground, you yourself conceive a bad opinion of him; for he wishes to keep his credit and reputation as much with you as with any one else. Each one may easily judge by himself, what prejudice he does hereby to his brother. Would you not be offended should another harbour a bad opinion of you, without having on your part, given occasion for his doing so. You offend him in the same manner, by judging disadvantageously of him without any just occasion offered. Judge of another by yourself; and let charity and justice make use of no other means than these, to measure your charity towards your neighbour.

You must, notwithstanding, observe that there is a very great difference between *having temptations* to judge rashly, and *suffering ourselves to be carried away by them.* For it is the same in this, as in all other things ; and as, for example, there is a great difference between having any temptations, and yielding to them ; for the crime consists not in being attacked, but in being overcome : in like manner the crime in this matter consists not in being tormented by thoughts of rash judgment. It would without doubt be much better, that we were so replenished with charity and esteem of our neighbour, and so taken up with the consideration of our own faults, that we should not be able to attend to those of our brother, nor imagine him to be guilty of any. " Yet after all," says St. Bernard, " a thought cannot render us guilty, so long as we give no consent," and are not overcome by the temptation. It is true, that in rash judgments, to become guilty of them, we must give our consent ; because, when we do so, we presently lose the good opinion we had of our brother, and begin to undervalue him, according to what we before quoted from St. Paul. In this case it is not sufficient, when we go to confession, to say, that there passed several rash judgments against our brethren in our minds; but we ought more fully to express that we consented to them ; and yielded to the temptation. Divines say, moreover, that we must take care not to speak of those suspicions that came into our minds against our brother, lest that should give occasion to another to have the same, or confirm him in that which perhaps he might before have had of him. For our inclination is so perverse, that it urges us to believe rather what is bad, than what is good of our neighbour; wherefore they forbid us even to name in confession, either the person of whom we made the rash judgment, or him who has given us an occasion of scandal, lest it should make on the mind of our confessor an impression which would lessen his esteem for them. See the length to which the holy doctors carry the circumspection they require we should have, in what concerns the honour and reputation of our neighbour. And yet, upon light conjectures, you would deprive him of the reputation he had before with you ; and which he is entitled to with all the world, until his actions give sufficient proof of the contrary.

But besides the injury we do in this to our neighbour, we also do a very great one to God, by usurping his jurisdiction, contrary to what our Saviour forbids in these words: "Judge not, and you shall not be judged ; condemn not, and you shall not be condemned." (Luke vi. 37.) St. Austin says, that by this the Son of God forbids all rash judgments ; such as, to judge the intention of the heart, and generally all other things that are hidden from us, because God has reserved the knowledge of these to himself ; and would not have men pretend to such a knowledge. But St. Paul explains this still more perfectly. " Who are you," says he, " that take upon you to judge the servant of another ? It belongs only to his master to absolve or condemn him." (Rom. xiv. 4.) " Wherefore, take care of judging before the time, until our Lord comes himself, who will illuminate even the thickest darkness, and discover the greatest secrets of hearts, and then every one shall receive praise from him." (1 Cor. iv. 5.) The reason he alleges why we should not judge is, because the things we judge are very uncertain, and very hidden and abstrnse. As therefore God is the only one able to penetrate them; and as it belongs only to him to judge, so whosoever takes upon him that office, usurps God's right, and trenches upon his divine jurisdiction. We read in the lives of the fathers, that a certain anchorite having upon slight grounds judged ill of another, heard presently a voice from heaven, that said to him : " Men usurp to themselves that right of judicature which I have reserved to myself, and encroach upon my jurisdiction."

But if it be criminal to judge ill of our neighbour, even when there is some appearance of evil; how far more must we believe it is, when the things he does are good in themselves ? And yet we presume to make an ill interpretation of them, and to judge that they are performed with a bad intention, or out of human respects? This is evidently to usurp God's jurisdiction, to pretend to penetrate the secrets of hearts, and to judge the most hidden thoughts and intentions. "This is to become judges, full of unjust thoughts." (Jam. ii. 4.) " That is like those who divine, and by vain conjectures would know what they are ignorant of." (Prov. xxiii. 7.)

————o————

CHAPTER XVI.

Of the Roots and Causes whence rash Judgments proceed, and the Remedies we must apply to them.

THE first root whence rash judgments commonly grow is pride, which, though it is the root of all other sins, yet it is much more particularly so of this. St. Bonaventure upon this subject remarks what is worthy to be considered : he says, that those who think themselves more advanced in a spiritual life, are more frequently tempted than others to judge and censure their neighbours : as if these words, which the apostle said in another sense, "the spiritual man judges all things" (2 Cor. ii. 15), had been said to give them power and right to judge all the world. They imagine themselves to possess the great gifts of God ; and instead of being the more humble thereby, they are puffed up with a greater pride, replenished with a good opinion of themselves, look contemptibly upon those who seem too much employed in exterior occupations, and becoming critics and reformers, they so far forget themselves, as to make it their only business to censure the lives of others. The saints say, that simplicity is the daughter of humility ; for he who is truly humble has not his eyes open to see the faults of his neighbour, but only to discern his own ; and finds so many things to consider and deplore in himself, that he never casts his eyes or thoughts on the faults of others. If therefore we were truly humble, we should be far from these kinds of judgments. It is also a very excellent remedy for this, as well as for many other defects, never to open our eyes but to behold our own infirmities ; that " we may know what we want" (Ps. xxxviii. 5) ; and to keep them shut to the defects of others, lest if we do otherwise, the same may be said to us that was said to the hypocrite in the gospel : " how come you to see a mote in your brother's eye, who have a beam in your own ?" (Matt. vii. 3.) We cannot sufficiently express how great an advantage it is to have our eyes always fixed upon our own defects; because this sight gives us humility and confusion—it augments the fear of God in the soul, keeps it in recollection, and produces in it the fruits of peace and tranquillity. On the contrary the practice of observing the faults of others is frequently the cause of many evils and inconveniences; it carries along with it pride, rash judgments, indignation against our neighbours, contempt of our brethren, remorse of conscience, indiscreet zeal, and a thousand other imperfections, which agitate and subvert the heart. Wherefore, if it happens that you discern any fault in your neighbour, endeavour to gather thence some fruit for your own amendment. When you perceive in your brother anything worthy of reprehension, turn your eyes upon yourself, says St. Bonaventure ; before you judge him, examine yourself well ; and if you find you are guilty of the same fault, pronounce the sentence against yourself, and condemn that in yourself, which you would have condemned in him, by saying with the Royal Prophet : " It is I who have sinned, it is I that have done evil." (2 Kings xxiv. 17.) I deserve not to kiss the ground he treads upon, and that which I perceive in him is nothing compared to what I find in myself. St. Bernard teaches us another means, which will aid us very much. "When you perceive in your neighbour," says he, "anything that pleases you, see if you possess the same ; and if you have it, think how to conserve it ; but if you have it not, endeavour to acquire it, and by this means you will make your profit in all things."

St. Thomas ascribes these rash judgments, of which we speak, to other causes, and says they proceed from some corruption within : and so judging the inclinations of our neighbour by our own, we easily think that to be in him, which we feel in ourselves. "A fool," says Ecclesiastes, "believes all he meets to be fools like himself" (Eccl. x. 3)—and it is a common saying, that " a robber believes all the world thieves." When one looks upon anything through a coloured glass, all things appear of the same colour of the glass ; so a wicked man judges all to be like himself ; he takes all things in the worst part, so that he views them through a false medium ; and as he has such or such a view in what he does, and governs himself by such and such a maxim, so he believes that all others govern themselves by the same motives and considerations. Yet you " do not consider," says St. Paul, "that you condemn yourself by the judgment you pass upon another, for that judgment is a sign that you, yourself, are guilty of the same thing you suspect in him." (Rom. ii. 1.) A virtuous man looks upon all things and puts on them the best construction, though sometimes he perceives something to doubt of ; and indeed when a thing admits of two interpretations, it is bad to give it the more unfavourable one. St. Dorotheus says, that as a man who is of good constitution, and has a good stomach, converts even those meats that are hard of digestion and unwholesome into good nourishment, and on the contrary, a bad stomach turns even the best meats into bile and bad humours, so he who has a good and upright heart, and practises virtue, interprets all things well ; whereas he who knows not what virtue is, poisons all things, and interprets them in the worst sense.

The saints add, moreover, that though there is no sin in judging that an action is bad, when it is evidently so ; yet should that which they see be manifestly culpable, it is still a virtue and perfection to endeavour, as far as in our power, to excuse our brother. " Excuse the intention if you cannot excuse the action," says St. Bernard, " believe it proceeds from ignorance, or surprise ; that it happens by chance, or is an effect of the first motion, which he could not help and was not master of." If we loved our brethren as ourselves, and looked upon them as our second selves, as in effect they really are, we should not want reasons or address to excuse them. Self love always furnishes us with an infinity of excuses ; it puts arms in our hands to defend ourselves, and teaches us how to lessen our own faults; and without doubt we should make use of the same means in behalf of our neighbour, if we loved him as well as we love ourselves. But if the fault should be so evident and criminal, that we cannot excuse it, believe then, says St. Bernard, and think thus with yourself ; " If I had been set upon with the same temptation, and God had permitted the devil to have the same power to tempt me, what might not have happened to me ?" We read of St. Ignatius, that when any action was so evidently bad, that when he found no way to excuse or colour it, he suspended his judgment, and adhering fast to the Holy Scripture, he said,

" take heed of judging before the time." (1 Cor. iv. 5.) "There is none but God who sees the heart." (1 Kings xvi. 7.) " A servant cannot be absolved or condemned but by his master." (Rom. xiv. 4.)

Besides all the causes already set down, St. Thomas still alleges another, and says that rash judgments often proceed from envy, jealousy, or some secret aversion. For as "we easily believe what is pleasing to us, so the bad disposition we are in in regard of our brother, is the reason why we find something to blame in all he does, and why we interpret, though we have but a slight knowledge of them, all his actions in the worst sense. This will be better conceived by quoting an example of the contrary. When we have a passionate affection for any one, we approve of all his actions, and are so far from giving them any bad interpretation, or taking them in ill part, that though we cannot but see his faults, yet we think of nothing else than how to palliate and diminish them as mnch as we are able. " Charity," says St. Paul, " never admits a thought to its neighbour's disadvantage." (1 Cor. xiii. 5.) The same fault, accompanied with the same circumstances and appearances, seems not to be the same in him we love as it does in him we have no affection for. And daily experience teaches us that there are some sorts of persons who displease and hurt us, whilst, at the same time, there are others who treat us perhaps worse, with whom we are not the least offended, nor do we take notice of what they do to us. It is this which the Wise Man prudently observes, when he says: " Hatred provokes quarrels, and charity covers all kinds of defects." (Prov. x. 12.) So that we may say with truth, that it is want of charity that makes us judge rashly. This want of charity is also the cause why we are shocked and very much troubled even at what is no fault at all in our brother. His air, his gesture, his conversation, his manner, and even his good qualities, become sometimes insupportable to us ; and this ought to show us, that as simplicity contributes very much to the preservation of mutual charity, so charity assists in preserving simplicity, and thus they assist one the other.

To guard against all these inconveniences we have mentioned, it will be of great advantage to us if we consider attentively the craft and malice of the devil, who, for matters of no moment, and for things which are not faults, or at least very slight and small ones, even such as none are exempted from, endeavours to make us divest ourselves of the affection and esteem we have for our brethren. For in this life no one is free from imperfections and venial sins : "If we say there is no sin in us," says St. John, "we deceive ourselves and there is no truth in us." (1 John i. 8.) And the Wise Man assures us, that "the just man shall fall seven times a day" (Prov. xxiv. 16): that is to say, many times, without ceasing notwithstanding to be still just. This being so, it is very unreasonable that what cannot take from him the grace of God, and the quality of being just, should make him forfeit our good will or esteem. For Christian charity has stronger ties and more solid foundations than worldly friendship. A mere bauble—the most trifling interest, the omission of a compliment, dissolves worldly friendship ; but Christian charity is founded on God alone, who can never fail. Wherefore, let us follow God's example, who, notwithstanding our defects and imperfections, ceases not to love us, and to have an uniform tenderness for us. He tolerates, out of his goodness, an infinity of faults we daily commit against him ; and yet without feeling resentment and ill-will against him, we cannot bear a small fault our brother commits against us. This shows that we do not truly love him for God; for if we loved him after this manner we should not be vexed or troubled for what God is not displeased at. If he who is master is not at all angry, why should we who are but servants be displeased ? He looks upon our brother as his son ; he tenderly loves and cherishes him ; it is, therefore, but just that we should have the same feelings for him that he has. "If God has loved us after such a manner as this, we ought in like manner to love one another." (1 John iv. 11.)

Let us attend to a thought of St. Gregory, and of many other saints, which is, that God sometimes refuses a lesser grace to those whom he has replenished with far greater, and thus, by the adorable order of his providence, leaves them to combat with slight and small imperfections, to the end that, by their constant endeavour to correct them, without ever being able to effect their intent, and feeling that notwithstanding all their care, and all their resolutions, they continually relapse into the same, they may the better be conserved in humility, and remain convinced, that of themselves they can never overcome great difficulties, since they are not able to surmount such small ones as these. Thus, the same man, at the same time, may have arrived to a high pitch of virtue, and a very eminent degree of sanctity, and yet be subject to some defects which God was pleased to leave in him, thereby to exercise him, that by humility he may keep himself in possession of those greater gifts he has received. The conclusion, therefore, we must draw from hence is, that we ought never to judge ill of our brother, nor contemn him for those small imperfections he may still retain, nor prefer ourselves before him, because we believe ourselves free from the like. Remember what St. Gregory says, that he who has these kinds of imperfections may for all this be perfect; and that, on the contrary, we may still be very imperfect, though we are free from them. This consideration will assist us not only to keep ourselves in the spirit of humility, but will also preserve in us those sentiments of charity we ought to have for our brother, and prevent our judging rashly of him.

———o———

CHAPTER XVII.

A Confirmation of the aforesaid Doctrine by Examples.

We read in the lives of the holy fathers, that Abbot Isaac, going one day to an assembly of religious in the desert, had a bad opinion of a certain person amongst them, and upon something he had seen amiss in him, judged him worthy of correction ; and having returned again to his cell, he there found an angel standing at the door who opposed his entrance. The holy abbot asking the cause, the angel answered, that our Lord had sent him to know what he would have done with that religious he had already condemned within himself. The abbot presently acknowledged his fault, and prostrated himself to ask pardon of God ; the angel told him that God pardoned him ; but for the future he should be more cautious in making himself judge of his brethren, and condemning those whom God, the universal Judge, had not condemned.

St. Gregory relates that Cassius, who was Bishop of Narni, and a very great servant of God, had naturally a red and fiery face, and that Totila, King of the Goths, having seen him, judged this to proceed from a great excess of drinking. But God took upon him the defence of his servant, by permitting the devil to seize upon an officer who bore Totila's sword, and to torment him on the spot in a most dreadful manner, in sight of all present, till at last being carried to the saint, he delivered him, by making the sign of the cross upon him ; whereupon Totila changed his opinion, and had ever after a very great esteem for the holy bishop.

In the lives of the holy fathers, mention is made of two holy religious, who lived together in very great union, and to whom God had granted this favour, that by a certain exterior mark, each one of them knew the interior state of his companion's soul. It happened that one of them going abroad upon a Friday morning, saw a religious eat something, and presently condemning him in his heart, without examining at all the necessity he might have of eating so soon, said to him in a chiding tone,— " What makes you eat thus early on a Friday morning ?" When he returned to his cell, his companion not perceiving the mark of the grace of God he was wont to have upon him, was extremely troubled thereat, and sighing, asked him what he had done since he went abroad ? I know not, answered the other, that I have done anything amiss. Whereupon the other desired him to think well, whether he had not spoken some idle word ; whereupon he remembered what he had said to the religious he met, and the rash judgment he had made ; but the mark of grace he was wont to have appeared not again, till after he and his companion had both fasted a fortnight together to expiate this fault.

In the Chronicles of St. Francis a wonderful vision is related, with which our Lord favoured one of the companions of this saint, called brother Leo. He saw one day a great company of the religious of his order, glittering with light and splendour, amongst whom there was one more bright than all the rest, out of whose eyes there came forth such resplendent rays that the good brother was not able to behold their lustre. He asked who that person was, and it was answered him, that he was blessed Bernard of Quintaval, the first companion of St. Francis ; and that the light which darted from his eyes proceeded from the good interpretation he gave to whatsoever he saw in his neighbour, and also, because he believed all the world better than himself. When he met the poor, all covered with rags and patches, " These," says he to himself, "observe poverty far better than I ;" and judged thus advantageously of them, as if in effect their poverty had been as voluntary as his own. When he saw persons of quality richly clad, he said in his heart—"Perhaps these perform greater austerities than I do; perhaps they wear a hair cloth underneath their rich clothes, and secretly chastise their flesh, and that it is to avoid being surprised with vainglory that they clothe themselves after this manner." In fine, of every object, he always looked at the most pleasing side, and the innocency of his eyes deserved to have such a recompense of glory bestowed upon them by God himself. Behold here after what manner we must judge of our neighbour ; and this is that spirit which St. Dorotheus requires of us, when he says, if entering into your brother's cell, you find it all in disorder, think that he is so absorbed in God, that he minds not exterior things ; but if, on the other hand, you perceive he takes care to keep it very neat and handsome, believe his interior is like the exterior.

The same Chronicles make mention also that St. Francis, going to preach in some parts of Italy, met in his way a poor man, who lay very sick ; and being touched with commiseration, he spoke to his companion with great signs of tenderness and compassion. Whereupon the good religious making this answer, that in truth he appeared very poor, but perhaps he was rich in desires, as even the rich men of the world were, St. Francis presently gave him a severe reprehension for this rash judgment he made, and told him that if he desired to remain with him, he must perform the penance he should impose upon him, for the fault committed against his neighbour. The good brother sub-mitting with great humility to what he should please to order, St. Francis commanded him to cast himself naked at the beggar's feet, to ask his pardon for the rash judgment he had made of him, and to beg that he would intercede by his prayers to God for him ; and the good religious presently obeyed the saint.

We read also in another part of the same Chronicles, that the same saint having for a time almost quite lost his sight by too much weeping, sought to divert himself with one of the religious, called brother Bernard, who had a very particular talent for discoursing of God, and with whom he sometimes spent whole nights in spiritual discourse. Having once sought him at his cell, which was in a remote part of the mountain ; and having called out to him, that he would come to a poor blind man ; brother Bernard was at the same time so wholly absorbed in God, that not hearing him call, he made no answer to the saint, who, having called him a second time, and finding he made no answer, returned very sad, murmuring within himself that brother Bernard would not admit him into his cell. In this anxiety of mind he went a little before his companion ; and having put himself in prayer, he heard a voice that said : "Why

art thou troubled? Is it reasonable that man should quit God
for a creature? Brother Bernard was with me when thou
calledst him, and could not go to meet thee, nor answer thee, because he did not hear thee." The saint getting up at these
words, returned presently to brother Bernard to accuse himself
of his fault, and to beg penance of him for it; and finding him
just risen from his prayer, he cast himself at his feet, declaring
the suspicion he had harboured of him, and the reprehension he
had received from God for it; commanding him, in virtue of
holy obedience, to punish him in the manner he should declare
to him. But brother Bernard, fearing that the saint, according
to his custom, should put himself upon some very extraordinary
humiliation, and desirous to find out some means to excuse
himself, answered: that he would do whatsoever he should
ordain, upon condition he would also perform what he should
desire of him. The saint, who was always readier to obey than
to command, easily accepted the condition; wherefore having
laid himself all along the ground upon his back, I command you,
says he, in virtue of holy obedience, that you first put one of
your feet upon my mouth, and then the other upon my neck,
and that you pass three times over me in this manner, saying:
"Remain here upon the ground, you wretched son of Peter
Bernardone; whence couldst thou conceive so much pride in
thyself, who art worthy to be contemned by all?" Brother
Bernard understanding what the saint required of him, doubted
for some time whether he should comply with his orders; but in
fine, both to observe obedience, and through fear of afflicting
him, he resolved to do it, but executed his commands with all
respect possible. After this the saint having bid him now to
command him, in his turn, what he thought fit: I command you
then, says the good religious, that, as often as we shall hereafter
be together, you severely reprehend me for my faults. The
saint, who had a very great veneration for brother Bernard, by
reason of his extraordinary virtue, was so mortified by the command he had received, that to avoid the occasion of reprehending
so holy a man, he durst not afterwards remain any long time in
his company, but every time he went to visit and to speak with
him of God, he took leave of him as soon as the conference
ended.

Surius relates that St. Arsenius being sick, a priest of a
neighbouring parish came to visit him, together with an ancient
hermit, and finding him lying upon a carpet and his head resting

upon a pillow, the hermit, who knew not what Arsenius had been in the world, was scandalized to see a man so famed for sanctity treat himself so tenderly, and with so much delicacy. The priest, who was a prudent man, perceived this very well, and taking him aside, I pray, father, tell me, says he, what kind of life you led before you embraced this of an hermit? The old man having answered him, that being always very poor, his life was much the same as that he lived at present. Know, then, replied the priest, that Arsenius, before he came to the desert, was a man of high rank, very rich, and a great favourite of the emperor, to whom he had also been tutor. Consider he has forsaken all these things to embrace poverty and humility, and judge, if in a man, who had all his life been brought up in abundance and pleasures, and who, at present, is worn out with age and sickness, it is too great nicety and delicacy to have a pillow and carpet to lie upon. The hermit, who with astonishment had heard all that he said, presently conceived a very high esteem of the sanctity of Arsenius, and a very great confusion for the rash judgment he had made of him.

Cassian relates, that the abbot Macquetius, desirous all should know that they ought not to judge hardly of any one, said, that heretofore he had taken the liberty to judge his neighbour, and that particularly in three things. The first was, that a certain religious man, having a swelling in his mouth, had recourse to surgeons, in order to get ease from his pain, he had ascribed this to impatience in him, and to a want of courage. The second was, that some others feeling themselves obliged to abate something of that austerity they lived in, and to make use of coverlets made of goats' hair, either to lie upon, or to cover themselves with, he had believed there was a certain delicacy or softness herein, that was contrary to the spirit of their profession. The third was, that, seeing religious bless the oil they gave to secular persons, who out of devotion had desired it, he thought there was a great deal of presumption in this, and a certain kind of ostentation of sanctity. But he confessed that God, in punishment of these rash judgments, let him afterwards be subject to the very same things, for which he had condemned others. For first—a swelling happening in his mouth, he was forced, by the command of his superiors, to cause himself to be dressed by surgeons; and this very incommodity forced him to make use of a coverlet; and in fine, yielding to the importunity of many secular persons, he had also given them oil which he had blessed.

In conclusion, he advised all his religious to take example by him, and to judge none lest they should be subjected, as he was, to the same things for which he had reprehended his brethren.

The abbot Anastasius, who flourished at the time of the sixth General Council, relates, that in the monastery of Mount Sinai, where he was abbot, there was a certain religious, who so easily dispensed with himself in the spiritual exercises of the community, that he passed amongst them for none of the most exemplary and religious persons. He fell sick, and the abbot perceiving that, instead of being troubled at the approach of death, he on the contrary, expressed a very great joy, severely reprehended him, saying; he was astonished that he who had lived after so loose a manner should have so great a peace and tranquillity of mind, when he was upon the point of rendering an account of all his defects to God. I pray, father, be not at all astonished, answered he. Our Lord has sent an angel to me with an assurance of my salvation, and that he will keep his word, and the promise he has given, when he said: "Judge not and you shall not be judged; condemn not, and you shall not be condemned." (Luke vi. 37.) For though it is very true, that either for want of health, or out of tepidity, I have not exactly complied with the duties of the community, yet I have never failed patiently to suffer the ill-treatment I have received for it, and to pardon it with all my heart; and have been so far from judging ill of those that thus treated me, that I have always taken it in good part, and judged well of all their words and actions : and this is what at present gives me so much joy and comfort.

——o——

CHAPTER XVIII.

Of these Sorts of particular Attachments and Friendships which are to be reprehended.

WE have hitherto treated of the attachments and friendships that are made by charity, now we will treat of such as are contrary both to the spirit of charity and religion. St. Basil, in his Monastical Constitutions, says, there ought to be a very great union amongst religious, but all sorts of particular ties or friendships between two or three persons only must be retrenched; for how holy soever these ties may appear, nevertheless this strict union with one particular person is a formal disunion from the rest. He takes notice also of this yet more precisely in his first sermon on the institution of monks, where, descending more to particulars, he says—" If any one be found, who upon any account whatsoever, either of kindred or anything else, seems to have a greater tie or affection to one religious than to another, he must be punished, as one who does an injury to common charity." He adds the reason also in the same place, and still more expressly in the following sermon, where he explains the injury we do in this to a religious community :— " Whoever," says he, " loves one of his brothers better than another, shows by this alone that he does not perfectly love the rest ; and consequently offends others, and injures the whole community." But if God feels so sensibly an offence given to an individual, that he says, " Whosoever touches him, touches the apple of his eye," how displeased will he be at the offence given a whole community ? Wherefore, the same saint expressly forbids all his religious to have any particular tie, affection, or familiarity, more with one than another, "through fear of giving any one the least occasion of offence," and desires that in imitation of the goodness of God, " who makes the sun shine as well upon the good as the bad, and makes it rain upon the just and unjust" (Matt. v. 45), we should have an equal charity for all our brethren. He adds, that these particular friendships in religion are an everlasting seed of envy, suspicions, distrusts, and enmities ; and give occasion of divisions, cabals, and secret assemblies ; which are the destruction and ruin of religion. For in them one discovers his particular designs ; another speaks of the judgments he has made; a third opens the subjects of his complaints ; a fourth reveals those secrets he should not speak of. In these cabals also they murmur, speak ill of one another, betray all sorts of defects, and spare not even the superior himself ; and by a most unhappy contagion they presently communicate all that is bad one to another. In fine, by means of these friendships, rules are often violated, and to follow the inclinations of friends, many things are done contrary to duty and profession.

St. Ephrem, speaking of this subject, says, that "these kinds of friendships and ties do great prejudice to the soul." (Eph. tom. i. p. 51.) We must, therefore, avoid them with a great deal of care, and act upon this principle—that in religion we must have no particular friend with whom we entertain any familiarities prejudicial to the community. Our friendships must be all spiritual ; they must not be founded upon flesh and blood, or any other human foundation, but on God alone ; and as we are all of us children of God, and brethren of Jesus Christ, we must also equally love one another, without suffering our hearts, which must be attached to none but God, to have any particular affection for creatures. We read in the Chronicles of the Order of St. Francis, that a holy religious, named brother John de Luques, very carefully avoided all sorts of conversations and particular friendships; and that another religious, who had a great esteem and affection for him, and had profited very much by his conversation, complaining one day to him of his manner of proceeding, and asking him why he behaved so coldly towards his friends? It is for your good I do so, answered the servant of God, for thereby I shall be more useful to those who also desire my good, for all particular friendships are so many amusements, that serve only to divert me from God, and consequently do harm to us both.

———o———

CHAPTER XIX.

Of the second Sort of Friendship we ought to avoid.

THERE is another sort of particular friendship, which differs from the former, because it has a different end; but it is often no less hurtful to the good of a community, and to union and fraternal charity, than the former: and it is when any one, desirous to distinguish himself from the rest of the community, to be advanced in employments, and to be held in consideration and esteem, does unite and join himself to those whom he thinks able to assist him to compass his ends. Cassian says that the great distempers of the soul are, like those of the body, formed by degrees. Wherefore I shall now explain how this distemper forms itself in the mind of a young religious; how it enters in, and by what means it afterwards comes to corrupt and destroy him. A religious, for example, having ended his noviceship, wherein by the mercy of God he had considerably advanced in virtue, leaves it with a high esteem and great affection for spiritual things; and thence is sent to a college to complete his studies. From this time, beginning, by means of the friendship he has contracted, to relent in his spiritual exercises, he either lops off part of them, or performs them through custom and negligently; and hence he gathers no fruit whereby to advance himself in perfection. Thus he continues for some time; and as, on the one hand, spiritual arms are wanting to him, because he discharges his duties of piety so ill, and as, on the other, science puffs him up, it happens that the esteem of human learning and reputation gaining on him daily, and increasing insensibly in him, the love of humility and of virtue decreases. Behold this is the gate through which all disorders commonly enter ; this is that which diverts young religious from the good way they were in ; this is what they cannot take too great precaution against. By little and little they permit the esteem they before had for humility, mortification, obedience, and whatever else regards their spiritual progress, to be destroyed in them. They are daily more and more prejudiced in favour of learning, and of the advantage there is in making themselves learned men—and think it is by this means they must advance and recommend themselves. Afterwards they begin to take measures for attaining the end they propose to themselves ; they do all they can to gain the esteem of men of letters; they think only of defending their *thesis* well, and of coming off with honour on every other public occasion—and aspiring only to things of this sort, they eternally seek occasions of distinguishing themselves, and perhaps of depreciating the knowledge and learning of their competitors. In fine, going still farther, they endeavour to gain the good will of those they imagine may be able to serve them, and maintain their esteem with superiors, and they contract with them particular friendships, for no other reason than to gain reputation, to advance themselves, and to secure their interest on all occasions.

This is one of the most pernicious friendships that can happen in religious, and which is most opposite to union and fraternal charity. For what can we imagine to be worse than to see ambition creep into our society ? And to hear it said, that every one must take care of himself, and help himself the best he can ; and that we must govern ourselves in religion as in the world, and consequently must exert ourselves, unless we wish to be forgotten and contemned ? God forbid that such discourses as these should ever be held amongst us, and that we should in religion meet with such unhappy persons, who begin to instil such poison as this into the hearts of such as live in all candour and innocency. Sentiments of this kind are far from the spirit of our institute, and from religious simplicity. And it is for this reason that St. Ignatius so strongly recommends to us in his Constitutions, to apply ourselves to solid virtues and spiritual things, and to set greater value on them than on human learning and all other endowments, either natural or acquired. Suffer not yourself, therefore, to be seduced by the old serpent, or to be persuaded that in breaking God's commandments, and in eating the forbidden fruit, "you shall become as gods." (Gen. iii. 5.) Take care of believing that hereby you shall be honoured and esteemed, though he tell you so, and promise you ever so much, for he lies as he is wont to do; and if you believe him, you will in the end gain nothing but contempt and confusion. But if you follow the path of virtue, and prefer your spiritual advancement before all other things, you will profit in every respect, because God then pouring down upon you in great abundance all sorts of his graces and favours, you will be better able to acquire at the same time both the perfections you aspire to, and the honour also you look not after. And thus you will be esteemed both by God and man.

We have a great example of this in the third Book of Kings. Here holy Scripture relates that God, appearing to Solomon, bid him ask whatsoever he desired, and he should obtain it. And Solomon having desired the spirit of wisdom and prudence, "this petition," says the Scripture, " so pleased our Lord, that he said to Solomon, because you have begged of me a thing of this nature, and have not asked a long life, nor great riches, nor the death of your enemies, but have only desired wisdom, to be the better able to judge, I grant you what you have desired, I give you the spirit of wisdom and understanding, in such a manner that none ever had the like before you, nor shall any person ever have the same after you." (3 Kings iii. 10.) But what makes particularly for our purpose is, that the choice which Solomon made in asking wisdom was so pleasing to God that he not only gave him the wisdom he asked, but also other advantages he had not demanded. " I give you also," says he, " other things that you did not ask of me, as riches and glory, and these after so ample a manner, that not any king in past ages ever equalled you." (Ibid.) Thus will God deal with you, if you make a good choice—if you apply yourself to ask true wisdom, that is to say, such virtues as are truly Christian and religious, he will assuredly grant them; because you cannot prefer a more pleasing petition. And he will also do more yet, and procure that you shall be esteemed and honoured by your brethren. We see every day by experience that those that take this way do equally gain both the grace of God and the esteem of men. For the promise of Jesus Christ is infallible : " He who humbles himself shall be exalted." (Luke xiv. 11.) The more you shall debase your-self the more you shall be exalted; and glory is annexed to sanctity of life as a shadow is to the body, which shadow never follows you more than when you fly from it. On the contrary, those who nourish and puff themselves up with vainglory, feed like chameleons upon the air, for the more they seek the esteem and approbation of men the less they obtain it. And it will happen that even what they thought would have contributed most to their elevation will serve only to debase them, and they will fall into disgrace by the same means whereby they hoped to have gained esteem and reputation. For they will be presently looked upon as proud and restless persons, who are good for nothing but to trouble the peace of religion; and then entirely to cover them with confusion, nothing more will be wanting than to cut them off as rotten members, lest they should infect and corrupt others.

But to return to our subject, I say, that as in religion we must divest ourselves entirely of all kind of ambition; so we must also divest ourselves of all particular friendships, contracted upon this account. We must not tie our affections to any one in particular, nor give occasion to have it said amongst us: " For my part, I am for Paul—for mine, I am for Apollo, and I am for Cephas." (1 Cor. i. 12.) We must not be for one person more than for another; we must adhere to the superior alone—it is with him alone we must unite; as for any other particular union, we are to admit of no such thing. In religion we have nothing to do with godfathers and protectors; we need not pay court to any one, nor insinuate ourselves into their favour by flatteries; and as we did not enter religion to make our fortune but to work out our salvation, so in it we ought to have no other object than this in view. Be a good religious, apply yourself seriously to your duty, and to that which regards the end for which you have renounced and forsaken the world, and you will have no business but what belongs to God and his service. It is only these that can taste peace and comfort in religion. To content and repose the others are strangers, and they themselves feel and confess the truth of these assertions. A religious ought to be ashamed to pass for a man that seeks patrons, and endeavours to insinuate himself into the grace or favour of this or that person, to be supported by them; for it is a sign he feels himself so weak, that he cannot without aid support himself. A house that wants a prop is in danger of falling, and a tree that must be upheld by poles, shows that it is very weak, and has not yet taken deep root in the earth : even so, if you take supporters—if you want people to hold you up, you are still very weak, and very ill grounded in virtue, or even in religion itself. Wherefore Father Acquiviva, general of our society, particularly admonishes our young religious not to seek the support or protection of the seniors ; and recommends particularly to these not to take upon them the protection of any person in particular. The seniors, he says, should not wish to be paid court to by those, who stand in need of their interest— nor should they offer their services or protection to others—nor are they to deem it an honour to have many applications made to them : and if but few applications of the sort are made to them, they are not to be offended, nor to imagine, that it is through arrogance or reserve the brothers have neglected or slighted them. They are not upon this account to find fault with a brother, who is so far from being culpable therein, that he deserves to be praised for it, as hereby he evinces that he has that detachment and liberty of spirit, which we ought to have in religion. To act otherwise, is to live like worldlings, and to govern ourselves by the maxims of the world. But if any one complains of you on this account, he will complain that you are virtuous, and that adhering to the rules of a good religious, you avoid what is opposite to the duties of religion ; and God grant they may never have any reason but this to complain of your conduct.

———o———

CHAPTER XX.

Of a third Sort of Union very prejudicial to Religion.

THE third sort of connexion and friendship is still worse than the two former, and far more contrary to union and fraternal charity. By this tie or union, we understand that which is made, when any particular persons cabal together, to change the institute of religion and such other things as are piously ordained and established therein. What St. Bernard says upon these words of the Canticles: "The children of my mother fought against me" (Cant. i. 5), is very much to our purpose. The spouse by these words makes her complaint, in the name of the Church, of the evil she had suffered from her children : " It is not," says this great saint, " that she did not very well remember all that the Jews, Gentiles and tyrants had made her suffer, but that which she most of all lamented, and which touched her most sensibly, and what she believed was with the greatest care imaginable to be avoided, was the internal and domestic war, as I may call it." (Bern. Serm. 29. Sup. Cant.) We must apply this to the religion into which we are entered ; and which being one of the principal members of the Church, walks in her footsteps. " My dear children," says he, " are revolted and risen up against me—those I have with so much care and pains brought up and instructed, that they may fight against the world, and convert souls to God, have turned against myself the arms I gave them ; and have used them to make war against me their mother." Behold now and judge, if this be not a very sensible affliction. But as sensible as it is, yet we must not wonder that such sorts of persecutions as these happen to us, because St. Francis, in his life-time, saw his order exposed to the same difficulty : and the holy Catholic Church, even while the apostles lived, was not exempted from the like persecution of her own children, who rose up against her, and by their errors endeavoured to destroy her. The members must follow their head, which is Jesus Christ ; he has led the way, through labours and sufferings ; therefore they must follow through the same ; in order that, as gold is refined in the crucible, so the elect may be tried and purified by labours and persecutions. " It is necessary," says St. Paul, " that there should be heresies to the end that those of sound principles may be the better known amongst you." (1 Cor. xi. 19.) " It is necessary," says Jesus Christ, "that scandal should happen ; but woe be to those, who are the cause thereof." (Matt. xviii. 7.)

St. Basil speaks very severely against these sorts of leagues. "If any of you," says he, " voluntarily separating yourselves from others, make particular cabals in the society you are of, these sorts of connexions are very pernicious : it is a sedition, it is a division ; and we cannot but form a bad opinion of those who are united after this manner ; because, under the pretence of reformation, under the shadow of the good and profit of religion, they think upon nothing else but how to change its rules, and derange the order of its first institute." (Eas. in Const. Mon. c. 30.) Wherefore, he should have such as these first of all admonished and reprehended in secret ; and afterwards in presence of all their brethren, as the gospel directs us ; but if all this, says he, does no good, " look upon them as heathens and publicans." (Matt. xviii. 17.) Separate them totally from the rest, as persons infected with the plague, lest the contagion spread itself, and infect the whole body. It is the very same that St. Ignatius ordains in his Constitutions ; it is also conformable to St. Paul's spirit, who, writing to the Galatians, says, " God grant that those who trouble you may be cut off from amongst you." (Ad. Gal. v. 12.)

It is so very easy a thing to know how great this evil is, of which we now speak, and how prejudicial it is to religion, that it is sufficient only to set it before you, to let you see its enormity, and it seems not worth our while to trouble ourselves by enlarging on it. But because this matter is of very great importance, I will dwell somewhat longer upon it, and state those reasons which I believe will be sufficient, not only to excite in us a detestation of these sorts of unions, but also make us conceive just horror of them, and always strengthen and urge us more and more to maintain our institute. Religious societies are not the invention of men ; but are an effect of the particular disposition and order of the divine Providence; so that the things which are instituted, whether they be for the conservation, or for the increase of these societies, must not be regarded as human inventions only ; and as the project of some particular person, but looked upon as the projects and inventions of God himself. For when God chose St. Francis, St. Dominick, St. Ignatius, and other saints to be founders of those orders which they instituted ; he, at the same time, inspired them to adopt the means they made use of to establish them. He has done also more than this; for " the works of God are always perfect." (Deut. xxxii. 4); which his institutions would not be, if they should be wanting in anything ; and because the founders, of themselves, could not foresee all things that should happen, he, therefore, discovered to them whatsoever he saw necessary for the maintaining, and for the spiritual progress of their orders. Thus we see in the Life of St. Ignatius, that to a very important point that concerned the establishment of our society, he made the same answer that father James Laynez had separately made on the same subject. This clearly proves that in more essential matters, which are as the foundation of our institute, God, who is the first author, has revealed or inspired all things to him, whom he has chosen to be our head, and chief founder after himself. The precaution St. Ignatius used in framing the Constitution which he left in writing, is also a proof of this truth. For how many prayers, how many tears must each word have cost him, since, in order to determine only, whether or not professed houses should have any particular rents allotted for the fabric of their churches, we read that for forty days together he offered his mass, and gave himself to more fervent prayer, than he was ordinarily accustomed to make? By this it is easy to perceive, that he concerted these his Constitutions with God— that he consulted with him, and that he received from him great lights, both to choose and resolve upon what was most pleasing to the divine majesty. But though what I have said is sufficient to prove our proposition, " yet we have still a greater testimony than this" (John v. 36), and lest it be objected that we give testimony of ourselves, it is good that I propose it here ; because it is of very great consequence to have this principle well established.

The rule of St. Francis, not having been yet approved of, but by the living voice of Innocent the III., and this great saint being about to write it and present it to the Pope, to obtain a bull for its confirmation, retired with two of his companions to a mountain near Reate. Fasting there on bread and water for forty days, and persevering day and night in continual prayer, he composed his rule, according to what God pleased to inspire him with ; and having brought it with him from the mountain, he gave it to keep to brother Elias, his vicar-general, a very prudent and experienced man as to worldly affairs. Elias finding it was founded upon too great a contempt of temporal things, and too excessive a poverty and humility, lost it on purpose, in order that this rule not having been confirmed, another should be made more consonant to his own ideas. St. Francis, who desired rather to follow the will of God than of man, and who would not rely upon the dictates of worldly wisdom, returned to the same mountain to make another retreat for forty days, and to obtain by his fasting and prayer that God would vouchsafe to inspire him anew to compose another rule. Brother Elias, knowing his intention, resolved to render it abortive ; and for this purpose, having assembled some of the chief and ablest men of their order, he told them that the saint would make so strict a rule that it would be impossible to observe it. Whereupon they begged of him, that as vicar-general he would go to the saint from them, and let him know that if he persisted in making too strict a rule, they would not feel themselves at all obliged to observe it. But brother Elias not daring to charge himself singly with such a commission, offered to go along with the rest; so all of them going together towards the mountain, when they came to it, and approached near the cell where the saint was in prayer, brother Elias called him. The saint, who knew him by his voice, went out to him, and perceiving so many religious assembled together, asked him what they desired? They are, answered Elias, the chief members of the order, who hearing you are about to make a new rule, and fearing you should make it too austere, they come to protest to you, that if it be so, you may keep it yourself, but as for them, they will not follow it. The saint, hearing these words, cast himself upon his knees, and lifting up his eyes to heaven, cried out; Lord, did 1 not tell you that these would not believe me? And presently they heard a voice from heaven that said : " Francis, there is nothing in the rule that is yours, all that is in it is mine, and I will have it observed, according to the letter, according to the letter, according to the letter, without gloss, without gloss, without gloss. I know what human weakness is capable of, and what succours I can and will give; let those that will not observe this rule quit your order, and permit others to observe it." Whereupon, St. Francis turning himself towards the religious; Have you heard, saye he, have you heard, have you heard? Do you desire that I should obtain of God, to have the words repeated again to you? Hereupon, brother Elias and all the rest, trembling, stunned, and full of confusion for their fault, returned without making any reply. The saint applied himself again to compose his rule, and made the very same with that which our Lord had before revealed to him; which being done, he carried it to Honorius the III. The pope said he found it very hard to be put in practice, by reason of the great austerity and extreme poverty to which it obliged. Holy Father, replied the saint, I have not put in this whole rule so much as one word of my own, but it is Jesus Christ who has composed it; and as it comes from him who alone knows all that is necessary for the salvation of souls, for the advantage of religious, and for the maintenance of this order; and that he only sees, as present to him, all things that shall happen to his Church in general, and to this order in particular; I ought not consequently to change anything he has once established. The pope being then touched by a particular inspiration from heaven, confirmed the saint's rule, and caused a bull to be issued for that end. Behold, then, in what manner

God is wont to prescribe to founders of religious, all that they are to insert into their rules. It is after this manner also that he prescribed the same to St. Ignatius, of which also we have a more authentic proof than of the preceding; because there are two apostolical bulls of Gregory the XIII., which make particular mention thereof. After having, in the one and the other, first declared what our institute is, and particularly those things that seemed to have the greatest difficulty; and because he knew several persons, and some of the society, would stick at them, he expressly adds, in formal terms; " Wherefore the same Ignatius, by Divine inspiration, judged that it was after this manner he ought to distribute the body of the society, into its members, its orders, and its degrees." Can any one more clearly declare, that St. Ignatius was inspired by God himself, in forming the rule ?

This being then supposed, let us come now to the point, and discuss it with those, who make these particular assemblies to alter the institute of our society, and such things as are established in it by our holy founder. Do you not perceive that it is an insupportable pride for an individual to presume of himself, out of his own judgment, to go so far as to dare to say, that the way St. Ignatius has marked out in his Constitutions is not good ? It were better we should take another way that seems to me far better. Without doubt, it would be a difficult thing to frame to one's self so great a folly as this. However, we shall comprehend this still more fully, if we reflect on a folly of another description. Heresy is, without doubt, one of the greatest evils, and the most enormous of sins, that can happen in the Church of God. I do not at present examine, whether there can be any other sin greater than this ; because it is certain that to hate God formally is still a crime of greater magnitude. But since it is very seldom that we meet with such sorts of sins as these amongst men ; and that in hell only such sins are committed ; I say, that of all sins to which man is commonly subject, heresy, whereby we separate ourselves still from the Church, is looked upon to be the greatest. And, without doubt, this opinion is very well grounded. For to say nothing of heresies overturning the foundation of the Christian religion, which is faith ; and without repeating many other reasons which are alleged ; it is not a pride that even passes imagination, to have so high an idea of ourselves, and to be so obstinate in our own opinion, that we inconsiderately believe whatever comes once into our heads to be a greater truth than all that is decided by the Roman Church; approved of by so many Councils ; received by so many persons, eminent both for sanctity and learning ; cemented together by the blood of so many thousand martyrs : and confirméd by so great a number of miracles? What folly can be greater than this—what pride more insupportable, and what greater blindness can one conceive, than to prefer before all these, either our own visions or fancies, or those of Luther ; and in good earnest to believe an apostate, a vicious man, a lewd, debauched, sacrilegious wretch, before God? We do very nigh as bad as this when we prefer our own particular judgment before his, whom God has chosen to be the head and founder of our society ; and persuade ourselves, that the way we have found out is far better than that which was inspired and revealed by God himself. This presumption is truly diabolical. What! Has God hid from St. Ignatius, whom he made choice of to be the head and founder of the society, the way which ought to be taken to govern it well, and has he discovered it to *you?* Is not this alone sufficient to convince you that it is a deceit and illusion of the devil, who would make use of you as his instrument to wage war against the society, of which he is an irreconcileable enemy, and to disturb the peace and union thereof, as he made use of an heretic to disturb the peace of the Church? But you, perhaps, will tell me you desire nothing else but the reform thereof. You deceive yourself ; and the devil, as father of lies, blinds you with a specious pretence. It is not a will or desire to reform the society, but it is a will to destroy and ruin it, and let what I say be well taken notice of ; for it is no exaggeration, but a very clear and infallible truth. We reform a religion, when, after it is fallen from its first institution, we endeavour to restore it to the purity of its first origin, and cause the rules that the founder left in it to be carefully observed. This kind of reform is holy and commendable, and has been practised with success in many orders, which have been re-established in the innocency and vigour of their origin. But to change the ancient institute—to quit the path which our founder, inspired by God, has marked out to us, and a desire to take a different one ; this is to wish not to reform an order, but to destroy and overthrow it ; this is to build upon its ruins, one after your own mode and fancy, as brother Elias pretended to do, in the order of St. Francis. A thought of this kind cannot come from the spirit of God, and can be nothing else but the effect and suggestion of the devil.

When in the Council of Trent they spoke of reforming religious orders, and when thereupon they had made some very profitable and holy decrees; Father James Laynez, general of our society, represented to the fathers of the council, that these decrees seemed not to have place in what regarded the society of Jesus, because it was a new body distinguished from other ancient bodies of religion, and had a mode of government peculiar to itself, and approved of also by the Holy See; that by the mercy of God, the society had not at all fallen off from the exact performance of its rule and first institute : and, therefore, if they comprehend it in these decrees, it would not be to reform, but to destroy it. The Council was pleased with and approved of this reason, and thereupon made this answer, which is set down in the twenty-fifth session in these terms :—" Nevertheless, the intention of the Council, by these decrees, is not to introduce any innovation into the religion of clerks of the society of Jesus, nor to hinder it from continuing to serve God and the Church according to their pious institute, approved of by the Holy See." (Conc. Trid. sess. xxv. decret. de refor. reg. c. 16.) Wherefore the Council of Trent would not undertake to change anything in the conduct and institution that God had prescribed the society of Jesus, by means of St. Ignatius ; but on the contrary, would hereby approve and confirm it as the Holy See had done. And will *you*, from some human reasons and considerations that you have admitted into your mind—will you meddle yourself so far as to wish to alter and change our constitutions ?

Marcellus Cervinus, Cardinal of the Holy Cross, who afterwards was Pope by the name of Marcellus II., esteemed our institute, and respected our founder, far otherwise indeed. A little before he was exalted to the supreme dignity, he had a grave debate with Father Olavius, one of the most famous divines of the society, upon that part of our constitutions, which forbids any one whomsoever amongst us to receive any dignity out of the society, if not obliged by the Pope to accept of it, by a precept of obedience under pain of sin. The general himself has no such power to oblige them to it, but by order from his Holiness ; and this constitution is so religiously observed amongst us, that every one who is professed makes a particular vow to observe it. The Cardinal therefore asserted, that the society would do a greater service to God's Church by giving it good bishops, than by giving it good preachers and confessors; and that the advantage derivable therefrom would be so much greater, inasmuch as the power of a bishop is greater than that of a simple priest. He also stated on this subject many other reasons, to which Father Olavius answered in substance—that the greatest service the society could do the Church was to maintain itself in the humility and purity of its first institute, thereby to be the longer capable to serve it well. And when, in fine, the Cardinal, judging his own reasons to be of greater weight, persisted still in his opinion :—If my reasons, replied Father Olavius, are not sufficient to convince and move you to change your opinion, at least the sole authority of our founder is sufficient to convince and make me believe that his opinion was far the better. I now yield to you, replied the Cardinal ; and confess you are right ; for though it seems to me that I have reason on my side, yet the authority of your founder is of far greater weight on this occasion, than all the reasons in the world; or to say better, it is reason itself, that would have it to be as it is. For, since he was chosen by God to establish in his Church such an order as yours is, to extend and spread itself over the whole world for the good of souls ; and to govern it with so much wisdom and prudence as it does ; it is also to be presumed, and it cannot be thought otherwise, but that God himself revealed to him the manner he would be served by this order, and after what manner it ought to be conserved and maintained. Now, if so great a person as this had so great a submission, even against the lights of his own reason ; with how much juster title ought we, who are religious, and consequently children of obedience, to submit our judgments, when we perceive anything to be established by the rule or constitutions of the society; or that it was ordained by him, whom God gave us for our head and founder ? But since all his constitutions and all his rules are also approved of and confirmed by all Popes since his time, and by the sacred Council of Trent ; and the society, since we have observed them, has received so many graces and favours from God, and produced such great fruits in the conversion of souls, who is there, after all this, that dare have the confidence or boldness, even so much as in thought, to desire to alter the statutes and constitutions ? " Transgress not," says the Wise Man, " the ancient bounds that your forefathers have established." (Prov. xxii. 28.)

But that the presumption of those that may form or entertain a thought of such an undertaking, may still be more crushed by what is the greatest and most inviolable authority in the Church, Gregory the XIII. in his bull, which begins *ascendente domino,* after having approved of and confirmed the new institute of the society, established the form for their conduct, and some other points in particular, which might give occasion to some disquiet spirits to make difficulties, expressly forbids all persons, of what condition or pre-eminence soever (under pain of excommunication *Latæ Sententiæ*, and incapacity or privation of office or benefice, *ipso facto*, without any declaration), to impugn or contradict even the least thing in the institute or constitutions of the society, either directly or indirectly, whether under colour or pretence of dispute, or from a desire to inform themselves more clearly of the truth. And in case any doubt should present itself upon this subject he declares that his will is, they should consult the Holy See, or the general of the society, or such as the general shall upon this account appoint ; and that no other person must intermeddle therein. Gregory the XIV. ordained the self-same thing in a more ample manner, and in more forcible and express terms, in his bull which he issued upon the same subject, which begins, *Ecclesiæ Catholicæ*. " Let them consider," says he, " that it would be a very great prejudice to spiritual discipline and perfection, and a great disturbance to religious orders, if that which was piously appointed by their founders, and very often received and approved of by the same religious orders, in their general congregations, and which is moreover established and confirmed by the Holy See, should, under any pretence whatsoever, either come to be quite changed, or the least altered, or impugned. Wherefore we, renewing the constitutions of our predecessor Gregory the XIII., and confirming all the privileges contained therein, by these presents, in virtue of holy obedience, do forbid all persons of what state or condition soever, whether ecclesiastic, secular, or religious, and even all of the same society of Jesus, under pain of excommunication *Latæ Sententiæ*, and of exclusion from all sorts of charges or ecclesiastical dignities, and privation of active and passive voice, which penalties are *ipso facto* incurred without any farther intimation : wherefore we reserve the decision and appeal to the Holy and Apostolical See, either to impugn or contradict anything of the institute, constitutions, or decrees of the society, either directly or indirectly, under colour of any greater good, shadow of zeal, or any other pretence whatsoever." To all this he yet adds a more essential point, which is, that he also forbids to propose anything, or any memorial upon this matter or subject, to add, diminish, or change anything in the institute, unless to the Pope himself, either immediately, or by his Nuncio, or Apostolical Legate ; or to the general, or to a general congregation of the society. Paul the V. in a bull published in the year 1606, for the confirmation of the institute, and the privileges of the society, makes particular mention of these two constitutions of Gregory the XIII. and Gregory the XIV., and approves and confirms anew what is contained in them. It is easy, then, to perceive how all things are founded and cemented together in the society, since neither any religious of the same company, nor any other religious; nor in fine, any clerk or layman, of what state, dignity, condition, or pre-eminence soever, may or can undertake to alter anything, without incurring instantly these penalties, together with the "greater excommunication." Let us now conclude with the same words wherewith St. Paul ends the second epistle to the Corinthians; "For the rest, brethren, rejoice, be perfect, encourage one another, be all of one mind and will, live in peace, and the God of peace and love will eternally remain with you." (2 Cor. xiii. 11.)

———o———

THE FIFTH TREATISE.

---o---

---o---

CHAPTER I.

Of the Merit and Excellency of Prayer.

ST. JOHN, in the fifth and eighth chapters of the Apocalypse, expresses admirably well the excellency and merit of prayer. He says in the eighth, "that there came an angel, and stood before the altar, having in his hand a thurible of gold, to whom was given a great quantity of incense, to the end he should offer up the prayers of all the saints upon the altar of God, which was before the throne of God ; and the smoke of the incense of the prayers raised itself from the hand of the angel to the presence of God." (Apoc. viii. 3, 4.) St. Chrysostom, speaking of this passage, tells us, that one proof of the merit of prayer is, that in the Holy Scripture it alone is compared to thymiama, which was a composition of incense of many admirable perfumes. For as the smell of well composed thymiama is very delicious ; so prayer also, when well made, is very acceptable to God, and gives great joy to the angels and inhabitants of the heavenly Jerusalem. Wherefore, St. John, speaking of the twenty-four elders, relates, " that they had golden cups, full of perfumes, which are prayers of saints." (Ibid. v. 8.) So that, says St. Austin, " what can be more excellent than prayer ? what is there more profitable in this life ? what more sweet to the mind ? and what in our whole religion more sublime ?" (Tract. de mis. tom. 10.) St. Gregory of Nice is of the same opinion, and says, " that of all things which we esteem in this life, none ought to be preferred before prayer." (De or. Dom.)

St. Bernard, the better, to make us understand the merit of it, says, that though it is certain the angels are often effectually (but invisibly) present with God's servants, to defend them from the deceits and ambushes of the devil, and more and more to raise their thoughts and desires to God ; yet nevertheless they more par-

ticularly favour us with this presence, when we are employed in
prayed. He proves this proposition by divers passages of
Scripture; as by this, " I will sing hymns to thee in the presence
of the angels" (Ps. cxxxvii. 2); and " the princes joining themselves to the musicians went before in the middle of young
damsels, who played upon timbrels." (Ps. lxvii. 26.) Understanding by the princes, the angels, who joined themselves to
those that are in prayer, as appears by these words of the angel
to Tobias : " When you were in prayer, and poured forth tears,
I offered your prayers to our Lord." (Tob. xii. 12.) We see by
this last passage, that prayers scarce go out of the mouth of him
that prays, but presently the angels who are by us receive and
present them to God. St. Hilary also assures us, that " the
angels preside at the prayers of the faithful, and continually
offer them to God." (Hil. can. 18 in Matt.) So that when we
are in prayer, we are surrounded by angels, and in effect we
perform their office; exercising at present what we must
practise with them for an eternity, Wherefore they already
look upon us as their companions, and beforehand beholding us
as in heaven, filling up the places of their fallen companions,
favour us more particularly during our prayer than at other
times.

St. Chrysostom, speaking of the excellency of prayer, and desirous to let us see its advantages, says ; " Consider to what a
degree of happiness you are raised by prayer, and how great
prerogatives are attributed to it. You thereby speak to God
himself, you entertain yourself and converse with Jesus Christ;
you therein desire what pleases you, and you ask whatsoever you
desire." (Lib. 2. de oran. Deum.) There is no tongue that is sufficiently able to express, of how great a value this communication
is, which man has with God, and what profit it brings along
with it. We see in the world, that those who ordinarily keep
company with wise and prudent persons, reform and improve
their minds and judgments by their conversation. If therefore
they become virtuous by frequenting the company of virtuous
persons : what advantage may we not believe we gain by a frequent communication with God ? " Approach him," says the
Royal Prophet, " and you shall be enlightened." (Ps. xxxiii. 7.)
In effect, with what lights, with what knowledge must we not
needs be filled? What good, what happiness, must we not
assuredly gain, by this kind of commerce? wherefore St. Chrysostom assures us, that nothing can so much contribute to our

progress in virtue, as frequent prayer, and conversation with God; so that by this means the heart of man comes to be filled and to relish the most noble thoughts; and is enabled to raise itself above all earthly things, and in fine, becomes spiritual and holy, and in a manner transforms itself into God.

———o———

CHAPTER II.

Of the Necessity of Prayer.

WE have but too much experience of the need we have of prayer; and would to God that this experience were less frequent than it is. But man being subject to so many frailties, finding himself encompassed by so many enemies, and standing in need of so many things, both for soul and body, ought to have a continual recourse to God, to implore his assistance, and to tell him, as King Josaphat did, when the Ammonites and Moabites were come against him; " Lord, in this extremity to which I am reduced, not knowing what to do, the only remedy I have left is to cast up my eyes unto thee." (2 Paral. xx. 11.) I know not, says Pope Celestine, speaking of the importance of prayer, how to say anything better to you upon this subject, than what Zosimus my predecessor said of it—" When is it that we stand not in need of the Divine assistance? Wherefore in all sorts of occasions and affairs let us always have recourse to his protection; for it would be an insupportable pride, should man dare to presume to do, or to think he can do anything of himself." (Celest. i. c. 9. cont. Pelag.)

St. Thomas, intending to prove the necessity of prayer, gives an excellent and most essential reason for it, which is taken from the doctrine of the holy fathers, and has this truth for its foundation—" That what God has from all eternity determined to give unto souls, he gives it in time, by the means and help of prayer." For as it is the order and disposition of the divine Providence, that mankind should increase and multiply by means of marriage; that the earth should become fruitful by the care that is taken to cultivate it; and lastly, that it is with materials, and by the help of workmen, that buildings are raised; so it is, says he, the order and disposition of the divine Providence, that by the means and help of prayer souls should obtain many graces and lights. For this reason Jesus Christ said in the gospel; "Ask, and it shall be given you; seek, and you shall find; knock, and it shall be opened unto you : because whosoever asks, receives; who searches, finds ; and the door is opened to him that knocks." (Matt. vii. 7, 8.) It is therefore very easy to perceive the need we have of having frequent recourse to prayer ; because it is the channel through which Jesus Christ communicates his favours, assists us in our necessities, and enriches us with his treasures. Some saints say, that it is like a chain of gold, fastened to heaven, and hanging down to the very earth, whereby the graces of God descend to us, and we are elevated and raised up unto him. We may also say, that it is Jacob's ladder, that reaches from earth to heaven, by which the angels continually ascend and descend, to carry our petitions to God, and bring back his blessings unto us. St. Austin calls it the *key of heaven* (Aug. Serm. 226) : and in effect, it is the key that opens all the gates, and by which all the coffers of the celestial treasures are opened. He says also, " that as natural food nourishes the body, so the word of God and prayer maintain and nourish the soul."

But one of the chief things that still shows what esteem we ought to have for prayer is, that it becomes a very efficacious means to regulate our life, and helps us to surmount all those obstacles we are to meet with in the way of virtue. Wherefore the saints say, that the whole conduct of our life depends upon it ; and that our life is well or ill regulated, according to our discharging well or ill the duty of prayer. " He who knows how to pray as he should, knows also how to live as he should" (Hom. iv. ex. 50), says St. Austin. And St. Climachus relates that a servant of God told him the following words, which are very remarkable—That in the morning he knew very well how the rest of the day would pass ; that is to say, that when he had made his prayer well, all the rest corresponded to this good beginning ; and when he had not well acquitted himself of this duty, he was disturbed and deranged all the day after. It is the same in order to our whole life in general ; for we often experience that when we have made our prayer well, we find ourselves in greater peace and tranquillity than ordinary ; and we feel the joy of our souls, as well as our holy resolutions, increased in us. But as soon as we come to relent, or neglect our prayer, we presently perceive the truth of what St. Bonaventure says, that " without that, religion is dry, imperfect, and near its ruin." (Bon. de prog. rel. c. 7.) Tepidity presently comes upon us, the soul grows weak by little and little, and insensibly loses the fervour and courage it before had for spiritual and heavenly things—its good desires and holy resolutions are dissipated and vanish away, and bad inclinations come in their place, and are again enkindled. In fine, we come at last to please ourselves in nothing but vain and unprofitable things, and to be transported with joy for such as are even ridiculous; and also fall into a shameful negligence. And what is still worse, the desire of vainglory, anger, envy, ambition, and those other dangerous inclinations which we thought we had overcome and extinguished, begin to revive anew in our hearts, and bring disorder and corruption along with them.

The abbot Nilus says that prayer ought to be the looking-glass of a religious; it is in this we daily must at leisure take a view of ourselves, both to know our faults, and the means to mend them. It is in this mirror that we consider the resplendent virtues of Jesus Christ, wherewith to adorn and embellish our souls. "A religious," says St. Francis, "ought to desire nothing so much as to obtain the grace and gift of prayer; for without this, we cannot hope to be able to make any progress in God's service; and with it, there is nothing we may not promise ourselves." (Hist. min. c. 7.) It is for this reason that St. Thomas of Aquin said, that a religious without prayer was like a soldier without arms in time of battle. And St. Thomas of Villanova was wont to say, that prayer was to the soul, as natural heat is to the stomach. And as without heat it is impossible that food should do a man any good, or even that he should be able to live; whereas by means of this heat, he converts it into good juice and nourishment, which disperse itself throughout the whole body, to furnish each part thereof with sufficient strength to perform its functions—in like manner our spiritual life cannot exist without prayer; for it is prayer that gives us strength to fulfil all the obligations of our profession, and to profit as we should do of even the most troublesome accidents—it is this that makes us easily digest all injuries and hardships, and makes them become easy and supportable; so that there is nothing can happen to a soul, of which it will not make its profit and advantage. In fine, if we make good use of prayer, we shall therein find a remedy for all our faults, and an assured help and means to maintain ourselves in the vigour and purity of religion. For if perhaps you have not been faithful in the observance of your rules; if you have given yourself too much liberty in anything; or in fine, if you feel some passions, which were before in a manner asleep, that begin to awake anew in you; have recourse presently to prayer, and by the grace of God you will therein find a speedy and efficacious remedy for all things. But if you should fall into remissness and tepidity during your prayer, it is still to prayer that you must have recourse; for it is this that will restore you that first state of fervour in which you were before. For prayer has proper remedies for all evils, and even for those faults that are committed in it. Wherefore they make a very just comparsion, who say, that prayer is to a spiritual life, what the hand is to the body. The hand serves for an instrument and help to the whole body in general, and to itself in particular; it labours for nourishment, for clothing, and all the other necessities of the body; and also labours for itself. For if the hand be indisposed, it is the hand that dresses it; if the hand be dirty, it is the hand that washes it; and if the hand be cold, it is the hand that warms itself again. In fine, as the hand does all things, so prayer does the same.

——o——

CHAPTER III.

Of the Obligations we have unto God, for bestowing upon us so easy, so excellent, and so necessary a Thing, as Prayer is.

PRAYER being a thing of so great value in itself, and of which we have so much need; it is just we should consider how much we are obliged to God for having rendered it so easy, that we may attend to it at any time, or in any place whatsoever. "It is in my power," says David, "to pray continually to our Lord, who has given me a being." (Ps. xli. 9.) The gates of God's mercy are never shut; they are always open to the whole world. We find him always at leisure, always well disposed to do good; and sometimes he even importunes us to ask graces and favours of him. Some make a most pious reflection hereupon, and say that if God should give audience only once a month, to all those that desired to speak with him, and give them a kind and favourable hearing; and moreover should bestow several graces on them; this without doubt would be what we could not sufficiently esteem: because we should repute it a greater happiness than if an earthly king should honour us after this manner. Now if this be so, what esteem ought we not to have of the offer which God makes us, by inviting us to address ourselves to him, not only once a month, but every day, and even every hour of the day? "At night, in the morning, and at noon, I will recount my afflictions to our Lord," says the Royal Prophet, "I will make my wants known unto him, and he will hear me." (Ps. liv. 18.) God is not like men, who reject the petitions offered to them; because by giving, he does not impoverish himself, as they do. A man has so much the less, by how much he bestows upon another; for he deprives himself of that which he gives, and grows the poorer by his liberality. It is for this reason, then, that men so easily refuse what is asked; and if they give once or twice with a good will, they grow angry the third time, and give nothing at all; or if they do, it is in so disobliging a manner, that thereby they take away all assurance or confidence of asking them anything another time. "But God," says the apostle, "is always rich, for such as implore his assistance" (Rom. x. 12): because he makes himself not the poorer by giving, nor is weary of being importuned, nor of seeing a great many continually employed in begging of him. He is rich enough to satisfy the whole world, and is able to enrich every one, without being in the least poorer than he was before. But as the fund of his riches is infinite, the source of his mercy is also inexhaustible. So that, as on the one hand, he abounds in all things to succour our necessities, so, on the other, he has a constant will to assist us, and would have us recur unto him. It is therefore very reasonable that we should have a most grateful sense of so great a favour; and that making our profit of so ample a permission, we should endeavour continually to apply ourselves to prayer. For as St. Austin says, upon these words of the Psalmist, "Blessed be our Lord, who has not deprived me of the spirit of prayer, nor of his mercy" (Ps. xv. 19), we must believe for certain, that if God withdraws not from us the spirit of prayer, he will neither withdraw that of his mercy; wherefore that his mercy may never forsake us, let us never leave off the exercise of prayer.

———o———

CHAPTER IV.

Of two Sorts of Mental Prayer.

To say nothing at present of vocal prayer, though the practice thereof is very holy, and much in use in the Church, we will now speak of mental prayer only, as the apostle St. Paul designed to do, when writing to the Corinthians, he said, "I will pray in spirit; I will pray within my heart; I will sing the praises of God in my mind, I will sing within my heart." (1 Cor. xiv. 15.) There are two sorts of mental prayer; the one is common and easy, the other is extraordinary and sublime; which, to speak with those who are most versed in it, we do not so much form in ourselves, as the Holy Ghost forms it in us. It is of this the great Areopagite speaks, when he says, that his master Hierotheus " suffered divine things" (Dion. c. ii. de div. nom.); that is, he was so absorbed in God, that what he did of himself was less his own production, than an impression which he received from God himself. There is a very great difference between these two sorts of prayer, for the first may in some sort be taught by words, but it is not the same of the second, because there are no words able to express it. " And no one can know what it is but who receives it" (Apoc. ii. 17), and experiences it in himself ; nor even then can he be able to express, or even know what it is, nor how it is made ; and it is this which Cassian very well takes notice of, when he relates that most heavenly and divine sentence of St. Anthony, very fit to our purpose : " that prayer is not wholly perfect, when he that prays has not entirely lost the knowledge of himself, or comprehends what he says." (Cass. Coll. ix. Ab. Isac. c. 31.) This kind of prayer is so high and sublime, that it does not permit us to think of ourselves, or to make any reflection upon what we then suffer. It sometimes happens, that a man has his mind so taken up and absorbed in some business, that he forgets himself. He knows not where he is, nor of what he thinks. It is the same in this kind of perfect prayer : wherein man is so ravished and lost in God, that he thinks no more of himself—he knows neither the things that pass within his heart, nor after what manner they pass; and without observing any method, without thinking of passing from one point to another, he loses himself in profound meditation. This is what happened to St. Anthony, of which Cassian makes mention, that oftentimes having gone to prayer overnight, he remained in it till the next day ; when the light falling upon his eyes, he complained that the sun rose too soon, to deprive him of those lights, which God interiorly communicated unto him. St. Bernard speaking of this kind of prayer, says, " that we very seldom find it, and when we do, its stay is very short." (Bern. ser. in Dom.) So that how long time soever it lasts, it seems to us only to have lasted a moment. And St.

Austin experiencing in himself the effect it produces; " Lord," says he, " you cause certain feelings of tenderness to arise in my mind, that are very extraordinary ; and I know no sweetness so great as this : but should it still increase, I know not what would happen." (Conf. lib. x. c. 40.)

But this last kind of prayer has also its subdivisions and degrees. St. Bernard makes mention of three, with reference to those words of the beloved in the Canticles : " Eat, my friends, drink, and be inebriated, my dearest ones." (Cant. v. 1.) He says, in the first place, *eat*, then *drink*, and last of all *inebriate yourselves* : and by these different gradations he leads us to that kind, which is most sublime of all ; though, nevertheless, all are most perfect, and are in us rather a suffering, or an effect of divine impression, than an action, or an effect that came from our own motion. Sometimes the gardener, to water his garden, is obliged to draw water out of a well by the strength of his arms; and sometimes with folded arms he sees the showers of heaven fall sweetly upon it, and water the earth, without his doing anything but letting it rain, or at most giving a little fall to the water that it may go in greater abundance to the root of the trees, that thereby they may bear the more fruit. The same may be said of the two first kinds of mental prayer we before spoke of ; the one is got by the care and diligence with which, by the mercy of God, we apply ourselves to it ; the other is purely given us, without our contributing anything to it. The first requires great labour and application ; and yet all that does not entirely satisfy you. But the second leads you to a table, that God himself has prepared for you, without your having taken any pains at all; a table very delicious, and a table abounding with all sorts of heavenly dainties. It is this which is signified by those words of the spouse : " The king has led me into his cellar, and replenished me with his love." (Cant. ii. 4.) And that which our Lord promises in Isaiah, when he says, " I will rejoice them in the house of prayer." (Is. lvi. 7.)

This last sort of prayer is a particular gift of God—a gift which he bestows upon whom he pleases, sometimes as a recompense for services done him, and for mortifications suffered for love of him ; at other times gratis, and as a free gift, without any regard to what is past. For it is a favour which proceeds from his pure liberality, and consequently he communicates it to whom he pleases, according to his own words in the gospel : " Is it not lawful for me to do what I please ?" (Matt. xx. 15.) And in fine, it is a thing so far above the reach and conception of the human mind, that we can never teach nor comprehend it. Wherefore, it is not without reason, that they have blamed and forbid certain authors, who imagining that there were rules to be found, whereby a man might infallibly be rendered a contemplative, would take upon them to teach what no one can ever apprehend, and reduce to art what is entirely above art and nature. Gerson, in a book he composed against Rusbrochius, severely reprehends him for this, and reproaches him for having separated the flower from the stalk. For, as a flower that we have pulled and carried in our hands fades presently, and loses its beauty ; so the most sublime things that God communicates interiorly to a soul, which he elevates to that high degree of contemplation, lose their beauty and lustre, when, taking them out of their true place, we will undertake to explain and communicate them to others. After all, these mysterious analogies, these transformations of the soul, this silence of all the faculties, this annihilation, this immediate union, this depth of Thaulerus, and all the other terms of this nature, what would they express ? Can any one comprehend anything by them ? For my own part, I must frankly confess I do not. There is therefore this difference between divine science and other sciences, as some say very well ; that in other sciences, before you can learn them, you must learn their terms, till you perfectly possess and are master of it. In others, the theory precedes the practice ; in this the practice goes before the theory.

I say still farther, that not only we cannot express what this prayer is, nor teach it to others ; but even no one must seek to raise himself unto it, if God himself does not elevate him thereunto. For otherwise it would be a thought of pride and presumption, whereby we should deserve to be deprived of the grace of ordinary prayer, and remain interiorly dry. " He has led me," says the spouse, " into his cellar" (Cant. i. 4) ; and this mode of acting which God adopts, this entrance which he gives to a soul, to inebriate it with the wine of his love, is a particular grace, and a special privilege, which he accords only to whom he pleases. Even the spouse herself enters not till her beloved takes her by the hand, and leads her in ; she dares not of herself take the liberty of kissing his lips ; she is too bashful and reserved to undertake so bold an enterprise as this : she begs this favour, "O that he would bestow upon me a kiss of his mouth !" (Ibid. i. 1.) As if she would say, says St. Bernard, as for me I cannot by my own

VOL. I.   R strength elevate myself to so high a perfection of love, to so glorious an union, to so sublime a contemplation, if he himself bestows not this favour upon me. It is, therefore, from him, and from his pure liberality, that we must expect such a grace and favour as this is—it is his goodness and bounty alone that must elevate us to the honour of kissing his mouth, to such a manner of prayer, to so sublime a contemplation, so far above our reach ; it is not what we are able to acquire of ourselves—and by ourselves we can neither learn it, nor must or can teach it to others.

——o——

CHAPTER V.

An Explanation of two Sorts of Prayer, taken from Holy Scripture.

THE two sorts of prayer, we are at present to take notice of, are clearly marked out by the Holy Scripture, when it says, that " the wise," that is, " the just man, will from break of day deliver up his heart to watch to our Lord who has made him, and will pray in the presence of the most High." (Ecclus. xxxix. 6.) The Scripture first speaks of the ordinary sort of prayer, and mentions the morning, as a time most proper for prayer ; which it takes notice of in divers other places. " I will present myself before you in the morning" (Ps. v. 5) ; " I made haste and I cried." (Ibid. cxviii. 147.) " My eyes have prevented the sun, that I might meditate upon your words." (Ibid. cxlviii.) " I sought you from the dawn of the day." (Ps. lxii. 1.) The Scripture says, that " the just man gave up his heart to watch;" to show that we must not be drowsy in prayer, or be present in body only, whilst our heart is wholly employed, or intent upon other things. It is this that the saints call " sleepiness, or drowsiness of heart ;" which is a very great obstacle to prayer ; for when the heart is thus heavy, it cannot remain in that respect it should have, while conversing with God. But what is it, that imprints this respect in the mind of the just? It is the reflection it makes, " that they are in the presence of our Lord who has made them, and that they pray before the most High !" And this reflection causes them to recollect themselves, and to have a most particular attention to all that he says. See from what has been said, with what preparation and attention we must apply ourselves to prayer. Let us now see also, what that prayer is, which the just man makes, when, as the Scripture says, " He will open his mouth in prayer, he will pray to obtain pardon of his sins." (Ecclus. xxxix. 7.) That is to say, he will be confounded for his sins; he will repent of them; and will make a firm purpose to fall no more into them. This is properly the prayer we must make, to deplore our sins and imperfections, and implore God's mercy. It is not sufficient to say, I have made a general confession in the beginning of my conversion, and then employed many days in lamenting, and weeping bitterly for my sins, and repenting of them. For it is not just that because we have confessed them, we should forget them; on the contrary, we must endeavour to set them always before our eyes, as the Royal Prophet did, according to his own words: "My sin is always against me" (Ps. l. 5); that is to say, always *before* me, and continually present in my mind.

St. Bernard, in his comments on those words of the Canticles, "Our bed is all covered with flowers" (Bern. Ser. lvi. sup. Cant. i. 15): Your bed, says he, which is your heart, is still very foul; it is still infected with the stench of vice, and the bad habits you brought with you from the world; and notwithstanding this, you venture to invite your spouse to lodge in it, you pretend to raise yourself to contemplation, and to the most sublime exercises of union with God; as if you had already acquired the highest degree of Christian perfection. Let your first study be to cleanse and wash your bed with your tears, as the Psalmist tells us he did " I will every night wash my bed with my tears." (Ps. vi. 7.) Think also how to adorn it with the flowers of all sorts of virtues; and then you may, like the spouse, invite your beloved to come and repose himself therein. Employ yourself in the mean time, in kissing his feet; in humbling yourself by true repentance for your sins; in kissing his hands, and offering to him all the good you can do; and in endeavouring to receive from him the grace of solid and true virtue. But as for approaching his mouth, to wit, this sublime and perfect union, attend and wait till God himself vouchsafes to elevate you thereunto. An ancient religious of the society of Jesus, very much esteemed for his piety, and very well versed in spirituality, remained, as it is said, for twenty years in the purgative way; and shall we, who have scarce begun, presently grow weary of it, and desire to pass to the exercises of the love of God? The foundations ought to be very deep and strong before we venture to raise so high a building. But that which is very particular in the exercise of the knowledge and sorrow for our faults is, that besides divers other advantages we draw from thence, of which we shall speak hereafter, there is not a more special remedy, nor a better preservative to keep us from falling into sin than this. For he who continually employs himself in detesting his sins ; who is always covered with a holy confusion for those he has committed ; and who continually exercises himself in a profound sorrow for having offended God, will be far from committing any new offence.   On the contrary, the saints take notice that the fall of some who seemed much devoted to contemplation and a spiritual life, has happened from a bare neglect of reflecting upon their past sins and imperfections, that they might give themselves to more sublime and pleasing exercises, and from the confidence they had in their own strength ; so that in not accustoming themselves to stand upon their guard, as they should have done, it caused them in the end miserably to run into disorders ; for by forgetting too soon their own baseness, they were on a sudden precipitated from the height of perfection, to which they thought themselves arrived.   Wherefore we must for a long time reduce our prayer to a sorrow for our sins ; and this must be our only exercise, till our Lord pleases to take us by the hand, and say unto us : " Friend, ascend higher." (Luke xiv. 10.)

But let us at present take notice, what that so sublime and particular prayer is, of which God bestows the grace when he pleases.   The holy Scripture informs what it is in these terms : " If our Lord pleases, he will fill him with the spirit of understanding."   (Ecc. xxxix. 8.)   It says, "If our Lord pleases ;" because it is not anything that is due unto us, or that he has any obligation to give us, but is a pure grace, and a pure effect of his liberality.   " If he pleases," then, when you are in prayer, that a sudden light from heaven should come upon you, and as it were a flash of lightning should strike upon the eyes of your understanding—you will then in a moment conceive that which you could not before comprehend.   Behold here what properly that gift of prayer is, of which we speak.   For how many times might the same thing have represented itself unto you, without your being touched, or at all struck with it ?   The reason, therefore, why the holy Scripture calls this " the spirit of understanding," is, because it gives us a knowledge of things, by a simple apprehension, without any assistance of the imagination, or any pains at all of the understanding.   It is in this manner, that a man who loves painting, meeting with an excellent piece, stops on a sudden, and fixes his eyes on it, without speaking a word ; and takes so much pleasure in viewing it that he can scarce take off his eyes. But to say better, this state in which a soul finds itself resembles that of the blessed in heaven. Beatitude consists in beholding and contemplating God ; and when we shall be placed in glory, we shall be entirely absorbed in this sole view of him for an eternity ; and thereby enjoy an everlasting felicity, without the least assistance from our reason, or without ever having any regard to ourselves. On the contrary, we shall continually be transported with a new joy—we shall find every moment a new relish in this heavenly manna ; and it will seem to us that we continually enjoy a new subject of admiration. The same thing happens in this kind of sublime and perfect prayer, which they call contemplation. When God pleases to elevate a soul thereunto, it never ceases to contemplate ; and without helping itself by discourse, or ever suffering any irksomeness, it perpetually has its sight fixed upon God. But the Scripture takes notice, that God will not only bestow this grace upon the just, but that he will also fill them with it ; because this grace is so abounding, that not being able to contain itself within so narrow a vessel, as the heart of man is, it necessarily overflows ; and, therefore, the Scripture presently adds, "That the discourses of him who is replenished with wisdom, will fall like showers from his mouth, and in prayer he will confess and praise our Lord." (Ecclus. xxxix. 9.) It is then that colloquies are made with God—when the soul is thus illuminated by this heavenly light, and elevated above its own force, then is the proper time to converse and entertain itself with God. Wherefore St. Ignatius admonishes us to " enter into these colloquies, when we find ourselves moved thereunto by an interior impulse of grace." (Lib. Exer. Spir. in Repet. 1 & 2.) These words deserve to be very well taken notice of, and do in substance inform us, that when we have applied all the powers of our soul to meditation, when our heart begins to be inflamed, and we feel ourselves secretly incited to treat familiarly with God ; it is then that we must have a very great trust and confidence in him ; since this is the proper time to ask and obtain all things. For the prayer that proceeds from the heart touched and inflamed by God, in this manner, is that which he hearkens unto ; because, as St. Austin says, when he himself moves us to ask anything of him, it is a sign that he intends to grant it. Behold then that kind of prayer that is so sublime, which God gives to whom he pleases, according to these words: " If our Lord pleases, he will fill him with the spirit of knowledge and understanding."

But if our Lord is not pleased to favour us with such a singular grace as this is, we must not therefore, as St. Bernard says, afflict ourselves, and lose courage; but rest contented with the practice of virtue, and believe ourselves happy, as long as God is pleased to keep us in his grace, and preserve us from falling into sin. "God grant," says this great saint, "that I may enjoy peace of soul, the sweetness and repose of a good conscience, the spirit of mercy, simplicity, and charity towards my neighbour, the gift of rejoicing with those that rejoice, and of weeping with those that weep, and I desire nothing else. All the rest I leave to the apostles and to men truly apostolical." (Bern. ser. xlviii. sup. Cant.) "The tops of the mountains serve for a retreat to stags, but the holes of the rocks for the irchens." (Ps. ciii. 18.) Let therefore these mountains of contemplation, that are so high and elevated, serve for a fit refuge to such as with an extraordinary facility run towards perfection; as for me, who am a sinner, and covered with the thorns of my sins, I will retire into the corner-stone of the rock, which is Jesus Christ; I will hide myself in his wounds; I will wash away my faults with his precious blood; and this shall be my prayer. If then so great a saint as St. Bernard contented himself with the practice of virtues, and a lively sorrow for his sins; and leaves this other kind of more sublime prayer for apostolical men, to whom it shall please God to communicate so signal a favour; it is very just that we also should content ourselves with the same —that we should apply ourselves to prayer, only to bewail our sins; to mortify our passions; to root out all our evil habits; and overcome and surmount all those obstacles and impediments that check us in the way of virtue. And as to this other kind of prayer, which is so much above our reach, we must leave it entirely to God to call and elevate us to it, whenever he himself pleases. Moreover, it will be very advantageous diligently to stand upon our guard, when he seems to call us to it; because there are often great abuses herein. We sometimes imagine that we are called to contemplation, because we find a certain sweetness and facility therein; yet, nevertheless, we deceive ourselves, for this is not a call from God, but an enterprise of man; it is an illusion of the devil, who carries you to contemplative life, thereby to withdraw you from the obligations of the active, and to occasion hereby that you fail in the performance both of the one and the other. A great master of a spiritual life says very well: as it would be a great boldness and an extreme imprudence, that a man whom a king had commanded to serve at his table, should presume to sit down without his invitation or permission; so it is also a very great indiscretion to abandon ourselves entirely to the sweet repose of contemplation, if we be not called thereunto by God himself. St. Bonaventure hereupon gives most excellent counsel, and says, that we must exercise ourselves in that which is for our assured profit; such as to get rid of our vicious habits and bad inclinations, and to gain solid virtues. And in this no abuse can be feared; because it is infallibly true, that the more we endeavour to mortify and humble ourselves or to be resigned to the will of God, the more pleasing we shall be to him, and we shall increase our merit in this world, and glory in the next. But the other sublime exercises, and matters so elevated, says the saint, may be deceits and illusions of the devil; because we often think that to come from God, which does not; and we count that a very great matter, which in effect is less than nothing. Wherefore in a spiritual life, we ought rather to choose and apply ourselves to those exercises that are most profitable, and not be carried away by the sweetness we find in them; but esteem them for the profit and advancement we receive thereby; and this opinion is entirely conformable to the general doctrine of saints, as we shall see in the following chapter.

———o———

CHAPTER VI.

In which this Doctrine is more particularly explained and confirmed.

FOR a more full and clear confirmation of this doctrine, the saints and the masters of a spiritual life affirm, that to arrive at this kind of prayer and high contemplation we speak of, we must in the first place apply ourselves to the mortification of our passions—to the laying a solid foundation of all Christian and moral virtues; and to the exercising ourselves a long time in their practice. Without this, say they, it is to no purpose to pretend to apply ourselves to contemplation, and to make a kind of particular profession thereof. " For we must wrestle like Jacob, before we can see God like Israel; and be able to say, I have seen God face to face." You must strive against your passions—you must overcome them together with all your bad habits, before you can attain this intimate union with God. Blosius says, that he who would raise himself to a most eminent degree of the love of God, and notwithstanding, does not carefully endeavour to correct and amend himself, by suppressing his vices, and freeing himself from the inordinate love of creatures, is like a man, who being loaded with iron and lead, and bound hand and foot, would attempt to climb up a high tree. Wherefore we ordinarily take notice, that such as are appointed for the spiritual direction of others, before they speak to them of contemplation, first teach them how to mortify thoroughly their passions, and to accustom themselves to patience, humility, and obedience; so that exercising them continually in all sorts of virtues of the active life of a Christian, they make them get a good and perfect habit therein. Many by not having observed this method, and by being elevated upon a sudden to a contemplative life, without having passed through the active, which ought to precede, find themselves, after many years of prayer, as defective in virtue, as impatient, as choleric, as proud as before; so that if they be in the least hurt, or admonished for any of their defects, they presently show their resentment in impatient and angry words; whereby they discover their imperfection, and the little command they have over themselves. Father Everard Mercurianus, general of the society of Jesus, explains this very well, in a letter he wrote upon this subject. Many, says he, hearing of another more sublime exercise of prayer, and of the love of God, than that which is ordinarily practised, as of certain anagogical acts, and of I know not what silence of all the faculties of the soul, would, more through want of insight and experience, than from any true desire of their spiritual advancement, raise themselves before their time to the exercise of the unitive life, as to the most heroic and most perfect exercise of all others; by means whereof they doubt not but to overcome their vices with less labour and pains, and to acquire virtues with greater facility. But because they are raised to it before their time, they lose a great deal of time therein to no purpose, and are so little advanced, that at the end of many years they find themselves as unmortified in their passions—as much tied to their own will and opinions—as wedded to their own ease as if they had never had any conversation or communication with God. In fine, when the superior would employ them in anything that does not please them, or is not according to their mind, they are as little docile and tractable, as they were the first day they entered religion; and have as great a repugnance as ever to submit their judgment to the will of their superiors. This happens, because they would needs fly before they had wings; and because instead of going in the highway they ought to have kept, they would shorten it, by unadvisedly taking a cross path. For they build not upon the solid foundation of mortifying their passions, and practising of virtues; so that they could do nothing that was substantial; and having built upon the sand, the building they raised with a great deal of pains falls down at the first blast of wind.

But that which still more evidently proves the truth of this doctrine, and how generally it is received, is, that it is commonly followed by all saints, when they establish the three sorts of prayer, according to the three sorts of ways that lead thereunto; which they call purgative, illuminative, and unitive. St. Gregory Nazianzen, and all those who have written of spirituality, have taken this doctrine from St. Denis the Areopagite, and they all agree herein, that before we apply ourselves to this kind of high prayer, which corresponds to the unitive, we ought to apply ourselves to what concerns the purgative and illuminative ways. We must first exercise ourselves a long time in gaining a lively sorrow for our sins; in labouring to root out our vices and bad inclinations; and we must endeavour, by imitating Jesus Christ, to acquire those true virtues that were most conspicuous in his life. But if acting otherwise, and without having travelled this road, we pretend to advance still farther, we shall but labour in vain, and be always deceived. We know that to raise ourselves to the knowledge of higher studies, we must exercise ourselves a long time in the lower; and to come to the top of the ladder, we must ascend by the first steps.

———o———

CHAPTER VII.

Of the ordinary Sort of Mental Prayer.

BUT we shall say no more of this more sublime prayer; since we cannot teach it, nor even explain what it is—nor is it in our power to attain it—neither does God command it; nor will he call us to account about it. We will, at present, therefore, speak of ordinary mental prayer, which after some manner may be taught, and which every one may attain; if they add, as they ought, their own care and endeavours to the counsel of their spiritual director, and to the assistance of God's grace.

Amongst divers other very considerable favours God has bestowed upon the society of Jesus, this is one, that he has given us a form and manner of prayer, confirmed by the Holy See, as may be seen by the bull in the beginning of the spiritual exercises of St. Ignatius. In this bull of Paul the III. it is expressly mentioned, that the Pope after having with great attention very strictly examined these exercises, does not only approve and confirm them, but exhorts all the faithful to make use of them as very profitable. This form of prayer was communicated to St. Ignatius by our Saviour ; and he afterwards communicated the same to us, as he had received it ; wherefore this being so, we have reason to hope, through his mercy, that Christ will bestow many favours upon us, by means of this prayer ; because it is he himself who has prescribed to us the manner thereof. It was by this that he drew to himself our blessed founder and his companions ; it was in the practice of this holy method that he made him conceive the design, and form the model of the society ; and this in the medium or means whereby he has gained so many other souls to Christ. Let us not, therefore, endeavour to go any other way than this ; let us not be attached to any extraordinary manner of prayer, but embracing this we have, let us endeavour to conform ourselves entirely thereunto, and like good children let us imitate the example of our father.

In the exercise of the three powers of the soul, which is the first of the exercises in the book we speak of, St. Ignatius teaches us the method we ought to observe in the rest. First, that having made choice of some spiritual point, we must exercise therein the three powers of our soul, which are the memory, understanding, and will. The memory, in setting before the eyes of our mind the point or mystery which ought to be the subject of our prayer—the understanding, in finding out and considering the things most likely to inflame the will—and finally the will, in producing those acts which depend upon her. The last point is the chief of all, and what we ought to aim at ; as it is the end of meditation and the fruit of all the reflections and discourses of the understanding. For these serve only to move the will to seek what is good, and to avoid what is evil. Moreover, this name of the *exercise* of the three powers of the soul is given to the said *exercise*, because it is the first, wherein this method of praying is taught ; for the three powers of the soul ought no less to be employed in the following exercises than in this.

This form of prayer which our holy founder has taught us, and which is practised in the society, is not singular, nor is it like others, filled with such inventions and novelties as savour of illusion. On the contrary, it is a very common method practised by the ancient fathers, and very conformable to human nature ; which being reasonable, governs itself by reason, and permits itself to be persuaded and convinced ; so that it is not to be doubted but that this manner must consequently be more easy, more secure, and more profitable than any other. For in prayer we must not be like statues, or like persons in an ecstasy ; but by means of thus exercising the powers of our soul, we must draw the spirit of God upon us ; and because he requires a co-operation of his creatures, we must take care to co-operate with him. This is what St. Ignatius teaches in his book of Exercises. All other kinds of prayer, where the discourse of the understanding has no place, where all the operations of the soul remain suspended and in silence ; these kinds of prayer, I say, which are taken out of mystical divinity, ought, commonly speaking, neither to be taught, nor sought after. And those who embrace them, being in a manner still novices, and little versed in spirituality, not having yet obtained a perfect knowledge of themselves, nor a victory over their passions, nor made any great progress in the practice of virtue, are subject to many deceits and illusions. For even when they think themselves much advanced, and to have gained the victory, they will find that their passions, which were only lulled by the charms and sweetness of prayer, will, to their very great danger, awake lively, strong, and violent as ever. Nay more, persons devoted to this wrapped-up and very particular kind of prayer, contract a certain obstinacy of opinion, and yet feel inclined to receive as essential truths the merest illusions and fabrications. It is for this reason St. Ignatius so much suspected this kind of prayer, and said, that those who applied themselves to it were commonly subject to inconveniences of this description.

I say, then, that the first thing we must do in prayer is to represent to ourselves by the help of our memory, the point or mystery which we make the subject of our prayer. Then the understanding must examine this point, review it, and consider all the particulars of it—finally, the will must produce acts according as the understanding has digested the matter which had been proposed to it by the memory. But *this discourse of the understanding*, being the source whence all our acts in prayer flow, and since we can make no act which does not necessarily spring from this our meditation, it follows that we must be particularly careful to make this well. The truth of this proposition is self-evident ; for there is no one that has the least tincture of philosophy, but knows that the will is a blind power, unable to attach itself to anything, unless the understanding guides it. Hence it is a maxim received by all philosophers, " that nothing

can be willed unless it is first known." The will, having of itself
no light, must borrow it from the understanding, which goes before to give it knowledge, and to discover what it ought to love
or hate.   It is this made St. Austin say, that " we may love the
things we never saw, but never those we have not known." (Aug.
lib. x. de Trin.) " No one," says St. Gregosy also, " can love
what he is entirely ignorant of." (Greg. hom. xxxvi. sup. Evan.)
And the reason of this is, that the object of the will being a
known good, we cannot love anything, but because we perceive
it is good, and deserving of love : just as, on the contrary, we do
not hate a thing, or fly from it, but because we conceive it is
bad, and deserving of hatred.   Hence it is, that when we wish
to make a man change his opinion, the mode we adopt to induce
him to give up his own and embrace ours is, to persuade and
convince him by reason, that what he proposes to himself is
not good, and what we propose to him is better and far more
salutary.   It is clear, therefore, that the operation of the understanding is the foundation of all our acts in prayer ; and consequently it is very truly said, that meditation is extremely necessary, as we shall show more particularly in the following
chapters.

————o————

CHAPTER VIII.

Of the necessity of Meditation.

HUGO of St. Victor says, prayer cannot be perfect unless meditation goes before or accompanies it ; and his doctrine is taken
from St. Austin, who says, prayer is tepid without meditation.
The proof of this proposition is easy ; for if we do not exert ourselves to know and examine our weakness and misery, we shall
be deceived and misinformed of our wants ; and hence it will
come to pass that in prayer we will not know what we ought to
ask, nor will we ask it with the requisite earnestness and fervour.
There are many who, from not reflecting upon themselves, and
from being ignorant of their own defects, presume too much upon
themselves, which they would not do if they had a right knowledge of themselves.   And hence, it happens that in prayer they
dwell on everything else, except what is most necessary for them.
If you wish, then, to learn to pray, and to beg of God what you
stand most in need of, employ yourself in considering exactly

your defects and weaknesses. Having obtained perfect knowledge of these, you will then know what you ought to ask of God ; and, as a man who feels himself pressed with necessity or misery, you will beg with all earnestness and fervour what is most proper for you. St. Bernard, speaking of the means of attaining perfection, says, " No one becomes perfect on a sudden, it is by mounting, and not by flying, that we come to the top of the ladder. Let us, therefore, ascend, and let meditation and prayer be the two feet we make use of to do so. For meditation lets us see our wants, and prayer obtains for us relief from God. The one shows us the way, and the other leads to him, and, in fine, meditation makes us clearly discern the dangers that surround us, and prayer makes us happily avoid and escape them." (Ber. serm. i. de S. Andrea.) But St. Austin goes yet farther, and says, that "meditation is the beginning and ground of all good." In effect we cannot consider how good God is in himself ; how good and merciful he is towards us ; how much he loves us, and how much he has done and suffered for us, without feeling ourselves inflamed with love of so good a master. We cannot perceive our faults and infirmities without humbling and conceiving a contempt for ourselves ; we cannot reflect upon our great negligence in the service of God, and the offences we have committed against him, without acknowledging, at the same time, that we deserve all kinds of chastisements. So that it is by the means and help of meditation that the soul comes to enrich herself with all the virtues that can render her agreeable in God's sight.

It is for this reason that the Holy Scriptures so particularly recommend meditation unto us : " Happy is the man," says the Royal Prophet, " who meditates day and night upon the law of our Lord. He shall be like a tree that is planted by the riverside, which brings forth its fruit in due season." (Ps. i. 3.) And in another place he says, " those who reflect upon his promises, show that they seek him with all their heart." (Ps. cxviii. 2.) Or rather, it is that which makes them seek him after this manner. The same prophet, also speaking to God, says, " Give me understanding ; I will make profound reflections upon your law, and I will observe it with all my heart." (Ps. cxviii. 34.) " But if," says he, in another place, " your law had not been the subject of my meditation, perhaps I had not remained in my humility, and I should have thereby perished " (Ps. cxviii. 92); that is to say, as St. Jerome interprets it, I should have remained in those pains and miseries that surrounded me. But that which still ought to give us a high esteem of meditation is, what the saints say of it, to wit, that it is a help to all virtues and good works. " It is," says Gerson, " the sister of spiritual reading ; the nurse of prayer ; the director of good actions, and in fine, the perfection and consummation of all heroic actions."

But to contrast it with the opposite vice, and thereby come to a better knowledge of it, we must know that the neglect of meditation is one of the chief causes of all the evils in the world, according to the words of the Prophet Jeremy: "The whole earth is desolate, because there is no one that makes reflection upon his heart." (Jer. xii. 11.) Would you know why the earth is desolate as to spiritual matters ? It is because there is scarce any one that enters into himself, and ruminates upon the ineffable mysteries of religion and the infinite bounties of God. For who is there that durst be so bold as to commit a sin, if he considered that God died for sin ; and that sin is so great an evil that it required God should become man, in order that by his death he might entirely make satisfaction for sin, even to the rigorous justice of his heavenly Father ? And who would sin, if he considered that one mortal sin is punished with the eternal pains of hell ? Or if he but seriously reflect upon these words—" Go ye cursed into everlasting fire ?" (Matt. xxv. 14.) If we considered seriously the everlasting duration of an unhappy eternity, and that as long as God is God, so long are we to burn in hell, would there be any one so mad or foolish, think you, as, for a moment of pleasure, to expose himself to such eternal torments ? St. Thomas of Aquin said, that he could not comprehend how a person in mortal sin could have any joy or repose. And without doubt the saint had a great deal of reason ; because man is not certain of the enjoyment of any one moment of his life, and yet knows infallibly, that should he die in this state, he would be for ever damned. We read that the most costly viands, and the most enchanting music, could not impart pleasure to Damocles, when he perceived a naked sword which was hanging over his head, and which was fastened by a single hair only ; for he trembled every moment lest the hair should break, and the sword fall, and cause his death. What fear, therefore, ought that man to have who, in the midst of the criminal delights and filthy pleasures of this world, knows that at every instant he is threatened not only with a temporal, but with an eternal death? That all depends upon the slender thread of life : that every

moment he may die suddenly; and that lying down in perfect
health, he may the next morning find himself buried in hell? A
great servant of God said very well upon this subject, that he
thought, in a Christian commonwealth, there ought to be only
two sorts of prisons ; the one for heretics, and the other for fools.
For either we do or do not believe that there is a hell destined
for the eternal punishment of sinners.   If we do not believe it,
we deserve to be cast into the inquisition as heretics ; and if we
believe it, and still remain in sin, we deserve to be ranked amongst
fools and madmen ; as having our understanding vitiated and infected with the greatest folly that can be imagined.   It is certain,
if we practised it as we might, that meditation would serve as a
bridle to restrain us from falling into sin.   It is for this reason
that the devil, who knows the advantage we would derive from
it, endeavours continually, by all sorts of means, to withdraw us
from meditation.   The first thing that the Philistines did to
Samson, after they had made him their prisoner, was to put out
his eyes.   It is the first thing the devil, in like manner, does to
sinners.   If he cannot entirely deprive them of the eyes of faith,
he endeavours at least to deprive them of their use; and to make
them believe in such a manner, as if they believed not at all—
" That seeing they may not see, and hearing they may not hear,
nor understand." (Matt. xiii. 13.)   He hinders them from reflecting upon what they believe ; and makes them think no more
on it than if they believed it not at all, which is all one for the
compassing his ends ; because, since he cannot put out their eyes,
he at least shuts them.   It is the same thing, whether we open
our eyes in the dark, or shut them in the light ; because, in
either case, we see nothing.   But meditation is of so great and
particular importance, that it not only opens the eyes of our
understanding, but also imparts light to discern the most obscure
mysteries of faith.

------o------

CHAPTER IX.

*Of the great Advantage we may derive from Meditation ; and how
we are to perform it.*

IT being very good during prayer to exercise ourselves in producing acts of the will, we will speak of *those* at present.   They
must be founded on reason.   For man being a rational being,

ought to be guided by reason ; and consequentiy it is necessary
that his understanding should be convinced, before his will can
be inflamed.   Wherefore, one of the chief things we should have
in view in meditation, is to disabuse ourselves of the errors of
the world ; to confirm ourselves in the belief of solid truths ; and
firmly to resolve upon what we design to do, and what we intend to avoid.   When a worldly man begins to conform himself
to a more Christian and regular life than ordinary, we are used
to say that he is disabused ; and to be thus disabused is one of
the chief advantages we ought to derive from prayer.   As this
point is of very great importance, so it is also very proper we
should particularly reflect upon it, and, above all, it is necessary
in the beginning, that we apply ourselves to it with great diligence, in order that, by means of an exact discussion of things,
we may be the more confirmed in the belief of essential truths.

Wherefore, that we may be able to gather much fruit from
meditation, we must not make it superficially, in haste, or after
a tepid and languishing manner, but with very great fervour,
and with all possible attention and peace of mind.   Consider
maturely the shortness of life, the frailty and vanity of all things
in the world, the little which will remain with you after death ;
and, thereby, you will soon contemn and undervalue all things
here below, and will fix your heart upon those things that will
last for ever.   Consider seriously, and frequently ponder, how
little solidity there is in the esteem and opinion of men, and how
ridiculous a thing it is, to torment yourself upon this account ;
because their esteem can neither give nor take anything from
you, nor render you either better or worse than you are ; and
by this means, you shall soon come to set no value at all on
them.   In fine, ruminate in like manner upon all other truths ;
and by this means you will, by little and little, disabuse yourself
of the chimeras and errors of the age—you will confirm yourself in true sentiments and principles of piety—you will resolve
upon what will conduce most to your salvation ; and you will
begin to become quite another man, and to lead a life altogether
spiritual.   " The solitary person will sit himself down," says
Jeremias, " and keep silence, because he is lifted above himself."
(Lamen. iii. 28.)   He will find that his heart is become greater
and larger than ordinary ; he will mount in his thoughts even to
heaven itself, contemning all earthly objects, and will say with
St. Paul—" That for love of Jesus Christ he looks upon them
all as hurtful and pernicious, and, in comparison of gaining

Jesus Christ, all other things are but as dirt and ordure." (Phil. iii. 8.)

There is a very great difference between meditating and meditating; between knowing and knowing: for the wise man knows things after one manner, and the ignorant man knows them after another. Wise men know what they are in effect, and ignorant persons know only what they are in appearance. If a simple clown finds a precious stone of great value, he will esteem it for its lustre and exterior beauty; but for nothing else, because he knows not the value of it. But if the same stone falls into the hands of a skilful lapidary, he esteems it not only for its exterior lustre, but because he knows its value. The same difference is found between him who knows how to meditate upon spiritual things, and another that knows it not : he who looks upon things superficially, and regards only the outside, though their exterior beauty pleases him, yet he feels not an ardent desire of them. But he who knows how to examine them as he ought—he who weighs and considers them attentively, will easily undeceive himself and reject such as are of no value, and will resolve to compass what he perceives to be excellent, and knowing perfectly well of how great a value the precious stone is he has found, he makes no account of anything else; "but goes and sells all he is worth to purchase it." (Mat. xiii. 46.)

This difference is pointed out to us by Jesus Christ, in his curing the woman of a bloody flux. Our Saviour went to raise to life the daughter of a prince of the synagogue, and was followed by a great crowd of people, who encompassed and pressed upon him on all sides. This poor woman, who, for twelve years together, had suffered this bloody flux, having spent all she was worth upon doctors to obtain a cure, and finding herself still in a worse condition than ever; seeing the Son of God pass by, the great desire she had to be cured made her break through the crowd with a wonderful faith and confidence : " For she said within herself, if I can come but so near him as to touch his garment, I shall be cured." (Mat. ix. 21.) In fine, she approaches him, touches him, and the flux of blood which she had suffered for many years wonderfully stopped upon a sudden. Whereupon, our Saviour turned about and asked, " who had touched him ?" And St. Peter said, " Master, the throng of people press upon you on all sides, and do you ask who touches you ?" " It is not that," replies our Saviour, " that I would know, but some one has touched me in a far different manner from the rest, for I find that virtue is gone out of me." (Luke viii. 45.) The chief point, then, is to touch Jesus in such a manner as to make him ask, who touched him? For it is nothing to touch him in the throng, as the common people did, and as all the rest of the world do. What is of importance, therefore, in meditation, is, to touch Jesus Christ and his mysteries after such a manner, that we may feel the fruit and virtue of them in ourselves; and for this purpose we must examine things with attention, in detail, and at our leisure. We find neither sweetness nor bitterness in things we give not ourselves time to taste. So the sinner feels not the bitterness of sin, death, judgment, nor of hell itself; because, imitating sick persons, he swallows down the pills whole and entire, lest he should feel their bad taste; he looks upon things only in the gross, and never ruminates upon them. The reason, then, why we relish not the Incarnation, Passion, Resurrection, and all other mysteries, is, because we consider them very superficially, and descend not to particulars, and dive not into them as we should do, by long continued and serious meditation. We taste not a grain of pepper or mustard-seed, if we swallow it whole; but if we break it in pieces with our teeth, it is pungent, it smarts, and even draws tears from our eyes.

—o—

CHAPTER X.

Of other Advantages found in Prayer.

THERE is another advantage in meditation, says St. Thomas— *i.e.*, it causes true devotion to spring up in our hearts, which is of very great importance in a spiritual life; and is very much sought after by those who are on the road of perfection. But this devotion is nothing else than a prompt and ardent disposition in the will to do good. Now this has two causes, the one and chief is from without, and is a God; the other is within us, and is meditation. For meditation is that which, next to the grace of God, most of all warms the heart and the will; and is what produces this so prompt disposition to do virtuous actions. So that true devotion and fervour of spirit consists not in a certain sensible sweetness which some feel and experience in prayer, but in having our will always disposed, and ready to execute

what may any ways conduce to God's glory and service. This is
the devotion which is lasting ; but as for the other, it quickly
vanishes, it being nothing else but an affectionate and sensible
motion that springs up upon a sudden, from a desire we have of
what is amiable—it is only the effect of our natural complexion—
it is found in those who, on every appeal made to their feelings,
express their sensibility by tears ; and scarce do the tears cease
to flow, but their devotion dries up with their tears, so that they
seldom remember the good resolutions they made.   In fine, this
devotion is only a love of tenderness, which is founded upon
sweetness and sensible consolations. While these last, their love
and devotion last also, and so long as they remain careful, punctual, and lovers of silence and retirement.   But when these
sweetnesses fail, all the rest also fail at the same time.   It is not
so with them whose devotion is grounded upon more solid foundations, and who, by the help of exact meditation, are disabused
and convinced as they should be.   Such as these always constantly persevere in virtue, and though they feel no longer the
usual sweetnesses or consolations, yet they remain always the
same ; because reason, which excited these sentiments in them,
always subsists.   A love of this nature is truly a vigorous and
manly love—it is the mark of the true servants of God ; and it
is from this mark, not from sweetness or sensible consolations,
that we must judge, whether we have effectually advanced in
virtue.   The passions of such as seek sensible comforts are, as
some say, like little dogs, that never cease to bark, till you throw
them a piece of bread to appease them ; they are quiet as long
as the consolation lasts, and for a time desire nothing ; but as
soon as the bread of consolation is gone, they begin to bark again;
and it is then that we come to know what each one effectually
is.   They compare also these sweetnesses and consolations to
moveable goods, which are soon worn out and dissipated ; and
solid virtues they compare to immoveable goods, which last
always, and of which consequently we ought to have a greater
esteem.

We shall likewise notice here, what is well known by experience, that, on the one hand, there are some, who receive great
consolations in prayer, and are yet afterwards very weak on occasions, and let themselves be easily overcome by temptations.
And on the other hand we see others, who, on the contrary, find
nothing but aridities in prayer, and know not what consolation
or sweetness is, and yet, notwithstanding, courageously resist

temptations, and behave themselves gloriously in the combat. The true cause of this is, as we have already stated, that the fervour of the one proceeds only from a certain sensible sweetness, which soon passes away, and leaves them dry; and the others have a devotion established upon solid foundations; that is, they have employed and made use of the light of true reason to undeceive and convince themselves ; and thus they remain constant and unshaken in the truths they have embraced, and the resolutions they have taken. One of the best means also with which we may help ourselves to remain constant in the practice of those good purposes we have made in prayer, and to put them the better into execution, is, that we endeavour to recollect the reason which had influenced us to form them; because that which occasioned the first thought will afterwards help us to conserve and put it in practice. From our being fully disabused and convinced by reason, in prayer, there arises this advantage also, that though we afterwards cannot call to mind the particular motives which influenced us to make this resolution, nevertheless we are thereby sufficiently moved to remain more constant therein ; because we know in general, that it was not made without reason ; and this certainly gives us strength to resist temptations, and to persevere in the way of virtue.

It was upon this account, that Gerson set so high a value on meditation, that being asked, what employment was most profitable for religious persons retired in their cells ; and what one of these four—spiritual reading, vocal prayer, manual work, or meditation, was most proper ? He answered, that obedience apart, they could do nothing better than apply themselves to meditation. The reason he gave was this ; that though in time of vocal prayer, or spiritual reading, we feel perhaps more fervour, and as it seems to us, greater profit than in meditation : yet, as soon as we cease to read or speak, our devotion, in like manner, ordinarily ceases. But meditation goes farther, and therefore is more profitable, since it disposes the mind for the future; and therefore he said we must accustom ourselves to it, in order that when our voice or books happen to be wanting, meditation may serve us instead of voice or books ; by which means true devotion will never be wanting or extinguished in us.

CHAPTER XI.

Of the Method to be observed in Prayer, and the advancement to be derived from it.

" My heart is inflamed within me," says the Royal Prophet, " and in my meditation this fire shall be kindled." (Ps. xxxviii. 4.) The method we must follow in prayer is prescribed us in these words, according to the interpretation of the holy fathers, who explain the fire here mentioned to be the fire of charity, and the love of God and of our neighbour, which was kindled in the bowels of the Holy Prophet, by meditating on heavenly things. " My heart," says he, "is inflamed within me ;" behold the effect of prayer. But by what is it inflamed ? By meditation : " And in meditation the fire shall be kindled ;" behold the means, and the instruments that served to light this fire. This manner of meditating, says St. Cyril of Alexandria, is like the striking a piece of steel upon a flint, to extract fire from it. It is therefore by meditation and reflections of the understanding, that we must continually strike the flint of our hard heart, till we extract fire from it, and till we inflame ourselves with the love of God and of our neighbour, and with an ardent desire of humility, mortification, and all other Christian virtues.

Nevertheless, though meditation be so profitable and necessary, yet we must not pass our prayer in reasoning and reflections only ; nor must we dwell and repose upon these ; because otherwise it would rather be study than prayer. But all the meditations we make must serve as so many helps to excite the desire of virtue in our hearts. For the perfection of a Christian and religious life, consists not either in good thoughts, or in the understanding of holy things, but in solid and true virtues ; and particularly in those acts of virtue we produce, which are, as St. Thomas says, the accomplishment of all perfection. It is this, therefore, we must insist upon, and it is to this we ought most apply ourselves in prayer.

On this occasion, it must be a first principle with us, " to apply ourselves to the study of virtue, and this also not only simply to know what virtue is, but to become virtuous." (Gerson sup. Magnif. Alph. 86. Littera D.) If we sew, we must have a needle ; but it is not the needle, but the thread that sews ; and it would be a ridiculous thing, and lost labour, for a man to busy himself all day long in sewing a cloth with a needle alone, without any thread in it. They act, however, nearly in the same manner, who meditate and make many reflections in prayer, without applying themselves to produce acts of the will; as acts of charity, humility, &c. For meditation must be like the needle, it must pass first, but it must carry after it the thread of love, and such affectionate acts as unite the will unto God.

St. Ignatius particularly advertises us of this, and repeats the same very often, in his book of Spiritual Exercises, wherein, after having established the point upon which we are to meditate, and having made some observations of less importance, he presently adds, that we must apply all to ourselves, in order to derive advantage from it. In effect, all the advantage of prayer consists in knowing how to apply to ourselves, and to our own profit, what we meditate on, according to the necessity we have thereof. As the sun, says St. Bernard, heats not all that it enlightens; so meditation, though it teaches us what we must do, does not always excite every one to practise what it teaches; nor does it excite affections in all persons. And as there is a great difference between knowing what great treasures are, and the possessing them; and as it is the possession only, and not the simple knowledge, that makes a man rich; so there is a great difference between knowing God, and between fearing and loving him. It is not the knowledge of what belongs to God, but it is his love and his fear that render us truly wise and rich. They make also another very just comparison upon the same subject. As it signifies nothing, say they, to a man almost dead with hunger, to be present at a table covered with all sorts of meats, if he be not permitted to eat thereof; so he that performs prayer profits little by the holy thoughts he receives in it, if he nourishes not himself therewith, nor applies them to himself, making firm and constant resolutions to put them in practice.

But still to examine things more particularly, I say, that the whole fruit we must derive from meditation consists in forming pious desires in the bottom of our hearts, that we may afterwards in due time put them in practice. And therefore St. Ambrose says, that "action is the end of the meditation of God's commandments." (Amb. sup. Ps. cxviii.) Amongst many other particulars, the Scripture informs us of, concerning these holy creatures that Ezechiel saw in his vision, it says, "that they had hands of men under their wings" (Ezech. i. 8); to let us know, that in meditation we must raise ourselves by the help of our understanding; that afterwards we may come to execute and practise by means of our will. In prayer, then, what we ought to have principally in view is, to excite in ourselves either acts of humility, by contemning ourselves, and desiring to be contemned by others—or an ardent will to suffer for the love of God, proposing to ourselves to suffer with joy the present pains and afflictions we lie under—or sentiments of affection to poverty of spirit, desiring to be rejected and contemned by all; and even sometimes to want such things as are very necessary. In fine, we must endeavour to bring with us to prayer a lively sorrow for our sins; a firm resolution rather to die than offend God; deep gratitude for his benefits; an entire resignation of ourselves into his hands; and an ardent desire to imitate our divine Master in the practice of those virtues of which he has given us an example. Behold here what ought to be the object and the end of our meditation, and the advantage we ought to derive from it.

From what has been already said, it follows, that because we make use of meditation and reflection, as means to excite our will to acts of affection, and to holy resolutions, and that this is our only aim and end, we consequently must not entertain ourselves in meditation any longer than is necessary to move our will. For the means must be proportionable to their end; so that when we find our will touched with any motion of piety, as for example, with a regret for our sins, contempt of the world, love of God, desire to suffer for him, and such like other motions; we must imitate skilful architects, who, as soon as the arch of a vault is finished, take away the frame of wood upon which it was formed; that is, we must presently interrupt our meditation, and dwell upon these affectionate acts, till our soul is quite penetrated therewith. This advice is very important, and is given us by St. Ignatius, in his book of Spiritual Exercises, where he says, the very moment we begin in our meditation to feel in ourselves these motions of fervour and devotion, we must stop and fix there, without being anxious to pass to other things till we are thereby very well penetrated and replenished. As a gardener who waters a bed in his garden, and perceiving the water not presently to enter into it, stops a little to let it be imbibed by the earth, and goes no farther till it has sunk to the very bottom, and that the earth is well watered; in like manner, when the water of these holy affections and desires begins to enter into our soul, which is, to speak with the Psalmist, "like earth without water" (Ps. cxlii. 6); we must suspend the operation of our understanding, and think only of receiving these salutary waters, and enjoying this effusion of the will, till our heart being filled, we feel its wants no more. The great St. Chrysostom explains the same thing by another comparison. Have you not taken notice, says he, of a lamb which would suck its dam? He first goes from side to side ; he takes, he leaves, and returns again divers times, sometimes to one, sometimes to the other teat; but when he finds that the milk begins to come, he presently stops, and does nothing else but receive it, and take it in large draughts. It is the same in prayer, as long as the dew of heaven does not fall, we turn from one side to another, by means of reasoning and reflections, but as soon as we begin to feel it we must stop, and think of nothing else than of receiving it into the bottom of our heart, and quietly enjoying those sweet and delicious draughts, whereby we may replenish and nourish our souls.

———o———

CHAPTER XII.

Of how great importance it is to dwell upon these Acts and affec-
tionate Motions of the Will.

IT is of so great importance to dwell a long time upon these affectionate motions of the will, that the masters of a spiritual life say, that prayer is then in its sovereign degree of perfection, when no longer recurring to meditation, in order to excite in us the love of God, our heart being penetrated with this love it sighs after it, enjoys it and reposes itself therein, as in the only end of its researches and desires. It is this the spouse teaches us, by her own example in the Canticles, when she says, "I have found him whom my soul loves ; I will hold him fast, and will not let him go " (Cant. iii. 4) : and what she intimates to us by these other words, "I sleep, but my heart is awake." (Ibid. v. 2.) For in perfect prayer, the understanding it as it were asleep, because all its functions are, in a manner suspended ; but the will and heart are awake, and melt with tenderness for the heavenly spouse. This sleep also of the spouse is so agreeable to her beloved, that "he conjures the daughters of Jerusalem not to dis-turb the repose of his spouse, and not to awake her till she awakes of herself." (Cant. iii. 5.) So that meditation, and all those other functions of the mind in prayer, are all made use of, and directed to contemplation, and are so many steps to help us to ascend to it. It is after this manner that St. Austin speaks of it, in his book he calls the Ladder of Paradise, where he says, that " we search by reading, we find by meditating, we ask by prayer, and we obtain by contemplation." (Lib. de Scala Parad.) And afterwards making mention of that passage proposed in the gospel, "Seek, and ye shall find, knock, and it shall be opened unto you" (Matt. vii. 7) ; he applies it to the same thought : "Seek," says he, " in reading, and you will find in meditating ; knock by the help of prayer, and the gate shall be opened unto you by means of contemplation." There is also, says Albertus Magnus, and many saints, this difference between the contemplation of the faithful and that of the heathen philosophers : that of the philosophers only perfected the understanding by the knowledge of truth, and stopped at that alone, as having no other end but to know daily more and more ; but the contemplation of the faithful goes farther, and tends to move the will, and to warm and inflame it with the love of God, according to these words of the spouse, " My heart melted with tenderness at the moment my beloved spoke." (Cant. v. 6.) St. Thomas understood very well this difference, when, speaking of contemplation, he says that though it essentially consists in the operations of the understanding, yet it oftentimes receives not its last perfection, but from affectionate motions, and acts of the love of God, produced by the will; so that these acts and motions must be the principal and chief end of contemplation.

This form of prayer, as St. Austin remarks, is taught us in the Gospel by Jesus Christ himself when he warns us " not to speak much in prayer." (Matt. vi. 7.) Whereupon the same saint adds, " that to employ ourselves in long discourses is quite a different thing from entertaining ourselves for a long time in affectionate thoughts ; and that in prayer we ought, as much as we can, to retrench the one, and let our prayer be always accompanied with the other. Because," says he, " it is a business that is better done by sighs than by words." (Lib. de oran. Deum, c. x.) The delicacy of thought, the force of argument, and the abundance of discourse, are all to little purpose when we treat with God. There are only the desires of the heart, sighs, moans, and tears, that we must employ ourselves in when we treat with him, according to the prophet Jeremias—" Let not the apple of your eye be silent." (Lamen. ii. 18.) St. Jerome hereupon proposes a question to himself, and after having asked how it was possible the apple of our eye should speak, because speaking is the proper office of the tongue only. " When we pour out our

tears," says he, " before God, then it is that the apples of our
eyes speak to him, make themselves understood by him in like
manner, though our mouth utter not a word, yet our heart
ceases not to make its cries be heard." This is what St. Paul
explains to us, when, writing to the Galatians, he says, " that
God has sent the spirit of his Son, which cries out in our hearts,
Father, Father." (Gal. iv. 6.) And it is this that God himself
gave us to understand when he asked Moses, " Wherefore do
you cry to me ?" (Exod. xiv. 15.) Though Moses had not so
much as opened his mouth, but instead thereof had made his
heart speak to him, praying with so much fervour and efficacy,
that God asked him why he cried out in such a manner. It is
thus we must raise our voices to God in our prayer—it is
thus we must speak to him with our eyes—it is thus "the apple of
our eye must not be silent"—and it is thus we must cry out to
him with the sighs, tears, sobs, and groans of our hearts.

———o———

CHAPTER XIII.

An Answer to the Complaints of such as say they are not capable
of meditating.

WHAT we have already said may serve as a sufficient answer to
those who complain they know not how to meditate ; because
nothing ever presenting itself to their minds to help them to
extend the points they have taken, they presently want matter.
There is nothing in this that should afflict them, for as we have
already said, meditation is an exercise that consists more in the
acts of the will than in the discourses of the understanding.
And even the masters of a spiritual life admonish us to take care
that the meditation be not too long ; because by this means, and
particularly when we entertain ourselves with curious and subtile reflections, we only check the motions and affections of the
will, which ought to be the chief end of prayer. The reason of
this is most clear and natural. For it is certain, if a supply
gives but one inch of water, and if it be distributed among
different pipes, the more there runs through one, the less there
will run through the other. Now the virtue of our soul is finite
and limited ; so that the more it effuses itself by the channel of
the understanding, the less it will be able to transmit by that of
the will ; and thus we see by experience, that when our heart is

filled with devotion, if the understanding lets itself be carried away with speculations and curious reflections, the devotion is presently spent, and our heart becomes dry. The reason of this is, because the spring flows entirely through the channel of the understanding, and therefore that of the will must necessarily be dried up. Hence it is, says Gerson, that those who are not learned are sometimes more devout, and make their prayer far better than others, because the understanding does not present to them so many objects to distract their attention, and without running after far-fetched speculations, they presently endeavour to move their wills by simple and familiar reflections, which make a deeper impression upon them than the most sublime and exquisite meditations can make upon others. We have an example of this in the cook I have already mentioned, who, from the material fire he had continually before his eyes, took occasion to call to mind the eternal fire of hell, and to be so deeply impressed with sentiments of devotion, that amidst his occupations he had continually the gift of tears.

What is to be farther observed is, provided the motions of the will and sentiments of the heart are very sublime, it is no matter whether the thoughts or the reflections that cause them be ever so mean and common. We have sufficient proofs and examples of this truth in Scripture, where the Holy Ghost, by simple and easy comparisons, is oftentimes pleased to explain the highest and most sublime mysteries. St. Ambrose, speaking of this verse of the Psalmist, " Who will give me the wings of a dove, that I may fly and be at rest ?" (Psal. liv. 7), asks the question why the prophet, desirous to fly and raise himself on high, should desire rather the wings of a dove than of any other fowl, since there are many more swift than a dove ? It is, says he, because the prophet knew very well that to fly to the highest pitch or summit of perfection, and to raise ourselves to what is most sublime in prayer, the wings of a dove are the best ; that is to say, that simplicity of heart is more proper and fit for it than the sublimity and refinement of the understanding, according to the words of the Wise Man—"The conversation of our Lord is with the simple." (Prov. iii. 32.)

We have no reason then, to be uneasy when, during prayer, we feel it difficult to make great or long discourses, when we find not reflections for enlarging on the points of our meditation. On the contrary, it is maintained with a great deal of reason, that in a spiritual life these are in the best state in whom God dries up the source of vague and diffuse speculation, and opens at the same time in them the source of the affections and feelings of the heart, in order that the understanding, remaining in a most profound tranquillity, the will may repose in God alone, and entirely employ itself in the love and enjoyment of the sovereign good. If our Lord bestows upon you this favour, that by the help of some simple reflection, or by the sole consideration of his being made man, of his being born for your sake in a stable, and dying for you upon a cross, you find and feel yourself inflamed with his love, and with a desire to humble and mortify yourself for his sake, and that you entertain yourself for a long time herein, this kind of prayer is without doubt far better and far more profitable than if you had busied yourself with long reflections and sublime discourses, because you dwelt upon that which is most exquisite and essential in prayer, and upon that which ought to be the end and fruit of it. This shews us how much these deceive themselves who imagine that not to make reflections is to pray ill, and to make them is to pray well.

We read in the Chronicles of St. Francis, that a holy religious, named brother Giles, said one day to St. Bonaventure, who was general of their order, " God has given great talents to you and other learned men, that you may serve and praise him ; but we simple and ignorant people, who have no light at all, what can we do to please God ?" " If nothing more," replied St. Bonaventure, " were given to a man than grace to love God, this would suffice to render him more pleasing to God, and to make him merit more than he would by using all other means together." " How," replied the good religious, " is it possible, then, that an ignorant and simple person should be able to love Jesus Christ as much as a wise and learned man ? " It is possible," replied St. Bonaventure, " that a poor, simple, ignorant woman may have as great love and charity as a very learned divine." Hereupon the good religious, transported with fervour, ran about that side of the garden next the town, and cried out with a loud voice, " Poor, simple woman, love but our Lord Jesus Christ, and you may have greater merit than brother Bonaventure ; " and he had scarce ended these words, but, as he frequently did, he fell into an ecstasy, and remained in it for three whole hours together.

CHAPTER XIV.

Two Advertisements, which may consderably help us to make our Prayer well, and to derive great advantage from it.

To make our prayer well, and to derive from it the benefit that we ought, it will be extremely profitable to us first to be assured that prayer is not the chief end we propose to ourselves in a spiritual life, but only a means and help we make use of to advance ourselves in perfection. We must not confine ourselves to prayer as to the end in which we are to repose. For our perfection consists not in consolations and sweetnesses of contemplation, but in acquiring a perfect mortification of sense—in obtaining a victory over ourselves—in surmounting our passions and appetites, and re-establishing ourselves as much as it is possible in the happy state of original justice wherein we are all created in the person of our first father Adam. For then the flesh and concupiscence were subject to reason, and reason was entirely subject and conformable to God. And it is to attain this so elevated an end, that we must help ourselves by prayer as a means most proper and profitable. Though iron is hard, yet fire softens it and renders it fit for any use we please. Prayer works the same effect upon our heart, which being naturally hard, has a repugnance to mortification and contempt, and feels it very difficult to submit to the will of another. We must, then, have recourse to prayer to overcome this hardness, and by the fire and heat of devotion, and the example of Jesus Christ, our heart will become so soft and pliable that we may afterwards very easily manage it, and form it to whatsoever shall be necessary for God's greater glory and service. See what prayer ought to work in us; behold the advantage we must derive from it. And as to those sweetnesses and interior consolations we sometimes receive from God therein, he does not send them that we may repose in them, but he gives them that thereby we may become more ready and ardent to run on in the way of virtue and perfection.

It is this the Holy Ghost would give us to understand by what happened to Moses descending from the mountain, where he conversed with God. The holy text says, that coming down, his face was resplendent with rays of light; and this light was formed into the shape of horns. For, as in Scripture, horns are a symbol of strength, so the Holy Ghost would thereby intimate

to us that we must rise from prayer with additional strength
and activity. The Son of God has also taught us this by his
own example, on the night of his passion. He put himself three
times in prayer, to prepare himself for the sufferings which
awaited him ; and as soon as he had ended it, he said to his disciples : " Arise, let us go, he who betrays me is at hand." (Mat.
xxvi. 46.) He himself offers and delivers up himself into the
hands of his enemies. " He was offered, because it was his pleasure." (Isai. liii. 7.) Yet it was not, as St. Ambrose well observes, because he wanted either preparation or succour that he
prayed, but because he would teach us, by his example, to recur
to prayer as a most proper means to surmount all difficulties
that occur in the way of virtue. St. Chrysostom compares our
heart to an instrument of music, and says, that prayer tunes all
the notes, to elicit thence an harmony very agreeable to God.
In effect what we must propose to ourselves in prayer is, so to
regulate all the motions of our heart, and all our actions and
passions, that they may accord very well with reason, and with
God. Wherefore we are every day admonished, in these exhortations that are made to us, that our prayer should be practical ;
that is to say, that it tend to the regulating of our life, the les-
sening difficulties, and removing the obstacles we shall meet
with in spiritual life. The Holy Ghost also gives the name of
" wisdom to the science of saints " (Prov. ix. 10) ; which is
nothing else than prayer ; because prudence teaches us to regulate our actions ; whereas human science terminates in the
simple knowledge of objects.

Theodoret, in his religious History, relates of a holy anchoret,
who was wont to say, that physicians ordinarily treat each corporal disease with a particular and proper remedy ; and frequently apply many remedies to the cure of one disease ; because
all medicines are weak, and have only a limited virtue in them :
but that prayer is an universal remedy, and is very efficacious
in all our necessities—that it is fit to repel and resist the attacks
of the devil, and to gain all the virtues ; so that to all the evils
of the soul it applies an infinite good, which is God himself,
from whom it borrows all its force and power. They also call
it omnipotent ; and it is a good title ; because it is in effect a
sovereign remedy, which the Saviour of the world has given
us against all sorts of temptations. " Watch and pray," says he,
" that ye enter not into temptation." (Mat. xxvi. 41.)

The second advertisement which will help us to reduce the

former to practice is, that as before we put ourselves in prayer, we should know the points upon which we are to meditate ; so we must also know the fruit we are to reap from it. But some may say, how shall we know beforehand what benefit to derive from the prayer we are about to make? This proposition requires to be explained; which I shall endeavour to do, and render it as intelligible as I can. Have I not just now said that when we have recourse to prayer, it is to find out a remedy for our spiritual infirmities, and to gain the victory over ourselves, and over our passions and bad habits ; and that prayer is a means we adopt, in order to amend and reform our lives ? This being so, we must consider for some time before we begin our prayer ; and ask ourselves what is the greatest spiritual infirmity I have ? What is the obstacle that most opposes itself to my progress in virtue ? And what enemies make the most open war against my soul? Let every one set this before his eyes ; let him beforehand call it to mind, that afterwards he may in his prayer, with greater fervour and earnestness, request some necessary remedy for this evil, wherewith he is molested ; and let all the preparation he makes for the disposing the points of his medita- tion be directed to this end only. You are, for example, tempted by an irregular desire of the esteem and praises of men ; and this renders you so very sensible to the least appearance of contempt, that sometimes you cannot forbear to let your resent- ment appear exteriorly. You perceive it is this which more violently wages war against you, and is the greatest obstacle and hindrance to your spiritual advancement—that it is this which most of all hinders the peace and quiet of your mind ; and in fine this is what occasions your falling into your most consider- able faults and imperfections. Since you know that this is your greatest fault, it is to overcome and root out this, that you must chiefly apply yourself; and consequently this is the fruit you must propose to yourself to reap from your prayer ; this is what you must always have before your eyes, and what you must insist on most constantly and earnestly.

Those, then, deceive themselves exceedingly, who think not upon what most imports them ; but, like a hunter that shoots always at random, go to prayer without any fixed desire to profit of what the Holy Ghost shall put into their minds. We go not to prayer to take all that comes to hand, but we go to find what is most necessary for us ; and to imitate the sick man who goes not to the apothecary's to take what drugs come next ; but to seek those he stands most in need of. One is puffed up with pride and vanity; another boils with anger and impatience; a third abounds in his own sense, being tied to his own will and opinion; every day we find ourselves guilty of faults, and yet in prayer we entertain ourselves with far-fetched speculations, and subtile reflections, taking hold of the first pleasing thing that presents itself; and, without directly stopping or fixing upon anything, let our minds wander to and fro on things which are not to the purpose. This is not the way to profit. We must continually think upon that which principally requires reformation in us, and endeavour to remedy it by prayer, since prayer was established for this end. St. Ephrem applies very well to this subject the example of the blind man in the gospel, who had recourse to Jesus Christ, crying out, and begging that he would take pity on him. Consider, says he, that our Saviour having asked him what he would have, the man presently mentions to him his greatest misery, which was his blindness, and said—" Lord, grant me my sight." (Luke xviii. 41.) He asked him for nothing else that he wanted; he mentioned not his poverty, his want of clothes, or anything else; but, not alluding to any of these, he thought only upon what was most pressing. It is after this manner, continues this great saint, that we must behave ourselves in prayer; we must regard that which we stand most in need of, and insist and persevere in our importunity till we have obtained it.

But to anticipate a difficulty which may be made, it is proper to observe, that though it be true, that to excite ourselves to a love of those particular virtues we stand most in need of, we must try whether the matter, and points we have chosen to meditate upon, be such as they ought to be, to move our will to produce fervorous acts; nevertheless, we may also affirm with truth, that any mystery or point we take for our meditation, may equally be applied to all sorts of necessities. For prayer is like the heavenly manna, that has that taste which each one desires. If you would find sentiments of humility, you will meet with them in the considerations you shall make upon sin, death, hell, the Passion of the Son of God, and upon the benefits you have thereby received. If you would excite in yourself a lively sorrow and extreme confusion for your faults, each one of these points will also conduce to this effect. If you would gain the spirit of sweetness and patience, they will, in the same manner, serve for the obtaining them. In fine, whatsoever you would seek in prayer, you will always infallibly find it therein.

CHAPTER XV.

How we are to understand, that in Prayer we must take to heart those things we stand most in need of, and insist on them till we have obtained them.

I DO not mean that in prayer we must always apply ourselves to one thing only ; because, though humility, for example, or any other virtue, be the most necessary for us, yet we may always in prayer exercise ourselves in any other virtues, and in forming or making acts of them. You are moved to make an act of conformity to the will of God, in whatsoever he shall please to ordain in your regard. Stop there as long as you can, and all the time you shall spend in it will be well spent ; and your prayer made in this manner will be so good, and be so far from diverting you from sentiments of humility, that it will even more and more excite you to them. You are moved to a grateful acknowledgment of all the benefits God has bestowed upon you, as well in general as in particular. Stop there as long as you are able, since it is just to thank God daily for all the favours you have received from him, and principally for that, which he bestowed upon you when he called you to religion. You are moved to a horror of your sins, and compunction for them, and to make a firm resolution rather to die a thousand times than offend God ; dwell a good while on this ; you cannot produce an act more profitable, and more conducive to your salvation. You are moved to a greater love of God, to a fervent zeal for the salvation of souls, and an ardent desire for this purpose to expose yourself to all sorts of labours and sufferings. Repose and rest herein ; and if you will, you may apply yourself, moreover, to beg the grace of God, as well for yourself as for your neighbour, and for the whole Church in general ; for this is one of the principal points in prayer ; and, by dwelling either on these, or those before mentioned, or any others of the same nature, you may make a very good and profitable prayer. Let us also take notice of the Psalms, which are a most perfect prayer, how they are replenished with an infinity of different affectionate acts ; and it is this that made Cassian say, that prayer is like a field enamelled with a thousand different odoriferous flowers ; a simile Isaac made use of when he said—" The smell of my son is like the smell of a fertile field, that our Lord has blessed." (Gen. xxvii. 27.) But there is also an advantage in this variety; which is, that it ordinarily helps to make prayer more easy and pleasant unto us, and consequently makes us persevere a longer time in it. For as frequent repetition of the same thing is wont to create tediousness; so variety, on the other hand, renders what we are about more pleasant and delightful.

What I wish to say, then, is, that it is of great importance for our spiritual advancement, to take to heart, for some time, some one thing in particular; and it must be precisely what we find ourselves stand most in need of. And in prayer we must chiefly insist upon this, and beg it of God with fervour several times, several days, nay even several months; making this our chief business, having it continually before our eyes, and lodging it in the very bottom of our hearts, till we come at last to obtain it. Even worldly affairs are performed after this manner: and, therefore we ordinarily say, "God preserve us from the man that has but one affair." St. Thomas, speaking of prayer, says, that the more the desire unites itself to one thing in particular, the more perfect and efficacious it is; and upon this subject, he recites the words of the Psalmist: "I desired one thing of our Lord, and I will not cease earnestly to beg it of him till I obtain it." (Ps. xxvi. 4.) Whoever wishes to distinguish himself in any art or science, begins not a thing one day, and another thing another, but he continues for some considerable time to make it his chief study, till he thoroughly understands what he undertook to learn. Whoever, therefore, wishes to acquire any virtue he stands in need of, must make it, in like manner, his chief business, and direct his prayer and all his spiritual exercises to this end; and this the more perseveringly, as all moral virtues, according to the doctrine of the same saint, are so inseparably united one with another, that whoever perfectly possesses one of them possesses all the rest. Root out of your heart pride, and plant humility in its place. As soon as you shall be truly humble, you will be obedient, you will be patient, you will complain of nothing, you will think nothing hard; and though anything should happen to you, very difficult to be borne with, yet it will always seem to you very little, in comparison of what you deserve. As soon also as you shall be humble, you will be charitable towards your brothers, because you will believe them all to be good, and that there is none bad but yourself; you will have a great simplicity of heart, and you will judge ill of nobody, because you will have so great sorrow and confusion for your own defects, that you will not at all reflect upon those of your neighbour. And what we say at present of these particular virtues may be in like manner extended to all others.

It is also very profitable to take for the subject of our particular examen, the same matter that we also take for the subject of our prayer; and to join prayer and examen together, because by this means all our exercises tending to the same end, we shall make a greater progress in virtue. But Cassian goes farther yet, and would have us not only insist in our prayer and examen, upon what we find most necessary for us, but would have us also elevate our minds to God several times in the day, by short and lively ejaculations, with sighs, and groans of our heart ; and that to these we also add penances, mortifications, and other particular devotions for the obtaining what we desire. For since the greatest business we have is to increase in virtue, and to root out that vice which most of all predominates within us ; and that bad inclination and propensity also, which carry us on, and cause us to fall into most grievous faults—and since by the overcoming and rooting out this vice, and the gaining this virtue, we overcome and root out all vices, and acquire all virtues ; whatsoever attention we devote to it, and what pains soever we take upon this account, our care and efforts can never be better applied.

St. Chrysostom says, that prayer is like a fountain in the middle of a garden, without which all things would become dry and barren ; and by means of which all things flourish and become fresh and pleasant. So that it is by prayer we must always keep the plants of obedience, humility, patience, mortification, silence, recollection, and all other virtues, in continual beauty and perfection. But as in a garden there is ordinarily one plant or flower that is cultivated with more care than all the rest, and for which we always find time and water sufficient, though we should want for the others; so in the spiritual garden of our souls, where all things must be refreshed with the wholesome water of prayer, there must always be something upon which we more particularly cast our eye, and for the cultivation of which we should always find leisure. I mean, we must take notice which is the virtue we want most, and apply ourselves more to attain that, than all the rest. Moreover, since it commonly happens, that before we go out of a garden we pluck one of those flowers that most of all pleases us ; so in prayer, we must apply ourselves not only to what pleases us most, but what is most necessary for us, and endeavour to take it along with us when we go from our prayer.

What we have here said may be a sufficient answer to those who ask, whether the fruit we reap from prayer must be conformable to the matter upon which we meditate? We have already taken notice, that though we ought always chiefly to apply ourselves to that which we find most necessary for us, yet we must exercise ourselves also in producing acts of other virtues, according to the point we have made choice of for our meditation. But in this there is one thing very essential to be observed, which is, that those affections which shall arise in us from the matter we meditate npon, must not be formed in haste and superficially; but though we should employ even the whole time of our prayer in them, yet we must make them at leisure, entertaining them in peace and tranquillity, till we feel our hearts very well filled and penetrated with them. For it is better without doubt to make and continue one sole act in this manner, than to produce many acts of different virtues in haste, and only, as I may say, take an imperfect sketch of them.

One of the things that most of all hinders some from deriving the advantage they ought is, that they slightly pass over all the acts they make. For they only touch the matter, and fly from one thing to another. A thought occurs to them to make an act of humility, they make it, and as soon as they have done they go to another. If it be to their purpose afterwards to make an act of obedience, they do the same without dwelling any longer upon it than upon the first—afterwards they make an act of patience, in which they spend no more time than in the former, and pass so quickly and lightly over all, that if they were running over burning coal they could not at all annoy themselves. Father Avila reprehends very severely those that thus go from one thing to another, and says, that in effect it proceeds from a deceit of the devil, who thus lays different matters before them, in order that like birds flying from one branch to another, they may not reap any considerable fruit from their prayer. It is therefore of great importance to dwell upon one thing, till the soul is filled and well penetrated with it. If you would, for example, make an act of contrition, and have a lively sorrow for your offences, you must persist so long in it, till, finding your soul seized with a horror of sin, you shall be able to say with the prophet, " I have hated iniquity, and had it in abomination." (Ps. cxviii. 163.) For this will cause you to make a firm resolution, rather to die a thousand deaths than mortally offend God. Wherefore, St. Austin very judiciously takes notice, that the horror which men have conceived of some certain sins, as parricide and such like, is the occasion that they very seldom fall into them. And on the contrary, there are other sins that the frequent habit of committing them has so taken away all fear or horror, and rendered them so small in appearance, that we permit ourselves to fall into them very easily. If you desire to exercise yourself in humility also, and to make acts of this virtue, you must entertain thoughts of self-contempt, till they have penetrated so to the bottom of your soul, that they chase from you all the smoke of vanity and pride ; and that you feel yourself ready to suffer contempt and reproaches with joy. And what we say here of contrition and humility, may in like manner be said of all the virtues, and of all pious motions of the soul.

By this we may see how much the taking some one thing to heart, and the persevering therein, according to the manner aforesaid, conduce to spiritual advancement; because if we entertain ourselves an hour in the morning and another in the evening, with a desire of being contemned, or in any other pious sentiment of this nature, and should continue many days together to do the same, it is certain, that this would work a quite different effect in our hearts, and this virtue would be imprinted in it after a quite different manner, than by thinking upon it only now and then, as if it were by chance, or only by a slight and passing thought. St. Chrysostom says, that though the soil be ever so good, yet to make it become fertile, it must be well watered with rain, and this not only once, but very often ; so our souls, in like manner, must be watered by prayer, if we desire they should bring forth the fruit of justice and sanctity. And he cites upon this subject those words of David, " I have sung your praises seven times a day." (Ps. cxviii. 164.) The Royal Prophet watered his soul seven times a-day by means of prayer; and the better to entertain himself in the same sentiments of devotion, he renewed it frequently in a short space of time. We see this in the hundred and thirty-fifth psalm, where he repeats twenty-seven times these words : " Because his mercy is for ever." (Ps. cxxxv. 1.) And in another psalm which contains only five verses, he invites us to praise God no less than eleven times. This manner of praying, in which the same words are repeated over and over again, and the persevering a good while therein, was taught us by our Saviour also in the Garden of Olives, where he returned to prayer three several times, " saying always the same words." (Matt. xxvi. 44.) By this he teaches us to insist often in prayer upon the same thing, and always with a new fervour : for, if we persevere a long while in this manner, we shall at last obtain the virtue and perfection we desire.

———o———

CHAPTER XVI.

Of the Means of exercising ourselves a long while in Prayer upon the same Subject ; and of a very profitable Manner or Form of Prayer which is made by our descending to Particulars.

HAVING shown that this is very profitable in prayer to dwell a long while upon interior acts of the same virtue, it remains that we point out the means requisite for effecting this. The most common, and what is ordinarily assigned, is to reproduce the same act in our heart, whether it be by helping ourselves with the first consideration that moved us to form it (as a man, by repeated strokes upon a wheel that hangs in the air upon its axletree, continues and augments its circular motion), and exciting ourselves by those words of the Prophet : " My soul return to thy repose, by remembering the benefits thou hast received of our Lord " (Ps. cxiv. 7) ; or by adding some other consideration to the first, when it is not sufficient to move us any longer—which is like casting fresh fuel upon the fire when we would preserve it from going out. But if, after all this, we feel not ourselves sufficiently excited, we must pass to another point ; for we must always have several points in readiness, in order when we have so much exhausted one, that we find nothing more in it to inflame our will, we may pass to another that is better able to awake and stir up the motions of our understanding, and carry our thoughts to what we chiefly desire and aim at. Moreover, when we would avoid the disgust we find in feeding constantly upon the same meat, we are accustomed to dress and season it after a different manner, which renders it as it were new, and that to excite in ourselves a new appetite ; so also to be able to dwell for a long time upon the same subject in prayer, which is the true food and nourishment of our soul, there is no better way than to season it after a different manner, by thinking of another consideration, or else upon some other point, as we have said before. So that as often as by any reflection different from the first, we produce the same act, it is as it were a different kind of seasoning that renders the thing in a manner new. We may also, without making use of any new reflection, vary the interior act of virtue different ways; as for example, if we would exercise ourselves upon humility, we may sometimes dwell upon the consideration and knowledge of our misery and weakness, and there find an ample subject of confusion and humiliation. Sometimes we may employ ourselves in desiring the contempt of men, considering that the esteem of the world is only mere vanity and smoke, and consequently we must make no account of it; sometimes we may conceive a wholesome shame and confusion for faults we find ourselves daily guilty of, and ask God's pardon, and beg a remedy for them. Sometimes we may enter into an admiration of the divine goodness, which tolerates us, notwithstanding all our imperfections, when frequently we are scarce able to tolerate or bear with ourselves; and, lastly, we may sometimes employ ourselves in giving him thanks that he has not permitted us to fall into greater faults. By this variety we avoid the disgust which the continuation of the same act ordinarily occasions; and the perseverance in the desire and exercise of the same virtue, becoming thus easy and pleasant, our hearts by this means will be more deeply penetrated therewith, and this virtue will take deeper root. For as every time the file goes over the iron, it takes something with it, so also every time we make an act of humility, or of any other virtue, we always diminish something of the contrary vice.

There is, besides this, another means to persevere many days in prayer upon the same subject; which means is both very easy and profitable, and consists in descending to several particulars of the things we meditate on. It is not sufficient, as all masters of a spiritual life tell us, to form in prayer a weak and wandering desire, or a general resolution to serve God—to make progress in virtue, and to render ourselves perfect; but we must, moreover, descend to the particulars of those things we know are most pleasing to God. Nor is it sufficient to conceive a desire in general of any virtue in particular, as of obedience, humility, patience or mortification, as this sort of general desire, or rather velleity, is formed in the hearts of even the most vicious persons. For virtue being a thing pleasant, honourable, and also most profitable, as well for this life as for the next, it is an easy thing to love it, or thus to desire it in general; but this is not enough—together with this we must enter into a detail of the particular circumstances which bear any relation to the very virtue we wish to acquire. If, for example, we propose to ourselves the gaining a perfect conformity to the will of God, we must set before us the different situations in which we may happen to find ourselves. We must look upon sickness as well as health ; the time of temptation as well as comfort, and life as well as death, with an entire resignation to the divine will. If we wish to acquire humility, we must in like manner descend to particulars, representing to ourselves those things in which we may have any occasion of exercising humility ; and it is the same with respect to all the other virtues. Because it is particular facts which most of all touch and move us ; it is in these what is most difficult in virtue consists ; it is by these virtue is not only proved but acquired. The method we are to observe herein is, in the beginning to propose to ourselves such examples and practices as are easy, and afterwards to image to ourselves such as are more hard and difficult, and then to image to ourselves such as are the most difficult of all ; and when we think we have mastered all these, we must endeavour after this manner still to raise ourselves by little and little, never ceasing to make one act after another, just as if the occasions had actually presented themselves, till there is nothing that opposes itself to our design, and till we have resisted and overcome all our difficulties with so much vigour that at last we become masters of the field. But if afterwards any new occasions offer themselves, we must also exercise ourselves in these, and excite ourselves to support them with patience, and make our profit of them. A certain servant of God, moreover, adds, that we must in prayer purpose to practise something of this kind each day; so true it is, that, in what concerns our perfection, we cannot descend too much to particulars.

Without doubt, this is one of the most profitable things in which we can exercise ourselves in time of prayer. For prayer, as we have said, ought to be practical : that is to say, it ought always tend to the practice of the virtue we aspire to; and it ought to smooth the difficulties we meet with in the practice of it. And for this purpose, it is requisite that we try and exercise ourselves beforehand, like soldiers who are trained in time of peace that they may be able to surmount the difficulties they meet in time of war. Cassian also particularly recommends this method. And even Seneca and Plutarch declare that the weak are the only persons who feel not how much the ills and afflictions of life are sweetened by often thinking upon them beforehand. It is very profitable, say they, often to fix our thoughts upon things that are hard and difficult; for as a man who employs his thoughts only upon those things that are pleasant, contracts a certain effeminacy that makes him afraid of any pain or labour, and therefore loses courage on the least occasion that presents itself; so he who is accustomed to propose to himself the pains of sickness, exile, prisons, and all other adversities that can happen in this life, will be the better prepared to bear them whenever they shall happen, and will experience that all these things cause a great deal more fear and apprehension in the beginning than they can do hurt in the end. "The darts we perceive afar off," says St. Gregory, "hurt us far less than others" (Greg. Hom. xxxv. sup. Evang.); the evil is, in a manner, half overcome when we have foreseen it; the enemies that surprise us fright us far more than those we courageously wait for.

We read in the life of St. Ignatius a thing very pertinent to this subject. He happened to be sick, and the physician having forbidden him to do anything that might give him any trouble of mind, or to dwell on any uneasy or disquieting thoughts, this circumstance led him to think with himself what accident could happen that was capable of afflicting him, or of disturbing the peace of his mind. After having cast his thoughts upon several, he found that the object most dear to his heart was the conservation of the society which he had but newly established, and that the dissolution thereof was the only thing that could give him any pain or trouble. He afterwards went on to examine himself how long this affliction would last, in case such a thing should happen; and it seemed to him, provided it happened not through his fault, he would require but a quarter of an hour's recollection and prayer, to free himself from all the trouble that this would give him, and to restore to his mind the peace and tranquillity it had before enjoyed. He added, moreover, that he should preserve the same joy and quiet, even though the society should come to be dissolved as complete as salt is in water. Behold here a most happy and a most profitable manner of praying.

" Is there any one of you afflicted?" says the apostle St. James, " let him have recourse to prayer" (James v. 13); it is there we find a comfort and a remedy for all evils; and this was what the Royal Prophet practised when he felt himself oppressed with any interior affliction or desolation : " My soul," says he, " refused to be comforted, I thought upon God, and I was delighted in him." (Ps. lxxvi. 4.) This is God's will, it is he that will have it thus, and this is enough for me ; because I ought to have no other will nor desire any other pleasure than his. Now if, in time of afflictions, prayer efficaciously assists us to bear them, and to derive advantage from them ; it is also an admirable preparative to render us more ready and better disposed to receive them. St. Chrysostom says, that one of the chief causes why Job remained so content and patient in all his adversities and sufferings was, that he had, in the manner described, prepared himself for them—representing them often to his mind, and making acts of resignation, as if these afflictions were very likely to happen to him. Job himself informs us of this in the following words : " The fear I had is truly fallen upon me, and that which I feared has happened unto me." (Job iii. 25.) But if you have not taken this salutary precaution, and if the bare representation of bad and troublesome accidents shock you at present, what will real afflictions do when they happen ? If whilst you are in prayer, and remote from any occasion, you feel not courage and vigour enough to accept of an humble and painful employment, or to suffer any contempt, what will you be able to do out of prayer, when deprived of that help which those reflections upon the example of Jesus Christ impart, and when you find yourself amidst the obstacles and difficulties which attend on the occasion ? And if, after having very great fervour in your prayer, you should afterwards, when the occasion happens, fail to execute your good purposes, what would you have done had you not been at all prepared for them, and if in prayer you had not had this fervour ? " If he who makes good resolutions," says Thomas á Kempis, "happens, notwithstanding, to fall, what will he do who makes none at all, or makes them very tepidly."

I have here furnished you with most ample and sufficient matter, to dwell a long time upon the same subject in prayer, and upon the same act of virtue. For the particular cases that may happen are numberless, and we must labour very hard, before we shall be able to resist all. But when you shall proceed so far as to find in yourself, as you imagine, sufficient strength to support with joy all that can happen to you, think not that you have gained the point, and that all is done. You are far from it ; for there is a great difference between saying and doing; and there are far more pains required to execute, than to resolve. In the action, the object is present, and acts by itself ; whereas the purpose has no force but what it borrows from the imagination. Hence it happens, that we very often feel ourselves so zealous and fervent in prayer, that we think nothing can be able to shake or move us ; and yet when the first occasion presents itself, and when we come to execute our good purposes, we experience to our shame and confusion, that we are far from being what we presumed and thought we had been.   It is not sufficient then, that you feel in yourself these good desires, but you must endeavour that these desires become efficacious, and that they be put in execution. For action is the true proof or trial of virtue; and if you perceive your actions correspond not with the resolutions you have made, but that, on the contrary, you find yourself in the occasion far from what you thought yourself in prayer : be truly confounded, that you have nothing else but weak and simple desires of what is good, or to say better, that they are no true desires at all, but only vain and flying imaginations; because when the least occasion gives you any trouble, you lose courage, and shamefully give way and fall back.   Imitate the smith, who, when the piece of iron he forges fails the first time, puts it into the fire a second time, in order to forge it again and give it a better form.   Put, therefore, these imperfect desires again into the fire of prayer, and there endeavour to render them efficacious, and do not give over till your actions are conformable to your purposes, and till there remains nothing which can render you wavering or inconstant in their execution.

But even after you have gained thus much over yourself, and you think you behave as you ought upon all occasions, be not persuaded that there remains nothing else for you to do.   For in the action itself there is a great many degrees of perfection that you must endeavour to compass.   First, you must support all things with patience : " Suffer with patience at least," says a holy man, "if you cannot suffer with joy." Behold the first degree of virtue, it will cost you some time and labour before you come to this, and when you are arrived thus far, you have still a considerable progress to make, before you attain perfection. For as the philosophers say very well, the true sign that we have gained any virtue in its perfection is, readily, easily, and with pleasure to produce its acts. See, therefore, whether you practise humility, poverty of spirit, patience, and other virtues, with this readiness, facility, and pleasure ; and thus you will know if you truly possess the virtue. See, according to the rule, which the gospel, as well as St. Ignatius prescribes, to examine yourself by ; whether contempt and reproaches impart as much joy and satisfaction to you, as praises and honours give unto worldly persons ? Whether, in want of all conveniences of this life, you are as well pleased and content, as the covetous man is amidst his riches, and plenty of all things? Whether the mortification you suffer be as pleasing to you as ease and pleasure are to worldlings? Now, if, in the practice of each virtue, we must endeavour to raise ourselves to this height of perfection, we shall have matter enough to employ ourselves in during our whole lives; since, in one virtue alone, we find sufficient employment not only for many days but even for many years.

———o———

CHAPTER XVII.

That we must meditate deliberately on the Mysteries of the Gospel. What will assist us to do so?

IT is also of very great importance to fathom things well, and not to pass over them lightly, in the meditations we make upon the mysteries of the gospel. For it will be of far greater profit to us, to examine only one deliberately, than to touch on many superficially. It is for this reason that St. Ignatius, in his book of the Spiritual Exercises, makes such an account of those repetitions that, at the end of each exercise, he wishes to repeat this exercise, twice or thrice over : " because, he who seeks, finds ; and the gate shall be opened to him that knocks." (Matt. vii. 8 ; Num. xx. 11.) Perseverance overcomes all difficulties, and attains its end. It was necessary that Moses should strike twice upon the rock, to make water issue forth. And even Jesus Christ himself did not immediately cure the blind man mentioned in the gospel : he first anointed his eyes with spittle, and asked him whether he saw anything? And the man who as yet could not see any objects distinctly, answered him : " I see men walk that seem to me like trees." (Matt. viii. 24.) Then our Saviour touched his eyes the second time with his hand, and perfected their cure. Behold here what ordinarily happens in prayer ; for by means of going over the same matter several times, and persevering therein, we discover those things which at first we did not perceive. Much after the same manner, as when we enter into a dark room ; at first we see nothing ; but if we remain for some time in it, we begin gradually to distinguish the objects. We must, therefore, dwell a good while in the consideration of the same matter, and not leave off till we find ourselves disabused of the errors of the age ; till we clearly behold these most important truths ; and find ourselves confirmed in our good resolutions. For this, as I have said before, is one of the greatest advantages we can derive from prayer, and to which we must chiefly apply ourselves.

Now to come to the means, which may help us to make long and salutary reflections upon these mysteries, I say, when God is pleased to impart his lights to a soul, and to open its eyes, it will find so many things to consider, and such a variety of things to dwell on, that it may say with the Psalmist: "Uncover my eyes, and I will consider the wonderful things of thy law." (Ps. cxviii. 18.) "I will rejoice in the consideration of thy promises, as he, who having gained a victory, finds a great quantity of rich spoils." (Ibid. 162.) St. Austin and St. Francis passed whole days and nights in repeating these words: Who are you, O Lord, and who am I? O that I could know you, O that I could know myself! You are my God, and all things to me." (Aug. Isa. vi. 3.) This manner of prayer is very conformable to that which the Prophet Isaias says the blessed make in heaven, when, ravished with the contemplation of the divine majesty, they incessantly sing: "Holy, holy, holy." The Apocalypse says the same of those holy and mysterious creatures, which were before God's throne: "They never ceased," says St. John, "to repeat day and night, holy, holy, holy, Lord God omnipotent, who was, and who is, and who is to come." (Apoc. iv. 8.)

But to attain this, it is necessary that we, on our part, perform our duty, by accustoming ourselves to reflect seriously upon those mysteries, and that we exercise ourselves in penetrating into their particular circumstances. Gerson says, the best means to succeed in this prayer *is to practise it;* and it is not a thing which is gained by the force or acuteness of arguing—nor is it learned by hearing it spoken of, nor by reading many treatises on prayer; but to acquire a knowledge of it, we must set our hand to work, and practise it a long time. When a mother wishes to teach an infant boy to walk, she holds not long discourses with him, to show him what he must do, but by practising him, she makes him form his steps, and thus, in a very short time, she teaches him to walk alone. It is this means, therefore, we must make use of, to gain the science of prayer. For though it be true, that it is a supernatural gift, and consequently not to be obtained by us, if it comes not from the liberal hand of God; "because it is our Lord who gives wisdom, and prudence; and knowledge proceeds from his mouth" (Prov. ii. 6);

yet it is very certain, that God wishes that we practise it as diligently, as if it were to be obtained by our own industry. He is
the eternal wisdom, " who powerfully reaches from end to end,
and disposes all things sweetly." (Wisd. viii. 1.) Wherefore he
acts in the order of grace, as he does in that of nature; and as
he would have all human arts and sciences acquired by practice;
so he would have us acquire the divine science of prayer, in
the same manner.   It is only because they do not practise contemplation, says Gerson, that there are now-a-days so few con-
templatives. Formerly monasteries were filled with them, and now
it is very hard to find in any convent a person that gives himself
to prayer; now-a-days we are so far from the practice of contemplation, that even if we speak of it, we are looked upon to
speak of some speculation, or of such metaphysical abstraction,
as is not to be understood. This difference, says he, proceeds from
our not following the method of the ancient fathers, who made
prayer their constant practice, and took care that it should be
practised likewise by such as they received into their monasteries, as we see in the rule of St Pacomius, and of other primitive founders of orders. Wherefore Gerson gives this counsel,
that in all religious houses there should be men of learning and
piety, long experienced in the exercise of prayer; and that they
should take care to form betimes the novices, by an assiduous
practice thereof.   And St. Ignatius has so punctually followed
this counsel, that in his Constitutions he not only ordains, that
in every house where novices are brought up, there should be one
put over them to instruct them in the exercise of prayer; but
he would, moreover, have a spiritual prefect appointed in all
colleges, who should have an eye upon what regards the practice
of prayer, and examine how every one acquits himself of that
duty.

There is still another thing which may help us to persevere a
long time in the exercise of prayer: and this is, to have an ardent love of God, and a very great affection for spiritual things.
" Because I love your law, O Lord," says the prophet, " it is the
subject of my meditation all the day long." (Ps. cxviii. 97.)
" And I meditate," says he, in another place, "upon your commandments, which I love." (Ibid. cxviii. 47.)   In effect, if we
loved God tenderly we should willingly pass whole days and
nights in thinking of him, and should never want matter to work
upon.   A mother that tenderly loves her son, wants no one to
put her in mind of him nor to urge her to think upon him. She

herself thinks often upon him ; and if anyone speaks ever so little of him, her heart is touched with a tender affection, and their words draw tears from her eyes. A widow also, that tenderly loved her husband, cannot hear him spoken of without shedding tears on his being recalled to her memory. If natural love, therefore, has so much power, what shall I say of supernatural. Nay, if the libertine's irregular love has so much influence over him, that it sets him, as it were, beside himself, and hinders him from thinking of anything but the object of his criminal passion, what wonders would not the supernatural love of the goodness and infinite beauty of God effect, since grace is incomparably more powerful than either nature or vice can be ? If God were your only good, and chief treasure, your heart would be continually wafted towards him ; " because where your treasure is, there is your heart also." (Matt. vi. 21.) Every one thinks very willingly of what he loves, and of what is most to his taste : and, therefore, the holy Scripture gives us this invitation : " Taste and see how sweet our Lord is." (Ps. xxxv. 9.) We must taste God before we see him ; that is to say, we must love him, to be able to think upon him, and the more we think upon him, the more we shall love him ; for love, according to the opinion of St. Thomas, augments itself by contemplation ; and as it is the beginning, so it is also the end. Hence it is that when we love God, we are easily induced to think upon him, and contemplate him ; and the more we contemplate and think upon him, the more we love him. Because that which is good excites us to love it, and the more we behold it, the more we love it ; as also the more we love it, the more joy and pleasure we feel in beholding and thinking of it.

———o———

CHAPTER XVIII.

That it is always in our Power to make our Prayer well, and to derive Advantage from it.

THE sublime and extraordinary prayer which I have before spoken of is in truth a very particular gift of God, which he bestows upon a few persons only ; but as to ordinary mental prayer, of which I speak at present, he refuses it to nobody. So that those who are not able to attain the other kind of prayer, and high contemplation, and who imagine that they cannot pray at all, and that they are unfit for this exercise, deceive themselves extremely. For the ordinary prayer I speak of is very holy and profitable ; because it is sufficient to render us perfect. And although God does not favour us at present with the other, yet this prayer is an excellent disposition to move him afterwards to bestow it. Wherefore, I shall now make it clearly appear, that with the assistance of God's grace, it is always in our power to perform well this last kind of prayer, and thereby to promote our salvation— which, without doubt, cannot but be a great comfort unto us.

This proposition is a consequence deduced from what I have already said in the preceding chapters, and may be proved two ways. We can prove it, first, from the form of prayer taught by St. Ignatius, which does not consist in our having certain sweetnesses and sensible comforts, but only in exercising the three powers of our soul. In this prayer, we first call to mind, by help of our memory, the point or mystery we should meditate on ; afterwards we reflect and meditate, by the means of our understanding, upon such things as may help us to excite our affections ; and lastly we produce acts of our will. Now, this exercise is always in our power, whatsoever state of dryness and aridity we may feel ourselves in. For let the aridity be ever so great, yet it is always in our power to produce an act of detestation and sorrow for our sins ; an act of the love of God, an act of patience, and an act of humility, that may even reach so far as to desire to be despised by the world, that we may the better imitate Jesus Christ, who was so kind as, for love of us, to become the reproach and scorn of men.

We must, moreover, call to mind, and believe it for a certain truth, that neither the merit nor fruit of prayer, nor the merit or fruit of these sorts of acts, consists in our having sweetness and comfort when making them ; nor in being very much touched by them ; it is in this many err and afflict themselves without cause, imagining they do nothing in prayer, because they feel not in themselves either so much sorrow for their sins as they would have, or so much love for virtue as they desire to possess. Sensible feelings of this kind are produced by the sensible appetite. But the will being a spiritual power depends not at all upon sense, and therefore it is not in the least necssary that we should have these sensible feelings ; it is enough that we produce the acts with a firm and resolute will. Wherefore, divines and holy persons, speaking of contrition and sorrow for sins, comfort their penitents, who, when they reflect upon the enormity of one mortal sin, are because they cannot shed tears, and because their hearts do not, as they could wish, even burst with sorrow. True contrition, say they, and true sorrow for sin, is not in the sensible appetite, but is in the will alone ; wherefore be sorry that you have sinned, because thereby you have offended God, who deserves to be loved above all things, and thus it will become true contrition. As for those other motions that proceed from the interior or sensitive part, when God pleases to send them, receive them with due thanks, but afflict not yourself at all when you have them not ; for God does not require them, nor does he desire anything of you that is not in your power to perform. These sensible affections you desire to have are nothing else but a certain kind of sweetness and sensible consolation, that depends not upon you at all, nor is it in your power, and therefore God does not require it of you. But what he exacts is in your power to perform, without any dependence at all upon our sensitive appetite ; and this is a grief that proceeds from a determined will never more to offend him. It is the same with respect to acts of the love of God. Love God above all things, with a firm and constant will, and this is that solid and true love of esteem which he requires. The other kind of love is such a tenderness of affection, as is not in our power, and the same may be said with respect to all other acts of virtue, and all other resolutions we make.

The truth of what I have here said may easily be inferred from such sinful acts as are contrary to the former. For if, for example, we consent to a mortal sin, it is certain that though at the same time we feel no sensible motion in ourselves, nor any pleasure at all therein, yet we cease not to offend mortally, and to deserve eternal damnation. By consequence, therefore, if we will and desire effectually what is good, though we feel not any sweetness in conceiving this will, yet, nevertheless, we fail not to please God, and merit heaven ; chiefly because God is always more ready to reward than he is to punish. I say yet more, that acts of this sort, which are made with an extreme dryness, and without any pleasure or sensible comfort, are more meritorious and pleasing to God than the others are ; because they are more pure, more strong, more lasting, more our own ; and because we take more pains in producing them, than when we are urged to them by fervour and devotion. And they are, moreover, a sign of a more solid virtue, and of a will more firm and constant in God's service ; because if we produce them without the help of spiritual consolations, what should we not do, had we them to help us? Such as produce no acts without the help of these sensible sweetnesses and comforts are, as Father Avila says, like infants that must be carried in persons' arms; but the others are like those who are able to walk alone. And Blosius says, that persons of this last description resemble those who serve their prince at their own expense. But it is of very great importance to accustom ourselves to these sorts of aridities in prayer; because these aridities are very frequent, and sensible comforts occur but seldom. And as galleys, when the wind fails, ply the oar, so when the favourable wind of Divine consolation is wanting to us in prayer, we must help ourselves by the powers of our soul, assisted by the succour of the Holy Ghost; and always continue our course, though the succours be less abundant, or less sensible than they were wont to be.

2ndly. What we advanced in the beginning of this chapter may also be proved in the following manner:—Prayer, as we have said elsewhere, is not the end we propose to ourselves in a spiritual life; it is only a means by which we help ourselves to make progress in virtue, and to obtain a victory over our passions and evil inclinations, in order that, having surmounted all the obstacles that hinder us from approaching God, and having made straight the path that leads to him, we may unite ourselves inseparably with him. When St. Paul had the eyes of his soul entirely opened by God, by that light which flashed on him from heaven, and by that divine voice that said to him, "I am Jesus whom you persecute" (Acts ix. 5), what a change was then made upon a sudden in him? With what promptitude, with what submission, did he then abandon himself to the will of God, as his own words testify—"Lord, what would you have me do?" (Acts ix. 6.) Behold here the fruit of a good prayer—behold the effect it ought to produce in us. I have also said that we must not content ourselves with forming general resolutions, but we must descend to such particular ones as are more necessary for us, and carefully prepare ourselves for such trials as may occur during the day, and in all things act with edification. Now, to apply this to our subject, I say it is always in our power to apply ourselves to that which is more necessary for us. Let us apply ourselves, one, for example, to humility, another to patience, another to obedience, another to the spirit of mortification and resignation, and let us endeavour to rise from prayer more humble, more patient, more obedient, and with a greater desire of mortification and of conformity to the will of God than we brought to it ; above all, let us endeavour to prevail with ourselves to live during the day in very great innocency, and with edification to our neighbour, each one according to his employment ; and by this means we shall have made a better prayer than if we had shed many tears and received very great lights and consolations.

This being so, we must not feel uneasy at our not being favoured with many reflections, or effusions of tenderness, or elevations, or raptures of devotion, for prayer consists not in these, but only in the fruit we reap from it. Nor must we be in pain about our distractions, or the thoughts that are wont to to disquiet us in prayer, of which the world do commonly complain. All required of you is, when you perceive them, and when you are come to yourself, to endeavour to employ your thoughts about what is most necessary ; that is to say, endeavour then to reap from your prayer the fruit you proposed to yourself, and thereby you will repair the time you have lost, and revenge yourself upon the devil, who tried to distract you by extravagant thoughts, which were either out of season, or which rendered your meditation unprofitable. And as a traveller who falls asleep upon the way, and is left behind by his companions, as soon as he awakes, presses forward to overtake them, and rides more in a quarter of an hour than, were it not that he slept, he would have done in an hour ; so, when you come to yourself after your distractions, you must so employ the remaining quarter of an hour, that therein you may perform what you might and should have done in the whole hour, had you been attentive. Wherefore call yourself to account ; ask yourself what the fruit was you designed to reap from your prayer, see whether it be either a profound humility, an extreme indifference to all things of this world, or an entire resignation to the will of God, and use your utmost endeavour to derive this advantage from your prayer, notwithstanding all the distractions the devil had been able to cause in you. But if indeed you should find that your whole time of prayer was spent without having reaped the fruit you desire, you must then, in the examining of your prayer, of which I shall afterwards treat, do that which I just now said, and thus you will make amends for your negligence in prayer, and will always reap fruit from it.

CHAPTER XIX.

Other Means of making our Mental Prayer well.

THERE are other things which enable us to pray well; and which, being easily practised, evince that it is always in our power to make mental prayer: that every man has talents sufficient for it; and that there is no one but may make it so as to derive advantage from it.

In the first place, several masters of a spiritual life give excellent advice on this head. They say we must not amuse ourselves with too many speculations in prayer; but we must imitate good merchants, who think only of their affairs, and of the means of improving them. It is thus a true servant of God ought to examine how he carries on the business of his spiritual advancement and of his eternal salvation. For, properly speaking, this is our only business, and we came into the world for no other purpose than to carry it on well. Let a religious, then, call himself to account, and say thus to himself:—How does the affair of my advancement and salvation succeed? What virtue have I gained during the space of ten, twenty, thirty, or forty years I have been in religion? What progress have I made in humility, in obedience, and the mortification of my senses? I would wish to see what account I shall be able to render to God for so many helps he has given me in religion, to increase the stock or talent he has trusted me with. But if, hitherto, I have spent my time badly and unprofitably, I will repair my past faults and negligences by a greater exactness for the time to come; and I will live in a manner entirely different from that wherein I have hitherto lived. Every person can, in the same manner, institute an inquiry, in order to discover whether or not he has fulfilled the obligations of his calling. He can ask himself, had he done what is requisite for leading a Christian life, for bringing up his family in the love and fear of God, and for enabling himself to support, like a Christian, all those troubles that his condition and employment are subject unto? If we ever so little apply ourselves to reflect upon these things, we shall find sufficient matter to meditate upon, and faults enough both to be sorry for, and to reform; and this will be a very profitable and a very excellent prayer.

Gerson makes mention of a servant of God, who was accustomed to say, that for forty years he had very diligently applied himself to prayer, but had not found a shorter or more easy method to make a good one, than to present himself before God as an infant, or as a man overwhelmed with miseries, blind, naked, destitute of all things, and abandoned by all the world. The Royal Prophet frequently makes use of this kind of prayer, which the psalms are full of in many places, wherein he styles himself, sometimes a sick person, sometimes an orphan, sometimes a blind man, and a poor beggar ; and many, adopting this method, have attained great perfection in prayer. Do you, therefore, adopt it, and God will give you the grace thereby to obtain what you desire. Gerson says, that the method adopted by any poor beggar man is an excellent method of praying. See with what humility, with what patience, he asks and expects an alms at the rich man's gate ; and what care he takes to go to those places where he knows alms are more frequently bestowed. We ought to act in the very same manner, in regard to God ; and as the poor man, when he casts himself at the rich man's feet, makes known his miseries with submission, expects assistance with patience, and a respectful countenance ; even so, when we present ourselves before God in prayer, we must discover and lay open all our wants, necessities, and miseries : and await, with respect and patience, the assistance of his liberality and goodness. " As the eyes of the servant are continually upon the hands of her mistress," when she expects a recompense from her, " so our eyes must be continually fixed upon our Lord, our God, and our master, till he has compassion upon us." (Ps. cxxii. 2.)

There is a very well known story related of Abbot Paphnucius, who, living in the farther part of the desert, and hearing of a famous courtesan, called Thais, that had occasioned the deplorable loss of many souls, and been the unhappy cause of many quarrels and murders, conceived within himself a design of converting her to God, and of bringing her back again into the way of salvation. For this end he put on secular clothes, took a considerable sum of money with him, and went to find her out. Coming to her house, he asked her to conduct him into a more retired and secret place than that she received him in ; she told him he was very private and secure in the place he was, where none but God could see him. He presently took this occasion to make known to her the sad and most unhappy state and condition she was in, and so touched her heart, that he entirely converted her. The story is very long ; but, to come to that part which is to my present purpose, this woman being converted, he led her into the desert, shut her up in a cell, and sealed up the door with a seal of lead ; leaving only a little hole open, through which they daily gave her a little allowance of bread and water. After this he resolved to leave her, and at his departure she asked him what kind of prayer she should make to God ? You deserve not, says the holy abbot, to pronounce the holy name of God, from a mouth so impure as yours is. Wherefore you shall make your prayer in this manner : you shall put yourself upon your knees, and, looking towards the east, you shall often repeat these words :— " Thou who hast made me, have mercy upon me." She lived three years in this manner, without ever daring to pronounce the sacred name of God, and did nothing else but continually set before her eyes the multitude and heinousness of her sins. and beg pardon of God for them, in the words the saint had taught her. At the end of three years the Abbot Paphnucius went to see St. Anthony, to know of him whether he believed that God had pardoned the sins of this woman. And the saint commanded his religious to put themselves in prayer all the night following, thereby to beg of God that he would please to reveal to some one of them what Paphnucius had so earnest a desire to know. There was one of these holy religious, named Paul, to whom this favour was granted. He thought he saw in heaven a bed very richly adorned, and guarded by four virgins : when, being surprised at the sight of a thing so rich and wonderful, he thought with himself that this could not be prepared for any one else but his spiritual father St. Anthony ; and, whilst he entertained this thought, he heard a voice that said to him : " This bed is not for your father Anthony, but it is destined for the sinner Thais." And within the space of fifteen days after, it pleased Almighty God to call her to himself, to make her enjoy the glory that awaited her, and that heavenly bed he had prepared for her. Wherefore content yourself with this prayer, believe you deserve not to make any other, and believe that perhaps you will render yourself hereby more pleasing to God, than by prayer of any other kind.

In a written treatise on Spiritual Communion, composed by a Carthusian monk, the author relates a story of St. Ignatius and his companions, which he assures us he received from a person most worthy of credit. He says that St. Ignatius and his companions going one day to Barcelona, on foot, as ordinarily they were wont to do, each one carrying his sack upon his back, they met upon the way a clown, who, being moved with compassion to see them travel in this condition, pressed them extremely to give him their bags to carry, alleging that he was stronger and better able to carry them than they were. After having a long time refused what he desired, at last they granted his request. They continued their journey in this manner ; and the good man, perceiving that as soon as the fathers came into the inn, each one sought out a corner, or some secret place, where upon his knees, he might recollect himself in prayer, he did so too, and put himself upon his knees as they did. They asked him one day what he did when he retired ? I do nothing else, says he, but this I now tell you—I say, " Lord, these persons are saints, and I am their sumpter horse ; what they do I desire to do also." Behold this is what I then offered to God. And the author remarks, that this man profited so much by means of this constant practice, that afterwards he very much excelled in the gift of prayer and spirituality. Now, who is there that cannot, if he will, make every day a prayer of this kind ?

I knew an ancient religious of the society, a very great preacher, whose prayer for a long time was no other than this :—" Lord, I am a beast. I know not how to make my prayer, teach me yourself to make it." And by this means he made great progress, and rendered himself perfect in this holy exercise ; fulfilling in himself what the Royal Prophet said, " I am become as a beast before thee, and I am always with thee." (Ps. lxxii. 23.) Humble yourself in the same manner—make yourself as a beast before God, and you will always be with him, and he will always be with you. Humility is very powerful before God ; it is a most proper means to obtain all things of his divine Majesty ; and the saints make an excellent remark upon this subject. They say that, as humility is a means to gain the gift of prayer, so prayer is a means to obtain and conserve humility ; and that we must never quit a good prayer without making an act of profound humility, and feeling very great confusion for our sins and ingratitude. Hence it follows that when we rise from prayer with a sort of satisfaction, or of vain complacency, or of self-esteem, imagining that we have already made great progress in spirituality, and are become very intelligent therein; we must, I say, when we find our-selves thus disposed, always suspect our prayer was not as it should have been. If you complain, therefore, that you are not capable of making many and great reflections, or of elevating yourself to high contemplation; humble yourself and reap at least this fruit from your prayer. This is entirely in your power; it admits of no excuse, and it is sufficient to render your prayer perfect.

That also is a very good means, which Father Avila wishes us to make use of, when we meet with distractions and desolations in prayer. Cast yourselves, says he, at the foot of your crucifix, as at the feet of Jesus Christ, and say to him; inasmuch as these, O Lord! happen to me, and through my fault, I am truly sorry, and feel extreme regret and trouble for the cause I have given; but inasmuch as it is your divine will, and a just punishment for my past sins, and present negligences, I accept them with all my heart; and it is with joy that I receive from you this dryness, this distraction, this mortification, and spiritual dere-liction. The acts of patience and humility you shall thus form on this occasion, are a sort of perfect prayer, which pleases God more than any you could have designed to make.

It is related of St. Francis Borgia, that when he thought he had not performed his duty well in prayer, he endeavoured that day to mortify himself more than usual, and to attend more par-ticularly to all that he did, thereby to make satisfaction for the faults he had committed in it. He counselled, moreover, all the religious of the society to do the same. And, without doubt, this is a very proper means and help, not only to make amends for negligence, but also to enable us to make a most perfect prayer. The Abbot Nilus says, that as it happens, when upon any day we have committed a fault, it seems as if God presently punished us for it in prayer; because he then retires from us, and leaves us in great dryness; so when we have mortified our senses, when in anything we have overcome ourselves, he pre-sently recompenses us for it in our prayer, communicating his favours unto us in greater abundance than he was used to do. "When you shall," says he, "patiently support some hard or bad usage, or any other affliction, you shall afterwards receive the fruit of it in your prayer."

The same saint teaches us, in the same place, another very proper means to dispose ourselves well for prayer, very like that which I mentioned last. "If you would make your prayer well do nothing," says he, " that is contrary to prayer, and by this means God will communicate himself unto you, and will go along with you." (Nil. de Orat. c. xxvii. & lxii.)

Moreover, let it be universally understood and felt, that the chief care of a true servant of God ought to be to mortify his senses, to purify his heart, to preserve himself from sin, to have always a firm resolution never to consent to offend God mortally in anything. This ought to be the foundation of prayer; and it is upon this we must particularly insist, confirming ourselves herein by many acts of our will. For there is nothing we have greater need of, than continually to take precautions, and strengthen ourselves against the weakness and inconstancy of our nature. But this foundation once laid, each one must afterwards endeavour to gain that virtue and perfection he afterwards desires; and if God be not pleased to raise him to a more sublime kind of prayer, instead of complaining or afflicting himself, he must daily return equal thanks to the Divine Goodness, because sanctity is not precisely annexed to the gift of prayer, but consists in performing God's will. "Fear God," says the Wise Man, " and observe his commandments, for in this the whole man does consist." (Eccl. xii. 13); that is to say, all the duty, all the obligations, all the perfection, and all the happiness of man.

I shall now conclude this chapter, by proposing a help or means that ought to impart comfort to all mankind. When you feel not in prayer that fervour you desire, and when you labour in vain to obtain an intimate union of your soul with God, exercise your will in conceiving an ardent desire thereof, and thereby you will supply and gain what you think you want. For, as St. Bartholomew of the martyrs says, " God contents himself no less with this will and holy desire, than if the soul, all languishing with devotion, should entirely unite itself unto him." (In. Comp. Spir. cap. xix.) This means, as Blosius relates, was taught to St. Gertrude by God himself, when once she complained that she could not always keep her heart so elevated towards God as she desired, and as she thought herself bound to do. She being assured from heaven, that when we feel not in ourselves any desire of heavenly things; or, at least feel but a very weak one, it suffices that we truly desire to have a very ardent one; because in the eyes of God the desire is always as great as we would have it to be. Blosius, moreover, adds, that in a heart which is impressed with this desire: *i.e.*, which wishes to be so impressed, God dwells with greater pleasure than that wherewith any man dwells in the most delightful place or palace in the world. In effect God does not want the sublimity of your prayer; he seeks only your heart, and will effect that all the good desires and sentiments thereof shall be accounted and rewarded as effects or good works. Offer yourself, therefore, entirely to him in prayer; give him your whole heart, and desire to have as much fervour as even the angels of the highest choir can have; he will receive that good will, and make the same account of it as of the action itself. This being so, it will be a most pious and profitable reflection, when we find ourselves tepid in prayer, to consider how many servants of God are then at their prayers, perhaps not only shedding tears of devotion, but even their blood in martyrdom; and in spirit we may join ourselves to them, and not only join ourselves to these, but even to the angels also, with intent to praise and love God, supplying after this manner by others, what you are not able to perform by yourself; and often repeating, both with mouth and heart, those words of the canon of the mass: "With whom, we beseech you to command, that our voices may be united and received; because we confess your holy name, and say with them, holy, holy, holy." We say, O Lord! what they say; and we would also willingly do what they do; and we earnestly desire we could love and glorify you in a manner equally perfect. It will also then be very good to call to mind those times in which we were most fervent and say:—"Lord, that which I then so earnestly desired, I desire at present; as then I made an entire oblation of myself unto you, so I now offer myself in the same manner; I have at present the same regret for my past sins I then had; and in the manner that I then desired, humility, patience, and obedience, I now desire the same, and earnestly beg them of you."

But above all, it is a most holy and profitable exercise, to unite our works with those of Jesus Christ, and thus to supply our defects and imperfections by his merits. Thus we may offer our prayer to the eternal Father, to be united to the prayer of Jesus Christ upon earth; and offer our sufferings also to be joined with his; begging of him that he would supply our impatience by his patience; our pride by his humility, and our malice by his innocency. Blosius says, that this exercise was revealed by God himself, to a great servant of his, that thereby we may render our actions more meritorious, and repair the miseries of our extreme poverty, by the infinite treasures of the merits of Jesus Christ.

——o——

CHAPTER XX.

That we must content ourselves with the form of Prayer I have now spoken of, and neither be afflicted, nor complain when we are not raised by God to more sublime Prayer.

ALBERTUS MAGNUS says, that he who is truly humble dares not raise his desires so high as to wish for the more sublime prayer, and those extraordinary favours that God sometimes communicates to his elect; for the humble man has such contempt of himself, that he thinks he is unworthy of them. But if it should happen, that without his having contributed anything to it by his desires, God should impart to him some particular consolation, yet he cannot receive it but with fear and trembling; because he thinks that he neither deserves it nor knows how to make use of it. If, therefore, we have true humility, we shall content ourselves with the common manner of praying, and shall even ascribe it to a special grace of God, that he is pleased to conduct us rather by this secure path of humility, than by any other way wherein perhaps we might go astray and lose ourselves. St. Bernard says, that God deals with us as fathers do with their children whilst they are young. For if a child asks of his father bread, he most willingly gives it to him, but if he asks a knife to cut with, the father refuses it, because the child may therewith do himself mischief. For this reason also, he cuts the bread himself for his child, whereby he both saves him labour, and preserves him from danger. God deals with you in the same manner—he gives you bread ready cut, and will not raise you to that more sublime kind of prayer, lest thereby you might do yourself hurt; that is, lest that other sort of prayer might, perhaps, do you a prejudice, by inducing you to entertain thoughts of vainglory—to believe yourself advanced in spirituality, and to prefer yourself before others. So that God does you a greater favour by cutting your bread himself, than by giving you a knife to cut it. And if in your ordinary prayer he bestows upon you so firm a resolution, as rather to die than offend him ; and in effect preserves you all your lifetime from mortal sin, what better prayer can you desire, or what greater fruit can you wish to reap from it ?

When the elder brother of the prodigal son understood the good reception his father had given him, he took it so very ill and so iudignantly that he would not so much as enter into his father's house. "Behold," says he, "how many years I have served you, and have never disobeyed you in anything, nevertheless you have never yet so much as given me a kid to eat with my friends; but as soon as your son returned, who has spent on bad women all the estate you gave him, you cause a fat calf to be killed for him." "Son," replied the good father, "you are always with me" (Luke xv. 29); as if he would have said, that which I have done to your brother is not because I love him better than you, for you are always in my house; and this particular favour deserves that you should well reflect upon it, and make great account of it. Let us now apply this to our present subject. Is it a small matter, think you, that you should be always with God? He does more for you by giving you the grace of perseverance, by hindering you from separating yourself from him, by preserving you from falling into mortal sin, than if, after you had fallen, he should stretch out his hand to help you up. For it is far more to hinder a man from being hurt, than to cure him after he is so. If, therefore, you derive from your ordinary prayer so considerable an advantage as this, what reason have you to complain? If, by the help of this prayer, God bestows upon you an ardent zeal for whatsoever belongs to his service, a general indifference to all other things in the world, and an absolute resignation and compliance with all that obedience shall command, what can you desire more? In fine if by the help of this prayer he preserves you in humility and in his fear—if he gives you a continual custody and watch over yourself, and defends you from all occasions of sin, what is there you can wish for more? Because this is all the fruit that can possibly be reaped from the most sublime prayer; for to what other end than this do all those sweetnesses and particular consolations serve that accompany the other prayer? And without this, what do they signify. But behold what God does to those who persevere in the common way of prayer; if he does not lead them as he does the others, by the way of sublime contemplation, he at least conducts them to the same end: and in this he bestows upon them a double favour, so that he makes them reap from ordinary prayer all the fruit and advantage that can be reaped from the other. Joseph spoke very harshly to his brethren when they appeared before him to buy bread; yet he omitted not to have their sacks filled with corn, and the money they paid for it put into them, and commanded his steward to treat them with all possible kindness. It is in this manner that God oftentimes deals with us.

We do not sufficiently comprehend in what prayer consists; or, to say better, we do not understand wherein consists our advancement and perfection, which is the end of prayer. Hence it comes to pass, that oftentimes we think we have done wonders, even when we have prayed ill. And, on the contrary, when we have diligently complied with our duties therein, we also believe that we have not made it well. Do but carry the fruit with you from prayer I have taught you to reap from it, and chiefly gain so much over yourself as to pass that day in extreme innocency, and with very great edification of your neighbour, and you will have made a very good prayer whatsoever dryness or hardness of heart you felt during it. As, on the other hand, if you do not profit in this manner by your prayer, assure yourself that it was not good, though you should have done nothing else but shed floods of tears the whole time of it, and though you even thought yourself, like St. Paul, rapt to the third heaven. Wherefore for the future complain not at all of your prayer, but turn your complaints against yourself, and say, I do not fortify myself enough; I am not so humble as I should be, nor have that patience I ought; I do not so exactly observe silence as the rule requires, nor do I sufficiently recollect myself. This complaint is very just; because it is to complain that you do not the things which you ought and could perform. But to complain of your prayer, and of the aridity you feel in it—to complain of your want of facility in making it, and that you find not that quiet and repose in it, nor those consolations you desire, is, in a manner, to complain of God himself, and is, as Judith said to the inhabitants of Bethulia, "a discourse that is more proper to excite him to anger and enkindle his fury, than to procure his mercy." (Judith viii. 12.) It is, moreover, very surprising to see how different our conduct is on this occasion to what it ought to be; for we never complain that we take no care to mortify, to humble, and to amend ourselves, which is what is in our power to do; but we complain of that which God has not left in our power to do, and which he has entirely reserved to himself. Apply yourself, then, seriously to mortify and overcome your passions; use your utmost endeavours in this, and leave the care of the rest unto God. He has a greater desire of our good than we ourselves can have; and if we do but perform what is required on our part, we may assure ourselves he will not be wanting on his, to

give us what is most expedient for us.   But I shall hereafter
treat this matter more at large in the treatise of Conformity to
the Will of God, where it shall be more fully proved that
this complaint is unfounded.

———o———

CHAPTER XXI.

*Of the Cause of Distractions in Prayer, and the Remedies to be
applied to them.*

DISTRACTIONS being a subject of very general complaint, several
saints have taken occasion to treat of them; and Cassian in particular has written at large of them.   Distractions, say they,
may proceed from three causes; first, from our own negligence;
because during the whole day we employ ourselves in a great
many unprofitable things ; and because we are not sufficiently
careful to place a guard over our heart and our senses.   He who
lives in this manner needs not ask the question, how he comes to
be distracted in prayer ?   Nor why he feels it so painful to apply
himself thereunto ? For it is certain, that the ideas of different objects, which had made an impression upon his mind, will not fail
afterwards to disquiet him, by representing themselves in time
of prayer.   The Abbot Moyses said, that though it is not in our
power to hinder ourselves from being perplexed by divers
thoughts, yet it is in our power to put them away when they
come, and adds, that it is even partly in our power to reform the
evil that our thoughts have in themselves, by procuring good
ones ; and to effect that only such as these should present themselves to our mind.   For if we apply ourselves to spiritual exercises, and works of piety, we shall have holy and pious thoughts ;
but if during the whole day we employ ourselves in vain and
extravagant things, the thoughts we shall have will be of the
same nature.   Cassian makes the same comparison that St.
Bernard and St. Anselm make upon this subject.   He says,
that though we cannot hinder a millstone in a mill from going
always about, whilst the wheel or sails move, yet it is in the
miller's power to make it go upon good or bad corn, and to make
it go only upon that which he puts under it ; so the heart of
man must always have something to think on.   It is like a millstone.   Whilst we live it is always in motion, but you may employ it upon what sort of grain you please ; and in fine, it will
work only upon what you cast into it.   According to this, then,
if in prayer you wish to be recollected, you must endeavour to

be so all day long, and must keep a strict guard over your senses; for God loves to converse with souls that are like a garden that is enclosed. "It was," says Cassian, "a maxim amongst the ancient fathers of the desert, that whoever wishes to pray well should prepare well for it, because the state and motion of the mind in prayer depend upon the state and disposition it was in before, and upon what impression it had before received." (Cass. Coll. 9. Abb. Ica.) "Such as the liquor is," says St. Bonaventure, "that we pour into a vessel, such will be the scent that it will give; and such as the seed is that you have received into your heart, such will be the fruit that it will bring forth." (Bonav. de prof. Rel. l. ii. c. lviii.) There is nothing more common or natural than to reflect frequently upon what we love; if therefore you would have your mind at repose in time of prayer, and not be distracted by vain thoughts, you must beforehand detach your heart from earthly, and attach it to nothing but heavenly things; and the greater progress you make in this, the greater will your application and attention be to prayer, which thereby will also become more easy.

The second cause of distraction proceeds from the malice of the devil; who perceiving, as St. Basil says, that prayer is the means whereby God replenishes us with all sorts of blessings, endeavours by all ways imaginable to withdraw us from it, and to raise to it a thousand obstacles and impediments; in order that, depriving us of these succours which accompany prayer, he may afterwards find a more easy passage and entrance into our souls. He does the same against us that Holofernes did against the city of Bethulia; when to facilitate the taking it, he broke the aquaducts through which the city was supplied with water. Prayer is the conduit or channel through which our souls receives the water of grace; and therefore the devil uses his utmost endeavours to break it, and render it useless. Wherefore St. John Climacus says, that when, at the sound of the bell, the faithful and religious visibly assemble to pray and praise God, our invisible enemies invisibly assemble to tempt us, and divert us from this pious occupation.

We read in the Spiritual Meadow, that Marcellus, an ancient father of the desert, having got up at midnight to make his prayer, and to sing psalms as his custom was, heard a noise like that of a trumpet when it sounds a charge, and being astonished how this noise should happen in so solitary a place, no soldiers being near it, the devil hereupon appeared to him, and told him, that this trumpet was the the signal that gave notice to the devils to prepare themselves for combat against the servants of God, and that if he would put himself out of danger he should go back again to rest; if not, that he must expect a severe attack. But the holy old man, confiding in our Saviour's help, put himself in prayer, and persevered in it, in spite of the devil's efforts.

One of the things which clearly show the merit and importance of this virtue (which the Abbot Nilus very well takes notice of) is, the particular hatred the devil conceives against those who apply themselves to prayer, and the continual war he makes against them. He suffers very patiently many other good works, as fasting, taking the discipline, and wearing the hair shirt; but he cannot suffer us to be a moment in prayer without using his utmost endeavours to hinder and molest us in it. Hence it is, that when we are in prayer we are far more tempted than at other times. It is then wicked thoughts pour in upon us, as if we put ourselves in prayer to be only a butt to all sorts of temptations; for in it he excites in our mind such strange and filthy ideas, that it seems as if he had reserved them all for that particular time. He knows very well that prayer is a sovereign remedy against all evil; an infinite source or fountain of all spiritual good, and the most efficacious means of attaining all the virtues, and, therefore, he makes use of all the power he has to deter us from it. Prayer, also, according to the language of the saints, is the "scourge and torment of the devils;" which consideration ought to give us a greater esteem of it, and urge us to apply ourselves to it with so much the greater care and diligence because we see the devil takes so much pains to withdraw us from it. St. Thomas and many other grave doctors say, that it is by reason of the war that the devil is accustomed to make against those that are in prayer, that the Church, directed by the Holy Ghost, ordains that we should begin all the canonical hours with this verse, " O God, incline unto my help, O Lord, make haste to assist me." (Ps. lxix. 1.) Whereby we implore God's assistance in prayer against the snares and temptations of the enemy.

In the third place, distractions sometimes proceed from man's natural weakness, without his being any way in fault; for sin has rendered us so weak and miserable, and our imagination chiefly partakes so much of the corruption of our nature, that we cannot be a moment in prayer, without having our mind distracted with a thousand thoughts. The remedy of this evil is to make them the subject of our prayer, and to humble ourselves upon the consideration and knowledge of our weakness; for this knowledge and humility is a very holy and profitable prayer. I shall, moreover, in the following chapters speak of some other remedies, which the saints and masters of a spiritual life prescribe us upon this subject.

———o———

CHAPTER XXII.

Of some other Helps to persevere with Attention and Respect in Prayer.

St. Basil asks what we should do to have our minds so recollected in prayer, as not to be molested with distractions? And he makes this answer, that the best and most proper means is, to consider that we are in God's presence, and that God beholds in what manner we pray unto him. For if before an earthly prince we take care to keep ourselves always in a profound respect—if we are exceedingly attentive to our words and actions, and if we conceive it a gross impropriety to turn our back whilst we are speaking to him, or to amuse or busy ourselves with anything else, how is it possible we should not be so much master of ourselves as to behave with the like respect when we reflect attentively that we are in God's presence, who takes notice not only of our exterior behaviour, but penetrates even to the bottom of our heart? And who is there that is fully persuaded of this truth that dares withdraw his eyes or heart, even for one moment, from what he is about; or as I may say, turn his back upon God, amusing himself not only with vain, but even sinful thoughts? Theodoret relates, that the Abbot Jacob was wont to make use of a reflection, similar to that just mentioned, in order to show how much ashamed and confounded he was to give way to distractions; and St. Austin also had the very same reflection. If I were in my master's service, says he, and instead of waiting upon him as I ought to do, I should busy myself in something else, he would have reason to chastise and punish me as I truly deserved. Moreover, should I come make a complaint to a judge of some injury done me, and should quit him on a sudden, turning my back upon him, to treat with some other person, would not the judge have reason to believe me very extravagant, and order me out of his presence? Yet see how far greater irreverence they daily fall into, who, putting themselves in prayer to God, permit their thoughts to be carried away with all sorts of distractions imaginable. St. Ignatius also, in one of his additions to mental prayer, points out to us the same remedy. He says, that a little before we go to prayer, we must raise our minds to heaven, by considering that God is present, and that he beholds us : and excite ourselves, by this consideration, to remain with a most profound respect, and keep ourselves in a diligent attention. Moreover, he would not have us lose the reflection upon *God's presence* all the time of our prayer, that we may say with the Psalmist : " The meditation of my heart is always in your presence." (Ps. xviii. 15.)

St. Chryostom says, " That when we go to prayer, we must imagine that we enter into the court of heaven, where the King of glory sits upon his throne, shining with bright stars, and surrounded by an infinite number of angels and saints, who all cast their eyes upon us " (Chrys. sup. Psal. iv.) ; according to the words of St. Paul : " We are become a spectacle to the world, to angels and to men." (1 Cor. iv. 9.) St. Bernard also gives us the same counsel in this point, which he himself followed : " When you go to the church," says he, " lay your hand upon your mouth, and say, stay here at the door, bad thoughts, criminal desires, irregular affections, and carnal concupiscences ; but you, my soul, enter into the joy of your Master, and of your God, that you may know the will of your Lord, and visit his holy temple." (Bern. Clim. in scala spir. grad. 4 et 18.) St. John Climacus says, that when we are in prayer, and make a serious reflection upon the presence of God, we are then like a firm and solid pillar, that nothing can shake. And he relates, that once taking notice that a certain religious was more attentive than the rest, whilst they were singing the psalms, and chiefly when they began the divine office : seeming by his countenance, and the motion of his lips, as if he had spoken to somebody ; he requested of him afterwards to tell him whence that happened ? It is, says he, because in the beginning of the divine office I am wont to recollect and call home all my thoughts, and all the powers of my soul, and speak to them in this manner :—Come, let us adore our Lord who has made us—let us prostrate ourselves and weep before him ; because he is our Master and our God ; because we are the people of his pasture, and sheep of his own making." (Ps. xciv. 6, 7.) All these methods and considerations are very good, and may very much help us to awake and stir up our attention to prayer, and cause us to remain in it with that respect we ought to have.

To attain the same end, others are wont to make their prayer, when they can, before the blessed sacrament; or at least to turn themselves towards the nearest place where it is kept, and to fix and unite their heart and thoughts to it. Others help themselves by looking upon pictures or images, whereby they find themselves excited to affection and respect. Others, by lifting up their eyes to heaven, find that this helps them to elevate and fix their minds. It is also a very good remedy against distractions and aridities, to represent our weakness to God, by short and lively ejaculations, imploring his help and assistance, saying, " Lord, I suffer violence, answer for me." (Isa. xxxviii. 14.) The blind man in the gospel, though Jesus Christ, as he thought, went on his way, and minded him not; and though all others endeavoured to make him hold his peace, yet ceased not to cry out still louder and louder, with all the strength he was able, " Jesus, Son of David, take compassion on me." (Mark x. 47.) You must do the same. Though God seems not to mind you, or not to think upon you, but rather retires from you, not vouchsafing you a visit; and though the multitude of thoughts and temptations that surround you, would stop your mouth, yet you must not hold your peace, but on the contrary, must raise your voice so much the higher, and cry out without ceasing :—" Jesus, Son of David, have compassion on me, fortify me, O Lord, at this present time" (Judith xiii. 9), that I may think only upon your divine self, and constantly persevere in prayer. This was the maxim of a very great saint, that when her heart was silent, she neglected not to speak with her lips, because thereby she renewed and enlivened the fervour of her heart; and she also confessed that sometimes, for want of making vocal prayer, when she found herself sleepy, she also omitted her mental prayer. This is but too often experienced; tepidity and drowsiness, to which we give way in time of prayer, are the cause why our lips are silent; but if we forced ourselves to speak, we should overcome these impediments, and should animate ourselves with new fervour.

Gerson says that it is also a very good remedy against distractions, to prepare ourselves well for prayer, and to choose several points to meditate upon. Because doing thus, when we come to be distracted in any point we have chosen, we no sooner perceive this distraction, but we have recourse to another point; and if we find not a facility in applying ourselves to that, we still go on to another; and thus we persevere with a great deal more ease in prayer. If we would but examine ourselves well, we should find that oftentimes those dissipations of mind, which we have in prayer, proceed from our not having resolved upon, nor prepared those points we should meditate on ; and from our having determined upon nothing for certain, whereupon we may fix our thoughts.

But to prepare well for prayer, there are also two things necessary ; and the first is what St. Ignatius recommends to us in these words : " It will be very profitable, before we begin our prayer, to call to mind the points we are to meditate upon, and determine the number of them." (Exerc. spir. nota 3, 4. Hebd.) And lest we should imagine that this was a duty attached to novices only, we read that it was his own practice, not only in the beginning, but even when he was well advanced in years and in perfection, to prepare himself with care, and read attentively over-night the subject of his meditation for the next day, just before he betook himself to rest.   Moreover, though we have heretofore meditated on any matter, and we believe it still remains very fresh in our memory ; yet it will be, nevertheless, very much to the purpose, especially when ordinarily we take any matter from the words of holy Scripture, which are dictated by the Holy Ghost, to read them with attention, which will give us fervour, and a new disposition for our meditation and spiritual advancement.

Another means that may in like manner be a very great help to us is, that as soon as we awake, we presently, without giving time to our thoughts to settle anywhere else, direct them to the subject we had prepared over-night and dispose ourselves for it by some strong reflection.   Cassian, St. Bonaventure, and St. Climacus, look upon it to be of very great importance, and say, that our praying well, and consequently our acting well, during the whole day depend on it.   And St. John Climacus, moreover, observes, that as the devil knows very well of how great consequence the good employment of those first moments are, so he always watches with great impatience for our first waking, that he may presently seize upon our imagination, and thus reap for himself the first fruits of the day.   He says also, that amongst the wicked spirits there is one called the *Precursor*, whose charge it is all night long to watch over us, that at the first moments of our waking, or even before we are quite awake, or come perfectly to ourselves, he may seize upon the avenues of our heart, by means of impure phantoms, and thereby take a kind of possession of us for the whole day ; figuring to himself that the imagination and heart, which he first seized upon, ought to belong to him as his right. We must then be extremely vigilant, in order that as soon as ever our eyes are open, our imaginations may be filled with the thoughts of God, and our memory and heart receive a similar impression, before any strange thought is able to make its entrance. St. Ignatius gives the same advice in his book of Spiritual Exercises, and adds, that when prayer is made at any other than the ordinary hour in the morning, the person so praying must, inasmuch as the time permits, do the same thing. He must pause and say to himself: What am I going to do? Before whom am I going to appear? And afterwards, like a man who tunes a musical instrument, he must repeat and run over very briefly the matter he resolves to meditate on. In fine, it was his opinion that upon the observance of these, and such other like advertisements, which he calls additions, the perfection and fruit of our prayer did in great part depend. Moreover, do we not daily experience that our prayer succeeds well or ill, according as we are well or ill prepared for it, or according as we practise or neglect these additions?

"Before prayer prepare your soul," says the Holy Ghost, by the mouth of the Wise Man, "and be not like a man who tempts God." (Eccl. xviii. 23.) St. Thomas, and St. Bonaventure, from these words draw this consequence, that, to go to prayer without preparation is in a manner to tempt God; for to tempt God, say they, is to desire to obtain something without adopting the means he has established for this end and effect. For example, if any one should say, I will not eat, because God who is all powerful can keep me alive without eating. This would be to tempt God; requiring he should work a miracle, without any necessity for it. Wherefore when the devil had transported our Saviour Christ to the top of the temple, and would have persuaded him to cast himself down, saying, "that God would send his angels to receive him in their arms," our Saviour answered him: "It is written you shall not tempt the Lord your God." (Matt. iv. 7.) Preparation, therefore, for prayer is so necessary a means to make it well that the Wise Man says, to pray without any preparation is to tempt God, and to desire he should work a miracle upon our account. Our Lord would have us make a good prayer, and that we should apply ourselves to it with great attention and respect; but he would have us to do this by help of the ordinary means, which consist in preparing ourselves beforehand, after the manner I have here set down.

CHAPTER XXIII.

Of the great Comfort and Consolation that those who are subject to Distractions in Prayer ought to have.

THOSE who are subject to distractions in prayer should derive great comfort from the words of St. Basil, who says that they are never imputed to us as faults, but when they are voluntary, and when, after we have perceived them, we continue in them, without respecting God in whose presence we are. He who in time of prayer freely and deliberately entertains thoughts of his studies or business, deserves that God should chastise him, instead of doing him any favour ; and we may very justly apply to such a one what St. Chrysostom says :—" You attend not to what you say yourself, and yet you would have God attend to you." (Chrys. hom. xvii.) But on the other hand, when with all sincerity we do all we can to recollect ourselves, and yet the natural weakness of our minds carries us, notwithstanding, to other things, and even our heart fails us, and forces us to cry out in the words of the Psalmist : " My heart has forsaken me ;" then God is not at all displeased ; but on the contrary, has compassion for us ; " and as a father pities his children, so our Lord has compassion on those that fear him, because he knows of what matter we are made." (Ps. cii. 13.) He knows our infirmities and weaknesses ; and as a father whose son is an idiot, is touched with compassion, when, after he had begun to speak to him in a peaceful and a respectful manner, he perceives him to fall upon a sudden into extravagant discourse ; so our heavenly Father pities and compassionates us, when he perceives that, after we have begun to treat with him in a rational and prudent manner, the weakness of our nature makes us fall into a thousand idle, vain, and ridiculous thoughts. Wherefore, though sometimes we feel no fervour at all in prayer, and pass the whole time of it in great aridities, amidst the embarrassment of innumerable fantastical ideas ; yet we may not only assure ourselves that this is a very meritorious condition in God's sight, but that what we suffer herein, through love of him, renders us far more pleasing and meritorious in his sight, than if we abounded in fervour and consolation. And as the jelly taken by a sick person fails not to nourish and strengthen him, though he takes it with disgust, nor perceives at present the good it does him ; so prayer fails not to nourish the soul, and to give it new strength to serve God.

though we find no sweetness at all whilst we make it, nor feel any benefit we receive by it.

To leave off praying, then, on account of the thoughts and temptations we are molested with at the time, is exceedingly improper. All we are to do, is to take care that tepidity and laziness do not introduce themselves under the cloak of natural weakness, of which I shall afterwards speak at large, whereby we come to yield too easily, let our mind take too much liberty and permit our imagination to wander from one thing to another. For we must take care, as Abraham did, to drive away the birds of prey that descend upon the sacrifice; that is to say, we must apply ourselves to the banishing all thoughts that hinder our prayer; and if we do but our endeavour, there will be no reason at all to disquiet ourselves. We read of St. Bridget, that once having a great many temptations to suffer in time of prayer, the blessed Virgin Mary appeared to her and said :—The devil, envying man's good, does all he can to trouble him in prayer, and to withdraw him from it; but, dear child, what temptation soever troubles you, and what pain soever you feel in resisting it, take care always to strengthen your good resolutions so much as you are able, and by this means your prayer will be of great merit in God's sight. I have in another place spoken of a very proper means to prepare and redeem the time we may fear to have lost in distractions, wherefore I shall say no more on that subject.

———o———

CHAPTER XXIV.

Of the Temptation of Sleep; whence it Comes; and the Remedies we may use to overcome it.

An inclination to sleep, which is another kind of distraction, may sometimes proceed from a natural cause; as, from our not having slept enough; from weariness and labour; from the heaviness and dulness of the air or weather; from the infirmity of old age; from excess in eating or drinking, though only of bread and water. At other times it may proceed from the malice of the devil, as is stated by some of the fathers of the desert, who, by God's permission, saw, in spirit, some devils sitting upon the heads of the religious, to oblige them to sleep; and others putting their fingers in their mouths to make them yawn. And sometimes it proceeds from our own negligence, by putting ourselves or continuing in such a posture, whilst we are at prayer, as easily provokes sleep.   The chief remedy for this is what I have already spoken of, which is to remember that we are in the presence of God.   For as we should not dare to sleep when we are in the presence of some great prince, so, if we consider well that in prayer we are before the infinite majesty of God, who beholds us, we shall be ashamed to sleep.   We may help ourselves also with many other remedies, as by standing upright without leaning against anything; to have a wet handkerchief to wipe our eyes with when we find ourselves most oppressed with drowsiness; to look now and then towards heaven; to hold a lighted candle in our hand; to make our prayer amongst others before the blessed sacrament; and, lastly, to take a discipline before we go to prayer, or to do some other thing that is painful during prayer itself, as to hold our arms across when we are alone.   We shall find great helps against sleep by reciting vocal prayer, as I have said elsewhere. Yet in helping ourselves by these, or other such like remedies, we must not neglect to beg God's assistance also, and that he would cure us of this infirmity.

Cæsarius, in his dialogues, says that a Cistercian monk being very subject to sleep in his prayer, our Saviour one time appeared to him, nailed to his cross, with his back towards him, and said thus—" Because you are tepid and drowsy you deserve not to see my face."   He makes mention in the same place of another religious that was treated more severely.   For falling asleep in the choir, as he was wont to do, the crucifix upon the altar unfastened itself from the cross, and flying to him, gave him such a stroke on the ear, that the third day after he died of it (Cæs. lib. 4. Dialog. c. 29 and 38): all of which gives us sufficiently to understand how much this laziness and tepidity displease God.   The lazy and tepid religious, says the same author, provokes God to vomit, according to the words of the apocalypse, "Because you are tepid, I begin to vomit you out." (Apoc. iii. 16.)

Peter Damian, speaking of that practice which St. Romuald, founder of the Camulduli, caused his religious to observe in prayer, says that it was a great fault in the opinion of this saint to sleep during that time, and he permitted no one who had fallen asleep in time of it to say mass that day, because of the little respect he had kept in his Master's presence, whom he was to receive.

CHAPTER XXV.

That besides the ordinary Times allotted for Prayer, it is very convenient to take some other Time to apply ourselves thereunto.

As secular persons, besides the ordinary meals they take every day for refection of their body, sometimes solace themselves also by particular feasts, wherein they have better cheer than ordinary, so it is very just that besides the ordinary time we daily employ in prayer, which is the food and nourishment of our souls, we should sometimes make spiritual feasts and banquets, in which the soul, taking more than its wonted allowance upon ordinary days, may fully satisfy itself with the abundant sweetness of God's graces and favours. Nature also teaches us this practice ; for we see that, besides the dew that falls every night, it sometimes rains whole weeks together without intermission, that the earth being well watered to the very bottom, neither the greatest heats nor the most violent winds might be able to dry it up. We must, therefore, according to this example, make choice of some particular times, in which, besides the dew which we procure for the soul by our ordinary prayer, we may also secure for it such large showers and effusions of many graces, that neither our exterior occupations nor the winds of temptations may ever be able to dry it up. This has been the practice of many saints and holy prelates of the Church, who laying aside their affairs and occupations for a time, gave themselves more freely to prayer and contemplation. And we read that St. Arsenius was wont every Saturday to remain in prayer from the evening till the next morning.

But this practice is not only of great importance for our spiritual advancement, but also hinders us from falling back ; because the frailty of man is so very great, and the inclinations we have to evil so powerful, that though we sometimes begin our spiritual exercises with a great deal of zeal and fervour, yet we soon, by little and little, come to relent therein, and to lose our first fervour; for we return to our first tepidity and natural remissness as easily as warm water returns to its first state of coldness after we have taken it off the fire, " For the mind of man," as the Scripture says, " is inclined to evil from its youth " (Gen. viii. 21) ; " and is like a perverse nation, to which malice has become natural." (Wisd. xii. 10.) Let us add to this, that being employed as we are, some in studies, others in domestic employments, and others in exercises and functions abroad, we have need to recollect ourselves sometimes by retirement, it being an axiom amongst philosophers, "that every agent suffers by its action ;" so that, though our employments are good and holy, yet as a knife grows blunt by daily use, and requires that it should be sharpened from time to time, so we grow dull by our continual action, and relent in the care of our own advancement by labouring to procure that of our neighbour. Therefore, it is of very great importance to make now and then a retreat, whereby, disengaging ourselves from all sorts of employments, we give leisure to our soul to recover her impaired strength, and regain new vigour to be able to continue in action ; for we are more obliged to ourselves than to our neighbour, and well-regulated charity begins at home.

But it is also for our neighbour's advantage that we do this ; since their progress depends upon the progress of those who are employed in the salvation of souls ; and therefore, it is so far from being a loss to our neighbour to take time for ourselves, that even he receives profit thereby. It is like the letting land lie fallow for a year, that afterwards it may become more fertile ; or to use Father Avila's comparison, it is like the taking off the millstone to pick it anew, thereby to make it grind the better. Our occupations, then, are so far from being a legitimate excuse, to dispense with ourselves sometimes from these retreats, that, on the contrary, the more we are employed and busied in affairs, the more we stand in need of having recourse to the ordinary remedy and help of prayer and recollection. Those who travel by sea must from time to time go ashore to lay in fresh provisions ; and in the same manner, those who are embarked in exterior employments, for the salvation of their neighbour, and who are continually encompassed with so many dangers, as the sea of this world is full of, have reason oftentimes to go ashore, and enter the harbour of solitude and recollection, to furnish themselves with fresh spiritual supplies, and thereby make provision of what is necessary for the continuation of their voyage. The gospel affords us an excellent example of this. Jesus Christ has sent his apostles to several places to preach ; and when they returned from missions, and had given account of them to the Son of God, he says to them, " Come aside to a place of solitude, and there repose and rest yourselves for a while." (Mark vi. 31.) If the Saviour of the world gave this counsel to his apostles ; and if such persons as these wanted repose and retirement, with how far greater reason ought we to believe, that we stand in need thereof ?

Those who have written of prayer say very well, that it is to the soul, what sleep is to the body ; and even in the Scripture itself, it is styled a sleep. " I sleep, but my heart watches." (Cant. v. 2.) " Ye daughters of Jerusalem, I conjure you not to awake my beloved, till she pleases to awake of herself." (Cant. viii. 4.) And the better to explain this comparison, he says as the body reposes and gathers new strength by sleep, so the soul reposes in prayer, and gathers thereby new vigour to serve God ; and as without sleep, though we should take the most exquisite food in the world, we should notwithstanding grow weaker, and be in danger of losing our senses ; so without this spiritual sleep of prayer, how holy soever our exterior employments are, the soul would become weak and sickly, and would even be in danger of being lost. It is for this reason that the spouse would not have his beloved wakened out of her sleep till she pleased ; for it is very troublesome to be wakened by any noise ; but very pleasant to wake of ourselves, after our bodies have taken all the repose they stood in need of, and that all the vapours that mounted to the head are quite dissipated and spent. God therefore would have no exterior thing disturb or awake our soul, when she reposes in prayer, but that she should awake of herself, when she has sufficiently reposed ; and she should exercise herself also in charitable employments ; because she is then far fitter for them than she was before.

Though, generally speaking, it is at any time whatsoever of great importance to apply ourselves to prayer, which we cannot do too often, yet there are some occasions and conjunctures in which it is particularly necessary that we should employ ourselves in it. When, for example, we perceive that we begin to relent in our spiritual duties, and reap not such fruit from them as we ought to do ; when we perceive that we are not as truly observant of our rules as we were wont to be, and set little or no value on small things ; when we find we have not sufficient interior recollection, and we are too much dissipated in the exterior, and too much taken up with affairs, into the management whereof we have intruded ourselves. It is good also to make a retreat for some days, when we perceive we cannot entirely overcome ourselves in some things, that we may endeavour to compass by prayer, what otherwise we could not effect. Because then it may happen, that in a happy moment we shall obtain more grace of God, and more strength to mortify and overcome ourselves, than we should have been able to do in many days, by the practice of our ordinary exercises. For then we would have employed a long time only in falling and getting up again ; but by the help of a few days' retreat, it will happen upon a sudden, that we shall feel ourselves disabused of our errors, confirmed in our good purposes, and absolutely resolved to change our lives. For after all, it is not to be doubted, but that to be sometimes alone, and to confer with God and ourselves, is a very good disposition to obtain of him to speak to our hearts, and to move him to bestow plentiful grace upon us. " The solitary person shall sit and keep silence," says the prophet, " because he is raised above himself." (Lamen. iii. 28.) By the help of a retreat, then, we elevate ourselves above ourselves, and become quite other men than we were before. And, hereby, very extraordinary changes have often happened : " The hand of God is not shortened "—(Isa. lix. 1)—his power is not at all diminished ; wherefore we must never lose courage nor neglect anything we are able to do. How do you know but that God may work great things in you in time of this retreat ? Perhaps it is to some one of those exercises during that time to which he has united your progress in perfection. Moreover, it is not less necessary, for the happy state of your soul, thus to retire after a long journey, or some great and distracting employments, than it is necessary for our corporal health, and for the regaining strength, to treat ourselves with more than ordinary care, after we have been exhausted by a long sickness. It is good, also, for the same reason, when we are about to engage ourselves in any great employments, to take our precautions in this manner, that we may afterwards perform our actions with more purity of mind, and defile ourselves less with the commerce and traffic of the world. The medicines that prevent diseases are better than those that cure them : and it was upon this account that St. Ignatius recommended to all superiors, that before they took their charge upon them, they should make eight days' retreat, to exercise themselves for that time in spiritual things. It is also very much to the purpose to do the same, when we are upon the point of being employed in any long mission, of which Jesus Christ himself has given us an example ; who, before he began to preach, retired forty days together in the desert. The time of affliction, also, is very proper for a retreat ; as well when the affliction regards ourselves in particular, as when it regards the society, or the whole Church in general. For it is an ordinary practice in the Church, to have recourse to prayer, penance, and mortification, for the appeasing God's wrath, and the obtaining his mercy and particular favours. All these occurrences may give us occasion to recollect ourselves in a retreat of some days. But is it not necessary to seek occasions? No! our own necessities, and our own interest also, furnish us with sufficient. Wherefore we ought not to pass a year without making such a spiritual retreat; and when we undertake it, we must perform it to the purpose; that is with a firm purpose to profit by it. For a matter of so great importance ought never to be made superficially, through custom, or condescension.

In fine, God has given this means particularly to the society, not only as a thing very proper for our own advancement in virtue, but also for the advancement of our neighbour. It is in this manner that the bulls of our institute speak; and St. Ignatius very particularly recommends it to the priests: "to the end," says he, "that thereby they make themselves skilful in the management of these sorts of spiritual arms, which, by the special grace of God, are so proper to gain souls to his service." (4 p. Const. c. viii. § 5. Reg. 7. Sacerd.) It was by this means that God drew to himself our blessed founder, and his companions; and it is by this means, also, that he will draw many others after the same example, and we have seen most wonderful effects of his holy grace in those he has conducted by these means; and we must hope that by our making use of the same he will give us the like assistance, and pour down the same blessings upon us.

I add to what I have already said, another thing still very considerable, which ought strongly to excite us to make use of these exercises. It is the favour which Paul V. has granted to all religious in general, in his bull, published in the year 1606, the 23rd of May—in which he grants a plenary indulgence and remission of all sins to those of any order whatsoever, who shall retire for eight or ten days to make the *spiritual exercises*. This evinces the esteem this great Pope had of them—an esteem, which we ought also to have. And that the whole world may be the better informed by the very words of the said bull, I shall here insert them :—"As to those who by the permission of their superiors, quitting their present affairs, and retiring for ten days in their cells, or in any other place, free from the commerce and conversation of men, shall employ themselves, during this time, in the reading of holy books, and in other spiritual exercises, to excite their hearts to piety and devotion; adding, at the same time, meditations upon the mysteries of our holy faith, upon the benefits received from God, upon the four ends of man, upon the

Passion of our Saviour, or at any other prayers, either ejaculatory or vocal, and applying themselves at least two hours a day in mental prayer; and after having at the same time made a general confession of their whole life, or of the year past, or only an ordinary confession, shall receive the holy sacrament of the Eucharist, or shall celebrate mass; every time that they shall make these exercises, we mercifully in our Lord grant them a plenary indulgence, or a remission of all their sins."

——o——

CHAPTER XXVI.

The Fruit we ought to reap from the Spiritual Exercise.

IN the spiritual exercise we must chiefly propose to ourselves three things. The first is, *to perform well our daily actions;* since all our advancement and perfection, as I have already signified, depend upon this. For we must not imagine that these exercises are instituted for no other end than that we should remain eight or ten days in retirement, constantly employed in prayer. No! but they were instituted that we may accustom ourselves to make our prayer and examens well, to hear or say mass with fervour, to recite the divine office with devotion, to profit by our spiritual reading, and so of the rest. It is to excite ourselves by many acts, and thereby to contract a habit to perform them as we should do, that we lay aside for some time all other employments; and it is for the same end that St. Ignatius would have us, during the time of these exercises (which in the beginning he ordained to last for a month, and would have all made in the same order he there appoints), wherein all the particular examens are to be made upon the observance of those rules or additions we are to follow, and upon the faults we also commit therein:—And this is frequently recommended to us, as a thing he knew to be of such great importance and profit. But it is not in our spiritual exercises only, which are the soul of the rest, that we ought to benefit in this retreat; but the fruit thereof must extend itself to our exterior offices and employments, that we may procure help and succour to perform them better, and to observe all our rules for the future more punctually. This is the advantage we must derive from these exercises in our retreat, and regards not only the present time but chiefly the time to come; and it is by our conduct after we have finished them, that we are to discern and judge the profit we have made by them.

The second thing we must propose to ourselves in the spiritual exercise or retreat, is to overcome ourselves, and to practise mortification for the defects and imperfections we are most subject to.   So that everyone ought to examine himself on the branch of duty he most frequently fails in—or that wherein he gives most frequent occasions of scandal and difficulty to his brethren ; and must employ himself chiefly in correcting these. He will have performed the spiritual exercise with profit ; because this is the chief end thereof. The title that St. Ignatius gives them marks this very expressly, because he calls them " spiritual meditations, to overcome ourselves, and to direct our thoughts, and all the actions of our life to the service of God." Wherefore we must make it our business in this retirement so to reform ourselves, that, at the end of it, each one may find himself " quite changed into another man " (1 Kings x. 6), as Samuel said to Saul, or as St. Paul says, "into a perfect man." (Eph. iv. 13.)   Now, it is amendment of our lives that will be the strongest proof of this change. Hence, if you loved hitherto to dissipate and divert yourselves, losing your time in frivolous conversations, it must appear that now you love silence and retirement ; if hitherto you love your own ease, it must appear that now you seek nothing else but your greater mortification and penance ; if hitherto you spoke harshly to your brethren, you must prove that now you speak to them with all imaginable sweetness ; if hitherto you relented in the observance of your rules, and neglected little things, it must appear that now you are become faithful in the very least observances, and most submissive and exact in following punctually whatsoever is prescribed, and in applying yourselves so to your duty that by God's assistance, you will not fall into any deliberate imperfection. See here what victory we ought to have gained over ourselves in this retreat ; for, if we depart from it no better than we entered into it, and bring out with us all the imperfections and defects we carried in, to what purpose have we made it ?

St. Ambrose mentions a circumstance we may very well here take notice of.   He says that a young man who was very much debauched had occasion to make a very long voyage, during which there was a complete reformation worked in him.   At his return to the city where he lived, he met in the street a person of his acquaintance of ill fame, with whom heretofore he had kept dishonest conversation ; and having passed her without saluting her, she was hereat very much surprised, and thinking he did not know her, went to him and told him she was such a one. I see very well, says he, who you are, but I am no longer the same you knew me heretofore. For he was so changed that he was become quite another man. We ought to effect in ourselves a similar reformation, that we may be able to say with the apostle : "I live, but after such a manner that it is no more I that live, but Christ that lives in me." (Gal. ii. 20.) And this, says St. Ambrose, is that happy change of which the Saviour of the world speaks, when he says, "whosoever will follow me, let him deny himself." (Matt. xvi. 24.) For, to renounce one's self, says this holy father, is to change one's self into another man, and to endeavour to be no more the same we were wont to be. When St. Francis Borgia accompanied the corpse of the Empress Isabella to Granada, God did him the favour so to convince him of the vanities of this world, by that constant spectacle of death he had always before his eyes, that at his return he affirmed, that the court appeared to him quite changed. The reason hereof was, that it was he himself was changed, when God had enlightened him. It is after this manner we should be changed ; and this is the end of the spiritual exercises, if we make good use of those lights and graces, which, during them, God is accustomed to communicate to souls.

The third thing we must take notice of, and which is only a consequence of the second, is, the gaining of that virtue which is most necessary for us. Because we root out vices only to plant virtues in their place : "And there are two means," says Thomas-a-Kempis, "that chiefly help to our spiritual advancement ; viz., violently to withdraw ourselves from what nature does viciously incline us unto, and fervently to set upon the gaining that virtue we stand most of all in need of" (1 Book, ch. xxv.) ; which is the thing in question. The directory also of the exercises, speaking of the conduct we ought to hold during the time of retreat, says, that we must not spend all the time of the first week in the practice of the first means ; but it is sufficient to employ only two or three days, in order that there may be sufficient space left, wherein we may proceed to some other means that may elevate us to a higher degree of perfection. Amongst others that are marked us as the most proper for this effect, the chief is, to select one out of our rules, in which we think all perfection we can desire is contained ; as, for example, the rule that says, "As those that are of the world, love and earnestly seek after honours, esteem and reputation of men, so we must love and earnestly seek after the contrary." Take to heart, during the time of your retirement, the gaining such a degree of humility, that all contempts, affronts, injuries, and false accusations may give you as much joy, as honour and praise give to worldlings. And thus raising yourselves above the temptations men ordinarily have of desiring to be esteemed—one for his learning, and another for the dignity of his employment—you will surmount what is a very great obstacle to your spiritual advancement. At another time propose to yourself the observance of the rule, which requires of us to be always "advancing ourselves in the service of God, purely to please him out of love of him; and rather through a grateful acknowledgment of his benefits, whereby he has prevented us, than through fear of punishment or hope of reward." Endeavour to purify your intention, that you seek your own interest in nothing, either little or great, in things temporal or eternal; but that in the one and the other you seek nothing but only the will and glory of God, so that you come at last even to forget yourself. At another time apply yourself to obtain a perfect conformity to the will of God in all things, that whatsoever may happen to you, or from whatsoever persons, you must still receive all as coming from his divine hand. Lastly, whatsoever virtue and perfection you shall propose to yourself to get in your retreat (for we may equally cast our eyes upon all, and see which we stand most in need of), you must never leave off till you have accomplished your object.

———o———

CHAPTER XXVII.

Of some Advertisements which will help us to derive still greater Advantage from the Spiritual Exercise.

THAT we may derive still greater profit from the spiritual exercise, and, as we have said, reap more fruit from it, we must know that before we set ourselves to prayer, we must not only prepare and resolve upon the points we are to meditate on, but upon the fruit also we ought to reap from thence. In the same manner, before we begin the exercise, we must beforehand foresee and determine the profit we ought to derive from it. For this end it is necessary, before we enter into any retreat, that we take an exact review of ourselves; and ponder at leisure, and

say each to himself: What is my greatest spiritual necessity?
To what does my corrupt nature feel the strongest inclination?
What is my most irregular passion, and the worst of those bad
habits I have contracted? Wherein have I most of all en-
dangered my soul? Which of my imperfections does most of
all offend or scandalise my brethren? Behold here an excellent
method to prepare ourselves for the spiritual exercise: and
when, after an exact discussion and examination, we have found
out what we sought for, we must always set it before our eyes,
either to procure it in perfection, if it be a virtue; or entirely
to correct it, if it be a vice. So that in these retreats, we must
not propose either the raising ourselves to a sublime contemplation, or imagine that therein our chief aim must be the enjoying
a strict communication with God; for it may so happen that,
even during this time, we may have more distractions, more
disquiet, and more frequent and violent temptations, than we
had amidst the impediments of worldly employments. We
must, therefore, chiefly have regard to the fruit we are to reap,
as I have before signified, and take all pains possible to gather
it; and, if we do this, we shall have made a profitable and pious
retreat, though perhaps, we have not felt therein all the fervour
and devotion we desired or expected. But if we do not compass
this, though we should be elevated to such a pitch of devotion,
as to be continually dissolved in tears, yet we shall find we shall
have lost our time; because it is not this feeling of tenderness,
but the care of our amendment, and progress in virtue, which
should have been our chief end and aim.

It will also conduce extremely to our advancement, if we help
ourselves by the method which St. Ignatius would have us always
make use of in prayer; which is, that having made our prayer
for an hour, we afterwards spend one quarter, or thereabouts,
standing or sitting, in making our reflection upon it, and taking
account how we have behaved ourselves the preceding hour.
When we find we have performed it ill, we must seek out the
cause and examine, whether it proceeds from our not having
prepared the points well? Whether we have not entertained
ourselves in vain and extravagant thoughts? Whether we have
not permitted ourselves to be overcome by sleep; or to fall into
a kind of drowsiness or languor of heart? Whether we have not
rested too long in speculations of the understanding, and
neglected to excite fervorous affections of the will? Whether
we performed it with all that purity of intention we ought; but

rather sought the sweetness of consolations, than the accomplishment of the divine will? After we have thus made an exact discussion or examen, and discovered in what we have failed, we must presently ask pardon for our defects, and make a firm resolution to correct them for the future ; and, on the contrary, if we find that our conscience does not reproach us with any neglect, we must give due thanks to God, and purpose hereafter to behave in prayer after the same manner. This instruction is of very great importance ; because, by means of this examen, we shall come to know by experience in what we are defective, and we shall correct it ; and in what we have been so happy as to succeed, that we may persevere therein ; and thus we shall gain the spirit of discretion and discipline which experience will teach us. On this account St. Ignatius considers this examen to be well calculated to form and make spiritual masters, not only in the science of prayer, but also in all other sciences which regard or relate to the direction of souls. For, in the fourth part of his Constitutions he says, that when a confessor has heard any one's confession, it will be a very great help to him, especially in the beginning, to reflect presently upon it, that he may see in what he has been defective ; and that, by correcting himself the next time, he may derive advantage from his own faults. The examen of prayer was appointed for the same end; and it is also the first thing we must do after we have ended it. The second thing, which is as important as this, is to take notice what the fruit is that we reap from our meditation ; and thereupon produce new acts of the will, by resuming, in a few words, the substance of what we had said in many ; whence we draw consequences and deductions, and make a kind of epilogue. Moreover, we cannot better know what opinion our holy founder had of prayer ; and of how great importance he thought it was to make it well, and carefully to correct the faults we commit in it, than by seeing that he was not content with our having only the ordinary help of our examens at noon and at night, but would have us also, immediately after prayer, to make a particular examen thereof. And this examen is of so great importance, that if we foresee we shall not have time to make it after our prayer, we must take part of the time of our prayer to make it in.

We may add here another very profitable advice, which is to write down very briefly the fruit we have reaped from prayer; the good thoughts we had ; the pious resolutions we made ; and the lights we received from God in it ; as well concerning those virtues we proposed to ourselves the gaining of, as about the mysteries upon which we meditated. This was the practice of St. Ignatius and Father Fabri, and we have even some of those things they wrote upon this subject. St. Francis Xaverius also advised us to practise the same method; the directory of the spiritual exercises counsels it; and Father Aquaviva, our general, in his writings has very particularly recommended the same. Besides, by this means the good desires and resolutions we make are more perfected, and take deeper root, and make deeper impression on our heart; and experience also will teach us, that when at another time we come to read them over again they will be of great profit to us; for being the very sentiments we had before, and which then touched and moved us, they will move us with a far greater facility afterwards than others, and we shall find ourselves excited to produce the same acts again with greater promptitude than before. But if we go not so far as heretofore we did, we shall have at least a greater confusion to find we are not the same now we were then, and that we go back instead of advancing; and by this means we either do our endeavours to come to the same point, or we supply our defects by that holy shame and confusion we suffer for coming so much short of our former perfection. Thus, either the one way or the other, it must needs be very profitable; but above all, in time of the spiritual exercise or retreat.

In the last place I say, if it be at all times good, as I shall have occasion to prove in another place, to render an account of conscience and prayer to some spiritual director, it is more particularly to be rendered in time of our retreat; and some persons, because they will not subject themselves hereunto, often reap not from the spiritual exercise that fruit which otherwise they would have reaped.

——o——

CHAPTER XXVIII.

Of Spiritual Reading; how important it is; how it is to be done properly.

SPIRITUAL reading is a very great help to prayer, and it is upon this account that St. Paul, writing to Timothy, recommended to him "to apply himself to reading." (1 Tim. iv. 13.) St. Athanasius esteems it so necessary for one who would walk in the path of God, that, in an exhortation he made to religious, he says—" You will see no one truly intent on God's service who is not also given to reading." (Exhor. ad. Relig.) We can neither practise nor leave it off without receiving profit or prejudice. St. Jerome also testifies the esteem he had of it, when writing to Eustochium—" Let sleep," says he, " surprise you with a book in your hand, and let the Holy Scripture receive your declining head." In fine, all saints in general recommend unto us spiritual reading, and experience, moreover, lets us clearly see the profit thereof ; because history records innumerable wonderful conversions that God has wrought by this means.

The founders of religious orders, relying upon the doctrine of St. Paul and upon the authority and experience of saints, have been so convinced of the importance and profit of this exercise, that all of them have prescribed the practice of it to their religious. Humbertus says that St. Bennet was not content with prescribing a time for the daily practice of it, but ordered, moreover, that at the time allotted for it, two of the ancient religious should make their visit round the monastery, to see if there were any that omitted this duty, or that withdrew or hindered others from it. By this we may see in what estimation it was held by this great saint ; and here it may be proper to observe that the visits daily made amongst us, whilst we are employed in our spiritual exercises, had their origin in the direction and experience of the most ancient saints. He ordered, moreover, that such as should be found faulty should, for the first and second time, be gently corrected ; but that afterwards, if they were found guilty, they should be severely punished, and be made examples to others. We have also in our society a rule for spiritual reading, which says—" That the religious should twice a day employ therein the time allotted for examen of conscience, for meditation, and spiritual reading, and with all possible care and diligence apply themselves thereunto in our Lord ; and the superior and spiritual prefect is to take care that each one daily employs therein the time allotted for these exercises." (Reg. 1 Com.) Lastly, spiritual reading is practised by all that make profession of piety ; whereupon I shall content myself to set down such things as may render the practice of it more profitable.

St. Ambrose, exhorting us to apply ourselves as much as we can to spiritual reading, says—" Wherefore do you not employ all the time you are out of the church in spiritual reading ?

Wherefore do you not return to take a view of Jesus Christ ? Why do you not speak to him ? And why do you not hearken to what he says to you ? For we speak to him whilst we are in prayer; and we hear him speak whilst we read the Holy Scripture." (Amb. l. i. Offic. c. xx.) Let this, therefore, be the first means we adopt to profit by spiritual reading; let us believe that it is God speaks to us, and that it is he who dictates to us what we there read. " Read the Holy Scripture in such a manner as always to bear in mind that all the words that are therein are the words of God, who would have us not only know his law, but also fulfil it." (Aug. ep. cxliii. ad. Virg. Demet.)

What the saint says elsewhere furnishes us with another very profitable means, and many most pious reflections. " The Holy Scripture," says he, " is like so many letters sent us from our own country" (Id. Serm. lvi. ad. frat. in Er.); let us, therefore, read them with the same eagerness that a man would read the letters he receives from his native country, from which he has been a very long time absent, and from which he is far away. Let us read them to see what news we receive from heaven, which is our true country; to see what they tell us of our fathers, brethren, and friends, that are there, to see what they say of that place, to which we so earnestly desire to go.

St. Gregory, writing upon the same subject, says, that the Holy Scripture is like a looking-glass, which we ought to set before the eyes of our soul, to behold our interior; and in which it is very easy to perceive what good or bad there is within us; and how near to, and how far off we are from perfection. For sometimes it sets before us the admirable exploits of the saints to excite us to imitate them, that the sight of their victories and triumphs may augment our courage in temptations and sufferings; sometimes it speaks also of their falls, that we may both know wherein we are to imitate them and what we ought to take care to avoid. Sometimes it sets before us the example of Job, whose virtue increased amidst temptations, as foam does amidst the waves and billows of the sea; sometimes also it represents David to us, who fell at the first attack. The constancy of the one helps to strengthen us in the greatest trials; and the frailty of the other teaches us always to have an humble fear, even in prosperity, and amidst the consolation that grace brings along with it; and never to presume upon ourselves, or our own strength, but to conduct ourselves always with all precaution imaginable. St. Austin speaks in the same manner as St. Gregory does—"You will make a good use," says he, " of Holy Scripture, if you use it as a looking-glass, that your soul beholding itself therein, may correct what is bad, and perfect what is good in her." (Id. ep. sup.) What the one and the other say of Holy Scripture, may also be applied to all kinds of spiritual reading.

But to descend more to particulars, and to declare what method we are to observe herein, we must take notice, that to profit by this sort of reading, we ought not to perform it in haste, as when we read something for the amusement of our minds ; but at leisure, and with very great application. For as violent and tempestuous rains do not penetrate the earth, or render it fruitful; but only gentle and continual showers do work this effect ; so to make our spiritual reading enter into our heart, and that it may be received therein, we must make it with tranquillity and attention. It is also very good, when we meet with any passage that strikes or moves us, to dwell a little longer upon it, than upon others ; and to pause a little and think upon what we have read, hereby to move the will ; in the same manner as we are wont to do in time of medita- tion. Yet we ought not, in our reading, to spend so much time on our thoughts and considerations, as we do in medita- tion : where things should be ruminated and digested at greater leisure ; but at least, we must give them some proportionable space. And this is what the saints counsel us to perform, when they say, we must in reading do as birds, who, whilst they drink, take different draughts, and every time they drink, lift up their eyes to heaven.

We see by this what connexion and resemblance there is between spiritual reading and prayer. In effect, this connexion is so great, that when we would train up any one to prayer, and would by little and little prepare him for it, agreeably to his genius and disposition ; the first thing we counsel him is to read good and pious books, and to stop now and then whilst he is reading ; and it often happens by this means, that God raises him to the exercise of mental prayer. We also direct such as have not a facility in prayer, and despair ever to com- pass it, by reason of their continual distractions, to join spiritual reading with prayer, reading a little at a time, and each time meditating upon what they have read. For the mind being thus collected, and fixed upon the things we read, has not so much occasion of spreading itself from side to side as when it is altogether free, or when the senses are not arrested by any object.

The facility of reading and praying together, is no doubt what induced the saints to set so high a value on spiritual reading, that they in a manner praise it as much as they do prayer. For they say that reading is the spiritual food of the soul, which fortifies, and renders it firm against all temptations; which inspires it with the only thoughts and desires of heaven; which enlightens the understanding; heats and inflames the will; comforts it in that irksomeness, occasioned by all the afflictions it meets with in this world; and produces that true and spiritual joy, that is found only in God.

St. Bernard gives us another instruction, how we may profit by spiritual reading—" He who sets himself to read," says he, " does not so much seek to learn, as to taste the things of God." (Bern. in spec. monach.) For the bare or simple knowledge of the understanding is dry and barren, if it warms not the will, and excites not that fervour, which renders the reading profitable and fruitful, and which is truly the end thereof. This advertisement is, moreover, of very great importance; for there is a very great difference between reading to learn, and reading to advance in virtue; between reading for others, and reading for ourselves; the one is a pure study, and the other is spiritual food. So that in reading, if you apply yourself only to the knowledge of things, or to gain something whereby to be better able to instruct others; this is not such a spiritual reading as is to be made for your own advancement; but it is a study you undertake to advance another. There are other times for this; " all things have their times." (Ecclus. iii. 1.) That of spiritual reading must not be employed in study, but in that which I have here set down.

It is for this reason that the saints recommend to us that we read not much at the time lest a long lecture should weary and tire out our mind, instead of fortifying it; and this counsel, which is very good for all persons, is most particularly necessary for those, who imagine that all consists in reading, or rather devouring, as I may say, a great many books. For as the nourishment of the body depends not upon the quantity of food, but upon the good digestion thereof; even so the nourishment of the soul consists not in reading much, but in ruminating and well digesting what we have read. And as hard matters rather tire us, than edify us ; and rather dry up devotion, than increase it ; therefore they counsel us to make our spiritual reading upon simple and easy matters, in which more and greater sentiments of piety rather than profoundness of learning, are contained. Hugo of St. Victor says upon this subject, that a servant of God was counselled by a revelation, to discontinue the reading of all sorts of intricate or hard matters, and to apply himself to read the lives of saints, and other books of the like nature ; and that by this means he made very great progress in piety.

St. Bernard more particularly teaches us, what we ought to observe herein : "We must," says he, " take care to keep in our minds all day long, some passage we have that day read ; that we may afterwards digest it the better ; by calling to mind, and often ruminating upon it. And this must be something also that agrees with the good purposes and resolutions you have made before, and that may be proper to strengthen them, and hinder your mind from distracting or dissipating itself upon other thoughts." (Bern. ep. ad frat. de mon Dei.) For as we do not eat, only to spend the time that is taken up therein, but that the food we take may sustain and nourish us all the day after ; so we must not apply ourselves to spiritual reading, which is the spiritual food of our souls, only to apply the time allotted for it ; but we must perform it so as to make our profit by it the whole day after. For this end it will be very advantageous to us, if we elevate our minds to God before we begin to read, and beg his grace, that our reading may become fruitful, that it may penetrate our heart, and take such root in it, and so fortify it, that it may render us more ardent and fervent in virtue, let us see the deceits of the world, and make us also more firm and constant in what regards our spiritual advancement and per- fection. St. Gregory was wont to make his spiritual reading after this manner, to which he never applied himself without being first prepared for it by prayer, and without having recited this verse of the Psalmist, " Retire from me, ye wicked spirits, and I will dive into, and penetrate the commandments of my God." (Ps. cxviii. 114.)

But that we may still conceive a greater esteem of spiritual reading, and have a greater desire to apply ourselves thereunto, the saints compare it to the preaching of the Word of God, and affirm, that it has all the force and energy that the voice of a preacher can have ; and has, moreover, a great many other ad- vantages that preaching has not. First, it is not so easy to have a preacher at hand at all times, as to have a spiritual book. Secondly, the best instruction of a preacher is soon over, and, therefore, cannot work all those good effects which this may ; for in this we may often turn to any place we have read that moved us ; we may examine and ponder it again and again, and insist and dwell so long upon it as we shall find necessary, to have it make a deep impression on our souls. Thirdly, in a spiritual book we have a good counsellor ; for as a great philosopher said very well, "a book says boldly, and without any fear, that which no person dares tell us ;" it tells the whole world their faults; exhorts and reprehends all with the same liberty. Moreover, by means of reading we converse with the greatest saints and the most famous doctors of the Church, and may entertain ourselves sometimes with one, sometimes with another, and hear them speak as if they were present with us, and as if we heard them pronounce the same words we read. Therefore, they had great reason who said, that spiritual and holy books were a public and inexhaustible treasure. For, in effect, there is no one who every moment may not draw immense benefits and infinite riches from them. In fine, the advantages we may derive from spiritual reading are so great, that St. Jerome, speaking of the interior fervour of the soul, says, that it is not to be doubted, but that it proceeds from holy and spiritual books, by the reading of which the soul, inflamed with divine fire, remains entirely purified from all its defects. To prove this, he alleges those words of the disciples going to Emmaus : "Was not our heart inflamed within us whilst he spoke unto us as we walked with him, and when he explained the Scripture unto us." (Luke xxiv. 32.) And that passage of the Psalmist : "The words of the Lord are chaste ; they are like silver that has been tried in the fire." (Ps. xi. 7.) St. Ambrose also says, that " the reading the Holy Scriptures is the life of the soul ;" and this was what our Lord himself testified in St. John, when he said : " The words which I have said are spirit and life." (Amb. serm. xxxv.; John vi. 63.) If, then, we would live a spiritual life ; if we would walk in the spirit of God, and be inflamed with his love ; let us apply ourselves to spiritual reading, and endeavour to make that good use of it which I have here noted.

What I have said shows us clearly that those are very much deceived, who, when they have read a book, never read it the second time, how good soever they find it to be. A good book ought not be read over only once ; wherefore, take it again into your hands, the second reading will touch and move you more than the first, and the third more than the second, and you will always feel new pleasure and satisfaction in it, as they experience who read with a real intention of reaping fruit from it. And, on the contrary, it is a very laudable and profitable custom those have who, when they meet in a pious book with anything affecting or impressive, take very great care to note it down, that they may have always something by them wherewith to nourish their souls when they stand in need thereof, and wherewith to excite themselves to fervour, and that which may be a comfort to them in the time of aridity and affliction.

What I have said of the many advantages derived from spiritual reading, I might confirm by a great many examples; but I shall content myself with selecting one, which is of very great edification, and which I relate on the authority of St. Austin. He says, that he was visited by an African gentleman, called Potitianus, who, beginning to speak of the wonders of St. Anthony, which all the world talked of, said, that one day the Emperor being at Triers, busy in beholding the sports of the circus, he himself (Potitianus) and three of his friends took a short walk out of the city—that two of them entering an hermitage, took up a book in which the life of St. Anthony was written, and that one of these had scarce begun to read, but he felt his heart inflamed with divine love, when, piously incensed against himself, he cried out to his companion : What do we aspire to, for all the services we have so many years rendered the Emperor? The most we can hope for is, to obtain his favour, and than this what can be more frail or dangerous ? For how much must we still encounter before we can arrive to any great fortune, which of itself is also very dangerous, and, therefore, is so much the more to be feared ? But, should I endeavour to gain the love of God, I can do it with ease—I may obtain it in a moment—it suffices that I only earnestly desire it. In saying this, the approaching pangs of his new birth to a new life caused such interior commotions in his soul, that he took up the book again, and the more he read the more he was disgusted with the things of the world, and the work of God was the more perfected in his heart, as the effect immediately after testified. For as soon as he had done reading, and that the storm which was raised in his heart became a little calm and appeased: " Now," says he to his friend with a sigh, " I am at ease ; my mind enjoys repose ; I renounce all hopes upon earth, to fix my thoughts only upon those of heaven; in short, I am resolved to serve God, and I declare that from this very moment I will never quit this habitation. For your part, if you desire not to make a similar resolution, at least lose not your time by going about to persuade me to no purpose to change the determination I have now made." The other answered, "that he was resolved never to leave or forsake him, especially in an enterprise where there were so great recompenses to be hoped for." And thus they both of them began together to raise a spiritual edifice of perfection, by abandoning all things to follow Jesus Christ. What is still no less wonderful and surprising is, that two young ladies to whom they were contracted, understanding the choice their lovers had made, consecrated their virginity to God. Behold here the example St. Austin relates, which, as he says, had so great influence upon himself, that turning to one of his friends, he cried out with a disgusted and agitated mind : "What will become of us? the ignorant rise, and take the kingdom of heaven by violence; and we, with all our learning, let ourselves be plunged into an abyss of misery." (Lib. viii. Conf. c. 16.) Being thus disquieted in mind, he retired into an adjacent garden, where sitting down under a fig tree, and melting into tears, in a transport of mind he cried out—" How long, O Lord ! how long will your anger against me continue ? Will your wrath, O Lord ! never have an end ? Remember not, O Lord ! my past iniquities." And as he repeated these words, "How long, O Lord ? how long ? To-morrow, to-morrow; and why not as well to-day ? Why may not my miseries find this day a happy end ?" He heard a voice that said, "Take up and read, take up and read." Whereupon he rose and took up the Epistles of St. Paul, to read the first passage he should light upon : for he had heard that the first thing that moved St. Anthony to leave all he had to follow Christ, was this passage of the gospel which he once heard by chance : "Go and sell all you have, and give it to the poor, and you shall have a treasure in heaven : and come and follow me." (Matt. xix. 21.) Excited, therefore, by this example, and far more by the voice he heard, he opened the book, and by the first words he read, he found himself struck with such a light from above, and so changed, that from thenceforward he absolutely renounced all things of this world, and gave himself entirely to God.

THE SIXTH TREATISE.

———o———

———o———

CHAPTER I.

*Of the Exercise of the Presence of God, and the great Advantages
included therein.*

"SEEK our Lord, and be confirmed, seek his face continually."
(Ps. civ. 4.) St. Austin says, that the face and presence of God
are one and the same thing; so that to seek continually God's
face, is to walk always in his presence, by turning all the desires
and motions of our heart towards him. Hesichius and St. Bonaventure affirm, "that to employ ourselves continually in the exercise of the presence of God, is to begin in this life to enjoy the
felicity of the blessed in the next." For though on earth we
cannot clearly see him as he is in himself, as the blessed do in
heaven; yet we may at least imitate them, as much as our frailty
will permit, by placing ourselves continually in his presence, by
acts of love and adoration. For his goodness was not satisfied
with having created us to enjoy him eternally in heaven only,
but would have us to enjoy a part of his beatitude even upon
earth, by always walking in his presence, and continually adoring, and beholding him through the clouds and obscurity of faith,
which make us at present "see him through a glass darkly," instead of seeing him as we shall hereafter, face to face. (1 Cor.
xiii. 12.) "The sight we have of God at present," says Hesichius,
"is that which causes our merit, but that which we shall then
have, will become our recompense." (Hesich. in cent. ult.)

That we may, therefore, merit so great a reward, let us continually do what will make us obtain it; let us view God in all our
actions, and as much as we can, let us always have him present before
our eyes. The angels who take care to guard and defend us, acquit
themselves in such manner of their charge, that they never lose
the sight of God. "I seemed," says the angel Raphael to Tobias, "as
though I had eaten and drunk with you; but I make use of an

invisible food, and of drink which men cannot perceive."(Tob. xii.
19.) The angels nourish themselves with God ; and the Son of
God himself tells us, "that they behold the face of his Father that
is in heaven." (Mat. xviii. 11.) Let us endeavour to imitate them in
this, that whether we eat, drink, or converse with men, it may appear that we have no other entertainment or nourishment but
God. Let us continually endeavour to partake of this invisible
food, and entertain ourselves with what we cannot see ; and this
nourishment and entertainment consist, in always beholding
God, in always loving him, and in always conforming to his
divine will.

The saints and patriarchs of the Old Testament took very
particular care to walk always in God's presence, and the Royal
Prophet was not contented with praising him only seven times
a day, but as he says—" I had always our Lord present before
my eyes, because I know that he is always at my right hand, to
hinder anything from troubling me." (Psal. xv. 8.) It was, in
fine, so familiar and customary a practice with them to place
themselves in God's presence, that they commonly had no other
way of expressing themselves than to say, " Our Lord beholds
me, in whose presence I am." (3 Kings xvii. 1.) And, without
doubt, their great attention to this devotion proceeded from the
perfect knowledge they had of the great advantage of walking
in God's presence, and of thinking that he continually beheld
them. This alone is sufficient to oblige us to be very particular
in all our actions ; for what servant is there so insolent as to
despise his master's orders, even in his presence ? But God is
our master ; he continually beholds us ; he is our judge ; he is
all-powerful ; he can make the earth to open, and cause hell to
swallow us up, as he has several times done to those that displeased him or provoked him to anger. Who, therefore, dares
to be so bold as to provoke him ? When I attentively consider,
O Lord, says St. Austin, that you have your eyes continually
fixed upon me, and that night and day you keep a continual
watch over me, with so great a care as if, neither in heaven nor
in earth, you had any other creature to govern besides myself—
when I think you behold all my actions, that you penetrate my
most hidden and secret thoughts, and that all my desires are
exposed to your view, I feel myself filled with confusion. Without doubt they ought to impose upon themselves a strict obligation to live well, who consider that all they do is done in the
presence of a judge who observes all, and from whom nothing

can be concealed. If the presence of a grave person is sufficient to keep us to our duty, what effect ought not the presence of the infinite majesty of God produce in us?

St. Jerome, upon the reproach which God made to Jerusalem, "because it had forgot him" (Ezech. xxii. 12), takes notice "that the remembrance of God banishes all sorts of sins." (Lib. de fide Resur. t. 4.) St. Ambrose says as much; and the same St. Jerome adds in another place, "that when we find ourselves tempted to commit any sin, if we would think that God beholds us, and that he is present with us, we should never consent to anything that were displeasing to him." (Ibid.) There needed no other consideration than this to oblige the sinner Thais to change her life, and to do penance in the remotest part of the desert. "Does not our Lord," says Job, "consider my paths, and does he not count all the steps I take?" (Job. xxxi. 4.) This being so, who dares be so bold as to sin, or to do anything that is displeasing to him?

On the contrary, the ruin and damnation of the wicked proceed from nothing else but because they forget that God is present and that he beholds them. "There is no one," say they, "that sees us." (Isaiah xlvii. 10.) "Our Lord shall not see our last end." (Jer. xii. 4.) And this St. Jerome takes notice of upon the twenty-second chapter of Ezechiel, where the prophet, after a long enumeration or catalogue of the crimes of Jerusalem, reproaches her in the end with her forgetfulness of God as the cause of all those disorders she had fallen into. A horse without a bridle casts himself headlong into a precipice, and a ship without a rudder cannot but perish. A man also that has not the bridle of God's presence, and is not governed by his fear, runs headlong to his own destruction, and abandons himself to all his irregular passions. "He has not God before his eyes," says the Royal Prophet, "and therefore he is defiled with all sorts of crimes." (Psal. ix. 26.)

The presence of God is that sovereign and universal remedy that St. Basil prescribes for the overcoming all the temptations of the devil and all the repugnances of nature. So that, if you desire a short and easy means to gain perfection, and such a one as contains within itself the force and efficacy of all others, make use of this, which God himself gave to Abraham, a very powerful one indeed—"Walk before me," says he, "and you shall be perfect." (Gen. xvii. 1.) Hereupon we must take notice, that though the text says "be you perfect," yet here, as in many other places of Scripture, the future is expresed by the imperative, thereby to let us see the infallibility of the success. It is, therefore, a thing so very certain, that you will become perfect by setting God before your eyes, that from the very moment you apply yourself with all attention to his presence, you may account that you are perfect. For as the stars borrow all their lustre and virtue from the sun, so the just, who are stars in God's church, derive from his presence, and from their continual elevation of heart to him, all that light with which they interiorly burn before him, and exteriorly before men; and also all the virtue they possess, in order to promote the general good of the whole world. There is nothing can better express the need we have always of God's presence than this simile. See how the moon depends upon the sun; see how necessary it is for her to keep her face always to it. Her light varies as her position with respect to the sun varies: she acts not upon sublunary bodies, but according to the light communicated to her by the sun; so that this action increases or diminishes according as her borrowed light increases or diminishes; and as soon as anything interposes between the sun and moon, the moon presently loses its light and force. The same thing happens between the soul and God, who is the sun; and it is for this reason that the saints so carefully recommend to us that we have the presence of God constantly before our eyes.

St. Ambrose and St. Bernard, speaking of the application we ought to have in calling it continually to mind, say:—"That, as there is not a moment in which man enjoys not the effects of God's goodness, so there ought not to be a moment but he should have God present in his thoughts." (Lib. de dig. con. humanæ, c. 2.) And St. Bernard adds, in another place, that "in all our thoughts and actions we ought to remember the presence of God, and make account that all the time is lost in which we think not of him." (Bern. in spec. Monach.) God never forgets us; it is very just, then, that we should endeavour never to forget him. St. Austin, upon these words of the Psalmist, "I will fix my eyes upon you" (Ps. xxx. 8), cries out, "I will never withdraw my eyes from beholding you; because you never take off yours from me; I will imitate the prophet." (Aug. sup. Ps. xxxi.) "My eyes shall always be fixed upon our Lord." St. Gregory of Nazianzen says, "that we ought not to breathe as often as we ought to think of God." (Greg. in 1 orat. Theol.) For as we every moment stand in need of breathing to refresh our heart, by tempering the natural heat and preserving our life; so we

stand in need of having recourse to God by prayer, to repress
the irregular heat of concupiscence that incites us continually
to sin, and thereby leads us to death.

———o———

CHAPTER II.

In what the Exercise of walking always in God's Presence consists.

THAT we may derive more profit from this exercise, I shall at
present explain in what it consists.   It consists in two points;
i.e., in two acts—the one of the understanding, and the other of
the will.   That of the understanding must precede, as being always required and presupposed for the producing any act of the
will.   Now this act is made by considering, that God is everywhere present; that he fills and replenishes the universe; that
he is all in all; and all in every part of each creature that has
a being. And hereupon we must produce an act of faith; because,
in effect, it is a truth that faith teaches us.   "For he is not far
from any one of us," says St. Paul: "in him we live, move, and
have our being." (Acts xvii. 27, 28.)   We must not imagine
God as far from us, or as if he were not present to us; for he is
within us.   "I sought you, O Lord," says St. Austin, "without
me, and you are within me."   God is present in us, and he is
within us after a more real manner than we are within ourselves.
It is he that gives life to all living creatures: he is the force
and motion of all things that move, and the being of all creatures
that are; he conserves all things by the power of his presence;
and, without the continual help and succour thereof, all things
would cease to be and return to their first nothing.   Consider,
therefore that you are filled with God, encompassed and surrounded by God, and that you, as it were, swim in God.   These
words, "the heavens and earth are full of thy glory," are words
which agree admirably well with the subject of this meditation.

Some, to render this consideration the more easy, represent the
whole world filled with God as it is, and themselves in the midst
of this infinite ocean of the divine immensity, as a sponge
plunged into the midst of the sea. This comparison at first sight,
seems to be very just and proper, and to be within the reach of
the human understanding; but at bottom, it is far from explaining sufficiently what we are speaking of. For this sponge in the
midst of the sea, if the sea be very high, keeps upon the very

surface of the waves ; if it descends low, it touches the bottom of
the sea ; and if it is carried either on the one side or the other,
it meets with the shore. But in God there is nothing of all this.
There is no end nor bounds in him, because he is immense, and
infinite. "If I ascend to heaven," says David, " you are there ; if I
descend to hell, you are present. If I take my wings early in the
morning, and dwell in the uttermost parts of the sea, even there
also shall your hand hold me." (Ps. cxxxviii. 8.) Moreover, as the
sponge is a body, so the water is a body also, which can never
penetrate all parts thereof ; but as to us, we are in all, and in all
parts penetrated by God, who is a pure spirit. Comparisons of
this kind, though very imperfect, are, notwithstanding, good and
profitable ; because in some manner they help us to conceive the
infinite immensity of God, and after what manner he is intimately present in all things ; and it is for this reason that St.
Austin makes use of them in sundry places.

Moreover, we must remember that, to place ourselves in the
presence of God, it is not necessary we should represent him as
by our side, or in this or that particular place, nor to imagine
him as under such or such a form. Some imagine Jesus Christ
to walk by their side, and continually to superintend all their
actions; and thus they keep themselves constantly in the presence
of God. And amongst those who practise this method, some
represent him hanging on the cross ; others as bound to the
pillar ; others as praying in the garden of Olives, and sweating
drops of blood ; or in some other stage of his passion. Several
represent him to themselves as in some other of the mysteries
and stages of his life, according to what touches them the most ;
or else they imagine him sometimes in one manner, sometimes
in another, according to the disposition their soul is in, or their
different feelings in devotion. All this is good, when it is performed well ; but commonly speaking, this is not what is most
expedient, because all those representations of sensible images
do nothing else but tire the mind and engage the head. St.
Bernard and St. Bonaventure without doubt knew, in this point,
secrets we are ignorant of ; which was the cause they felt therein
so great a facility and sweetness. For sometimes they imagined
they heard those words of the spouse in the Canticles, "Arise, my
beloved ; arise, my fair one ; come, my dove, enter into the clifts
of the rock, into the hollow places of the wall." (Cant. ii. 13.)
So they hid themselves in spirit in the wounds of Jesus Christ,
entered into his holy side, and there found an assured refuge in

all their afflictions, a sovereign remedy in all their infirmities, and an infallible ease and comfort in all their pains. Another time applying to themselves those words of Isaias : " You shall drink with joy the waters of the fountains of our Saviour " (Isa. xii. 3), they imagined the foot of the cross to be fixed in their hearts, and with an extreme satisfaction received into their mouths those drops of blood which ran from the precious wounds of the Saviour of the world. These great saints found the benefit of this practice ; but if we should apply ourselves to exercise the presence of God in this manner, it might indeed succeed well for a day, or for a month, but would perhaps hinder us from praying the whole year after, and we should do nothing more than bewilder ourselves to no purpose.

We shall easily perceive how necessary this advertisement is, if we consider that the best writers on prayer, when they speak of the *representation of the place or subject*—which is only one of the preambles of meditation, whereby we endeavour to render things as present to us, as if in effect they passed before our eyes—admonish us not to insist too much upon fictions and representations of this kind, because from them many inconveniences and illusions may arise. Now if a simple prelude, which takes up so very little time to make it, and is also made when we have nothing else to do, requires so painful and dangerous an attention of mind, what difficulty and prejudice would the applying ourselves all day long to preserve these images we have formed to ourselves in prayer, even whilst we are busy about other affairs, occasion in us ? The presence of God, which we now speak of, is entirely free from all these sort of fictions ; because we mean to speak of his presence, as he is God ; and in this there is no reason to feign or imagine that he is here or there ; all we are to do is to believe as a certain truth that he is really and effectually everywhere. Jesus Christ, as he is man, is in heaven and in the blessed sacrament of the altar ; but he is not so in all places, and therefore when we imagine Jesus Christ present, as he is man, it is in effect a pure work of our imagination ; but as he is God, he is always present within us, and everywhere without us. " The spirit of our Lord fills the whole earth." (Wisdom i. 7.) And there is no need to imagine to ourselves that which is not ; but to make acts of faith of that which is. Secondly, we may form an idea of the humanity of Jesus Christ, and figure it to ourselves, because he has a body, and a figure ; but we cannot represent to ourselves God, as he is God, or conceive any figure of him, or of what he is, because he has neither body nor figure, but is a pure Spirit. For the same reason we cannot represent to ourselves, even an angel as he is, nor our own soul as it is ; how far less, therefore, can we represent God to ourselves, after such manner as he is, or make any portrait of him in our imagination ?

But you will say, how then must we consider God present? I answer, by forming a simple act of faith hereupon ; supposing that he is actually and effectually present ; because faith assures us that he is so, without searching any farther how he is present. Thus Moses did, who, as St. Paul relates, " considered God, invisible as he was, and had him always present in his mind, as if he had beheld him with his eyes." (Heb. xi. 27.) Thus when we speak to a friend in the dark, we think of nothing else but of entertaining him, and of that satisfaction we have, by his being present with us, without amusing our selves in painting him to our imagination ; in the same manner we ought simply to repose in this consideration, that God is present ; and content ourselves with enjoying the fruit we can reap from his presence. Because if we will amuse ourselves in representing him to our mind as he is, we shall never be able to acccomplish it. It is yet too dark a night to see him in this manner ; let us, therefore, wait till the morning clears up, and till the broad daylight of the next life appears. " For when he shall discover himself to us in his glory, we shall be like him ; because we shall see him as he is." (1 John iii. 2.) At present our sight is too weak ; and his apparition in a cloud to Moses, teaches us that he wishes his presence to be so concealed from us here below, that we cannot see him but with the eyes of a faith blind and perfectly submissive.

All that I have said regards the first act, which is that of the understanding. But this is not the chief point in the matter we treat of ; for we must not only employ our understanding to consider God as present, but we must afterwards exercise our will in loving him, and in uniting ourselves to him as present ; and it is in this, that the chief exercise of the presence of God consists, as we shall make appear in the following chapter.

CHAPTER III.

Of the Acts of the Will in which this Exercise chiefly consists, and after what Manner they are to be produced.

ST. BONAVENTURE, in his Mystical Divinity, says, that the act of the will, whereby we must elevate our hearts to God, in this exercise of which I speak at present, consists in the ardent desires of the soul to unite itself to God, by the bands of perfect charity. It consists, he says, in the deep sighs, which love prompts the soul to heave, in order to call her beloved to her, and in the tender and affectionate motions, which serve her as wings to fly up, and to make her approaches nearer and nearer unto him. These motions and desires are by the saints styled aspirations ; because they make the soul raise itself to God, which is the same thing as to aspire to him ; and because, as the action of continually repelling from our lungs the air that we draw into them, is made without any previous reflection or resolution to respire or draw breath ; so these burning desires proceed so suddenly from the bottom of our hearts, that we sometimes make them, without having had beforehand so much time as to think of them, or to design or purpose with ourselves to produce them. These aspirations and these desires are· expressed by short and frequent prayers which are called " ejaculatory," that is to say, according to St. Austin, " suddenly shot forth" (Epis. ad Prob.) ; because they are like inflamed darts or arrows, which the heart shoots one after another towards God. Cassian likewise says, that they were very much in esteem, and as much in use amongst the primitive monks in Egypt ; because, " being short they did not weary the mind" (Lib. ii. de instit. renunt.) ; and being full of zeal and fervour, they approached God's presence before the devil could have leisure to trouble him that made them, or to oppose any obstacle to them. St. Austin says upon this subject, what ought to be very much taken notice of by those who give themselves to prayer—" We must take care," says he, " that this ardent and lively attention which is necessary for him that prays, be not weakened by the length of our prayer." (Epis. ad Prob.) But this is not so much to be feared in ejaculatory prayers, and therefore the saints in the desert ordinarily made use of them, endeavouring, by a continual elevation of their hearts to God, to entertain themselves always in his presence.

And indeed there is no means more fit to attain this end; nor any more easy or profitable: but we shall first explain its practice more fully. Cassian establishes it in that verse which the Church repeats in the beginning of each canonical hour: "Incline unto my aid, O God; O Lord, make haste to help me" (Psal. lxix. 1.) Do we begin any hard or difficult employment, let us first of all by these words beg grace that we may perform it well; and as in all things we stand in need of his assistance, so let us continually have recourse unto him. This verse, says the same Cassian, wonderfully expresses all our desires, in whatsoever state or condition we may be. By this we beg God's assistance; by this we humble ourselves, and acknowledge our wants and miseries; and by it, we inflame ourselves with his love, considering that he is our protector and refuge. In fine, whatsoever combats or assaults of the enemy we have to sustain or resist, we have in these words an impenetrable buckler, a coat of mail that is proof, and an assured rampart of defence. Wherefore we must have these words always in our heart, and in our mouth—we must make them our constant prayer and avail ourselves of them, in order to put ourselves in the presence of God.

St. Basil makes the practice of this exercise to consist in taking occasion from all things to call God to mind. If we eat, let us give thanks to God; if we clothe or dress ourselves, let us always render him thanks; if we look up to the heavens, or behold the sun or stars, let us praise God who created them; and as often as we awake in the night, let us never fail to elevate our hearts to God.

But because there are are three states in a spiritual life—the purgative, for those that begin; the illuminative, for those that are advanced; and the unitive, for such as are perfect—some, therefore, judge three sorts of aspirations or ejaculatory prayers necessary. Aspirations of the first kind regard the purgative way, and help to obtain pardon of our sins, to purify the soul from vices, and to withdraw it from all terrene affections. Those of the second kind conduce to the obtaining of virtues, the overcoming temptations, the gaining courage to embrace all sorts of labours for God; and these belong to the illuminative way. The third, in fine, appertain to the unitive, and have for their end, the union of the soul with God, by the bond of perfect charity. The object of this distribution is, that each one should find wherewith to employ himself in that exercise which is most conformable to the present state of his soul. But after all, let us be ever so perfect, there cannot be an exercise more agreeable to God, than to employ ourselves in conceiving a lively sorrow for our sins, and in begging grace that we may never offend him. So, also, those that still labour to overcome their imperfections, and the bad habits they have contracted, or to gain those virtues they stand in need of, though they should not yet be in the state of perfection, yet may also exercise themselves in making acts of the love of God, that they may render their enterprise more easy and pleasant. And all in general may sometimes apply themselves to make the following acts : O my God, happy are they that have never offended your divine goodness ! Never permit me, O Lord ! to be so unhappy as to displease you. Let me rather die than sin. Nay, grant that I may rather die a thousand deaths, than ever commit one mortal sin. At another time we may elevate our hearts to God, either by returning him thanks for the general or particular benefits we have received, or by begging of him to grant us some particular virtue ; as profound humility, perfect obedience, ardent charity, or firm and unshaken patience. At another time we may make acts of the love of God, of conformity to his divine will—pronouncing these words, taken from divers places of Scripture : " My beloved is all mine, and I am all his." (Cant. ii. 16.) " Let not my will, but your will, O Lord ! be done." (Luke xxii. 42.) " What is there I pretend to in heaven, besides you ; and what do I desire upon earth, in comparison of you ?" (Ps. lxxii. 25.) All these sorts of aspirations or ejaculatory prayers are very proper to keep ourselves in the presence of God. But the best and most efficacious of all (though, perhaps, they cannot be conceived in such proper and expressive terms as those we have just now mentioned) are such as the heart produces of its own accord when touched by God. Oftentimes a bare repetition of the same act with fervour, is sufficient to keep us many days in his presence, or to entertain ourselves with, even for our whole life. You may, therefore, if you think good, often repeat those words of St. Paul : " Lord, what would you have me to do ?" (Acts ix. 6.) Or those of the Spouse : " My beloved is all mine, and I am all his." Or this verse of the Psalmist : " What is there that I pretend to in heaven, besides the enjoyment of yourself,

O Lord? And what is there I desire upon earth in comparison of you?" You need no other than these; wherefore entertain yourself with them, let them be your continual exercise, and the constant means you make use of, to keep and maintain the presence of God in your heart.

-----o-----

CHAPTER IV.

In which this Exercise is more particularly explained, and a very easy, profitable, and perfect Means is prescribed, of walking always in the presence of God.

AMONGST the many aspirations and ejaculatory prayers we may make use of, for the practice of this exercise, one of the chief and most proper is, that which St. Paul prescribes in the first Epistle to the Corinthians—" Whether you eat," says he, " or drink, or whatever you do, do all to the greater glory of God." (1 Cor. x. 31.) Endeavour, in all things you do, to elevate your heart to him, saying to him: Lord, it is for your sake I do this; it is to please you, it is because you will have it so. Your will, O Lord! is mine, and I have no other comfort or satisfaction but yours. I know not what to desire, or what not to desire, but what is your holy will I should, or should not desire. All my joy, all my satisfaction, is the fulfilling your will; and so that I do but please you, I desire nothing more; there is nothing in heaven nor upon earth that I desire to behold but yourself—and provided I can but please and satisfy you, I have all that can please, or be a satisfaction to myself. This is a most excellent and most perfect way of walking in God's presence; because it is to entertain ourselves in a continual exercise of the love of God. But since I have already spoken of it, and shall again speak of it elsewhere, I will here only add one thing more, which I think, will complete its eulogy. It is this, that of all the means we can imagine, there is no one better nor more profitable than this, to keep ourselves always in that continual prayer, which the Saviour of the world requires we should practise, when he says, " It behoves us to pray always without ceasing." (Luke xviii. 1.) For what better prayer can we make, than continually to desire the greater glory of God, to conform ourselves continually in all things to his Divine will, and to place all our joy and contentment in the joy and contentment of God?

It was this that gave occasion to a famous doctor to say with a great deal of reason, that whosoever continued constant in this exercise, would reap so much fruit from it, that, in a short time, he would find his heart quite changed, and should feel in it an exceedingly great hatred of the world, and an inconceivable love of God. If, as you ought, you observe this so holy a method, "you are no longer guests or strangers, but you are fellow-citizens with the saints, and domestics of God." (Eph. ii. 19.) It is of such as adopt this method St. John speaks in the apocalypse, when he says, that the servants of God "shall behold him face to face, and his name shall be written in their foreheads." (Apoc. xxii. 4.) Those who live in this manner, properly speaking, have no more commerce or conversation with the world. "All their conversation is in heaven." (Phil. iii. 20.) "They consider not the things they see, but those they see not, because those they see are temporal, but those they see not are eternal." (2 Cor. iv. 18.)

Moreover, we must take notice, that when we make these acts which I have now spoken of, and say, Lord, it is for you that I do this; it is because you will have it so, and such like things of this nature, we must say them, not as elevating our heart, or raising our thoughts to something without us, but as speaking to God present within us, for this is properly to walk in the presence of God, and this is what will render this more sweet, pleasant, easy, and profitable to us than any other sort of prayer whatsoever. For if, for example, when we meditate upon Jesus Christ hanging upon a cross or bound to a pillar, those that have written of prayer observe, that we are not to imagine this is a thing that happened in Jerusalem so many ages since, because our imagination is hereby tired, and our heart is less moved and excited : but we must imagine it as a thing present, that passes before us, and as if we heard the blows of the hammer and the strokes of the whips. If we also meditate upon death, they say, we must, in like manner, imagine, that we are in present danger of death ; that the physicians despair of us, and that we already have the hallowed candle or the crucifix in our hands. With far greater reason, therefore, is it fit that, in the exercise of the presence of God, we should make such acts as I have here mentioned; not as if we were speaking to one absent or far distant from us, but as speaking to God present, because it is properly herein that this exercise consists, and, in effect, his presence is thus really and truly enjoyed by us.

CHAPTER V.

How different this Mode of walking in the Presence of God is from other Modes that are practised, and the Advantages that this has above all others.

To show more clearly how perfect and advantageous this manner of walking in God's presence is, and to explain it more fully, I shall point out in what this manner excels all others. First, in most of those other ways, it seems that all is reduced to a simple act of the understanding, and ends only in imagining that God is present; but this presupposes this act of the understanding, and of faith also, touching the presence of God, and wholly employs itself in making acts of the love of God; and consequently there is no doubt, but that it is the most excellent and most profitable of all others. For, as in prayer, we must not content ourselves with forming acts of the understanding only, which consist in the meditation and reflections we make upon things, but must proceed also to make acts of our will, which are affectionate motions and inclinations to virtue, and vehement desires to imitate Jesus Christ—and it is upon these last acts the fruit of prayer depends—so likewise all the fruit of the exercise of the presence of God is contained in the acts of the will, and therefore, it is upon these we must more particularly insist.

In the second place, this practice is more easy and pleasant than the others; because in the others the understanding and imagination must take a great deal of pains to represent things, which exceedingly engages the brain; but in this, there is no want of the assistance of the imagination; nothing but the affectionate motions of the will are required, which are produced without any pain or difficulty at all. For though it is very true, that the presence of God, upon which this exercise is grounded, cannot be conceived but by an act of the understanding, yet even when we are before the blessed sacrament we content ourselves, supposing by faith that Jesus Christ is there present, and we reduce all our attention to adore him, to love him, and to beg those graces of him we stand most in need of. So in the exercise of the presence of God, we must also regard this presence, as a thing supposed by faith, and without insisting upon acts of the understanding, we must pass to those of the will. But as these are easy to produce, so we may persevere a long time in them ; and hence it is that when sick persons are able to make no other kind of prayer, they are advised often to elevate their hearts to God by acts of the will, because it is a thing easily done at all times. So that if there were no other advantage in the practice we have proposed than this, to be able to persevere longer in it than in others, this alone were sufficient to make us prefer it before them ; because this as far surpasses all others, as real and essential things surpass imaginary.

But that which is most of all considerable, and which we must very particularly take notice of, is, that when we put ourselves in the presence of God, it is not to remain or rest there ; but that this presence may serve as a means or help to perform all our actions. For if we content ourselves with barely attending to the presence of God, and so become negligent in our actions, and commit thereby several faults in them, this attention would be no profitable devotion, but a very hurtful illusion. Whilst, therefore, we have one eye engaged in contemplating God, we must engage the other in seeing how to do all things well for his love ; so that the consideration of our being in his presence may be a means to oblige us to do all our actions better. And it is for this reason, that the method we speak of is far more proper than all others ; for in the others the understanding is taken up, either in forming sensible images of those things it would represent to itself, or in deriving from those images some good thoughts conformable to them ; so that the soul giving all her attention to this, and retaining none for other things, she consequently produces only imperfect and defective actions. But here, the imagination having nothing to do, there is nothing to prevent that application, which is so necessary for the due performance of our actions. But, on the contrary, we here find great help and succour to perform them as we should ; because by thinking that we do them for God, and in the presence of God, we endeavour to perform them in such a manner, that they may be worthy to appear before his Divine majesty ; and I have spoken in another place of an excellent means to walk always before God ; but since I have sufficiently explained it there, I shall not repeat here what I have before said of it.

———o———

THE SEVENTH TREATISE.

---o---

---o---

CHAPTER I.

Of how great Importance this Examen of Conscience is.

ONE of the chief and most efficacious means we have for our spiritual advancement, is that of examen of conscience, and it is for this reason the saints recommend so earnestly the practice of it. St. Basil, one of the most ancient of those that have made rules for religious persons, ordained that they should every night make this examen. St. Austin in his rule enjoins the same. St. Anthony taught also the same to his followers, by his own example; and St. Bernard, St. Bonaventure, Cassian, and generally all the founders of religious orders, as well as all masters of a spiritual life, would have us daily apply ourselves to this exercise. St. Chrysostom, writing upon the words of the Psalmist, "in your beds excite yourselves to compunction and sorrow of heart" (Ps. iv. 5), declares, that we should make this examen before we go to bed; and gives two good reasons for it. First, that the day following we may be the better disposed to preserve ourselves from those faults we committed the day before: for if we examine ourselves well overnight, and conceive a great sorrow for our defects, and propose firmly to correct them, it is certain that this will serve as a curb, to hinder us from falling again into them the day following. Secondly, the examining ourselves at night will be an occasion of greater moderation and recollection all the day long: for the knowledge we have, that on the very same day we must render an account of what we have done, will make us stand more upon our guard, and pay greater attention to what we do. And as a nobleman, says St. Chrysostom, who preserves order in his family, lets no day pass, without calling his steward to an account, to prevent him from being careless and confused therein; even so it is

good that we also daily make up our accounts, lest our negligence and forgetfulness should cause great disorder in them. St.
Ephrem and St. John Climacus, moreover, add, that as merchants set down their gains and losses every day; and when
they find they have suffered any loss, they presently endeavour
to repair it: so we must daily examine the gains and losses that
happen to us in the great affair of our salvation, that by
presently repairing our losses, we may prevent them from being
so great as to bring on our total ruin. St. Dorotheus takes
notice of another very considerable advantage we derive from
this examen—it is that by accustoming ourselves to make it well
every day, and by daily repenting of our faults, we hinder them
from taking deeper root in our heart, and prevent our bad
habits from growing stronger.

But it is not so with those who are not careful to examine
themselves, and whose consciences are compared by the saints
to the field and vineyard mentioned by the Wise Man, when he
says—"I passed by the field of idle persons, and the vineyard
of the fool, and all was overgrown with nettles, all was covered
with thorns, and the dry wall about it was thrown down."
(Prov. xxiv. 30.) The conscience of those who do not examine
themselves, is like a neglected vineyard, which, because it is not
cultivated, is presently overgrown with thorns and brambles.
For our corrupt nature is so bad a soil, that of itself it produces
nothing but weeds: and therefore we must always have our
pruning-hook in our hand, and employ ourselves in cutting or
rooting them out. Now this is done by means of our examen—
it is this that cuts up vice effectually, that plucks up our bad
inclinations as soon as they begin to appear, and hinders bad
habits from taking root.

But the importance and efficacy of this means have been made
known not only to the saints, but also to many pagan philosophers, who were illuminated by the light of nature only. St.
Jerome and St. Thomas relate, that one of the chief instructions
Pythagoras was wont to give his disciples was, that they should
daily, morning and evening, employ some time in examining
themselves upon these three questions—What have I done?
How have I done it? And what have I omitted to do? Rejoicing at what they found they had done well; and repenting
and being sorry for what they had done amiss. Seneca, Plutarch,
Epictetus, and many others, recommended the same thing.

St. Ignatius, resting upon the doctrine of the holy fathers, upon the light of reason, and upon the authority of experience, made so great an account of this examen, that he affirms, as St. Bonaventure had done before him, that it is one of the best and most profitable means we can help ourselves with to make great progress in spirituality, and has also given us particular rules concerning it. Let all the society, says he in one place, take care to examine their consciences every day. In another place he ordains, that this examen should be made twice a day; and in some measure prefers this examen even before prayer itself. Because what we only purposed to do in prayer, ought to be put in execution in our examen; wherein the extirpation of vices, and the mortification of our passions, are what we must chiefly employ ourselves in. Wherefore this examen is held in so great esteem amongst us, that the religious are twice a day called to it by sound of bell—in the morning before we go to dinner, and and at night before we go to bed; and lest any should fail in the observance of it, all are visited at that time, as at the time of prayer. But St. Ignatius is not content with establishing this examen in the society only, but would have those of the society to persuade, as much as they can, all seculars with whom they converse to practise the same. Hence it is that, amongst us, those who are good labourers in our Lord's vineyard fail not, as soon as any one puts himself into their hands, presently to teach him to make his general and particular examen of conscience; thereby to break and overcome more easily any evil habits he may have contracted; as that of swearing, lying, backbiting, and the like. Behold the use to which our first founders applied it. Father Fabri recommended nothing more to those whose consciences he governed. And when St. Ignatius had undertaken the cure of any person that was spiritually sick, he was not content with giving him the wholesome remedy of the particular examen only; but he, moreover, assigned some pious person, in whom the patient had great confidence, and obliged the patient, every noon and night, to go to him, to give him an account if he had made his particular examen; and whether he had observed what was prescribed for the due performance of it. We know also that for a long time together, whilst he employed himself in the spiritual conduct and instruction of his companions, he did nothing else but exhort them to prayer, examen of conscience, and frequenting the sacraments; believing that if they acquitted themselves well of these, this was sufficient to preserve and maintain them in virtue.

All this ought to give us a great esteem of this exercise, and make us consider and look upon it as the most efficacious means for our advancement in perfection, and move us to be very exact in making our examens twice a day, and convince us that we cannot neglect them without neglecting, at the same time, the chief obligations of a religious life. Nothing should divert us from so holy an exercise; or if any indispensable occupation hinders us from making it at the time appointed, we must endeavour afterwards to fulfil this obligation as soon as possible. And sickness itself, which dispenses with our ordinary hour of mental prayer, dispenses not with our general or particular examens. We must hold it, therefore, for an infallible maxim, that we must never exempt ourselves from it upon any account whatsoever. The sick person, moreover, has daily sufficient matter for his particular examen, either by conforming himself in pains and sickness, which God sends him, to his divine will, and also to the remedies he is obliged to take, which are sometimes more troublesome than the disease itself; or else by supporting with patience the want of several things he imagines he stands in need of; or, in fine, by resigning himself entirely into the hands of God, to live or to die, as it shall please the divine providence to ordain.

———o———

CHAPTER II.

Upon what the particular Examen ought to be made.

THE examen practised in the society is twofold—one particular, the other general. The particular is made upon one subject only, and hence it is called particular. The general is made upon all the faults and imperfections we have that day committed, in thoughts, words, or deeds, and it is called the general examen, because it embraces all things in general. I shall speak first of the particular examen, and afterwards briefly touch on what shall be necessary to add concerning the general; because almost the same method we are to practise in the particular must also be practised in the general examen; so that what I say of the one will, in like manner, serve for the other. There are two things to be considered in the particular examen; the one, upon what subject it is to be made; the other, how it ought to be made. As to the first, that we may the better know upon what we ought chiefly to make this examen, we must very well imprint in our minds an advertisement that St. Ignatius gives us in his Spiritual Exercises and which he himself extracted from the works of St. Bonaventure. He says that the devil deals with us as a general of an army deals with a town he designs to take. The general first endeavours to know the weakest part thereof, to raise his batteries against it, and bring all his troops to bear on it; because he knows that as soon as he has gained that post, he will presently become master of the town. The devil, in like manner, takes all care imaginable to know the most feeble part of our souls, to make his attack afterwards in that part, that thereby he may more easily reduce us to his subjection. Let us make use of this admonition to keep ourselves upon our guard, and to take precaution against our enemies. Let us attentively seek and find out which is the weakest part of our soul and the most naked of virtue; let us see where our natural inclination renders an attack more easy, and what part is most of all decayed and ruined by ill habits; and let us labour everywhere to repair and fortify the weakest places by strong ramparts. See here what the masters of a spiritual life would chiefly have us do, that we should endeavour to tame our irregular inclinations and root out our bad habits; and since this is what is most of all necessary, it is also this to which we must chiefly apply our particular examen.

Cassian gives two reasons of the necessity we have thus to begin to combat with our bad habits. The first, because it is from them our chief and greatest dangers arise, they being the occasion of our greatest and most grievous falls, and, therefore, it is very just to take care of them before all other things. The second, because having once overcome the most formidable enemies, and those that make fierce war against us, the rest becoming more weak by the defeat of these, will afterwards be more easily overcome by us, since our soul becomes more strong and more courageous by this first victory. On this subject he relates what was heretofore practised at Rome in the combats with wild beasts, where those who desired to signalize themselves in an extraordinary manner, and to give the emperor a greater pleasure and amusement, presently set upon that beast that seemed most fierce, because, having killed that, they easily despatched all the rest. He says we must act in the same manner. We see by experience that, ordinarily speaking, each one has a particular vice or predominant passion which masters him, and causes him to commit those things which otherwise he would not. Hence it is a common saying amongst people, if I had not this or that bad inclination, I think there is nothing could hinder, trouble, or give me any pain. Behold here the very thing we must first of all set upon and fight against; see here what we must make choice of for our particular examen.

In the war which the King of Assyria waged against the King of Israel, he commanded all his captains " not to fight against any one, little or great, but only against the King of Israel " (2 Para. xviii. 30) ; promising himself that the death of the king would give him an easy victory over the whole army ; as happened in effect. For King Achab being killed by an arrow, which was shot at random, they all retreated, and the war was presently ended. Let us follow this example, let us overcome that vice which in us is king of the rest, and we shall easily tame and vanquish all the others. Let us cut off the head of Goliath, and all the other Philistines will soon be defeated and entirely routed. We cannot prescribe a better general rule or direction, upon what every one ought chiefly to make his examen, than this. But what may still be added to this subject is, that it is very good that every one confer with his spiritual director, after having first given him an exact account of the present state of his conscience, of his inclinations, passions, propensities, and bad habits; acquainting him with everything without exception ; for the necessity of each one being hereby perfectly known, it will be very easy for the director afterwards to determine upon what matter or subject the penitent ought to make his particular examen. One of the things we ought chiefly to observe, when we render an account of conscience, is, to declare upon what subject we make our particular examen, and in what manner we profit by it. For it is of serious consequence that this examen be effectually made upon that subject which each one finds of greatest importance. For as a physician has made no small advance in his cure, when he has found out the true cause of the disease, because he then applies proper remedies, which fail not of their effect ; so we may look upon ourselves to have gained a very considerable point, if we succeed in finding out the true source of all our spiritual infirmities; because then we shall have discovered the true means of curing them ; *i.e.*, applying the salutary remedy of the particular examen. The reason in some degree why many persons derive but little advantage from what they do, is, because they apply not to what they ought. If you cut away the root the tree withers, grows dry, and dies presently ; but if you only lop the branches, it will soon shoot out new ones, and will become larger than ever.

CHAPTER III.

Two very important Advices to be followed in making Choice of a proper Subject for the particular Examen.

To treat this matter more particularly, I say there are two things chiefly to be observed, of which the first is, that when we have any exterior defects, that offend and scandalize our neighbour, it is these we must begin to retrench by means of our particular examen ; though we should have interior defects far more considerable. For example, if one speaks too much, or too hastily, or too sharply to his brethren, or lets himself be carried so far as to say things that affect their reputation ; and in fine, if one is subject to other failings that may hurt the neighbour, reason and charity oblige us first to correct ourselves in what may give pain or trouble to our brethren, that we may endeavour to live with them in such manner as to give no occasion of complaint or scandal. The gospel, speaking of the father and mother of St. John the Baptist, says, "that they were both just before God, walking according to all the commandments and ordinances of our Lord, without giving any one occasion of complaint." (Luke i. 6.) This was a very great praise for a servant of God, and it is what every religious person that lives in a community ought particularly to aim at. It is not sufficient to be just before God, but it is, moreover, necessary so to live in religion as to give no one occasion of complaint ; and if one finds anything in himself, that is any way offensive to his neighbour, it is upon this he must begin to make his particular examen.

But the second advice is, that we take care not to be so intent on making our examen on exterior things of this sort, as to pass our whole life therein ; for it is far easier to overcome ourselves in these exterior than in our interior defects. I command my hand, says St. Austin, and the hand obeys ; I command my foot, and it obeys ; but I command my appetite, and it obeys not. The reason is, because neither hand nor foot have in themselves any inclination contrary to the will ; but the appetite has its own inclination, which is often opposite to the will ; and, therefore, it is necessary that we endeavour to free ourselves from exterior things as soon as possible, that we may be more at leisure to attend to those which are more essential and of greater importance. To obtain, for example, a profound humility of heart, which reaches not only to a contempt of ourselves, but also to be glad that others despise us ; to gain so much upon ourselves as to do all things purely for the love of God, and always to have before our eyes that it is God and not man we serve ; to attain entire conformity to the divine will, or to gain, in fine, any other virtue or interior perfection.   For though the particular examen was chiefly established for retrenching our defects and imperfections, and this would be a sufficient employment during our whole life, because we can never be quite free and exempt from venial sins, nevertheless it were very unfit that all our time should be employed in this alone.   He who is engaged in weeding a garden is well employed, but yet, must he never do anything else but this ? The object in plucking up the weeds is, that flowers and fruit may grow in their place.   The time, therefore, of the particular examen is, in like manner, well employed when we exercise ourselves in rooting out of our souls vicious and bad inclinations ; but all this must be done with intent to plant the odoriferous flowers of virtue in their place : " I have established and appointed you," says our Lord to Jeremias, " that you pluck up and destroy ; that you should pull down and dissipate, in order that you should build and plant anew." (Jerem. i. 10.) We must first demolish and pluck up ; but afterwards we must build and plant again.

But what should oblige us still more to observe this method is, that even for the correcting those exterior faults to which we are subject, oftentimes the sweetest, shortest, and most efficacious means is, to take for our particular examen the perfection most opposite to those defects.   Do you speak passionately and authoritatively to your brethren ? During your examen employ yourself in looking upon them as being superior to you in all things, and look upon yourself as the least and most unworthy of them all, and by this you will soon learn both how to speak to them, and how to answer them ; and if you acquire but true humility you may assure yourself you will never say anything to them rude or mortifying.   Do you feel a repugnance to do anything?   Do you feel pain in submitting to what happens to you ?   Let your examen be on receiving all things as coming from the hand of God ; as emanating from a particular disposition of his divine Providence, and as being sent you for your good ; and thus you will be able easily to submit to whatsoever shall happen.   Do you sometimes fail in the observance of modesty and reserve ?   Do you often look about you on every side ?

Or have you a violent curiosity to know all that passes ? Let your examen be upon the presence of God, and upon the obligation you have of doing all your actions so as they may appear before him, and by this means you will soon, without pain, or even so much as thinking of it, be modest in all your deportment; you will be recollected and wholly given to spirituality and devotion. For do you not experience that when you have made your prayer with fervour you feel not on rising from it any vain curiosity ? The reason is plain ; it is because the commerce and conversation you have had with God make you easily despise all other things. But should you undertake to correct all your exterior faults, one after another, the task will be very tedious. Moreover, while you direct all your attention to one point—to keeping a guard on your eyes, for example—it will often happen that you will not succeed, and that the violence of your exertion will impair your intellect. Hence a grave doctor had good reason to blame those directors who endeavour to correct the exterior only, whilst their chief care ought to be to reform the interior. But a true pastor of souls ought to imitate Moses, " who led his flock to the inmost part of the desert " (Exod. iii. 1) ; that is, he ought to make them enter into themselves, and employ themselves wholly in correcting their interior, which being done, their exterior will afterwards easily reform itself.

———o———

CHAPTER IV.

That the particular Examen must be made only on one Thing at a Time.

THE particular examen must be made only upon one subject, as I have already said; and the reason is, that hereby it is far more efficacious, than if we should take several subjects at once. For it is certain, and the very light of nature teaches us this truth, that we are better able to resist one vice alone, than many vices together. It is a common saying—*that he who grasps at too much holds fast but little*—the sense which is spread upon divers objects, acts more weakly upon any one of them in particular. By attacking them one by one, we easily overcome our enemies, whom we could not vanquish in an entire body. Cassian says that this way of overcoming our enemies, that is to say, our vices and passions, was taught us by the Holy Ghost, when he instructed the children of Israel how they were to act in order to overcome the seven nations their enemies in the land of promise. "The Lord your God," says he, "will by little and little consume these nations before your face; you cannot exterminate them all together." (Deut. vii. 22.)

The same Cassian, as although he answered an objection that might be made, takes further notice upon this point, that we must not be afraid, that by being employed against one vice alone, and by using our whole endeavours to overcome it, we shall receive any prejudice from the rest. First, because the attention we exercise in overcoming one particular vice will excite in the soul a general horror of all the rest; by reason of that malice which is common to them all; and therefore when we shall be well armed and fortified against one vice, we shall also be fortified against all others, and be in a condition to make vigorous resistance to them all. Secondly, because the care we take in our particular examen, to root out of our hearts any evil habit, cuts by degrees the root of all the rest; which root is nothing else than the too great facility with which we suffer ourselves to embrace whatever we feel an inclination for. So that to endeavour in our examen to overcome one vice, is to overcome all; because the means we make use of, to secure ourselves from that, will secure us from all the others; just as pulling in and correcting a stubborn horse will prevent him from being stubborn on other occasions. To these add another reason, which is, that we daily make a general examen comprehending all vices; and therefore there is no reason to fear, that endeavouring in our particular examen to correct one vice in ourselves, will occasion the rest to fortify themselves against us.

It is, moreover, of such importance, to make our particular examen upon one vice alone, that very often when we would examine ourselves, either upon a vice, or upon a virtue, it is very profitable to divide the matter into several parts or degrees, and to make our particular examen first upon one part, and then upon another, that we may be the better able to attain what we aim at; because if we should undertake it only in the gross, we should never be able to come off with success. If we would, for example, apply our particular examen to the rooting pride out of our souls, and the gaining humility, it is not sufficient to propose to ourselves in general, not to take pride in anything, and to be humble in all things; because this purpose being of as great extent, as if we should make our examen upon three or four different matters, we should infallibly profit nothing by it; but we must divide our matter into different points; and our enemies being thus divided, and separately attacked by us one after another, it will be more easy to overcome them, and attain our object.

But that this may be the better put in practice, I shall here, by way of example, divide some of the chief matters upon which we make our particular examen into different degrees; and though I have observed the same method where I have treated of some virtues in particular, yet that all the things relating to this exercise may be collected and connected together, and because this is the proper place to speak of them, I shall make an abridgment, which may serve us for a glass or model, to see how far we are advanced in virtue, and what is still wanting to our perfection.

———o———

CHAPTER V.

How we ought to divide the Examen, accordingly to the Parts and Degrees of Virtue.

I.—Of Humility.

1. NEVER to speak a word that may tend to our own praise.

2. Not to take pleasure in being praised or spoken well of; but, on the contrary to embrace the opportunity thus offered of humbling ourselves and covering ourselves with shame and confusion, to see we are so far from being such as we are thought, or such as we should be. To this we may add, to rejoice on hearing others well spoken of; and if we find ourselves displeased thereat, or feel any secret envy within ourselves, to note it as a fault, as well as when we find we feel pleasure in the good things that are said of us.

3. To do nothing through human respects, nor to attract the eyes or esteem of men, but to do all things purely to please God.

4. Never to excuse our faults, much less to cast them upon others, either interiorly or exteriorly.

5. To drive away all thoughts of vainglory and pride, occasioned by whatever brings reputation and esteem along with it.

6. To prefer all the world before ourselves, not only in opinion, but in practice; behaving to all our brethren with the same humility and respect as if they were our superiors.

7. To receive as from the hand of God, all the occasions which shall offer of humbling ourselves, and to advance daily therein, mounting, as it were, by three steps, of which the first is to bear crosses with patience; the second, to accept them promptly and readily; and the third, to embrace them with joy; because we must not stop till we are come to be glad to suffer affronts and contempts, the better to resemble Jesus Christ, who for love of us, vouchsafed to become " the reproach of men, and the outcast of the people." (Psal. xxi. 7.)

8. In the last place, both in this matter and in all others of the like nature, we must apply ourselves to produce interior and exterior acts of humility, or of any other virtue we have made choice of for the subject of our particular examen, exercising ourselves therein a certain number of times, morning and evening, and daily argumenting this number till we have obtained a perfect habit of this virtue.

II.—Of Fraternal Charity.

1. Never to detract our neighbour or to speak ill of him; not to discover his defects, though ever so small or apparent. Never to do him any prejudice, or let the least contempt of him appear, either in his presence, or in his absence, but to act so well that at least, it will not be owing to our testimony if each one does not pass for a person of merit and virtue.

2. Never tell any one what has been said of him when the thing may give him the least discontent; because this is to sow discord or *cockle* amongst our brethren.

3. Never to break out into passionate words, nor say anything mortifying to our neighbour; not to be obstinate in our own opinion, nor dispute or contest with heat, nor reprehend any one over whom we have no authority.

4. To behave sweetly and charitably to every one, doing everything in our power to serve others and to make them happy: and if by our office we are in a more special manner bound to serve the neighbour, and to take care of him, we must apply ourselves to it still more particularly, and endeavour, by sweetness of manners, of words and answers, to supply whatever is not in our power to do for him.

5. To harbour no aversion against our neighbour; not to shew even the least sign thereof, either by contemptuously abstaining from speaking to him, or by neglecting to succour him in his

necessities, or letting it in any way appear that we are not well satisfied with him.

6. Not to be too much attached to any one; to shun familiarities or particular friendships, which are opposite to the spirit of religion.

7. Never to judge the neighbour, but to endeavour to excuse the faults he commits against others and against ourselves, and, in general, to have a good opinion of every one.

III.—Of Mortification.

1. To mortify ourselves in such occasions as present themselves, whether they come immediately from God, from our superiors, from our brethren, or in any other way whatsoever; and to endeavour both to receive them well and to make our profit of them.

2. To mortify and overcome ourselves in all things that hinder us from observing our rules, or from performing as we ought the ordinary actions of the day, as well spiritual and interior as exterior; for all the faults committed in them proceed from our not being so much masters over ourselves as either to suffer some pain or to deprive ourselves of some pleasure required for their due performance.

3. To mortify ourselves by obliging ourselves to observe in all things the modesty which a religious person ought to observe, and chiefly by guarding our eyes and tongue, especially when we find that we are subject to fail in this point.

4. To mortify ourselves in such things as are permitted, as not to go out of our chamber; not to see anything that is curious or extraordinary; not to hearken to what does not belong to us to know; nor to say what we have a desire to say, and to curb ourselves in the same manner, in other things of the like nature. It will be good, in what concerns this matter, to determine in our examen to mortify ourselves thus a certain number of times in the morning and afternoon; beginning with what will be easiest to us, and continuing daily to increase the number; for the practice of those voluntary mortifications, though they be only in little things, is always very profitable.

5. To mortify ourselves even in things of necessity and duty —thus in going to eat, sleep, or study, to teach, preach, or to exercise any other function that is pleasing to us, we must mortify our senses, and our will also; saying from the bottom of our heart; it is not, O Lord! for my own satisfaction I do this; but I do it, because you will it.

IV.—*Of Abstinence and Sobriety.*

1. Never to eat or drink before or after the community-hour: or out of the refectory.

2. To content ourselves with what is given to the community, without desiring any other meat, or any other way of dressing it, without seeking any other particular seasonings, unless through such necessity as is known to all.

3. Never to exceed the rules of temperance, either in eating or drinking.

4. Not to eat greedily, or too fast, but with all moderation and decency ; not yielding too much to our appetite.

5. Never to speak about eating, much less complain of our diet.

6. To banish from us all thoughts of gluttony.

V.—*Of Patience.*

1. Never to let the least mark of impatience appear ; but on the contrary, in all our words, in all our actions, and in our countenance, to show signs of great tranquillity and peace of mind ; and to suppress all such motions as are opposite thereto.

2. To let nothing enter into our hearts that may any ways trouble its peace, or cause any sadness, or indignation ; and not to permit any desire of revenge to steal into it, though it should be ever so small a thing we desire to do to the person that has injured us.

3. To receive all things in general, and trials of every kind, as so many presents from the hand of God: and this in whatsoever manner, or by whatsoever means they come to us.

4. To exercise ourselves in making acts thereon according to these three degrees—first, bearing all crosses with patience—secondly, accepting of sufferings with promptitude and ease—thirdly, embracing them with joy ; because it is the will of God.

VI.—*Of Obedience.*

1. To be punctual in exterior obedience to that degree, as not to leave even a single letter half-formed. As soon as we know the will of the superior, never to wait for his express command.

2. To submit our will to that of our superior, having no other will but his.

3. To submit our understanding and judgment to his—to be ever of the same sentiments with our superior, rejecting all lights to the contrary.

4. To hear the voice of our superior, and the sound of the bell, as

the voice of God : and to obey our superior, whosoever he is, and those that command under him, as Jesus Christ himself.

5. To have a blind obedience, that is, to obey in such manner as not so examine wherefore such a thing is commanded, but let it suffice and be a stronger reason to us than all others, that the superior ordains, and obedience enjoins it.

6. To pass often to acts of our will, by accustoming ourselves to think, that when we obey, it is the will of God we perform, and that, therefore, we should place all our joy and satisfaction in obedience.

VII.—*Of Poverty.*

1. Not to give anything away, nor to receive anything from any one in the house, or out of it, without permission.

2. Not to lend, or take anything belonging to the house, or to the chamber of any religious, without leave.

3. To have nothing superfluous, and to give up all things we have that are not necessary, whether books, moveables, clothes, or anything else whatsoever.

4. To seek occasions to appear poor, even in the things most necessary to preserve life, endeavouring in all things we make use of, that they be always the worst and meanest of the house. —So that the poverty we profess may not only appear in our chambers, in our habits, in our meat, and in all other things ; but that we make it also shine forth in ourselves ; desiring for our greater mortification, and for our greater spiritual advancement, to have never any other things given us for our use, but such as are the worst in the house.

5. To be glad to be in want of anything that is necessary, even for the preservation of life ; for this is the character of one that is truly poor in spirit, and of a perfect imitator of Jesus Christ ; who, being rich and powerful, became poor for love of us, and wished to be in want of even necesssaries ; suffering hunger and thirst, heat and cold, weariness and nakedness.

VIII.—*Of Chastity.*

1. To place a strict guard on our eyes—never to direct our looks to what may cause the flesh to rebel against the spirit.

2. Neither to speak nor hearken to any words, or to read any books, that may excite in us any thoughts or motions against purity.

3. Not to entertain any impure thoughts, but promptly to reject all those that present themselves.

4. To touch nobody either in their hands or face, nor permit them to touch us.

5. To observe all possible decency and delicacy towards ourselves ; never looking at or touching ourselves without absolute necessity.

6. Never to entertain any particular affection, nor give or receive presents ; and as to those persons who may give us occasions of falling, and for whom we feel any particular inclination, to avoid their company and conversation by a prudent flight, which ordinarily is the only remedy on such occasions.

IX.—*To perform our ordinary Actions well.*

1. Never to let a day pass without performing all our duties ; to spend faithfully therein, the whole time allotted for them ; and when we shall be prevented from doing so, by any indispensable employment, to supply it afterwards as soon as possibly we can.

2. To make our mental prayer well, and diligently observe all the additions in it ; to make our general and particular examen : and do well less on examining exactly the number of our defects, than on exciting a lively sorrow and extreme confusion for them ; and making a firm resolution to correct them : for it is in this that all the virtue and fruit of our examen consist; and some, because they neglect to adopt this method, receive not the advantages which otherwise they might and would receive.

3. To perform well all our other spiritual exercises—as, to hear or say mass—to attend to vocal prayer, and spiritual reading—to perform our ordinary penances—to practise both our public and private mortifications ; and to derive from them all the advantages each was destined to confer—and to do nothing through custom, human respects, or by way of task.

4. To perform exactly whatsoever belongs to our office and employment, and to use all possible care and application therein, as performing all things for God, and in his presence.

5. Not to commit deliberately any fault, how little soever it may be.

6. To set great value on even the least things.

7. And since our whole spiritual advancement depends upon the due performance of our ordinary actions, we must from time to time, as soon as we perceive we begin to relent in any one, take care to make it the subject of our particular examen ; to renew by this means our fervour and attention, and to put

ourselves again in the way of performing exactly even the smallest things.

X.—*To do all Things purely for God.*

1. Not to do anything through human respects—not to be seen and esteemed by men—nor for our own particular ease, glory, or satisfaction.

2. To perform all our actions purely for God, and to accustom ourselves to refer all of them to him alone ; first, in the morning as soon as we awake; secondly, in the beginning of every action ; and lastly, whilst we perform the action itself; by often elevating our hearts to God, saying to him : Lord, it is for you that I do this, it is for your glory, it is because you would have me do it.

3. To bind ourselves to make a certain number of these acts every day, both in the morning and afternoon ; beginning at first with a small number, and afterwards always augmenting it, till we find we have got a habit of frequently elevating our hearts to God in all our actions, and till we regard nothing in them but God himself.

4. We ought not discontinue this exercise, till we come to perform all our actions as if it were God himself and not man whom we serve; and till we perform them in such manner, that whilst we do them we find ourselves penetrated with the love of God, so that placing all our joy and comfort in the accomplishment of his divine will, it may appear that our actions are performed much less by ourselves, than by the love of God which reigns within us.

5. Behold what the presence of God is, which we ought always to have before our eyes ; and that continual prayer with which we ought to entertain ourselves. Nothing can be of greater profit, or conduce more to our spiritual advancement, than this, or be a greater help to us to do all things in perfection.

XI.—*Of Conformity to the will of God.*

1. To receive all things, of what nature, in what way, or what manner soever they happen to us, as coming from the hand of God, who sends them with the tender love and compassionate bowels of a father, for our greater good ; and to conform ourselves in this so entirely to his divine will, as if we saw Jesus Christ himself, and heard him say to us :—"Child, I would have you do or suffer this for love of me."

2. To endeavour to be always increasing in conformity to the will of God : first, supporting with patience whatsoever evils

shall happen unto us; secondly, accepting them promptly and willingly; and in the last place, embracing them with joy, because this is the will of God.

3. To persevere in this exercise, till we are arrived so far, as to be glad that the will of God is accomplished in us, by means of afflictions, contempts, and sufferings; and till such time as this accomplishment becomes all our joy and content.

4. Never to omit anything we know to be the will of God, or to be for his glory or service; endeavouring in this to imitate the Saviour of the world, "who did continually what was most pleasing to his Father." (John viii. 19.)

5. The practice of this exercise will be an excellent means always to keep us in the presence of God, and in continual prayer.

6. What has been said of mortification, may be the better practised, if we apply it to the exercise of conformity to the will of God by taking all things as coming from the hand of God. For by this means the practice will not only become more easy, but it will be more pleasing and profitable, because it will be an exercise of the love of God.

7. Lastly, I pretend not that the order here prescribed, whether concerning any virtue, or concerning the degrees of it, should be the rule each one is to observe in his particular examen. For the true rule is, that each one choose a virtue he has most need of, and that he begin to exercise himself therein, by that degree he perceives most necessary for him, and having gained that point, he afterwards is to apply himself to that, which shall be most convenient for him, till he comes perfectly to possess it.

———o———

CHAPTER VI.

That we ought not readily change the Matter of our particular Examen; and how long it is to be continued on the same Subject.

It is good here to observe, that we ought not easily or lightly change the matter of our examen, sometimes taking one, sometimes another subject; for this would be to go round and round, without advancing; but we must pursue our object to the very goal; and afterwards prepare to pursue another, and then another, with equal constancy. The reason why some reap so little fruit from their examen is, that they make it by starts; so that having pursued an object for ten or fifteen days, or for a month at most, they grow weary, and without having succeeded, they break off and pursue another. This pursuit too they give up, and commence a third, in which they are as unsuccessful as in the two former. If a man that had undertaken to carry a stone to the top of a high mountain, having carried it a considerable way up, should let it fall down again, and should often do the same ; it is certain that what pains soever he takes, he will never carry the stone to the top of the mountain. It is just so with those who embrace one matter for their examen, and before they have finished it, leave it there and take up another, and then another. They can never attain the end they propose to themselves—they fatigue themselves, yet do nothing : " They are always learning," as the apostle says, " and never attain true knowledge." (2 Tim. viii. 7.) The affair of perfection is not an affair that is gained by sudden starts—it requires long perseverance—we must take it to heart—we must insist upon it—we must fully resolve to compass it whatever it costs us.

It is a thought of St. John Chrysostom, that as those who dig for a treasure, or a mine of gold or silver, continue to work and to remove every obstacle, till they find the object sought for ; so we who seek after true spiritual riches, and the rich treasure of virtue and perfection, must persevere in our search, till we have overcome those difficulties that oppose us, and have found what we seek after. " I will pursue my enemies," says the Royal Prophet, " till I overtake them ; and I will not return or leave them, till they are wholly defeated." (Psalm xvii. 38.)   It is by this strong and constant resolution, and not by short sallies, or weak endeavours, that vice is overcome, and virtue obtained.

Let us, then, for a moment inspect the account. How long is it since you commenced your examen ?   How many objects has it comprised ?   Had you succeeded in them all you would have been long since perfect ; and if there be any one point in which you have not succeeded, why did you leave it off?   You will perhaps tell me, it is because you found you failed in it. But do you know why you failed ?   It is because you changed your design every moment ; and because you did not persevere long enough, in order to crown your efforts with success.   Moreover, if even while you directed your examen and your attention to one object only, you did not attain it, is it not plain, that without this examen and this attention, you would be much farther from attaining the object in question ?   For if he who makes good resolutions is, as we have said elsewhere, liable to fall, how will he be, who either makes none, or at least makes them too late? At all events, three times a-day to resolve against your usual failings must be a curb on you; and though after some time you think you are not more advanced than you were in the beginning, yet lose not courage, nor leave off what you have undertaken, but humble yourself in your examen, conceive a great confusion for your weakness, and make new resolutions to correct and amend yourself. God permits our failings; he always suffered a Jebusite in the land of promise: that is he permits some defect or vice to remain in us, that we may resist and fight it; that being thereby fully convinced that of ourselves we can do nothing, and that it is from God alone we must expect strength and succour, we should always have recourse to him and be always attached to him. And it often happens that from the difficulty we feel in perfectly overcoming our passions, we take greater care, and become more fervent in our spiritual advancement, than if God had presently granted us the victory we begged of him.

But you will ask me, how long then must I continue in my examen upon the same matter? St. Bernard, and Hugo of St. Victor, ask almost the same question: that is, How long we ought to fight any vice? And they answer, that we must fight it till we find we have got so much ground and advantage over our enemy, that as soon as he dares shew himself, we are presently able to overcome him, and subject him to reason. So that we must not stay till the passion is quite extinguished, and till we feel no repugnance at all, for this we must never expect in this life; and Hugo says, this is rather what is bestowed upon angels than men. It is sufficient that the passion we propose to ourselves to overcome gives us not much trouble, and that it is of so little hindrance to us, that as soon as it rises we are able easily and certainly to overcome it; and then we may attack other enemies, and take another subject for our examen. Seneca himself teaches us how we are to behave ourselves in this matter. "We fight," says he, "against vices, not that we may entirely overcome them, but that we may not be overcome by them." (Senec. lib. iii. de ira.) It is not necessary, therefore, that we should wait till the vice is so dead in us, that we feel nothing at all of it; it is sufficient that we have so weakened and so disarmed it, that it is no hindrance to us in the performance of what conduces to our salvation.

The surest means, notwithstanding, not to deceive ourselves in this, is to confer with our spiritual director, it being in effect one of the chief things in which we stand most of all in need of counsel. There are some things upon which it is sufficient to examine ourselves only for a short time ; and there are others in which an examen of many years would be well employed ; "for we should soon become perfect men, if every year we extirpated some one vice or imperfection." (Thomas a Kempis, l. i. c. 11. n. 5.) And there are other virtues also, in the gaining of which our whole lives would be very well spent ; since the gaining one of these alone is sufficient to render us perfect. We have the example of some persons, who having taken one thing only to heart, and made it their whole life the matter and subject to their examen, have very much signalized themselves ; one in patience, another in humility, and others in a perfect conformity to the will of God, and in performing all things purely for his sake. We must, therefore, after the same manner, endeavour to excel in some one virtue, persevering in our undertaking, till we have completely attained our object. But this, however, hinders us not from interrupting sometimes the examen we have purposed to make every day upon this matter ; but on the contrary, it will even be very profitable sometimes to discontinue it for ten or fifteen days, taking for that time the observance of silence—the performing well our spiritual exercises—the speaking advantageously of all persons—the saying nothing that may anyways offend any one—the reforming and amending ourselves in many things of this kind, and in many other faults which spring up, unless from time to time we take care to eradicate them. But after this interruption we must return to our first and chief affair and undertaking, and continue so to apply ourselves to it, that at length we may accomplish our object.

-----o-----

CHAPTER VII.

How we ought to make our particular Examen.

THE second thing of importance, which I proposed to treat of, is the manner we ought to observe in our particular examen. There are three times for this examen ; and of these three, there are only two, in which we can examine ourselves. The first is in the morning when we awake; at which time we have nothing else to do, but to make a firm purpose to abstain, during the day, from what vice or imperfection we aim at correcting. The second time is at noon before dinner; when we are to make our first examen, which is reduced to three points. The first is, to beg grace of God, to know how often we have fallen into the vice or defect we have taken for the subject of our examen; the second is, to bring ourselves to an exact account, by revolving in our mind what has happened to us from the moment of our awaking and making the last resolution to the present moment; to see how many times we have offended; marking down upon a paper or table-book so many points as we find we have committed faults. The last is, to conceive a deep sorrow and regret for the faults we have fallen into, to beg pardon of God, and to make a firm resolution, by the assistance of his divine grace, not to fall any more into them during that day. The third time is at night, before we go to bed; and then we must renew the examen we made at noon, keeping the same order, and running over the time from that examen to this we are about; and noting upon a different line from the former, so many points as we find ourselves to have failed in, since that time. But to root out still more readily any vice or defect, which we wish to free ourselves from, St. Ignatius gives us four excellent instructions, which he calls Additions. The first is, that every time we fall into the defect or vice, we presently make an act of repentance, laying our hand upon our breast; for though we should be in company, this may easily be done without any one taking notice of it. Secondly, that after the examen of night, we compare the points we have noted, with those noted in the morning; to see if after dinner there be any amendment. The third and fourth, that in like manner we compare for the same end, the points of the day with those of the day before, and those of that week with those of the week before.

This whole doctrine is taken from the writings and practice of the saints. Ecclesiastical history states, that St. Anthony counselled his religious, in their examen, to note down in writing those faults they found themselves guilty of; that on reading them afterwards they might conceive greater confusion, and endeavour to correct them with more fervour. St. John Climacus would have us imitate a good merchant, who as soon as he has bought or sold anything, presently notes it down in his day-book, that he may forget nothing, and be better able to make up his accounts at night : even so, he says, as soon as we have committed any fault, we should presently note it down, to be able to make our examen at night with greater facility. St Basil and St. Bernard expressly counsel us, to compare one day with another, that we may the better see how far we advance or go back in virtue, and that we may be more zealous in our efforts to live better every day ; and be so more like unto the angels. St. Dorotheus is also of the same opinion, that we should compare week with week, and month with month.

As for the method prescribed by St. Ignatius for the correcting any fault—which is, that we should undertake this amendment by degrees at different times, and for some hours only at a time ; it is a method that St. Chrysostom, St. Ephrem, and St. Bernard approve of as being efficacious to root out any vice whatsoever. And even Plutarch recommends the same as very profitable, and relates an example very much to the purpose, of a man who being naturally of an exceeding choleric temper, and finding it difficult to overcome his passion, imposed the task upon himself to remain a whole day without flying out into anger, and he succeeded ; when, seeing he was able so long to refrain, he resolved the day following to keep the same guard over himself, and this enterprise succeeded as well as the former ; wherefore, doing the same for several days he, by this means, so entirely overcame himself that he at length became of a very sweet temper. Behold here the very method St. Ignatius would have us observe in our particular examen, thereby to render the combat and victory the more easy. When a sick person is disgusted with all sorts of meat, and still needs something for his nourishment, we set not before him the whole of what we would have him to eat, because the sight of so much would give him still a greater repugnance, and it is to prevent this that we give it but by little and little, and thus induce him to take so much as is necessary for his sustenance. St. Ignatius acts in the same manner. In the affair of our particular examen he treats us as patients ; he wishes that we should propose to ourselves only one thing at a time, and that for a short space, for some few hours only. For if we should undertake many things, or one thing for a long time together ; if we should, for example, keep silence for a whole year together, or keep guard on our eyes during our whole life, the bare idea thereof would, perhaps, dispirit us, and induce us to believe that it is impossible to overcome ourselves so far as to subject ourselves to such reserve and such restraint, and, perhaps, we would conclude that such a life would be too melancholy and too painful. But when we think that it is but for a morning, we look upon it as a small matter, and there is no one who is not able to overcome himself so far as to keep guard on his eyes and tongue for so short a space. In the afternoon we make the same purpose till night, for God will take care and provide for the next day ; and how do we know whether we shall live to see it ? But suppose we do, it will be but another day, and on rising in the morn, we shall feel no regret at having spent the preceding day in so Christian a manner, nor shall we feel what we had imposed on ourselves to be a constraint ; but, on the contrary, we shall experience a greater facility, and perceive ourselves better disposed to continue it. When I reflect upon this, I think that many are wrong in not fixing their resolution at half a day only, for that would conduce much to the efficacy of their resolutions.

It is related in the Chronicles of St. Francis that brother Juniper, notwithstanding he was always very sparing of his words, and, therefore, needed not to restrain himself, once kept silence for six months together, adopting the following method : He resolved to keep silence the first day, in honour of God the Father, the second in honour of God the Son, and the third in honour of God the Holy Ghost, the fourth in honour of the Virgin, and so every day following to the end of the six months in honour of some particular saint or other. Going on thus by degrees we shall be not only more excited to correct the fault, whose correction we aim at, but on relapsing into it we shall feel more shame and confusion when we perceive we cannot overcome ourselves for even so short a time. So that we must needs think it very good and profitable to put this method in practice.

------o------

CHAPTER VIII.

That in our Examens we must chiefly dwell upon making Acts of Sorrow for our Faults and Resolutions of Amendment.

WE must take particular notice that, in our examens which contain three points, the two last are the principal ones, and that these consist in exciting in our hearts deep sorrow and extreme

regret for our faults and negligences, and in making a firm resolution to correct them.   "Excite yourselves to sorrow and
compunction on your beds," (Ps. iv. 5,) says the Psalmist; and
since all the virtue and efficacy of our examen consist in compunction and true repentance for our faults, and in a firm resolution not to relapse into them, it is therefore to this that we
ought particularly to apply ourselves. One of the chief reasons
why very many profit so little by their examens is, that in a
manner they only apply themselves to find out how often they
failed in their duty; and they have scarce done this, but the time
of the examen being almost at an end, they pass over very
superficially all the rest; and they have no time at all left to
repent of their defects; to ask God pardon for them; to make a
purpose of correcting them either in the afternoon or in the
morning, or to beg grace and strength for this effect. Hence it
happens that the next day they fall into as many defects as they
did the day before, because, having done nothing else but called
to mind the number of them, they sought not the means of
amending them, which is, to raise a lively sorrow in their hearts
for them, firmly to purpose not to fall again into them, and to
beg the grace of God to fulfil this purpose.   Without this we
can never hope to correct ourselves; for amendment for the
future so much depends upon sorrow for the past that the
one is regulated by the other; it being certain that the care we
take to avoid anything will be in proportion to the horror we
have of it.

    We daily preach to seculars that morality which we ourselves
ought to practise. How does, it happen, say we, that persons in
the world so easily fall again into the same sins, after so many
confessions? It ordinarily happens from their not having a true
sorrow for their sins, and because they brought not with them
to confession a firm resolution of not relapsing for the future; so
that their heart not being entirely converted to God, and having
renounced vice only by halves, they easily return to what they
never entirely deserted. But had they had an efficacious sorrow
and regret, and a true horror of their sin, and had they made
a firm resolution of not relapsing into it, they would not commit
it so soon after, nor with as much facility as if they had never confessed it. Let us, therefore, examine ourselves by this rule, and
we shall find that what causes us to commit in the afternoon, and
the day following, the sins we committed the day before, is, that
we had not a true repentance, that we did not abhor them with

our whole heart, that we did not dwell long enough, during our examen, in the exercise of these acts. For did we but acquit ourselves well of this duty, our relapses would not be so frequent, because we are not wont to permit ourselves to be carried away easily, by things which we detest, and which we regret our having done.

When the repentance is true, it is not only a remedy for what is past, but also a preservative against what is to come. For whosoever has a horror of sin, is far from falling into it. The efficacy of this remedy was not unknown to that ancient philosopher, who, when a bad woman asked a great deal of money to abandon herself to his desires : " I buy not repentance," says he, " at so dear a rate." And if we take notice of this answer, we shall find it to be worthy not only of a philosopher, but of a Christian and religious also. I sometimes set myself to consider the strange folly or rather madness of these, who resolve to commit sin, saying, I will afterwards repent, and God will pardon me. Is there common sense in imagining, that for the satisfying an irregular appetite, and for a moment's pleasure, you should resolve to purchase trouble and regret all your life long, and a continual repentance ? For I grant, as you say, that God afterwards pardons your sins ; but if you do wish him to pardon it, you must have true repentance, you must have a real and entire sorrow for having committed it. This seems to me a most powerful reason, which, morally speaking, ought to take place, though that of the love of God, which should be our chief motive, moves us not ; and though we had in view only ourselves, and our own satisfaction. I will not do that which I know I shall be extremely sorry for. The pleasure of gratifying myself will pass away in a moment ; but the sorrow for not having been able to overcome myself will last during my whole life. I cannot, then, feel any satisfaction in committing sin—" I will not purchase repentance at so dear a rate :" I cannot suffer that pleasure so transient should cost me sorrow so durable. This idea is still better expressed by St. Paul in these words : " What fruit have you gathered from the things you now blush to think on ? " (Rom. vi. 21.) What proportion is there between so short a satisfaction, and so long a sorrow, which we must afterwards undergo ? All that I have said ought maturely to be considered beforehand ; and when, after this, we are attacked by any temptation, let us say to ourselves, I will not do that which will give me shame and regret all my life long. When you would dissuade any one from any undertaking, you say, Take care of what you are about to do; you will, hereafter, heartily repent it, and if he will persist in his design, he will make answer that he shall not repent it. Hence, if he feel persuaded that he must repent, there is no one would be guilty of so great a folly, as to do what he knew would afterwards cause him great sorrow and confusion.

I have enlarged somewhat upon this matter, to show evidently that a real compunction and true repentance of our faults is a powerful remedy to hinder us from relapsing; and also that we may know of how great importance it is to dwell some time and remain hereupon in our examens. It is true, that though we may have conceived a lively sorrow for our sins, and a firm resolution of amendment, yet, notwithstanding, we may be subject to a relapse; because when all is done we are not angels but weak men, formed of clay, and consequently of a matter which may be easily broken and dissolved, and as easily mended and made whole again. But as, when a secular person, as soon as he goes from confession permits himself to be overcome by the same passions and sins he but just came from confessing; we ordinarily say he had not a true sorrow for them, and had not made a firm purpose of amendment, because he returns so soon to his former manner of living: so it is a great mark, that a religious, in his examen at noon or night, has neither truly repented his having broken silence, nor firmly resolved to break it no more; when the very same day, or the next day at least, he is not more careful of keeping it, than if he had made no examen at all. And what I say of silence may be applied to all other things, upon which the particular examen is made. You would be ashamed to own before your brethren, or to hear yourself reproached in their presence, with a fault which you had three or four times accused yourself of before them. How far greater confusion, therefore, ought you to have, to be reproached with it in God's presence, if you had before heartily accused yourself of it unto him—if you had truly and from the bottom of your heart repented it, had asked him pardon, and promised amendment; and that not only three or four times, but even thirty or forty times? There is no doubt but we should soon grow better, and should advance in perfection in a very different manner, if we truly repented, and made a firm purpose and resolution of amendment.

CHAPTER IX.

That it is very profitable to add some Penance to our Examen.

ST. IGNATIUS contents not himself with our only having a lively sorrow in our hearts for our faults, or with our making a firm purpose not to relapse ; for to ensure our thorough amendment, he desires that we add some corporal penance to our particular examen ; and that we afterwards inflict it upon ourselves, as often as we fall into the imperfection we wish to amend. Father Lewis Granada recounts the example of several servants of God, with whom he was acquainted, who praised this method ; and amongst others he speaks of one, who was wont to bite his tongue very severely, when in his examen he found he had during the day let drop any improper expression. He mentions another who disciplined himself at night very rigorously for all the faults he found he had fallen into that day. The holy Abbot Agatho carried a pebble stone in his mouth for three whole years together, thereby to obtain the virtue of silence. For as a hair-cloth serves to mortify the flesh, and is a perpetual admonition to observe chastity ; so this pebble stone served him as a bridle to curb his tongue, and a continual admonition not to give himself too much liberty in speaking. We read also that St. Ignatius, being in the beginning of his conversion subject to laugh very much, overcame this difficulty by disciplining himself as often as he found himself faulty herein ; inflicting as many strokes at night as he found he had transgressed during the whole day. And without doubt, it cannot but be a very great help, thus to add some penance to our examen ; because the fear of chastisement makes us stand more upon our guard. Let a horse be ever so lazy, the spur will make him go forwards ; and if he knows we have one, it is enough to make him go, though we never spur him with it. If every time we break silence, we were obliged to take a public discipline, or to fast three days on bread and water, which was the ancient practice of religious, we should certainly be far more reserved in speaking than we are.

Besides this advantage, and the merit that penance carries along with it, and that it serves for satisfaction and expiation of our faults, it still contains another advantage, which is, that God is wont to hear the prayers and desires of those who mortify themselves, and afflict their bodies. And this is one of the effects which the saints attribute to exterior penance and mortification which St. Ignatius takes particular notice of in his book of Spiritual Exercises. "From the first day," says the angel to Daniel, "that you applied your mind to the understanding of spiritual things, by your afflicting your body in God's presence, your prayers were heard." (Dan. x. 12.) So that Daniel added fasting and other austerities to his prayer, whereby he obtained the liberty of his people, and merited that God should reveal to him several great mysteries, and bestow many signal graces and favours upon him. We see also that it is a means, always very much practised by the Church, for the imploring God's assistance in those public calamities it has suffered, and in all the wants and necessities of the faithful. When an infant expresses not its desire of the breast by pressing and earnest signs, the nurse oftentimes refuses it, or makes it stay the longer. But when by cries and sobs it asks it she cannot refuse the giving it presently. God treats us after the same manner, when we ask the virtue of humility, patience, chastity, or a victory over some particular temptation, or any other thing whatsoever; and when we only offer up our desires and prayers to him, he often does not grant us what we ask; or at least he defers it for a long time. But when we join penance to prayer, when we mortify our flesh, and afflict ourselves before him, then we more easily and more certainly obtain all that we desire or wish for. God loves the just very tenderly, and when he sees them torment and afflict their bodies to obtain anything of him, he has compassion on them, and shows great mercy to them. If the Scripture says, that Joseph, seeing the tears and affliction of his brethren, could not refrain any longer from discovering himself to them, what will God do to those whom he loves far more tenderly than Joseph loved his brethren? what will Jesus Christ our brother do, when he sees our mortification and the sorrow we suffer? It is, therefore, a means which cannot but be of great advantage and profit to us in every respect.

All this agrees very well with what Cassian says, when he describes the manner wherein we ought to behave ourselves in the spiritual war we make against ourselves in our particular examen. Because the chief thing we aim at is the obtaining what we stand most in need of, and what is most necessary for us. For our examen is made, in order to extirpate that passion and bad inclination which chiefly domineers over us—which draws us after it with greater violence—which exposes us to greater dangers, and causes us to fall into the most grevious sins: and because hereby also we endeavour to overcome that vice whose defeat gives us an assurance of a victory over all the rest; and to gain that virtue the possession of which will help us to gain all others. What care, therefore, what precaution, and what application ought not a religious take, in a thing that is of so great importance as this is to him ? "He ought," says Cassian, " to make it his chief endeavour, he ought to apply his whole study and attention to obtain it. He must offer up all his fasts, all the sighs and earnest desires of his heart to accomplish this object." (Cass. coll. v. Abb. Serap. cap. xiv.) But it is not only in our particular examen that we are seriously to apply ourselves to this : we must do the same in our prayer ; and not only in the ordinary time prescribed for prayer, but also very often throughout the whole day by elevating our hearts to God, saying with sighs and groans—Lord, give me humility; Lord, give me chastity; Lord, give me patience. We must also, for this end, often visit the blessed sacrament, begging with fervour of Jesus Christ the grace we stand most in need of, and have recourse also to the intercession of the Blessed Virgin, and of the saints, in order to obtain it. Our fasts, disciplines, all our austerities, and all the particular devotions we practise, must tend to nothing else but to the attainment of this. And lastly, it being a business of so great importance to us, we must continually have it in our mind and in our thoughts. And if in this manner we take it to heart, we shall soon perceive the great profit we get by our examens; because God beholding our afflictions, will hear our prayers, and grant the acccomplishment of our desires. And this, moreover, deserves to be so much the more taken notice of ; because we may hereby help ourselves upon all occasions, and in all temptations. St. Bonaventure relates that the Blessed Virgin appearing once to St. Elizabeth of Hungary, told her that God did not ordinarily grant any particular grace or favour to a soul, but by means of prayer and corporal mortifications.

———o———

CHAPTER X.

Of the General Examen of Conscience.

THERE are five points in the general examen of conscience. The first is to give thanks to God for the benefits we have received; and this put in the first place, that by afterwards comparing his benefits with our sins, we may be moved to greater sorrow and confusion. Thus when Nathan would make David conceive a great horror and regret for his crime of adultery, he first laid before him those many benefits God's liberal hand had heaped upon him. The second point is, to beg grace to obtain a perfect knowledge of all the sins we have committed. The third, to call ourselves to account how often we have sinned, since the last resolution and good purpose we made ; beginning with the examination of our thoughts, and afterwards continuing it on our words and actions. The fourth is, to beg pardon of God for all those sins into which we find we have fallen, and to repent and conceive a great sorrow for them. The fifth is, to purpose a firm amendment, and afterwards end with reciting a *Pater Noster* or the *Lord's Prayer*.

This general examen ought always to be joined to the particular ; and to this end, the first thing we ought to do every morning when we get up, is to offer to God all the actions we shall do during the day. For though, in speaking of the particular examen, I have said that as soon as we awake we should purpose to abstain from that vice we have undertaken to correct ; and that in this we should employ the beginning of our examen ; yet this ought not to be done, till after we have offered up to God all our thoughts, words, and actions ; referring them all beforehand to his greater glory ; and having made a firm purpose and resolution not to offend him, and having begged his grace for this end we must afterwards twice a-day, at noon and night, join the general examen with the particular. And this is what, according to our constitutions, all are to practise in the society, agreeably to the first of the common rules ; which says, " that twice a-day all should take care to examine their consciences at the time appointed for it." (4 p. Const. c. iv.) For as, to make a clock go well, they ordinarily wind it up twice a-day, in the morning and at night ; so to give a regular motion to our heart, we must help ourselves twice a-day, by our general and particular examen at noon, bringing ourselves to a strict account for all our faults since we awoke— as well as those we committed in thought, word, and deed, as those which regard the matter of our particular examen. After this we must excite in ourselves and conceive a lively sorrow for the one and the other, and purpose not to fall into the same during the afternoon. And the same must be observed in the same manner in our examen at night before we go to bed.

But the most important advice that can be given concerning

the mode of making our general examen is that already mentioned in the particular examen, namely, that all the force and efficacy, as well of the one as of the other, consist in the two last points. That is to say, in a lively sorrow for the faults we have committed, and in a firm purpose and resolution to correct them. Father Avila, treating of this general examen, says : "You ought to imagine that you have a young prince committed to your charge, whom you are to take constant care to teach good breeding, and to break off those bad habits and propensities you perceive he has got, or find him inclined unto, and whom you are obliged to give every day an account of his behaviour." (Av. c. xlii. audi filia.) It is very certain that, in such a case as this is, you would not build the chief hopes you have of his improvement upon the exact account he himself should give of how often he has failed to observe your directions ; but, upon the knowledge you have, that you use your utmost endeavours to make him sensible of his faults by reprehending him for them ; and that you take all care to teach him his duty, by your constant counsels and advice, and that you perceive he takes to heart both your reprehensions and advice, by the care you see him take to amend his faults and to put in practice your counsels. You ought to act in the same manner with your own soul, of which God has given you the charge ; and therefore, it is not the calling to mind the number of your sins, to which in your examen you are chiefly to apply yourself, nor does your amendment consist therein ; but it consists in a great confusion for having committed them ; in repenting of them from the bottom of your heart ; in reprehending yourself for them in the same manner you would reprehend another whose education was entrusted to you, and in making a firm purpose and resolution never more to relapse into them.

Another thing which ought more particularly excite us to put what I have said in practice is, that the general examen is a most proper and profitable disposition for confession, as may be inferred from the title St. Ignatius gives it in the book of Spiritual Exercises, where he calls it "a general examen of conscience, very proper for the curing of souls and for the confession of our sins." The reason of this is very clear.   For two things are chiefly required for confession, the examen of our sins and sorrow for having committed them, both which are included in the examen of conscience ; so that if we make this examen well we may be assured that we shall also make our confession well.

Moreover, according to the Council of Trent, we must take notice that the repentance necessarily required to make it well contains two things, a sorrow for our past offences, and a resolution not to commit them any more ; so that wanting one of these two the disposition for confession is not sufficient.   Some may think that their confessions are only then invalid, when, through a sinful bashfulness, they omit to accuse themselves of some sin. But I hold those confessions far more invalid and sacrilegious, which are made without true repentance of the sins we have committed, and without a firm resolution of not falling into them any more.   By this we may see now necessary the preparation we speak of is for confession, and how much it imports us to accustom ourselves, in our examen, to practise and dwell particularly upon those two points.   Wherefore I say, that of the three chief points contained in our examen (for the other two are but as it were preambles to it) that which consists in calling to mind our faults, is that in which we are to employ least of our time, and that the third part of a quarter of an hour designed for our examen is sufficient for it.   But as to the two others, which consist in begging pardon of God for our sins and defects, and conceiving sorrow and confusion for them, to these we must allow two parts of the time, because hereupon depend the efficacy of our examen, and the fruit we are to reap from it.

But how is it possible, some may object, that in the third part of a quarter of an hour we will be able to find out how often we have failed, as well in the matter of our particular examen, which is limited to one thing, as in that of our general, which comprehends all our thoughts, words, and actions, since even a quarter seems not sufficient to do this in ?   The best and surest means is, to endeavour beforehand to settle this point. And it is related that St. Ignatius for this end was wont, as often as he happened to commit any fault, which regarded the subject of his particular examen, to tie a knot upon a string which he wore at his girdle ; and afterwards by seeing the number of knots, he easily saw the number of his faults.   As to what concerns the general examen, he took care to let no hour pass throughout the day, in which he did not recollect himself, leaving off whatsoever he was about, to take a short reflection and examen of conscience.   And if by chance he was so taken up, and pressed with business of importance, or so employed in any other indispensable occupation, that he could not observe so good and holy a practice, he failed not to repair it the next hour, or as soon as he could have leisure. It would, without doubt, be a very laudable and profitable custom, thus, for the twinkling of an eye, to look upon our conscience whilst the clock strikes. Some others extend this practice so far, as to examine themselves at the end of every action they do. But if you think it too great a subjection to examine yourself every hour of the day, or after every action, it will at least not be amiss to practice it at the end of your chief actions. Because there are some of them, as that of prayer, which, as I have said before, we are to examine ourselves about, as soon as we have performed them. St. Bonaventure says, that a true servant of God ought to examine himself seven times a day. And if we diligently observe this addition in our particular examen, which requires that as often as we fail in the matter it is about, we lay our hand upon our breast, we shall easily remember all the faults we have committed. It is true that this addition was not made by St. Ignatius, that we should call to mind our defects, but that we should repent of them; and therefore he enjoins us to lay our hand upon our breast, as if we would say, *Lord, I have sinned*; yet, after all, if we exactly practise this addition, it will extremely help us to remember the number of times we shall have fallen. What is still to be added upon this subject is, that when we attend to ourselves, and thus take to heart our advancement, we shall scarce have committed any fault, but presently we shall have a remorse of conscience, which will assuredly make us remember it.

This may serve as an answer to two sorts of persons; for there are some to whom a quarter of an hour seems too little time to call to mind the number of their faults; and to these we have already prescribed a means, which is to bring with them this point almost already made, so that they may have more time to apply themselves to the two last. There are others, on the contrary, that in a quarter of an hour find a great deal of time to spare, and know not in what to employ it;—and it is therefore far easier to satisfy these by giving them some employment. For this end I need only repeat here what I have said before, that the general examen must be joined with the particular, and after we have run over the faults we have committed, as well in the matter of the one as of the other, we must stop to conceive a confusion and regret, and to beg God's pardon for them, purposing firmly to correct them; and to beg with fervour that he would grant us sufficient grace to do this. Let us apply ourselves to this; let us employ our time in it, and we shall find what to do; and we cannot employ our time better than in this.

St. Dorotheus adds to this, another very profitable and important advice. He says, that in our examen we must seek out not only the faults we have committed, as well in the matter, but chiefly the roots of them also, applying ourselves to examine the cause and the occasion, to keep ourselves from falling into them again. As for example, if for having gone out of my chamber I happened to break silence, or to fall into the sin of detraction, I must purpose for the time to come not to go out without necessity; and every time I shall be under a necessity of going out, to stand extremely upon my guard. To do otherwise, would be acting like one who having stumbled against a stone, and not shunning it, should stumble on it again the very next moment; or like him who pretending to give life and health to a dry or sick tree, contents himself with cutting off a few rotten branches, or plucking off some of the rotten fruit that hang upon it. But if we make our examens with the attention I have now spoken of, the time appointed for it will be so far from appearing too long, that it will infallibly appear unto us too short.

---o---

CHAPTER XI.

That the Examen of Conscience is a Means to assist us in practising all other Helps that regard our Spiritual Progress; and that the Reason why we profit so little by it is, because we take not sufficient Care to make it well.

ST. BASIL, after he had given several spiritual advices to his religious, concludes all by earnestly recommending to them the making their examen of conscience every night before they went to bed. This great saint judged this practice sufficient to keep them in the observance of all other things, which he had recommended them. I intend, therefore, to finish this treatise in the same manner, by recommending to all persons to apply themselves seriously to this examen of conscience; since, by the grace of God, it is sufficient to enable us to put in practice all other spiritual advices, and to repair all our defects. If you relax and grow tepid in your prayer; if you are become negligent in what regards obedience; if you give yourself too great a freedom of speech; if you begin to take too many liberties, this examen of conscience will easily check the progress of these evils, and will apply a speedy remedy unto them.   Whoever takes care daily to make his examen of conscience well, may be assured that he carries with him a director, a master of novices, and a superior that continually requires of him an account of what state and condition his soul is in—who instructs him in what he is to do, and reprehends him when he is faulty in any-thing.   You will not remain long in your ill habits, says father Avila, if you are diligent in making your examen after this manner, in exacting an account of your behaviour, in reprehend-ing yourself for your faults ; but if you always persevere in them, and at the end of many days, yea at the end of many years, you find yourself very little or not at all mortified, but your passions as lively, strong, and violent as ever they were ; it is because you have not made use of those remedies given for this end.   For if you had undertaken to correct any ill habit, or to acquire any particular virtue, and for this end had endeavoured three times a-day, morning, evening, and night, to renew the purpose and resolution of amendment, and compared the faults of the night with those of the day, and those of each week with those of the week before ; and made as many acts of confusion and sorrow, as you found yourself faulty, and lastly implored God's and the saints' assistance, to be able to correct your faults, it would be impossible you should not, after so long a time, have gained a perfect victory over yourself, in what you aimed at.   But if we make our examens negligently and out of custom, without having any true sorrow for our faults or making any firm purpose to amend them; this is no true examen, but only a piece of formality and a mere empty ceremony that signifies nothing at all.   Hence it happens, that after many years spent in religion, oftentimes we retain the same defects, the same vicious inclinations we brought out of the world with us ; and if then we were subject to pride and vanity, we are so still ; if we were then impatient and choleric, we are still the same ; if we were easily provoked to give sharp and mortifying language, we give the same still ; and, in fine, we are still as irregular as we were the first day, as much addicted to our own will, and attached to our own ease and convenience.   And God grant that many, instead of correcting themselves and making progress in virtue, have not grown worse, and even increased their vicious habits ; and that the long time they spent in religion serves them not to become more irregular and unruly ; and that instead of being more humble than others, they are not become arrogant and presumptuous, and give not cause to have those words of St. Bernard applied to them : "What is to be lamented," says he, " is that many who would have been despicable had they stayed in their own houses, cannot suffer the least contempt even in God's house. And such as would have even wanted necessaries in the world, in religion often seek superfluities and delicacies." (Hom. iv. sup. missus est.)

We may also easily perceive, by what has been said, how little those persons are to be excused who cast the fault of their irregular life upon their natural temper and constitution, or inclination ; for on the contrary, they deserve a more severe check than others, because knowing to what sins the viciousness of their nature inclines them, and being obliged to fortify themselves against this weakness they find in their nature, whereby the devil gets more free and easy entrance into their souls ; yet neglecting this, after many years, they are as irregular, and as little masters of themselves, as they were the first day they entered religion.

Let all, therefore, who seriously resolve to serve God (for here we speak as well to secular as religious persons) reflect upon themselves, and let them begin again seriously to apply themselves anew, and to endeavour, for the time to come, to make their examen of conscience so well that the fruit they will reap from it may be visible to all. We are men, and consequently have our defects, and shall have them as long as we live ; but notwithstanding we must endeavour to gain three things by the help of our examen. The first is, that if hitherto we have had a great many faults, we should henceforward have fewer. The second, if hitherto they were great, they must in future be smaller. The third, that we do not relapse daily into the same faults ; because that is a mark of great want of application and of negligence.

Evagrius, in one of the books he composed, on the *conversation of religious persons, and their corporal exercises,* makes mention of a holy hermit, that said he did not remember that the devil had ever made him fall twice into the same fault. Without doubt, this man made his examen of conscience very well ; he had true repentance ; and also firm resolutions of amendment. It is thus we ought to do ; and it was by this means that St. Ignatius raised himself to such a high degree of perfection. We read in his life a very remarkable passage, which is, that comparing one day with another, and the present state of his soul with the past, he found that he had daily made a greater progress in virtue, and in the gaining of heaven, insomuch that he said in his old age, that the state in which his soul was in at Manrese (for the time of his studies he ordinarily styled his primitive church) was as it were his noviceship, and that God, by the lively colours of his grace, beautified and perfected the picture in his soul, of which he had at Manrese only made a rough draught, or drawn the outlines. Let us, therefore, make good use of so profitable a means, that God has vouchsafed to bestow upon us ; let us have a firm confidence, that hereby he will lead us to that height of perfection, to which, by the assistance of his grace, we aspire.

THE EIGHTH TREATISE.

——o——

OF CONFORMITY TO THE WILL OF GOD.

——o——

CHAPTER I.

In which two Principles are established concerning Conformity to the Will of God.

" Not as I will, but as you will." (Matt. xxvi. 39.)   The Son of God, according to the holy fathers, descended from heaven, and clothed himself with our flesh for two reasons; the one to redeem us by his blood ; the other, to teach us by his doctrine the way to heaven, and to instruct us by his example.   For, as it would have been to little or no purpose, says St. Bernard, to have known the way had we been kept in prison, so it would have been to as little purpose to take us out of prison, had we remained ignorant of the way.   Wherefore, since God is invisible, it was necessary for our being able to follow and imitate him, that he should render himself visible, and clothe himself with our humanity, as shepherds are wont to clothe themselves with the skins of their sheep, that on seeing their own resemblance, the sheep may follow the more willingly.   " If he were not truly God," says St Leo, " he could not have given us a remedy ; and if he were not truly man, he had not given us an example." (Ser. i. Nat. Dom.)   He has expressed in one and the other of these two things, the excess of his love towards man. " The grace of his redemption has been very plentiful " (Ps. cxxix. 7), and his instructions have abounded as much.   Because he has instructed us not only by the doctrine of his words, but far more by the example of his deeds.   " Jesus began to do and teach " (Acts i. 1), says St. Luke.   He began first to act, and continued to do so throughout his whole life, and afterwards he employed two or three of the last years of his life in teaching.

But amongst many other instructions he has given us, one of the chief is, that we should have an entire conformity to the will of God. This is a doctrine which he taught us not only in words, when he bid us to say to his Eternal Father, " Let your will be done on earth as it is in heaven " (Matt. vi. 10); but what he has confirmed by his own example, because he himself tells us, " I descended from heaven not to do my own will, but to do the will of him who sent me." (John vi. 38.) Wherefore, in his prayer in the garden, when he was upon the point of finishing the work of our salvation, though as man he had a great horror of death, to manifest which, as well as his humanity, he said, " Father, if it be possible, let this chalice pass from me." (Matt. xxvi.) Yet his will always remained in a perfect submission to the will of his Father, and, therefore, he presently adds : " Yet let not my will but thine be done." (Ibid.)

To treat this matter clearly, and to establish firmly this exercise of conformity, we must suppose two principles or truths, upon which this doctrine is founded. The first is, that our advancement and perfection consist in this conformity to the will of God ; and that the greater this conformity is, the greater also will be our perfection. This truth is clear and easy to comprehend ; because, beyond all doubt, perfection essentially consists in the charity and love of God ; and the more we love God, the more perfect we shall consequently be. The four Gospels are full of this doctrine, as well as the Epistles of St Paul as also the works of the holy fathers. "The love of God is the greatest, and the first of all the commandments." (Matt. xxii. 38.) "Charity is the bond of perfection." (Col. iii. 14.) "Charity is above all other virtues." (1 Cor. xiii. 13.) But as the love of God is the most elevated and most perfect of all virtues, so the most sublime, the most pure, and the most excellent practice of this love is an absolute conformity to the divine will, and to have no other will in all things but the will of God. "For that friendship only," says St. Jerome (as the Roman orator had said before him), "is firm and solid, when we can neither will or not will anything, but what our friend wills or not wills." (Ep. ad Demet.) And, therefore, the more we shall conform and submit our wills to the will of God, the more perfect, without doubt, we shall find ourselves. Moreover, it is certain that there is nothing better or more perfect than the will of God ; and, consequently, we shall become better and more perfect according to the proportion of our greater union with this will, according to the reasoning of the philosopher, who said, "if God be the most perfect of all things, it is infallibly true, that the more anything shall resemble him, the more perfect it will be."

The second principle or truth is, that there can nothing happen in this world, but by the order and will of God. And this is always to be understood except in sin, of which he is neither the cause nor author. Insomuch that as it is against the nature of fire to cool, and of light to darken, so it is more repugnant to the infinite goodness of God, either to love, or be the cause of evil. "Your eyes are pure, O Lord!" says the prophet Habacuc; "you cannot look upon evil, nor behold iniquity." (Hab. i. 13.) As in the world, when we would express the aversion we have for anything, we ordinarily say, "we can not endure the sight of it;" so the prophet says here, that God cannot endure the sight of iniquity, to express how great a horror he has of it. "You are not a God who are pleased with iniquity" (Ps. v. 4), says David in a certain place; and in another: "You have loved justice and hated iniquity." (Ps. liv. 8.) Lastly, the Scripture speaks in innumerable places of the hatred that God bears to sin, and, therefore, it is certain he can neither be the cause nor author thereof. But, sin only excepted, all other things, as suffering, pains, and afflictions, happen by the order, and by the will of God. This is a truth not to be called in question. For what the pagans suppose concerning fortune is a mere chimæra or impossibility, since fortune is nothing; and, consequently, it is not she who bestows those goods upon us, which are commonly called the goods of fortune. It is God alone who distributes them, and the Holy Ghost teaches us this truth by the mouth of the Wise Man. "Both good and bad, life and death, poverty and riches, come all equally from the hand of God." (Eccl. xi. 14.)

For though all these things proceed from second causes, yet it is certain that there is nothing done throughout the universe, but by the command and will of our sovereign master, that orders and governs it. There is nothing in respect of God, that happens by chance. He has regulated all things, and appointed everything from all eternity. He has taken an account of every hair of your head, and not one of them shall fall to the ground without his order. But why do I speak of men, since his providence extends itself over all other creatures? "Are not two sparrows," says Jesus Christ, "sold for a farthing? and not one of them falls to the ground without the permission of your heavenly Father." (Matt. x. 29.) No; there is not a leaf that moves upon a tree but by his will. And it is by this very will that those things are regulated in which chance

seems to have a greater share. "They draw lots," says the
Wise Man, "but it is by God they are directed." (Prov. xvi. 33.)
We must not imagine that there is anything of this kind that
happens by chance. What seems most of all to depend upon
chance is, an effect of his unalterable providence, which adjusts
all things for his proper ends. "The lot fell upon Matthias"
(Acts i. 26), says St. Luke, and without doubt it was not by
chance the lot fell on him, but by a particular disposition of
the divine Providence, which from all eternity, had destined
him for an apostleship, and would make use of this means.

The light of nature alone has been sufficient to make philosophers themselves come to the knowledge of this truth, and forced
them to declare that, though in regard to second causes, some
things might happen by chance, yet, in regard of the first cause,
nothing happened but by order of providence. Which happens,
say they, as when a master, having sent his servant about some
business, should afterwards send another to the same place upon
a different errand, yet with intention that they should meet with
one another upon the way. Their meeting in regard to themselves, would be purely by chance ; but in regard to their master,
it would be a premediated design. It is the very same with things
which seem to happen here below by chance. In respect of
men, who see these accidents happen contrary to their inclination, and without ever having so much as thought of them, it is
an effect of chance ; but in regard of God, it is a necessary consequence, and an execution of the eternal order of his providence, who would have it thus for secret and hidden ends, which
are known to none but himself.

What we ought to infer from these two truths is, what we
have before spoken of, that since all things come to us from the
hand of God, and that all our perfection consists in conforming
ourselves to what he wills ; we must receive all things as coming
from him, and in them conform ourselves entirely to his divine
will. We must look upon nothing to happen by chance, or by the
conduct or malice of man, for this is what ordinarily is wont to
give us most trouble and pain ; nor must we imagine that this
or that thing has happened to us because such or such a one had
a hand in it; nor that if such and such an accident had happened things would have fallen out after a different manner.
This is not what we are to amuse or trouble ourselves about ;
but what way or what manner soever anything happens to us
we must always receive it as coming from the hand of God,

because it is he, in effect, who by these means sends these things to us.

An ancient father of the desert was wont to say, that man should never enjoy true peace and satisfaction in this life till he could persuade himself that there were none but God and he in this world. And St. Dorotheus relates that the ancient fathers so accustomed themselves to receive all things as coming from the hand of God, of what nature soever they were, and after what manner soever they happened, that by this means they enjoyed a profound tranquillity and peace of mind, and always led a heavenly life upon earth.

———o———

CHAPTER II.

In which the Second Truth or Principle is more particularly explained.

IT is a truth so firmly supported by the authority of Holy Scripture, that all misfortunes and sufferings come from the hands of God, that it would not be necessary to stop any longer to prove it, if the devil, by his vain subtleties, did not endeavour to obscure it, and render it doubtful. For, from that other truth I before proposed, that God is neither the cause nor author of sin, he endeavours to draw a false conclusion, making some believe that, though the evils which happen by natural causes, or from irrational creatures, as sickness, hunger, thirst, heat, and cold, come from the hand of God, because the causes from which they proceed are incapable of sin ; yet the evils which happen by means of man, as, to be robbed, to be wounded, to be dishonoured, come not from God's hand, nor are directed by the order of his providence, but proceed only from the malice and sinful will of man. We cannot hold this opinion without falling into a dangerous error ; and St. Dorotheus discourses very well upon this subject, whilst he reprehends those who receive all things as not coming from the hands of God. "When we have anything said against us," says he, " we imitate dogs, who, when a stone is thrown at them, run to bite it, and take no notice of him that threw it ; so we take no notice of God who sends us these mortifications for the expiating our sins, but run after the stone, and make an attack upon our neighbour, endeavouring to revenge ourselves upon him." (Doc. vii.)

To destroy entirely this error, and solidly establish the contrary truth, divines take notice, that in every sin we commit, there are two things that occur to it. The one is, the motion or exterior act; the other is the irregularity of the will, whereby we transgress what the commandments of God prescribe. God is the cause and author of the first;—man only is the cause and author of the second. Let us put the case, for example, that a man fights against another and kills him. To kill him he must have a sword in his hand, he must lift up and stretch out his arm, and make a thrust, and perform several other natural motions, which may be considered in themselves, and are quite distinct from that irregular will which caused him to kill the man. God is the cause of the motions considered in the first place; and it is he who properly produces them, as he produces all other effects that proceed from irrational creatures. For, as they cannot move themselves or act without God; so neither can man without his help be able to move his arms, or put his hand to his sword. Moreover, these kinds of natural motions or actions have nothing in them that is bad; because if a man should make use of them, either for his own defence, or in a just war, or as a minister of justice should kill another, it is certain he would not commit any sin at all. But as to what makes the action sinful, that is to say, as to the irregularity of the will that moves or determines him to commit a murder, and puts the mind out of the right way of reason, though this be what God permits by a secret judgment of his providence, because when he might he does not hinder it, yet for all this we may say with truth, that he is not the cause of it. The truth of this is explained by the following comparison :—One has received a hurt in his foot which makes him lame. What causes him to walk is the faculty and power he has to move himself; but what causes him to halt is his hurt in his foot. It is the same in every vicious or sinful action. The cause of the action is God; but the cause of the sin mixed with the action, proceeds from the free will of man.

So that God neither is nor can be the cause or author of sin. But as to other evils, whether they proceed from natural causes, and irrational creatures, or whether they come from men, or from what other source soever they spring, or after whatsoever manner they happen, we must hold for certain that they proceed from the hand of God, and happen to us by his divine Providence. It is God that moved the hand of him that struck you—it is

God that gave motion to his tongue who gave you injurious
language. " And there is no evil in a city," says the Prophet
Amos, " which our Lord has not done." (Amos iii. 1.)   Which
truth the holy Scripture frequently takes notice of, often attri-
buting to man the evil which one man does to another, and
says that it is God himself that has done it.

In the second book of Kings, God, speaking of the chastisement wherewith he resolved to punish the crimes of David,
makes himself the author of all those evils which were to happen
by the means of his son Absalom. "It shall be, " says he, " from
your own family, that I will raise up evil upon you. I will take
away your wives before your face, and will deliver them up to
your neighbours. You have sinned in private, but I will accomplish what I have said in the presence of all the people of Israel,
and in the sight of the sun." (2 Kings xii.) It is for this reason,
and upon this very account, that impious kings who exercise
most unheard-of cruelties on the people of God, are termed in
holy Scripture the instruments of the divine justice. " Woe be
to Assur, the instrument of my fury " (Is. x. 5), says our Lord
by the Prophet Isaias.   And speaking of Cyrus, whom he intended to make use of in punishing the Chaldæans, he says, "that
he conducted him by the hand to subdue all nations before him,"
(Isa. xlv. 1.) St. Austin treating this matter says : that " their
impiety and wickedness was, as it were, an axe in the hand of
God.   They were the instruments of God moved to indignation,
but were not any share of the kingdom of God appeased and
mitigated.   For God does, in things of this nature, as a man
ordinarily does. A father being angry with his child, lays hold
of the first twig he finds, gives him some strokes, and then casting the twig in the fire, he designs for this his child the inheritance that belongs to him.   Just so does God make use sometimes of wicked people for the chastisement and correction of
the good." (Sup. Ps. lxxiii.)

We read in ecclesiastical history, how, after the taking of
Jerusalem, Titus making a tour about the walls of the city, and
seeing the ditches filled with the carcasses of the slain, whose
stench infected the whole country, lifted up his hands to heaven,
calling God for his witness, that it was not he himself who was
the cause of that bloody massacre and woeful desolation.   The
same history affirms also that Alaricus, King of the Goths,
marching with an innumerable army to sack Rome ; and meeting
with a certain holy person, who conjured him not to be the cause

of those so great calamities and miseries which would ensue : It is not my own inclination, said he, which carries me on in this enterprise, but I find myself pushed on and forced to it by a certain spirit, or ghost, that haunts and torments me, and even compels me day and night, by a constant repetition of these words, " Go, and destroy Rome." So that hereby we may see all things come from the hand of God, and are sent us by his holy will and appointment. Wherefore when Semei cursed and reviled King David, and flung stones at him ; David hindering those who were resolute in taking revenge upon the wretch for this affront, made answer, " Our Lord has ordered him to curse David ; and who is he that dares dispute or ask, why it is our Lord's pleasure to have done so ? " (2 Kings xvi. 10.) That is, our Lord has chosen him as an instrument whereby to chastise me.

But we must not look upon it so surprising a thing, that men are made the instruments of God's justice and providence, since even the devils themselves, who are obdurate in their malice, and so ardently desirous of our ruin and destruction, are also here upon earth sometimes made the instruments and ministers of the same providence and justice. St. Gregory, upon these words of the first book of Kings, " The evil spirit of our Lord seized upon Saul," (1 Kings xvi. 23), takes notice, that the same spirit is called the spirit of our Lord, and an evil spirit. *Evil*, by reason of its bad intent; and *of the Lord*, to show that God made use of it to punish Saul. This the holy text declares more openly in the same place when it says, "that the evil spirit was sent by our Lord to torment Saul." (1 Kings xvi. 14.) It is for the same reason, says this great saint, that the devils who afflict and persecute the just, are styled in Holy Writ, the *thieves* of God. They are called *thieves*, to denote the desire they have of doing us an injury ; and *of God* to let us understand that they receive from him the power of hurting us. St. Austin makes a very just observation upon this point : Job, as he takes notice, did not say, " the Lord gave, and the devil took away ; " but knowing for certain the devil could do him no harm, but only what God permitted him, he refers all equally to God, and says, " the Lord gave, and the Lord took away." (Job. i. 21.) So that, continues the same saint, refer all your grievances and afflictions to God ; for the devil can do nothing to you, without the permission of him who has his power from above. They could not enter into the swine of the Gerasenians without first asking leave of Jesus Christ. How then can they afflict, how can they tempt you without this same licence and permission ? They who without this could not touch the swine, how should they touch the children or hurt them ?

————o————

CHAPTER III.

Of the great Advantages we receive from a Conformity to the Will of God.

St. Basil affirms, that all the sanctity and all the perfection of a Christian life consist in ascribing to God the cause of all things whatever in general, and in conforming ourselves thereupon entirely to his holy will. But that we may the better comprehend the merit and importance of this conformity, and that we may aspire to it with a fervent desire, and also that we may apply ourselves with more diligence to the attaining it, we will explain in particular the great helps and advantages annexed to it. First, then, it produces a true resignation, or rather it is itself this perfect and entire resignation, which the saints and masters of a spiritual life prize at so high a rate as to esteem it the very foundation and beginning of all the peace and tranquillity of our soul. For by this resignation a man places himself in the hands of God, as a piece of clay in the hands of the potter, that is, that divine Providence may dispose of him at pleasure ; not desiring anything for the future in order to himself, nor to live for himself, neither to eat, sleep, or work for himself, but to do all things for God alone, and for his service and glory. A conformity to the divine will works the same effect ; for thereby a man delivers up his whole self in such manner to this holy will, that he cannot seek or covet any other thing, than to see this will totally accomplished in him, not only in all the actions he does, but also in all accidents whatever which can occur ; and this not only in prosperity and consolation, but even in adversity and affliction. This sort of submission is so acceptable to God, that for this very one reason he calls David a man according to his own heart. " I have found," says he, " a man according to my own heart, who will comply with all my desires." (1 Kings xiii. 14.) The reason indeed was, that David had that submission of his own will to the orders of Providence, as that his heart was always disposed to receive all sorts of impressions alike from the hand of God, as a piece of softened wax is disposed to receive any figure that is given it ; insomuch that he repeated it in a certain place : " My heart is disposed, O God, my heart is disposed." (Ps. lvi. 8.)

Secondly, he who has an entire and perfect conformity to the will of God, will have also a perfect mortification of all his passions, and all evil inclinations whatever. It is sufficiently evident how necessary this mortification is for a Christian, and how much it is recommended and inculcated to us by the holy Scripture and the saints. Yet before we can attain a perfect conformity to the divine will, this mortification is necessary to be presupposed ; since conformity is considered as the end, and mortification but as the means to attain this end, and as all know, the end is always more perfect and noble than the means. That this mortification is a necessary means to acquire a real conformity to the will of God, nothing can be more evident. For it is most certain that our own will and our own irregular appetite are the chief things which oppose this conformity ; and by consequence, the more we renounce ourselves, and the more we mortify and keep in subjection this will and appetite of ours, the more we unite and conform ourselves to the divine will. To join a piece of rough and unshaped timber, and another piece which is brought into form, we must first plane it and bring it into the same figure, without which it is impossible ever to join them together. We may see by this what effects mortification produces in us. It retrenches and cuts off all that which may any ways hinder us from this union with God ; to the end we may join ourselves to him by a more strict tie, in conforming ourselves to the divine will. And the more we mortify ourselves, the more strictly we unite ourselves to God, and when we shall have gained an absolute victory over our passions in all things, then shall we attain a perfect union with him.

Hence flows a consequence, which may be looked upon as a third advantage, which is, that this resignation and entire conformity to the divine will, is the most grateful and most acceptable sacrifice that a man can possibly offer to God out of his own stock and treasure. For in other sacrifices, he only offers up something appertaining to him ; but in this, he offers and delivers his whole self. In other sacrifices, and other mortifications, he only mortifies himself in some particular thing ; for example, in temperance, in humility, in modesty, and in patience, he offers but a part of himself to God ; but in this, he offers himself, an entire holocaust, that the Divine Majesty may determine and dispose of him in what it shall please, and when it shall please, without any the least exception or any the least reserve. So that as much as the man himself is superior to his property—the whole to a part; by so much is this sacrifice superior to whatever is found in other sacrifices and mortifications.

Moreover, God sets so high a value and esteem upon this holocaust of our heart, that it is this very one thing precisely he demands of us. " My son," says he, " give me your heart." (Prov. xxiii. 26.) As the eagle, the prince of birds, feeds only upon the heart, so what God most regards is the heart : and in case you bestow not this upon him, it is not in your power to bestow any other present which can give him satisfaction. Nor is it indeed any great thing he demands of us. For, if we, who are but dust and ashes, cannot be fully satisfied with all things God has created; and if there is nothing, except God alone, can fill this heart of ours, as little as it is; how do you imagine, you can satisfy God in giving him but a part of your heart, and reserving the rest to yourself ? To pretend this, is only to abuse him ; since our heart cannot be divided in this manner. " For the bed is so narrow," says Isaias, " that the one or the other must necessarily fall out ; and the cloak so short that it cannot cover both at once." (Isa. xxviii. 20.) The heart of a man is a narrow bed, it cannot contain any, besides God alone. And it is for this reason that the spouse calls it a little bed. " I will search," says she, " all night in my little bed him whom my heart loves." (Cant. iii. 1.) She has made the bed of her heart so narrow, that there is only place left for her beloved. And, on the contrary, he who enlarges his heart to that extent, as to admit place for another, at the same time leaves no room for God, and expels him thence. It is of this division of our heart, which God complains in the Prophet Isaias, when he says, " You have discovered yourself near me to receive an adulterer ; you have enlarged your bed, and have contracted an alliance with others." (Isa. lvii. 8.) Had we a thousand hearts, we ought to offer them all to God; and look upon it as but little, in regard of what we stand indebted to him.

In the fourth place, whosoever has a perfect conformity, to the will of God, will also have, as we have said before, a perfect charity : and the more he advances in this conformity, the more will he also advance in charity and the love of God ; and consequently in perfection, which consists of this charity and of this love. Besides our having sufficiently established this truth in the first chapter, what we have said in the preceding article may serve again for a confirmation; since the love of God consists not in words but in actions. "The proof or trial of love," says St. Gregory, "is the performance of deeds" (Hom. xxx. in Evan.); and the more painful and difficult the works are, the more they testify love. Wherefore St. John, explaining the excess of love which God had for the world, says, that "he so loved the world, as to give his only begotten Son." (John iii. 16.) And Jesus Christ, speaking himself of the love he bore his heavenly Father, says thus, "That the world may know that I love my Father, and that I perform what my Father has commanded me, rise let us go hence." (John xiv. 31.) But where was it he went? He went to suffer death on a cross; and by fulfilling so rigorous an injunction, he clearly proved to the world the love he bore his eternal Father. Insomuch that hereby we see, that love proves itself by actions; and the greater and more difficult the actions are, the greater does the love appear. Moreover, this entire conformity to the divine will is, as we said before, the greatest sacrifice we can make of ourselves. Because it presupposes a perfect mortification of all our senses, and absolute resignation, whereby we offer up ourselves to God, and put ourselves into his hands, to be disposed of at his pleasure. We may hence, therefore, conclude, that there is nothing whereby we can testify our love to God more than by this conformity; since by this means we give and resign up to him all things in general we have, and all things whatever we are in prospect of enjoying or desiring, and in case we enjoyed more, or if it were in our power, we would offer it up wholly in like manner.

---o---

CHAPTER IV.

That a perfect conforming ourselves to God's Will is to enjoy Beatitude upon Earth.

He who is arrived to that degree as to have an entire conformity to the divine will, taking all things as sent by the order of Providence, will have obtained the supreme felicity of the servants of God upon earth; since he will fully possess the profound peace and interior joy in which the real happiness of this life consists. "For the kingdom of God," as the apostle says, "is

not of either meat or drink ; it is justice, it is peace, and joy in
the Holy Ghost." (Rom. xiv. 17.) Here we may see what is
the kingdom of heaven on earth, and what that paradise of delights
is, which we may purchase to ourselves on earth : and we may
well call it a blessing, since thereby we resemble in some degree
the blessed in heaven. For as there is no vicissitude or change
in heaven, and the saints persist perpetually in the same state,
by a constant fruition and enjoyment of God ; even so, on earth,
those who have attained a perfect conformity to the divine will,
and who establish their own contentment in that of God, never
suffer themselves to be disquieted or any ways discontented at
the inconstancy of things, and the divers accidents of this life.
Their will is so totally subjected to that of God, that the very
assurance they have, that all things come as sent by him, and
that his holy will is accomplished in whatever adversity happens
to them, makes them, by preferring his will to their own, look
upon all their tribulations and sufferings as so many joys : and
all their griefs and sorrows as so much sweetness and consolation.
Hence it is, that nothing can trouble them. For as trouble can
come only from crosses, misfortunes, or affronts ; and as *these,*
through respect for the hand which sends them are received by
them as so many favours, it follows, that there is nothing which
can change or diminish the peace or tranquillity of their soul.

Behold here the source of that tranquillity and joy which
always appeared in the countenance, in the discourse and comportment of the saints—of St. Anthony, of St. Dominick, St.
Francis, and several other most eminent models of sanctity in
past ages. The same is also said of our holy father St. Ignatius ;
and the same was frequent amongst the true servants of God.
But perhaps these great saints were wholly exempt from the
miseries of this life ; perhaps they were not subject to corporal
infirmities ; and had no temptations to suffer, no conflict to
undergo ; and in fine, perhaps no painful accident ever befel
them. It is certain they had their griefs and mortifications, and
those greater than what we have to suffer. For afflictions, contempts, and sufferings are the portion and lot of saints ; and
those who are in most singular favour with God, and most beloved
by him, are frequently the very persons he makes a trial of, by
sending them crosses of this kind. How then is it possible they
should constantly remain in the same state of mind, that they
should always retain so great a tranquillity and peace, both
interiorly and exteriorly, and have such an abundance of joy in

heart and countenance, as if each day of their life were a day of jubilee and exultation? It is because they had attained a perfect conformity to the divine will : and because they placed their whole happiness in seeing it accomplished ; and thus they met everywhere sources of content and satisfaction. " All things work together unto the good of those who love God." (Rom. viii. 28.) Let what will happen, the just shall not be annoyed." (Prov. xii. 21.) All their pains, temptations, mortifications, and every adversity, become matter of joy ; because they are satisfied that these happen by the appointment of God, and proceed from his holy will, in which they have established their felicity ; and possessing in this manner all the happiness which can be found here upon earth, they have a taste of that charm and sweetness of glory, wherewith they are to be satiated hereafter in heaven. St. Catherine of Sienna speaks admirably well upon this point, in comparing the just to our Saviour Jesus Christ. For as Jesus Christ never lost the beatitude of his soul amidst all the torments, sorrows, and anguishes he underwent ; so the just, whatever afflictions, whatever adversities happen, never lost that beatitude, which consists in a conformity to the divine will. Because the accomplishment of that will in them is always a new subject of joy. This sort of perfection is so elevated and sublime, that the apostle, wishing it the Philippians, says: " The peace of God, which infinitely surpasses all sense, preserve your hearts and your souls in Jesus Christ." (Phil. iv. 7.) He says, this peace is infinitely above all sense, and surpasses all imagination. For, in reality, it is a gift so supernatural, that human understanding of itself is never able to comprehend how it is possible a heart can remain so unconcerned and quiet, amidst the storms and tempests of temptation and sufferings wherewith it is daily tossed and assaulted in this life. There seems to be some affinity between it and the miracle of the bush, that burned and was not consumed ; and with that of the three children, who were not in the least hurt amidst the scorching flames of the Babylonian furnace, but sung forth praises incessantly to the Almighty. This was also what made Job cry out in speaking to God ; " You torment me, O Lord ! after a most wonderful manner." (Job x. 16.) As though he would thereby express on one hand the pains and afflictions he underwent ; and on the other, the joy and satisfaction he received in suffering them ; since it was the divine Providence that had so ordered it.

Cassian relates, that a holy man being once in Alexandria,

was surrounded by a great number of infidels, who loaded him with affronts and injuries; who beat and pushed him, and committed on him many other contumelious outrages. The holy man remained, nevertheless, amongst them, like a lamb, suffering and not uttering the least word or complaint; and some of the multitude present, asking him in scorn, what miracles had Jesus Christ ever wrought? he answered, The miracles he has done, are, that whatever injuries you commit against me, and in what rude manner soever you treat me, I am not moved with the least anger against you, nor concerned at so hard usage. See here most admirable patience, see a perfection most excellent and sublime.

The ancient authors have left us in writing, and St. Austin mentions it after them in several places of his works, that the mountain Olympus, in Macedonia, is of so excessive height that it surpasses by much the first region of the air. Cloud, wind, or rain never touches its top; because these are formed only of thick and gross air, and the air of this place is exceedingly pure. Even the birds cannot mount here, by reason of its height; and in case they do, they cannot remain any time, no more than men and other animals, who cannot live there by reason the air is so subtile, that it cannot be breathed. This was experienced by some persons, who ascending every year to perform certain sacrifices, carried with them sponges full of water, that when they found the air too fine to be breathed, they might apply the sponges to their nose, and inhaling the air through them, by this means have it more condensed. They were accustomed also, before they descended, to write on the summit certain characters in the sand, which, at their arrival the year following, they found as entire and perfect as when they were first written; which could never have been, had there come the least blast of wind, or had the smallest drop of rain fallen upon them. See here the symbol or type of perfection to which those are arrived who have an entire conformity to the divine will. For as Olympus is elevated above the clouds, and its top enjoys a continual serenity; so these are elevated above the things of this world; and the birds of prey, that is to say, their irregular desires and passions, not being able to take wing so high, their peace and tranquillity of mind is never disturbed by any commotion or agitation of the world.

St. Austin, writing on these words of our Saviour, in St. Matthew, "Blessed are the peacemakers, for they shall be called the children of God" (Matt. v. 9), says, that the Saviour of the world called the peacemakers blessed and the children of God, because there is nothing found in them opposite to the divine will; and that, on the contrary, they conform themselves in all things as good children, who endeavour to render themselves like to their father, in all they are able—who have no other will or desire, no other content and satisfaction, but in the content and satisfaction of their father. This is one of the most considerable points in a spiritual life; and he who has attained this conformity in all things to God's will, so as to receive all things as coming from his holy hand, and to place all his joy and content in the performance of what is God's pleasure, will find a paradise upon earth. " All things enjoy peace about him, and his habitation is on Mount Sion." (Ps. lxxv. 3.) He may justly, says St. Bernard, sing with all confidence that canticle of the Wise Man: " I have sought my content and repose in all things, and will abide in the inheritance of our Lord." (Eccl. xxiv. 11.) For he will find in effect a true repose; he will find " this joy entire and complete, which no one shall ever be able to dispossess him of." (John xvi. 24.)

How happy should we be, could we gain so much upon ourselves, as to place all our joy and content in the accomplishing God's will, and could we arrive so far, as in all things to have no other will but his. So that we may truly say to him : Grant, O Lord! that I may never will, or not will, but according to your pleasure. Grant that this may be my only desire and comfort. " For my only happiness consists in adhering so to God, as to build all my trust and confidence upon him." (Ps. lxxii. 28.) Moreover, how happy should we be, if we were so united with God, that in all our actions, all our afflictions and sufferings, we have regard to nothing but the fulfilling his holy will in us ? This made a certain devout person say, " That he who has only one thing in prospect, who refers all to one thing, and in this one thing contemplates all things, will always preserve his heart in a peaceful state, and will rest and repose in peace, in the bosom of God." (Imit. Chr.)

CHAPTER V.

That there is no true Content but in God alone ; and that it is not to be obtained by any other Means.

THOSE who establish their content in God, and his holy will, enjoy a perpetual satisfaction, because clinging to the immoveable pillar of the divine will, they participate of the immutability of this will, and remain, by this means, always constant and firm, always immoveable, and always in the same state of heart and mind. But those who are attached to the things of this life, who have settled their heart, and fixed their affections and content therein, can never receive any satisfaction that is constant and durable. For they follow the impression and nature of the objects they embrace ; and in the same manner, are exposed to all the vicissitudes and revolutions to which the objects are. St. Austin explains this admirably well, speaking of those words of the Psalmist : "He has conceived sorrow, and brought forth iniquity" (Ps. vii. 15) : "You will never see," says he, "a term of your sufferings and discontents, unless you bend all your affections upon one only thing, which, in spite of yourself, you cannot be deprived of."

When St. Francis Borgia, being as yet in the world, arrived at Granada with the corpse of the Empress Isabella ; and being to deliver it up to those charged to receive it, was, according to his orders, to open the coffin of lead where it lay, and expose the face of this princess ; the dreadful change and deformity which caused such a horror in all present, struck him so in particular, that the grace of God touching his heart at the same time, and giving him a lively sense of the vanity of this life, he made from that very moment a firm resolution in himself to renounce and forsake the world ; and elevating his soul to God, "I promise, O Lord !" said he, "never to serve a master more, who is subject to death:" let us imitate him in this—let us form the like resolution, and say to God ; Yes, O Lord ! I promise for the future, never to place my affection upon anything that is mortal, upon anything that is subject to perish, or anything which can be taken from me against my own will and desire. Without this we can never have true content. "For when we love anything, which can be taken from us against our will," says St. Austin, "we must necessarily meet with a thousand discontents and afflictions." (Tract. xxiv. Sup. Joan.) For either the apprehension we have of losing it makes us uneasy, and disquiets our thoughts; or sorrow for having lost it afflicts and torments us. It is with grief we see ourselves deprived of what we are much attached to; and the more close the attachment, the more violent and sensible will be our grief. He confirms this in another place, where he says, " He who seeks his content in himself shall be contristated." (Ibid.) If you seek your content in administering such a charge, or in such an employ, or in living in such a place, or in any other thing of this nature, it is a content which your superior can rob you of, and thus you will never feel real satisfaction. If you make it depend on objects, which please you for the present—if you place it in the accomplishment of your temporal desires; these are things easily subject to change; and supposing they do not change, yet you will change of yourself, and what was pleasing to you to-day, will be displeasing to-morrow. Were not the Israelites disgusted with the *manna*, though delicious and extremely nourishing? When they shook off the Egyptian yoke, did they not grow weary of liberty—did they not long again for bondage and for the onions and flesh-pots of Egypt? You will never feel thorough satisfaction, as long as you build it upon things that have no solid foundation, and are subject to change. " But he," continues the saint, " who places his joy in God, shall have an eternal joy, because God is eternal. And if you desire your joy should be eternal, apply yourself to God who is eternal, to God who admits of no change, and who remains ever immoveable in the same state and condition." (Tract. xxiv. sup. Joan.)

The difference which the Holy Ghost makes between a fool and a wise and just man is, " that the fool changes like the moon, and the just man in his prudence is like the sun." (Ecclus. xxvii. 12.) In reality, there is not more change in the body of the moon than there is in the mind of the fool. He is to-day in his increase, to-morrow in his decrease; to-day transported with joy, to-morrow oppressed with grief. In fine, he is sometimes in one temper, sometimes in another, because he seeks his content in things of this world, which, by reason of their inconstancy and vicissitude, make him variable as themselves, and according to the diversity of his success, he is carried away by different emotions. But, as for the just man, like the sun, he is ever in the same state. He has neither increase nor decrease; he is always composed, always at peace, always satisfied, because, having fixed his content and happiness in God, and in the performance of his holy will, he partakes of a good which never changes, and which he cannot be despoiled of. The holy abbot Deicola, is said to have always had a smile on his countenance, and being once asked, why he was uniformly so cheerful, he answered, that it was " because no one could deprive him of Jesus Christ." He had experienced a real content, since he had placed all his felicity in that which could never fail, and which could never be taken from him. Let us do the same, and " let the just rejoice in our Lord." (Ps. xxxii. 1.) Take notice, says St. Basil, of these words. The Prophet bids us not rejoice in the abundance of temporal goods, nor in the attaining a great capacity and learning, nor in the enjoyment of perfect health, or of a strong constitution and bodily strength, nor, in fine, in being esteemed by others. But he says, rejoice in our Lord, that you have placed all your joy and hope in him, and that you make all your satisfaction and content consist in the accomplishing of his will. In effect, it is but this can give us entire satisfaction—everything else is incapable thereof.

St. Bernard, in a sermon made upon those words of St. Peter, " Behold we have left all things and followed thee " (Matt. xix. 17), sufficiently proves this truth. " A rational soul," says he, " may well be employed and taken up in things of this life, but can never be satisfied with them." (Sup. illud Matt.) They can only inflame its thirst ; they are not able to allay it. " The covetous man," says Ecclesiasticus, " shall never have his fill of riches." (Eccles. v. 9.) The more he has the more he desires, and never says " enough." The same may be said of all transitory goods. And learn, says St. Bernard, the cause why they cannot satisfy him : " Because they are not the proper and natural food of his soul." For, as the air and wind can never serve for a nourishment to our bodies ; and he would be looked upon as a madman who, being just upon the point of dying of hunger, would open his mouth, like a cameleon, to suck in the air, thinking thereby to get new food and sustenance ; just so, says the saint, it would be a notable piece of folly to imagine a rational soul, which is a pure spirit, can be satiated with sensible or corporal things. " It may be puffed up, but can never be filled," because it receives not a nourishment adapted to its nature. Give everything what is proper for it : to the body a corporal refection ; to the soul a spiritual one, since justice and perfection is the soul's bread, " and none can be happy but they who have a hunger after it, because they only shall be filled."

St. Austin explains this more at large in his soliloquies, where, treating of a rational soul, he addresses himself to God in these terms: "You have made it capable," says he, "of containing your Infinite Majesty, that you alone may be able to satiate it." (Cap. xxx. Solil.) Enchase a ring for the reception of a particular diamond, and you will see that no other diamond will fit the enchasing. If the work is of a triangular form, no object whatsoever of a different form will correspond to it. Our soul has been created to the image of the blessed Trinity, and adorned with enchasing, as I may say, which is designed and formed for God alone, so that it is impossible any other thing should fill the void exactly. Not all the earth, nor all we can conceive, except God, will ever be able to fill it. "You have created us, O Lord! for yourself, and our heart will never be at rest till it reposes in you." (Conf. cap. 1.) The comparison usually made of the needle of a compass is very applicable, and explains exceedingly well the words of St. Austin. The property of this needle, when touched on the loadstone, is, to turn always to the north ; and the impression and virtue it receives by this touch is so forcible that, move it what way you please, it never ceases to be in agitation till it has recovered its first direction. It is the same with us in respect of God. He has inspired into us a natural inclination. which carries us continually to him as to our north pole and last end. So that as long as our heart turns not to God, so long, like this needle, shall we be in continual motion and disquiet. Of all the moveable parts of heaven, whatever part it beholds in its motion, yet it rests not. But as soon as it has found the fixed and immoveable north pole it stands still and immoveable. Just so, as long as your eyes and heart are cast upon the things of this world, which are subject to daily alterations and changes, you will never have repose and satisfaction ; but turn them towards God, who is unalterable and still the same, and you will obtain a perfect joy and tranquillity.

Though we were influenced by no other motive, we should at least, in consideration of our own interest, make it our chief end to seek God. "For we know well, my brethren," says St. Austin, "that the world seeks its content; but unfortunately it seeks not where it should." (Ser. xxx. de sanctis.) The principal thing is to be able to discern between true and false content ; and it is our misery, that we suffer ourselves more frequently to be deceived by the vain representations of pleasure, and false appearances of good. The covetous, the ambitious, the proud, the gluttonous, and the carnal man, each seeks his content. But the one makes it consist in amassing riches; the other in climbing up to the highest degree of dignity and preferment; another in being respected and honoured by men; another in making good cheer; and the carnal man in complying with and satisfying his impure and unlawful desires. None of all these seek their content where they ought; and therefore shall never find it. Because whatever they covet, and whatever the world can afford them, is not capable of satiating their soul, and giving it true joy and satisfaction. "Wherefore then, imprudent as you are," continues the same saint, " do you torment yourselves in an unprofitable search after these goods, with which you would satisfy your soul and body? Love and seek one only good, which comprehends all other goods, and that suffices." (De spir. & an. cap. lxiv.) Aspire to one only good, which is both sovereign and universal, and it is enough. And you, " O my soul, bless our Lord, who satisfies your desires with his heavenly treasures." (Ps. cii. 5.)

----o----

CHAPTER VI.

Another Proof that Conformity to the Will of God is a Means of Content.

St. Austin, writing upon these words of our Saviour, in St. John : " All you shall ask my Father in my name, I will grant " (John xiv. 13); says, we are not to think that all the peace and tranquillity of our souls consist in doing our own will, and in obtaining whatsoever we desire. Because we frequently will and covet that which is not convenient for us ; and the very accomplishing of our own desires turns often to our no small prejudice. But we must endeavour to find our satisfaction in whatsoever God shall ordain, and it is that alone we are to petition at his hands. "For whensoever our own will and desire carry us to things that are hurtful, and hinder us from good, we are," says he, "to petition God, not that he would grant what is hurtful, but that he would make us take a delight in what is good." (Aug. sup. Joan.) In a word if we take less pleasure in performing his divine will, than in performing our own, we ought to ask of God, not to grant us our own, for that may turn to our prejudice and misfortune ; but that he would order it so, that we accommodate ourselves in his, which can never be but for our greater good and advantage. He quotes on this subject, what the holy Scripture relates of the Israelites, who, disgusted with the manna sent them from heaven, desired and asked for flesh. They obtained indeed their desire, but to their misfortune. " They had even the very meat in their mouths, when the anger of God seized upon them, destroyed the chief amongst them, and overthrew the elect people of Israel." (Ps. lxxvii. 30.) It is certain the manna God sent them from heaven excelled all the meats they desired; and surpassed the onions of Egypt, after which they so much sighed ; and consequently that was not the thing, adds St. Austin, that they should have demanded. They should have begged of God to rectify their taste that they may relish the manna of heaven, and so there had been no need of petitioning other food; since in the manna alone they had the taste of all the meats they could desire or imagine. Whensoever, then, it happens, that either by the devil's temptations, or your own irregular appetite, you have lost the taste and savour of virtue, and like a sick person, you seek and demand what is dangerous for you; you must by no means, yield to your inordinate appetite, nor endeavour to attain what you desire. For instead of purchasing solid content, you will only find dissatisfaction and trouble. What you should desire, and what you should ask of God, is, that he would cure your palate, and take away that disgust and bitterness, which hinder you from tasting delicious sweetness in accomplishing his will. And by this means you will come to possess true content, and real tranquillity and peace of soul.

St. Dorotheus points out to us another road for arriving at this point; or rather he explains this same thing in another manner. Whosoever, says he, submits his will to that of God, in such manner, as not to know what to will or not to will, but what God wills or not wills, comes to do always his own will, and to possess a constant repose, and peace of mind. Let us put the case in what appertains to religious obedience; and so shall more evidently demonstrate what we intend here to establish ; and as it is said, we shall attain two objects at once. We say very frequently to such as wish to enter into religion, and to walk in the paths of obedience ; " Take care, I pray, of what you undertake; for after you are engaged in religion, you must never think of doing your own will in the least thing." But St. Dorotheus affirms the contrary ; Go, says he, don't trouble yourselves ;

you may if you please always do your own will; and I will show
you how this may be done, not only without any fault, but even
after a most holy and perfect manner. Do you know how ? It
is thus: " He who has not a will of his own, always performs his
own will. A religious who has a mind pliant and subjected in all
things to obedience, who is not at all tied to his own will, never
does anything contrary to his own will; because he does his own,
in that of his superior." It is after this manner, that, by renounc-
ing our own will, we do it daily. Endeavour to have no other
will than that of your superior ; and thus, you may have your
own will all the day long, and gain merit thereby at the same
time. By this means you shall sleep as long as you please, because you desire not to sleep longer than obedience permits.
You shall eat what you please; because you would not eat but
what is put before you. In fine, you shall pray no more, read no
more, but what you will ; you shall perform no penance, but what
you will; have no other employment but what you will; and
hence, generally speaking, you shall do nothing but what is enjoined you by your rules and obedience. Thus a true religious,
by never desiring to perform his own will, performs it always;
and receives thereby this satisfaction and content of mind, which
cannot be purchased in religion, but by making his own will
consist in that of the superior, and in the rules.

Moreover, it is in this alone that all the facility or difficulty
of a religious life consists ; and it is on this all the content or
uneasiness of those who have embraced this state depends. If
you are resolved to give up your own will, and to take upon you
that of your superior, you will find all things easy and pleasant
in religion; and you will live in peace and content of mind. But
if you retain any will contrary to that of your superior, you will
never go on in that state, without difficulty and vexation; for
two opposite wills in the same person are incompatible. And
we ourselves, although we have only one will, nevertheless, because we have a sensual appetite, which always opposes this our
will and our reason; what pain and difficulty does it not cost us
to subdue it, although it be so much inferior and subordinate to
the will? How then is it possible to reconcile in religion two
contrary wills, whereof each lays claims to superiority? "No
one can serve two masters." (Matt. vi. 24.) The difficulty we
feel in a religious life proceeds not so much from exterior mortifications, as from the perversity and repugnance of our will;
and from the fault of our imagination, which renders things

painful and difficult, from the manner wherein it conceives them. We see this clearly in the difference we find in ourselves, either when we are molested with temptations, or when we are free from them. When we are free, we experience all things easy and delightful. But if there rises a temptation, we perceive ourselves presently seized with trouble and melancholy—what before seemed so pleasing and grateful now becomes insupportable, and appears to us impossible to be practised. The difficulty consists not in the thing itself, since it is ever the same it was heretofore; but it consists in the evil disposition of our mind: so, when a sick person has an aversion for wholesome and proper meats; it is not his fault, but the fault of that peccant and vicious humour, which makes all food seem bitter and ill-tasted.

The most signal and eminent favour God confers on those he calls to a religious state, is that he makes it a pleasure to them to follow the will of another. This is properly the grace of vocation, whereby we excel our brethren that are in the world. For what is it that has given you this facility in divesting yourself of your own will to embrace that of another? What has created in you a new heart, to abjure the things of this world, that you might love retirement, prayer, and mortification? It is not any natural inclination you have brought with you into this life; nature itself has given quite contrary sentiments: "For the sense and inclination of man are propense to evil from his very youth" (Gen. viii. 21), says Holy Writ. It is a gift which comes from God, and it is he, who, that you might be disgusted with the things of this world, wherein you would otherwise perceive such a sweetness, has rendered them bitter; and that he might give us a liking to the things of heaven, which before seemed so ungrateful to our palate, has seasoned them with all sweetness and delight. "I give you infinite thanks, my Lord God," says St. Agatha, "thay you have protected me from my infancy, and have rooted out of my heart all worldly affections." For it is not we that confer any great obligation on God, by our entrance into religion; but it is he has conferred upon us singular grace and favour in calling us to this state, there to be nourished with the bread of heaven; whilst persons of the world feed upon the garlick and onions of Egypt.

I have several times considered with myself, how those who live in the world, from the highest to the lowest, renounce their own will, and subject themselves to that of another; and this for a small interest of honour or profit. They accommodate their eating and their sleeping to the appetite and sleep of others, and they are so brought to this, they are so conformed to another's will, that they feel pleasure in this sort of life, contract an agreeable habit, " and, nevertheless, they do this only to obtain a temporal reward; when, on the contrary, we hope for an eternal and permanent one." (1 Cor. ix. 25.)   What wonder then is it, that we take pleasure and delight in a life so regulated as this of religion, and that we make our will that of the superior, which is better than ours can possibly be, when persons of the world conform themselves so entirely to the irregular practice of others, and make it their happiness to comply with them, by changing day into night, and night into day ? What wonder is it, that we act purely for the love of God, and to purchase eternal life, when they do the same for a poor consideration of glory and profit ? Wherefore, let us for the future make a firm resolution with ourselves to change our will into that of our superiors, and so we shall always perform our own.   We shall live in religion to our perfect satisfaction, and all our joy and content shall turn to our spiritual profit, and be in itself pure and perfect.

But let us return to what we said before, and apply it to what we have in hand.   Let us always make the will of God ours, and conform ourselves in all things to him by neither accepting or refusing, but what we know he would accept or refuse ; and by this means we shall come always to follow our own will, and live in perfect peace and tranquillity of mind.   It is certain, if you never desire anything but what God desires, you will always attain the object of your desires, because God's holy will can never fail of being entirely performed.   Seneca, himself, was sufficiently convinced of this truth, by the light of natural reason : " What is our main point," says he, " is to be able to support adversities and crosses with joy and cheerfulness ; " and to receive whatever occurs as though we desired it should happen. For we would have felt it our duty to desire it, if we were persuaded that nothing happens but by order of Divine Providence. How happy should we be, could we but so make our will the will of God, and never covet anything but what he pleases ? And how happy ought we deem ourselves, not only because our own will would be accomplished, but because we would see the will of God, whom we love, accomplished in us and in all things ? For though we make use of the first consideration, nevertheless, it is the second upon which we ought chiefly to dwell ; and it is only in the contentment of God, and in the execution of his holy will, wherein we ought to ground and establish all our joy and satisfaction. "Whatever it has pleased our Lord, he has done in heaven and on earth; in the sea, and the abyss of the deep" (Ps. cxxxiv. 6): and will do, whatever it shall please him. "For, O Lord! you can perform what you please." (Wisd. xii. 18.) "All things are subjected to your power; and there is no one can resist your holy will." (Esth. xiii. 9).

---o---

CHAPTER VII.

Of some other Advantages we derive from Conformity to the Will of God.

ANOTHER advantage in this exercise we speak of is, that this conformity and this absolute resignation to the divine will is one of the best dispositions we can possibly have on our part to oblige Almighty God to confer upon us his graces and favours, and enrich us with his blessing. So when he wished that St. Paul, of a persecutor of Christians, should become a preacher of his gospel, and an apostle of the Gentiles, he prepared him by the like disposition. He struck him on a sudden with a vivid light, which dazzling his eyes, and casting him off his horse upon the ground, opened at the same time the eyes of his soul, and made him cry out: "Lord, what would you have me do?" Behold me as a piece of clay in your hands, ready to receive whatsoever impression you shall give me. It was by this means that he began to merit so highly as to be chosen of our Lord, and made "a vessel of election, to bear the name of God before nations, before kings, and before the children of Israel." (Acts ix. 15.) It is related of St. Gertrude, that our Lord appearing to her, told her, that those who desired he should freely reside and live in their hearts, ought first to put into his hands the key of their own will, without ever pretending to demand it back. It is according to this holy sentiment, that St. Ignatius sets down an absolute resignation as a chief disposition to receive all sorts of graces from God; and expressly orders we should begin our spiritual exercises after this manner. For the foundation he establishes for their due performance, is to have so great an indifference for things of this world, and to be so entirely resigned, that not desiring one thing or another, we limit all our inclina-

tions to the accomplishing God's holy will in us.   He says also,
in the rules he prescribes those who give the spiritual exercises,
and in the rules of those who perform them, that it conduces extremely to the help of the latter, to place themselves in the hands
of divine Providence, to dispose of them, and what belongs to
them, as it shall please and judge expedient. The reason, moreover, why this resignation draws down upon us so many graces
and favours from God is, that on the one hand it destroys in us
whatsoever may put an obstacle to grace, and on the other, the
more assurance and confidence we place in God, by committing
ourselves wholly to his conduct, and refraining from willing any
other thing but what he wills, the more we oblige him to take us
under his protection, and confer upon us new helps and benefits.

This conformity to the will of God is always a very efficacious
means for the attaining all other virtues; because the things appertaining to grace, following for the most part those which are of
nature, the habit of virtue, as all other habits, cannot be acquired
but by frequent and assiduous practice.   And whilst you exercise yourself in this total conformity to the divine will, you exercise yourself at the same time in all other virtues; because
occasions occur every moment of practising sometimes humility,
sometimes obedience, at other times poverty, patience, and so of
the rest.   So that the more you practise this resignation, and
the more perfect you are therein, the greater also will be the
increase of all other virtues.   "Attach yourself to God," says
the Wise Man; or as another version has it, "Bind yourself to
God as it were with glue, that you may still increase even to the
end of your life." (Eccl. ii. 3.)   The masters of a spiritual life
advise us to cast our eyes upon some eminent virtue which in-
cludes in it all the rest: constantly to insist upon it in all our
prayers and meditations, and to direct all our spiritual duties to
the acquisition of it.   This counsel is doubtless the most profitable, and the most advantageous that can be given; inasmuch as
by applying our whole endeavours to the attaining this one
thing, we shall compass our end with more facility ; and it is
enough if we possess but one of this nature, to possess the rest.
But amongst all those we can choose for this effect, one of the
chief is an entire resignation and conformity to the will of
God. So that whatever time we spend in obtaining this,
though we devoted all our life, all our examens, and all our
prayers to it, we would do well; since the obtaining this one
virtue alone would put us in possession of all the rest.

St. Bernard, explaining these words of the apostle : " Lord, what is it you would have me do ? " cries out, " O short prayer, but full of sense, efficacious, and worthy of all esteem and recompense ! " If you desire an easy and compendious way of attaining perfection, here you have it. Say daily with the apostle, " Lord, what would you have me do ? " and with the Psalmist : " My heart is disposed, O God, my heart is disposed to whatsoever you please to ordain." Have always these words in your mouth, have them in your heart : and according as you strengthen yourself in these holy sentiments, so will you increase in the perfection you aim at.

There is another advantage and profit in this exercise; which is, that we find here a remedy against a certain temptation which molests us but too frequently, and which consists in thoughts and questions with which the devil disturbs us, by suggesting, for example, suppose one should speak so and so to you, what answer would you make ? If such a thing should happen, what would you do ? How would you conduct yourself on such or such an occasion. Malicious and wicked in himself, he represents all this to us after this manner, that to what side soever we turn, we know not how to escape the snares wherewith we are beset. For he troubles not himself if what he makes use of to ensnare us be real difficulty or a mere illusion ; and so that he can but gain his point, which is to force from us some consent to what is evil, he is content. As for the rest, it is equal to him what means he adopts, provided he attains his object. The ordinary opinion is, that on these occasions, and during the temptation, we are not obliged to return or frame an answer either yes or no ; and that it is even better not to answer at all, especially if we are of a scrupulous disposition. Because, if with such disposition we enter into discourse with the devil, and listen to his arguments, and make our replies, which is what he chiefly desires, he will never want reasons; and we can never rise from the dispute, without receiving some injury or other. But in my opinion, there is one answer which may serve for all these sorts of temptations, and that so just and so inculpably virituous, that I think it is better to make it, than to say nothing at all. It is all at once, without deliberating on the propositions of the devil, to say, if such is the divine will I am content. If it please God, it also pleases me; I have no will of my own, but what is his ; I remit myself entirely to his; I would endeavour to comply with what is my duty ; I hope God will afford me that grace that sufficient and necessary to keep me from offending him, and to do that which may be most acceptable to him. These general answers are abundantly sufficient; and cause no trouble of mind, or inconveniency. For whatever God wills, must of necessity be good; and if he wills anything, it must assuredly be that which is for our good. In fine, we must with all safety commit ourselves entirely to his holy will; and by this means the devil will receive nothing but the confusion and shame of having attacked us; and besides the satisfaction we shall feel in having overcome him, we shall, moreover, gain strength and courage to subdue him for the future. As in temptations which assault us in matters of faith, it is the common advice, especially to persons who are scrupulous, not to answer anything in particular, and to stick to general terms, saying: I believe all the Church believes; so in these temptations we now speak of, the best way is, not to enter upon any one thing, but always to have recourse to the divine will, which is sovereignly good and sovereignly perfect.

————o————

CHAPTER VIII.

Wherein it is proved by several Examples, how pleasing to God Conformity to the Divine Will is.

CÆSARIUS relates that in a certain monastery there was a religious, upon whom God had so abundantly conferred the gift of miracles, that he cured the sick by the very touch of his habit or girdle. The abbot of the monastery taking notice of it, and not discerning any particular mark of sanctity in the religious, took him aside, and forced him to discover whence it came, that God worked so many miracles by his means. I cannot conceive the reason, answered the religious; for I do not fast more than others; I practise no more austerities and penances than others; I neither work nor watch, nor do I spend more time in prayer and meditation than others do. All in reality I can say of myself is, that I am neither puffed up with prosperity, nor dejected with adversity; so that whatsoever happens, I am never discomposed, or troubled in mind; and in all the misfortunes which are annexed to this life, whether they fall upon me in particular, or my brethren in general, I always, notwithstanding, retain equal temper and peace of mind as before. But were you not somewhat concerned, replied the abbot, when the enemy put fire

to our farm, and burnt it down? Not in the least, said the
religious; I was not at all troubled thereat; because I have long
since resigned all things into the hands of God; and so let whatever happen, whether good or bad, great or small, I receive
them with equal thanksgiving, as coming from the hand of the
Almighty. By this, the abbot clearly understood that doubtless
this resignation was the cause of the many miracles which God
wrought by this holy man.

Blosius relates, that a certain poor man, living in great sanctity
of life, was asked by a grave divine, how and by what means he
had arrived to so great perfection? In making a firm resolution,
answered the poor man, to attach myself to nothing but the will
of God; to which I have so conformed my own will, that whatever he wills, I will the same. When I am pinched with hunger,
or shivering with cold, I praise God. And whether it be foul
or fair, sunshine or stormy, what weather soever it be, I always
bless God for it. Whether he sends me of himself some fortunate
or unfortunate accident, or permits it to happen, I receive all
from his hand with joy; since nothing can come from him but
good; and I resign myself with profound humility into the arms
of his fatherly care and providence. All that is not God, can
never give me content; and as soon as I find God I rejoice in
continual comfort and tranquillity.

The same Blosius makes mention of a holy virgin who, being
asked how she arrived to so high a pitch of perfection, answered,
by conforming myself in all things to the will of God, and receiving all things as sent me by him; by endeavouring always to
render good for evil, and never complaining to any one of my sufferings when I receive any injury from others; but still having
recourse to God alone, of whom I receive new vigour and comfort. The same author affirms, that the like question being proposed to another holy virgin, she replied with humility, that she
never yet had suffered so much but that she could have wished
to suffer more for the love of God, and that she received all the
afflictions sent her by God as a most singular favour, of which
she judged herself wholly unworthy.

Taulerus relates, that several persons came from divers parts
to recommend the good success of their affairs to a holy virgin
who lived in perfect resignation to God's will. She promised
them all to remember their demands in her prayers; but frequently forgot what she promised. Nevertheless, all that was recommended to her succeeded happily, and all attributed the event

to her prayers, so that she received thanks and acknowledgments from all parts, to which she answered she had contributed nothing on her part, and that they were to thank God only. Several people coming to thank her in this manner, she complained one day to God most tenderly for his having been pleased to give success to all those undertakings recommended to her, which, though she had not so much as thought of in her prayers, yet she received all the thanks. My daughter, answered our Saviour, from the first moment you put your will into my hands, I put also mine into yours, so, though you asked me nothing in particular, I never omitted to perform all things to your intention by the knowledge I have of what you desired.

There is mention made in the lives of the holy fathers, of a husbandman, whose grounds brought forth much more fruit than those of others, and his neighbours asking him the reason, he replied, Do not be amazed that I reap a far greater crop from my lands than you from yours, since I have all sorts of seasons, all weathers at my wish. This answer surprised them more than the former; and having urged him earnestly to declare to them the reason; it is, said he, because I never wish nor seek for any other weather than what God pleases; and as I never desire anything but what he wills, he gives me an income as good as I could desire.

Severus Sulpicius, in the life of St. Martin, relates, that all the time he knew this holy bishop he never saw him transported with the least passion of anger or discontent; but, on the contrary, his very countenance bespoke content and satisfaction. The cause of this, says he, is, that whatever happened to this great saint he looked upon as immediately sent him from God, and that he conformed himself to the divine will with an entire abnegation and perfect resignation.

———o———

CHAPTER IX.

Of some other Helps that will make this Practice of Conformity more sweet and easy to us.

THAT this exercise of conforming ourselves to the will of God may become more easy and pleasant to us, we must in the first place, set continually before our eyes the principle we established in the beginning of this treatise, that nothing painful can happen to us which has not first passed through the hands of God, and been decreed and determined by his holy will and pleasure. Jesus Christ himself teaches us this truth, not only by his words, but also by his example. For when, in the night of his passion, he commanded St. Peter to put up his sword into the scabbard, he added these words, " Will you not let me drink the chalice my Father has given me ? " (John xviii. 11.) He says not, the chalice prepared for me by Judas, or by the Scribes and Phari-sees. Because he knew they only executed the will of his eter-nal Father ; and what they perpetrated through hatred and malice was ordained him from all eternity, by the goodness and wisdom of his eternal Father, for the redemption of man. So, when Pilate said he had power to crucify him, or power to deliver him, he answered, " You would not have any power over me if it were not given you from above." (John xix. 11.) Which is as much as to say, as the saints explain it, if the divine Providence had not ordered it so. So that everything comes from above, and is an effect of the disposition and ordina-tion of God.

St. Peter takes notice of this admirably well in the Acts of the Apostles, where, explaining this passage of the Psalmist : " Why did the Gentiles rage, and people meditate vain things ? The kings of the earth stood up, and the princes assembled together against our Lord, and against his Christ. (Ps. ii. 1.) We see," says he, " clearly that Herod and Pontius Pilate assembled together with the Gentiles and Israelites in this city, against your holy Son Jesus, upon whom you have poured forth your holy unction, and that they were met together to execute what your eternal power and providence has decreed. (Acts iv. 27.) The princes and great persons of the earth are combined together against our divine Saviour, to execute only what was resolved on in the sacred assembly of the most Blessed Trinity ; for their power was of no more extent. And in effect we see that Herod's power, and all the stratagems he used to destroy Jesus in his infancy, were not capable of depriving him of his life ; since it was not the will of God he should die. To murder all the children of those parts, who were under the age of two years, availed this tyrant but little. He could never amongst them all find him whom he sought; because our Saviour's hour, prescribed by himself, was not then come. Would not the Jews and Phari-sees have laid hands several times upon him, and put him to death ? The people of Nazareth once led him out of the town to precipitate him down a great rock, upon which their city was built; and the Holy Scripture says, " He passed through the midst of them and retired." (Luke iv. 30.) He passed safely through the midst of them, because not having determined upon this sort of death, it was not in their power to inflict it upon him.   At another time those of Jerusalem would have stoned him, and had even the stones ready, and their hands lifted up ; but he, unconcerned, only answered them, "I have done you many good works in the name of my Father : and for which of all these is it you would stone me ? " (John x. 32.) And by this means he tied their hands, and permitted them not to execute their design ; "because his hour was not yet come." (John vii. 30.) But no sooner was it come, as he had before marked out to himself, but they had all power and force to handle and treat him after the manner he had resolved to suffer; because it was his holy will, and he gave them permission. " This is your hour," said he to them, when they assaulted him at first, " and this the time of the powers of darkness." (Luke xxii. 53.)   I was daily with you in the temple, and you seized me not, because this hour was not come.   But now it is come, here you have me, do with me in whatever the eternal providence of my Father has commissioned you.   Did not Saul use the like endeavours to take David ?   What arts and stratagems did he not practise to arrest him.   What pains and labours did not this great and potent king undergo to destroy one particular person, and " catch," as David himself said, " one little flea? " (1 Kings xxvi. 20.)   Notwithstanding he could never compass his designs; and the reason the Holy Scripture gives is, that " our Lord had not delivered David into his hands." (Ibid. xxiii. 14.) It is for this reason that St. Cyprian, writing upon these words, "and lead us not into temptation " (Matt. vi. 13), says that in all our temptations and adversities we ought to turn all our attention, and all our apprehension and fear to God; because neither the devil nor anything whatsoever can hurt us in the least, unless God gives previous permission.

But though this truth, being once well imprinted in our hearts, may effectually suffice to oblige us to an absolute conformity to the will of God ; nevertheless we are not to content ourselves with this single consideration, but we must proceed farther, even to the knowledge of another truth, which is deduced from the former, and which is very particularly inculcated to us by the saints. It is, that considering all things as sent us from the hand of God, we are to consider, at the same time, that they are sent us for our good. The pains of the damned in hell come from God; and yet they are not sent for their good, but purely for their punishment. But as to the pains which either the just or sinners suffer in this life, we are always to presume so far upon the infinite goodness and mercy of God, as to assure ourselves they happen for their greater good, and they are positively such as are most proper, and most conducive to their salvation. So that, when Judith harangued the citizens of Bethulia, besieged by Holofernes, and reduced to extremity, "Let us be convinced," said she, "that all this has happened for our amendment, not for our destruction." (Judith viii. 27.) In reality, the intention of God is so good, and his love so tender, that we may safely confide, what he does is for the best; and what he orders is what is most expedient for us; as we shall demonstrate more at large in the sequel of this treatise.

It is not, for all this, sufficient that we know by mere speculative knowledge, that all things comes from the hand of God; nor that we believe it in general terms, because faith teaches us so, or because we have read it, or heard it delivered in sermons. But to derive more advantage from this truth, and by this means to arrive to a perfect conformity to the divine will, we must in the third place have a strong and lively belief, and so apply this belief to whatever can happen to us, that we accept it, as if we beheld our Saviour Jesus Christ who spoke thus to us :—Receive this, my son; it is I send it you; and it is I who would have you do this, or suffer this and that difficulty. So that, in this manner, it will be exceedingly easy and pleasant to conform ourselves in all things to the divine will. For if Jesus Christ himself should appear to you, and say, Consider, my son, it is I who request this of you; it is I would have you undergo this affliction or this sickness for the love of me: it is I who would have you serve me in such a function, or such a charge or employ—and although what he demanded were the most painful and difficult task imaginable, would you not, I do not say only submit yourself most willingly to execute it during your whole life, but even look upon yourself happy, that God would please to accept of your service? Would you not in this case easily persuade yourself, that whatsoever he appointed you was for the best, and of the greatest advantage to your salvation? And would you, even for a moment, entertain a doubt or a thought contrary to this persuasion?

We must, in the last place, endeavour in our prayers to reduce, by frequent acts, this exercise to practice, and never cease searching this rich vein of God's fatherly providence over us, till we have found the inestimable treasure of a perfect conformity to his holy will.

———o———

CHAPTER X.

Of God's fatherly and special Providence over us; and the filial Confidence we are to have in Him.

ONE of the greatest benefits enjoyed by the faithful, is a confidence in the providence of God, and an assurance they have that nothing can happen them, which is not an effect of his unalterable decree, and a present bestowed by his own hand. Wherefore, the Royal Prophet said : " Lord, thou hast crowned us with the shield of thy holy will." (Ps. xxvi. 9.) And it is certain, we are so surrounded and protected on all sides with the love which God bears us, that nothing can approach or molest us, which has not first passed this guard. Hence there is nothing can put us in fear, since it is clear he lets nothing pass but what contributes, in a special manner, to our greater good and profit. "He has hidden me under his tabernacle in the day of afflictions," says the same prophet, " and has offered me sanctuary, in the inmost retreat of his tabernacle." (Ps. v. 13.) He does more yet ; he hides us under his wings. And as though this were not enough still, "you shall conceal them," says this great king, "in the secret of your face." (Ps. xxx. 21.) And as another version has it, "in the very eyes of your face." And the care he still takes of us makes him go so far, as to hide us in the very apples of his eyes. This accords well with what is said elsewhere by the same prophet, who begs of God " to protect him as the apple of his eye " (Ibid. xvi. 8) ; and with what our Lord himself says by the prophet Zachary, where he assures us, " he who touches us, touches the apple of his eye." (Zach. ii. 8.) Can any one conceive a thing more precious than protection so signal and tender ?

What a singular comfort should we receive in all our adversities, and what strong confidence and ease in the midst of our greatest afflictions and pressing calamities should we have, were we but thoroughly convinced of this truth ! If a son saw his father invested with great titles, abounding in wealth, and one of the chief favourites of his king; what assurance would he not have, that the credit and power of his father would never be wanting to him in his most important affairs? With how much greater reason, then, ought we to have this assurance, when we consider we have him for a father, who is absolute Lord of heaven and earth; and that nothing can happen to us without his order and permission? And with how much more reason ought we to have a thorough confidence in the special providence of Him, who is by a thousand degrees, more our father, than all carnal fathers, who in comparison of him deserve not even the name of fathers? For there is no tenderness or affection can come near to that which God bears us. It infinitely exceeds all that nature imprints in the hearts of fathers. So that we may rest satisfied, that whatever such a father ordains, he ordains it us for our greater advancement and greater good. The love he bears us in his only Son, will never permit him to be backward in procuring the good of those, for whose sake he gave up this Son of his to the sufferings and ignominy of the cross. "He who has not spared his own Son, but delivered him over for us all; has he not also given us all things, in giving us him?" (Rom. viii. 32.) And he who has so freely given us all whatever he had most precious and dear, will he not also give us whatever else we stand in need of? If, then, all the world ought to have this confidence in God, how much more ought religious, whom he has been pleased to adopt in so particular a manner— whom he has inspired with those real sentiments, which a son should have for his father, and who has made them forsake and renounce their carnal fathers, to assume him for their only and real one? What affection, what tenderness of a father, ought they not assure themselves he bears them? And what care ought they not believe he will take of them? "My father and mother have you forsaken me; but our Lord has received me." (Ps. xxvi. 16.) What a happy exchange have you made? And what a good father have you made choice of, in place of him who has cast you off? Henceforward you may say with more reason and confidence than others: "Our Lord rules me, and I shall want for nothing." (Ibid. xxii. 1) "It is true, I am poor and destitute of all things; but our Lord is solicitous and careful of me." (Ibid. xxxix. 23.) Who is there that may not comfort himself, and who is there that feels not in his heart an extraordinary expansion of tenderness for God; when he reflects that it is God himself who has care of him, and protects him with so much goodness and vigilance, as if, in the whole extent of his eternal providence, he had not any other creature to preserve? What motives should we not find of loving God, and giving up ourselves without reserve to him, if we only considered as we ought, his paternal providence and the tender affection he has for us?

Hence arises that filial confidence which the true servants of God have in him; and this is so great in some, that there is no child reposes greater in the protection of his own father. Since they know God has more than the bowels of a father towards them; and not only more than those of a father, but even more than those of a mother; and even more tender a thousand times than those of the most tender mother on earth. It is he himself assures us of this, speaking to his people by the prophet, Isaias:— " Can a mother," says he, " so far forget her own child, as not to have any pity or commiseration on him she bore in her womb? Yet though she forgot him, yet will I never forget you; I bear you, O Sion! engraven in my hands, and your walls always in my sight." (Is. xlix. 15.) As though he should say, I carry you in my hands, and have my eyes continually fixed upon you, for your safety and defence. He explains this in another place, by the same prophet, using another comparison full of tenderness:—" Hearken," says he, " children of Israel, who are borne up by my womb." (Ibid. xlvi. 3.) As if he would let us understand thereby, that, as the entrails of a mother serve for a place of habitation, and of nourishment, and of whatever else to the infant she bears; so the entrails of the divine mercy and goodness are all things to us, and supply us in all our necessities. Hence it is, that the just in all their crosses feel so sure of his assistance, that nothing of all the afflictions which can possibly happen to them in this life is able to discompose or molest them. He who puts his confidence in our Lord, says Jeremias, is as a tree planted by the river side. " In the time of drought, he shall not be solicitous " (Jer. xvii. 1); that is to say, that nothing shall touch his heart, and he shall not be dejected by all the misfortunes of this life; because he is certain nothing can happen but by the will and appointment of his father; in whose tenderness and affection he so much confides, as to be persuaded nothing can occur but for his greater good; and whatsoever he takes from him in one respect, he will, in another, repay with usury.

From the filial confidence the just repose in God there arises that peace of mind, and that happy tranquillity described by Isaias, when he says: " My people shall repose in the beauty of

peace, and in the tabernacles of confidence, and in the peaceable
abundance of all sorts of good." (Is. xxxii. 8.) The prophet
joins peace and confidence together. Because, in reality, peace
of mind is but a necessary effect of confidence : and he who
confides in God, fears nothing, nor troubles himself at whatever
occurs, since he knows God is his protector. "I will repose and
sleep in peace," says the Psalmist, " because it is you, O Lord !
who, out of your singular goodness, have confirmed me in hope."
(Ps. iv. 9.) But the confidence we speak of affords us not only
tranquillity; but it also replenishes us with the joy of the faithful.
" The God of all hope," says the apostle, "fill you with all joy,
and bless you with his peace in your belief; to the end you may
still increase in hope, and in the virtue of the Holy Ghost."
(Rom. xv. 13.) The firm belief we have, that God knows what
is for our good, better than we ourselves, is the reason that we are
not only exempt from all those troubles, and all those anxieties
incident to those who view things with the eyes of flesh and
blood ; but that even in the most unexpected accidents, we enjoy an entire content and satisfaction. And the more perfect
this confidence is, the greater also will be the joy and tranquillity. Because the more we love God, and confide in him, the
more assured shall we be that all which comes from him will
turn to our profit and advantage ; it being impossible we can
expect anything else from the goodness and tenderness of affection he always had for us.

It is this animated the saints—it is this gave them such interior peace and confidence in their sufferings and trials, that
they feared neither men nor devils, neither savage beasts nor
anything which could happen to them from creatures ; because
they were satisfied, that without the permission of God there
was no power to hurt them. St Athanasius, in the Life of St.
Anthony, relates how the devils appeared to this great saint
under the several figures of lions, tigers, bulls, and serpents ;
surrounding him on all sides, and endeavouring to terrify him,
some with their teeth and talons ; others with their dreadful
bellowings and hissings. The saint all this time laughed at
them, and said : "If you have any power, any one of you
would be strong enough to encounter a man ; but because
God has robbed you of your force, and you are but weak and
feeble, you come thus in a crowd to frighten me with your
numbers. If God has given you any power over me, here I am,
devour me. But if he has not given you permission, why do you
make so many vain attempts upon me ? The knowledge this

great saint had, that these could not of themselves do him any
injury, and his entire resignation to the will of God, gave him
this constancy and courage of mind.   Ecclesiastical history
abounds with passages of this nature, and the life of St. Ignatius
furnishes us with the like examples. But not to repeat the same
thing twice, I will content myself with relating what is found in
the second book of his life.   One day, whilst he sailed towards
Rome, there arose a tempest so violent, that it carried away the
mast, and rent all the tackling of the vessel.   Those who were
aboard being in a consternation, and imagining their last hour
was come, expected nothing but death. In this extremity, and in
the terror which the approach of death causes in all persons, the
saint was not seized with the least apprehension or fear. The only
trouble he had was, that he had not served God as he ought to
have done. But as to anything else he was not concerned, knowing
that " the winds and the seas obey our Lord " (Matt. viii. 27);
that the tempests arose not but by his command, and the waves
swallowed not any but by his permission. This is the confidence,
this the tranquillity and composure of mind we ought to aspire to
by constantly making acts of conformity and resignation to the
divine will, and by making our way, through prayer and meditation, to the treasure of the all-fatherly providence of God over us.
I am certain nothing can happen to me without his orders ; and
that neither men nor devils, nor any other creature whatever, can
effect anything contrary to his holy pleasure. Let then his orders
be executed upon me.   I must refuse nothing he sends, and I
desire nothing but the accomplishing his holy will.

We read in the life of St. Gertrude, that neither dangers, nor
crosses, neither loss of her goods nor even her own sins and faults,
were ever able to diminish that firm confidence and trust she had
in the mercy of God. Insomuch, that she was strongly persuaded,
whatever fell out, either according or contrary to her desire, was
equally designed for her greater good, by the disposition of Providence. As this holy virgin had frequent revelations, God appeared
once to her, and said to her: Whosoever has a firm confidence in
me, and believes I can and will assist him in all things, so pierces
my heart, that in some degree I can neither determine myself to
bestow my comforts upon him, by reason of the satisfaction I take
in seeing in him this absolute conformity which augments his
merit ; nor to withhold my assistance, as I must satisfy the
obligations of my infinite bounty, and the extreme affection and
tenderness I have for him. He uses our mode of speaking, and

expresses himself as a person, whose excess of love transports him so far, as to leave him undecided on what is to be done.

It is related also of St. Mechthildis, that God thus said to her : I am very well pleased that men rely upon, and trust in my mercy ; and whoever has an humble and firm confidence in me, I will favour him in this life, and will reward him in the next, with more than he merits.   The more they confide in me, the more graces shall they receive from me; for it is impossible they should not obtain of me all they hope for, by relying on the fidelity of my promises.   Wherefore it is very expedient for those who expect great things from me, to confide entirely in me. At another time this saint, asking of God what she ought chiefly believe, and what expect from his unspeakable goodness, Believe, said he to her, that after your death, I will receive you as a father receives his dearest child ; and that there yet never was any father who has so liberally imparted all his goods to his only son, as I will impart to you the inexhaustible treasures of my grace, in bestowing myself upon you.   Whosoever has this confidence in my infinite goodness, and resigns himself into my hands with the spirit of charity and humility, shall be eternally happy.

———o———

CHAPTER XI.

Some Examples taken from Holy Scripture to help us to attain perfect Confidence in God.

IT conduces much to our advantage, if, in the first place, we cast our eyes upon the custom that all the ancient patriarchs had, of always ascribing to God each event, of what nature, and by what means soever it occurred.   The sons of Jacob having gone to buy corn in Egypt, Joseph, their brother, who ruled under Pharao, as yet unknown to them, ordered their sacks to be filled, and the price they paid to be secretly put therein. On their return, one of them going to refresh his beast in the inn, found his money in the mouth of the sack, and having shown it to his brothers, they were all seized with a fright, and said, " What is this the Lord has done to us ?" (Gen. xlii. 28.) Here we must take notice, they did not say : Is not this a snare laid for us ?   Has not the master of the inn left this by mistake here ?   Shall we look upon it a charity he has done us ?   But they referred it all to God, and said ; " What is this the Lord has done to us?" And by this they confessed, that as a leaf falls not from the tree without the permission of God, this could not happen without a most particular disposition of his providence. When Jacob caused himself afterwards to be carried into Egypt, and fell sick there, Joseph brought before him his two sons ; and the holy man asking him whose they were, he answered "These are the children God has given me in this country." (Gen. xlviii. 9.) Jacob had made the same answer to his brother Esau ; and urging him to accept the presents he offered him, said : " Accept this blessing I have brought you, and which God, the sovereign dispenser of all good, has bestowed upon me." (Gen. xxxiii. 11.) He calls his present a blessing of God. Because, in reality, to bless and to do good are the same thing in God ; and he refers all to God without ascribing any the least to himself. When David, incensed against Nabal, marched with his soldiers to pillage and sack the house, and Abigail met him with presents to appease him ; " Blessed," said he, " be the Lord God of Israel, who has sent you this day to meet me, and hinder me from shedding blood." (1 Kings xxv. 32.) As if he had said, You are not come of your own accord, but it is God has sent you to hinder me from sinning. It is to him I owe this favour, and his name be blessed for ever. This was the ordinary language of these great patriarchs ; and ought also to be ours.

But to contemplate their miracles of providence more particularly, we are only to consider the above-mentioned history of Joseph. The hatred and envy the recital of the dreams which presaged his future greatness had excited in the hearts of his brothers, were their motives for resolving on his death; and being dissuaded by the reasons and arguments of Ruben, they sold him for a slave to some Ismaelite merchants. Now the very means they took to prevent the effect of his dreams, were those which Providence made use of to make him lord over them and all Egypt. So that when he discovered himself to his brothers, and they, seized with fear and knew not what to reply : " Fear not," said he, " do not trouble and afflict yourselves for having sold me into this country. For it is for your good, that God has sent me before you into Egypt. He has sent me here, for your preservation on earth, and that you may have food whereon to live. It has not happened by your counsel, but by the will of God alone that I am sent here." (Gen. xlv. 5-8.) " Can we," says he in another place, " resist the will of God ? You have had a bad design against me, but God has turned it to the best, to raise me to this degree of dignity wherein you now behold me, for the preservation of many people." (Ibid. 1. 19.) Who then is there that, considering this, will not have confidence in God? Who will fear the evil designs of men, and unfortunate accidents of this world? Since nothing happens without the unchangeable order of his providence, which adjusts all things to their end; and which turns to our good and to our glory, these very means the world made use of to persecute and destroy us. "What I have determined," says our Lord to the Prophet Isaias, "shall remain firm and immoveable; and my will shall be executed in all things." (Is. lxvi. 10.) Act you as you please; nevertheless the will of God must be performed; and he will easily turn to his designs everything you do to frustrate them.

St. Chrysostom makes an apposite reflection upon another particular passage of the same story. The interpretation Joseph gave the dream of Pharao's cup-bearer having had its effect, by the re-establishment of this officer in his former dignity, two years passed without any remembrance of Joseph, who had most earnestly desired he would be mindful of him. But do you think, says the saint, this forgetfulness was only an effect of chance, or any ingratitude in the cup-bearer? Not at all; it was an effect of the divine disposition, which would wait a more proper season and a more favourable conjuncture, to free Joseph from prison with more splendour and glory. For supposing the cup-bearer had remembered him, he might perhaps have found means to get him out in some obscure manner, and without its being known who he was. But because God would not have him come out in that manner, and had resolved to elevate him with honour, he permitted the cup-bearer to forget him for two whole years, in order that, when the time of Pharao's dreams had come, the king should make him come forth gloriously out of prison, to be invested afterwards with the command of all Egypt. God, adds the great saint, is a most prudent artificer, who knows perfectly well how long the gold is to be in the fire, and when it must be taken out.

We have in the first book of Kings another history, where the divine Providence shines brightly even in the most minute things. Wishing to describe to Samuel the person whom he had chosen to reign over Israel, God said: "To-morrow, at this very same hour, I will send to you a man of the tribe of Benjamin; and you shall consecrate him king over the people of Israel." (1 Kings

ix. 16.) But let us see in what manner he sent this man, who was Saul. The asses of Cis, Saul's father, had strayed from home, and Cis commanded his son to seek and bring them back. Saul takes a servant with him. They both seek everywhere, but to no purpose; and Saul about to return, lest his father should be in pain at his absence, the servant who accompanied him said, there was a man of God in the next city who could inform him of what he sought. They go to find this man, who was Samuel, and being arrived in his sight; " Behold," says our Lord, " the man I spoke to you of; it is he shall rule over my people." (Ibid. ix. 17.) O incomprehensible depth of the judgments of God! Cis sends Saul to find the asses that had broke out of their bounds, and God sends Samuel to consecrate him king. How far was Saul and his father from ever imagining he went to be anointed king? It is the same with most part of the projects parents design with respect to their children. They are often far from the ends God proposes himself; but notwithstanding he directs things so to the execution of his orders, that even such things as seem to have little or no relation thereto serve to accomplish his designs. For it was not by chance that the asses of Cis were lost, nor that Cis sent Saul to seek them; nor that they could not be found; nor that the servant who was with Saul advised him to consult the prophet. All this was decreed in this manner by providence, which availed itself of these means to send Saul to Samuel, and make Samuel anoint him king, as God had ordered. Perhaps your parents sent you for no other end to a college or university, but for your advancement in learning, and that afterwards you may be able to fill some office or possess some benefice. But God sent you there with another intent; and made use of your parents, to draw you to him and make you enter into religion. When St. Austin left Rome to go to Milan, where Symmachus the governor sent him, both he and the governor thought it was only to teach rhetoric. But they were both deceived; God, who had other designs, sent him to Milan, there to be converted by St. Ambrose.

Let us consider a little the different sorts of vocations, and their so many particular means, and even those sometimes so apparently remote, by which God has drawn an infinity of persons to religion. It is a thing that will appear very surprising. For we shall oftentimes see that unless something or other had happened, and had it not been for some trifle, or some affair of no moment or consideration, we should never have been religious.

And these very things, notwithstanding how small and incon-siderable soever they seem in themselves, were the preparations and instruments God had resolved on always whereby to move you to enter religion. Let us take notice of this in short—it is a reflection which may prove very advantageous to some persons, who imagine with themselves their vocation comes not from God, because it has been brought about by things of this nature. This imagination is nothing but a mere deceit and dangerous illusion of the devil your enemy; who, envious of the state you are in, makes every effort to disturb you. For, with respect to God, it is his custom to use these means to effect his own ends : that is, for his own greater glory, and our greater good; and of this we have abundance of examples in the lives of the saints. God's intent then terminated not at what appeared then to you, and he sent not you more than Saul to seek the asses; " for has God any care of the oxen?" (1 Cor. ix. 9.) But his pleasure was that by this indirect way you should come to reign with Saul; since, "to serve God is to reign."

When Samuel went in the name of God to reprimand Saul severely for his disobedience, in not destroying the Amalecites as God had ordered him; Saul acknowledging his fault, and seeing the prophet upon the point of departing, would have retained him by laying hold of his cloak, to request he would intercede with God for him; and in the strife a piece of Samuel's cloak was rent, and remained in Saul's hand. Who would have thought but this might have happened by pure accident; and that the cloak was torn as being old and rotten, or that Saul had pulled too hard? Notwithstanding, it happened not but by a peculiar order and disposition of providence; to signify, that God had deprived Saul of his kingdom for this his sin. Wherefore Samuel seeing his cloak rent, " Understand by this," said he, " that God has cut off and separated the kingdom of Israel from you, and has transferred it over to your neighbour, who is a better man than you are." (1 Kings xv. 28.)

In the same book of Kings it is related that Saul had once surrounded David and his followers, as it were in a circle; so that David despaired of making his escape. Whilst he was in this extremity, there come a courtier to Saul, who told him the Philistines were entered with fire and sword into his dominions, pillaging and destroying all in their way. Saul obliged to attend to what was of greater moment and concern, abandoned his enterprise; and David by this means escaped. The irruption of the Philistines was not casual and by mere chance; but it was the execution of those measures God had taken to set David at liberty.

At another time the princes and nobility of the Philistines arranged it so with their king Achis, that he commanded David, who took refuge some time before in his court, and was then in the army with him, to return to the place assigned him for his retirement. Achis indeed had a great esteem of David's valour and courage; and for that reason brought him along in the expedition he undertook against Saul. "But David did not please the nobles." (Ibid. xxix. 6.) The accusations they brought against him were not a pure effect of their jealousy and ill-will, and had more than the end they proposed themselves. It was a plan of the divine Providence; which disposed things for other ends than those of men. For David, at his return found, that the Amalecites, taking advantage of the Philistines' absence, had poured into the country with sword in hand; and taking Siceleg, the place of David's retirement, had led away captive all the inhabitants : " From the least to the biggest " (Ibid. xxx. 2) :—and amongst the rest even two of his wives, and then set fire to the town. He followed them with what men he had, over-took, and defeated them, and rescued the prisoners, making him-self master of all the spoils and prey they had carried away. So that had not the nobles and courtiers of Achis forced him out of their army, he had never been in a possibility of executing all those achievements. And it was for this end the divine Providence, which had thus decreed from all eternity, directed their counsel to the effecting what it had before projected; although they at the same time had another design in the matter.

We see also throughout the whole history of Esther, that this particular providence of God is very perspicuous and evident even in the most minute things. What means did not God use in delivering the Jews from the cruel and bloody sentence of King Assuerus ? And what strange and unheard of ways did he not take to make Vasthi fall into disgrace, and raise Esther to the throne in her place, in order that being herself a Jew, she might undertake the patronage, and plead the cause of her nation ? That Mardocheus should come to discover the con-spiracy laid by two eunuchs against the king's person—that some time after the king, not being able to sleep in the night, should call for the annals of his reign, and causing them to be read before him, should wonderfully light upon the place wherein was registered the service Mardocheus had done him on this occasion—all this seems but pure accident ; and nevertheless it happened not but by the special order of Providence, which by a most hidden way, and a manner surpassing the capacity of man, disposed thus all these different means of saving his people from the danger they were in. So when Esther declared to Mardocheus, she durst not venture to go to the king, without his sending for her : " Who knows," said Mardocheus, " but you were raised to the throne for the help and protection of your people on this occasion ? " (Esther iv. 14.)

Ecclesiastical history abounds with the like examples, which teach us to refer all to God, and receive all as sent us from his hands, for our greater good and advantage. St. Clement recounts of himself to this purpose a very remarkable passage. He says, that having been converted to the faith by St. Barnaby, at the time that Simon Magus was most vigorously opposed by the doctrine and miracles of St. Peter, he went to this prince of the apostles, gave him an account of his conversion, and desired to be amply instructed by him in matters of faith. St. Peter told him, he came very opportunely, since the day following was the very time assigned for a public dispute between him and Simon Magus ; and that then he might hear what he desired. It happened at that very moment there came two of Simon Magus's disciples, who told St. Peter they were sent to him by their master, to acquaint him that some urgent business had occurred, and that their master desired the dispute might be put off for three days. St. Peter answered, he was content ; and when they were gone, seeing this deferring the dispute had somewhat troubled St. Clement, he asked him : " What is the matter with you, my son, that makes you melancholy ?" I assure you, father, answered St. Clement, I am very sorry that this dispute is deferred; and could heartily wish it would be to-morrow. The saint, hereupon, taking an opportunity of speaking to him on submission to Providence, said to him : Amongst the Gentiles, indeed, when things succeed not according to their desires, there may be found disquiet of mind and vexation ; but for us, who are persuaded and convinced that all things are regulated and governed by God himself, there ought to be more content of mind and resignation. Know that this has not thus happened, but for your greater good. For suppose the dispute were to have been to-morrow, you would not have comprehended it so well : but after three days' space you will be more capable to conceive it; for in this time I shall make it my business to instruct you so as to make you profit hereby.

I will conclude with the means God took to send St. Francis Xavier to the East Indies; and without all doubt it is a thing worth our serious consideration; and wherein the divine Providence signalized itself most wonderfully. St. Ignatius had named for this mission the fathers, Simon Rodriguez, and Nicholas Bobadilla; and although the former, who was then at Rome, had a quartan ague, he prepared himself, notwithstanding, to embark for Portugal, with Don Pedro Mascarenas, the ambassador, who was on the point of returning. Bobadilla was sent for, who presently set out from Calabria for Rome; and came so tired and harassed with the fatigue of his journey, and so incommoded in one of his legs, that the ambassador just departing, and not able to stay till Bobadilla could be cured, and unwilling to go without the other father that was named for the Indies, it was thought fit, in the place of Bobadilla, to substitute St. Francis Xavier, who embarked immediately and set sail with the ambassador. If we consider these things humanly speaking, this substituting of St. Xavier at so short a warning might seem to have been done by chance; however, it was not so; but it was an execution of the orders of Providence, which had from eternity designed St. Francis Xavier an apostle of the Indies. Moreover, when he and Father Simon Rodriguez were arrived in Portugal, they made so plentiful a harvest of souls, that they had been almost stopped there; and the determination came to this, that one of them was to remain, and the other to prosecute his journey. See here the design in a manner broken off, and the affair reduced to a new uncertainty. But in respect of God, there was nothing uncertain. St. Xavier at last was pitched upon and sent to the Indies; it being the will of God who had thus ordered it, for the good of innumerable souls, and his own greater honour and glory. Men, therefore, may project and purpose to themselves what they please—they may use what means they will to compass their designs: God, notwithstanding, can turn all to his own ends, and perform what conduces most to his glory, and our advancement. All these examples, and such also as experience daily furnishes us with, may serve, by the help of prayer and meditation, to imprint in our hearts a filial confidence in God: and we must not discontinue this holy exercise, till we feel this confidence firmly established within us. The more we resign ourselves into the hands of God, the more secure we are ; and on the contrary, without this confidence, all things will seem troublesome, and make you lose courage ; and till you have entirely purchased it, you will never find solid peace, nor true content and repose. Let us then contemplate this absolute resignation of ourselves into the hands of God, with a full confidence. " Let us commit our care to our Lord, and cast them upon him, and he will nourish us." (Ps. liv. 23.) "And since he takes care of us, let us cast all our troubles and solicitudes into his bosom." (1 Pet. v. 7.) What ! O Lord ! you have loved me so tenderly, that for the love of me you delivered yourself into the hands of the executioners, to do with you as they pleased. Is it extraordinary, then, that I should give up myself absolutely into your merciful hands, to be disposed of as you shall judge fit; since I am certain you do nothing but what is for my good? Let us accept of the offer made by our Saviour Jesus Christ to St. Catherine of Sienna. He bestowed upon her many signal graces and favours, and amongst the rest appearing once to her, " My daughter," said he, " think on me, and I will always think on you." What a happy compact ! What a blessed exchange ! And what an immense gain for our souls ! Nevertheless, God makes the same compact with all the world. Forget yourselves, forget the care and solicitude of what belongs to you, and lay aside all your own designs ; and the more you cast off the remembrance of yourselves, to think and meditate of God, and to place all your confidence in him, the more care will he take of you. Who would not accept so profitable a condition? It is the same the spouse made to her beloved : " I think not," says she, " but of my beloved ; and all his thoughts are also of me." (Cant. vii. 10.)

———o———

CHAPTER XII.

How profitable it is to join Prayer with this Exercise of Conformity, and how we are to descend to Particulars till we arrive to the third Degree of Conformity.

RUSHROCHIUS, a man very learned, and excellently well versed in spirituality, relates that a holy virgin, explaining to her director, who was a great servant of God, the method she used in prayer, told him she was accustomed to make her meditation upon the passion of our Lord Jesus Christ ; and the fruit she reaped thence was to have a knowledge of herself, of her own faults, and her vicious inclinations; and above all, to have a great compassion and sorrow for the sufferings of the Son of God. The director answered her, what she said was very good, but that any one might, without attaining any great perfection, be extremely touched with the sufferings of Jesus Christ; even as amongst men, the very sentiments of nature make them feel for the afflictions and calamities of their neighbour. But the holy virgin who desired to know the opinion of her confessor, thereby to regulate her way of proceeding, demanded if a continual lamenting her sins were not a profitable devotion? Yes, my daughter, replied the confessor; but still that is not what is the most perfect; because naturally what is evil in itself causes in us dissatisfaction and regret. Would it then be, answered she, a perfect devotion to exercise ourselves in meditating on the pains of the damned, and the glory of the blessed? Nor is that, replied he, what is the most sublime in perfection. For nature itself abhors all that causes it any grief or pain, and is always inclined to what affords it joy and content. At last, seeing she could get no other answer from her director, she departed in tears and very much troubled, that she could not understand to what she should more particularly apply herself in her meditations, to render them more acceptable to God. A while after, as she was still in the same affliction, there appeared to her a young child, of surprising beauty, to whom, after she had discovered the cause of her affliction, and that she could find no one capable of giving her any comfort—Not so, said the child, for I both can and will comfort you. Go seek your spiritual father, and tell him that true and real devotion consists in an entire renunciation of one's self, and an absolute resignation into the hands of God, by a strict union with him in love, and a perfect conformity in all things to his divine will. The holy woman, abundantly satisfied with this, told it her director; who answered, that that very thing in reality was the essential point to which she ought most particularly to apply herself in meditation. Because in this consists true charity, and love of God, and consequently all our advancement and perfection

Blosius tells us of another saint who was instructed by God himself, that in reciting our Lord's prayer, she should dwell particularly upon these words: "Your will be done on earth, as it is in heaven." (Matt. vi. 10.) And it is related of St. Gertrude, that by divine inspiration, she recited in one day these words of our Saviour in the garden, three hundred and sixty-five times : " Not my will, but thine be done" (Luke xxii. 42) ; and that afterwards she knew it was extremely acceptable to God. Let us copy these examples, and apply ourselves particularly to this exercise in our prayers and meditations.

But that we may practise it with more facility and profit, we must presuppose two things. The first is, that this exercise is chiefly necessary in time of adversity, and when we are in difficult circumstances, and such as are more repugnant to the dictates of nature. For on these occasions we stand in need of more solid virtue ; and it is then the love we bear God shews itself in a more special manner than at other times. As the affection a king has for his subjects is more manifestly shown in the time of peace, by the gifts and recompenses he makes them ; and as the zeal and solicitude the soldiers have for their king is demonstrated in time of war, by fighting and sacrificing their lives in his service ; so the love and tenderness the sovereign King of kings has for us, is most apparent in times of graces and consolations ; and the excess of love and affection we bear him is chiefly evinced in time of aridities and tribulations. It is a common thing, says father Avila, with all people to thank God for favours and comforts received ; but it is peculiar only to the just to pay thanks and acknowledgments for afflictions and adversities. The thanks they then return are as a melodious harmony in his ears ; and one acknowledgment made him then from the bottom of their heart, is more grateful to him, than infinity of others returned in time of prosperity. Hence it is, that the holy Scripture compares the just man to a carbuncle. For as the carbuncle casts forth more rays of light in the night than in the day ; so the virtue of the just man and the true servant of God is more resplendent in sufferings and crosses, than in comforts and prosperities. It is for this entire resignation in time of afflictions, that the holy Scripture praises very particularly the virtue of Tobias, when it says of him, that amongst other calamities which befel him, being deprived of his sight, " he did not murmur nor repine against our Lord ; but remaining constant in the fear of our Lord, he continued to bless his holy name all the remainder of his life." (Tob. ii. 14.) It was what Job had done before, amidst all the misfortunes and sufferings it pleased God to send him : " And see here," says St. Austin, " what we must endeavour to imitate. Resolve with yourself, to be ever the same as well in adversity as prosperity ; as a hand is always the same whether it be open or shut." (Serm. iv. ad Frat. in Erem.) For the servant of God ought always to be the same interiorly in his soul, although exteriorly he seems to be touched with affliction. " Socrates is said to have never been either more merry or melancholy at one time than at another ; and amidst all his changes of fortune, he kept himself constantly in an equal temper to the last moment of his life." It will not seem any great work, if we, who are Christians and religious, propose to gain so much over ourselves by the assistance of grace, as this heathen did by the help of reason only.

In the second place we must understand, it is not enough to conform ourselves to God's holy will in general. For this indeterminate sort of conformity, which is applied to nothing in particular, is no very hard business ; and in fact there is scarce any one who does not say, he wishes the will of God accomplished in all things. The good and the bad use herein the same language, and say daily alike to God, " Your will be done on earth as it is in heaven." But we must come to somewhat more than this—we must proceed to particulars—we must descend to each part of what would give us any dissatisfaction, in case it should happen ; and continue constantly herein, till we have surpassed the difficulty, and till we find no more enemies to overcome. In fine, we must encounter whatever occurs, and not lay down our arms, till we have thoroughly vanquished all that can any ways oppose our union and absolute conformity to the will of God.

But this is not yet sufficient ; we must pass on still farther, and never stop till we come to conceive interiorly an immense joy in ourselves, on beholding the will of God accomplished in us, even by the means of sufferings and injuries ; and this is the third degree of conformity. For in this virtue as well as in others, there are several degrees, which may all be reduced to three ; according to the distinction of degrees the saints note in the virtue of patience. The first degree is, when we are far from desiring or taking a pleasure in misfortunes that befall us, but on the contrary, we avoid and shun them, as far as we are able ; yet we would rather suffer and undergo them, than incur any sin in avoiding them. And this is the lowest degree, and what precisely is of indispensable obligation. So that supposing we are sensibly touched with any mischances or accidents ; that we groan and sigh in our sickness, that we cry out in the violence of our pain; that we mourn and lament at the death of our parents or friends, we may, notwithstanding all this, have conformity to the divine will. The second degree is, when although of ourselves we have no inclination to desire pains and afflictions, nevertheless when they happen we receive and bear them most willingly; because we know the will of God is thereby executed. And in what this degree surpasses the former is, that it makes us in some manner love afflictions for God's sake, and that we are willing to suffer them not only with patience, inasmuch as we are obliged thereto under sin, but also with a sort of joy, inasmuch as we are convinced it is a thing very pleasing to God. The first degree makes us suffer things with patience. The second, makes us suffer them with a prompt and cheerful disposition of mind towards what God ordains. But the third, and most perfect degree of all, is, when out of an excess of love towards God, we do not only suffer and accept willingly all the afflictions and pains he sends, but we even prevent him by our desires, and rejoice; because we know they happen not but by the adorable decree of his holy will. So the apostles, after they had been publicly beaten with whips, "went out of the assembly of Jews, rejoicing that they were thought fit to be treated ignominiously for the name of Jesus Christ." (Acts v. 41.) And St. Paul said : "He was replenished with comfort, and abounded with joy, amidst his pains and sufferings." (1 Cor. vii. 4.) The same apostle praises the Hebrews upon the same account, when in his epistle to them he says :—"You have received with joy the loss of your goods ; knowing you have in store far better and more solid riches." (Heb. x. 34.) Let us make it our endeavour to become, by God's holy grace, so as to receive with joy and satisfaction whatever misfortune happens ; and as St. James says, in his first canonical epistle : "Look upon all the different afflictions which befal you, my brethren, as a great subject of joy and consolation." (James i. 2.) We ought to find so great a satisfaction in whatever proceeds from the divine will, as thereby to sweeten all the bitterness of this life, and make whatsoever is hard and difficult, easy and delightful. "If our hearts are fixed on God," says St, Gregory, "whatever is bitter and afflicting in this life becomes sweet and pleasant to them. They find their repose and tranquillity in pains and afflictions, and desire death with impatience, to obtain their joy and felicity in the life to come."

St. Catherine of Sienna, in a dialogue she composed on

Christian perfection, says, that amongst many other things her beloved taught her, one was, that she ought to shut herself up in the divine will, as in a most secure retreat, and live there as a pearl in the shell, or a bee in the hive, without ever coming forth upon any occasion. That in the beginning, perhaps, she would find the place very narrow, but afterwards it would be larger; and without once coming forth, she might walk there as in the habitations of the blessed; and obtain, in a short time, what out of that retirement she would not be able to compass in a long term of years. Let us make use of this in such a manner, as to make it our continual practice. "My beloved to me, and I to him." (Cant. ii. 16.) These few words may easily administer sufficient matter for our whole lives: wherefore we ought to have them perpetually in our mouths and hearts.

———o———

CHAPTER XIII.

Of the Conformity a religious Person should have to the Divine Will, so as to go and live in what Part of the World Obedience shall assign him.

THAT we may reap more fruit from this exercise of resignation to the will of God, and put in practice what we said: we will lay down some principal points, wherein we may exercise ourselves. And after having treated of those which appertain more particularly to our constitutions, since in this it is more fit a religious should show in a special manner his virtue and submission, we will proceed to some in general, which concern every one. Nevertheless, what we say here may be applied to all in the like occasions, according to their state and profession. In the seventh part of our constitutions, St. Ignatius, speaking of missions, which are the chief end of our institute, says, that those of the society ought to have such an indifference of mind for whatever place obedience shall allot them, as to be equally prepared, and ready to go and live in whatever part of the world obedience shall send them; amongst Christians or infidels, amongst Catholics or heretics. Wherefore the professed religious of our society make a fourth solemn vow of obedience to the Pope, whereby they promise to go where he shall please, without delay, excuse, or repugnance; on foot or horseback; with, or without money for their charges, and living in their journey on alms, as the Pope shall judge it most expedient. The end proposed in establishing this vow, says St. Ignatius, is to be the better able by this means to find the will of God. So that as the first fathers, of the society were of different nations, and knew not in what part of the world they should be most acceptable to God, whether amongst Christians or infidels ; they judged it fit, for taking away all grounds of mistake, in following their own choice, to make a fourth vow in the hands of Christ's vicar, that he may send them throughout the world, as he should judge it most conducive to his service, and the greater glory of God. Wherefore, says he, no religious of the society is to use any means whereby he may go or stay in this place more than another ; but must have such an indifference herein, that not respecting anything but the greater service and glory of God, he must leave himself wholly in the hands of the superior who holds God's place.

To show how far our holy founder would have this our indifference extend itself of going to any place of the world, where obedience shall call us, it will be sufficient to assign the following example : Father Laynez having once signified to him, he had a desire of going to the Indies, there to procure the salvation of those infidels, who, for want of evangelical labourers to assist them, ran to their perdition in the blindness of idolatry. And I, replied the saint, find not any desire or inclination in myself that way. Father Laynez asked him the reason. The saint replied, that having made to the Pope a vow of obedience, for the purpose of being sent, on God's service, wherever he pleased, we ought to retain this absolute indifference, without inclining more to one side than the other. And for myself, said he, if I thought I had any inclination for the Indies, I would oppose it with all my might ; in order to put myself in the balance of a just equality and indifference of mind, as I ought to be, to attain the perfection of obedience.

We do not adduce this, with a view to censure the desires of the Indian Mission, for they are much to be commended, and are very holy in themselves ; and St. Ignatius would have all superiors rejoice, when they find any of those in their charge who have such a desire, because it is ordinarily the mark and assurance of a vocation from God, and a means whereby things are done with more facility and satisfaction. But we would show by this, what an indifference St. Ignatius recommends to us for all sorts of places and employs ; since he would not have us retain attachment to even a thing so important to God's service, and so difficult in itself ; lest hereby we destroy in our selves that indifference we ought always to have for whatever obedience designs us.

Hence follows some consequences, which show more evidently what we here speak of. First, if the desire any one has of going to the Indies so engages him, as to diminish or hinder his indifference and disposition to whatever obedience may otherwise enjoin him ; this sort of desire is absolutely to be condemned. For example, if the desire of going to the Indies, or any other place in the world, makes me uneasy or dissatisfied in the place I am sent to ; or if it makes me more tepid and remiss in the functions of that charge imposed upon me ; it is certain this desire is culpable, and comes not from God, because it is opposite to his will and pleasure. For God cannot be contrary to himself ; and the inspirations of the Holy Ghost are not accompanied with discontents and troubles ; on the contrary, they bring all peace and tranquillity to the mind. And this is one of the signs the masters of a spiritual life give to distinguish those desires which come from God, and those that come from man.

In the second place, it follows, that he who has a disposition equally inclined for all places and all things obedience assigns him, must not trouble and afflict himself if he finds not a particular inclination for foreign missions. For this disposition of mind is not less good than the other ; on the contrary, it is rather better, since that which St. Ignatius wishes us to have in the society is, that we be not biassed by any particular inclination to one thing more than another, and that we be as the needle of a balance without inclining to either side. He had once a thought of sending father Natalis upon some mission ; but that things might be done with all sweetness imaginable, he would first see if his inclination tended that way. Father Natalis answered him in writing, that he had no other inclination than to have no inclination to anything at all. And this was what our holy founder esteemed the greatest thing in a religious, and most consistent with reason. So that whoever has an affection to any particular thing, seems to be tied and wedded to that thing only ; but he who is equally and indifferently disposed to whatsoever is enjoined, embraces all things in general. And as God looks upon the heart, and esteems the will for the deed, so in respect of God, it is the same as though he had performed all in general.

For the better understanding this point, I say, if either through tepidity or pusillanimity, any one feels not a desire of going to the Indies, if it be through fear of losing those conveniences and satisfactions he finds in the place he is in, or because he apprehends such fatigues and dangers as are frequent in such missions, then it is an imperfection and self-love. But supposing it be not any tepidity that hinders this desire in him, nor any backwardness in being willing to undergo all things for the love of God and the good of souls; that he is only uncertain whether it be the will of God, and at the same time finds himself equally disposed to whatever he understands to be his holy will, and is wholly prepared to go to the Indies, with as much or more joy than if he had ardently desired it; because he is assured it is not his own will, but the will of God which he fulfils; in this case, there is no doubt but such an one is in the best disposition possible. So we see superiors freely make choice of such as they know have this universal and equal disposition.

But to come to our principal point, St. Ignatius wishes we all had so great an indifference and resignation to remain and live as well in one place as another, that even the consideration of our health should not have that influence on us, as to make us change our sentiments. He says in the third part of the Constitutions: It is our vocation and our institute to go to all places, where we shall be judged more profitable to God's service, and the good of our neighbour. Yet, however, supposing it is found by experience that the air of such a climate agrees not with the constitution of such religious, and that he enjoys not his health; the superior upon this must consider, if it be necessary to send him to some other place, where he may enjoy better health, and employ himself with more fruit in the service of God and neighbour. "Notwithstanding," says he, "it is not for the indisposed person to petition his removal, or show in himself any such inclination; but he must commit this affair totally and absolutely to his superior." What is here required of us is not, I assure you, a thing of no value; for it must be a great abnegation of ourselves, when we see our health called in question—when we see it daily on the decline, to be able not only to refrain from desiring change of air, but even abstain from showing any inclination that way. So that forasmuch as relates to the mission amongst heathens or heretics; it is allowed any one to propose his thoughts and desires, provided it be with entire resignation of himself into the hands of his superior. But in point of health to be recovered by change of place, it is not permitted either to demand this change, or to show any desire thereof. All that can be done is, when we are in such condition, and we feel we are no longer able to fulfil the obligations and duties of our charge, to signify it to the superior; and this is prescribed by our rules. But after this, the subject has no more to do; and it is the superior's business to see if it be necessary to send him anywhere else, to recover strength, and to do the society more service; or although he be wholly unprofitable where he is, if it be not more expedient, and to the greater glory of God, for him to remain there. However, it is not for the subject to judge, but for the superior, who governs in the place of God; and to whom the inferior ought so far to deliver the disposal of himself, as to be assured whatever the superior orders touching his concerns, is what is most for God's service, and his own good. How many persons are there who live in countries remote from their own, and in such as agree not with their health and constitution, and this only to secure a livelihood? How many cross the seas, how many go to Constantinople, to Africa, to the Indies, and for an inconsiderable gain, run the risk, not only of their health, but of life, itself? What greater wonder, then, if we, who are religious, should perform for the love of God, and through obedience, what men of the world do for the sake of some inconsiderable lucre, and temporal interest. Suppose, then, you should chance to think the indisposition caused in you by the place you live in makes you unserviceable, and that in another place you could labour with some success in the service of God; remember, at the same time, that it is better you remain, though unprofitable where you are, submitting yourself to the will of God, than to perform great things in following your own inclinations and desires; and conform yourself herein to the divine will, which requires this of you, for reasons best known to itself, which ought not to be manifested to you.

We read in the chronicles of St. Francis, that blessed brother Giles, having obtained leave of the saint to go and reside in what province, and what convent of the order he pleased, had scarce enjoyed four days this liberty, when, finding the former peace and tranquillity of his mind disturbed and troubled, he begged earnestly of the saint to assign him some house for his abode, and not leave it any longer to his own choice; because this sort of liberty so undetermined, and of so great extent, contributed only to disturb his repose of spirit, and disquiet his content of mind. Good and true religious feel not any peace or satisfaction of mind in doing their own will, and set not their affection upon one place more than another ; but look upon that place where obedience sends them as the best, because they know it is that which the divine will has allotted them ; and it is in the divine will they place all their content and satisfaction.

---o---

CHAPTER XIV.

Of the Indifference a Religious is to have for all Charges and Functions wherein Obedience employs him.

THE indifference and resignation we here speak of must extend itself also to all those offices to which it shall please obedience to attach us. It is easy to know their number and functions. Let every person take a view of them in his mind, one after another, till he feels an equal inclination to them all. As to such offices as are more humble and contemptible, and to which, consequently, there is greater repugnance ; our constitution will have us apply ourselves to such with all promptitude and readiness, when obedience calls. There is never more need of resignation than in these sort of employs ; because our natural pride gives us an aversion to them, and so there is more virtue and perfection in readily subjecting ourselves to them for the love of God, than in desiring such offices as are of greater note, and more honourable. If a person should bind himself to any great lord for all his life, to be willing to serve him in the lowest and basest offices of his family, if there were need ; he would show doubtless in this a greater zeal and affection for his service, than if he would only engage himself in the more honourable employs, which carry along with them in some manner their recompense. And the more talents he would have for those higher posts, the more affection would he show in employing himself in these servile occupations. It is the very same in religion. If you offer yourself to serve God only in the quality of a preacher or master of divinity, you would not do any great thing, nor would you testify any great zeal and fervour for his service ; since these employs carry a sufficient recommendation to be desired for sake of them-

selves. But supposing you offer yourself for your whole life
to his service, in the lowest and vilest ministries and charges
which are most opposite to the pride of our nature, and most
repugnant to our feelings ; then it is you give a signal token of
the zeal you have for his service. And the greater your talents
are for high and sublime offices the greater and more acceptable
is this proof of your love. This very one thing might suffice to
oblige us always to desire those charges which are more mean
and subject ; since in the house of God there are no offices of
that nature. It is ordinarily said, that there are no mean
persons about a king ; because, in what quality soever they serve
him, there is some honour annexed. How much greater, then,
is it to serve God in any manner whatsoever, " since to serve
him is to reign with him ? "

St. Basil, endeavouring to excite us to love servile and humble
offices, adduces the example of our Saviour Jesus Christ, who
exercised himself not once only in washing the feet of his
apostles, but throughout his whole life, in obeying his blessed
mother and St. Joseph in all things they enjoined him. For
although the holy Scripture mentions nothing concerning him
from the age of twelve years to thirty, only that " he was subjected to them " (Luke ii. 51),—it is nevertheless inferred thence,
and from their extreme poverty, that he doubtless submitted
himself to divers servile employs. " Let not, then, a Christian,"
says St. Austin, " think it beneath him, to do what Jesus Christ
himself has done before him." Since the Son of God disdained
not for the love of us to exercise himself in the most humble
and abject offices ; let us not look upon it below us, to exercise
ourselves in the same for his love, although it were for the
durance of life.

Bnt to come yet nearer to our object, I say, one of the chief
motives which should oblige us to embrace most willingly what
is imposed upon us by obedience, is, that we rest assured, this
employ is absolutely that which God exacts at the present of us.
For as we said before, it ought to be a subject of great joy and
comfort to us in all our occupations prescribed by obedience,
to rest convinced that it is the will of God we then perform.
Nothing affords our soul more content than this thought ; God
will have me at present do this, it is his holy will ; we must not
entertain any farther doubt, and must desire nothing more, since
nothing can be better than the performing his divine will. Those
who view objects in this manner are not at all solicitous when

they are commanded one thing rather than another, or whether they are designed for any mean employ, or one of more note, since both are alike acceptable to them.

St. Jerome relates an example very applicable to our purpose. He says, that visiting upon an occasion the religious of the desert, he saw one, who, by the superior's order, bore upon his shoulders twice a day a great stone for the space of a league, for no other end, than that his superior, who had another design in the thing, would teach him and others by his example, to obey with submission, and to mortify their own judgment. He had at that time spent eight years in this practice. And to those, says this same saint, who knew not the price and merit of obedience, and whose pride and self-conceit hindered them from attaining the purity and simplicity of this virtue, it seemed but a childish business. Many asked him how he could bear this subjection; and even I myself, desirous to know what were his thoughts and sentiments during the time of this employ, proposed some questions to him concerning it. He answered me, that when he had finished his labour, he felt such joy and satisfaction in himself, as if he had performed the most important and honourable thing that could be enjoined him. And this answer made such an impression upon me, that from thenceforth I began to live as a true religious person ought. In fine, it is the part of a good and true religious to embrace things which appear most despicable in the exterior, and to imagine that in performing them we perform the will of God. And those who have this esteem of whatever obedience assigns them make great progress in virtue; because they nourish themselves with what is more pure. The performance of the divine will, which they make their daily food, is that "fat of corn, wherewith they are satiated." (Ps. cxlvii. 14.)

But some one will say, that to do the will of God in all things is indeed a great perfection; and in reality, I am always ready to do it in whatever office is assigned me; however, I could wish to do it in an honourable office. This is to err in the very principles themselves; because at the bottom it is nothing else than to desire that God should do your will, and not that you should accommodate yourself to his. It is not for you to prescribe conditions to God, and to desire him to grant you what you judge most agreeable; you must receive with blind obedience those he shall please to impose upon you, and conform yourself entirely to all he requires of you. "He, O Lord!" says St. Austin, " serves you as he ought, who desires not that you enjoin him what he pleases; but who makes it his business to desire, and accommodate himself to what you enjoin." And the holy abbot Nilus, writing upon prayer : " Do not pray," says he, " that what you desire may be done ; but rather pray as you are taught to pray, that the will of God be accomplished in you."

Let us reflect upon this—it is a very profitable point, and may be applied to any affliction whatever that befalls us. It is not for us, it is for God only to choose how and what we ought to suffer. Nor is it for you to choose what kind of temptation you would have; nor to say, I could have borne it with ease had it been any other; but for this, I am in no wise able to support it. The pains we suffer would not be pains, if they were such as depended upon our choice; and if you desire entirely to please God, you ought to entreat him, that he would guide and govern you as he pleases, and not as you please. If he assigns you what is most repugnant, and what you have the greatest difficulty to undergo ; and nevertheless, you receive it, and support it with a perfect resignation ; it is then you show yourself a true imitator of Jesus Christ, who desired not that his own will, but the will of his Eternal Father, might be done. We cannot say we have a real conformity to God's will, unless we commit ourselves totally into his hands, that he may dispose of us as he shall think fit, when and how he shall think fit, without any the least opposition or reserve on our part.

Blosius relates that St. Gertrude, being once in prayer for one who bore with great impatience the sufferings and temptations it pleased God to send her; our Lord said to her, Go and tell the person you pray for, that since the kingdom of heaven is not to be purchased but by sufferings, and those which I have sent her are not to her liking, she may choose such as are more to her desire. The holy virgin understood clearly by these words, and by the manner wherewith our Saviour uttered them, that it is a dangerous sort of impatience to wish to have sufferings of our own choice, and to say we cannot bear those sent from God, and that they are not conducive to our good. For all must be convinced, that what comes from God is precisely what is most for our advantage ; and so we are to receive it with patience, by absolutely conforming ourselves to the divine will. To apply this more particularly to our present subject, as it is not for us to choose what pains and temptations we ought to suffer, but must receive, as from the hands of God, whatsoever he designs us; and be assured, at the same time, what he assigns us is for our greater good; so, in like manner, it is not for us to make choice of what charge or office we would undertake; but we must accept, as from the hands of God, the charge assigned us by obedience, and be thoroughly convinced it is that in reality which is most useful and profitable to us.

We may add here another point, which appertains to very great perfection. It is to resign ourselves to the will of God, with such confidence as not to have the least curiosity to know what it shall please him to do with us. As it is the greatest sign of confidence a master can put in his servant, to rely so far upon him, as to deliver up to him the charge of all he has, without taking account of anything himself—" See," says Joseph, " my prince has intrusted all he has so in my care, that he knows not what he has himself" (Gen. xxxix. 8) : so it is a proof of a great confidence in God, not to be desirous of knowing in what manner he designs to dispose of us. I am in good hands, and that is sufficient : " My destiny, O Lord, is in your hands." (Ps. xxx. 16.) With this I live in peace and security, nor do I desire to know more.

As to the persons who are ambitious of posts and employs more honourable than those they are in, imagining they could do God greater service, and the neighbour greater good; they deceive themselves mightily, in believing these desires take rise from the zeal they have of God's glory, and of the neighbour's salvation. No ! but these sentiments spring from their ambition, from their desire of being esteemed and honoured, from the love of their own convenience, and because the employ they seek after is either of great dignity, or more conformable to their own inclinations than that they at present are in. Were you in the world and independent of others, you would be at liberty to change one thing for another, in regard of its greater conveniency and good, because you could not do both. But it is not so in religion. We cannot leave one thing to undertake another; both must be performed. Every one must do his part, and if you occupy the higher office, another must take upon him the lower. But were you truly humble, you would endeavour to have others charged with the higher duties; because you would believe that they would perform them better than you could; and there would be less danger of your being carried away by sentiments of pride, and thoughts of vainglory.

In order to point out to us the grounds of election, in such matters as depend on our choice, St. Ignatius has left us profitable doctrine, quite applicable to the subject we treat of, and to several others of the like nature. He says there are three degrees of humility ; the most perfect of which is always, when offered two occasions of equally serving God, to choose that wherein we judge there is more abnegation of ourselves, and more subject of contempt; the better to imitate Jesus Christ, who, for the love of us, would subject himself to the scorn and contempt of men. Another advantage we may yet draw hence is, that in these lowly functions there is less self-interest found than in the others; and so we have fewer occasions of seeking ourselves, and are less exposed to temptations of vainglory. In these lower offices we exercise, at one and the same time, the virtues of charity and humility; and particularly of humility, since it is by these things humility is preserved. But in higher and more important charges we only practise charity, with some risk of our humility; and this should suffice, not only to hinder us from aspiring to higher things, but should also make us dread them.

——o——

CHAPTER XV.

Of the Conformity we ought to have to the Will of God in the Distribution of natural Gifts and Talents.

WE must all be content with the talents we have received from God, without envying others who are possessed of superior abilities. All persons stand in need of this instruction. For although several seem to surpass in some things, they have, notwithstanding, their defects, which counterpoise these advantages, and which render necessary to them the moderation and conformity we here speak of. It is our duty, then, to take precautions in this particular, and the more so, as the devil attacks many persons herein. You are, for example, in the course of your studies ; and if, at the public exhibitions, others signalise themselves more than you do, you will be apt presently to conceive in yourself a secret sort of envy. This envy, it is true, may not influence you so far as to afflict and torment yourself at your neighbour's good, yet you will feel ashamed and chagrined on seeing that others have the precedence. Hence, will arise dejection and discontent, which may at last work so far upon you as to tempt you to quit your studies, and sometimes even religion itself ; as in reality this temptation had made some do, because they had not laid strong foundations of humility. Some imagined they would become eminent for their studies, and acquire a great name and reputation ; but the issue not answering their expectations, they conceive such shame and confusion that the devil, embracing this opportunity, fails not to suggest to them, that unless they quit religion they will never be free from the disgrace and confusion they have incurred.

This sort of temptation is not of a new date. We read in the chronicles of St. Dominick something like it, in the example of Albertus Magnus, who was master to St. Thomas of Aquin. This Albertus, as the history relates, had from his very infancy been a great client of the Blessed Virgin ; recited some prayer daily in her honour, and, by her intercession, had been received at the age of sixteen into the order of St. Dominick. His talents at the time were by no means splendid ; he seemed rather incapable of prosecuting his studies. In a word, seeing himself backward while many of his fellow-students were making very considerable progress, he became so dissatisfied with himself, and the temptation pressed so heavily on him, that he was on the point of forsaking religion ; and had certainly done it had he not, in this trouble of mind, received comfort from a miraculous vision. One night, in his sleep he fancied he had reared a ladder to the wall of the monastery to make his escape, and as he mounted, he beheld on the top of the wall four venerable matrons, of whom one seemed to be the chief. Having now approached them, one of the four gave him a violent push and threw him down to the bottom. He got up again, and was treated by another in the same manner : and being now ready to make the third attempt, one of them asked him what he intended, and upon what account he resolved to leave the order ? He answered, quite confused, that he saw his fellow-students daily making great progress in their studies, that all his own application and industry were to little purpose, and that it was shame made him leave religion. Whereupon the matron showing him the Blessed Virgin ; behold here present, said she, the mother of God and queen of heaven, whose servants only we are ; recommend yourself to her, and we will also join our petitions with yours, that she will please to obtain of her Son those necessary qualities and helps for your success in your studies. Having said this she presented him to the Blessed Virgin, who, receiving him with a tender affection, asked what he desired ? He told her it was to learn philosophy, wherein he had spent some time without any success. The Blessed Virgin exhorted him to take courage and continue his studies, and that he should become a learned and famous man. But to let you know it is to me you owe this favour, and not to your own capacity and parts, I here foretell you, upon a certain time, whilst you are in the public chair, you shall forget on a sudden all you knew before. He was extremely comforted at this vision ; and after that time became so eminent not only in philosophy but in divinity also, and in holy Scripture, as is sufficiently attested and evinced by his writings left to posterity. Three years before his death, as he taught publicly at Cologne, he so far forgot all he knew before as not to retain a single idea of all he had formerly learned ; and it may be that God permitted it to fall out so, in punishment of his want of conformity to his holy will, in the distribution of those talents he had received. When remembering the vision he had, when he designed to leave the order, he related the whole matter to his auditors, took leave of them, and retired to his monastery, where he employed the rest of his life in prayer and contemplation.

But lest we fall into the like inconveniences, we must necessarily take some precaution. Now what we stand most in need of is profound humility. For it is through want of humility that we content not ourselves with those few qualities and talents we have ; it is for this reason we cannot bear that any one should consider us as possessed of less ability and capacity than our companions. How then would it be, if on account of your incapacity, you were not allowed to continue your studies, and at the same time to see others advanced in the most sublime sciences, and become great divines, or famous preachers? For such a trial as this, you will stand very much in need of humility and resignation : nor must you have less need thereof at the end of your studies, if you see yourself not qualified for those employs which are assigned others ; and if you have not parts or talents, either for the chair or exterior functions, or for the management of business at home. Those who have never studied are not to stand less upon their guard ; for they may feel regret ; one, that he knows not Latin ; another, that he is not a priest ; and a third, that he has not sufficient knowledge and science to take part in the conversion of souls. And these temptations may come to work so upon them, and prove so strong and violent, as to make them lose the esteem of their vocation as it sometimes happens, and even to endanger their salvation.

What we speak of here regards all in general ; and each person in particular may apply it to his own state and condition, according to the circumstances he is in. For it is the duty of every one to conform himself to the divine will, to rest contented with the talents God has given him, and the condition he has placed him in; and not to desire and seek after any other thing, but what God pleases. St. Austin upon this passage of the Psalmist: "Incline my heart to the practice of your commandments, and not to avarice" (Ps. cxviii. 36), says, that avarice, by which name we understand all sorts of irregular desires, has been the occasion of all our misfortunes. What banished our first parents from paradise and robbed them of those great advantages they enjoyed was, that they wished to be more than what God had made them, and sought after more than God had bestowed upon them. "You shall become," says the serpent, "as gods; having the knowledge of good and evil." (Gen. iii. 5.) This was the bait and allurement he made use of to delude them, and to work their destruction; and we have inherited this their desire of becoming gods, that is their folly, or rather their madness, in striving to be greater than we really are. This enemy of ours was, by his argument, so successful against our first parents, that he makes use of the same even to this day against us; persuading and pushing us on, inasmuch as he is able, to desire to be more and greater than what God would have us be; and not to rest satisfied with the talents God has given us or the condition he has placed us in. It is for this reason, says St. Austin, the Royal Prophet asks of God, that he will give him a heart wholly disinterested, and a heart which is faithfully inclined to all that shall please the divine will, and that is entirely void of self-satisfaction, and self-interest. For by this word avarice, as we said before, he understands not only desire of riches, but also of honours, of glory, of pleasure, and all cupidity in general. And it is in this sense the apostle takes it, saying, "covetousness, or avarice, is the root of all evil."

But though we had no other motive of contenting ourselves with those talents God has conferred upon us, and the state and condition wherein he has placed us, but purely that of the divine will; this motive alone might suffice to oblige us to a perfect conformity to the orders of his Providence. "All those things," says St. Paul, "are the work of one and the same spirit, which gives and allots each one his share as it pleases." (1 Cor. xii. 11.) The apostle in this place makes use of the metaphor of a man's body; of which we have spoken elsewhere when treating of the union which ought to be amongst religious persons : and he says, that as in the body of a man, God has placed the members as he pleased ; and the feet have not murmured because they were not the head ; nor the hands, because they were not the eyes : so in the body of the Church (the same may also be said of that of religion) God has ranged and placed the faithful as he pleased. It is not by pure chance that some are given one charge, some another : but it is by a special order of his Providence. So that if it please God you should be the feet, by what right would you aspire to be the head ? And if he would have you be the hands, by what title would you endeavour to be the eyes ? Oh, how profound are the judgments of God—how incomprehensible are they ? " And what man is there who can penetrate into the secret designs of God ?" All things, O Lord, come from you ; and consequently we ought to praise you in all. You know what is most proper and expedient for each one, and why you confer more upon one than another; and it is not for us to search into the reason. For who knows what would become of us, had we received more knowledge and capacity ? How do you know if you had been some great preacher, and had been followed and esteemed, but this would prove utter ruin to you, as to many others, whose pride and vanity precipitated them into their final perdition ? The persons of great learning and parts are soonest carried away with a desire of being known and esteemed. If with the little capacity and knowledge you have, and that mean science, and perhaps less than mean, you are so presumptuous as to compare, and even prefer yourselves to others ; and look upon it an injury done you, not to be selected for the most honourable functions ; what would you do, if in reality you were masters of these rare qualities, and those so sublime and extraordinary talents and endowments ? " Wings are not granted the ant," as the saying is, " but for her ruin :" and perhaps these great talents would not have been conferred upon you, but for your ruin. If we seriously reflect upon these things as we should do, and not look upon them through a disordered imagination, we should find sufficient reason to thank God all our life-time, for having placed us in this state of subjection and humility, and given us so scanty a portion of talents : and we might say with the pious à Kempis, " Lord, I look upon it as a most signal favour and happiness, not to have received a great many things, which might have gained the applause and esteem of men." The saints knew very well the danger which accompanied these great gifts and advantages ; and so, they not only abstained from desiring, but even dreaded them, as those possessed of them are so much exposed to the danger of vainglory ; and thus the saints became more pleasing to God, who prefers humility of heart to sublimity of genius. Were we but well convinced that all things, except the accomplishment of God's holy will, are but pure vanity, and could we persuade ourselves to repose, and place our satisfaction and content in that of God, we should find nothing else worth our desiring or seeking after. If you, with those mean talents you have, and your limited science, can find wherewith to be more pleasing to God, why do you trouble yourself in seeking what you have not? If you have any reason for doing so, it is that you may please God more; but if, on the contrary, it pleases him more, that you remain in your ignorance, and poverty of knowledge, as certainly it must be that which pleases him most; since it is he who disposes of his gifts as he thinks best; why are you so concerned? Wherefore do you endeavour to be what God never designed you for, and what is not convenient you should be? The great and magnificent sacrifices of Saul were no wise grateful to God; because they were not conformable to his holy will. And those great and aspiring desires you conceive in yourself, will be as little pleasing to him; since our spiritual advancement consists not in being learned divines, or able preachers, nor in receiving great lights and helps, great talents, and great employs; but it consists in performing the will of God, in giving a faithful and just account of what he has committed to our charge, in improving well the talent he has been pleased to intrust us with. It is to this point only we are to direct our course; since it is only this God demands of us.

In order to elucidate this matter still more, let us compare men in the different states of life, to players on the stage. It is not from the character assigned him, but it is from the natural manner wherein he performs his part, that a player derives praise. So that if he who acts the peasant, represents him better than he who acts the emperor, he will be certainly more applauded and esteemed. It is the same with us in respect to God. What he regards in us during this life, which, properly speaking, is but a long comedy, and God grant to some of us it never prove a tragedy, is, not the character we bear in religion, one a superior, another a preacher, this a porter, that a sacristan; but it is the manner wherein each acquits himself of his charge. If the inferior acquits himself better, and acts his part more to the life than the superior, he shall be more esteemed in the sight of God, and receive greater recompense and glory. This actor, perhaps, who succeeded ill in the part of a king, had he represented the shepherd, might have gained more honour, and been looked upon as the chief. So you may fail in the part of the preacher, or superior, and have good success in that of an infirmarian, or spiritual father. God knows very well how to mark out to all the part most proper for them ; and distributes his talents, " to every one according to his capacity " (Matt. xxv. 15.) Wherefore we are to desire no part but what we already have. Our chief affair is to do to the life the part assigned us, and to give a good account of the talent we are entrusted with ; for so we shall please God the more, and receive from him greater merit and recompense.

——o——

CHAPTER XVI.

Of the Conformity we are to have to the Will of God in Time of Sickness.

As health is a gift of God, so is sickness also ; and God sends it us to try and correct us—to make us sensible of our weakness—to disabuse us of our high notions—to detach us from the love of terrene things, and the pleasures of our senses—to check the impetuosity and diminish the strength of our greatest enemy, our own flesh ; to put us in mind that we are here in a place of exile, and that heaven is our real country ; and in fine, to procure to us all the advantages which flow therefrom, when it is received as a present from his hand. " A grievous sickness maketh the soul sober." (Eccles. xxxi. 2.) And hence an ancient father of the desert said to one of his disciples, who was sick : My son, be not troubled at this sickness ; on the contrary give God thanks : for it is a fire which purges all your rust, if you are iron ; and purifies you, if you are gold. It is a sign of great piety and perfect virtue, to thank God for all the infirmities he pleases to send us.

We read in the life of St. Clare, that for the space of twenty-eight years she was a martyr to several grievous infirmities ; and instead of murmuring or making her complaints, she constantly gave God thanks. But in her last sickness in particular, her pains were so acute, that she could take nothing ; and her confessor endeavouring to comfort and exhort her to bear this long martyrdom with patience ; she said, that since by means of the great St. Francis, she had come to know the grace of Jesus Christ our Saviour, she found no difficulty in her infirmities, nothing insupportable in her sufferings, nothing hard or painful in the practice of penance. The life of St. Lidwina is also a most wonderful example in this respect, and well calculated for the comfort and encouragement of persons in their sickness. This holy virgin lay sick for thirty-eight years, in unspeakable pain and torture; she was bed-ridden for thirty, without being able, all this time, to set her foot upon the ground. And she supported all these afflictions with that patience and humility, as to merit thereby that God should show her daily some notable sign of his favour and kindness.

But because, in these trials, there occur to the mind some particular reasons, which, under pretence and appearance of good, impede our entire resignation to the divine will; we will endeavour to give a full and satisfactory answer to all. First, one will say, inasmuch as it regards myself, I should be wholly indifferent whether I were visited with sickness, or enjoyed my health; but what troubles me most is, that I feel myself a burden to religion, and a charge to the house. To this I answer, that you hereby tax the superiors with want of charity and of submission to the will of God; that you ought to believe that they endeavour, as well as you, to conform themselves to his will, and to accept all things as coming from his hand; and consequently, if it be his pleasure to employ them for some space of time in providing for your necessities, and taking care of you, it is but what he requires of them. And as you bear patiently the crosses and afflictions he sends you; so they will accept the share and part assigned.

But I see clearly, you will say, the great charity and tenderness of the society; yet I feel uneasy, when I consider, that if God gave me health, I could improve myself—I could preach— I could teach or employ my time in the direction of souls; and all this while I must lie in bed, and be prevented by sickness. St. Austin solves this very satisfactorily. We do not know, says he, whether it is expedient or not to obtain what we desire. Let us therefore think on this in all the designs we frame to ourselves; and then, if they succeed, we may rejoice; not because we have attained what we desired, but what has been the will of God. But if, on the contrary, our designs succeed not to our expectation, we are not therefore to afflict ourselves, and lose our peace of mind. "For it is more reasonable we comply with, and accommodate ourselves to the will of God, than that he accommodate himself to ours." In fine, as this great saint concludes, "no one can ever be better regulated in his actions, than he who is more disposed, not to perform what the divine power forbids, than he is to do what human reason urges him to project." We must therefore have such an indifference of mind to whatsoever we take in hand, that, supposing it pleases not God to bring it to the end we propose to ourselves, we remain always ready and prepared to exercise an entire conformity to his holy will. So that if sickness or anything else prevents us from executing our resolutions, we are not therefore to trouble or disquiet our thoughts; how profitable soever, and conducive this our design might have been to the service of God, and the good of souls. Father Avila, writing to a certain priest that lay sick, advised him not to consider what he would do were he in good health, but how acceptable he would be to God in taking his sickness patiently. And provided you seek only the will of God, as I question not but you do, whatmatter is it whether you are sick or well, since this divine will, whence springs all our good, is equally accomplished?

St. Chrysostom affirms, that Job merited more by these words: " As it pleased our Lord, so it has happened : blessed be the name of our Lord " (Job i. 21) ; and by his submission to the divine will in his afflictions and sufferings, than by all the actions he performed in his health and prosperity. You will merit also more, and become more pleasing to God, by conforming yourself wholly to his will in time of sickness, than in all you can do in perfect health. St. Bonaventure is of the same opinion. " There is more perfection," says he, " in supporting adversities with patience, than in seriously applying ourselves to good works." For God stands not in need of you or me to produce in his Church the fruit he desires. " I have said to our Lord, you are my God, since you stand not in need of what I have." (Ps. xv. 1.) It is he who preaches to you at present by means of sickness, and who teaches you patience and submission. Let him go on without interruption ; he knows what is expedient for you, and you are ignorant of it yourself. Were we to desire health upon any account, it would be to employ it in serving and pleasing him ; but if he is better pleased that I be sick, and if I please him more, by my suffering patiently all the pains of a troublesome disease, his holy will be done. It is what is more for my profit and advantage, and what may be most expedient for me. God permitted the apostle of nations, St. Paul, to lie in prison two whole years, at a time wherein the primitive

Church had so great a need of persons to preach the gospel. Do not look upon it much if God detains you as it were in prison, by a sickness of two months or two years, or even of your whole life, if it be his pleasure; since you are not so necessary to his Church as this great apostle was.

There are also some others, whose constant infirmity prevents them from being regular to the community hour, and forces them to singularity of conduct on many occasions. These persons feel quite distressed and mortified; for they fancy that not discharging the requisite duties, they either are not true religious, or that their singularities are, at least, disedifying. And this chiefly, if their sickness is not considerable externally— if it is known only to God, while every one sees them dispensed with in their rules. To this I answer, that their sentiments are very just and laudable; yet, nevertheless, they are to take care that none of these considerations any way diminish the conformity they ought to have to the divine will in their afflictions. On the contrary, they ought hence to take an occasion of increasing their merit, whether it be by an absolute resignation of themselves to God, in all the dispositions he is pleased to send them; whether it be that of an ardent desire of being able to perform with exactness and punctuality all the exercises of religion, or that of feeling in themselves an extreme sorrow at not being able to be present as others are. In this manner, besides the merit they have on one hand in supporting their infirmity with patience and resignation; they merit on the other as much, if not more, than those who are in health, and live in the regular observance of all their rules.

St. Austin, preaching on the obligation all Christians have of fasting during the time of Lent, and coming to speak of those who by reason of indisposition were exempted from this duty, says of them, that since they are not able to fast, it is sufficient they sigh and lament in their hearts to see others fast, and themselves at the same time constrained to eat. A courageous and valiant soldier being carried off wounded in the engagement, is more concerned that he cannot fight and distinguish himself in the service of his prince in the battle, than that he suffers the pain of his wounds, and is to undergo the operations of the chirurgeon. This ought to be the case of a true and perfect religious, when, by sickness, he is hindered from performing the exercises and rules of the order and community. This hindrance ought to be a more sensible affliction to him than the distemper. But after all, neither this impediment, nor anything else, should ever hinder us from maintaining an entire conformity in our hearts to the divine will, during our sickness; but on the contrary, we are to receive it as coming from his hand, as sent us for his greater glory and our greater profit and advantage.

St. Jerome relates that holy Abbot John the Egyptian was once very much importuned by a certain religious, to cure him of a fever wherewith he was afflicted. "You desire," said the abbot, "to be freed from a thing which is very necessary for you. For as the body is cleansed from sweat and noisome evaporations, by soap, and other such detersive ointments; so is the soul purified, and cleansed from all its defects, by corporal infirmities and afflictions."

———o———

CHAPTER XVII.

That during our Sickness, we are not to repose our Trust and Hope in the Assistance and Knowledge of Physicians, but in God alone; and that we are to conform ourselves to his Will, not only as to the Sickness in general, but also to every and each particular painful Circumstance that accompanies it.

WHAT we have already said concerning sickness in general must also be understood concerning every particular circumstance during the same. St. Basil, upon this point, gives a very profitable instruction. He says, we are so to apply ourselves to physicians and remedies, as not to place therein all our hopes and confidence; as King Asa did, who was reprimanded by the holy Scripture: "For that in his sickness he had not recourse to our Lord; and confided more in the science of physicians." (2 Paral. xvi. 12.) We must not attribute to them the good or bad success of remedies, but to God alone, who makes them operate as he pleases. And in case you are destitute of physicians and remedies, you are not, says this holy father, to despair therefore of your recovery. When our Saviour conversed upon earth, he cured the sick sometimes by his will only; as when he healed the leper, saying, "It is my will, be cured." (Mat. viii. 3.) Sometimes he applied some certain things, as when he made clay with his spittle, and anointed the eyes of the blind man, commanding him to wash them in the pond of Siloe. At other times he left them in their diseases, and would not cure them, whatever expenses they had been at in procuring physicians and remedies. God does the very same ; sometimes he confers health, without any help of remedies or physicians ; sometimes he operates by the means of things applied; and at other times he renders all the consultations, and all the remedies useless ; to teach us thereby, that we are to put our confidence in him alone. Ezechias ascribed not his cure to the plaister of figs applied to him by the prophet Isaias, but to God only. You are to ascribe your cure, in like manner, not to the care and diligence of the physicians, or the efficaciousness of remedies, but to the goodness of God, who has power to cure all sorts of diseases. " For it is not herbs or fomentations which wrought the cure," says the Wise Man, " but, O Lord, it is your word which has the virtue to heal all diseases." (Wisd. xvi. 12.) But if, on the contrary, you recover not your health, you are not therefore to lay the fault on the physicians or their remedies; but must reflect that all comes from God, and it is his pleasure you shall not recover from this sickness.

When it likewise happens, that either the physician under-stands not your distemper, or has not used that diligence he ought; or the infirmarian has not had due care of you; you are to ascribe the cause to the sole will of God. And so you are not to say, it was through their defect you relapsed into your fever; but you must be convinced, God made use of them to occasion your relapse; and you must receive all as coming from his hand. For although, inasmuch as regards those who have the care of you, these things may be culpable; nevertheless, in respect of God who permits them so to happen, and with whom nothing happens by pure chance, it is an effect of his providence which has determined it after that manner. It was not merely casual that old Tobias slept under the swallow's nest, and that the dung which fell into his eyes struck him blind, but it was by an un-alterable ordination of the divine will. " The Lord," says the holy Scripture, " permitted this temptation to befall him; that posterity might have an example of patience, as it had in the person of Job." (Tob. ii. 12.) And the angel himself, speaking to Tobias after his cure said: " Because you were acceptable to God, it was requisite you should be proved by temptation." (Ibid. xii. 13.)

It is recounted in the lives of the holy fathers, that Abbot Stephen falling sick, the brother infirmarian would needs make him a little cake ; and by a mistake, instead of making it with sweet oil, he poured in the oil of linseed, which is extremely bitter. Having prepared, he offered it to the holy abbot; who perceiving by the taste what had happened, nevertheless eat some part thereof without taking the least notice. The brother made him a second cake in the same manner; and seeing the holy abbot, after he had tasted it, eat no more, being very urgent with him to eat, took a piece himself, thereby to excite him and show him the way; but he had scarce put it in his mouth, when perceiving the bitterness, he was very sensibly troubled and afflicted thereat, calling himself a poisoner, and that he had poisoned the abbot. Trouble not yourself, my son, said the holy man; if it had not been God's will that you should mistake one pot for another, this had not happened. We have several other examples of saints who submitted with wonderful patience and resignation to all the physicians' prescriptions and remedies, although they were contrary to the nature of their distemper. And it is in this manner we are to consider the defects of the physicians, and negligence of infirmarians, and those who have care of us, without complaining of them, or casting the fault upon them, if any accidents befall us.

Our virtue never appears more than in trials of this sort; and a religious in his sickness edifies the whole community, when he receives all things as coming from the hand of God, with an equal temper and tranquillity of mind; and forgetting in a manner himself, delivers up himself to be entirely governed by his superiors, and such as have charge of him in his infirmity. You confide in your superiors, says St. Basil, in things appertaining to your soul; and why not also in things that regard your body? You put into his hands the care of your salvation; and why do you not commit to him the care of your health? Our rules permit, and even command us, in our sickness, not to be solicitous for our body; and since they acquit us of that trouble, we should most willingly embrace so profitable a permission, and so advantageous a command. But on the contrary, that religious person extremely disedifies a community, when he assumes to himself an over-great care of his body during his sickness; when he takes not patiently what is ordered him, nor after the manner it is ordered; and fails not to complain, and sometimes even murmur, if all things be not done as he desires.

Cassian says very well that the indisposition of the body is not prejudicial to the good disposition of the soul; but on the contrary, that it contributes very much to it, provided it be received as it ought. But take care, says he, lest the infirmity of the body goes so far as to infect the soul ; and it will certainly communicate itself, and will cause the superior to be more concerned at your spiritual than at your corporal disease, if you behave so in your sickness, as to take occasion of doing nothing but your own will, and according to your own inclinations, and if you cast off all docility and obedience. We do not cease to be a religious, by being sick ; and we must not think we are exempt from our obligations, when we are indisposed ; and that then we have nothing to do but to think of our health and ease ; and that we are for that time dispensed with making progress in our spiritual advancement. A sick person, says St. Ignatius, ought to endeavour, by showing great humility and patience, to edify his brethren no less in time of sickness than in time of health. St. Chrysostom, upon these words of the Psalmist, "O Lord, you have covered us with your good will, as it were with a buckler" (Ps. v. 13), says, "This life is a perpetual warfare, where we are always to be in readiness to give battle ;" and adds—"as well sick persons, as those who are in health, are equally bound to the engagement. And the most proper time for this combat is the time of sickness, when our soul is assaulted on all sides with pains and afflictions, when it is seized with grief, and the devil incites us each moment to vent forth some complaining words, and lash out into some impatient expressions" (Chrys. in Ps. v.) It is then we are chiefly to give more evident proofs of our virtue. In our very bed, says Seneca, amidst the torments and pains of a violent disease, we have as great an opportunity of exercising our courage in suffering, as, in the field of battle, of fighting. The main part of our force consists in rather bearing with constancy, than in making a vigorous attack. This the Wise Man signifies in these words : "A patient man is better than the man of courage ; and he who has a command over himself excels him who takes cities by force." (Prov. xvi. 32.)

———C———

CHAPTER XVIII.

What has been said in the preceding Chapter is confirmed by Examples.

BLOSIUS, in the life of St. Gertrude, relates that our Saviour upon a time appearing to her, and telling her he left both health and sickness at her disposal, to make choice of what was more pleasing to her ; " What I desire, O Lord ! " said she, " is that you have no respect to my desire and choice, but that you effect and accomplish what is most conducive to your honour and glory."

A certain person who had a particular devotion to St. Thomas of Canterbury, falling sick, made a pilgrimage to the saint's tomb, in order that, by his intercession, God would cure him of his infirmity. He obtained his petition, and being upon his journey home in perfect health, he began seriously to meditate and consider whether, perhaps, he had not done himself an injury in desiring to be cured of his disease, since he was not certain but it might have been for his greater good to have remained still therein. This thought had so great an influence upon him, that he returned again to the sepulchre of the saint, and there earnestly desired he would demand of God for him, what would most promote his salvation. It pleased God to cast him again into the same infirmity, which he received with a sensible joy and comfort, understanding thereby that sickness was most expedient for him.

We read in the Life of St. Vedastus, Bishop of Arras, an example somewhat similar, of a blind man who, being present at the translation of this saint's relics, was very desirous of recovering his sight, that he might see them. His petition was granted, he saw what he desired, and presently put himself in prayer to God, that if the sight he newly obtained were not for his greater good, he might become blind again ; and having finished his prayer, he became blind as before.

St. Athanasius having sent for St. Anthony to Alexandria, to help and assist him in confuting and extirpating the heresies which were spreading there, a learned man who was blind, called Didimus, conferred with the holy abbot concerning several passages of Scripture. At the end of the conference

St. Anthony asked him if he looked not upon it a sensible affliction to be blind? Didimus having some difficulty to own it, at first made no answer. But being pressed even a third time, he confessed at last ingenuously, that the loss of his sight was a very sensible mortification to him. I am amazed, said the saint, that so prudent and learned a man as you, should be so concerned and troubled at the loss of a thing which is common to flies and ants; and that you rejoice not in possessing what the apostles only, and most eminent saints have merited.

We find in the history of the order of St. Dominick, that this great saint being at Rome, was accustomed sometimes to visit a holy person, who, falling sick of a most dangerous distemper, had retired to the gate of St. John Lateran, and there immured herself in a tower between four walls. This holy woman was called Bona; and her life was so conformable to her name, that being instructed by the sovereign Master of all, she had learned amidst the most sharp pangs and torments of her sickness, and now almost reduced to the point of death, to preserve a perpetual joy and tranquility of mind. Her disease was a cancer, that eat away and consumed her breast, which was so putrefied and corrupted that it was almost turned into worms, which were bred there in great abundance; and yet she bore this cross with such patience, as to render it a continual subject of her comfort and thanksgiving. St. Dominick, seeing, amidst her grievous torments, she still retained so much virtue and resignation, had so tender an affection, and so ardent a charity and love for her, as to go very frequently to hear her confession, and administer to her the blessed sacrament. One day, after having confessed and communicated her, he had a great desire to see her noisome and painful sore, the very sight of which was enough to excite horror in the spectators; and at last with much difficulty obtained his request. When she had opened her breast, and he beheld on one side the loathsomeness, the corruption, and worms; on the other, the patience and content of mind, wherewith the holy woman suffered this infirmity, he felt himself touched with extreme compassion; and, preferring the noisomeness of the disease to all the riches of this world, he earnestly entreated she should bestow one of these worms upon him, to keep as a precious relic. To this she would by no means consent, until he had promised to restore it to her again; because she took so great a pleasure in seeing these worms eat and in a manner consume her alive, that when any of them chanced to drop to the ground, she presently took it up with great care, and put it again into the hole it had fallen from. Upon these terms she at last gave him one; which he scarce had received into his hand, when on a sudden it was changed into a pearl of inestimable value. The other religious who were present with the saint, astonished at the circumstance, would needs have him keep it; the sick person at the same time desired her worm, demanding of him back her pearl; which the saint restored, and immediately it was changed into its former shape, and restored by the holy woman to the place it had been taken from, and where it had been engendered and nourished for so long a time. Whereupon St. Dominick, praying for her, and giving her his blessing, departed. And as he was descending the tower, all the loathsome impostume and corruption of the holy woman's breast, together with the worms, fell off, and the flesh closing by degrees, she was entirely healed in a few days, and testified to the world the wonders and miracles God has wrought in her by the means of his servant St. Dominick.

It is recounted in the same history that a certain religious, called Brother Reginald, being as yet a secular, came to St. Dominick to desire the habit of the order; and at the very time he was to have been received he fell sick of a fever, which the physicians judged mortal. The saint, very solicitous for the sick person's recovery, offered up fervent prayers to this effect; and as well the one as the other invoked incessantly the assistance of the Blessed Virgin with great fervour and devotion. One day, whilst they were both in prayer for this intention, the Queen of Angels, all resplendent with rays of glory, and accompanied with two other virgins, who appeared to be St. Cecily and St. Catherine, entered the sick man's chamber, and drawing nigh to his bed, asked of him, "What he desired at her hands? I am come to know," said she, "what it is you would hane me do for you; tell me, and I will grant it." The sick person, somewhat surprised at so strange an apparition, and seized with fear and respect, knew not what to do or say. But one of the saints that were with the glorious virgin soon freed him from his embarrassment, bidding him ask nothing in particular, and put himself entirely in the hands of the mother of God, who knew what was necessary for him better than he himself. He embraced this prudent advice; and addressing himself to the Blessed Virgin, said, I demand nothing; I have no will but yours, and I deliver up all I have to your disposal. Whereupon the Blessed Virgin, taking the oil the other two saints had brought with them, anointed him after the manner of Extreme Unction. And the very touch of her sacred hands had such virtue, that the sick man found himself wholly cured in an instant, and in as perfect health as though he had never had the least fit of fever. But what is yet more is, that this benefit conferred upon his body, communicating itself even to his soul, left therein such an impression of purity, as from that very moment he never found in himself at any time, or in any place or occasion, the least motion or inclination to the contrary.

Church history relates, that amongst the many great and eminent persons who flourished in the fourth age, there was a certain religious, named Benjamin, who had received of God the grace of curing diseases by the imposition of hands, or by praying for the diseased party, and anointing them with some oil that had been blessed. This gift, however, of curing others, did not prevent him from falling sick himself of a dropsy, whereby his body became swelled to that degree, that he could no longer enter the door of his cell. After being eight months in this condition, he died; and having all the time of his sickness healed all sorts of infirmities in others, yet he never complained that he could not heal himself. He also endeavoured to comfort such as were sick of the same distemper, and desired they would pray to God for his soul, and not concern themselves for his body; "For," said he, "when I was in good health, it profited and availed me little or nothing at all."

We read in the book called the Spiritual Meadow, of a certain religious, called Barnaby, who having by chance run a splinter of wood into his foot, would not for some time either pull it out himself or permit others to do it: "That," said he, "I may have something to suffer for the love of God." He frequently said to those who came to visit him: "The more the exterior man is mortified and weakened by sufferings, the more the interior is strengthened."

It is recorded in the Life of St. Pachomius, that a religious person named Zacheus, falling sick of an epilepsy, never abated anything of his accustomed abstinence, which was never to eat more than a piece of bread with a little salt, and never to dispense with himself in attending choir, and in fulfilling all the other obligations of his fellow-religious. All the spare time he could find, was taken up in making mats, baskets, and cords ; and the rushes he used being rough and hard, his hands were galled and cut in several places, so that the blood issued forth daily. At night, before he betook himself to rest, he meditated upon some passage of the Scripture; and then making the sign of the cross upon his body, he reposed till matins; after which he remained in prayer and contemplation till morning. This was his ordinary distribution of time, and this the holy man practised in sickness. It chanced once, that another religious coming to pay him a visit, and seeing his hands all cut, and the skin off, advised him to anoint them with oil, and assured him he would get ease thereby. He followed his counsel, and made use of the remedy, which instead of mitigating, doubled his pain. Having represented his suffering to St. Pachomius; And do you think, my son, replied the saint, that God sees not our infirmities, and cannot heal them when he pleases ? And if, on the contrary, he permits us to suffer, why, do you think, does he deal so with us, unless he would have us wholly resigned in putting all the care of ourselves, and all our confidence into his hands; that having thus offered us a greater occasion of merit by sufferings, he may afterwards recompense the small mortifications and afflictions he sends us in this life, with a celestial crown for eternity? Zacheus was so moved with these words of the saint, that he replied : " Forgive me, my dear father, and pray to God that he would pardon in me this over-eager desire of being cured, and my little confidence in, and conformity to his divine will." He afterwards performed so rigorous penance, for this trivial fault, that he took sustenance, and that but little, every second day, for the space of a year, weeping and lamenting continually all the time. The great Pachomius was often accustomed to relate this example to his religious, to instruct them how to suffer with resignation, and have always an entire confidence in God, during their sufferings, and also to amend and correct in themselves the least faults and imperfections.

———o———

CHAPTER XIX.

Of the Conformity we are to have to the Will of God, as well in order to Death as to Life.

OUR conformity to the will of God ought to extend itself as well to what appertains to dying as what appertains to living. For although, generally speaking, this is one of the most difficult points, inasmuch as nothing is more terrible, nothing more dreadful than death; nevertheless, this difficulty is greatly diminished for religious people, because they have already advanced halfway, or rather surmounted almost all the obstacles. First, one of the motives which makes worldly persons have such an apprehension and horror of death, and tremble at its approach, is, that death deprives them of their riches, their honours, their pleasures, their amusements, and all the conveniences they enjoyed in this life. It is by death they are separated from kindred and friends; some are snatched away from the wife they passionately love, and others from children for whose subsistence and maintenance they have not as yet provided. But a religious is free from all these ties and obligations; and as he has nothing to part with, so there is nothing to afflict and torment him at that hour. We easily pluck out a tooth, when we have loosened it beforehand from the gums; but if we endeavour to pluck it out violently, without using the means aforesaid, we shall feel pain and torment. It is the same with a religious person who is disengaged from the things of this life. He feels no difficulty in parting with them at his death, because he parted with them before on his voluntary and meritorious entrance into religion. But people of the world, forsaking these things only through constraint and necessity, forsake them consequently with great difficulty and reluctance; and sometimes even without any merit; since we may justly say they do not so much forsake these things, as these things forsake them. Amongst many other advantages we receive from a religious life, this certainty is not the least; for persons of the world, as St. Chrysostom well remarks, being attached to their wealth, to their pleasures, and to their conveniences of life, find death very dreadful. "O death, how bitter is thy memory to a man that has peace in his riches?" (Ecclus. xli. 1.) If, whilst they contemplate it but at a distance, it is so terrible, what will it be, when they behold it present? and if the very thought of it be so frightful, what will it prove, when they come to experience it? It is not so with religious; who, as they have heretofore divested themselves of all things, instead of finding afflictions and miseries in death, feel comfort and content. They look upon it as the term of all their sufferings, and as a passage whereby they are to go to receive the reward and recompense of all they hitherto forsook for the love of God.

Another thing that still troubles those of the world at their death, and makes it more dreadful, is, says St. Ambrose, the bad state of their conscience, and the want of the dispositions requisite to die well. A religious is far from being thus embarrassed : all his life is but a continual preparation for death ; and to prove this, the example of a great saint is happily cited, who, being desired by the physicians to prepare himself for death, " I have done nothing else," answered the holy man, "since I took the habit of religion." This ought to be the exercise of a religious ; and he cannot comply with the obligations of his state unless he be always in the disposition wherein our Saviour Jesus Christ would have us await his coming. " Let your loins be girt, and burning lamps in your hands." St. Gregory says, girding the loins, is a sign of chastity; and burning lamps in your hands denote the performance of good works: and as these are the most perspicuous things in a religious life, so a true religious has no reason to fear death.

We must take notice here of one thing very suitable to our present purpose, and which we touched on elsewhere. It is that one of the chief signs of a good conscience, and of our having made our peace with God, is, to be entirely conformed to his divine will in all things touching the hour of our death, and to expect it, "as they who expect their master's return from the marriage." (Luke xii. 35.) On the contrary, it is a bad sign, not to have the submission we here speak of, and to feel pain at the idea of death. A sheep is led to the shambles without any resistance; and therefore the holy Scripture, speaking of the death of our Saviour Jesus Christ, says—" He was led like a sheep to the slaughter." (Isa. liii. 7.) But the swine, which is an unclean creature, makes a most hideous noise when it is to be killed, and struggles with all its force against the approach of death. The same difference is found between the just, who are signified by the sheep, and the wicked and the carnal man, who is designed by the swine. A criminal condemned to die, and who knows he is not to leave the prison, unless to be brought to execution, trembles every time he hears the prison door opened ; but he who is declared innocent feels joy and comfort when he hears the same door opened, because he imagines it is to restore him to his liberty. In like manner, a bad Christian, when he is brought to his agony, and feels in his body the approaching pangs of death, is troubled and afflicted, and even sometimes falls into despair; because having a conscience charged and guilty, he fancies each moment he is to be precipitated into eternal flames; while he who has his conscience clear, and sees his end approach, finds in himself a joy and delight, as being persuaded that the time of his deliverance is arrived, and his eternal repose at hand. Let us act, therefore, as becomes true religious, and we shall find that we will not only feel no repugnance in conforming ourselves to God's holy will as to the hour of our death; but, on the contrary, shall rejoice when it is at hand. We shall even prevent it by our wishes, and say with the Psalmist: " Deliver, O Lord ! my soul out of its prison." (Ps. cxli. 8.)

St. Gregory, upon these words of Job, " And you shall not fear the beasts of the earth," (Job v. 22), says, " the security of a soul at the moment of death, is the beginning of a just man's recompense." He begins then to enjoy that spiritual peace and tranquillity, which he is soon after to enjoy for eternity; and he then feels, as it were, a foretaste of his felicity. While, on the contrary, the wicked man begins, from that very moment, to feel the torments of hell, by reason of the fears which torment him, and the remorse of conscience, which then tortures him. It is a very laudable practice, says St. John Climacus, to expect death continually; but it belongs only to the just to long for it every moment. And St. Ambrose commends mightily such as are in so holy a disposition. It is the same wherein the ancient patriarchs were, " when they declared themselves as pilgrims and strangers upon earth." For as the apostle very well takes notice : " Those who speak in this manner show manifestly they tend to their own country." (Heb. xi. 13.) This it was occasioned so many sighs and aspirations in the Royal Prophet, when, complaining to God in a most tender and affectionate manner, he said : " Miserable man that I am, why is my habitation prolonged ?" (Ps. cxix. 5.) If, then the ancient patriarchs of the old law used this manner of speaking, and were of these sentiments, when as yet the gates of heaven were not open ; nor could they then enter there by death; what may not we at present say, when these gates are so opened to us, that at the very moment our soul is purified of its faults and imperfections, it shall be admitted to the fruition of God.

CHAPTER XX.

Some Reasons why we may lawfully and piously wish for Death.

THAT we may attain a more perfect conformity to the will of
God, as well in order to death, as to life, we will here advance
some reasons for which we may desire death; and every one
may take to himself, and make use of what he likes best, and is
most to his purpose. The first reason why we may with all
justice desire death, is to be free from the miseries of this mortal
life. " For death," says the Wise Man, " is to be preferred to a
miserable life." (Ecclus. xxx. 17.) It is thus persons of the
world oftentimes desire death, and request it of God. And unquestionably they may do this without sin, since the miseries of
this life are such and so numerous that they are permitted to
desire death, the better to avoid them. The saints say, one
reason why God heaped upon men so many afflictions and
tribulations is, to hinder them from being too much attached to
the things of this world; and that, instead of loving this life,
which is transient, they may direct all their thoughts to the life
to come, which is eternal; "where there are no sighs, no clamours,
no sorrows or afflictions." (Apoc. xxi. 4.) St. Austin says, God
out of his boundless mercy, has ordered that this present life,
which is so painful and difficult, should also be short, and that
the next should be eternal, in order that this, with its pains and
afflictions, may pass away speedily, and that the joy and happiness of the next may continue for eternity. "This life," says
St. Ambrose, "is so full of evils, that death in comparison of it
seems rather a remedy than a punishment." (Sup. Job c. vii.)
And if God had not ordained death as a penalty, we should have
had reason to desire him to grant it us as a favour, that we may
be freed from our crosses and afflictions. It is true, indeed,
worldly persons often offend God in this point, by the impatience
wherewith they receive afflictions, and by their repinings and
complaints in demanding it of God. But supposing they desired
it with a most entire submission of mind, and said: Lord, if it
be your holy pleasure, free me from this miserable condition I
am in; I have lived long enough: without doubt they would not
commit any offence herein.

In the second place, we may desire death in a still more lawful
and more perfect manner; which is, that we may not behold the
persecutions of the Church, and the daily offences committed
against God's sovereign majesty. It was thus the prophet Elias

desired it, during the persecution of Achab and Jezebel. For seeing that both the one and the other, after having demolished the temples and altars, and killed the rest of the prophets, sought also after him to put him to death; and that he could not any way prevent so great violence, and so horrid sacrileges, full of sorrow and indignation, he betook himself to the desert; and sitting down under a tree, " he desired to die," and said : " It is enough, O Lord, take away my life, since I am not better than my forefathers." (3 Kings xix. 4.) The great Judas Machabeus, captain of God's people, animating his men to battle :— "It is better," says he, "to die in the field, than to be spectators of the miseries of our country, and the profanation of holy things," (1 Mac. iii. 59.) When the city of Hippo in Africa was besieged by the Vandals, who came from Spain, and put all to fire and sword, without respect to sex or age, St. Austin, who was then bishop of the place, beholding a desolation so lamentable, the towns ruined and deserted, churches pillaged, and the people wandering without prelate or pastor, ceased not to implore the mercy of God by continual tears and supplications. One day, assembling together his clergy : " I have desired of our Lord," said he, "either to free you from the present calamities, or to give you the grace to support them with patience and constancy, or else to take me out of this life, that I may not be forced to behold such great miseries and afflictions ; and it has pleased him to grant me the last petition." In fine, he fell sick immediately upon it, and died of the same sickness, in the third month of the siege. The like is related of St. Ignatius, and without doubt it is a perfection peculiar to saints, to be so much afflicted and touched with the calamities of the Church, and the offences committed against the divine majesty, as to desire rather to die than to be eye-witness of them.

It is also a very laudable and pious practice, to desire death, and even to beg it of God, in order that we may no longer have it in our power to offend him. For it is certain, as long as we live, we cannot be sure of ourselves ; it is certain we are capable of falling into mortal sin ; since others who had attained a higher pitch of perfection, who had received greater talents and gifts of God, and who were really saints, and saints in an eminent degree, were yet so unfortunate as to fall. This is one of the principal reasons that makes the true servants of God tremble, and makes them desire with more earnestness to be freed from the bond of this mortal life. We may also with a holy fervour of zeal, desire we had never been born, that so we might never have fallen into sin; since sin is a greater evil, than never to have been; and it would have been better we never had been born than to have sinned. With how greater reason may we then wish to die, not to sin any more? Our Lord Jesus Christ, speaking of him who was to betray him, said : "It were better for that man he had never been born." (Matt. xxi. 24.) And St. Ambrose, explaining on this subject those words of Ecclesiasticus, "I have preferred the condition of the dead to that of the living, and have esteemed him who is not yet born, more happy than either." (Ecclus. iv. 2.) "The dead," says he, "are preferred to the living; because they have ceased to sin. And he who is not yet born, is in a better state than he who is dead; because he has never sinned." It is therefore a very commendable exercise, to produce frequently, in time of prayer, acts of this sort, saying : Lord, let not sin separate me from you. If I am to be miserable in offending you for the future, let me rather die; for I desire not life unless it be to employ it in your service ; nor would I live longer unless I could behave as I ought in your service, and not fail in acquitting myself of my duty. This is a very holy and useful practice, because it implies an extreme horror of sin, and great sentiments of humility, and of the love of God, and herein we prefer the most acceptable petition to God we possibly can. We find in the life of St. Lewis, king of France, that Queen Blanche, his mother, was accustomed to tell him, "She would rather see him dead, than see him fall once into mortal sin ;" which holy desire of hers was so pleasing to God, and drew down so great a blessing upon this prince, that, as it is recorded, he never once offended God mortally. Perhaps the same desires may produce in us the same effects.

But it is not to avoid mortal sin only, that we can wish for death. We may wish for it, to avoid even venial sins, which are so frequently committed ; and this motive is very holy and laudable; for a true servant of God ought to be resolutely determined rather to die than to commit not only a mortal sin, but even than to tell a lie, which may be but a venial one. And it is certain, that be the time we have to live ever so short, it is impossible for us not to fall into many venial sins. "For the just man falls seven times a-day" (Prov. xxiv. 16) ; that is to say, frequently ; and the longer he lives, the more numerous will his falls be. But the zealous servants of God stop not here ; they go so far as to petition to die, that they may not be subject to so many defects, so many imperfections, so many temptations and frailties wherewith man's life is replenished. "O Lord, what do I suffer," says a holy man, "when in prayer and meditation of heavenly things, I have a thousand carnal and worldly thoughts, which present themselves to my imagination in crowds" (Thomas à Kempis). It is the misfortune of this life, that it is never entirely free from miseries and afflictions. It is beset with ambushes, and surrounded with enemies ; one temptation is scarce over, when a new one succeeds ; and sometimes we have scarce time to overcome one, when we are assaulted suddenly by several others we did not foresee. How can we be enamoured with a life so full of anguish and labour, and so obnoxious to accidents and calamities ? How can we call it life, which produces so many kinds of deaths ? A great saint was accustomed to say, that were it left to his choice, he would choose death, as the only means of putting his soul out of apprehension of ever being capable of doing anything contrary to the love of God. It is a mark of greater perfection to desire death in order to avoid venial sins, and such faults and imperfections as are of less moment, than to desire it in order to avoid mortal. For *in this* there may be rather a certain fear of hell, and more of self-love than of the love of God. But to love God so ardently, that in order to avoid venial sin, and the most trivial imperfection, we wish for death, is doubtless a very pure intention and a consummate virtue.

But some may say, it is for the expiation of my sins and faults that I desire to live. To this I answer, that if by living longer we diminish daily the number of our faults, and add not new ones to the old, this desire would be good. But if, instead of cancelling your old debts, you still add new, and if the longer you live, the more you have to answer for to God, then this objection is unreasonable. "Wherefore do we desire life so earnestly," says St. Bernard, " since the longer we live the more we offend God ; and the number of our days increase not, unless to increase our offences?" (Bern. c. ii. Med.) St. Jerome, speaking of the same point : "What difference do you think, says he, " is there between him who dies in his youth, and him who dies in old age, unless the old man, being more burdened with sins than the young man, has a larger account to settle with God ? " It is a very holy resolution made by St. Bernard upon this subject, when his extreme humility suggested him words more applicable to us, than to him. "I am ashamed of living," says

he, " because I profit so little ; I am afraid of dying, because I
am not prepared.   But after all, I had rather die, and commit
myself to the mercy of God, which is infinitely good, than be a
subject of scandal to my neighbour, by the ill-example of my
life." (De inter. Dom. ca. xxxv.)   Father Avila affirms, whosoever finds in himself but an indifferent disposition to virtue,
ought rather to desire death, than life, since he lives in continual
danger, which would cease entirely by death.   " For what is
death," says St. Ambrose, " but the burial of our vices, and the
resurrection of our virtues." (De bon. mor.)

The reasons we have here alleged for wishing to die, are
good and holy ; but the most perfect of all, is that which made
St. Paul "desire to be dissolved, and be with Christ." (Phil. i.
23.)   What is it you say, O great saint ?   Why do you desire
to be delivered from the prison of your body ?   Is it not
perhaps to avoid sufferings ?   Not at all ; " For it is in afflictions and sufferings we place our glory." (Rom. v. 2.)   Is it
for fear of falling into sin ?   Still less : " For I am certain,"
you will tell us, " neither death nor life can ever separate us
from the love of God." (Rom. viii. 38.)   This great saint was
so confirmed in grace, that he was assured of never losing it ;
and so he had nothing to fear on that side.   But why do you
desire death with so much earnestness ?   " To be with Jesus
Christ, and because I languish with love." (Cant. ii. 5.)   He
was sick with love ; he sighed after his beloved ; and in the
impatience he was in of enjoying the divine presence, the least
delay seemed long and tedious.

It is in this St. Bonaventure establishes the highest degree
of the love of God ; and says, there are three of these degrees.
The first is to love God above all things, so that nothing in
the world can have that power over us as to make us offend
him once mortally, and violate any one of his commandments.
It is this our Saviour gave as a rule to the young man in the
gospel, when he said to him : " If you desire to enter into life
eternal, keep the commandments." (Mat. xix. 17.)   And it is
this which is the general duty and obligation of the whole
world.   The second degree of the love of God is to add the
practice of his counsels to the observance of his precepts.   And
this belongs properly to religious, who apply themselves not
only to what is good, but still aim at what is better, and more
perfect, according to these words of the apostle : " In order
that you seek in the will of God what pleases him most, and

what is most perfect." (Rom. xii. 2.) But the third degree of love and charity, as St. Bonaventure adds, is " To be in such a manner transported with the love of God, as not to be able even to live without him ; " to desire earnestly to see yourself freed from the prison of this mortal life, and to be with Jesus Christ ; and continually to wish to be recalled from your banishment, and to return to your native country ; and also to make daily aspirations and petitions, for the dissolution of this prison of your body, which hinders you from enjoying the sight of God. All that persons in this state can do, says the same saint, is to bear with patience their life, which is a burden and impediment to them, and thereby they desire nothing more than to be freed from it. ,

We read in the life of St. Ignatius, that he was inflamed with an ardent desire of quitting the prison of his body, and wished with so great fervour to enjoy the sight of God, that as often as he reflected upon death he could not but shed tears of joy. But in the same place it is very justly observed, that it was not the consideration of his own happiness, but it was the ardent love wherewith he was inflamed by the humanity of Jesus Christ, that urged him to wish for death. As the Royal Prophet placed all his joy " in contemplating the joy of our Lord " (Ps. xxvi. 4) ; and as in the world, when we sincerely love any one, we feel great satisfaction in seeing him obtain an honourable post : so this great saint from pure principle, and pure excess of love, longed to behold his dear master in all the splendour of his glory. He wished to behold him in it, that he might rejoice with him, without any regard to his own interest and felicity ; and, without question, this was the most perfect and sublime act of love any man could produce.

When we consider things in the manner we have here spoken of, the idea of death will be so far from afflicting and troubling us, that it will replenish us with joy and satisfaction. Reflect but a little upon what terrifies you ; think only that in a short space of time you shall be in heaven, and that there you shall enjoy a happiness which is superior to sense ; which the eye has never seen, the ear not heard, and which infinitely surpasses the reach of understanding ; and by this means all your fears and apprehensions will be changed into delight and joy. For how is it possible we should not rejoice at our recal from banishment, and at the termination of our pains and sufferings ? How can we not but rejoice on attaining the end for which we were

created, on entering upon our inheritance—an inheritance so
ample and glorious? It is by death only we can take possession
of the inheritance of heaven. "When he shall send sleep to his
beloved, behold then the inheritance of our Lord." (Ps. cxxvi.
2.)   It is death, then, which puts us in possession; and hence
the Wise Man says: "The just man hopes and confides in death."
(Ps. xiv. 32.)   Because, in reality, it is death that opens the
passage to heaven, and affords him matter of comfort during
the time of his exile.   St. Austin, explaining the words of the
Psalmist: "I will make it my business to march on in the pure
way; and will sing, when is it you will come to me?" (Ps. c.
2.)   All my endeavours, O Lord! says he, shall be to preserve
myself without spot or blemish during my life; I will have a
continual guard on my eyes, and will sing daily, when is it, O
Lord! you will put a term to my banishment? When will you
come and bring me to you? "When shall I come to you, and
when shall I appear in your sight?" (Ps. xli. 2.) O how long and
tedious is the time; and how glad shall I be when I hear it is
arrived! "I rejoiced when I heard we should go to the house
of our Lord; and should enter very soon into your gates, O
Jerusalem!" (Ps. cxxi. 1, 2.)   Yes, O Lord! I imagine that I
am already in heaven, and in the company of the angels, rejoicing in your divine presence, and blessing your holy name
for all eternity.

———o———

CHAPTER XXI.

*What has been said in the preceding Chapter, confirmed by
Examples.*

SIMON METAPHRASTES, in the Life of St. John, the almoner,
Archbishop of Alexandria, relates that a rich and great man,
who had an only son, recommended him to the prayers of this
great saint, entreating him very urgently to offer them up for
the preservation of his son; and gave withal a great quantity of
money into the holy man's hands, to be distributed amongst the
poor for this intention.   The saint did what the other desired of
him; and at the end of a month, the child died.   Whereupon
the father was very sensibly afflicted, imagining the alms he had
given, and the prayers he had obtained, were of no effect.   This
coming to the knowledge of the archbishop, he betook himself
to prayer for the distressed father, requesting of God that he

would be pleased to afford him some comfort. Some time after an angel appeared by night to the father of the child, and told him the prayers for his son were heard ; that he lived now in heaven ; and had he remained longer upon earth he would have been perverted, and rendered unworthy of the eternal happiness he now possessed. He added, that he ought to be assured, nothing happened in this life, but by a just judgment of God, although the causes of these his judgments were unknown to men, and consequently he had done very ill, in permitting himself to be transported with so excessive grief ; that on the contrary, he ought to receive with the spirit of submission and gratitude whatever it pleased God to send him. This celestial vision comforted entirely the afflicted father, and encouraged him to serve God with more fervour than ever.

It is recounted in the history of Thebais, that a certain lady having a great devotion to St. Maurice, who had been Captain to the Theban legion, received thereby a singular grace and favour. This lady had an only son ; who had scarce passed his infancy, when, in order to train him up in piety from his tender years, she consecrated him to God in the monastery of St. Maurice, according to the custom of these times. It was thus, that in the days of St. Bennet, several persons of quality in Rome, and amongst the rest St. Maurice and St. Placidus, were placed by their parents in the monastery of Mount Cassian ; and many years after, St. Thomas of Aquin was sent there by his mother Theodora, and his brothers the Counts of Aquin. The child being settled in the monastery, was taught the belles-lettres, morality, and religious discipline, and had been in the practice of singing in choir with the rest, when it pleased God to visit him with a violent fever which carried him off in a short time. His sorrowful mother came to the church, and there in tears and grief accompanied the corpse of her son to the grave ; over which she came every day to lament—feeling her grief revive particularly at the time of the divine office, when she reflected with herself that she should never again hear the voice of her son. While she persevered in sorrow, weeping by day in the church, and by night at home, she happened once to be so overwhelmed with grief, that she lay down to take her repose ; when behold St. Maurice appeared to her, and having asked her, why she lamented the death of her son so incessantly ? The remainder of my life, said she, is not sufficient to dry up the source of my tears, nor to afford me the least comfort in my sorrows. Wherefore I firmly resolve to lament the death of my only and dear child as long as I live; and my tears shall never cease flowing till death closes my eyes, and separates my soul from my body. Woman, answered the saint, trouble not yourself, and lament not your son is dead; for at present he is with us, where he enjoys eternal felicity, and as a proof of this rise at next matins and go to the church; there you shall hear the voice of your son, who sings with the religious; and you shall have this satisfaction not only to-morrow, but also as often as you shall assist at the divine office. Comfort yourself, therefore, and dry up your tears, since you have much more reason to rejoice than lament. The afflicted lady waking hereupon, and not knowing for certain whether this apparition were a dream or not, waited with impatience the hour of matins, that she might go to the church and there solve her doubts. But scarce had she entered the church, when she heard her son's voice, who intoned an Antiphon, and then firmly persuaded that he enjoyed the glory of the blessed, she banished all grief, and gave thanks to God; who having comforted her in this manner, continued the same favour to her till the end of her life.

We read in a grave author (Flor. de Henriq. gran. l. 4. c. lxviii.), that a certain nobleman was one day a-hunting, and his attendants having rode different ways, in pursuit of the game, he pursued a wild beast into a wood; and as he was eager in the pursuit, he heard the voice of a man, who sung most charmingly. Surprised to hear so sweet voice in so solitary a place, and knowing it could not be the voice of any of his company, or of any inhabitants of the place, he was curious to know whose it could be. When breaking through the thickets, he perceived a man in a most wretched condition, and so disfigured with leprosy all over his body, that his corrupted flesh fell in pieces to the ground. The nobleman was seized with horror at the sight; yet, doing violence to himself, he approached the leper, saluted him very courteously, and asked him if it was he who had sung, and how he could have so melodious a voice? The leper answered him, it was he who sung, and the voice he used was his natural one. But how can you, replied the nobleman, rejoice in the miserable condition you are in at present? I will tell you, answered the leper: the only separation between God and me is this wall of clay, this body of mine—when this is broken down and removed, then shall I enjoy securely the sight of my Saviour: and as I daily behold it go to ruin, the excess of joy I conceive thereat makes me sing, still awaiting the happy hour when it will fall utterly to pieces ; and when my soul, being separated from my body, I will enjoy my God, who is the living fountain, and the inexhaustible source of all sorts of happiness.

St. Cyprian relates that a certain bishop being in the agony of death, and having begged of God to prolong his life. there appeared to him a young man environed with resplendent light, who said to him in a grave and severe tone: "You fear the sufferings and difficulties to which you are exposed in the world, and yet you desire not to be freed from them—what would you have me to do with you ? By which he signified to him abundantly that the repugnance he had of quitting this life was in no wise acceptable to God. And St. Cyprian adds, that the angel spoke in these terms to the bishop, in order that being related to others, they might serve for their instruction.

Simon Metaphrastes, cited by Surius, says that the holy Abbot Theodosius, knowing well how profitable the remembrance of death is for a Christian, and endeavouring to excite his religious by this means to virtue, ordered them one day to dig a grave; and assembling the community who stood round it, see here, said he, the grave finished : but who amongst us all will be the first whose funeral rites will be here performed ? At which one of the religious called Basil, who was priest, and whose eminent virtue kept him always prepared for death, stepped forth and falling upon his knees, before him, said, " Give me your blessing, my father, for if you please, I will be the first for whom the funeral office shall be here performed." Having urged what he proposed, the saint granted his petition, and ordered presently the prayers and ceremonies used by the Church in the office of the dead to be performed. The office was sung the first day, the third, and the ninth. At the end of forty days, and as soon as ever the obsequies were totally finished, Basil, who was in perfect health, without so much as a small fever, the least pain of the head, or any other sign of sickness whatsoever, passed on a sudden from this life to the other, like one who had fallen into a weak and easy sleep ; and went to receive the recompense due to his virtue, and to the earnest desire he had of being re-united to his Saviour. But that we may more clearly see, how pleasing his zeal had been to God, the first miracle was accompanied with another ; and for forty days after his death the holy abbot saw him daily assist at vespers, and sing in the choir with the other religious. There was no one either heard or saw him, except one religious named Aetius ; who, hearing, but not seeing him, acquainted the abbot, and asked him if he heard not Basil singing? I hear him, replied the abbot ; and what is yet more, I see him : and if you will, you may see him in the same manner I do. Next day, whilst all the religious were at their office in choir, the abbot beheld again Basil, who sung with the rest according to his custom ; and pointing his finger, shewed him to Aetius ; whereupon they both fell to their prayers, that God would permit Aetius to have a sight of him. Aetius no sooner discerned him, but ran to embrace him ; but Basil disappeared immediately, saying with a loud voice, insomuch that all present heard him, " Farewell, my fathers and brothers, farewell ; for you will see me no more for the future."

We read in the history of the Order of St. Austin, that young St. Columban, nephew and disciple to St. Columban the abbot, falling sick and from the holy confidence he had in God, desiring with all earnestness to die, there appeared to him a young man, all glittering with rays of glory, who said : " Know that the prayers of the abbot, and the tears he daily sheds for your recovery, hinder your passage hence." The sick person, complaining in most tender and affectionate terms to his abbot, and his eyes bathed in tears, said to him : " Why do you detain me in a life so miserable as this is, and hinder me from enjoying that which is eternal?" These words so touched the abbot, that he ceased praying and shedding tears for his nephew, who, after he had received all the sacraments of the Church, and embraced all the religious, reposed happily in our Lord.

St. Ambrose affirms that the people of Thrace were accustomed to weep at the birth of their friends, and to rejoice at their death ; esteeming with good reason, says he, that those who entered the world, where there is nothing but misery and affliction, were worthy of compassion ; and that on leaving the world, they were happy, as being recalled from exile, and released from so many evils and calamities. If barbarians who lived in the ignorance and obscurity of paganism, and who had no knowledge of the glory that awaits us after death, behaved themselves in this manner, how ought we behave who are enlightened with the rays of the true faith, and know for certain the happiness laid up in store for us, provided we depart this life in the grace and favour of God? This made the Wise

Man say, " The hour of death is to be preferred to that of our nativity." And that was the reason, says St. Jerome, why the Son of God, on leaving this world to return to his heavenly Father, comforted his disciples, who were troubled and afflicted thereat, by saying, " If you truly loved me, you would rejoice that I go to my Father." (John xiv. 28.)   But when he determined to raise Lazarus, he wept.   He wept not, says the saint, ·for the death of Lazarus, since he knew he was to be raised to life again : but he wept, because he whom he loved so affectionately was to be exposed anew to the miseries of this life, and to all the calamities of this deplorable exile.

———o———

CHAPTER XXII.

Of the Conformity we are to have to the Will of God in all public Calamities.

BUT it is not only in what regards ourselves, and our own particular sufferings, that we are to be entirely conformed to the will of God ; we must have this conformity in public calamities also ; for example, in famine, war, plague, and all the other scourges of divine vengeance.   For this end we must establish as a fundamental point, that as a just judge, seeing himself obliged to condemn to death a criminal at the bar, is not any ways hindered either by natural compassion, or the bonds of friendship from pronouncing the fatal sentence, and effectually resolving on the death of the criminal ; because justice so orders, and the good of the commonwealth requires it ; in like manner, the compassion we have for others, whom we see lie under the chastisements of the divine justice, should not hinder us from conforming ourselves to what pleases Almighty God.   For we are to look upon these chastisements as the effects of his holy will ; which, by a secret and hidden judgment, has thus decreed it, for certain purposes, conducive to his greater glory and service.   For although it is true, that the conformity he requires of us to his holy will in all these accidents, does not oblige us to love them positively ; and that it is sufficient we bear them with patience, without murmuring at the orders of Providence; nevertheless, we must assure ourselves there is more merit and perfection, not only in suffering, but even loving and embracing them, inasmuch as they are the effects of his will and justice, and conduce to his greater glory. St. Thomas says, that it is thus the blessed in heaven conform themselves in all things to the will of God; and St. Anselm says, that the will of God and our will shall be conformed in heaven as two eyes in the same body. It is one motion governs both eyes—one cannot look upon anything, but the other looks upon it also; and although both are fixed upon the same object, they present, however, but one image to the brain. Now, as the conformity of the blessed to the will of God sees in all things only what pleases him and tends to his greater glory, to which they are all directed; so we cannot do better than to follow the example of the blessed in heaven, by viewing in all things only the execution of the orders of his providence, and the accomplishment of the divine will. We can never be in a better disposition, than when we only will what God wills, and will it for the same end, and in the same manner as he wills it.

Possidonias, in the Life of St. Austin, says, that the city of Hippo, of which he was bishop, being besieged by the Vandals, who wasted and destroyed all Africa, filling it with blood and slaughter, this great saint comforted himself with these words of an ancient person : "It is not for a great man to think it strange that wood and stone decay, and mortals die." (Possid. in ejusvita.) But in all calamities of this kind we have a still juster reason of consoling ourselves, if we consider all as coming from the hand of God : that it is his holy will ; and although the reason why he afflicts us lies hidden, yet that it never can be but just. "The judgments of God are an abyss" (Ps. xxxv. 7), says the Royal Prophet. It would be great temerity in us, with this weak and limited capacity of ours, to dive into the secrets and reasons of God. "For who was there that comprehended the design of God, or who was ever made his counsellor?" (Rom. xi. 34.) We must reverence the judgments of God with profound humility, and believe that since we are governed by wisdom, infinite as his is, nothing can befall us which tends not to our greater good and profit. Upon this foundation we are to rest, and rely so far upon his goodness and mercy as to be persuaded he would not permit any such calamities to befall us were it not to draw thence a greater good. God conducts to heaven, by sufferings, an infinity of souls which would perish by any other way. How many are there who, in their crosses and tribulations, turn to God with their whole heart, and die sincere penitents? How many have been saved by this means, who otherwise had been damned? So that what seems to us a scourge and chastisement, is oftentimes a great favour and singular mercy conferred upon us.

In the second book of Machabees, the author, having described the horrid persecution the Jews suffered under King Antiochus, the massacres committed without any regard to age, sex, or quality, the pillaging or profanation of the temple, and the abominations committed therein by this impious and wicked king, adds: "And I conjure those who shall read this book not to be shocked at so many calamities; but let them imagine those befell us for our chastisement, and not for our destruction." (2 Mach. vi. 11.) The leech sucks the blood of the sick man, says St. Gregory, with intent to glut itself, and draw out, if it were in its power, the very last drop. But the intention of the physician is only hereby to take from the patient the corrupted blood and to cure him. That of God is the very same in the afflictions he sends us. And as that patient would be guilty of great folly who, considering more the greediness of the leech than the good design of the physician, should hinder the taking away the corrupted blood : in like manner, when any misfortune or affliction happens to us, whether by the means of others or by any creature whatever; we are in this case not to consider those other persons, or any creatures, but the sovereign physician only, who makes use of them as of leeches to purify our blood, and restore us to our perfect health. We must also be convinced that he orders us nothing but for our greater good : and supposing he had no other end herein than to punish us as his children in this world, instead of reserving our punishment for the next; he would nevertheless do us a great favour, and our obligations to him would be most considerable.

It is related of St. Catherine of Sienna, that being once extremely troubled by reason of several calumnies raised against her honour and reputation : our Saviour appeared to her with a crown of gold, all inlaid with pearls and precious stones in his right hand : and in his left a crown of thorns, and said to her : "Know, my dear daughter, that of necessity you must be crowned with one of these two, some time or other. Wherefore take your choice ; either the crown of thorns in this transitory life, and have the other reserved for you in the next ; or the crown of gold at present, and have that of thorns hereafter." It is a long time, O Lord ! answered the holy virgin, since I have made an entire renunciation of my own will to follow but yours; and consequently, it is not for me to choose. But if, notwithstanding, you will have me answer, I desire to choose that which will be most acceptable to you; and the better to imitate your example, I accept with my whole heart of sufferings. Having said this she took the crown of thorns from our Saviour's hand, and putting it upon her head, she pressed it down with such force, that from that time she always had a great pain in her head, caused by the thorns that pierced it.

———o———

CHAPTER XXIII.

That a View of our Sins, and a true Repentance, help us to support with all Resignation both general and particular Afflictions sent us from God.

WITH all holy men it is a general opinion, wherein they are confirmed by several passages of holy Scripture, that ordinarily speaking, public calamities are sent from God in punishment of our sins. "It is upon account of our sins," said Azarias, in the flaming furnace, "that you have heaped all these afflictions upon us. For we have sinned, we have done ill, we have separated ourselves from you, we have erred in all points. We have neither heard nor obeyed your commands; nor have we performed what you enjoined us for our happiness. Wherefore we have justly deserved all the miseries you have sent us; and in general, whatever you have done against us, you have done with all justice." (Dan. iii. 28.) We see by this, that God chastises his people, and delivers them into the hands of their enemies, because they offend him. We read also in several places, that he freed them when they repented and were sincerely converted. Hence Achoir, general of the Ammonites, having told Holofernes, that God took the children of Israel under his protection, but that he chastised them if they performed not their duty; added, that before he attacked them he should send to know, if at present they had offended God in anything; and in case they had, that then he might easily gain the victory over them. But if they had not any way offended God, he should desist from his enterprise, lest it would turn to his disgrace and shame; since God, whom no one can oppose, would infallibly fight in the cause of his people. When our Saviour cured the paralytic who had been sick twenty-eight years : "See," says he, "you are now cured : sin no more lest a worse thing befall you " (John v. 14) : and the holy doctors observe that these words of our Saviour convey this truth most fully. According, then, to this doctrine, one of the means which may enable us to conform ourselves to God's will in all our adversities, as well general as particular, and to bear them with patience, is presently to enter into ourselves, by a reflection upon our sins, and to think how justly we merit the punishment sent us from God. For thus, whatever misfortune shall befall us, we shall bear it patiently, and shall consider the punishment to be less than it ought to be.

St. Bernard and St. Gregory treat of this matter exceedingly well. " Whosoever has a lively feeling and sense of his faults in the interior," says St. Bernard, " will feel little or no pain in the exterior." Hence David was not so moved at the curses given him by his subjects, when he saw his own son up in arms against him. " My son," says he, " who received his being from me, seeks to take my life away : with how much more reason may the son of Jemini revile and curse me ?" (2 Kings xvi. 11). St. Gregory, writing upon these words of Job—" that you may know you have received a less punishment from him than your sins have deserved," makes use of a comparison which clearly explains this doctrine. As, says he, in wounds and impostumes, the greater and more dangerous the sore is, the more patiently we endure the lancet and searing-iron ; so as soon as we have a lively feeling of the wound caused in us by sin, we easily and willingly admit of the lancing and searing of mortification, of sufferings and of humiliations sent by God, to enable us to bear this wound, and cure it effectually. For the pain of our chastisement is less felt when we come to acknowledge our past fault, says the same saint. But if you bear not patiently the afflictions and evils that befal you, it is a sign you see not the danger of the wound given you by sin ; and so, not knowing that an abscess is forming within you, you are not able to bear the requisite operations.

Holy men, and true servants of God, not only receive their pains and afflictions with willingness, but even desire and beg them earnestly at the hands of God. " I wish I may obtain my petition," says Job, " that he who began would crush me ; that he would extend his hand and cut me off ; and this be my comfort not to be spared in the sufferings wherewith he afflicts me !" (Job viii.) The Royal Prophet had similar sentiments when he said : " Try me, O Lord, and tempt me." (Ps. xxv. 2.) " For I am prepared to receive all sorts of corrections." (Ps. xxxvii. 18.) " It is well for me that thou hast humbled me." (Ps. cxviii. 71.) The true servants of God beg ardently, says St. Gregory, of God to chastise and humble them ; and they are even afflicted when they consider their faults and defects, and see they are not punished by God. For then they fear that he will reserve them for a more severe correction in the other world ; and it is to this end Job adds : "and that I may have the comfort not to be spared in the sufferings, wherewith he afflicts me." Which is as if he said : there are some whom God spares in this world, to punish them afterwards more severely in the next ; but let him not spare me in this manner, that he may spare me for eternity—I desire he would correct me now like a charitable father, that he may not chastise me hereafter like a rigorous judge—I shall not murmur, nor shall I even complain, "nor will I oppose myself in the least to his holy decrees" (Job vi. 10) ; but on the contrary, I shall find a subject of comfort in my sufferings. This was St. Austin's sentiment also, when he cried out, " Burn me, O Lord, cut me, and spare me not in anything belonging to this life, that you may spare me for eternity." (Aug.)

It is an effect of our stupidity to be so little sensible to the evils of our souls, and be so solicitous as to those of our body. For we ought to be more touched at our sins, than at an other thing whatsoever ; and did we but rightly conceive the enormity of our sins, we should look upon the most rigid punishment that could be inflicted as too little, and should say with Job : "I have sinned, I have indeed offended ; and have not as yet received the punishment my crimes have deserved." (Job xxxiii. 27.) We ought to have these words always in our hearts and mouths ; for all we can suffer in this world is nothing in comparison of what one mortal sin deserves. "And so you will come to see you have not received less punishment of him, than your crimes deserved." Whoever seriously reflects that he has offended God, and that consequently he merits eternal damnation ; what affronts, what injuries, what contumelies would he not suffer joyfully in expiation of all the faults committed against the divine majesty ? " Permit him," said David to those who would have punished Semei for cursing him, " perhaps our Lord will regard my affliction, and our Lord will render me good for the present curses." 2 Kings xvi. 12.) Perhaps after his indignation he may be appeased, he may pardon my offences and have compassion on me ; and so I shall be happy in being thus affronted. It is with the same disposition we are to embrace whatsoever injuri s and affronts are offered to us. Let us be ill-treated ; what matter! perhaps God, in consideration of our patience, will receive our sufferings as a deduction of those pains due to our sins ; and what we esteem as evil, may prove one of the greatest advantages that can be conferred on us. If, instead of wasting our time on complaints and resentments, we spent it in entering into ourselves, we should please God the more, and should feel greater comfort in our afflictions.

The saints made use of this means so frequently on similar occasions, and this practice was so familiar to them, that as we read of some of them, they ascribed all the persecutions and calamities which befel the Church to their own sins ; and judging their offences merited a still greater punishment, they cried out—It is my sins which are the cause of so many wars ; they are my sins which are the cause of so many plagues and other calamities sent from God. What may contribute much to confirm any one in these sentiments is, that in reality God punishes oftentimes his people for the sins of one single person : as we see he did for the sin of David, when he sent upon the Israelites a violent plague, of which died threescore and ten thousand persons in the space of three days. It may be answered, David was king, and God frequently punishes the faults of the prince in the people. But what will be said to the example of Achan, who was only a private man ? And yet because he, contrary to orders, conveyed away secretly some part of the booty taken at Jericho, God revenged this transgression upon all the people, by permitting three thousand of the bravest men in the whole army to fly most shamefully from the enemy, and not to escape without having experienced great loss. It is not then for the sins of commanders only, but also for those of every particular person, that God sometimes extends his punishment upon a whole multitude. It is in this sense the saints explain what is so often repeated in holy Scripture, that "God punished the sins of the parents upon their children to the third and fourth generation." (Exod. xxxiv. 7.) For inasmuch as appertains to the sin alone, it assures us the sin of the father shall not be imputed to the son, nor the sin of the son be imputed to the father ; " He who shall have sinned shall die; the son shall not bear the iniquity of his father, and the father shall not bear the iniquity of his son."

(Ez. xviii. 29.) But as to the pain, God acts in a different manner—he oftentimes chastises one person for another; and so, perhaps for your sins and for mine, God will chastise a whole community, and perhaps the whole society.

Let us have always before our eyes, on the one hand, this consideration, and on the other the will of God; and so we shall conform ourselves with these to all the afflictions it shall please him to send us. "He is the master and Lord, who can do what seems to him best. As it pleases him in heaven, so let it be done." (1 Mach. iii. 60.) "I held my peace; and did not so much as open my mouth; because it was you, O Lord, who caused whatever I suffer." (Ps. xxxviii. 10.) This is what we ought to say—this is what ought to be our comfort in the most difficult occurrences. God wills it; God ordains it; God has caused it; God has sent it; we must receive all things as coming from his hands; nor do we want any other motive to make us bear all things with patience and joy. The holy doctors, explaining these words of the Psalmist: "And my beloved is to me as the young unicorn" (Ps. xxviii. 6); take notice that God compares himself to the unicorn, because this animal having its horn lower than its eyes, sees better how to aim its stroke, whereas the bull having his above the eyes, pushes at random. Moreover, the unicorn cures with the same horn wherewith he gave the wound. And so in the same manner God strikes not but with the same weapons which serve for our cure.

In fine, this conformity and this humble submission to our punishment is so grateful to God, that sometimes it is a means to appease him, and to hinder him from inflicting chastisement. It is related in ecclesiastical history, that Attila, King of the Huns, who overran and destroyed so many provinces, and made himself be called "the terror of the world, and scourge of God" (Nauclerus, 2 vol.), approaching the city of Troyes, in Champaigne, St. Lupus, who was then bishop of the place, went forth to meet him in his pontifical habit, accompanied by all the clergy; and being come up to him, "Who are you," said he, "who waste and ruin the whole earth?" Attila answered, "I am the scourge of God." The holy bishop having replied: "The scourge of God is welcome," commanded the gates of the city to be opened to him. But as the soldiers entered the city, God blinded them so, that they passed through without doing the least injury. For although Attila were indeed the scourge of God, yet, notwithstanding, God employed him not as such against those who with so much submission received him as his scourge.

CHAPTER XXIV.

The Conformity we are to have to the Will of God in Aridity of Prayer ; and what we understand by the word Aridity.

IT is not only in exterior, natural, and human things, we are to practise a perfect conformity to the will of God ; we must submit to it likewise in such things as would, in the opinion of many, imply sanctity, to wish daily more and more for them. The things I allude to are spiritual and supernatural—for example, divine consolations, and even virtues ; the gift of prayer ; the interior peace and tranquillity of the soul; and in fine, all the advantages of grace.   But some one will ask, how is it possible, in things of this sort, there should be any irregularity of the will, or self-love, so as to need moderation herein ?   I answer, this may happen ; and here we see how dangerous and subtile self-love is, and how easily it is found in the most holy and pious things.   Spiritual sweetness and consolations are very profitable to a soul, because they give it a loathing and horror of all earthly satisfactions, which are the bait and nourishment of vice ; and also because they make us go on with more alacrity in the service of God.   " I have run on in the ways of your commandments," says the Psalmist, " when you dilated my heart." (Ps. cxviii. 32.)   As the heart is straitened by sorrow, so is it dilated by joy.   And it was for this reason the Royal Prophet said in this place, that when his heart was dilated with the joy of spiritual consolations, he ran with more swiftness in the way of virtue, and in the commandments of our Lord.   Spiritual consolations likewise prompt us forcibly to put down our own will, to curb our appetites, to mortify the flesh, and to support with constancy all afflictions which occur.   So that when God intends to send us crosses, he is accustomed to prepare our souls beforehand by sweetnesses and comforts, which fortify us, and put us in a right disposition to make good use of those afflictions which befall us.   It was thus our Saviour comforted his apostles by his glorious transfiguration, that they might not be troubled afterwards in seeing him die upon a cross.   And in like manner, we see God ordinarily sends comforts to those who begin to embrace virtue, in order to draw them off totally from all affections to this world.   But when they are once inflamed with divine love, and their virtues have struck deep root within their hearts, then it is he sends them aridities, that they may increase in patience and humility ; and that serving God purely for his own sake, and without any sensible comfort, they may merit a greater increase of grace and glory. Hence it comes to pass, that many find when they are newly entered into religion, and even before they are entered, and have only a desire of entering, that they had many more consolations than they have afterwards. And the reason is, because God treats them according to their age, that is, according to their age in virtue. In order to detach them from the world, and cause them a disgust and horror of all its vanities, he nourishes them with milk like children, and with a spiritual sort of milk, which is more sweet and pleasant than all the sweetness of the world. But when they are advanced in virtue, there is no need of their being treated so delicately, so that he feeds them with more solid and substantial food. It is then for these ends he imparts spiritual delights and comforts ; and hence the saints advise us in time of consolation to prepare and arm ourselves for temptation, as in time of peace we make preparations for war ; it being a truth almost infallible, that comforts are a presage of approaching affliction.

Spiritual consolations, therefore, are very profitable if we knew but the right way to make use of them. And when it pleases God to bestow them upon us, we must receive them with acts of gratitude and acts of thanksgiving. But if any one regards them inasmuch as they are sensible, and desires them only for the satisfaction and delight the soul finds therein ; this desire of his would be vicious, as coming from an irregular self-love. As we should commit sin, if in things necessary for the preservation of life—if in eating, drinking, sleeping, we propose no other end but the pleasure we enjoy therein ; so, if in prayer we propose to ourselves nothing but consolations and sweetnesses, it would be a sin of spiritual intemperance. We must not either desire or receive things of this sort for our own content only, but we must look upon them as a means which helps us to attain those ends we have spoken of. As a sick person who has lost his appetite for all sorts of necessary meats, is glad to find some taste, not only for the pleasure he has in eating, but because it excites in him an appetite, and causes him to take so much nourishment as suffices for recovering his health and strength ; in like manner a servant of God ought to wish for spiritual consolations, not for the delight he finds, but inasmuch as they are a spiritual refreshing which gives him courage and strength to advance in the difficult way of virtue, and to persevere therein with constancy. In this manner spiritual consolations are not to be desired as they are consolations, but only for the greater glory of God, and inasmuch as they contribute thereunto.

But still I say, that even suppose we desire them not but with this intention, which is very laudable and holy : yet we may commit an excess in desires of this kind, and find some tincture of self-love therein. If, for example, we desire these consolations without measure, and with a certain impatience and importunity, that supposing we receive them not, we are less satisfied in the interior, and less conformed to God's will, and cease not to complain and be out of humour; then I say, this so violent an affection is nothing else than an inordinate spiritual covetousness. For we must not long so much for sweetnesses of this sort, and if it pleases God not to send us them, we lose the peace of our soul thereby, and that conformity we ought to have to the divine will; because this will is to be preferred to all things, and our most important duty is to submit to the will of God.

What I say here of spiritual consolations and delights, I say also of the gift of prayer and of the facility we desire therein, of the interior peace and tranquillity of the soul, and of all other spiritual advantages. For there may be want of moderation in these things, if they are desired with so much impatience and earnestness, that in case of failing in the pursuit, we are discontented and troubled, and in nowise conformed to the will of God. Wherefore by these words, " spiritual consolations," and " delights," we understand not only sensible pleasure of devotion, but even the very substance of prayer, and the gift of being able to persevere therein with all the attention and recollection of mind we could wish or desire. Or rather it is chiefly of this we speak at present, and concerning which we design to show, that we must absolutely conform ourselves to the divine will without being carried away with too much earnestness and solicitude. For inasmuch as appertains to sensible sweetnesses and consolations, there is no one who does not easily renounce them, provided he can but certainly have what is most essential to prayer, and feel the fruit thereof in himself. All know that the essence of prayer consists not in a tender and a sensible devotion ; and that to consent to be deprived of this, we need not offer ourselves any great violence, or be possessed of sublime virtue. But when it happens that, in time of prayer we find ourselves in so great a desolation that it would seem God had retired from us, and we felt in effect the curse wherewith he threatened his people when he said : " I will make the heavens to be of iron for you, and the earth of brass " (Lev. xxvi. 19) : then it is we stand in need of an extraordinary virtue and strength to undergo all this with due resignation.   For the heavens seem of iron and the earth of brass, to such as are in this state.   They feel not only a continual aridity and barrenness, without the least drop of water for their comfort, but they are sometimes molested with perpetual distractions, and a mutiplicity of such strange and improper thoughts, that they seem to place themselves in prayer for no other end than to be exposed to all sorts of temptations.   If you desire then in this case to think of death, of Jesus Christ crucified, and tell them these are the chief remedies for recollection of mind ; they will answer you, they know very well they are good remedies, and could they but practise them they desired nothing more ; but their misery is, they are not masters of their own imagination ; and when they endeavour most to apply themselves to their points, nothing moves them, nor makes any impression upon their heart.   This is what in spiritual things we call desolation or aridity; and we are to make it our business to conform ourselves to God as well in this as in all other things.

This is a point of great consequence, as being the most common subject of complaint, and one of the greatest mortifications which can befall those who are given to prayer.   For, informed on the one hand, that their conduct throughout the day, and consequently that of their life, depends upon the manner wherein they perform their prayer ; and that it is one of the chief means we have, as well for our own spiritual advancement, as for the edification of our neighbour : and on the other hand, thinking they are far from doing their duty, they fall to tears and sighs, as if God had abandoned them.   And seeing whilst they have no success in their undertakings, others make great progress with ease ; they fear they have lost God's grace, since they feel no greater effects of his presence.   Hence arise in them other temptations more dangerous, as for example, to complain of God for treating them in this manner, and an intention of discontinuing their exercise of prayer, looking upon themselves as not fit for it, since they succeed so indifferently.   In fine, what adds to their affliction is, that the devil represents to them that it is on account of their sins God has abandoned them; and there are some who by this consideration are cast into such dejection of mind, that they come from prayer as from a torture, and with a fretfulness which is insupportable to themselves and to those they converse with. We will endeavour, by the help of God's grace, to give a satisfactory answer to all the complaints and objections those who are molested with this temptation can possibly make.

———o———

CHAPTER XXV.

Wherein are fully answered the Objection and Complaints of those who are troubled with Aridity and Desolations in Prayer.

FIRST, I do not here pretend to deny but that we are to rejoice when God approaches us, and be sorry when he withdraws himself from us. For it is impossible a soul should not feel a sensible joy in the presence of her beloved, and be sensibly afflicted at his absence, since by this she is left to desolations and temptations. Jesus Christ himself was sensibly affected on seeing himself forsaken by his eternal Father, when on the cross he cried out: "My God, my God, why hast thou forsaken me?" (Matt. xxvii. 46.) But what I desire is, that we make our profit of this hard proof and trial which God sometimes sends his elect; and that we endeavour to fortify our souls, in conforming ourselves to the divine will, saying: "Nevertheless, O Lord, not as I will, but as you will." (Matt. xxvi. 39.) We must make use of this means the more readily, as Christian perfection consists neither in the sweetness of consolations, nor in sublime prayer: and as our advancement is not measured thereby, but only according to the rule of charity, which is independent of all other things, and which consists in a perfect union and submission to the divine will, as well in adversity and desolation, as in prosperity and comfort. Wherefore upon this account it is, that spiritual crosses and aridities ought to be received from the hand of God, as well as consolations and favours; and we must thank him equally for both. If it be your pleasure, O Lord! that I remain in darkness, blessed be your holy name; if you will have me enjoy the light, blessed be your holy name; if you confer comforts upon me, blessed be your holy name; and if you will have me suffer afflictions, blessed be your holy name. This is the advice of the apostle when, writing to the Thessalonians, he says : "In all this give God thanks ; for this is what God would have all do in Jesus Christ." (1 Thes. v. 18.) If this be the will of God, what can we desire more ? I have nothing else to do but to please him ; my life is given only for this end ; and how obscure and tedious soever are the paths by which it pleases him to conduct me, my business is not to desire more plain and easy ways. God leads some through pleasant fields, where there are infinite delights ; I march through forlorn and frightful deserts, where I am deprived of all comfort. I would not change the pains and difficulties of my road, for all the satisfaction and pleasure others find in theirs. This is the language of those whose eyes are open to discern things, and thus they comfort themselves upon all occasions. O that it but pleased God to open our eyes, says father Avila, we should see more clear than the day, that there is nothing upon earth nor in heaven which deserves to be desired or possessed, if the will of God be not annexed thereto ; and that, on the contrary, there is nothing so contemptible, so painful, which becomes not of inestimable value, if joined to the will of God. It were without comparison much better to suffer afflictions, pains, aridities, and temptations, if it were his will, than to enjoy all consolations imaginable, and the most sublime contemplations, if you exclude God's will.

But you will say ; If I knew that such was the will of God, and that this was what in effect pleased him most, I could conform myself with ease. And although I were to pass my whole life in this manner, I could submit with satisfaction and content ; because I know there is nothing in this world more to be desired, than to please God, and that my life has been given me for no other end. But on the contrary it seems to me that God would keep me more attentive and recollected in prayer, provided I brought on my part a better disposition. And what troubles me is, that I believe my aridities proceed from my tepidity and sloth. For if I could but satisfy myself in this point, that I had performed all on my part, and were but assured it is not my fault, I should be at ease. This complaint is very well formed ; there can be nothing added ; since it comprehends all that can be alleged : so that we will look upon it a great point gained, if we give it a full and satisfactory answer ; since it is a common complaint, and there is not a soul, how holy and perfect soever it be, which feels not sometimes these desolations and spiritual afflictions. St. Francis and St. Catherine of Sienna were not exempt from them, although otherwise they were great servants of God. The great St. Anthony likewise, who, often having passed whole nights in prayer, thought he had been but a moment, complaining the sun rose too soon, was yet so tormented with a multiplicity of evil thoughts, that not being able to repel them, he cried out : " Lord, I desire to be perfect, but my extravagant thoughts will not permit me." St. Bernard complained of the same thing, when he said : " My heart is dried up ; it is curdled like milk ; it is become like parched earth without water ; and it is so hardened that I cannot excite it either to tears or compunction. I take no more pleasure in singing the divine office ; I have no inclination to spiritual reading nor prayer ; nor do I find now those holy meditations I was accustomed to make. Where are now those spiritual flames ? Where that tranquillity and peace of mind ? Where that content and repose in the Holy Ghost ?" So that the matter we here speak of concerns in general the whole world, and I hope, with God's grace, I shall reply satisfactorily to the complaints and objections of all.

I begin, then, in the first place, to grant you that all the distractions and desolations you find in prayer, and that all the difficulty you find therein, proceed from your own fault ; it is requisite also that you persuade yourself, and in reality acknowledge, that in punishment of your past sins and your present negligence, God permits you to have no facility in prayer, no attention in it, no recollection of spirit, no tranquillity. Nevertheless it follows not from thence that instead of conforming yourself therein to God's will, you have a right to complain. Shall I answer you once for all ? " I condemn you from your own words." (Luke xix. 22.) Do not you acknowledge that you deserve great punishment from God for your past sins and negligences ? You own it, doubtless ; and grant you have several times deserved hell itself ; that there cannot be found in the world any punishment great enough for you ; that in comparison of what you deserve, whatever you otherwise can suffer will be an effect of the divine mercy and goodness ; and, in fine, that you will receive as a singular favour the chastisements he shall please to send you in this life, because you will rest assured thereby he will pardon your sins, and not punish you in the life to some. This is sufficient ; I desire no more. But let us come to the application of all that has been said. All your distractions, all your desolations, your afflictions, your spiritual dereliction ; the heaven becoming iron, and the earth brass to you ; your

little or no facility in prayer, as often as you apply yourself to
it, and God, in fine, who seems to retire from you ; all this, I
say, is a chastisement sent from God for the expiation of your
past sins and present faults.   Do you not find both the one and
the other deserve their punishment alike ?   Yes, doubtless you
find it so.   Unquestionably you own the punishment to be but
little in consideration of what you deserve, and it is equally full
of justice and mercy.   Of justice, because having so often shut
the gate of your heart against God, and having been deaf to him
when he knocked at it by so many holy aspirations ; and, having
rejected them so often, it is but just that now he hears you not ;
when you call upon him that he answers you not ; and that
instead of opening the door he shuts it upon you.   You cannot
disagree with me in this ; and thus, in fine, the justice of the
punishment you receive is entirely established.   Nor will you
likewise disown but that it is little, when compared to what you
deserve, and that it is full also of mercy.   Conform yourself,
then, to God in the chastisement sent you, and receive it with
thanksgiving for his having punished you with so much mercy
and sweetness.   Have you not owned you deserved hell ?   With
what face then dare you expect to receive consolations and
favours in your prayers ?   To have free access therein to God,
to entertain yourself familiarly with him, and enjoy peace and
tranquillity, which only his beloved children enjoy ?   How dare
you complain you have not what you so little deserved ?   Is not
this a sign of too much boldness and presumption ?   Content
yourself that God suffers you in his house, and permits you to
remain in his presence.   This is so great a favour, and so considerable a benefit, that you can never have too great an esteem of
it, nor never acknowledge it as you ought.   Were we really
humble of heart, we should never open our mouth to complain
in what maner soever it pleases God to deal with us : and thus
all temptations proceeding from these causes would immediately
cease.

————o————

CHAPTER XXVI.

How we may convert Aridities and Desolations into a good profitable Prayer.

IT is not enough that we make no complaint of the aridities and desolations, but we must endeavour to profit by them, and to convert them into an excellent prayer. And the first thing that will help us to do this, is to address ourselves to God, and say to him : Lord, inasmuch as this aridity proceeds from my fault or negligence, I am truly sorry, and troubled for the cause I have given of it, but inasmuch as it is your holy will, and a just pain and punishment which my sins have merited, I accept it with all my heart, and not only submit to this cross, and embrace it for the present, but even to the end of my life, giving you infinite thanks for it. This spirit of patience, humility, and resignation to the will of God is infinitely more pleasing to him, than those complaints and disquiets which proceed from the difficulties we find in prayer, and from the multiplicity of distractions we meet with therein. Which of his two sons do you think a father would love better; him who is contented with whatsoever he shall bestow upon him, or the other, who is contented with nothing that he gives him, but murmurs and complains continually, and thinks all that he gives him too little in comparison of what he thinks he deserves ? It is not to be doubted but you will say the first is more pleasing to him. It is the same with us in regard of God. We are all his children ; he who is of a peaceable and complying humour, and conforms himself in all things to the will of his heavenly Father, and is content with whatsoever he sends him, how hard and troublesome soever, pleases God far more than the other who is so hard to be pleased, and does nothing else but murmur and complain because what is given him is not to his liking. Moreover, which of the two beggars do you think makes better use of what is given him, or more excites charity and compassion ; he who grumbles at the gate, because he receives not presently an answer, or because nothing is given him ; or the other, who stays patiently at the door, after he knows they hear him, without farther importunity, and without making any complaint waits with patience in the cold and rain to see whether they will bestow anything upon him ? It is very certain that the humility of the latter inspires feelings of pity and compassion ; and the pride of the former excites motions of anger and indignation. The same thing happens between God and us.

But that we may better know the excellency and profit of this kind of prayer, and how pleasing it is to God, I ask, what greater fruit can be reaped from prayer than that of great patience in afflictions, of an entire conformity to the divine will, and of an extreme love of God? Is not this what we ought to propose to ourselves in prayer? This being so, when therefore God shall send you dryness and desolation in prayer, conform yourself to his will in this spiritual dereliction, in which he leaves you, and this will be one of the greatest acts of patience and of the love of God, which it is possible for you to perform. Nothing shows more clearly the excess of our love than the greatness of pain and labour which we bear for the sake of the beloved. But it is certain that the aridities and derelictions of which we speak, are the greatest sufferings, most sensible mortifications, and the most painful crosses of the true servants of God. For all temporal afflictions that regard our goods, health, or reputation, are nothing compared to them. So that to conform ourselves in these entirely to the will of God, by imitating Jesus Christ in that dereliction he found upon the cross; and to accept purely from the sole desire of pleasing God so great a cross as this, during our whole lives, is certainly one of the greatest acts of patience and of the love of God; a sort of most sublime and profitable prayer, and an effect of the most consummate perfection. There is so much virtue and merit herein, that those who thus submit themselves to these afflictions are styled by some the greatest of martyrs.

Moreover, why do you betake yourself to prayer but to obtain a profound humility, and an entire knowledge of yourself? How often have you begged of God that he would let you see how miserable a creature you are? And behold he gives you a sight and knowledge of this, by means of these aridities and disgusts. Some think the knowledge of themselves consists in having a great sorrow and regret for their sins, and in bitterly deploring them. But they are deceived; for this compunction is from God, and not from themselves, and consequently it is God, not themselves, they come to know thereby. That which is purely from yourself, is that hardness of heart, such an insensibility, as is like a rock from which a drop of water cannot issue unless God strikes it. It is in this the knowledge of ourselves consists, and consequently this is the source of all happiness, which you may very easily gain amidst those aridities you complain of; so that if you do but reap this fruit from your prayer, your prayer will become most profitable.

CHAPTER XXVII.

Of some other Reasons that ought to move us to comfort ourselves, and conform to the Divine Will, in these Aridities and Desolations in Prayer.

THOUGH for the entertaining ourselves so much the more in profound sentiments of humility and confusion, it is very good that we should think our sins to be the cause of the aridities we suffer, yet we must also think that they are not always a punishment of our offences, but sometimes they are a pure effect of the impenetrable providence of God, who bestows his favours and graces, how and to whom he pleases.   As the human body consists of different members, the Church also consists of different members. So that all those that compose this mystical body ought not to be raised to this kind of high prayer, of which we have spoken in the Fifth Treatise. However, we are not hereupon to conclude, that those upon whom God confers not this grace are unworthy of it ; but it is because he knows they will be able to reap more profit another way, and therefore he bestows a greater and more signal favour in bestowing rather another grace than this upon them. There have been very great saints that have never been able to obtain this grace, or if they have, they have said with St. Paul : "Far be it from me to glory, except in the cross of my Lord Jesus Christ." (Gal. vi. 14.)

Father Avila, on this subject, makes a declaration which cannot but afford us very great comfort. God, says he, sometimes leaves certain persons in an entire privation of all sorts of spiritual comforts, during many years together, and sometimes even for their whole lives; but their portion, in my opinion, says he, is far better if they have but faith as lively as not to judge ill of the order of providence, and patience so courageous as constantly to support so great and sensible a dereliction.   All the world would in this easily conform themselves to the will of God, if each one were well persuaded that this state were more for his advantage than any other. The saints and masters of a spiritual life assign many reasons to prove this truth ; but I will content myself with relating a principal one, which St. Austin, St. Jerome, and St. Gregory, and generally all those that treat of this matter, propose to us. It is, that all persons are not able to preserve humility amidst the favours of an elevated contemplation.   We find we have scarce shed a tear in our prayer, but we think ourselves already advanced

to a high pitch of spirituality and contemplation, and dare compare, if not prefer ourselves to those who are perfect. It seems as if
St. Paul himself stood in need of the counterpoise of temptations,
not to let himself be carried away with vanity which thereupon
might arise to him. "Lest," says he, "the greatness of my revelations should puff me up, there was given me a sting of my flesh,
the angel of Satan to buffet me." (2 Cor. xii. 7.) God permits the
apostle to be disquieted with a temptation that humbled him,
and made him sensible of his weakness, lest the circumstance of
his being rapt to the third heavens, and the greatness of his revelations, should give him any vainglory. Of all the ways of a
spiritual life, that of contemplation is most elevated, but it is not
the most secure; and it is for this reason God, who has created us
all for the same end, which is the enjoyment of himself, conducts
us all by that way which he sees most suitable to each one. Perhaps, if you found in prayer that facility, and all those sweetnesses
you desire, you would thereby be puffed up with pride; whereas,
finding nothing therein but aridities, you may always be kept in
humility, and a contempt of yourself; and therefore this way is far
better and more secure for you; but if you desire to go any other
way, it is because "you know not what you ask." (Matt. xx. 22.)

St. Gregory, writing upon these words of Job: "If he comes to
me I will see him; and if he goes away from me, I will take no
notice of his departure" (Job ix. 11), says, man is become so blind
by his fall, that he neither knows when God approaches, or when
he leaves him. But, on the contrary, what he thinks to be a particular favour, and a means of approaching nearer unto God, sometimes increases the divine anger, and causes God to go farther
from him; and what we believe to be a mark of God's indignation,
and which repels us farther from him, is a particular favour that
inseparably unites us unto him. For who is there that, perceiving
himself elevated to a high degree of sublime prayer, and receiving
every day in it some new favour, does not imagine that hereby he
continually more and more approaches unto God? The effect,
however, produced by favours of this kind, is, that they give an
occasion of pride and presumption, and so the same things that we
think should raise us higher and bring us nearer unto God, are
those the devil frequently uses to make us fall into the precipice.
And when, on the contrary, we see ourselves deprived of all
spiritual comfort, and tormented with thoughts either against
purity, or against faith, we imagine ourselves forsaken by God;
that he is angry with us and withdraws himself from us. However,

it is then he comes nearest to us; because we then most of all humble ourselves, and have a lower opinion of our own strength. It is then we have recourse unto him with greater fervour, put all our confidence in him, and so intimately unite ourselves unto him that we can never be separated from him. It is not therefore certain, that the way you think best is best for you, but that way which God is pleased to lead you is that which is most convenient and profitable for you.

Moreover, your very sorrow at the idea of not performing your duty as you ought to do in prayer, is a subject of comfort, because it is a particular grace of God, and a proof that you love him. For grief supposes love, and we have no regret for serving him ill, but because we desire to serve him well. Certainly if you were not troubled that you serve him ill, and that you perform not your prayer and other exercises well, it would in effect be a very bad sign; but to be displeased, because you think you perform not your duty as you ought, is a very bad sign. Wherefore, since the pain you suffer hereby is an effect of the divine will, it follows that, on the one hand, this consideration should serve to allay your displeasure, conforming yourself to all that is God's will; and on the other hand, you must give him thanks for this, that if there be any tepidity in your actions, you have at least at the same time a very great desire to perform them better.

Moreover, as the bare assiduity of courtiers in the prince's palace, is a service done the prince; even so if you do nothing else in your prayer but keep yourself diligently in God's presence, you continually do him service. " Blessed is he who gives ear to me," says the holy Scripture by the mouth of the Wise Man, "and always waits at my gate, and waits till I open to him." (Prov. viii. 34.) It is very fit, both in respect of the greatness of the infinite majesty of God, and the lowliness of our own condition, as well as in respect of the important affair we have in hand, that we should go often to wait at his gate. If he pleases to open it, give him thanks; if he opens it not, acknowledge that you do not deserve he should open it; and this will be a very good and profitable kind of prayer. We must help ourselves with these kinds of considerations, and divers others of the like nature, to obtain a conformity to the will of God, in the aridities he sends us, and in the spiritual dereliction and desolation in which he leaves us; and receiving all from his hands with thanksgiving, we must say with Bartholomew of the martyrs: " Hail, O bitterness; because how unpleasant soever thou art, yet thou art replenished with all sorts of grace."

CHAPTER XXVIII.

That it is very improper to discontinue Prayer upon account of the Desolation and Aridities we find therein.

FROM what we have already said, it follows that it is a very great illusion to discontinue our prayer or to pray less than usual; because, feeling nothing but aridity therein, we therefore imagine we do nothing but lose our time. This thought is a very dangerous temptation, that has made not only many secular persons leave off the exercise of prayer, but many religious also; and though it causes not some to leave off entirely this exercise, yet it lessens their affection to it, and hinders them from spending therein all the time they could. Many in the beginning give themselves to prayer with great fervour, and continue to do so long as they find comfort and sweetness in it; but when aridities and distractions molest them, they imagine they do not pray, but rather commit a fault, by being in God's presence with so little attention and respect; and think they might serve him better by some other spiritual exercise, and therefore apply themselves less than usual to that of prayer. The devil, who sees their weakness and inconstancy, seizes this occasion, and endeavours to disquiet them so much in time of prayer, by all sorts of thoughts and temptations, that being at last quite discouraged, and persuading themselves the time thus spent in prayer to be very ill employed, they abandon it entirely, and therewith the desire of their perfection, and sometimes even the care of the salvation of their souls. Thus a great many persons ruin and destroy themselves. "These are friends and guests at our table, who leave us in time of necessity." (Eccl. vi. 10.) There is no one who would not desire to be happy with God; but the true mark of love is the desire to suffer with him. It is no very great matter to persevere a long time in prayer, when we receive sweetnesses and consolations; the very satisfaction we feel therein is sufficient to oblige us thereunto. And if we leave off prayer, when we find this wanting, it is a sign we act only from this motive. But when God sends us desolations, aridities, and distractions, it is then we show ourselves true friends of God, and his faithful servants, who seek not our own interest, but regard only his holy will and pleasure. For this reason we ought at such a time as this persevere with the spirit of humility and patience, and give the whole time to prayer, nay, even more than is appointed, as St. Ignatius counsels us; that we may better surmount the temptation, and testify our constancy and courage in resisting the devil.

Palladius relates of himself, that being shut up in his cell, the better to give himself to prayer, contemplation, and other spiritual duties, he found himself in so great an aridity, and was disquieted with such a number of thoughts, that it came into his mind to discontinue his prayer, being able to make no progress in it. Whereupon he went to find out the great Macarius of Alexandria, whom he acquainted with his temptation, and asked his counsel what to do in it. When these thoughts, replied the saint, tell you to go away, and that you do but lose your time, answer them ; " It is for the love of Jesus Christ I keep within the walls of my cell." This was telling him plainly that his duty was to persevere, and though he reaped no other fruit from this exercise than to continue in it for the love of Jesus Christ, this alone was sufficient. We may avail ourselves of the same answer in the like temptations. For our own satisfaction is not the end we must aim at, or ought to have in prayer ; and it is not upon this account we are to apply ourselves to it. What we are to propose to ourselves in prayer is, to perform an action that is pleasing to God, whereby we may in some measure acquit ourselves of a part of our duty to him, as he is our God ; and a part of the obligations we have to him, as our benefactor. And this being so, though in the midst of aridities and distractions you think you are not able to derive advantage from prayer, yet you do not fail to persevere in it, because it is this that pleases him.

We read of St. Catherine of Sienna, that for many days together she was deprived of all sorts of spiritual comfort, feeling nothing at all of her wonted fervour, but daily tormented with a multiplicity of impure thoughts which she was not able to banish. Yet, nevertheless, she no day failed to make her accustomed prayer, in which she persevered as well as she was able, speaking thus to herself : " Alas! miserable sinner as you are, do you deserve any comfort? Would it not be a greater happiness than you deserve, to pass your whole life in darkness and in the desolate afflictions you are in, so you might but be freed from eternal damnation ? You were not called to the service of God, to have sweetness and comforts in this life, but eternally to enjoy them with him in the next. Take courage, therefore ; continue in your exercise, and persevere with that fidelity you owe your sovereign master."

Let us imitate those two examples, and fortify ourselves with the words of Thomas-à-Kempis. "Let my consolation, O Lord! be to be always willing to want all human comfort, and if your comfort also be wanting in me, let your will and pleasure thus to try

me, be to me the greatest of all comforts." When we shall become
so much masters over ourselves, as thus to unite our satisfaction
to the divine will, so that it shall even be a joy unto us to have
no comfort, if God pleases to deprive us of it; then we shall
enjoy so perfect a peace and contentment, that nothing in this
world shall be able to take it from us, or give us any trouble.

——o——

CHAPTER XXIX.

What has been already said is confirmed by divers Examples.

In the Chronicles of the Order of St. Dominick, it is related, that
one of the most distinguished persons of the order lived therein
many years, leading a life pure, holy, and exemplary, without
having felt any spiritual consolation in the discharge of his religious duties. But when he heard the religious speak of those
favours God did to others, and of those spiritual sweetnesses with
which he filled them, he became so sensibly afflicted, that at last,
staying one night in the church after matins, being overwhelmed
with grief, he prostrated himself before a crucifix, where, weeping very bitterly, and almost beside himself, he was moved to
make this complaint : " O Lord, I have been always persuaded
that you surpass all your creatures in goodness and liberality.
Behold me here prostrate who have served you so many years :
and, for love of you, have suffered so many grievous afflictions,
having made an entire sacrifice of myself unto your divine
majesty. Had I served a tyrant for the fourth part of that time I
have served you, he would before this have given me some mark
or testimony of his good will, either by a kind word, a smile, or
a favourable look. But you, O Lord, have not bestowed upon me
even the least of those favours, that you are accustomed to give
to others; and you, who are sweetness itself, of all the world are
harder and more cruel to me than the greatest tyrant in the world
would be. Whence proceeds this, O Lord? And why do you
treat me after so cruel a manner?" (Hist. Ord. Prædic. i. p. lib.
l. c. lx. He had scarce pronounced these words, when on a sudden
he heard as dreadful a noise as if the whole church was thrown
down; when, seized with fear, and turning his head to see
what was the matter, he perceived a devil behind him, who,
holding a bar of iron in his hands, gave him such a blow on
his body, that he fell with his face upon the ground, without
being able to raise himself from it; yet, nevertheless, he had

so much strength and courage left as to creep to an altar hard by, where, not being able to move by reason of the great pain he felt, he there remained stretched out as if he had been all over bruised and broken in pieces by the force of the blows. The religious coming afterwards to the office of prime, finding him half dead, carried him to the infirmary, without knowing how or why this strange accident had happened to him. He remained there three whole weeks, suffered most grievous pains, and his body emitted so intolerable a stench, that the infirmarians were scarce able to come near him to dress or assist him. At the end of three weeks he began to recover some strength, and as soon as he was able to rise, being desirous to cure himself entirely of his pride and presumption, he went to seek a remedy in the same place where he had committed the fault. Here, full of shame and confusion, bathed in tears, he made a very different prayer from that he made before—confessing his guilt, that he deserved no favour from God, and that he had not received the punishment he deserved. At which time he heard a voice from heaven, that said to him, " If you desire sweetness and comforts, you must know your own baseness, and remember that you are more vile and contemptible than the very dirt or worms." He profited so well by this instruction, and from what had happened unto him, that from that time forward he became a most perfect religious.

We read another example, very different from the former, in the Life of St. Ignatius. It is related that this saint, considering his faults, and weeping bitterly for them, said : he wished with all his heart God would punish them, by depriving him for some time of all sweetness, and of his divine consolations, that this chastisement might render him more careful and zealous in his service But he owned at the same time, that God had always so great mercy and compassion for him, and treated him with so much sweetness, that the more faults he committed, and the more he thus desired to be punished for them, the more goodness our Lord showed towards him, and poured down upon him with greater abundance the treasures of his infinite liberality. So that he said he thought there was no person in the world in whom two things so opposite were to be found in so great excess as in himself; first, to fall so often into imperfection, and continue so ungrateful to God ; the second, to receive so great and continual favours from his divine hand.

Blosius relates that a holy man, to whom our Lord did many favours, and communicated great lights in prayer, begged one day of God, out of great excess of humility, and from an ardent desire of pleasing him more, that he would deprive him of those favours he bestowed upon him, if this would render him more pleasing in his sight. God heard his prayer, and withdrew from him all his consolations in such manner, that for the space of five years together, he tried him with continual temptations, aridities, and bitterness. One day, being oppressed with sorrow, he wept bitterly ; at which time two angels appeared and comforted him; but the good man, refusing the consolations they came to give him, said to them, " I desire no comfort; for the accomplishment of the will of God in me is all the comfort I desire."

The same Blosius relates also, that Jesus Christ appearing one day to St. Bridget, who was in great desolation and affliction of mind, asked her why she was afflicted ?   And the saint having answered him, that it was because she was tormented with an infinity of bad thoughts, which gave her cause to apprehend his just judgments might fall upon her :   " It is just," replied our Saviour, " that as you have taken pleasure in the vanities of the world against my will, so you should also now suffer against your own many vain and bad thoughts ; and as to what concerns my judgments, it is good also that you fear them ; but this must be with moderation, and with a firm confidence in me, who am your God."   For you must hold for a certain truth, that bad thoughts which are resisted and rejected as much as possible, are the purgatory of a soul in this world, and a subject of recompense in heaven.   But if you cannot entirely banish them, be contented that you desire all you can to resist them, and then suffer them with patience.   But to take care also that you do not attribute this resistance to your own strength, and that pride be not the occasion of your fall ; because no one can remain constant in virtue, but so far as he is supported and strengthened by the grace of God.

Taulerus says, that many persons addressing themselves to him in their spiritual afflictions, and complaining that they were in a deplorable condition, because they suffered continual pain and trouble of mind, he gave this answer—That all things went very well with them, and that even the very things they complained of was a favour God bestowed upon them.   And when they replied they believed the contrary, and that this happened to them in punishment of their sins ; Whether it be for your sins or not, replied he, yet still believe this cross comes from God, and therefore willingly embrace it, gave him thanks for it, and resign yourselves entirely into his hands. But if they told him they felt themselves quite consumed with the aridities and tediousness they felt in prayer, he answered; Suffer with patience, and thereby you will receive more favours than if you felt in yourselves the transports of a tender and fervent devotion.

A great servant of God was wont to say that for forty years together, which he had spent in God's service, and in application to prayer, he had never yet received any sweetness or comfort ; yet notwithstanding as often as he made his prayer, he felt afterwards greater strength to acquit himself of his spiritual duties, and when he neglected it he found himself in so weak and languishing a condition, that he was scarce able to undertake anything that was either good or virtuous.

———o———

CHAPTER XXX.

Of the Conformity we ought to have to the Will of God in the Participation of all other Virtues and supernatural Gifts.

THE same submission we ought to have to the will of God, in what manner soever he treats us in prayer, we must also have in regard of all the other advantages of grace. It is good to desire virtue, to be carried towards it with fervour, and to offer violence to ourselves to obtain it ; but we must govern ourselves in this in such a manner, that if we attain not that height of perfection we aim at, yet we must not fail to keep our minds in peace, and content ourselves with what God pleases ; conforming ourselves entirely to his divine will. If God will not bestow upon you the purity of an angel—if he will humble and try you by continual temptations against chastity, it is better you should humbly submit to his divine will, than disquiet yourself, or complain that you are not so pure as an angel. If God will not confer upon you so profound an humility as he gave to St. Francis, such a spirit of meekness as he gave to Moses and David, nor so great and constant a patience as he gave to Job, and if it is his pleasure you should be continually disquieted with temptations, contrary to these virtues, it is good to take occasion hereby to acknowledge your baseness ; but you ought not upon this account to lose the peace of your mind, and give yourself over to grief or complaints, because he is not pleased to do you the same favours he has done to great saints. I do not believe, says Father Avila, that there were ever any saints so perfect as not to desire still greater perfection; yet this did not at all disturb their peace of mind, because it was not a desire that proceeded from insatiable avarice, but from a thought with which the love of God only inspired them. So that they were contented with the part given them, and would have been contented with less, had God not been so liberal to them ; knowing very well, that it is a mere illusion of self-love to desire great gifts in order to be thereby the better able to render services to God; and that true love consists in being satisfied with what is given us.

This discourse, it will be objected, seems to tend to the establishing in us so great an error as to think we ought not fervently desire to be more perfect than we are, but that we ought to leave to God as well the care of our souls as of our bodies ; which would be to open a gap to all kind of liberty and disorder, to give rise to tepidity. and to hinder us from endeavouring to become perfect. This objection deserves to be taken notice of, and marks out the sole inconvenience that is to be feared in the matter we treat of, There is no doctrine so holy that may not be abused, when we know not how duly to put it in practice ; and lest that happen here, as well in regard to prayer in particular as to what concerns all virtues in general, it is fit I here should more clearly explain this point. Wherefore take notice, that I do not say we ought not daily to render ourselves more perfect in virtue, and to imitate the most perfect ; for, it is for this reason we entered into religion, and without it we can never be good religious; but what I here say is, that as in corporal and exterior things, we must take such care as is free from disquiet and solicitude, so also our care in interior and spiritual things ought not to disturb our peace, or hinder our entire conformity to the will of God. When Jesus Christ said to his apostles, " Be not solicitous what you shall eat or drink, nor for your body with what you shall be clothed " (Mat. vi. 25) ; what he intended hereby to forbid, say the holy fathers, was only the too great avidity and solicitude for temporal conveniences. For as to what concerns a reasonable care and labour, we are so far from being forbidden it, that we are even commanded it; nay, it is a punishment God has imposed upon us, as his words to Adam express:— " You shall eat your bread in the sweat of your brow " (Gen. iii. 19) ; and it would be to tempt God to neglect it. It is the same in spiritual things. We must seek them with care, and do all we can to obtain them; but if in doing all that lies in your power, you are not able to arrive to the point of perfection you aim at, yet you ought not upon this account, even though you should find yourself defective, to give way to any thoughts of impatience, which would be a greater imperfection than the fault itself, which was the cause thereof. Take care, therefore, you neglect nothing that is in your power to perform ; and if, after all your careful endeavours, it happens you fall into some defects, wonder not hereat, nor let this make you lose courage, because we are all prone and subject to fall. We are neither angels, nor saints confirmed in grace—we are poor weak men, and God, who knows our weakness and misery, who knows the frail matter of which we are made " (Ps. cii. 13), would not have us be discouraged hereat. But what he requires of us is, that after we have fallen, we be sorry and confounded, and endeavour presently to rise again that we beg of him new force and courage, and that we study to preserve both our interior and exterior peace. For it is far better you should rise presently with a holy confidence in his goodness, and that you redouble your courage for his service, than to permit your mind to be cast down and discouraged, believing you weep for your sins out of love for him ; and to displease him by your disquiet and chagrin, by the languishing manner you serve him, and by a thousand other things that issue from the same source.

The only thing we are here to dread is, as I have taken notice of before, lest negligence and tepidity steal hereby into our minds, and we fail to do what we are able, under a pretence that God ought first to bestow his grace npon us, that all things ought to come from his hands, and that it is not in our power to do more than we do. We must make it our care to defend ourselves from the same thing I mentioned while treating of prayer, and take heed, that under the same pretence, idleness and negligence do not get the better of us. But when this passage shall once be well shut, and when on your side you do all you can, it is certain the patience and humility you shall exercise in your feelings and weakness, will be far more pleasing to God than the troubles, disquiets, and complaints to which we are too apt to give ourselves, when we imagine we make not such progress in prayer and virtue as we desire. For the gift of prayer and perfection is not a grace to be obtained by force or by chagrin. It is a favour which God bestows, on whom, how, and when he pleases. After all, it is certain, that those who shall be saved shall not be all equal in virtue; and therefore we ought not to lose courage if we be not in the rank of the most perfect, nor even among the middle sort; but we must in all things conform ourselves to the will of God, and render him thanks that he has given us hopes through his infinite mercy we may save our souls. If we cannot become so perfect as to commit no voluntary faults, let us give God thanks at least that he gives us his grace to know and be sorry for those we commit; and since in the way to heaven the most high and sublime paths of virtue are trodden by very few, and are too high for us, let us content ourselves to tread the path of the knowledge and sorrow of our sins, which is beaten by a great number of persons. Each one, says St. Jerome, offers what he is able in the temple of God. The one offers gold, silver, and precious stones; the other makes a present of linen, of purple or scarlet cloth; for my part I must content myself with giving some goat-skins, they being the only thing I have to give. Let them, therefore, who are arrived to perfection, offer their eminent virtues and sublime contemplations to Almighty God; as for me, it is enough I offer him my baseness, acknowledge myself to be a sinner, owning myself to be full of faults and imperfections, and presenting myself to his divine majesty as one in want of all things. We must take an interior joy in these thoughts, and give God thanks who bestows them upon us, lest if we be not grateful for them, he should perhaps take them from us.

St. Bonaventure, Gerson, and many others, add one thing more, which confirms what I have spoken of. They say, that there are many whom the privation of the virtue they wish for renders more fervent in God's service than they would have been had they enjoyed it; because, by wanting it they become more humble, fervent, and careful, forcing and pushing on themselves to great perfection, and having continual recourse to God. But, perhaps, had they acquired the virtue they aimed at, they would have become proud thereof, or have grown more careless and tepid in his service; and imagining they wanted nothing, would not have exerted themselves to make new progress in perfection. All this gives us sufficiently to understand that on our part we must do what we can to become perfect; but when we have done what we are able, we must be contented with what God bestows upon us, neither afflicting ourselves nor complaining that there are several things beyond our reach. For this, says father Avila, were as if we should be troubled because we had not wings to fly.

CHAPTER XXXI.

Of the Conformity we are to have to the Will of God in the Gifts of Glory.

WE are not only to conform ourselves to the will of God, in what regards the gifts of grace, but must also submit in what concerns the gifts of glory. A true servant of God ought even in this life to be so entirely disengaged from his own private interest that the accomplishment of the divine will may afford him more joy and satisfaction than his own happiness. It is a sign of a consummate perfection, says a holy man, not to seek our own private interest either in little things or in great, in things temporal or eternal; since your will, O Lord! and the desire of your glory, ought always to be of more weight with us, than any other motive whatsoever; and we ought to feel more comfort and content in this alone, than in all the benefits we have received or possibly can receive from your hands.

This is what chiefly causes the joy and content of the blessed. They rejoice more at the will of God fulfilled in them, than at their own reception into glory. They are so transformed into God, and so united to his holy will, that it is not so much by the act of reflecting upon their own happiness, as by an effusion of love for God, they are enamoured of the felicity they enjoy. Whence it happens, that each and every one of them is so satisfied with the degree of glory wherein he is, that he covets no more, and is not in the least concerned at another's being advanced before him. For, from the moment they enjoy the sight of God, they are so changed into him, that ceasing to will by their own sentiments, they will only by those of God. So that to whatsoever they find the divine will inclined, they incline theirs also to the same point, and place herein their content. This perfection has been very eminent in some great saints, as in Moses and St. Paul; who were so far transported with the zeal of the salvation of souls, and the greater glory of God, as to forget themselves, and not regard their own happiness. "Either pardon this fault," says the guide and conductor of the people of God, "or if you do not, blot me rather out of the book of life, where you have written me." (Exod. xxxii. 31.) "I desire," says the apostle of the Gentiles, "to become myself an anathema, and separated from

Jesus Christ, for my brethren." (Rom. ix. 3.)   And it is hence
St. Martin and other great saints learned to say; Lord if I
am still anyways necessary to your people, I refuse not any
pains or labours whatever."   The most willing prefer sufferings
and hardships for the glory and service of God, to the eternal
repose and happiness they were in prospect of enjoying.   And
this is really to perform the will of God upon earth as it is
performed in heaven; which is to place all our content in seeing
it fulfilled, and to prefer that of God to any interest of our own,
and even to the possession of heaven and earth.

Hence we may conceive what perfection it is which requires
this exercise of conformity to the divine will, since if we are not
to consider even the gifts of grace and glory, to attend only to
the pleasure and will of God, how far disengaged ought we to
be from all sorts of temporal interest and human respect ?   We
may at the same time understand by this, how far we are from
perfection in feeling it difficult to conform ourselves to the divine
will, in the things we spoke of in the beginning; which are, in
living in this or that place, in undertaking this or that employ,
in enjoying health, or suffering sickness, in being contemned, or
esteemed.   We say, therefore, we are to make a greater account
of the pleasure and will of God, than of all the advantages of
grace and glory : and you, notwithstanding wed yourself to
things which are nothing in comparison of these.   When we
conceive so earnest a desire of the accomplishment of God's will,
that from this sole principle, and not from any motive of tepidity
or want of courage, we can willingly renounce all pre-eminence
in happiness, and content ourselves with the least share of glory,
it is easy to sacrifice the rest upon the same consideration, having before sacrificed a good which infinitely surpasses all others.
This is the last effort we can make to conform ourselves to the
divine will.   If it pleases God that I die at present, and that I
possess a less degree of beatitude than what I should possess,
were I to live yet twenty or thirty years, I would rather desire
a fulfilling of the divine will than a higher degree of glory.
And if, on the contrary, it were God's holy pleasure I should live
yet for a longer time in the prison of this my body, in pains and
sufferings, I prefer even this to the advantage of enjoying from
this moment an eternal felicity, because I place all my happiness
and all my glory in the content of God, and the performance
of his holy will.   "You are my glory, O Lord, and it is from
you all my exaltation proceeds " (Ps. iii. 4.)

In the Life of St. Ignatius, we read a passage which is very remarkable, and quite apposite to our present subject. Being one day in company with Father Laynez and some others, what think you, said he, you would do in case God should say to you, If you desire to die this moment, I will free you from the prison of this your body, and place you in the fruition of eternal happiness ; but if you have a mind to live longer, I assure you of nothing ; unless that upon condition you persevere in virtue, I will bestow upon you your recompense : and if you deviate from the path of righteousness, I will judge you according to your works ? If, then, our Saviour should speak thus to you, and you knew at the same time that your life being prolonged for some years, you could do some great service, which would you choose ? As for me, replied Father Laynez, I declare I should not doubt a moment in choosing to enjoy God, to assure my eternal happiness, and deliver myself from all danger in an affair of so great importance as this is. As to me, replied the saint, I should not be of your opinion. For if I judged that by living longer upon earth, I could do God greater service, I would desire earnestly of him to grant me a longer time of life for that very end : and herein I should not consider anything but him, without any the least regard to myself, and without any the least respect, either to an infallible assurance of my salvation, or danger of not obtaining it. He was, notwithstanding, fully persuaded in this case, not only of the certainty of his salvation, but also, as he preferred the service of God to the consideration of his own happiness, that his recompense in heaven would be increased. For, said he, if a prince saw any of his subjects deprive himself of the enjoyment of those favours offered him, from the pure motive of performing some great action in his service, would he not look upon himself obliged to such a person, and confer upon him afterwards not only the favours and honours he had designed him, but also add new ones, since his refusal proceeded only from the excess of love he bore to him, and desire of signalizing his loyalty in his service If, then, we may justly assure ourselves that even the most ungrateful persons would do the same, what ought we not to believe God would do, who so liberally prevents us with his holy grace, and from whom we daily receive so many benefits? How can we fear he will abandon us, and permit us to fall into a precipice, since for the love of him we deferred the enjoying him ? It is impossible we should conceive any such opinion of so good a master.

CHAPTER XXXII.

Of the Conformity and Union with God by the Means of a perfect
Love and the Practice we are to observe in this Exercise.

THAT we may better understand what perfection is included
in this exercise of conformity to the will of God, and that we
may clearly show how far we may advance by this means, I
intend to conclude this treatise, by speaking briefly of the
exercise acknowledged by the saints and masters of a spiritual
life to be the most sublime of all. This exercise is that of the
love of God; and without doubt it is not foreign to our purpose
to speak of it in this place, since one of the principal effects of
love being, according to St. Denis, to endeavour that those who
love have but one will in all things, it follows by consequence,
the more we love God, the more we conform ourselves to his
divine will; and again, the more strict this conformity is, the
more perfect is also our love. The better to explain this point,
it is requisite we elevate ourselves in thought up to heaven, and
there behold that the continual occupation of the blessed is to
love God, to conform themselves entirely to his holy will, and to
have no other will but his; inasmuch as the nearer we approach
this idea, the greater will our perfection be in this exercise. St.
John, in his first canonical epistle, says, that the sight of God
makes the blessed like to him: " When he shall appear to us in
glory, we shall be like to him, because we shall see him as he
is." (1 John iii. 2.) And this, because at the same instant they
see God, they are so transformed into him, that their will becomes one and the same thing with his. Let us then see what
is his will, and what he most of all loves, that so by knowing
what is the will and the love of the blessed in heaven, we may
also know at the same time what will and love we ought to have
in ourselves. The will and supreme love in God is the will
of his own glory, and the love of his own being sovereignly perfect, and sovereignly amiable. The will and love of the blessed
is the same thing with the will and love of God; so that their
love is a continual act, by which they are moved incessantly to
will, with all their force, that God may be what he is; that he
be equally good, equally perfect, equally happy, equally worthy
of honour and praise, as he in himself is. And as they see in
him all they can wish may be, they thence feel an inconceivable
joy on seeing that he whom they love is so complete in perfection,

and so replenished with all good. What we see sometimes happen in this life, may give us some faint idea or representation of that supreme and all divine joy which the blessed receive herein. Consider how sensible the joy of a son is, who, loving his father with all affection and tenderness, sees him rich, wise, powerful, honoured and esteemed by the whole world, and particularly favoured by his prince. There are children, doubtless, so nobly born as not to feel any joy comparable to that of seeing their parents so highly esteemed, and in so sublime a post and degree of dignity. If then in the world, where the sentiments of love are so weak, and where all happiness is so contemptible, this joy, notwithstanding, arrives to such a greatness, what must that of the blessed be in beholding their sovereign Master, their Creator, and their heavenly Father, into whom they are wholly transformed by love, to be infinitely good, infinitely holy, infinitely perfect, and infinitely powerful; in beholding all things created to receive their being and perfection from his holy will only; and that not so much as one leaf falls from the tree without his permission? It is of this joy the apostle speaks when he says: " Neither eye has seen, nor ear heard, nor has the heart of man been able to conceive what God has designed for those who love him." (1 Cor. ii. 9.) This is that "river of living water which St. John saw, issuing forth from the throne of God and the Lamb." (Apoc. xxii. 1.) " That river whose impetuous stream rejoiced the city of God." (Ps. xlv. 5.) That river, in which the blessed continually quench their thirst, and inebriate themselves with divine love; blessing God eternally, and singing perpetually, " Bless God, because the Lord our God Omnipotent is entered into his kingdom; let us rejoice and exult, and give him the glory." (Apoc. xix. 6, 7.) They rejoice at the glory and greatness of God; they make themselves happy incessantly, and as it were, animating one the other, they all say, " Blessing, splendour, wisdom, thanksgiving, honour, power and strength be to our God for ever. Amen." (Apoc. vii. 12.)

See here, to speak according to the weak extent of human capacity, what is the continual exercise and love of the blessed in heaven, and how great the conformity and union to the divine will; and see consequently what we are to endeavour to imitate as far as in our power, in order that this will may be performed on earth as it is in heaven. When God ordered Moses to make him a tabernacle : " Take notice," says he, " and make it according to the model and pattern shown you upon the mountain." (Exod. xxv. 40.) It is thus that, in imitation of what is performed upon this high-mountain of glory, we are to exercise ourselves always in loving and willing what the blessed love and will in heaven, and what God himself loves and wills; that is to say, the grandeur of his glory, and the immensity of his being sovereignly perfect and sovereignly happy.

But that all may perform with more facility what we here have laid down, we will show in short in what the practice of this exercise consists. When we are in prayer, let us elevate our understanding to the consideration of the infinite being of God, his eternity, his wisdom, his omnipotence, his beauty, his glory, and his happiness; and at the same time, form acts of our will, by which we may conceive in ourselves a content and joy that God is what he is; that he is God, that he has no dependence on anything but himself, the immensity of his own being, and the infinite good he possesses. For if he stands in need of nothing whatsoever, and all things stand in need of him, he is therefore all powerful, and all replenished with goodness, with sanctity, and glory, and all other perfections, which are found in him without number or limit. St. Thomas, and other divines say, this is the greatest and most perfect act of love we can produce, and the most sublime exercise of conformity we are capable of practising. For there is no more excellent love of God than that which God bears himself; which is the love of his own glory, and of his sovereignly perfect being: nor a will more holy than his. By consequence, then, the more the manner wherein we love God resembles that wherein he loves himself, the more perfect is our love and our union and conformity to the divine will. Moreover, if it be true what philosophy, or rather what nature itself teaches us, that to love is to wish well to the persons we love, it follows of necessity the more we wish another well, the more we love him. But the greatest good we can wish God, is that which he already possesses—the immensity of his being, of his goodness, his wisdom, his omnipotence, and his glory. For we may well rejoice when we love any creature, not only in the gifts it possesses, but also wish it possessed many more; inasmuch as all creatures want many things. But as to God, we cannot wish him anything but he possesses; because, his immensity including all things, and being infinite in himself, it is impossible he should receive more glory, power, and goodness than he already has. Wherefore the greatest good we can wish him, and by consequence, the greatest and most perfect love we can bear him, is to rejoice at the infinite good he possesses, and to take a holy delight therein.

The sacred humanity of Jesus Christ, the glorious Virgin, all the saints in heaven, and all the choirs of angels, rejoice incessantly on beholding God so replenished with all perfection and good, and eternally manifest their joy by continual songs of gladness and by the eternal praises they give him. "Blessed are those, O Lord! who live in your habitations. They shall praise you for ever and ever." (Ps. lxxxiii. 5.) Let us endeavour to imitate them, according as the Church teaches us, "in joining our voices and hearts with theirs, and saying with an humble and sincere confession : Holy, holy, holy, Lord God of Hosts ! the heavens and the earth are full of your glory." Let us exercise ourselves continually, at least as oft as we are able, in praising and glorifying God, in rejoicing with him at the immensity of that great good he possesses ; and so we shall become in some manner like to the blessed, and to God himself, and shall hereby have the most sublime love of God, and the most perfect conformity to the divine will, we are capable of.

---o---

CHAPTER XXXIII.

How much this Exercise is recommended to us in holy Scripture.

THE diligence the holy Scripture uses in frequently recommending to us this exercise, may serve to show the merit and excellency of it, and affords us at the same time matter to practise it, and to employ ourselves more therein. The Psalmist expressly invites us, in these words, "Rejoice ye just in our Lord, and conceive a joy and gladness ; and be glorified in him all ye who have an upright heart." (Ps. xxxi. 11.) "Let the just exult in our Lord." (Ps. xxxii. 1.) "Place your joy in our Lord, and he will grant you the petitions of your heart." (Ps. xxxvi. 4.) Or rather, he will grant you all you can desire, and all you stand in need of. For it is a sort of prayer wherein, though you demand nothing, he hears and grants whatever your heart can covet or petition. The apostle writing to the

Philippians, says : " Rejoice without intermission in the Lord "
(Phil. iv. 4) : and imagining it a point worthy of being inculcated more than once, he immediately adds : " I tell you again
rejoice." It was with such holy joy the Blessed Virgin found
herself replenished, when she said : " My soul is ravished with
joy in God my Saviour." (Luke i. 47.) And it was with this
sort of joy wherewith our Lord Jesus Christ was transported,
when his disciples being returned from the mission upon which
he had sent him, the gospel ssys, " He rejoiced in the Holy
Ghost." (Luke x. 21.) The Royal Prophet affirms, that when
he considered the immensity of God's glory, and how worthy
God is, that all the world should rejoice at the infinite good
he possesses, the joy he felt in his soul passed even to his body.
" My heart and my flesh," says he in one place, " are transported
with joy in the living God." (Ps. lxxxiii. 2.) And in another
place, taking more particular notice of the superabundance of
joy : " My soul," says he, " shall rejoice in our Lord, and shall
delight itself in my Saviour. All my bones shall say, O Lord !
who is like to you ? " (Ps. xxxiv. 9, 10.) In like manner the
Church, which is governed and directed by the Holy Ghost,
knowing how sublime this love of God is, invites us at the
beginning of the canonical hours to love him in this manner,
using for this end the words of David : " Come let us rejoice in
our Lord ; let us sing forth hymns to God our Saviour ; let us
present ourselves in his sight, by acknowledging the benefits
we have received from him, and let us sing canticles of praise.
For our God is a great Lord and a great King above all other
gods. Because the sea is his and he created it, and the dry
land his hands have founded." (Ps. xiv. 1.) It is also for this
very same reason, and with the same intent, that at the end of
every psalm the Church adds always this verse : " Glory be to
the Father, and to the Son, and to the Holy Ghost : as it was
in the beginning, is now, and ever shall be, world without end.
Amen." See here what is meant by these words, " enter into
the joy of your Lord," (Matt. xxv. 21) : which is to participate
in this manner of the infinite joy of God, and to rejoice with
him at his glory, his power, his wisdom, and all the other attri-
butes he possesses.

For the better entertaining ourselves in this spiritual joy, and
the more to incite us to the love of this exercise, it is very requisite to apply ourselves to consider how great the goodness,
the beauty, and the glory of God are : which are in themselves

such, that we only want the sight thereof to make us happy. And in case the damned could but have a sight thereof, all their pains would cease at the same moment, and hell would become a paradise. " For eternal life," as Jesus Christ himself affirms, "consists in the knowledge of God." (John xvii. 3.)   It is this knowledge and this sight which makes the happiness of the blessed ; and which make it not for a day only, or a year, but for all eternity.   So that without ever being tired of the sight of God, they feel therein a content and satisfaction, according to the words of St. John in the Apocalypse—" And they shall sing as it were a new song." (Apoc. xiv. 3.)   It seems that this conveys a sufficient idea of the goodness, beauty, and infinite perfection of God ; and yet, notwithstanding, more, and a great deal more, may be said upon the subject.   God is so beautiful, so perfect, and so full of glory and majesty, that he renders himself happy in contemplating himself ; and that because he contemplates and loves himself.   Let us now consider, whether we have not sufficient reason to place all our joy in one only thing, which causes the eternal happiness of the blessed ; and which also causes that of God himself, by reason of the knowledge he has of his own being, and the love he bears himself.

———o———

CHAPTER XXXIV.

How we may still enlarge upon this Exercise.

WE may extend this exercise still farther by descending from the contemplation of the divine nature, to the consideration of the sacred humanity of Jesus Christ, and exciting ourselves thereby to produce the same acts of love and joy.   We will consider for this effect, the excellency and the perfections of this most sacred humanity.   We may well rejoice that it has been elevated to the honour of being united to the divine person, and replenished with grace and glory ; that it is the instrument of the divinity to sanctify and glorify the elect, and in general, to operate all those graces, and distribute all those supernatural gifts God imparts to men ; and in fine we will conceive an interior delight in all that concerns the perfection and glory of the soul and body of Jesus Christ.   To dwell the more hereupon and to excite in ourselves the deepest sentiments of love and joy we possibly can, we may propose to ourselves, either the joy the Blessed Virgin felt on the day of our Saviour's resurrection, when she beheld him triumph most gloriously over death—or the joy wherewith the holy Scripture affirms the patriarch Jacob was transported on hearing that his son Joseph lived, and was made superintendent of all Egypt. The excess of his joy was such, that, " receiving as it were a new life, I am satisfied," said he, "since my son Joseph is yet alive. I will go and see him before I die." (Gen. xlv. 27, 28.)

We may also apply this exercise to what relates to the glory of the Blessed Virgin and that of the saints: and this will be a very laudable devotion, if we employ therein a part of our prayer upon the day of their feast. For this is to give them the greatest testimony they can receive from us, when we rejoice with them at the felicity they possess. Wherefore the Church, upon the feast of the Blessed Virgin's assumption, proposes to us this exercise in these words : " To-day the Blessed Virgin Mary mounted the heavens ; rejoice that she reigns with Jesus Christ for all eternity." And upon the day of the same feast and several others, the same Church begins the office of the mass by inviting us to the same practice, and exciting us to the example of the angels : " Let us all rejoice in our Lord, in celebrating this feast in honour of the Blessed Virgin Mary ; at whose assumption the angels rejoice and praise the Son of God." There is also another advantage in practising this exercise in respect of the saints, and chiefly of the sacred humanity of Jesus Christ : since hereby we come to elevate ourselves to the exercise which relates to the divinity, and we make it easy. For our Saviour himself teaches us, that he is the way and the gate whereby we must have access to his eternal Father.

This exercise has also its different degrees, even when we practise it in reference to God as he is God. We may also bring it more within our reach, by descending to the consideration of things here below. For although it is true that God in himself increaseth not, because he is infinite, and that we cannot wish him any good he possesses not already, he may, nevertheless, receive an exterior addition from his creatures, inasmuch as they come to know him, to love and glorify him the more ; and by consequence we may exercise this sort of love towards him in wishing him ardently this kind of exterior good. To this end, when in our prayer we come to consider how worthy God is of being loved and served by all his creatures, we must then apply ourselves to wish that all men present and to come may know him, love and glorify him in all things. How happy should we be, O my God! were we able to convert all the infidels and sinners throughout the whole world; that we could not hinder all persons from ever offending you, and make all obey you, and study nothing else for the future but to serve you! "Hallowed be thy name." (Matt. vi. 9.) "Let all the earth adore you, and chant forth your praises. Let it sing canticles of praise to your holy name!" (Ps. lxv. 4.) We can entertain ourselves thus in this exercise; and by representing to ourselves a thousand sorts of services which creatures can render God, we shall find sufficient matter to dilate our wishes upon.

Thence each one coming to reflect upon himself, ought to apply his thoughts to an earnest desire of accomplishing the will of God, and promoting his glory in whatsoever depends upon him; and from henceforth imitating Jesus Christ, "who always performed such things as were acceptable to his eternal Father" (John viii. 29), he may form a determined resolution of embracing with joy whatsoever he knows to be according to the will and glory of God. For, "he who says he knows God, and nevertheless, keeps not his commandments, is a liar, and has not truth in him; but he who keeps his words, in this man the love of God perfectly abides." (1 John ii. 4, 5.) In like manner, to attain a real love of God, and an entire conformity to his holy will, it suffices not that by considering the infinite good God possesses, we turn it into a subject of joy, and so wish all creatures to love and glorify him. We must wholly devote ourselves and employ our whole force to the fulfilling the divine will; since we cannot say from our heart we desire the greater glory of God, unless we contribute all we are able to the accomplishing of it. It is in this sort of love our soul is exercised, when in time of prayer it conceives a real desire, and a firm resolution of performing the will of God in things proposed to it at that time, and in whatever may afterwards occur; and this exercise is what we ought more frequently to use in all our prayers.

We have here opened a field wide enough to employ ourselves a long time in this exercise, and have sufficiently explained the perfection included therein, and the profit we may hence receive. There is nothing now remaining but that we lay our hand to the work, and begin from this moment to repeat upon earth what we are hereafter to repeat for eternity in heaven. It is here we must begin to enkindle in ourselves the fire of the love of God.   But since this " divine fire has its source in Sion, and its furnace in Jerusalem " (Isa. xxxi. 9), it will never attain the perfection of a full blaze till we arrive in the heavenly Jerusalem, *i.e.*, till we attain the felicity of glory.

END OF VOLUME FIRST.

Printed by EDMUND BURKE & Co.,
61 & 62 Great Strand Street and 70 Jervis Street, Dublin.

Other Books by St Athanasius Press

Terra Incognita or Convents of the United Kingdom by John Nicholas Murphy. 757 pages. Hardcover. Unedited Reprint of 1873 book. Catholic. CLOSEOUT Now available ONLY for Retail Customers $34.99

Church Ornaments of our Manufacture. 1910 Benziger Bros Catalog. Softcover. Unedited Reprint of Benziger's 1910 catalog. Fully Illustrated. Catholic. Retail $24.99

Vera Sapentia Or True Wisdom by Thomas A Kempis. Softcover. Unedited Reprint of 1904 book. Catholic 204 pages. Retail $19.99

The Raccolta: Prayers and Devotions enriched with Indulgences. 1957 Unedited Softcover edition. Mostly English with some prayers in Latin & English. Timeless Book. 720+ pages. Retail $29.99

The History of Heresies and Their Refutation by St Alphonsus Liguori. Softcover. Unedited reprint of 1857 book. 642 pages. Retail $29.99

For Ordering info, please email melwaller@gmail.com or call 1-608-763-4097. Mailing address in front of book.

Visit our Web site: http://www.stathanasiuspress.com and Click on the link to find "Stores Near You". If your local Bookstore doesn't carry our titles, please ask them to or at least order a copy for you! Thanks!

Bookstore inquiries are always welcome!